CAMBRIDGE STUDIES IN
ANGLO-SAXON ENGLAND
25

THE INTELLECTUAL FOUNDATIONS OF
THE ENGLISH BENEDICTINE REFORM

CAMBRIDGE STUDIES IN ANGLO-SAXON ENGLAND

Founding General Editors

MICHAEL LAPIDGE AND SIMON KEYNES

Current General Editors

SIMON KEYNES AND ANDY ORCHARD

THE INTELLECTUAL
FOUNDATIONS OF THE ENGLISH
BENEDICTINE REFORM

MECHTHILD GRETSCH

Institut für Englische Philologie
University of Munich

CAMBRIDGE
UNIVERSITY PRESS

PUBLISHED BY THE PRESS SYNDICATE OF THE UNIVERSITY OF CAMBRIDGE
The Pitt Building, Trumpington Street, Cambridge CB2 1RP, United Kingdom

CAMBRIDGE UNIVERSITY PRESS
The Edinburgh Building, Cambridge CB2 2RU, UK   http://www.cup.cam.ac.uk
40 West 20th Street, New York, NY 10011–4211, USA   http://www.cup.org
10 Stamford Road, Oakleigh, Melbourne 3166, Australia

First published 1999

Printed in the United Kingdom at the University Press, Cambridge

Typeset in Garamond 11/13pt   CE

A catalogue record for this book is available from the British Library

ISBN 0 521 58155 9 hardback

Contents

Preface

Writing this book has been a fascinating and challenging scholarly experience. Three years ago, I set about what I then thought would be a longish article on the Old English interlinear gloss in the Royal Psalter, its impressive quality and its origin in Bishop Æthelwold's circle, an origin which I had been suspecting for quite a number of years. As my work proceeded, I soon discovered that another important corpus of glosses – those to Aldhelm's prose *De uirginitate* – showed unmistakable verbal links with the Royal Psalter gloss and with Æthelwold's translation of the *Regula Sancti Benedicti*, thereby indicating a common origin for all three texts. At that point it became clear that I would have to write a short monograph in order to deal adequately with the three texts and their relationships. I then intended to discuss primarily philological aspects of the three texts and to demonstrate their common origin chiefly by means of philological methods. However, within a few months I had become convinced that such a restricted approach would not be sufficient to draw a comprehensive picture of the three texts and their relevance to Anglo-Saxon literary culture, and that for this I would need to assemble and assess what evidence might be gleaned from neighbouring disciplines. By the same token, I realized that this wider approach would present me with an opportunity to demonstrate the role and importance of philology in our attempts to recreate the Anglo-Saxon past. As a result of such discoveries and considerations, the present book gained its final form.

In the course of writing this book I incurred many debts, which I here gratefully acknowledge. For help and advice on various points I should like to thank Professor Peter Clemoes(†), Dr Birgit Ebersperger, Helene Feulner, Dr Walter Hofstetter (even a cursory glance at ch. 4 will reveal how much I am indebted to his magisterial study of the Winchester vocabulary), Ursula Kalbhen, Dr Michael Korhammer, Dr Lucia Kornexl, Dr Ursula Lenker (whose sound scepticism on occasions saved me from getting lost in Æthelwold's world), Dr Andy Orchard, Clare Orchard and Dr Roland Torkar. I should also like to thank the students of my Old English classes who taught me that I could get them interested in Old English sound shifts and noun declensions only by telling them who the people were who spoke that language. Since I did not enjoy the privilege of a sabbatical leave (a privilege which in the system of the wonderful German universities is not deemed appropriate for the majority of their academic staff), I had to rely on student help in order to complete the book within a reasonable span of time. For competent word-processing of my manuscript I should like to thank Carolin Schreiber and, especially, Svenja Weidinger. In the tradition of vigilant medieval scribes they were also my first critics.

My greatest debt, however, is to three scholars without whom this book would not have been written: I have had the expert guidance and the critical but unflagging support of Professor Helmut Gneuss over many years. In the case of the present book this support included access to the invaluable files for his revised handlist of Anglo-Saxon manuscripts, housed in the study next door. I am proud and grateful to be a product of his 'Munich school'. Dr Simon Keynes expertly guided my forays into Anglo-Saxon history; and it is with pleasure that I recall our many discussions about King Æthelstan and his charters. Professor Michael Lapidge, through his attempts to recreate the Anglo-Saxon world of learning and literature, prompted me to return to Anglo-Saxon studies after the lapse of many years. I had his encouragement at every stage of this book's production, and he generously laid his immense erudition at my disposal, patiently answering innumerable queries. I am also deeply indebted to him for help in matters of English style and for suggesting that the book should be included in Cambridge Studies in Anglo-Saxon England. I can only hope that the book in its printed form will be a fitting token of my gratitude to these three scholars, and that it would also have pleased the redoubtable bishop of Winchester.

M. G.
July 1997

Abbreviations

ASC	the Anglo-Saxon Chronicle; see *Two of the Saxon Chronicles Parallel*, ed. C. Plummer, 2 vols. (Oxford, 1892–9, rev. D. Whitelock, 1952)
ASE	*Anglo-Saxon England*
ASPR	The Anglo-Saxon Poetic Records, ed. G. P. Krapp and E. V. K. Dobbie, 6 vols. (New York, 1931–42)
BCS	W. de G. Birch, *Cartularium Saxonicum*, 3 vols. (London, 1885–93) with index (1899)
BR	the Old English Benedictine Rule, quoted by page and line from the edition by Schröer
BT, BTS	J. Bosworth and T. N. Toller, *An Anglo-Saxon Dictionary* (Oxford, 1882-98); T. N. Toller, *An Anglo-Saxon Dictionary: Supplement* (Oxford, 1908–21)
Campbell	A. Campbell, *Old English Grammar* (Oxford, 1959)
cant.	Canticle, numbered according to J. Mearns, *The Canticles of the Church, Eastern and Western, in Early and Medieval Times* (Cambridge, 1914) (the numbers used there agree with those in Roeder's edition of the Royal Psalter)
Cassiodorus, *Expositio*	ed. Adriaen
CCM	Corpus Consuetudinum Monasticarum (Siegburg)
CCSL	Corpus Christianorum Series Latina (Turnhout)
CHM	J. R. Clark Hall, *A Concise Anglo-Saxon*

	Dictionary, 4th ed. with suppl. by H. D. Meritt (Cambridge, 1960)
Cleo I	the First Cleopatra Glossary (London, British Library, Cotton Cleopatra A. iii, fols. 5–75v), ptd WW I (line 21)–535
Cleo III	the Third Cleopatra Glossary (London, British Library, Cotton Cleopatra A. iii, fols. 92–117), ptd WW I, 485 (line 21)–535
CPL	*Clauis Patrum Latinorum*, ed. E. Dekkers and A. Gaar, 3rd ed., CCSL (Steenbrugge, 1995)
CS	*Councils & Synods with other Documents relating to the English Church I: A. D. 871–1204*, ed. D. Whitelock, M. Brett and C. N. L. Brooke (Oxford, 1981) I, pt 1: 871–1066
CSASE	Cambridge Studies in Anglo-Saxon England
CSEL	Corpus Scriptorum Ecclesiasticorum Latinorum (Vienna)
DACL	*Dictionnaire d'archéologie chrétienne et de liturgie*, ed. F. Cabrol and H. Leclercq, 15 vols. in 30 (Paris, 1907–53)
DOE	*Dictionary of Old English*, ed. A. Cameron *et al.* (Toronto, 1986–)
DTC	*Dictionnaire de théologie catholique*, ed. A. Vacant, E. Mangenot and E. Amann, 15 vols. (Paris, 1903–50)
EEM	'Edgar's Establishment of Monasteries' (the Preface to the Old English Rule), ptd and transl. in *CS* I.1, pp. 142–54 (no. 33)
EEMF	Early English Manuscripts in Facsimile (Copenhagen)
EETS	Early English Text Society (London)
OS	Original Series
SS	Supplementary Series
EHD	*English Historical Documents c. 500–1042*, ed. D. Whitelock, English Historical Documents 1, 2nd ed. (London, 1979)
G	*The Old English Glosses of MS Brussels, Royal Library, 1650*, ed. Goossens

HBS	Henry Bradshaw Society Publications (London)
HE	*Historia ecclesiastica*
ICL	D. Schaller and E. Könsgen, *Initia carminum Latinorum saeculo undecimo antiquiorum* (Göttingen, 1977)
Isidore, *Etymologiae*	ed. Lindsay
LkMA	*Lexikon des Mittelalters* (Munich, 1977–98)
LThK	*Lexikon für Theologie und Kirche*, 2nd ed. by J. Höfer and K. Rahner, 10 vols. and Index (Freiburg, 1957–67)
MED	*Middle English Dictionary*, ed. H. Kurath, S. M. Kuhn *et al.* (Ann Arbor, MI, 1952–)
MGH	Monumenta Germaniae Historica
MHG	Middle High German
Microfiche Concordance	A. di Paolo Healey and R. L. Venezky, *A Microfiche Concordance to Old English*, Publ. of the Dictionary of Old English 1 (Toronto, 1980)
NT	the New Testament
ODCC	*The Oxford Dictionary of the Christian Church*, ed. F. L. Cross, 3rd ed. by E. A. Livingstone (Oxford, 1997)
OE	Old English
OED	*The Oxford English Dictionary*, ed. J. A. H. Murray *et al.* (Oxford, 1884–1928; 2nd ed. in 20 vols., prep. by J.A. Simpson and A. S. C. Weiner, Oxford, 1989)
OEG	*Old English Glosses*, ed. Napier
OF	Old French
OHG	Old High German
ON	Old Norse
OS	Old Saxon
OT	the Old Testament
PL	Patrologia Latina, ed. J. P. Migne, 221 vols. (Paris, 1844–64)
RSB	*Regula Sancti Benedicti*, quoted by chapter and verse number from the edition by Hanslik
S	P. H. Sawyer, *Anglo-Saxon Charters: an Annotated List and Bibliography*, Royal

	Historical Society Guides and Handbooks 8 (London, 1968)
SB	K. Brunner, *Altenglische Grammatik. Nach der Angelsächsischen Grammatik von E. Sievers*, 3rd ed. (Tübingen, 1965)
TCBS	*Transactions of the Cambridge Bibliographical Society*
TUEPh	Texte und Untersuchungen zur Englischen Philologie (Munich)
Wulfstan: Life	ed. Lapidge and Winterbottom
WW	T. Wright, *Anglo-Saxon and Old English Vocabularies*, 2 vols., 2nd ed., rev. R. P. Wülcker (London, 1884)

For a list of the sigla of psalters with Old English glosses, see below, pp. 18–21. Roman numerals for the psalms have been used in conformity with CSASE series style.

1

Introduction

1 Inclitus pastor populique rector,
Cuius insignem colimus triumphum,
Nunc Adeluuoldus sine fine letus
Regnat in astris.

2 Qui pater noster fuit et magister
Exhibens sacre documenta uite,
Et Deo semper satagens placere
Corde benigno.

. . .

(1) Æthelwold, the excellent shepherd and ruler of the people, whose glorious triumph we celebrate, now rules joyous in heaven without end. (2) He was our father and teacher, showing us the pattern of the holy life, and always concerned to please God in his kindly heart.[1]

On 10 September, one thousand years ago, this hymn was chanted, perhaps for the first time, at the celebration of Vespers in the Old Minster at Winchester. It had been composed, probably, by Wulfstan the precentor of the Old Minster and one of Bishop Æthelwold's most distinguished pupils, perhaps on the occasion of the first liturgical commemoration of Æthelwold's translation which had taken place on 10 September 996, twelve years after the bishop's death on 1 August 984, and while he will still have been vividly remembered by many of the minster's *familia*.[2]

---

[1] *Analecta Hymnica Medii Aevi*, ed. G. M. Dreves and C. Blume, 55 vols. (Leipzig, 1886–1922) XXIII, 126 (no. 209) and XLIII, 68 (no. 107). The hymn is also printed and translated by Lapidge, *Wulfstan: Life*, ed. Lapidge and Winterbottom, pp. cxiii–cxiv (the above translation is as given there).

[2] On the cult of St Æthelwold, the liturgical pieces pertaining thereto which are still

Wulfstan's hymn is not a unique testimony to Bishop Æthelwold's role as a teacher. No school in Anglo-Saxon England has been praised more warmly by its pupils than the school established by Æthelwold at the Old Minster (his cathedral church) after 963.[3] The distinction of Æthelwold's school emerges from the fact (proudly reported by Wulfstan) that many of his students 'fierent sacerdotes atque abbates et honorabiles episcopi, quidam etiam archiepiscopi, in gente Anglorum.'[4] The exacting standard of tuition provided by the Old Minster school is further revealed in Wulfstan himself, as well as in Ælfric, abbot of Eynsham, two of the foremost scholars and authors in late Anglo-Saxon England. In their writings, Wulfstan and Ælfric represent the two pillars on which Æthelwold's school rested: instruction in Latin and Old English. Instruction in Latin apparently comprised grammar, metrics and the careful study of a wide range of Latin authors, including even Horace, as well as late classical and patristic writers and Aldhelm. Instruction in English seems to have encompassed the translation of Latin texts and attempts to standardize the terminology within certain semantic fields in the vernacular, inasmuch as a number of translation equivalents were taught for certain Latin terms. (Many of these Latin terms stand for key concepts of Christianity, such as *ecclesia* or *superbia*.) Such Old English words were employed with great consistency and to the exclusion of any native synonyms in the works of Ælfric and in some other anonymous works which (on grounds other than vocabulary) can be linked with Winchester.[5]

Æthelwold's own writings which hitherto have been identified also

---

extant, and the role played by Wulfstan in the promotion of Æthelwold's cult, see Lapidge, *Wulfstan: Life*, pp. xxiii–xxvii, xcix–ci and cxii–cxliii. For a table of biographical events in Æthelwold's life as they are related in Wulfstan's *Vita S. Æthelwoldi*, see below, Appendix I.

[3] See below, pp. 262–3 for further testimonies from Æthelwold's pupils, revealing their love for their master and praising the high standard of his tuition.

[4] *Wulfstan: Life*, ch. 31 (p. 48): '[Many of his pupils] became priests, abbots, and notable bishops, some even archbishops, in England' (*ibid.*, p. 49; all translations from Wulfstan's *Vita* are taken from this edition).

[5] Wulfstan's *Vita*, ch. 31 (ed. Lapidge and Winterbottom pp. 47–8), is our primary (unfortunately not very specific) witness for the curriculum in Æthelwold's school. On the subjects and authors presumably taught at Æthelwold's school (and the difficulties involved in establishing that school's curriculum), see Lapidge, *ibid.*, pp. xcii–xcix, and *idem*, 'Æthelwold as Scholar and Teacher', pp. 201–6. On the so-called 'Winchester

attest to his preoccupation with both languages: works in Latin and English are attributable to his pen. Æthelwold's corpus of Latin works is not large: a couple of charters (including the renowned document commemorating the introduction of Benedictines to the New Minster, Winchester, in 964), a letter to a continental duke, perhaps a few prayers, and (most voluminous) the *Regularis concordia*, a monastic consuetudinary produced to regulate daily routine and liturgical observation in the English reformed monasteries.[6] As a Latin author, Æthelwold reveals a pronounced penchant for the hermeneutic style.

Thus far, only one work in Old English has been ascribed to Æthelwold: a translation into Old English prose of the *Regula S. Benedicti*. The translation is attributed to Æthelwold in a late-tenth-century source; that it must have circulated widely, is clear from the number of surviving manuscripts (nine in total, several of these presenting later revisions).[7] The translation is accompanied by a lengthy preface in Old English (preserved in one manuscript), which relates the history of the conversion of the English and the origin and progress of the English Benedictine reform. This text (commonly referred to as 'Edgar's Establishment of Monasteries') closely agrees in vocabulary and wording with the Old English Rule; from this, and from a number of points in its narrative, it is clear that Æthelwold is also the author of this piece of original Old English prose.[8] The translation of the *Regula S. Benedicti* and its English preface reveal Æthelwold as a proficient Latinist as well as a powerful author of Old English prose.

The *Regula S. Benedicti* is not merely a monastic consuetudinary (such as the *Regularis concordia*), meticulously regulating the daily routine in a monastery: it is one of the great texts of western spirituality. Throughout its pages, instructions for organizing the daily life and spiritual guidance are inextricably intertwined; nearly every chapter makes its readers aware that, in following their monastic vocation, they have chosen a distinctive if austere way of life, and at every turn St Benedict stresses that he composed his *Regula* as an elementary daily and spiritual guide for his *dominici scola seruitii* (*RSB*, prol. 45), to help his followers to attain

---

vocabulary', see Hofstetter, *Winchester und Sprachgebrauch*, and *idem*, 'Winchester and the Standardization of Old English Vocabulary'; and see below, pp. 93–113.

[6] On these works, see below, pp. 125–7.

[7] For a list of these manuscripts, see below, p. 227.

[8] On the Rule and its preface, see below, pp. 121–4 and 230–3.

perfection in their pursuit of a life devoted to God. Apart from Æthelwold's translation, no prose version of the *Regula S. Benedicti* in any European vernacular has survived from the early Middle Ages. The Old English Rule is therefore a testimony to Æthelwold's deep spirituality, as it is to the confidence he placed in the resourcefulness of the English language and its potential for being forged into an instrument for conveying complex ideas.

In the light of modern research it is possible that more surviving writings can be attributed to Æthelwold. In the following chapters, we shall examine two massive Old English gloss corpora (of paramount importance for late Old English glossography), and explore how these corpora can be related to Æthelwold and his circle. The glosses in question are the continuous interlinear version of the psalter, preserved in London, BL, Royal 2. B. V, and the interlinear and marginal glosses to Aldhelm's principal work, the prose *De uirginitate*, preserved in Brussels, Bibliothèque Royale, 1650. The Old English gloss in the Royal Psalter is a fresh interlinear translation of the entire psalter, the first to be undertaken in English since the Vespasian psalter gloss (in London, BL, Cotton Vespasian A. i) in the early ninth century. The subsequent influence of the Royal Psalter gloss was very considerable: it was to become the exemplar for one of the two Old English families of psalter glosses, the so-called D-type glosses. The Royal Psalter gloss is of striking quality, revealing the glossator's proficiency in Latin as well as his remarkable competence and resourcefulness in choosing and coining his Old English *interpretamenta*.

By the same token, many of the Aldhelm glosses in Brussels 1650 are distinguished by their aptness and their recherché or learned character. However, although vast, the Brussels gloss corpus does not amount to a continuous interlinear version, and as it is transmitted, it is clearly composite, having attracted accretions in the course of its transmission (to what extent is no longer definable) before being copied into Brussels 1650 in the first half of the eleventh century. In spite of this complex state of transmission, lexical evidence suggests that the core of these Aldhelm glosses originated in the same circle as the Royal Psalter gloss, and, on grounds of lexical evidence again, the psalter and the Aldhelm glosses appear to be linked to the Old English Rule, composed by Æthelwold.

Acceptance of a common origin of the three works would dramatically broaden our textual base for evaluating the reputation which Æthelwold's scholarship and teaching enjoyed in the later tenth and in the eleventh century. Various evidence such as the mid-tenth-century date of Royal 2. B. V (which is itself a copy of the original psalter gloss) points to an origin of all three works not much later than (say) 950; in other words, it points to the period of prolonged study which Æthelwold spent (together with Dunstan) at Glastonbury *c.* 939–*c.* 954, and on which we are informed, again, by Æthelwold's biographer Wulfstan.[9] In the Royal Psalter, the Aldhelm glosses and the Rule we would therefore have tangible and precious evidence that the seeds of the intellectual renaissance in late Anglo-Saxon England, which is marked by the Benedictine reform, were being sown many years before the actual ecclesiastical reforms got under way, and many years before close contacts with continental reformed monasteries such as Fleury or Corbie were established. Furthermore, the Royal Psalter, the Aldhelm glosses and the Rule attest that the literary culture nurtured by the Benedictine reform, even in its nascent stage, based itself decisively on the pivotal role of the vernacular and on a fervent enthusiasm for the hermeneutic style in Latin.

In the first five of the following chapters we shall focus our attention on the place taken by the Royal Psalter and the Brussels glosses to the prose *De uirginitate* in the textual history of Old English psalter glosses and Aldhelm glosses respectively; we shall further try to form some notion of how the glossator, or glossators, did their work, what their aims were and how they strove to achieve these aims; and we shall scrutinize the lexical evidence which can be found to point to a common origin of the Old English Rule and the glosses. We shall then turn our attention to the question of what evidence, other than philological, can be adduced to substantiate the claim that the three texts originated in the same circle, evidence, that is, of a historical, art historical, palaeographical and liturgical nature. In the concluding chapter we shall aim to trace possible reflexes of the social and intellectual world in which the three texts had their origin by analysing some of the loanwords or loan formations employed in these texts.

[9] See *Vita*, ch. 9 (ed. Lapidge and Winterbottom, pp. 14–16).

2

Psalters and psalter glosses in Anglo-Saxon England

Owing to its paramount importance in the liturgy of the Christian Church, the transmission of the psalter has always been distinct from the transmission of other books of the Old Testament (OT). Such a distinction is most evident in the number of surviving manuscripts. In his study of the transmission of the OT (apart from the psalter) in Anglo-Saxon England, Richard Marsden has listed thirteen Bibles or part-Bibles containing OT books, written or owned in pre-Conquest England, nine of these being fragments, often no more than single folios (which leaves us without a means of estimating the amount of text originally contained in the manuscripts in question). In addition, individual OT books (or extracts from them) have been preserved in three more non-biblical manuscripts.[1]

By contrast, we still have thirty-seven psalter manuscripts from Anglo-Saxon England. Of these, eight are minor fragments, twenty-nine complete (or almost complete) psalters; twenty-seven of the twenty-nine complete psalters were arguably used for liturgical purposes. A liturgical use is traditionally assumed if a manuscript, in addition to the psalter, contains the ten canticles from the Old and the New Testament (to be sung at Lauds, Vespers and Compline in the monastic and secular Office), and (from the tenth century onwards) the *Gloria in excelsis*, the *Credo in Deum patrem* (or 'Apostles' Creed') and the *Quicumque uult* (or 'Athanasian Creed'), texts also chanted in the liturgy. The employment of large or

---

[1] See Marsden, *Text of the Old Testament*, pp. 2–3 and 40–8; cf. also *idem*, 'The Old Testament in Late Anglo-Saxon England', pp. 101–6 and 123–4, and Gneuss, 'Liturgical Books', p. 122.

decorated initials for subdividing the 150 psalms is a further pointer to the liturgical use of a manuscript.[2]

THE BOOKS OF THE OLD TESTAMENT

The books of the OT were carefully read (as was the psalter) in private study and classroom instruction. In the case of the Pentateuch we are now in a position to assess the astonishing heights which such instruction achieved in one particular classroom, namely that of Archbishop Theodore and Abbot Hadrian at Canterbury from 669 onwards (see below). In the liturgy, however, the OT books figure much less prominently than the psalter. On certain days, lessons from the OT were (and are) prescribed for the first reading, or 'epistle', in the mass, but on most days, these lessons are taken from the epistles of the NT (whence their name).[3] In the Divine Office, readings from OT books have their place in Nocturns where they were instituted by St Benedict himself:

Codices autem legantur in uigiliis diuinae auctoritatis tam ueteris testamenti quam noui; sed et expositiones earum, quae a nominatis et orthodoxis catholicis patribus factae sunt.[4]

Concerning private reading or reading aloud to the monastic community

---

[2] See Gneuss, 'Liturgical Books', pp. 114–16, for such indications of liturgical use in a psalter manuscript, and for a list of the psalter manuscripts with canticles, as well as references to those manuscripts and fragments for which a liturgical use cannot be established. For a list of psalters from Anglo-Saxon England and description of their contents, see also Pulsiano, 'Psalters', pp. 61–84. For the subdivision of psalms for use in monastic and secular Office, see also Sisam, *Salisbury Psalter*, pp. 4–5, and see below, pp. 226–7 and 272; for the tenth-century liturgical pieces, see below, pp. 89, 273–4 and 276.

[3] See Harper, *Forms and Orders*, pp. 116–17, Hughes, *Medieval Manuscripts for Mass and Office*, p. 85, and Gneuss, 'Liturgical Books', pp. 105–6 and 110.

[4] *RSB* 9.8. All quotations from *RSB* are (by ch. and verse number) from *Benedicti Regula*, ed. Hanslik. English translations are from *RB 1980*, ed. Fry *et al.*: 'Besides the inspired books of the Old and New Testaments, the works read at Vigils should include explanations of Scripture by reputable and orthodox catholic Fathers.' (p. 205). Note that *uigiliae* ('Vigils') is Benedict's term for the Night Office, called 'Nocturns' or 'Matins' in the medieval liturgy. At various other points Benedict refers to OT lessons at Nocturns; cf., for example, *RSB* 10.2, 11.2, 11.5 and 11.7. For the readings (in general) pertaining to the secular and monastic Night Office and the books needed for such purposes, see Gneuss, 'Liturgical Books', pp. 120–7, and Hughes, *Medieval Manuscripts for Mass and Office*, pp. 60–2.

during meals or at other times,[5] it is noteworthy that Benedict twice expressly encourages the private study of psalms,[6] but that he straightforwardly forbids reading passages from the Heptateuch or the Books of Kings after Vespers or the evening meal. It is worthwhile quoting St Benedict's verdict on these OT books in full, together with Bishop Æthelwold's translation made approximately 400 years later, since a comparison of both passages highlights Æthelwold's penchant for interpretative translation by adding brief explanatory remarks to the original text. By the same token, Æthelwold's translation may serve to highlight the change in the intellectual climate from a Canterbury classroom in the 670s to a Winchester classroom in the 960s. The text of the *Regula* is as follows:

[legat] non autem eptaticum aut regum, quia infirmis intellectibus non erit utile illa hora hanc scripturam audire; aliis uero horis legantur.[7]

This is translated by Æthelwold as follows:

Ne ræde him mon nauðer ne Moyses boc, ne Regum, forðæm þæm unandgytfullum þæt gastlice an[d]gyt is earfoþe to understanden[n]e butan haligra manna trahtnunge; ræde hy mon þeah oþrum tidum on cirican, þonne hit togebyrige.[8]

In other words, Bishop Æthelwold has Benedict say that certain books of the OT should *only* be read during Nocturns, where (according to *RSB* 9.8) such dangerous lessons are to be followed by readings from orthodox catholic Fathers, expounding the allegorical sense of the OT

---

[5] *RSB* provides for extensive periods of study and private reading (for those capable of such an undertaking), as well as enjoining the reading of sacred or edifying texts to the community by a *lector* during meals or at other times; cf., for instance, chs. 38, 48.13–18, or 73.2–6.

[6] Cf. *RSB* 8.3 and 48.13.

[7] *RSB* 42.4; 'but not the Heptateuch or the Books of Kings, because it will not be good for those of weak understanding to hear these writings at that hour; they should be read at other times'. (*RB 1980*, p. 243).

[8] BR 66.18–67.2; quotations from the Old English Rule are (by page and line) from *Benediktinerregel*, ed. Schröer. In a few instances where (in my view) the reading printed by Schröer is erroneous I have provided an emendation, indicated by square brackets. Modern English translations are my own. 'One shall not read to them [*scil.* the brethren] either the book of Moses or the Books of Kings, because for the simple-minded [or: ignorant] the spiritual sense is difficult to understand without an exposition by holy men. These books shall be read, however, at other times, in divine service, where they pertain.'

passages.[9] In fact, Benedict says nothing of the sort; on the contrary, it is even possible that, at one point in his *Regula*, he expressly encourages private reading of the OT. In the passage in question, he prescribes that, during Lent, the monks should receive *singulos codices de bibliotheca* which they should diligently peruse (cf. *RSB* 48.15). It is possible – but not certain – that by *bibliotheca* he refers to the complete Bible, its books (or groups of books such as the Pentateuch) bound in separate volumes (*singuli codices*).[10]

If, for his interpretative translation of *RSB* 42.4, Æthelwold consulted the commentary on the *Regula* by Smaragdus of Saint-Mihiel (as he occasionally did for his Old English version),[11] he chose to ignore important points in Smaragdus's lengthy exposition of this passage.[12] In Smaragdus, he would have found a remark to the effect that OT books required allegorical interpretations. But he would have found there as well that Smaragdus regarded the ban on the Heptateuch or the Books of Kings as valid only for *infirmis intellectibus*, and that, in his view, Benedict had not forbidden the serious, sober-minded and intelligent monks (who were in a position to discern the allegorical meanings and prefigurations hidden away in the OT narrative) to read those books, or indeed any other book of the Bible at any time they wished to read them:

---

[9] In this connection it is probably significant that the passage concerning the lessons from the OT at Nocturns (*RSB* 9.8, quoted above) is translated verbatim by Æthelwold: 'Æt þam uhtsange ræde man þære godcundan lare bec, ægðer ge of þære ealdan cyðnesse ge of þære niwan, and eac swa þa haligan trahtas [þe] fram namcuþum fæderum and rihtgelyfedum geworhte synt.' (BR 33.17–21). Here, only the authority of Benedict's *expositiones* is emphasized by an added adjective: *þa haligan trahtas*.

[10] See A. Mundó, 'Bibliotheca, Bible et lecture de carême d'après S. Benoît', *Revue Bénédictine* 60 (1950), 65–92. But the wording is ambiguous. Benedict may well have referred to individual books (*codices*) held in the monastery's library (*bibliotheca*); see the remarks (with further references) by de Vogüé, *Règle de Saint Benôit*, ed. Vogüé and Neufville II, 602–3, n. 15. It may be noteworthy in respect of Æthelwold's understanding of the passage in question that the loanword *biblioðeca* (rarely attested in Old English) once refers unambiguously to the Bible; cf. Gneuss, 'Liturgical Books', p. 122. It may further be noteworthy that when translating the passage, Æthelwold chose to retain the ambiguous *bibliotheca* (*sume boc of þære bibliothecan*, BR 74.12–13).

[11] See Gretsch, *Regula*, pp. 257–62, and *idem*, 'Æthelwold's Translation', pp. 144–6; and see below, pp. 255–9.

[12] Cf. *Smaragdi Abbatis Expositio in Regulam S. Benedicti*, ed. Spannagel and Engelbert, pp. 262–3.

Sinceris autem, sanis et acutis intellectibus nullo tempore uetatur Eptaticum aut Regum uel quamcumque historiam diuinarum legere scripturarum, quia possunt in eis figuras et sensus dinoscere et exemplum salutis ab illis legendo recipere.[13]

Similarly, Æthelwold's statement that those OT books were to be read at their proper time in divine service (*on cirican, þonne hit togebyrige*) could have been lifted from Smaragdus's commentary; but if so, Æthelwold saw no occasion to refer in his translation to Smaragdus's ensuing remark, that those books should not only be read *in ecclesia*, but that they should be studied by *every* monk at school ('aut unusquisque pro legendi doctrina debet eos legere in scola').[14]

Æthelwold saw fit on a second occasion to stress the importance of allegorical exegesis of the Bible: in the tract which goes by the name 'Edgar's Establishment of Monasteries', and which was manifestly composed by Æthelwold to serve as a preface to his translation of the *Regula*, he, somewhat unexpectedly in the context, draws attention to the various levels of biblical exegesis:

þeah þa scearpþanclan witan þe þone twydæledan wisdom hlutorlice tocnawaþ – þæt is andweardra þinga 7 gastlicre wisdom – 7 þara ægþer eft on þrim todalum gelyfedlice wunaþ – þisse engliscan geþeodnesse ne behofien . . .[15]

Bishop Æthelwold's verdict on the OT books and his emphasis on the necessity of allegorical exegesis will recall Ælfric's verbose description of the embarrassment he felt when translating the book of Genesis, and of the difficulties he saw involved in such an undertaking. Here, the pupil has manifestly and thoroughly been imbued with the master's teaching. The master's reason for banning certain OT books from extra-liturgical reading, succinctly couched in terms of paronomasia (*forðæm þæm unandgytfullan þæt gastlice andgyt is earfoþe to understandenne*), recurs as a sort of leitmotif in the pupil's 'Preface to Genesis', as will become clear from the following (sample) quotations:

---

[13] *Ibid.*, p. 262. [14] *Ibid.*, p. 263.

[15] 'Although keen-witted scholars who understand clearly the two-fold wisdom – that is, the wisdom of things actual and spiritual – and each of those again admittedly consists of three divisions – do not require this English translation . . .'; printed *CS*, p. 151. Translations from the Preface are as given there. For the Preface itself, see below, pp. 121–4 and 230–3.

ac hi [*scil.* ða ungelæredan preostas] ne cunnon swa þeah þæt gastlice andgit þærto [*scil.* þære ealdan æ], 7 hu seo ealde æ wæs getacnung toweardra þinga.[16]

þonne þincþ þam ungelæredum þæt eall þæt andgit beo belocen on þære anfealdan gerecednisse, ac hit ys swiþe feor þam.[17]

Be ðisum lytlan man mæg understandan, hu deop seo boc is on gastlicum andgyte, ðeah ðe heo mid leohtum wordum awriten sy.[18]

It is interesting to remark that the expression *þæt gastlice andgit*, signifying allegorical biblical exegesis, and so constantly reiterated by Ælfric, here and throughout his writings, seems to have been coined by Æthelwold himself (see below, pp. 233 and 378).

By contrast, there is not much exegesis concerning *þæt gastlice andgit* to be found in the Canterbury biblical commentaries on the Pentateuch. From their first-hand knowledge of the Byzantine East, Archbishop Theodore and Abbot Hadrian were able to expound to their students the literal meaning of the sacred texts. Such teaching embraced the realia of OT life, such as the flora, fauna and topography of the Holy Land, as well as information about biblical weights or measures or remarks on illnesses and their cures. The commentaries are further distinctive by their concern with Greek philosophy and rhetoric and with what we would now call philological exegesis, comprising explanations of the etymology of words, or attempts to elucidate the meanings of words through their context, as well as assessments of the relative merits of textual variants.[19]

Even from these cursory remarks the utterly different attitude towards the OT, prevalent in the two most important schools in Anglo-Saxon England, will have become clear. There can be no doubt that, in spite of his ban on extra-liturgical, unguided reading of the OT, Bishop Æthelwold did, in fact, expound the OT at his school (or had it expounded there by his teachers) to his more mature and his *andgitfullran* students.

---

[16] Ælfric, 'Preface to Genesis', ed. Crawford, p. 77.25–7. 'But the ignorant priests know nothing about the spiritual sense of the OT, and how the OT signified future events'.

[17] *Ibid.*, p. 77.43–5. 'Then the uneducated people believe that the whole sense of the text is encompassed within the simple narrative, but this is far from true.'

[18] *Ibid.*, pp. 78.72–79.1. 'These few examples may teach one, how profound the spiritual sense in this book is, even though it may be written in words which are easy to understand.'

[19] For the nature of the Canterbury commentaries, see Lapidge, *Biblical Commentaries*, ed. Bischoff and Lapidge, pp. 243–74, and the texts of the commentaries themselves. For the Antiochene background and orientation of the exegetical method employed in the commentaries, see *ibid.*, pp. 14–25.

Ælfric's 'Preface to Genesis' bears unambiguous testimony to this (as does his 'Treatise on the Old and New Testament').[20] Such exposition, however, will have been almost exclusively allegorical and typological in explaining the OT as a prefiguration of events in the NT. This much is clear again from Ælfric's 'Preface' and the 'Treatise'.[21] But such a preponderance of allegorical exposition was only to be expected in a tenth-century Anglo-Saxon school. What has been called 'the intellectual highpoint of Anglo-Saxon literary culture',[22] the Canterbury school of biblical scholarship in the late seventh century, was made possible only by extraordinarily fortunate historical coincidences, and, by its very nature, could not be upheld and continued even within the generation of Theodore's and Hadrian's students. Even if some of these students had a sound knowledge of Greek (as Bede asserts),[23] they would have lacked their masters' familiarity with the civilization of the Byzantine East. Apart from this, in a culture intellectually dominated by the Latin West, there would have been little incentive to pass on the knowledge of Greek, and, given the universal preponderance of an allegorical interpretation of the OT in the Latin West, Anglo-Saxon scholars would simply have lacked the books and the intellectual stimulus necessary for continuing Theodore's and Hadrian's form of literal biblical exegesis.

Nonetheless, Æthelwold's and Ælfric's concern with the typological interpretation of the OT in order to avert any threat to orthodox Christian doctrine, which might follow from a literal reading, seems remarkable. We shall have occasion to return to the overall importance which allegorical exegesis had in Bishop Æthelwold's school, in the context of the Royal Psalter. For the moment, one wonders whether the extreme scarcity of Bibles and part-Bibles, from the period of the Benedictine reform onwards (only four out of thirteen surviving manuscripts date from the second half of the tenth to the mid-eleventh century, as opposed to nine, dated s. vi–viii/ix),[24] might somehow be related to the strong aversion to unguided OT reading,

---

[20] The 'Treatise' is printed by Crawford, pp. 15–75.

[21] For the role of allegorical and typological exegesis in the 'Preface', see, for example, the passages quoted above, p. 11; for relevant passages from the 'Treatise', see Crawford's edition, pp. 23–4, 32 or 36.

[22] Lapidge, *Biblical Commentaries*, ed. Bischoff and Lapidge, p. 274.

[23] See *HE* IV.2 (ed. Colgrave and Mynors, p. 334).

[24] See Marsden, *Text of the Old Testament*, pp. 40–1.

discernible in the most influential school in late Anglo-Saxon England. In this connection it may be relevant to mention that on the testimony of the anonymous author of the *Vita S. Ceolfridi*, Abbot Ceolfrith (689–716) expressly aimed to encourage private study of either of the Testaments by the inmates of Wearmouth and Jarrow when he commissioned three pandects, or complete Bibles (the 'Codex Amiatinus' among them),[25] to be produced in his scriptorium. According to his biographer, Ceolfrith gave orders that one each of these pandects should be placed in the two monastery churches so that any monk who wished to read a ch. of either Testament should be in a position to do so without difficulty.[26]

However, against the hypothesis of potential Æthelwoldian influence in discouraging the production of copies of the OT on a significant scale, one must weigh the fact that (for whatever reasons), Bibles or part-Bibles (containing books of the OT) of the Latin Vulgate do not seem to have survived in substantial numbers from anywhere in early medieval Europe.[27] Still, the scarcity of Bible manuscripts from post-reform Anglo-Saxon England is striking, especially in view of the fact that a far greater number of witnesses is still extant from the period prior to the ninth century.

THE PSALTER

But the psalter was different. Whatever the attitude towards other OT books may have been, or whatever reasons there were to account for the scarcity of manuscript witnesses, the psalms had always had their place in

---

[25] Cf. also below, p. 23.

[26] 'tres Pandectes faceret describi, quorum duo per totidem sua monasteria posuit in aecclesiis, ut cunctis qui aliquod capitulum de utrolibet Testamento legere uoluissent, in promtu esset inuenire quod cuperent.' *Vita S. Ceolfridi*, ch. 20, printed in *Venerabilis Baedae Opera Historica*, ed. C. Plummer, 2 vols. (Oxford, 1896) I, 388–404, at 395; translation in *EHD*, pp. 758–70 (no. 155). For the production of the Wearmouth–Jarrow pandects, see most recently Marsden, *Text of the Old Testament*, pp. 76–106.

[27] See Fischer, 'Bibelausgaben des frühen Mittelalters', in his *Lateinische Bibelhandschriften*, pp. 35–100, esp. at 97–100. For the paucity of early manuscripts of the Vulgate in comparison with the far greater number of early Septuagint manuscripts which have survived, see Lapidge, *Biblical Commentaries*, ed. Bischoff and Lapidge, pp. 198–9 and n. 29 (with further references). For the scarcity of Latin Bibles from early medieval Ireland, see McNamara, 'The Text of the Latin Bible in the Early Irish Church', pp. 33–4.

the sung parts of the mass, and above all, the chant of psalms was at the core of the Divine Office.[28] The pivotal role which the psalms played in monastic life shows clearly in the vast number of surviving manuscripts of the psalter, from Anglo-Saxon England as from elsewhere in medieval Europe. Benedict had given most explicit instructions (in chs. 9–18 of the *Regula*) concerning the distribution of the psalms of the entire psalter over the canonical hours during the week. Although he was not dogmatic about the arrangement of the psalms for the individual days and hours which he had adopted in his *Regula*, he was utterly uncompromising concerning his injunction that the full psalter should be chanted once a week:

Hoc praecipue commonentes, ut, si cui forte haec distributio psalmorum displicuerit, ordinet, si melius aliter iudicauerit, dum omnimodis id adtendat, ut omni ebdomada psalterium ex integro numero centum quinquaginta psalmorum psallatur et dominico die semper a caput reprendatur ad uigilias, quia nimis inertem deuotionis suae seruitium ostendunt monachi, qui minus a psalterio cum canticis consuetudinariis per septimanae circulum psallunt.[29]

It is in accordance with this central place taken by the psalter in the Divine Office that the entire 150 psalms had to be memorized by the monks and nuns. On two occasions (*RSB* 8.3 and 48.13), Benedict expressly enjoins the memorizing and study of psalms on those who were in need of it, during the periods he had assigned to private study. Such emphasis on psalmody (strong as it had been ever since the foundation of the Benedictine Order) as one of the foremost duties of a monk or nun, was even increased to a considerable degree in the wake of the tenth-century monastic reforms. For Anglo-Saxon England our primary witness to this increased emphasis on psalmody is the *Regularis concordia*, a monastic consuetudinary drafted by Bishop Æthelwold *c*. 973 to establish uniformity in liturgical practice in the English reformed monasteries, in

---

[28] For a brief introduction to the chant of psalms in mass and Office, see Harper, *Forms and Orders*, pp. 69–72; for their use in the Office, see also the introductory remarks by Hughes, *Medieval Manuscripts for Mass and Office*, pp. 50–1.

[29] *RSB* 18.22–4. 'Above all else we urge that if anyone finds this distribution of the psalms unsatisfactory, he should arrange whatever he judges better, provided that the full complement of one hundred and fifty psalms is by all means carefully maintained every week, and that the series begins anew each Sunday at Vigils. For monks who in a week's time say less than the full psalter with the customary canticles betray extreme indolence and lack of devotion in their service' (*RSB 1980*, p. 215).

keeping with the usage of the most distinguished continental monasteries such as Fleury, Corbie or Ghent.[30] In the *Regularis concordia* the additional chant of psalms features prominently among the numerous and substantial liturgical accretions to the established Benedictine *cursus*. Thus, five psalms for the dead had to be recited every day after the Chapter Office (ch. 25). The prayers for the king, the queen and the benefactors of the house (one of the hallmarks of the *Concordia*, to be said daily after each of the Hours, except Prime, and after mass) were to be accompanied by the chant of two psalms varying at each performance (see, for instance, chs. 20, 24 and 25). Every night, before Nocturns, the seven Penitential psalms (pss. VI, XXXI, XXXVII, L, CI, CXXIX and CXLII) and the fifteen Gradual psalms (pss. CXIX–CXXXIII) had to be sung; the Penitential psalms were to be repeated after Prime (cf. chs. 16, 17 and 19). During the three days before Easter, the entire psalter had to be recited every day after Prime, a stipulation which appears to be peculiar to the *Regularis concordia*.[31] Psalms or the entire psalter had to be recited if one of the brethren had died (ch. 67); and so on.[32] In addition to such accretions to

[30] The standard edition (Latin text and facing English translation) is by Symons, *Regularis Concordia* (London, 1953). I quote from this edition by reference to the sub-ch. numbers given there. The more recent edition (1984), *Regularis Concordia*, ed. Symons and Spath, has not superseded the earlier one, *inter alia* because it follows the less reliable of the two manuscripts of the *Regularis concordia*, while, at the same time, being heavily dependent on the earlier edition by Symons. (See Kornexl, *Die 'Regularis Concordia' und ihre altenglische Interlinearversion*, p. clxvi, for a brief evaluation of the 1984 edition, and *ibid.*, pp. cii–cxi, for the textual idiosyncrasies in London, BL Cotton Faustina B. iii, the base for this edition.) A statement to the effect that uniformity in liturgical practice was aimed at by the *Concordia* is found, for instance, in ch. 4, where it is said that King Edgar 'urged all to be of one mind as regards monastic usage' (*concordes aequali consuetudinis usu*, p. 3). For Æthelwold as author and compiler of the *Regularis concordia*, see most recently Lapidge, *Wulfstan: Life*, pp. lviii–lx, and Kornexl, *Die 'Regularis Concordia' und ihre altenglische Interlinearversion*, pp. xxxi–l. For the date of the *Concordia*, see Symons, 'History and Derivation', pp. 40–2, where the latest views of that expert on the text are stated. For the pervasive importance of the monastic customs of Fleury on the compilation of the *Concordia*, see Lapidge, 'Æthelwold as Scholar and Teacher', p. 193, and *idem*, *Wulfstan: Life*, pp. lix–lx (and the references given there).

[31] Cf. *Regularis Concordia*, ed. Symons, ch. 40, and see Symons's remark *ibid.*, p. 38, n. 13.

[32] For a representation of the monastic time-table, as it can be extracted from the information given in the *Concordia* and set out in tabular form, see Knowles, *Monastic Order*, Appendix xviii, pp. 714–15 (the tables are also printed by Symons, *Regularis Concordia*, pp. xliii–xliv; see also *ibid.*, pp. xxxi–xxxii). See now also M. Berry, 'What

the communal liturgy, monks and nuns are exhorted by the *Regularis concordia* to recite the psalter privately, while performing the manual labour assigned to them (ch. 25).

It is difficult to estimate to what extent the stipulations of the *Regularis concordia*, which resulted in an immensely augmented monastic liturgy, were enacted in the daily performance of the mass and the Divine Office at Æthelwold's Winchester and other reformed monasteries. This difficulty arises because so very few liturgical manuscripts from the late tenth century have survived.[33] However, for our purposes it is sufficient to note that the stipulations of the *Concordia* show clearly and explicitly that Bishop Æthelwold and his colleagues had in mind (in keeping with continental practice) an elaboration of the mass and the Divine Office by which *inter alia* the chant of psalms was enormously increased.[34] Furthermore, some interesting pieces of first-hand evidence for the actual performance by Æthelwold's own monks of such accretions to the established Benedictine *cursus* have come to light recently. Such evidence is in the form of two supplementary Offices which Æthelwold prescribed for additional and private recitation by his monks at the Old Minster, and which were identified in Anglo-Saxon manuscripts latterly. The Offices in question are an Office for the Virgin and an Office for All Saints and (in accordance with the established canonical hours) both Offices stipulate the chant of a number of psalms.[35]

There was yet a further factor, which added to the dominant role played by the psalter in the life of a monk. For those monks who were not native speakers of Latin, memorizing the psalms would have gone hand in hand with learning the language in which they were transmitted. Therefore the psalter was of primary importance in acquiring a knowledge of

the Saxon Monks Sang. Music in Winchester in the Late Tenth Century', in *Bishop Æthelwold*, ed. Yorke, pp. 149–60, esp. 150–2.

[33] For a survey of what meagre information concerning liturgical performance in late-tenth-century Winchester can be gleaned from the few surviving liturgical manuscripts, see Lapidge, *Wulfstan: Life*, pp. lx–lxvii.

[34] See also below, pp. 270–3, for the pivotal role played by the psalter in the elaborate liturgy which characterizes the tenth-century Benedictine reform, and the bearing this may have had on the Royal Psalter gloss.

[35] See Lapidge, *Wulfstan: Life*, pp. lxviii–lxxvii, for an edition and discussion of the Offices in question. See also Gneuss, *Hymnar und Hymnen*, pp. 109–13, for such additional Offices in eleventh-century manuscripts and an evaluation of their evidence for the performance of the liturgy.

Latin – hair-raising as such an approach to language aquisition might appear to modern language teachers in view of the difficult and often arcane language of the psalms.[36] Both these factors, the paramount importance of the psalms in the liturgy and the perduring prominence of the psalter as a textbook for learning Latin, reasonably account for the vast amount of continuous interlinear glossing in psalter manuscripts which must have been going on in Anglo-Saxon England. However, as we shall see in due course, the Old English interlinear versions (in their original form, not in the sometimes garbled and deficient later copies) could exceed by far the purposes of elementary language teaching, and might well have served as a tool for mature students in their scrutiny of the language and the meaning of the psalms.[37] Ample evidence of such glossing activity is still available in the ten psalters with interlinear Old English glosses which have survived from the pre-Conquest period. It is to these psalters from Anglo-Saxon England that we may now turn.

PSALTERS WITH OLD ENGLISH GLOSSES

The manuscripts

Of the twenty-nine psalters of Anglo-Saxon origin or provenance and written before 1100, the ten manuscripts listed below are provided with a continuous interlinear gloss in Old English. The list printed here is intended simply for convenient reference in the following discussion of the place taken by the Royal Psalter in the textual history of the Old English psalter glosses. In the case of a psalter being treated more specifically in this connection, relevant bibliographical references for the psalter in question will be given in their appropriate place. For full

---

[36] For the use of the psalter as a Latin primer, see, for example, P. Riché, *Les écoles et l'enseignement dans l'Occident de la fin du v*[e] *siècle au milieu du xi*[e] *siècle* (Paris, 1979), pp. 227–8. In fact, the psalter was in universal use throughout the Middle Ages for teaching oblates and young nobles how to read, and not only in (originally) Latin-speaking parts of Europe; see *ibid.*, pp. 223–4. See further P. Riché, 'Le Livre Psautier, livre de lecture élémentaire d'après les vies des saints mérovingiens', *Études Mérovingiennes. Actes des Journées de Poitiers 1952* (Paris, 1953), pp. 253–6, and B. Bischoff, 'Elementarunterricht und Probationes Pennae in der ersten Hälfte des Mittelalters', in his *Mittelalterliche Studien* I, 74–8, at 75–6.

[37] For the use of continuous interlinear glosses for teaching at elementary as well as at advanced levels, see Gneuss, 'Language Contact', pp. 146–8.

descriptions of the manuscripts with Old English glosses, see Ker, *Catalogue*.[38] At the head of each of the following entries, I give the siglum (a capital letter) and the name by which the psalter in question is traditionally referred to in scholarly literature. Indications of the date and origin are usually taken from Gneuss, 'Handlist'. References are always to the (presumed) origin of a manuscript; no specification concerning later provenance is given. Unless otherwise stated, the date refers to Latin text and Old English gloss. I provide in each case the pertinent numbers from Ker, *Catalogue* and Gneuss, 'Handlist'. An asterisk indicates that the Latin text is a *Psalterium Romanum*; unmarked manuscripts contain the *Psalterium Gallicanum* (on both versions see below).

*A   Vespasian Psalter. London, British Library, Cotton Vespasian A. i; s. viii $^{2/4}$; OE gloss s. ix; probably Canterbury (St Augustine's); Ker, no. 203; Gneuss, no. 381. Facsimile: *Vespasian Psalter*, ed. Wright; edition: *Vespasian Psalter*, ed. Kuhn.

*B   Junius Psalter. Oxford, Bodleian Library, Junius 27; s. x^1 (probably in the 920s); Winchester (?); Ker, no. 335; Gneuss, no. 641. Edition: *Junius Psalter*, ed. Brenner.

*C   Cambridge Psalter. Cambridge, University Library, Ff. 1. 23; *c.* 1000; Ramsey (?); Ker, no. 13; Gneuss, no. 4. Edition: *Cambridger Psalter*, ed. Wildhagen.

*D   Royal Psalter or Regius Psalter. London, British Library, Royal 2. B. V; s. x^{med}; Ker, no. 249; Gneuss, no. 451. Edition: *Regius Psalter*, ed. Roeder.

F   Stowe Psalter or Spelman Psalter. London, British Library, Stowe 2; s. xi^{med} or s. xi$^{3/4}$; southwest England, probably Winchester (New Minster); Ker, no. 271; Gneuss, no. 499. Edition: *The Stowe Psalter*, ed. A. Kimmens (Toronto, 1979).[39]

---

[38] For complete inventories of psalter manuscripts surviving from Anglo-Saxon England, see Gneuss, 'Liturgical Books', pp. 115–16, and Pulsiano, 'Psalters', pp. 61–84 (with brief descriptions of the manuscripts and some bibliographical references).

[39] Two fragments (binding strips) seem to be closely related to the Stowe Psalter: Cambridge, Pembroke College 312 C, nos. 1 and 2 (with Haarlem Stadsbibliotheek, 188 F. 53); 'Psalter N'; s. xi^{med}; south (?) England; Ker, no. 79 (and Ker, *Supplement*, p. 122); Gneuss, no. 141. Edition: K. Dietz, 'Die altenglischen Psalterglossen der Hs. Cambridge, Pembroke College 312', *Anglia* 86 (1968), 273–9, and (for Haarlem) R. Derolez, 'A New Psalter Fragment with Old English Glosses', *English Studies* 53 (1972), 401–8. For the close relation with the Stowe Psalter, see *Salisbury*

G   Vitellius Psalter. London, British Library, Cotton Vitellius E. xviii; s. xi^{med}; Winchester (New Minster or Old Minster?); Ker, no. 224; Gneuss, no. 407. Edition: *The Vitellius Psalter, Edited from British Museum MS Cotton Vitellius E. xviii*, ed. J. L. Rosier (Ithaca, NY, 1962).

H   Tiberius Psalter. London, British Library, Cotton Tiberius C. vi; s. xi^{med} or s. xi$^{3/4}$; Winchester (Old Minster?); Ker, no. 199; Gneuss, no. 378. Edition: *The Tiberius Psalter, Edited from British Museum MS Cotton Tiberius C. vi*, ed. A. P. Campbell (Ottawa, 1974).

I   Lambeth Psalter. London, Lambeth Palace Library 427; s. xi^1; southwest England (Winchester?); Ker, no. 280; Gneuss, no. 517. Edition: *Lambeth-Psalter*, ed. Lindelöf.

J   Arundel Psalter. London, British Library, Arundel 60; s. xi^2; Winchester (New Minster?); Ker, no. 134; Gneuss, no. 304; Edition: *Der altenglische Arundel-Psalter. Eine Interlinearversion in der Handschrift Arundel 60 des Britischen Museums*, ed. G. Oess (Heidelberg, 1910).

K   Salisbury Psalter. Salisbury, Cathedral Library, 150; s. x^2 (969 × 978); OE gloss s. xi/xii; southwest England (Shaftesbury?); Ker, no. 379; Gneuss, no. 740. Edition: *Salisbury Psalter*, ed. Sisam and Sisam.

In addition to these ten psalters with continuous interlinear glosses, substantial portions of the following psalter have been glossed in Old English:

*L   Bosworth Psalter. London, British Library, Add. 37517; s. x$^{3/4}$; OE gloss s. xi^{in}; Canterbury (Christ Church?); Ker, no. 129; Gneuss,

---

Psalter, ed. Sisam and Sisam, p. 67, n. 1 (but cf. Derolez, 'Psalter Fragment', who opts for G as N's closest relative). Recently, a further glossed psalter fragment has come to light in Thuringia, containing pss. VI.9–VII.9 on the recto and verso of one folio (Schlossmuseum Sondershausen, Br. 1). The absurdly inadequate edition of this fragment by H. Pilch, 'The Sondershäuser Psalter: a Newly Discovered Old English Interlinear Gloss', in *Germanic Studies in Honor of Anatoly Libermann*, ed. K. G. Goblirsch *et al.* [= *NOWELE* 31–2] (Odense, 1997), pp. 313–23, has now been superseded by the edition and discussion by H. Gneuss, 'A Newly-Found Fragment of an Anglo-Saxon Psalter', *ASE* 27 (1998), pp. 273–87. Gneuss identified the Sondershausen leaf as a further fragment from the manuscript from which the Pembroke and Haarlem strips have survived. See *ibid.*, pp. 278–81, for the textual relationships with other psalters.

no. 291. Edition: Lindelöf, 'Die altenglischen Glossen im Bosworth-Psalter'. The following psalms (or psalm verses) are provided with a continuous Old English gloss: XL.5, L.6–21, LIII, LXIII, LXVI, LXVIII–LXX, LXXXV, CI, CXVIII–CXXXIII, CXXXIX.2 and 9, CXL.1–4 and CXLII.

One further psalter contains a substantial amount of Old English glosses (approximately 700), dispersed throughout its text:

*M Blickling Psalter or Blickling Glosses. New York, Pierpont Morgan Library, 776; s. viii^med; Ker, no. 287; Gneuss, no. 862. Two layers of Old English glosses can be distinguished: first, twenty-one glosses in the Mercian dialect, dated (by Ker) to the ninth century, and second, 653 predominantly West Saxon glosses dated (again by Ker) to the later part of the tenth century. Both layers of glosses were printed (in alphabetical order) by E. Brock as an appendix to *The Blickling Homilies*, ed. R. Morris, EETS OS 58, 63 and 73 (1874–80; repr. in one volume 1967), 251–63. (The Blickling glosses were originally printed in vol. 73.) Some additional glosses were printed by R. Collins, 'A Reexamination of the Old English Glosses in the *Blickling Psalter*', *Anglia* 81 (1963), 124–8. The older glosses were also printed by H. Sweet, *The Oldest English Texts*, EETS OS 183 (1885), 122–3. In addition, the manuscript contains some ninety-six scattered glosses and scholia in Latin, most of these apparently written by the same (late-tenth-century) scribe who wrote the second stratum of Old English glosses. The Latin glosses are printed by P. Pulsiano, 'The Latin and Old English Glosses in the "Blickling" and "Regius" Psalters', *Traditio* 41 (1985), 79–115, at 83–96. The later Old English glosses and the Latin glosses and scholia in the Blickling Psalter are very closely related to those in Royal 2. B. V, from which manuscript they may actually have been copied; see Pulsiano, 'The Latin and Old English Glosses', esp. pp. 112–15; on the Latin scholia in Royal 2. B. V, see below, pp. 28–32.

One post-Conquest glossed psalter must be mentioned here, because, again, parts of its gloss are closely related to the Royal Psalter:

E Eadwine Psalter or Canterbury Psalter. Cambridge, Trinity College R. 17. 1; *c.* 1155 × 1160; Canterbury (Christ Church); Ker, no. 91.

Facsimile: *The Canterbury Psalter*, ed. M. R. James (London, 1935). The Eadwine Psalter is a *psalterium triplex* containing the three Latin recensions of the psalter (*Romanum*, *Gallicanum* and *Hebraicum*) in parallel columns. It has a continuous and contemporary Old English gloss to its *Romanum* text. The first part of this gloss (up to and including ps. LXXVII) was heavily corrected and supplemented by another contemporary hand. The manuscript from which the corrections were made was arguably Royal 2. B. V.[40] The Old English gloss is printed by F. Harsley, *Eadwine's Canterbury Psalter*, EETS OS 92 (1889).

Finally mention should be made of a manuscript which contains, not a glossed psalter, but a Latin *Romanum* text accompanied by a facing Old English translation in prose and verse:

*P Paris Psalter. Paris, Bibliothèque Nationale, lat. 8824; s. xi^med.; origin unknown; Ker, no. 367; Gneuss, no. 891. Psalms I–L are accompanied by an early West Saxon prose translation which has been convincingly assigned to King Alfred.[41] The Old English 'Prose Psalter' is printed by Bright and Ramsay, *The West Saxon Psalms*. Psalms LI–CL are faced by a translation into Old English verse ('Metrical Psalter'), tentatively dated to the mid-tenth century (or somewhat later). The 'Metrical Psalter' is printed by G. P. Krapp, *The Paris Psalter and the Meters of Boethius*, ASPR 5 (New York, 1932), 1–150. For a facsimile of the entire manuscript, see *The Paris Psalter*, ed. Colgrave *et al.*

The textual recensions of the psalter

The Latin text in Royal 2. B. V is a *Psalterium Romanum*, as are all psalters originating in England before the middle of the tenth century. Two main

---

[40] For the close agreement between the corrections in the Eadwine Psalter and the gloss transmitted in Royal 2. B. V (which gives rise to the suspicion that Royal 2. B. V may have been the manuscript from which these corrections were made), see for example *Salisbury Psalter*, ed. Sisam and Sisam, p. 57, and P. S. Baker, 'A Little-Known Variant Text of the Old English Metrical Psalms', *Speculum* 59 (1984), 263–81, at 265, n. 7; but cf. O'Neill, 'The English Version', p. 132.

[41] See J. M. Bately, 'Lexical Evidence for the Authorship of the Prose Psalms in the Paris Psalter', *ASE* 10 (1982), 69–95.

versions of the Latin psalter text must be distinguished: the *Psalterium Romanum* and the *Psalterium Gallicanum*. The *Romanum* forms a distinctive textual tradition among the often widely divergent manuscripts of the *Vetus Latina* or 'Old Latin' translation of the psalms, inasmuch as it represents a version which was slightly revised after fresh consultation of the Greek Septuagint, from which the psalter (like the other books of the OT) had orginally been translated.

The *Gallicanum* is a more thorough revision of the *Vetus Latina* text, made by St Jerome between approximately 389×392, based on the Septuagint and (occasionally) the Hebrew text as found in the Hexapla. (The Hexapla was a huge one-volume edition of the OT which was compiled by Origen (*c*. 185–253), the foremost proponent of the Alexandrine school of exegesis; it was compiled *c*. 231×245, and consisted of the Hebrew text of the OT in Hebrew and Greek characters, and four Greek translations (the Septuagint among them), arranged in six parallel columns.)[42]

The two psalter versions came to be referred to by the names of *Romanum* and *Gallicanum* respectively in manuscripts from the ninth century onwards. These designations are usually taken to indicate that the respective versions were in use in the churches of Rome and Francia by that time. Subsequently, the *Romanum* remained the psalter in official use in the churches all over Italy up to the time of Pope Pius V (1566–72), when it was replaced by the *Gallicanum* (except for St Peter's in Rome, where it is still employed). Remnants of the liturgical use of the *Romanum* can still be found in certain components of the Roman breviary, such as antiphons or responsories consisting of psalm verses. The *Gallicanum* was the version to be incorporated in the Vulgate text of the Bible from the ninth century onwards, it has been thought through the agency of Alcuin.

A fresh translation of the entire psalter (subsequent to his *Gallicanum* revision) made by Jerome after the Hebrew original (the *psalterium iuxta Hebraeos* or *Hebraicum*, 392×393) never gained general currency, presumably because of conservative adherence to an already established textual

---

[42] On the Hexapla, see conveniently, Lapidge, *Biblical Commentaries*, ed. Bischoff and Lapidge, pp. 430–1 (with further references). It is interesting to note in passing that Theodore and Hadrian provided their Canterbury students with fairly detailed explanations concerning the composition and intention of the Hexapla and concerning the authors of the four Greek translations; see *ibid.*, pp. 298–301.

form of a book of the OT which had always been of utmost importance in the liturgy. However, the version *iuxta Hebraeos* is found in early pandects (complete Bibles), such as the 'Codex Amiatinus', s. viii[in], of English (Wearmouth–Jarrow) origin, now Florence, Biblioteca Medicea Laurenziana, Amiatino 1. In connection with the origin of the Amiatinus (and that of its two sister pandects),[43] it may be worth mentioning that Bede, who usually quotes from the *Romanum* version of the psalms, on one occasion (in a discussion of the rhetorical figure of paronomasia) expressly points out that one of his quotations is taken from a psalm *iuxta Hebraicam ueritatem*.[44] Otherwise, in English psalter manuscripts (as opposed to Bibles) the *Romanum* text is found invariably in books written up to the middle of the tenth century, the *Gallicanum* becoming established only gradually in the wake of the Benedictine reform with its close contacts with continental reformed monasteries. There is, however, ample manuscript evidence (in the form of psalters imported to England), that the *Gallicanum* was known in England long before it became the established recension in the liturgy of the Anglo-Saxon church.[45] It is interesting to note that the *Romanum* version seems to have been in liturgical use at Christ Church, Canterbury as late as the first half of the eleventh century, as is witnessed by the psalter in London, BL, Arundel 155, dated s. xi[1/4], of Christ Church origin and in use there as an official service book.[46]

---

[43] Cf. above, p. 13.

[44] Cf. Bede, *De schematibus et tropis*, ed. Kendall, pp. 147–8. For Bede's usual adherence to the *Romanum* text, see his *De arte metrica*, ed. Kendall, p. 175, n. 4.

[45] On these imported psalters, see below, pp. 274–7; on the special importance of the *Romanum* for the Anglo-Saxon church, see below, pp. 287–96.

[46] For the three recensions of the psalter (*Romanum*, *Gallicanum* and *Hebraicum*), see (briefly) *ODCC*, pp. 1344 ('Psalter'), 1410 ('Roman Psalter') and 652 ('Gallican Psalter'); see further E. F. Sutcliffe, 'Jerome', in *Cambridge History of the Bible*, ed. Lampe, pp. 84–5 and 88, Leclercq, 'Psautier', *DACL* XIV.2 (1948), 1950–67, at 1951–4, P. Synave, 'Psaumes', *DTC* XIII (1936), 1093–1149, at 1106–8, and Fischer, 'Zur Überlieferung altlateinischer Bibeltexte im Mittelalter', pp. 407–15. For the substitution of the *Romanum* by the *Gallicanum* in Francia and a sceptical view of the role allegedly played by Alcuin in this, see Fischer, 'Bibeltext und Bibelreform unter Karl dem Großen', pp. 164–7. The critical edition of the *Romanum* is: *Le Psautier Romain*, ed. Weber (as is noted *ibid.*, p. ix, the oldest extant manuscripts of this version come from England). The critical edition of the *Gallicanum* has appeared as vol. 10 of the comprehensive critical edition of the Latin Vulgate published by the Benedictines of S. Girolamo in Rome: *Biblia Sacra iuxta Latinam Vulgatam Versionem*, ed. Quentin *et*

By contrast, the *Gallicanum* was well established in the Irish church from an early date onwards. Here, the *Hebraicum* must also have been disseminated early and widely in psalter manuscripts (not only in pandects), as can be seen from the manuscripts still extant.[47] This situation would explain why (according to Stephen of Ripon) the Irish-taught young Wilfrid, future bishop of York (669–78), who previously had known only the *Psalterium Gallicanum* (*psalmos ... secundum Hieronymi emendationem*), had to learn the *Romanum* during his stay at Canterbury in the early 650s, *en route* to Rome (*psalmos ... more Romanorum ... memoraliter transmetuit*).[48]

al. X: *Liber Psalmorum*. The edition of the *Hebraicum* is: *Sancti Hieronymi Psalterium iuxta Hebraeos*, ed. de Sainte-Marie. Facing texts of the *Gallicanum* and the *Hebraicum* may be consulted conveniently in the one-volume edition (with variants from selected manuscripts) of the Vulgate: *Biblia Sacra iuxta Vulgatam Versionem*, ed. Weber *et al.* A critical edition of the remnants of the unrevised 'Old Latin' psalter texts will appear as vol. 9 of the comprehensive edition prepared by the Erzabtei Beuron: *Vetus Latina. Die Reste der altlateinischen Bibel nach Petrus Sabatier neu gesammelt und ... herausgegeben von der Erzabtei Beuron* (Freiburg, 1949–). Until this volume has appeared, for the 'Old Latin' psalter texts one has to refer to *Bibliorum Sacrorum Latinae Versiones antiquae seu Vetus Italica*, ed. P. Sabatier II (Rheims, 1743). Concerning the origin of the *Psalterium Romanum*, it was traditionally held that this recension, as well, should be attributed to St Jerome, representing his first, somewhat cursory revision of the *Vetus Latina* texts. This view, however, has been challenged by D. de Bruyne, 'Le problème du Psautier Romain', *Revue Bénédictine* 42 (1930), 101–26, but his arguments have not gained general acceptance; see, for example, *Le Psautier Romain*, ed. Weber, pp. viii–ix, and Sutcliffe, 'Jerome', pp. 84–5. The question of the relationship between the archetype of Jerome's first revision and the transmitted *Romanum* texts is complicated; see Fischer, 'Zur Überlieferung altlateinischer Bibeltexte im Mittelalter', p. 407. For the three recensions of the psalter with special reference to their transmission in Anglo-Saxon England, there is a convenient synopsis by K. Sisam, *The Salisbury Psalter*, Appendix I: 'Latin Texts of the Psalter' (pp. 47–52); for Arundel 155 in official use at Christ Church, see *ibid.*, p. 49, n. 1. For the sustained use of the *Romanum* at Christ Church, see also Brooks, *Early History*, pp. 261–5. For the transmissional history of the *Romanum* and *Gallicanum* in Anglo-Saxon England (including their Old English interlinear glosses), see also the pioneering, somewhat adventurous but still valuable studies by Wildhagen, 'Studien zum *Psalterium Romanum*' and 'Das *Psalterium Gallicanum* in England'.

[47] See McNamara, 'The Text of the Latin Bible in the Early Irish Church', pp. 39–41, and *idem*, 'Psalter Text and Psalter Study in the Early Irish Church (A. D. 600–1200)', *Proceedings of the Royal Irish Academy* 73 C (1973), 201–76.

[48] See *The Life of Bishop Wilfrid by Eddius Stephanus*, ed. and transl. B. Colgrave (Cambridge, 1927), ch. 3 (p. 8).

It should be stressed, however, that the differences between the two principal Latin text forms, the *Romanum* and the *Gallicanum*, although numerous, are by no means dramatic, since both derive (preponderantly) from the Septuagint (unlike the *iuxta Hebraeos* version). Apart from aiming at more accurate translation of the Greek text in general, the *Gallicanum* quite often presents a more 'modern' phraseology, replacing rare, difficult or obsolete words in the *Romanum*. The following short list of textual variants, randomly lifted from a few consecutive verses of one psalm (and not complete for the verses in question), will give some impression of the nature of these variants and the frequency with which they occur.[49]

	Romanum	*Gallicanum*
IX.4	perient	peribunt
IX.8	sedem suam	t(h)ronum suum
IX.13	memoratus est	recordatus est
IX.13	orationem	clamorem
IX.15	laudes	laudationes
IX.16	occultauerunt	absconderunt
IX.18	dominum	deum
IX.19	pauperum (1)	pauperis
IX.20	praeualeat	confortetur
IX.21	ut	*omitted*
IX.23	in cogitationibus suis quas cogitant	in consiliis quibus cogitant

In any event, an interlinear Old English gloss, originally designed for a *Romanum* text, could be copied into a *Gallicanum* psalter without causing major difficulties. (Many of the textual variants would only cause a change of inflexional endings or not show at all in a vernacular gloss.) Such copying has, for example, been done in the case of the Old English gloss in the Salisbury Psalter (K, *Gallicanum*) which is very closely dependent on the gloss in the Royal Psalter (D, *Romanum*).[50]

---

[49] The typically *Gallicanum* variants are conveniently listed in the *apparatus criticus* of *Le Psautier Romain*, ed. Weber.

[50] For the close relationship between the Royal and the Salisbury psalters, see K. Sisam, *Salisbury Psalter*, esp. pp. 39–47.

The textual affiliations of the Old English psalter glosses

Among the Anglo-Saxon glossed psalters, the versions in the Vespasian Psalter (A), the Royal Psalter (D), and the Lambeth Psalter (I), each stand out as the oldest witnesses of distinctive gloss traditions.[51]

Dependent[52] on the Vespasian gloss (A) are the A-type glosses in the following psalters:

The glosses to all the psalms in the Junius (B) and the Cambridge (C) psalters.

The glosses to psalms L, LIII, LXIII, LXVIII, CI, CXVIII–CXXXIII and CXLII in the Bosworth Psalter (L).

The glosses to psalms I–XVII.35 in the Vitellius Psalter (G).

The glosses to psalms VIII.10–IX.10, XIII, XXVI.6–8(?) and XXVIII.5–8 in the Tiberius Psalter (H).

The glosses to psalms I–LI and LXIII–LXXV in the Arundel Psalter (J).

The A-type gloss is of Mercian origin.

Dependent on the Royal gloss (D) are the D-type glosses in the following psalters:

The glosses to all the psalms in the Stowe Psalter (F)[53] and in the Salisbury Psalter (K).

---

[51] For a brief discussion of scholarly opinions concerning the textual affiliations of the D-type glosses, see below, pp. 33–4. For a convenient conspectus of the affiliations of the individual glossed psalters with A- or D-type glosses, see K. Sisam, *Salisbury Psalter*, pp. 52–75. Sisam's account includes the results of previous research in the field, undertaken principally by K. Wildhagen, U. Lindelöf and O. Heinzel (cf. below). See also the summary of the psalter affiliations by Schabram, *Superbia*, pp. 21–8. The following, somewhat simplified, lists of A- and D-type psalters are based primarily on these two accounts.

[52] It should be noted that the assertion that a psalter gloss is dependent on the Vespasian gloss is not tantamount to saying that this gloss was copied from Vespasian A. i in the flesh. Such assertion means no more than that the gloss in question belongs to the A-type family of glosses of which Vespasian A. i is the oldest and (for all we know) the purest witness. The same holds true for the D-type glosses. In some cases, however, direct copying of a gloss from one manuscript into another is highly likely. Thus, we have seen (above, p. 20–1) that the Blickling glosses (M) and the corrections in the Eadwine Psalter (E) may well have been copied from Royal 2. B. V (D).

[53] Cf., however, Hofstetter, *Winchester und Sprachgebrauch*, pp. 73–5, who points out a

The glosses to psalms XL.5, LXVI, LXVII, LXIX, LXX, LXXXV, CXXXIX.2 and 9 and CXL.1–2 in the Bosworth Psalter (L).

The glosses to all psalms, except I–XVII.35 in the Vitellius Psalter (G).

The glosses to all psalms, except VIII.10–IX.10, XIII, XXVI.6–8(?) and XXVIII.5–8 in the Tiberius Psalter (H).

The glosses to psalms LII–LXII and LXXVI–CL in the Arundel Psalter (J).

The Blickling glosses (M) except for the earliest layer of twenty-one Mercian glosses (see above, p. 20).

The numerous corrections of the original glosses to psalms I–LXXVII in the twelfth-century Eadwine Psalter (E).[54]

The D-type gloss is of Late West Saxon origin, exhibiting an early form of this dialectal variety.

The Lambeth Psalter gloss (I) is of Late West Saxon origin. It is a fresh and highly competent interlinear version of the *Gallicanum* text (A- and D-type glosses were originally devised for the *Romanum*), which, however, freely adopts A- and D-type gloss material. This, in turn, accounts for the encyclopaedic character of its vocabulary, with a huge number (almost 1500) of double or even triple glosses for one Latin lemma. The Lambeth gloss is an important witness of the so-called Winchester vocabulary (presumably taught at Bishop Æthelwold's school at the Old Minster).[55] Unlike the Vespasian and Royal Psalter glosses, the Lambeth gloss did not become the ancestor of a sizeable family of psalter glosses, although a number of its *interpretamenta* (in particular 'Winchester' words) seem to have been adopted by the Vitellius (G), Arundel (J) and, above all, the Stowe (F) psalters.[56]

---

number of A-type glosses in Stowe which had not been noted previously; see *ibid.*, pp. 70–3, for I-type (Lambeth) glosses in Stowe.

[54] The uncorrected parts of the Eadwine Psalter still await a thorough analysis. They belong neither with the A- nor with the D-type families (although they have some links with the A-type group), and in substantial portions they may derive from an Anglian gloss, otherwise lost. See Schabram, *Superbia*, pp. 27–8, and, most recently, the survey (with further references) by O'Neill, 'The English Version', pp. 123–38. A new critical edition of that psalter gloss is an urgent desideratum.

[55] See Hofstetter, *Winchester und Sprachgebrauch*, pp. 84–8, and cf. below, p. 40 for the extraordinary vocabulary of the Lambeth Psalter.

[56] See Hofstetter, *Winchester und Sprachgebrauch*, pp. 70–3, and (for F) K. Sisam, *Salisbury Psalter*, pp. 73–4.

The marginal commentary in Royal 2. B. V

The gloss as it is transmitted in Royal 2. B. V is not only the earliest and purest witness of the D-type psalter glosses, very close to the original of that gloss itself;[57] Royal 2. B. V also stands out as unique among psalter manuscripts with Old English glosses inasmuch as its psalter text is accompanied by a Latin commentary, written in the margins and (occasionally) between the lines, and referred to in the psalter text by a rather sophisticated system of *signes de renvoie*. Thus, at the outset, the physical appearance of the manuscript gives rise to the suspicion that in his vernacular gloss, the Glossator might somehow have been aiming at a more ambitious goal than the provision of an elementary understanding aid for beginners in Latin. Latin psalter text, commentary and Old English gloss were all written by the same scribe, at some point near the mid-tenth century.[58]

It is a matter of great interest that presumably this same scribe also produced a copy of St Jerome's *Tractatus .lix. in psalmos* (*CPL*, no. 592) which is preserved, in fragmentary form, in London, BL, Royal 4. A. XIV, 3r–105r.[59] This betrays a deep concern with psalm exegesis in the centre where both manuscripts originated. However, Jerome's homilies on the

---

[57] For the relationship of the text in Royal 2. B. V to the original gloss, see K. Sisam, *Salisbury Psalter*, pp. 54–5, 71–2 and 71, n. 2.

[58] Cf. Ker, *Catalogue*, p. 320 (no. 249), and see below, pp. 264–6.

[59] Royal 4. A. XIV contains Jerome's homilies on psalms CIX–CXLIX; some of the psalms in this sequence are not expounded. On the whole, such omissions correspond to those psalms which were not expounded in Jerome's *Tractatus*. However, in his *Tractatus* Jerome did interpret a number of psalms anterior to ps. CIX; these homilies are not preserved in Royal 4. A. XIV. They may have been lost from the manuscript, and the series of Jerome's 59 *Tractatus* may once have been (almost) complete, since the manuscript is described as defective at the beginning by Warner and Gilson, *Catalogue* I, 82. Jerome's homilies on the psalter were edited by G. Morin, *S. Hieronymi Presbyteri tractatus .lix. in psalmos*, Anecdota Maredsolana III, part ii (Oxford, 1897); repr. in CCSL 78 (Turnhout, 1958), 3–352. The matter is complicated further by the circumstance that in Royal 4. A. XIV, Jerome's *Tractatus* present some interpolations from the pseudo-Hieronymian *Breuiarium in psalmos* (*CPL*, no. 629; ptd PL 26, 871–1346), an anonymous psalm commentary which possibly originated in Ireland before 800: cf. Wright, 'Hiberno-Latin Commentaries', pp. 98–9, and the references given there. For the insertions from the *Breuiarium* in the text of Jerome's *Tractatus*, see also Warner and Gilson, *Catalogue* I, 81, and Morin, CCSL 78, pp. xvi–xvii. The scribal link between the *Tractatus* in Royal 4. A. XIV and Royal 2. B. V was first noted

psalms were only a very minor source (if a direct source at all) for the marginal commentary in Royal 2. B. V, as William Davey has shown.[60] Apparently *c.* 75 per cent of these comments are derived from the *Expositio psalmorum* by Cassiodorus (b. *c.* 485, d. *c.* 580), one of the most important and influential exegetical works on the psalms in early medieval Europe.[61] The Royal Psalter's marginal explanations are derived from Cassiodorus either verbatim or (more often) in a rigidly abbreviated form, no doubt prompted by the restricted space available in the margins of the manuscript. Such abbreviation of Cassiodorus's usually lengthy exegesis of a psalm verse (often only the gist or part of his interpretation is given) leaves us without a means of deciding whether it was the complete *Expositio* or some form of abridged version of that text which was laid under contribution by the Royal Glossator.[62]

In England, the *Expositio* was known and laid under contribution by Anglo-Saxon authors from an early date onwards. Bede, for example, draws freely on the *Expositio* in his *De schematibus et tropis*.[63] Furthermore, the oldest surviving manuscript of the *Expositio* is of Northumbrian origin (s. viii, probably second quarter): Durham, Cathedral Library, B. II. 30; and it is interesting to note that this manuscript presents a much-abridged version of the text.[64] Of the approximately 4280 marginal or

---

by K. Sisam, *Salisbury Psalter*, pp. 52–3 and 53, n. 1; cf. also Ker, *Catalogue*, p. 320 (nos. 249 and 250), and see below, pp. 265–7, on the origin of both manuscripts.

[60] See W. Davey, 'An Edition of the Regius Psalter and its Latin Commentary' (unpubl. PhD dissertation, Carleton Univ., Ottawa, 1979). Davey's edition has never appeared in print, and I am very grateful to him for having made available his work for scholarly use at Munich. The principal results of Davey's work are published in his article 'Commentary of the Regius Psalter'.

[61] The standard edition is *Expositio psalmorum*, ed. Adriaen; for a translation, see Walsh, *Cassiodorus*; on Cassiodorus in general, see, for example, J.-M. Alonso-Núñez and J. Gruber, 'Cassiodor(us)', *LkMA* II (1983), 1551–3, A. van de Vyver, 'Cassiodore et son œuvre', *Speculum* 6 (1931), 244–92, and J. J. O'Donnell, *Cassiodorus* (Berkeley, CA, 1979).

[62] Cf. Davey, 'Commentary of the Regius Psalter', p. 338.

[63] See the numerous references to the *Expositio* in the *apparatus fontium* of *De schematibus*, ed. Kendall. For further testimonies to the extensive use which Anglo-Saxon authors made of the *Expositio*, see Knappe, *Traditionen der klassischen Rhetorik*, pp. 217–29.

[64] See Lowe, *Codices Latini Antiquiores* II, 11, 49 and 57 (no. 152), and *Expositio psalmorum*, ed. Adriaen, pp. xv–xvi. On the decoration of the Durham breviate version and its implication for the origin of the manuscript, see R. N. Bailey, 'The Durham Cassiodorus', in *Bede and his World: The Jarrow Lectures 1958–1993*, ed. M. Lapidge, 2

interlinear scholia which Davey counted in Royal 2. B. V, some 3242 can be traced back to Cassiodorus's *Expositio*.[65] Most of these comments pertain to allegorical and typological exegesis, interpreting the text of the psalms in the light of the New Testament. By the same token, explanatory quotations of parallel passages from the Bible, principally from the New Testament (as given by Cassiodorus), are adduced to reinforce the overall typological interpretation. The scholia which do not pertain to such allegorical exposition are concerned *inter alia* with clarifying the grammatical construction of a psalm verse or with providing etymological explanations (principally of Hebrew names).[66] It is interesting that the emphasis on the indispensability of allegorical exposition for the OT books which we have noted in the Old English Rule is paralleled in some ways by the selective method in which Cassiodorus's commentary was laid under contribution for the scholia in Royal 2. B. V. No doubt allegorical and typological exposition is pervasive in Cassiodorus, but his *Expositio* was also an important vehicle for the transmission of the late classical tradition of rhetoric, inasmuch as an imposing number of explanatory remarks on rhetorical figures and tropes (drawn from the text of the psalms) are embedded in this voluminous work.[67] It was these explanations of figures and tropes that were drawn on by Bede in his *De schematibus* and that were excerpted in a section of the Leiden Glossary,[68] but not a single one of such

---

vols. (Aldershot, 1994) I, 463–90 [Jarrow Lecture, 1978]. It has been suggested that the manuscript was at York in the late eighth century, since Alcuin quotes from the *Expositio* in the breviate form as preserved in B. II. 30: see D. Bullough, 'Alcuin and the Kingdom of Heaven: Liturgy, Theology and the Carolingian Age', in his *Carolingian Renewal* (Manchester, 1991), pp. 161–240, at 172–4. An abridged version is also found in one of the two surviving fragments of the *Expositio* of English origin and eighth-century date: Düsseldorf, Universitätsbibliothek, fragment K. 19: Z8/8, s. viii[1], Northumbria; Gneuss, 'Handlist', no. 822. (The other fragment is Cambridge, St John's College Aa. 5. 1, fol. 67; s. viii[1]; Gneuss, 'Handlist', no. 154). For a list of all surviving manuscripts of the *Expositio*, see J. W. Halporn, 'The Manuscripts of Cassiodorus' "Expositio Psalmorum"', *Traditio* 37 (1981), 388–96.

[65] Cf. Davey, 'Commentary of the Regius Psalter', p. 338.

[66] See *ibid.*, pp. 336–8.

[67] The figures and tropes explained and referred to in the *Expositio* are conveniently indexed by Knappe, *Traditionen der klassischen Rhetorik*, pp. 491–9.

[68] On the historical context of the Leiden Glossary, see below, pp. 196–8 and 244–5; for the section on the rhetorical figures drawn from Cassiodorus, see Knappe, *Traditionen der klassischen Rhetorik*, pp. 220–9.

explanations found its way into the marginal commentary in Royal 2. B. V. It is, however, difficult to evaluate this piece of evidence, since the vernacular gloss in Royal 2. B. V does reveal an interest in rhetorical effects, as we shall see. No doubt the amount of space available for the Latin gloss should be borne in mind in an estimation of the contents of the scholia.

The remaining *c.* 25 per cent of the scholia which cannot be traced back to Cassiodorus contain to a large extent what have been called 'traditional or commonplace interpretations of the Psalms',[69] which means that such interpretations occur in various commentaries on the psalms, or in other reference works such as Isidore's *Etymologiae*, and therefore are difficult to attribute to a single source.[70] In providing such a massive corpus of Latin scholia, Royal 2. B. V is not only unique among glossed psalters from Anglo-Saxon England:[71] the manuscript stands out as well among all other surviving psalters from that time. Only one further manuscript bears a comparable amount of scholia which were written in England before 1100: Cambridge, Corpus Christi College 272. Here, however, the scholia are later by about a century (s. xi^{med}) than the Royal commentary; they are not related to that commentary.[72]

---

[69] Davey, 'Commentary of the Regius Psalter', p. 340.

[70] See *ibid.*, pp. 340–3. Davey (p. 340) tentatively suggests Jerome's *Tractatus .lix. in psalmos* (see above) and the anonymous (and composite) *In psalmorum librum exegesis* (wrongly attributed *in toto* to Bede, cf. *CPL*, no. 1384, ptd PL 93, 477–1098) as possible direct sources for the scholia in Royal 2. B. V.

[71] The extensive Latin glosses to some of the psalms in the Bosworth Psalter (BL Add. 37517 (L)) date from the twelfth century; cf., for example, Ker, *Catalogue*, p. 161 (no. 129). The approximately ninety-six Latin glosses in the Blickling Psalter (Pierpont Morgan 776 (M)) are derived from the Royal Psalter (see above).

[72] The psalter in CCCC 272 was written at Rheims, s. ix^{ex} (on the manuscript and the possible circumstances of its arrival in England, see below, pp. 275–7). The marginal comments in CCCC 272 are usually more extensive than those in Royal 2. B. V; again, they seem to be drawn principally from Cassiodorus's *Expositio*. The scholia are written in Anglo-Caroline minuscule, Style IV, probably s. xi^{med}. I am grateful to Michael Lapidge for inspecting this manuscript for me, providing me with excerpts from its Latin commentary and letting me have his expert advice on the script of the scholia. A further witness to an Anglo-Saxon psalter bearing a Latin gloss is a fragment, now Worcester, Cathedral Library, F. 173, fol. 1 (Gneuss, 'Handlist', no. 764.5). The fragment is dated s. x^2 and is therefore more or less contemporary with the Royal Psalter, and it is a matter of great regret that no more than a single folio has survived. This leaves us without a means of estimating the amount of glossing done throughout

In the present state of our knowledge, it is not possible to say whether the Latin commentary in Royal 2. B. V was originally compiled (from Cassiodorus and various other sources) in the circle where that manuscript was written, or whether an exemplar of the commentary more or less in its present form (some kind of *catena* on the psalms) was already available there, and was subsequently copied out in the margins of Royal 2. B. V. Psalters with extensive marginal commentaries in Latin were produced on the Continent from the early ninth century onwards; and (in view of their respective links with Anglo-Saxon England) it is interesting to note that St Gallen from the ninth century and Fleury from the tenth century onwards appear to have been centres where such books were produced in substantial numbers. However, it should also be noted that the space alloted to such scholia in the continental manuscripts is usually much larger than that in Royal 2. B. V.[73]

In the case of the Royal Psalter, it can be shown that psalm exegesis also played a role in the choice of a number of English *interpretamenta*, either via the scholia as found in the manuscript itself, or through resort the Glossator must have had to other commentaries. The commentary in question in such cases, again, is almost invariably Cassiodorus's *Expositio*.[74]

In sum, it would appear that Kenneth Sisam's dictum that the Royal Psalter is 'a book for study, not a service book'[75] is amply borne out by a close inspection of the layout of the manuscript and of the interactions between the Latin text, marginal commentary and Old English gloss;

the entire psalter, since it is a frequent feature in annotated manuscripts that even comparatively dense glossing is sustained no longer than a few folios (on this feature, see Lapidge, 'Study of Latin Texts', p. 495); note that the twelfth-century Latin gloss in the Bosworth Psalter does not extend to all the psalms (cf. above, n. 71). The Worcester leaf is of great interest, furthermore, as arguably the earliest witness of a *Psalterium Gallicanum* written in England.

[73] See M. Gibson, 'Carolingian Glossed Psalters', in *Early Medieval Bible*, ed. Gameson, pp. 78–100, esp. at 80 (and *passim*), for St Gallen, and 90–1, for Fleury; for specimen plates from some of the psalters in question, see also *ibid.*

[74] Cf. Davey, 'Commentary of the Regius Psalter', pp. 343–9. The influence of psalm exegesis on the Old English vocabulary of the Royal Psalter (and the Vespasian and Lambeth psalters) has also been dealt with recently by Wiesenekker, *Translation Performance*, esp. pp. 201–10. Such influence had been noted as early as 1955: see Gneuss, *Lehnbildungen*, pp. 47–8 and *passim*.

[75] *Salisbury Psalter*, p. 52.

interactions of an amount and quality which (since they can scarcely be dealt with adequately in a printed edition)[76] should have earned Royal 2. B. V a place of honour among the *Early English Manuscripts in Facsimile* long ago. In the present book our principal concern with the marginal scholia in Royal 2. B. V will be with their impact on the Old English gloss. From the following discussion of the nature and quality of the Royal Psalter's Old English vocabulary some notion may be formed of the influence which psalm exegesis (in various forms) exercised on the Glossator's choice of words. Before we can proceed to an evaluation of the Old English gloss, however, we must briefly concern ourselves with the question of whether some sort of relationship can be established between the Royal Psalter gloss (the ancestor of the D-type glosses) and the A-type glosses, the only psalter gloss which (to our knowledge) was in existence by the time the Royal Glossator devised his fresh interlinear version of the psalms.

The Royal Psalter gloss and the A-type glosses

The relationships between the psalters with Old English glosses have always been the foremost preoccupation of scholars in that field. Yet, after more than a century of research in psalter glossing, many questions pertaining to textual affiliations and dependencies of the glosses cannot be regarded as definitely settled. One of these still vexed questions which we must briefly address here concerns the relationship between the Royal Psalter (D) and the A-type glosses, as represented by the Vespasian Psalter (A) in its purest form, and in a more or less uncontaminated form also by the Junius (B) and the Cambridge (C) psalters, both closely dependent on A.[77] Did the Royal Glossator draw in some way on the A-type gloss? There is no need here for an extended review of scholarly opinions on the subject; it will be enough to note that among the older scholars Uno Lindelöf did

---

[76] There is no edition comprising all three components of the psalter. Roeder (*Der altenglische Regius-Psalter*) prints only the Latin text of the psalms and its Old English gloss. The facsimile reproduction of the manuscript on microfiche, published recently, is useful but unsatisfactory as far as the marginal commentary is concerned, since the scholia are in many places partly illegible on the microfilm from which the microfiches apparently were produced; cf. *Anglo-Saxon Manuscripts in Microfiche Facsimile* II, *Psalters I*, ed. P. Pulsiano, A. N. Doane and R. E. Buckalew (Binghamton, NY, 1994).

[77] For other glossed psalters containing A-type material, cf. above, p. 26.

not believe that the Royal Psalter was in any way dependent on the A-type gloss, whereas Karl Wildhagen and Otto Heinzel were convinced of the contrary.[78] Among more recent scholarship, the opinion that the Royal Psalter gloss originated in complete independence from an A-type exemplar seems to prevail.[79] However, any opinion concerning a relationship or non-relationship between the A-type glosses and the Royal Psalter must be regarded as preliminary. We have as yet no complete list of lexical variants between the Royal Psalter and the Vespasian Psalter (to say nothing of the Junius and Cambridge Psalters). A first step towards such a collation has recently been taken by Phillip Pulsiano, who has listed all divergent glosses in A and D for the first thirty psalms.[80]

I doubt, however, whether a purely statistical evaluation of such a collation (or even one along the traditional lines of textual criticism) would conclusively answer the question of a potential dependence of the Royal Psalter on the Vespasian gloss. It is quite obvious, and has in fact never been disputed, that the Anglo-Saxon scholar responsible for the Royal gloss did not content himself with copying out an existing gloss, but aimed to create a fresh interlinear version of the psalms. What has not sufficiently been taken into consideration, however, is that for that very reason, the traditional means of textual criticism for establishing relationships between any two texts can be applied only to a limited extent. A high percentage of agreement between the Royal and Vespasian psalters

---

[78] See Lindelöf, *Studien zu altenglischen Psalterglossen*, pp. 102–3, Wildhagen, 'Studien zum *Psalterium Romanum*', p. 449, and Heinzel, *Entstehungsgeschichte des ags. Interlinear-Psalters*, pp. 64 (stemma) and 113 (summary). Note that Heinzel, in his elaborate stemma, assumed a more distant relationship between the A-type glosses and the Royal Psalter than did Wildhagen. For recent brief surveys of scholarly opinions on the subject, see Pulsiano, 'Defining the A-type and D-type Traditions', pp. 308–11, and *idem*, 'Psalters', pp. 74–7.

[79] See, for example, K. Sisam, *Salisbury Psalter*, pp. 55–6, Bierbaumer, 'Interrelationships of Psalter-Glosses', pp. 124–5, Berghaus, *Verwandtschaftsverhältnisse der Interlinear-versionen*, esp. at pp. 92, 108 and 133, and Pulsiano, 'Defining the A-type and D-type Traditions', pp. 309–10.

[80] See Pulsiano, 'Defining the A-type and D-type Traditions', pp. 311–12 and 315–27. Note that Berghaus (*Verwandtschaftsverhältnisse der Interlinearversionen*, pp. 30–1 and 132) claims to have based his investigations on a complete collation of all glossed psalters comprising some 14,000 variants in total. However, since those variants have never been made available in any form, the reader is in no position to verify Berghaus's results and his ensuing stemma (for the stemma, cf. *ibid.*, p. 135).

in the translation of so-called 'commonplace' words has been noted (by
Kenneth Sisam and others) whereas both psalters often disagree 'in the
rendering of difficult words and phrases'.[81] While Sisam thought it
'unreasonable to suppose that a competent glossator would use a gloss in
this way',[82] it might well be asked whether such 'difficult' lemmata were
not just the ones where a scholar, intent on glossing the psalter afresh,
would be apt to disagree with a glossed manuscript which he regularly
consulted while composing his own gloss.[83] In other words, a divergent
gloss in the Royal Psalter does not imply *a priori* that the Glossator had
no knowledge of the corresponding A-type gloss.

By the same token, disagreement between the Mercian Vespasian
Psalter gloss and the West Saxon Royal gloss is to be expected in those
cases where Vespasian employs an Anglian dialect word (as opposed to the
frequent retention of such Anglian words in the West Saxon Junius and
Cambridge psalter glosses, which derive in direct line from Vespasian).
For the Royal Psalter, it is rather the sporadic agreement with the
Vespasian Psalter in the employment of such a dialect word which might
well point to the use of an A-type exemplar.[84] Similarly, the exceedingly
numerous minor lexical variants between the Royal gloss and the A-type
glosses, such as prefixed versus unprefixed forms (e. g. A: *gefallan* and D:

---

[81] K. Sisam, *Salisbury Psalter*, pp. 55–6; cf. also Pulsiano, 'Defining the A-type and D-
type Traditions', pp. 309–10.

[82] *Salisbury Psalter*, p. 56.

[83] Apart from that, it has never been stated precisely what 'commonplace' and 'difficult'
words are. For example, the five variants in ps. II (adduced by Pulsiano from a sample
collation of that psalm and as corroborative evidence for Sisam's view) where the
Vespasian and the Royal psalters disagree could be called 'difficult' only by some
stretch of the meaning of that word; cf. 'Defining the A-type and D-type Traditions',
pp. 309–10.

[84] Cf., for example, the occurrence in the Royal Psalter of Anglian *leoran* and *aleoran* for
praeterire, transire (pss. LVI.2 and CXLVIII.6), or Anglian *feogan* for *odisse* (in five out of
thirty-five occurrences of the Latin lemma, e. g. pss. XVII.41 and LXXXVIII.24). For
the Anglian character of both words, see Wenisch, *Spezifisch anglisches Wortgut*,
pp. 134–7 and 175–8 (with a survey of previous scholarly opinions). A complete list
of putative Anglian dialect words in the Royal Psalter can be compiled from the
references in Wenisch's index (p. 349, s. v. 'PsD'). For the words in question, the
adoption of an A-type *interpretamentum* by the Royal Glossator seems decidedly more
likely than his consultation of unspecified glossaries with a dialectally heterogeneous
vocabulary which has been presumed by Berghaus in explanation of such Anglian
words in the Royal Psalter; cf. *Verwandtschaftsverhältnisse der Interlinearversionen*, p. 108.

feallan), or the affixation of different prefixes to identical Old English simplexes (e. g. A: *onlesan* and D: *tolysan*) should not be assigned the same status as variants consisting of completely different words (e. g. A: *fallan* and D: *hreosan*). Such minor variants are exactly what one would expect if a glossator set out to 're-write' an existing gloss.[85]

All this makes rather slippery ground for any pronouncement on a relationship between the Royal Psalter and the A-type gloss. In some cases (as in his avoidance of Anglian dialect words) it is easy to see the Royal Glossator's rationale for disagreeing with the A-type gloss. By the same token, it is, for example, not difficult to uncover the Glossator's reasons for his frequent translation of *christus* as *cyning*,[86] and *tabernaculum* as *eardung(stow)* 'habitation',[87] whereas Vespasian has *Crist* and *geteld*. Such D-type glosses are explanatory and exegetical; therefore we should not think for a moment that the Royal Glossator intended them in any way as synonyms for the literal A-type glosses. However, in many more cases, no such reasons for the Royal Glossator's choice of a word different from Vespasian can be detected. Aside from this, understanding the reasons for the Glossator's choice, usually (as in the case of *cyning* and *eardung(stow)*) neither proves nor disproves the assumption that he did not consult an A-type psalter before he decided on his *interpretamentum*.

Nevertheless, when working through the Royal Psalter (open-mindedly, as I hope I did) and checking its vocabulary against the Vespasian Psalter, I became increasingly convinced that the Glossator worked with a copy of the A-type gloss on his desk. Often the relationship is not straightforward, a matter of simple agreement between both psalters. In such cases one rather suspects that the Glossator chose his own *interpretamentum*, starting from what he found in his A-type exemplar. In the following exploration of the Royal Psalter's vocabulary, we shall have occasion to observe such subtle and often elusive links between the Royal and the Vespasian gloss. For the moment, it will be sufficient to draw attention to a few agreements of a more general and obvious nature between both psalters.

---

[85] See Bierbaumer, 'Interrelationships of Psalter-Glosses', p. 126 and Berghaus, *Verwandtschaftsverhältnisse der Interlinearversionen*, p. 29, where any such classifying of variants is rejected. Here again (as in the case of 'commonplace' and 'difficult' words), it would be extremely difficult to decide precisely what kind of morphological variation such a group of 'minor' lexical variants would comprise.

[86] Cf. e. g. pss. XVII.51 or XIX.7; for this gloss, see below, pp. 73–9.

[87] Cf. e. g. pss. XIV.1, XVIII.6 or XXVI.5, and see below, pp. 71–3.

Two important points have already been mentioned: the high percentage of agreement in the use of 'commonplace' words or phrases, and the sporadic use of Anglian dialect words in the Royal Psalter in precisely the verses where the Vespasian Psalter employs them. Furthermore, it is striking that in more than one third of the Royal Psalter's approximately 120 double glosses for one Latin lemma, one of the gloss words (very often the first one) is the A-type *interpretamentum*.[88] The number of such double glosses presenting the A-type word is noteworthy *per se*, but even more remarkable are those doublets in the Royal Psalter where the A-type gloss appearing in the doublet does not properly fit its context, in most cases because Vespasian's Old English word translates a sense of the Latin lemma which is not applicable in the psalm verse in question. In such cases D's alternative gloss usually provides a contextually adequate rendering of the Latin lemma. For example, in ps. LXXXVIII.39, the meaning of *differe* which is most appropriate in the context is 'to spread about, scatter, disperse, separate'; Vespasian's gloss is *ældan* which renders another attested meaning of *differe*, namely 'to defer, put off, delay'. The doublet in the Royal Psalter is *yldan* ł *tobrædan*, the (phonologically) Saxonized form of the A-type gloss (*ældan*) plus a verb which translates the meaning *differe* has in that particular context. Note that in the one further occurrence of *differe* in the psalter (ps. LXXVII.21), the lemma means 'to defer, delay'. Here, the Royal Psalter agrees with the A-type gloss (*ældan*) in presenting Saxonized *geyldan* as a single gloss. In ps. LXVIII.32 *uitulum nouellum* is glossed *cælf niowe* in A, whereas D has *cealf neowe* ł *geong*; and in ps. IX.34, the A-gloss *soecan* for *requirere* translates the meaning 'to seek or search for', which is not the sense required by the context. D has *secan* ł *myndgian*, the latter gloss matching the contextual meaning of *requirere*: 'to look for, inquire after; care for'.[89] Interestingly, doublets of that type occur principally in the more difficult passages of the psalter. They possibly reveal the scholarly habit of a glossator who had realized that the translation provided by his exemplar, although not appropriate in the passage in question, was nonetheless a correct

---

[88] Cf., for example, ps. XIV.5 *commouere*: *drefan* ł *astyran* (D): *onstyran* (A); this doublet in D, as against single *onstyran* in A, occurs four times throughout the psalter; ps. LIX.14 *tribulare*: *swencan* ł *dreccan* (D): *swencan* (A); ps. XCIV.9 *temptare*: *costian* ł *fandian* (D): *costian* (A); for further examples, see the doublets in pss. XXII.4, XXIV.4, LXXVII.42, CXVIII.57 or CXXXVIII.23.

[89] For further examples, see the doublets in pss. XV.5, XXIV.21 or LXVIII.5.

rendering of the lemma and should therefore be retained (for lexico-graphical purposes, as it were).

By the same token, the Royal Glossator occasionally employs the A-type word for certain Latin lemmata which are frequently attested in the psalter and in the rendering of which he usually disagrees with the A-type gloss. For example, *adtendere, intendere* are almost invariably glossed by *bihaldan* in A and usually by *begiman* in D.[90] However, on very rare occasions, the A-type gloss also appears in D, Saxonized as *behealdan*.[91] Here one suspects that a momentary lapse in the Glossator's attention made him adopt a gloss from his consultation copy of which he otherwise would not have approved.

Finally, a striking orthographical (and, quite possibly, also phono-logical) link between the Royal and the Vespasian psalters should be mentioned. The ten occurrences of *meditatio* in the psalter are invariably glossed by <smeang>in the Vespasian Psalter. The Royal Psalter has the same gloss for eight occurrences of the lemma, spelled in five instances exactly as in the Vespasian Psalter.[92] The spelling <smeang> does not occur in any other psalter gloss (not even in the Cambridge or Junius psalters, closely dependent on Vespasian); here the word is spelled <smeaung> (as it is in the remaining three instances in the Royal gloss), or <smeagung>. According to the *Microfiche Concordance*, there is only one further occurrence of the spelling <smeang> outside the psalter glosses A and D (namely in the Old English *Regula pastoralis*), which makes the peculiar agreement between the Royal and Vespasian psalters (in a frequently attested word) stand out even more prominently. Perhaps the most economical and natural explanation for all these verbal and orthographical ties between the two psalters would be that the Royal Glossator, while working on his interlinear version, constantly had recourse to an A-type gloss.

There are further grounds for suspecting that the Royal Glossator might have drawn on an A-type gloss. But these are historical grounds, such as usually are sublimely disregarded by textual critics working on psalter relationships.[93] The A-type gloss in Junius 27 predates the Royal

---

[90] See, for example, pss. V.3, XVI.1, LXV.19, LXXVII.1, LXXVII.9 or LXXXV.6.

[91] Cf. pss. LXIX.2 and LXXX.12.   [92] Cf. e. g. ps. CXVIII.97 or CXVIII.143.

[93] Wildhagen's 'Studien zum *Psalterium Romanum*' is an ingenious exception to this universal and exclusive preoccupation of textual critics with variant readings only.

gloss;[94] the Junius manuscript was probably written in the 920s and has traditionally been assigned to Winchester on palaeographical and art historical grounds,[95] that is, to the centre which in pre-reform times was of vital importance for the intellectual formation of the Royal Glossator, as we shall see in due course.[96] This traditional ascription to Winchester has recently been challenged by David Dumville.[97] But irrespective of whether the Junius Psalter was written at Winchester or not, it is beyond question that an A-type gloss was available in post-reform Winchester by the middle of the eleventh century. More important, it obviously was still looked upon as a kind of model version, in spite of the fact that by this time the Royal Psalter gloss had already established a new tradition, the D-type psalter glosses. All this emerges from the glosses in the Winchester psalters in Vitellius E. xviii (G), Tiberius C. vi (H) and Arundel 60 (J), as well as from the gloss in the Stowe Psalter (Stowe 2 (F)), of probable Winchester origin.[98] The interlinear versions in these psalters are all predominantly D-type glosses, but all present an admixture of A-type material in varying degrees and in different parts of their gloss.[99]

We should also be aware that Winchester was not the only place where the A-type gloss was available and still laid under contribution for the

[94] For the very close dependence of Junius 27 on Vespasian A. i, see Brenner, *Junius Psalter*, pp. xiii–xv, and, most recently, Pulsiano, 'The Originality of the Vespasian Psalter'.

[95] See Ker, *Catalogue*, pp. 408–9 (no. 335), and K. Sisam, *Salisbury Psalter*, p. 48. See further Bishop, 'Early Example of Square Minuscule', p. 247, Parkes, 'The Palaeography of the Parker Manuscript', pp. 150–60, Temple, *Anglo-Saxon Manuscripts*, pp. 38–9 (no. 7), and Lapidge, 'Tenth-Century Metrical Calendar', pp. 361–2.

[96] For the relationship between the Junius Psalter and the Royal Psalter, see below, pp. 315–31.

[97] See Dumville, 'The Anglo-Saxon Chronicle', pp. 73–5, 77–8, 87–8, 92–3 and 104–6; see also *idem*, 'Kalendar of the Junius Psalter', esp. pp. 1 and 37–8. For the script in Junius 27 as a specimen of Square minuscule, Phase I, see *idem*, 'English Square Minuscule' [*ASE* 16], pp. 169–73.

[98] See Ker, *Catalogue*, pp. 298–301 (no. 224) for G, p. 262 (no. 199) for H, pp. 166–7 (no. 134) for J, and pp. 336–7 (no. 271) for F. For the probable Winchester (New Minster) origin of F, see *Missal of the New Minster*, ed. Turner, pp. xi–xiii, and Bishop, *English Caroline Minuscule*, p. xvi, n. 2.

[99] For a listing of A-type and D-type material in these psalters, see above, pp. 26–7. For a convenient summary of the textual affiliations of G, H and J, see K. Sisam, *Salisbury Psalter*, pp. 59–66. For the D-type character of F, see *ibid.*, pp. 66–8; for the A-type element in F (not previously noted), see Hofstetter, *Winchester und Sprachgebrauch*, pp. 73–5.

production of glossed psalters in the later tenth and eleventh centuries, that is, subsequent to the heyday of reform. The Cambridge Psalter (Cambridge, University Library, Ff. 1. 23 (C)), dating from *c.* 1000 (Latin text and gloss) and arguably originating from Bishop Oswald's model reform monastery at Ramsey, presents an almost uncontaminated A-type gloss.[100] A-type material is found in the Bosworth Psalter (BL Add. 37517 (L)) where the gloss was inserted at the beginning of the eleventh century between the lines of a *Psalterium Romanum* dating from the third quarter of the tenth century; the psalter was probably written at Christ Church, Canterbury, but it is not clear whether the gloss was copied out there as well.[101] Significantly, A-type material is one of the components of the Lambeth Psalter (Lambeth Palace 427 (I)), dating from the first half of the eleventh century and of unknown (perhaps Winchester) origin, a fresh interlinear version, which is famous for its highly competent glossator and the encyclopaedic character of its vocabulary. That a glossator of such competence should have drawn on the A-type gloss throws interesting light on the esteem in which this gloss (by then some two hundred years old) was held in an eminent centre of learning where the Lambeth glossator must have done his work.[102]

Like the glossator of the Lambeth Psalter, the Royal Glossator has been praised for the resourcefulness and richness of his vocabulary and for his

---

[100] For the date, see Dumville, 'On the Dating', pp. 40–1, and Lapidge, 'Abbot Germanus', p. 415 (note that Ker, *Catalogue*, pp. 11–12 (no. 13) had posited a date 's. xi^med'). The Cambridge Psalter had been traditionally associated with Winchombe: cf. Ker, *Catalogue*, p. 12, and Lapidge, 'Abbot Germanus', p. 390. For the ascription to Ramsey, see Lapidge, *ibid.*, esp. pp. 403–4 and 414–17. Note, however, that Dumville assigns the manuscript to Canterbury (St Augustine's); cf. Dumville, 'On the Dating', pp. 40–1, and *idem*, *English Caroline Script*, pp. 79–85. For the Cambridge Psalter as a pure A-type gloss, see *Cambridger Psalter*, ed. Wildhagen, pp. xiv–xv; on this psalter, see also below, pp. 283–5.

[101] For date and origin of manuscript and gloss, see Ker, *Catalogue*, pp. 161–2 (no. 129), Korhammer, 'The Origin of the Bosworth Psalter', pp. 173–87, and Brooks, *Early History*, pp. 252–3. For the textual affiliation of the gloss, see K. Sisam, *Salisbury Psalter*, p. 56. On this psalter, see also below, pp. 282–3.

[102] For the date of the psalter, cf. Ker, *Catalogue*, pp. 342–3 (no. 280); for textual affiliations, see K. Sisam, *Salisbury Psalter*, pp. 72–4, and *Lambeth Psalter*, ed. Lindelöf II, 34–6. For the opulence of I's vocabulary, see Lindelöf, *ibid.*, pp. 30–4 and 47–56. For the affinity of part of I's vocabulary with the Winchester group of texts, see Hofstetter, *Winchester und Sprachgebrauch*, pp. 84–8. For the ascription of the manuscript to Winchester, cf. O'Neill, 'Latin Learning', pp. 143–66.

scholarly habit of regularly consulting psalter exegesis for his Old English *interpretamenta*.[103] Bearing in mind the apparently wide circulation of the A-type gloss, the esteem in which this gloss was evidently held, and the indubitable verbal links between the Royal Psalter and the earlier gloss – how reasonable is it to assume that a first-rate Anglo-Saxon scholar who set about the task of providing a fresh continuous gloss to the psalter, a gloss which at every turn betrays his ingrained interest in English words, should have shut his eyes (deliberately, as it were) to an already existing psalter gloss? However, when in the following discussion of the Royal Psalter's vocabulary I regularly refer to the A-type gloss as it is represented in the Vespasian Psalter, it is not with the aim of providing irrefutable proof that that gloss type was laid under contribution by the Glossator – the matter is not settled and deserves a detailed and comprehensive treatment. Rather, I refer to the Vespasian gloss as a kind of lexical backdrop which may furnish us with some information about what alternatives there would have been for the Glossator's choice of words, and which may, at least in some instances, suggest why he chose a specific glossword. Still, by referring regularly to the Vespasian Psalter gloss, I am arguing that any pronouncement on psalter relationship resulting from a meticulous but undiscriminating count of thousands of variant readings cannot capture in an adequate fashion the links between individual glossed psalters, at least not in those cases where glossators were at work who must be reckoned among the intellectual elite of their generation; an elite who, in their Latin writings, can be shown to have drawn in a confident and flexible manner on a wide range of written sources.

---

[103] Cf. above, p. 32, and see below, pp. 42–3.

3

The vocabulary of the Royal Psalter

The remarkable richness and variety of the Royal Psalter's vocabulary and the unusual character of part of that vocabulary have been noted ever since Fritz Roeder's edition of its text became available for scholarly study.[1] As Kenneth Sisam has aptly put it: 'The original glossator was a man of considerable learning. His vocabulary is rich and varied; and if allowance is made for the difficulty of the language of the psalms, he makes few gross errors'.[2] When referring to the Royal Psalter's vocabulary, scholars have regularly pointed out two salient features of the gloss: first, the fact that its glossator is much inclined to use a variety of Old English *interpretamenta* for a given Latin lemma (an inclination which, for example, is utterly distinct from that of the glossator of the Vespasian Psalter) and, second, the Glossator's extraordinary penchant for choosing rare words, many of which are not recorded outside the Royal Psalter (or attested in directly dependent glosses only), and no doubt many of which were coined by the Glossator himself. A substantial number of these

---

[1] See, for example, the appreciative remarks by Roeder himself in the preface to his edition (*Der altenglische Regius-Psalter*, pp. vii–viii). In an appendix (*ibid.*, pp. 303–5), Roeder supplied a list of words from the gloss which were not recorded in the dictionaries by Bosworth and Toller (BT, BTS) and H. Sweet (*A Student's Dictionary of Anglo-Saxon* (Oxford, 1896)). See also Schlutter, 'Zum Wortschatz des Regius Psalters', pp. 10–27, and Wildhagen, 'Studien zum *Psalterium Romanum*', p. 449, who expand Roeder's list of rare words or *hapax legomena*. Similarly, A. S. Napier, 'Contributions to Old English Lexicography', lists rare words from the Royal gloss among his collection, from Old English texts, of words of unusual character or hitherto unrecorded.

[2] *Salisbury Psalter*, p. 55; see also *ibid.*, p. 44, and cf. the similar remarks by Wildhagen, 'Studien zum *Psalterium Romanum*', pp. 448–9. The most recent and most comprehensive study of the Royal Psalter's vocabulary (undertaken again primarily by compiling word-lists), is by Wiesenekker, *Translation Performance*, pp. 135–217.

42

unusual words belong to the register of poetry.[3] It is interesting to remark that these extravagant idiosyncrasies of the Glossator often are not adopted by the other D-type psalters, which tend to choose a more common gloss word instead of one of the Glossator's rarities and to cut down his exuberant lexical variation with the aim of producing (again) a stable relationship between Latin lemma and Old English *interpretamentum*.[4]

In previous discussions of the Royal Psalter's vocabulary, the focus has been primarily on the Old English lexicon as a whole and the Psalter's position within this lexicon. Accordingly, it has duly been noted which words are unusual or not yet recorded (and should therefore be added to the Old English dictionaries),[5] where the Royal gloss agrees or disagrees with other psalter glosses,[6] which new loan formations or semantic loans can be found in the Royal Psalter,[7] which of its words are restricted to certain dialects in Old English[8] or whether part of its vocabulary can be attributed to a certain school.[9] The importance and utility of such lists and discussions are beyond question, but what is needed now is an

---

[3] See the lists compiled by Wiesenekker, *Translation Performance*, pp. 192–201 (for variation in the rendering of a given Latin lemma) and 210–13 (for poetical words). Additional material (especially for rare words) can be found in his list of loan formations and semantic loans in the Royal Psalter, pp. 136–60. See also the articles by Schlutter, Wildhagen and Napier, listed above, n. 1.

[4] See, for example, K. Sisam, *Salisbury Psalter*, p. 44, for this tendency in the Salisbury Psalter (K) which otherwise is very closely dependent on the Royal gloss.

[5] Cf. above, n. 1. [6] Cf. above, pp. 33–4.

[7] See Wiesenekker, *Translation Performance*, pp. 136–60.

[8] See Schabram, *Superbia* (pp. 30–1, and table at the end of the book) who discusses the dialectal relevance of the renderings for *superbia*, *superbus* and *superbire* in the Royal Psalter in the wider perspective of his study of the dialectal and chronological distribution of the Old English terminology for the concept of *superbia*. (For the terms for *superbia* etc. with regard to Æthelwold's school, see also below, pp. 410–23). See also Wenisch, *Spezifisch anglisches Wortgut*, *passim*, for Anglian dialect words in the Royal Psalter.

[9] See Hofstetter, *Winchester und Sprachgebrauch*, pp. 462–4, and cf. E. Seebold, 'Die ae. Entsprechungen von lat. *sapiens* und *prudens*: Eine Untersuchung über die mundartliche Gliederung der ae. Literatur', *Anglia* 92 (1974), 291–333, who includes the Royal Psalter in a group of texts in some way connected with the Benedictine reform (his 'Benediktinergruppe'), which agree in their renditions of *sapiens* and *prudens*. For further discussion of the Royal Psalter and the vocabulary of Æthelwold's school, see below, pp. 90–113.

analysis of the gloss words within their immediate contexts, that is to say within the context of their Latin lemmata as well as within the context of the surrounding English glosses. Such an analysis, undertaken from a semantic and stylistic point of view, would enable us to determine to what extent word choice is conditioned by the context and to what extent the Glossator conceived of his interlinear version, not as a haphazard assemblage of Latin–Old English word pairs, but as a text form intermediate between discontinuous glossing and prose translation. I am well aware that such a contextual approach is not normally brought to bear upon Old English interlinear versions,[10] whose glossators are, more often than not, seen as the crude forbears of Dr Johnson's 'harmless drudge', the lexicographer.[11] I am equally aware that a full analysis of the vast gloss corpus of the Psalter is beyond the scope of the present book. In what follows, I shall do no more than tentatively point out in what way the choice of Old English glosses shapes the overall appearance of the Royal Psalter. This in turn may help us to form a better impression of the personality and intellectual stance of a glossator whom thus far we have come to know as a man of an ambitiously innovative and scholarly disposition, inasmuch as he set out to produce a fresh interlinear translation of the psalms to be accompanied by an explanatory and exegetical commentary in Latin.

LEXICAL VARIATION AND DOUBLE GLOSSES

Lexical variation, that is the translation of a given Latin lemma (which occurs more than once in the psalter) by a number of different Old English words, is a hallmark of the Royal Psalter. A first notion of this feature may be gained from the following short list of examples. In each

---

[10] The short monograph by H. Götz ('Zur Bedeutungsanalyse und Darstellung althochdeutscher Glossen', in R. Grosse, S. Blum and H. Götz, *Beiträge zur Bedeutungserschließung im althochdeutschen Wortschatz*, Sitzungsberichte der sächsischen Akademie der Wissenschaften zu Leipzig, Phil.-hist. Klasse 118/1 (Berlin, 1977), 53–208) analyses a great number of Old High German glosses (from a variety of sources) by having resort to the context of their Latin lemmata on a hitherto unprecedented scale. However, this is done not with a view to providing a picture of the translation performance in a given interlinear version, but with the primary aim of establishing the full range of meanings of the *interpretamentum* in question to be entered in a comprehensive dictionary of Old High German.

[11] See S. Johnson, *A Dictionary of the English Language* (London, 1755), s. v. *lexicographer*.

case the glosses from the Vespasian Psalter (A) are recorded by way of providing information about the *interpretamenta* the Glossator would have found in the A-type gloss which he arguably consulted.[12]

A conspicuous example is the rendering of *honor* by no less than five Old English equivalents: *arweorþness, arweorþung, wyrþmynt, weorþscipe* and *weorþung*. (The Vespasian Psalter invariably has *ar*.)[13] Further examples would be: *forbryttan, forgnidan, tobrecan* and *tobrytan* for *conterere* (A: *forðræstan*); *gewilnung* and *gyrning* for *desiderium* (A: *lust*); *wiþercwedolnis* and *wiþersæc* for *contradictio* (A: *wiðcwednis*); *cirice, gesomning, gesomnung, getreowful gesomnung, haligu gesomnung* for *ecclesia* (A: *circe*);[14] *ablysian, areodigan, aryderian, ascamian, sceamian* and *aswarnian* for *erubescere* (A: *scamian*); *bilewit, geþwære, manþwære* and *manswæse* for *mansuetus* (A: *monðwære*); *miltsung* and *ofearmung* for *miseratio* (A: *milds*);[15] *unsped* and *wædlung* for *inopia* (A: *weðelnis*); *hlynnan* and *swegan* for *intonare* (A: *hleoðrian*); and *behealdan, beseon, geseon, gelocian* for *respicere* (A: *gelocian*).[16] What does not emerge from an uncommented listing of such examples of lexical variation is that in the case of these glosses (as in the case of innumerable similar instances), there is no question of helpless or awkward uncertainty about an adequate rendering of the lemma being the reason for such multiple gloss words. On the contrary, such lexical variation tends to confirm one's overall impression when working one's way through the gloss, namely that the Glossator had a firm command of the resources and the resourcefulness of his native language, especially its wealth of (near-)synonyms and the ease with which new compounds and derivatives could be coined. He adeptly employs such resources and resourcefulness in search of an equivalent for the lemma which would be most adequate in its context or through which certain stylistic effects could be achieved. In chs. 4 and 6 below, we will have occasion to inspect some such cases of lexical variation and possible explanations for them more closely; for the moment – and in order to flesh out the skeletal information provided by the foregoing list of examples – let us consider just one case of lexical variation in some detail.

---

[12] For the possibility that the Glossator drew on the A-type gloss, see above, pp. 33–41.

[13] See below, pp. 203–5, for an assessment of these (near-)synonyms and lexical variants.

[14] For these glosses, see below, pp. 104–13.

[15] For these glosses, see below, pp. 399–403.

[16] Further material for a study of lexical variation can be drawn from the list provided by Wiesenekker, *Translation Performance*, pp. 192–201; cf. also the list in Pulsiano, 'Defining the A-type and D-type Traditions', pp. 316–27.

The glosses for refugium

Latin *refugium* occurs fourteen times in the psalter and (with one exception) always refers to God as the refuge or protection of mortals. The lemma is invariably glossed by *geberg* 'protection, defence, refuge' in the Vespasian Psalter. The Royal Psalter has *frofor* eight times, the doublets *rotsung* ɫ *frofor* and *frofor* ɫ *gener* once each, and also once each, the glosses *rotnis*, *tohyht*, *tofleam* and *help*, which gives us a total of no less than seven *interpretamenta* for *refugium*. From a consideration of these glosses in their respective contexts, several interesting points concerning the method of the Glossator emerge: first, the word employed most frequently, namely *frofor*, usually means 'consolation', which implies that the Royal Glossator preferred an abstract and allegorical rather than a literal rendering of the lemma. (Most of his alternative glosses translate the lemma in a similar abstract fashion.) Such inclination to translate *refugium* by a word meaning 'consolation' could well have been prompted by psalm exegesis such as Cassiodorus's: '*Refugium* ergo fidelium est, quando eos de animae periculo liberat'.[17] It is probably significant that this explanation provided by Cassiodorus is copied verbatim in the margin of Royal 2. B. V (57v) as a scholion on *refugium* in ps. XLV.2. On two further occasions, *refugium* is explained typologically as *resurrectio* in the marginal commentary,[18] which again may be indebted to Cassiodorus.

The second point of interest revealed by a scrutiny of these glosses is that the three earliest occurrences of *refugium* in the psalter show the Glossator experimenting with various possibilities for translating the lemma. Here we meet one of the two doublets, namely *rotsung* ɫ *frofr* (ps. IX.10), as well as a second derivative from the adjective *rot*, namely *rotnis* (ps. XXX.3), and a prefix formation: *tohyht* (ps. XVII.3). Old English *tohyht* 'hope, consolation' is extremely rare and possibly belongs to the register of poetry (it occurs in the *Rune Poem*). In any event, stylistic considerations may have played a role in the Glossator's choice of *tohyht* at this specific point, as will become clear from a glance at text and gloss of ps. XVII.3:

	trumnes	min	tohyht		ic hyhte	on	hine
dominus	*firmamentum*	*meum*	*et refugium*	*meum . . .*	*et sperabo*	*in*	*eum*

---

[17] 'He is a *refugium* for the faithful when he liberates them from the danger their souls are in.' *Expositio* I, 415; cf. also *ibid.* I, 528, II, 822, 830 and 1282.

[18] On 37r and 108v as scholia to pss. XXX.4 and XC.9.

By his choice of *tohyht* the Glossator achieves alliteration with *trumnes* and a *figura etymologica* with *hyhte*, stylistic embellishments for which he has a great predilection, as we shall see presently. No such rhetorical effects occur in the Latin psalm verse.

Rotsung and *rotnis*, derivatives from the adjective *rot* 'glad, cheerful' or 'noble, excellent', are equally rare and may be *ad hoc* formations of the Glossator. However, after experimenting with them in two places (not far apart) he discarded them.[19] We can only speculate what his reasons for this were. Perhaps they were semantic reasons, because he did not consider the senses of the base adjective (which would also be manifest in the derivatives) wholly appropriate for translating *refugium*. Perhaps he was also dissatisfied with *rotsung* and *rotnis* because of their phonetic similarity with *rot* 'root' and, above all, with *rotung* 'corruption, ulcer', *rotian* 'to rot, putrefy' and *(h)rot* 'scum'. It is true that the stressed vowel in *rotsung* and *rotnis* was originally long, that in *rotung*, *rotian* and *(h)rot* originally short; however, the 'Middle English' shortening of long vowels before two consonants, and in the first syllable of a three-syllable word, is attested already in texts from the eleventh century and may have been in effect in spoken language much earlier.[20] In any event, a glossator given as much to sound effects as ours is could not have been too happy with a phonetic similarity between glosses for *refugium* (which in turn referred to the Deity) and words for scum and putrefaction.

A third point emerges from our close inspection of the seven glosses for *refugium* in their contexts: after some experimenting in the first thirty psalms of the psalter, *frofor*, which thus far had been only one of four possible choices, becomes established as the almost exclusive gloss word for *refugium*. It occurs eight times as a single gloss,[21] plus once in a doublet *frofr* l *gener* (ps. LXX.3). After ps. XXX, there are only three instances where *refugium* is not glossed by *frofor* alone, and these can all be explained by reference to their contexts. Let us first consider the aforementioned doublet *frofr* l *gener* (ps. LXX.3). Old English *gener* is derived from the verb *nerian* 'to save, rescue, defend, protect'. Accordingly, the meaning for the noun given by the dictionaries is 'refuge,

---

[19] There is one further occurrence of *rotnis* in the Royal gloss: in ps. LXV.12, *refrigerium* 'succour, comfort, consolation' is glossed *rotnis* l *frofr*. Note that here again, the word occurs in a doublet and in the first part of the psalter.

[20] Cf. SB, § 138.2 and 4, and Campbell, § 329.1.

[21] Cf. pss. XXX.4, XXXI.7, XLV.2, LVIII.17, LXXXIX.1, XC.2, XC.9 and CXLIII.2.

protection'. *Gener* was to become the dominant gloss word for *refugium* in the Lambeth Psalter, whose glossator thus decided on a more literal rendering of the lemma (similar to Vespasian's *geberg*).[22] By choosing *gener* as an alternative gloss in a doublet at this specific point, the Glossator again links two Latin words by *figura etymologica* in his gloss: *eripe me* in the foregoing psalm verse (ps. LXX.2) is glossed: *nere*. Appropriately, *gener* in the following doublet stresses the literal aspects of *refugium* in this context. Note that, again, such paronomasia is not found in the Latin.

In the second instance with a gloss other than *frofor* after ps. XXX, *refugium* is translated by *tofleam* 'refuge' (ps. XCIII.22). This is a most intriguing gloss. It is a *hapax legomenon* which has not even been adopted by the psalters most closely dependent on the Royal gloss. It is clearly a loan rendition of Latin *refugium* (*fleam* meaning 'flight'), and morphologically corresponds precisely to Old High German *zuofluht* (German *Zuflucht*), employed to translate *refugium* in Old High German glosses.[23] The correspondence between *tofleam* and *zuofluht* is all the more striking, since the prefix in both words is not an exact rendering of Latin *re-* 'backwards', which gives rise to the suspicion that Old English *tofleam* was modelled on the German word. Such a coinage would not be without parallel in the Royal Psalter. German (that is Old High German or Old Saxon) influence may be suspected in a number of other words employed in the Royal Psalter (and in the Old English Rule). We shall consider several of these and the implications of their presence in ch. 10, below. At this point in the psalter the use of *tofleam* instead of *frofor* may be attributable to the circumstance that *consolationes* had been translated by *frofra* shortly before (ps. XCIII.19). It should also be noted that by his choice of *tofleam*, the Glossator achieves *f*-alliteration with the next gloss for a noun in the same verse: *fultum* for *auxilium*.[24]

The third and last instance where a gloss other than *frofor* has been chosen after ps. XXX is the one point in the psalter where *refugium* does not refer to God. In the verse in question, it is stated that 'the high

---

[22] It will be recalled that the Lambeth gloss is a fresh interlinear version which nevertheless draws freely on A- and D-type gloss material; cf. above, p. 27.

[23] Cf. Schützeichel, *Althochdeutsches Wörterbuch* and Wells, *Althochdeutsches Glossenwörterbuch*, s. v. *zuofluht*.

[24] The main stress in *tofleam* would have been on the first syllable (as in German *Zuflucht*); for alliteration on syllables bearing a secondary stress only, see *Homilies of Ælfric*, ed. Pope I, 124–8.

48

mountains are the *refugium* for the harts and the stone for the hedgehogs' (*montes excelsi ceruis petra refugium herenacis*; ps. CIII.18). Apparently the Glossator felt that his usual abstract or allegorical translation of *refugium* by *frofor* (or *rotsung, rotnis, tohyht* or *tofleam*) would not be appropriate here and therefore had resort to a plain English noun: *help*. By comparison, the Vespasian and Lambeth psalters employ their standard (and more literal) glosses (*geberg* and *gener*) on this occasion as well.

To sum up: a close analysis of the glosses for *refugium* throughout the psalter reveals a thoroughly competent and sensitive glossator at work. He is given to experimenting, thereby making ample use of synonyms and employing new or unusual coinages and words belonging to the poetic register. Despite all this versatility, his glossing method is by no means haphazard. It is guided by the firm principle of establishing one more or less standard translation for the lemma (*frofor*), while keeping open an avenue of choosing (partial) synonyms for this standard term for purposes of stressing specific semantic connotations or achieving stylistic effects in a given context.

Double glosses

In his glosses for *refugium* we have observed the Glossator resorting twice to double glosses. Such doublets are a conspicuous stylistic feature of the Royal gloss, some 120 of them occurring throughout the psalter. In its employment of doublets, the Royal Psalter stands about midway between the Vespasian gloss, where practically no doublets occur,[25] and the Lambeth Psalter which presents approximately 1,400 double, more than sixty triple and three fourfold glosses.[26] The difference between the

---

[25] The second glosses in the doublets occurring occasionally in the Vespasian Psalter were almost all entered by an eleventh-century hand (probably s. xi[1]) with the purpose of bringing the original Vespasian gloss into conformity with the D-type gloss for the lemma in question. For a list and discussion of the doublets in Vespasian A. i, see Campbell, 'The Glosses', pp. 90–2. As far as the Vespasian gloss is concerned, the study (often quoted with respect to doublets) by I. Koskenniemi, *Repetitive Word Pairs in Old and Early Middle English Prose* (Turku, 1968) is utterly misleading. All the 'doublets' under discussion there and taken from the Vespasian Psalter (pp. 24–7) translate word pairs which occur already in the Latin text of the psalter (and not single lemmata). The Vespasian Psalter is the only interlinear text analysed in Koskenniemi's study.

[26] Cf. *Lambeth-Psalter*, ed. Lindelöf, pp. 30–1.

Lambeth Psalter and our gloss is striking, not only on grounds of arithmetic but more so on grounds of style. While one can scarcely escape the conclusion that the Lambeth Glossator compiled his double and triple glosses with the habit and resolution of a lexicographer who had set himself the task of producing some sort of *Roget's Thesaurus* for Old English, the Royal Glossator seems to have conceived of his doublets more in terms of style.

There may be doublets, such as *rotsung ł frofr* (ps. IX.10) noted above, which may have been chosen primarily by way of experimenting with various translation equivalents for the lemma; or there may be doublets chosen for purposes of grammatical clarification, as when *non erat* is translated *he næs ł na wæs* (ps. XXXVI.36), or when the Latin imperative *psallite* is glossed *syngan ge ł singað ge* (ps. XLVI.7; *singað* being the Old English imperative proper, and *syngan* probably to be taken as a subjunctive form 'you should sing', which would be appropriate in the context).[27] There may also be double glosses, the components of which are – at least to our eyes – more or less completely synonymous such as *ic gange ł fare* for *ambulem* (ps. XXII.41) or *cwicra ł lifiendra* for *uiuorum* (ps. CXIV.9). However, the majority of the double glosses seem to have been employed for more specifically stylistic purposes,[28] either to display different semantic aspects of a lemma, both relevant to the lemma in its context as we have seen in the case of *frofr ł gener* (ps. LXX.3); cf. also *beorht ł mære* for *praeclarum* (ps. XXII.5) or *þicnes ł fætnes* for *crassitudo* (ps. CXL.7, referring to clods of earth). Or a literal and a free rendering (which might better suit the context) of a lemma are coupled in a doublet as in *ablysien* ('blush') *ł forscamien* for *erubescant* (ps. XXXIX.15) or *hy gesomniað ł hydaþ* ('they assemble or hide') for *conlocabunt* (ps. CIII.22). Or a common Old English word is joined to one which is decidedly rare, as

---

[27] Cf. SB, § 361, n. 1, and Campbell, § 735 (f), for forms of the present subjunctive in *-an*.

[28] Doublets were employed for stylistic reasons prior to the Royal gloss, albeit in prose texts only. For their use in works connected with King Alfred's translation programme, see Bately, 'Old English Prose', pp. 123–5 and the references given there. For the frequent occurrence of tautological word pairs as a feature of style in the Old English *Letter of Alexander to Aristotle* (arguably dating from the same period as the Royal Psalter), see Orchard, *Pride and Prodigies*, pp. 132–3. For the frequent employment of doublets as a stylistic device in the Old English Benedictine Rule, see Gretsch, *Regula*, pp. 263–8, and cf. below, pp. 113–14.

anunga ł *in sceortnisse* for *in breui* (ps. II.13), *ðystro* ł *swarcunga* for *tenebras* (ps. XVII.29), *awyrp* ł *ascyhh* for *proicias* (ps. L.13) or *ongalnis* ł *sang* for *decantatio* (ps. LXX.6). (In each case the unusual word in the pair has been underlined.) Apparently psalm exegesis was drawn on for some of these doublets: in the aforementioned pair *gesomniað* ł *hydað* (for *conlocabunt*), the gloss *hydað* is almost certainly indebted to Cassiodorus.[29]

In other words, the double glosses in the Royal Psalter are not a makeshift employed by a glossator who is inept at conveying the meaning of a lemma by a single Old English word;[30] nor were they conceived of as convenient listings of Old English synonyms for translation or teaching purposes (as they arguably were in the Lambeth Psalter). Rather, they should be jugded in terms of rhetoric, as a form of hendiadys (striking as this may appear in an interlinear version). As such they are an integral and important part of lexical variation in the Royal Psalter.

LOANWORDS

The Royal Glossator deploys his vast lexicological resources and his keen interest in language also by the Latin loanwords he uses. His gloss presents several loans which, by the mid-tenth century, must have been newcomers to the English language. For some of these we may well suspect that the Glossator himself had a hand in their introduction and dissemination. For example, all occurrences of *canticum* 'song of praise' in the psalter (ten in total) are glossed by *cantic*, a word which, prior to the Royal gloss, is extremely rare.[31] All occurrences of the verb *scrutari* 'to investigate' (nine in total), plus the sole occurrence of the noun *scrutinium*, are glossed by *scrudnian* and *scrudnung*, loans not recorded anterior to the Royal Psalter. The consistent and frequent use of *scrudnian*, *scrudnung* and *cantic* establishes close verbal links between the Royal Psalter and the Old English Benedictine Rule.[32] Such links stand in view even more prominently when we consider that the psalter glosses dependent on the

---

[29] Cf. *Expositio* II, 935: 'in suis se trepidi cubilibus *abdiderunt*'.

[30] For the (widespread) opinion that double glosses in interlinear versions are called forth by a state of indecision on the glossator's part as to how to render the lemma in question, see, for example, S. M. Kuhn, 'Synonyms in the Old English Bede', *JEGP* 46 (1947), 168–76, at 168–70.

[31] Cf. Gretsch, 'Der liturgische Wortschatz', p. 344 and n. 142.

[32] For a discussion of the links between the two texts in the case of *cantic*, see Gretsch,

Royal gloss (as well as the Lambeth Psalter) do not strictly adhere to their model for the glosses in question.

Further links between the Psalter and the Rule are established by their use of *chor* (for Latin *chorus*), a loan which is first attested in these two texts,[33] as well as by their use of *alter* (Royal Psalter) or *altare* (Rule) for Latin *altare*.[34] The form *alter* is infrequently attested in Alfredian texts, but it was introduced into psalter glossing by the Royal Glossator. It should also be noted that in both texts, the Psalter and the Rule, the native synonym *weofod* occurs with approximately equal frequency as the loan.[35]

The loanword *son* (from Latin *sonus* 'sound') forms another link between the Psalter and the Rule. The word occurs extremely rarely in Alfredian texts. *Son* must have been rather unfamiliar to the scribe of Oxford, Bodleian Library, Hatton 20 (s. ix[ex], one of the two earliest manuscripts of the Old English *Regula pastoralis*), because in one of its two occurrences in that text, this scribe replaced *son* by native *song*.[36] The somewhat exotic character of *son* may also be deduced from the Royal Psalter itself, where *sonus* is glossed three times by native *sweg*, once by a doublet where the loan is coupled with a native synonym: *son ł hlisa* (ps. XVIII.5) and once only by *son* alone (ps. LXIV.8). Note also that the Vespasian and the Lambeth psalters employ *sweg* and that the Royal Psalter's closest relative, the Salisbury Psalter, has *son* only once (ps. LXIV.8). The Glossator's taste for *son* is matched, however, by the apparent familiarity with that word revealed by the translator of the Rule: he uses *son* only once, but, interestingly, in one of his frequent and minute additions to the Latin text (as a term for Latin *antiphona*).[37]

In the case of *cantic* and *scrudnian* we have noted the Glossator's inclination consistently to employ the loanword at every occurrence of the Latin lemma from which the loan derives. Such a procedure is not restricted to loans which arguably were introduced by the Glossator

---

'Der liturgische Wortschatz', pp. 329–33 and 342–8, and cf. below, pp. 92–3. For *scrudnian*, see below, pp. 211–18 and 407–10.

[33] See Funke, *Die gelehrten lateinischen Lehn- und Fremdwörter*, pp. 160 and 164.

[34] See *ibid.*, and pp. 141–2.

[35] Cf. Gneuss, *Lehnbildungen*, p. 85 and Gretsch, *Regula*, pp. 361–2.

[36] See *Pastoral Care*, ed. Sweet I, 175.9; see also Funke, *Die gelehrten lateinischen Lehn- und Fremdwörter*, p. 50.

[37] BR 41.9; cf. *RSB* 17.7.

himself; the same tendency makes itself felt with regard to loanwords of long standing. For example, *mons* is always glossed by *munt* (here the Royal gloss agrees with the Vespasian Psalter, whereas Lambeth uses *munt*, *dun* or *munt* ɫ *dun* indiscriminately). Latin *puteus* and *fouea* are more or less synonyms in the psalter, both meaning 'pit, abyss'. The Glossator has *pytt* only for *puteus* and employs native *seað* for *fouea*. By comparison, Vespasian has *seað* only, for both *puteus* and *fouea*, and Lambeth, again, uses *pytt* or *pytt* ɫ *seað* indiscriminately for both lemmata. A third example would be *ceaster*, adopted from Latin *castra* at an early date (as is clear from the presence of palatalization and assibilation of initial /k/ and the palatal diphthongization (*ea*) of early Old English *æ*, which in turn is the reflex of Latin *a* in Primitive Old English). In accordance with the Vespasian and the Lambeth psalters, the Glossator employs *ceaster* regularly as a gloss to *ciuitas* 'town, city', which obviously had become the usual meaning of *ceaster* in Old English.[38] In the Royal gloss, however, *ceaster* is also used to translate two of the three occurrences of *castra* in the psalter and where this bears the sense of 'army camp' (pss. LXXVII.28 and CV.16; Vespasian and Lambeth use *fyrdwic*). Here it seems likely that the Glossator chose *ceaster* because he wished to couple loanword and Latin etymon in his gloss, even if this implied a clearly unusual meaning for the long-established loanword *ceaster*.[39]

What is striking about these examples of established loans being consistently paired with their etyma is that the Glossator evidently saw no difficulty in coupling them, despite the manifest phonetic differences, which had been effected by Vulgar Latin, Germanic or Old English sound changes, between *mons* and *munt*, *puteus* and *pytt* or *castra* and *ceaster* (/tʃɛɑstər/). Perhaps in some such cases it was not so much a clear notion that the Latin and the Old English word were identical, but rather the unmistakable phonetic similarity between both words which brought the Glossator to couple them. In connection with lexical variation, we have already observed the Glossator's penchant for word-play and sound effects. We should recall, however, that medieval scholars often took phonetic similarity between any two words to point to a common etymology for

---

[38] Cf. the relevant entry in *DOE*.

[39] In the third instance of *castra* in the psalter, the Glossator took the lemma to mean 'army' (a sense of *castra* well-attested in Medieval Latin), which he accordingly translated by *werod*. Perhaps he felt that the semantic range of *ceaster* could not be stretched to encompass the meaning 'army'.

these words.[40] Other examples can be found where Latin lemmata are glossed by Old English words bearing some phonological resemblance to them, although there is no question of such glosses being loanwords deriving from their lemmata. Consider, for example, *manswæs* for *mansuetus* 'mild, humble' (ps. XXIV.9) or *on sealtsyleðan* for *in salsilaginem* 'on salty ground' (ps. CVI.34),[41] and the consistent and frequent translation of *nubes* by *genipu* (e. g. pss. XVII.12, XXXV.6 and LXVII.35, in distinction to the Vespasian and Lambeth glosses). In some such cases the Glossator may have presumed a common etymological origin of lemma and gloss, a presumption which is not borne out by modern philology; in others, especially in those where the Old English words were his own coinages (as possibly were *manswæs* and *sealtsyleða*), he was perhaps content and even delighted that part of the phonological structure of the lemma could be retained in its Old English gloss.

At all events, this various evidence provided by the loanwords in the Royal Psalter points again to the Glossator's acute interest in the fabric of language, in etymological and phonological links between Latin and English, and in the enrichment of English by the agency of Latin, the language of unparalleled prestige.

UNUSUAL WORDS AND STYLISTIC EMBELLISHMENTS

The Latin psalms are difficult texts, and they are poetic texts.[42] The difficulty of their language results from various circumstances of which

---

[40] For such etymologies based on phonetic similarity and for a comprehensive survey of the etymological methods and handbooks available in Anglo-Saxon England, see Gneuss, 'The Study of Language', pp. 22–5. For the pervasive importance of the study of etymology in the Latin Middle Ages, see also E. R. Curtius, 'Etymologie als Denkform' in his *Europäische Literatur und Lateinisches Mittelalter*, 2nd ed. (Bern, 1954), pp. 486–90 (transl. W. R. Trask, *European Literature and the Latin Middle Ages* (New York, 1953), pp. 495–500).

[41] For a discussion of the translations of *salsilago* in the Royal and other psalter glosses, see Gneuss, *Lehnbildungen*, p. 126.

[42] For surveys of the origins, transmission, literary forms and use of the original Hebrew psalms (and further references on the subject), see *The Oxford Companion to the Bible*, ed. B. M. Metzger and M. D. Coogan (Oxford, 1993), pp. 626–9, *DTC* XIII (1936), 1093–1114 and 1148–9, *Die Religion in Geschichte und Gegenwart*, 3rd ed. by K. Galling, 6 vols. (Tübingen, 1957–63) V (1961), 672–86, *LThK* VIII, 851–7, *Dictionnaire encyclopédique de la Bible*, ed. P.-M. Bogaert *et al.*, 2nd ed. (Turnhout,

only the most obvious need briefly to be set out here. The psalms were originally translated into Latin, not directly from the Hebrew, but via the Greek Septuagint. Concerning the Greek text it is relevant to note that this is marred to some extent by corruptions found already in the Hebrew exemplar which lay behind the Greek translation. Such corruptions as well as frequent textual variants in the Hebrew original result from the fact that the psalter is not a homogeneous text composed at a given time, but that, in its transmitted form, it rather represents an agglomeration of earlier collections of poems and songs which were composed over a period spanning at least 600 years (perhaps even stretching from the era of King David (*c.* 1000 B. C.) to the time of the Maccabees (second century B. C.)). The textual corruptions and variants in the Hebrew psalter testify to this long and complicated transmissional history of the majority of the 150 psalms, a history which in many cases almost certainly included periods and branches of oral transmission.

The subsequent translation from the Septuagint into Latin aggravated the problem of textual cruces and corruptions. We have seen (above, pp. 21–4) that because of the unsatisfactory state of the Latin text, by the time of St Jerome, three revisions of the oldest Latin translation from the Greek had been deemed necessary, which gave us the *Romanum*, *Gallicanum* and *Hebraicum* psalter texts. Of these revisions, only the last was based entirely on the Hebrew and was in effect a fresh translation, but this version *iuxta hebraeos* was, as we have also seen, not widely current. The Hebrew text itself would have been beyond the compass of most medieval scholars. We certainly know of no Anglo-Saxon scholar who would have been in a position to consult the Hebrew text in cases where he was puzzled by a passage in his Latin psalter.[43] In any event, the

---

1987), pp. 1068–74, R. Smend, *Die Entstehung des Alten Testaments*, 3rd ed. (Stuttgart, 1984), pp. 188–201. For an evaluation of the psalms in terms of specific literary genres, see especially the seminal study by H. Gunkel and J. Begrich, *Einleitung in die Psalmen. Die Gattungen der religiösen Lyrik Israels*, 2nd ed. (Göttingen, 1975); see further, R. Alter, 'Psalms', in *A Literary Guide to the Bible*, ed. R. Alter and F. Kermode (Cambridge, MA, 1987), pp. 244–62.

[43] See Gneuss, 'Language Contact', pp. 123–5, for remarks on the complete absence of any reading knowledge of Hebrew in Anglo-Saxon England and for a survey of the sources available to the Anglo-Saxons for the Hebrew alphabets which they copied into their manuscripts and for the etymological explanations of Hebrew words or names which they paraded in their writings. The situation in Anglo-Saxon England is consonant with the situation obtaining on the Continent; for knowledge of Hebrew in

version to be glossed by the Royal Glossator, and the version which was in almost universal use in England before the second half of the tenth century was the *Romanum*, the version with the slightest amount of revision and hence the greatest number of textual problems.[44]

Further difficulties would have presented themselves in the form of the many references to Jewish customs and the paraphernalia of Old Testament life throughout the psalter. Such references had often been translated incomprehendingly into Latin (as in fact they sometimes were into Greek). We may, however, scarcely expect a sensible English gloss for what was a garbled rendering in Latin.[45] Psalm exegesis, as it was available to the Glossator, was (as we have seen above, pp. 28–31) primarily allegorical and typological. It does not provide much philological commentary, let alone any detailed explanations of *realia*. Finally, we have to bear in mind that the psalms are poetry, a circumstance to which a great number of philological difficulties are attributable, and a point likely to be overlooked by modern-day Anglo-Saxonists with their predominant concern for psalm glossing or the role of the psalter in the Christian liturgy. Among Old Testament scholars, a basic classification of the psalms into three literary genres, namely hymns or songs of praise, laments and poems of thanksgiving

---

early medieval Europe, see M. Thiel, *Grundlagen und Gestalt der Hebräischkenntisse des frühen Mittelalters*, Biblioteca degli 'Studi Medievali' 4 (Spoleto, 1973). For an attempt to copy the Hebrew original of a few psalms (in Latin transcription) into a tenth-century *psalterium triplex* (that is a psalter containing all three Latin versions), see *ibid.*, p. 206 and n. 764.

[44] It would have been possible for the Royal Glossator to consult a *Gallicanum* text, since such psalters were imported from the Continent and available in England by the mid-tenth century; see below, pp. 274–7. The *Hebraicum* could have been available to the Glossator in a *psalterium triplex* or as part of a pandect; cf. above, p. 23.

[45] For example, in ps. CXVII.27, the *Romanum* reading *in confrequentationibus* is translated *on gelomlecnessum* 'in a numerous assembly' by the Royal Glossator (a translation which is very close to the A-type gloss, *in gelomlicnissum*). This makes perfect sense for the Latin lemma *per se* (and is in broad agreement with the explanation given by Cassiodorus for the Latin word, cf. *Expositio* II, 1057) but is nonsense in the context. The original Hebrew word means 'twigs providing shade' (the passage refers to the feast of the Tabernacles); the *Hebraicum* appropriately has *frondosus* 'densely leaved' in lieu of *confrequentatio* in the *Romanum*; the *Gallicanum* reading is also more to the point by employing *condensus* 'dense, densely leaved'. For the literal sense of this passage, see Hoberg, *Die Psalmen der Vulgata*, p. 419; for the Old English glosses, cf. Gneuss, *Lehnbildungen*, pp. 129–30.

has been widely accepted.[46] As poetic compositions the psalms often employ a circumlocutory, dark or metaphorical wording, the language of a poetic tradition[47] which had not much in common with the diction of Latin or Old English poetry known or composed in Anglo-Saxon England. In other words, for the Anglo-Saxons (as for us), the psalms were texts of an utterly alien culture.

How then did the Royal Glossator respond to the immense difficulties presented by the language of the psalms? He was not the first Anglo-Saxon scholar to undertake the task of providing an interlinear gloss for the psalter, and he probably was aware of that fact. As we have seen, he seems to have had a copy of his predecessor's work, the A-type gloss, on his desk. This A-type gloss is a competent interlinear version, based on the original glossator's firm command of Latin and of the resources of the Old English vocabulary, and drawing occasionally on patristic exegesis of the psalms.[48] It is a version which would have served perfectly the purposes of classroom instruction as well as those of private study of the psalms. The Royal Glossator adopted its method of glossing in many places, not only where he has the same *interpretamentum* as the Vespasian Psalter (perhaps taken over from that gloss), but also in those numerous instances where he replaced the A-type gloss by another plain English term, because he aimed at a more modern word or a word without an Anglian dialect colouring or for whatever other reasons. However, his

---

[46] This classification was first suggested by Gunkel; he has stated his views comprehensively in the first edition (1933) of his *Einleitung in die Psalmen*; cf. above, n. 42. Some thoughts pointing in the direction of such a classification can already be found in the late eighteenth century in Johann Gottfried Herder's *Vom Geist der Ebräischen Poesie* (1782–3); see *Herders Sämtliche Werke*, ed. B. Suphan *et al.*, 33 vols. (Berlin, 1877–1913) XII, 1–308 *passim*. Although several modifications of Gunkel's classification have been proposed, it is the point of departure for all recent research on the literary types of the psalms; cf. the reference works cited above, n. 42, and the bibliographies contained therein.

[47] For a comprehensive introduction to the close relations between the imagery and metaphorical language of the psalms and the iconography and the architecture of the Old Testament East, see O. Keel, *Die Welt der altorientalischen Bildsymbolik und das Alte Testament; am Beispiel der Psalmen* (Zürich, 1972).

[48] For a brief evaluation of the Vespasian gloss, see Wiesenekker, *Translation Performance*, pp. 132–4 (based on his word-lists); for the recourse to patristic exegesis, see Gneuss, *Lehnbildungen*, pp. 47–8, 63 and *passim*, and Wiesenekker, *Translation Performance*, pp. 131–2.

ambitions did not come to an end here. He did not content himself with revising and updating an existing interlinear version; he intended to create a fresh translation designed on a grander scale. He achieved his goal in two ways: first, by basing himself to a much larger degree on psalm exegesis when selecting his *interpretamenta*, and second, by liberally sprinkling his version with words belonging to the register of Old English poetry, as well as with unusual terms, among them many which he apparently had coined himself with a view to creating exotic, arcane or poetic expressions to emulate the difficult and recherché Latin of the psalms (and we have seen already that he had a taste for linking several of his glosses by means of paronomasia or other sound effects such as alliteration). The first of these strategies might be called the Glossator's scholarly response to the language of the psalms while the second would be his stylistic response. It is this stylistic response which must next concern us.[49] It is important to stress, however, and from the examples discussed below and in the following chs. it will become abundantly clear, that the Glossator's stylistic and scholarly responses are often inextricably intertwined, a symbiosis which forms one of the most characteristic features of the Royal Psalter gloss.

There can scarcely be any doubt that the Glossator was aware of the poetic nature of the psalms. In his *De arte metrica*, Bede had expressly stated that the psalms were metrical compositions in their original language;[50] and in the introduction to his *De schematibus et tropis*, he was concerned to point out that it was not the Greeks (as they had boasted) who had invented rhetorical *ornatus*, but that a rich hoard of rhetorical figures and tropes could be found much earlier in Scripture, and that therefore he had chosen the examples in his treatise principally from among the sacred texts.[51] As will be seen from any random opening of Bede's rhetorical handbook, a very large portion of his examples for the various figures of speech has been taken from the psalms.[52] It is highly likely that the Royal Glossator, given his interest in rhetoric and style,

---

[49] See Gneuss, 'Language Contact', pp. 144–8, for the methods and aims of compilers of Old English interlinear versions, including a survey of recent scholarship in that field. A sustained attempt to emulate the stylistic level of the original has, to my knowledge, not so far been noted for any Old English gloss.

[50] Cf. *De arte metrica*, ed. Kendall, p. 140.

[51] Cf. *De schematibus et tropis*, ed. Kendall, pp. 142–3.

[52] Cf. e. g. *ibid.*, pp. 147–8, the examples under *epanalepsis*, *epizeuxis* or *paronomasia*.

would have known Bede's treatises, which by the mid-tenth century had already become the standard medieval textbooks on the subject.[53] Furthermore, Bede is not unique in claiming for Scripture, and especially the psalms, priority and greater perfection in metre and figures of speech, but he rehearses an argument well-established by the time he composed his textbooks, and which he could have found *inter alia* in Cassiodorus's *Expositio psalmorum*, one of the sources for his *De schematibus et tropis*, and a text of paramount importance for the Royal Glossator as well.[54]

We have already noted that lists (albeit not with the aim of completeness) of rare or poetic words have been compiled from Roeder's edition of Royal 2. B. V on several occasions;[55] we have also noted that for various reasons such uncommented lists draw only an unsatisfactory picture of the Glossator's lexical and stylistic performance. As in the case of lexical variation (above, p. 45), therefore, it is simply with the intention of forming a preliminary notion of a salient feature of the Royal gloss that I record the following examples of rare or poetic verbs, adjectives and nouns, before we proceed in this and the subsequent chs. to examine a number of such words in greater detail. Most of the rare words are either *hapax legomena* or not attested in texts earlier than the Royal Psalter and

---

[53] For the circulation of Bede's treatises, see Manitius, *Geschichte der lateinischen Literatur des Mittelalters* I, 74–5, and R. B. Palmer, 'Bede as Textbook Writer: a Study of his *De arte metrica*', *Speculum* 34 (1959), 573–84. In his edition of both texts, Kendall lists some ninety-six manuscripts containing either both or one of the two texts (pp. 60–72). Surviving manuscripts from Anglo-Saxon England comprise one complete copy of both treatises (now Worcester, Cathedral Library, Q. 5, written at Christ Church, Canterbury, s. x^ex, Gneuss, 'Handlist', no. 765) and three fragments or excerpts from *De arte metrica*, Gneuss, 'Handlist', nos. 418.8, s. x/xi; 489, s. ix/x (on this manuscript, London, BL Royal 15. A. XVI, see below, p. 333, n. 4), and 784, s. x–xi. In the early eleventh century, *De arte metrica* and *De schematibus et tropis* were among the sources drawn on by Byrhtferth for his *Enchiridion*; cf. *Byrhtferth's Enchiridion*, ed. Baker and Lapidge, pp. lxxx–lxxxi. For an evaluation of *De schematibus et tropis* and its place in the rhetorical tradition, see now also Knappe, *Traditionen der klassischen Rhetorik*, pp. 234–43, as well as M. Irvine, *The Making of Textual Culture* (Cambridge, 1994), pp. 288–97.

[54] On Bede's sources for the *De schematibus et tropis*, see especially U. Schindel, 'Die Quellen von Bedas Figurenlehre', *Classica et Medievalia* 29 (1968), 169–86; see also M. Irvine, 'Bede the Grammarian and the Scope of Grammatical Studies in Eighth-Century Northumbria', *ASE* 15 (1986), 15–44, at 33–8, and the meticulous identification of sources in the *apparatus fontium* in Kendall's edition.

[55] Cf. above, nn. 1 and 3.

hence possibly coined by the Glossator. They comprise verbs like *(ge)angian* 'to be in anguish'[56] (pss. LX.3 and CXLII.4, for *anxiare*), *aryderian* 'to blush, be ashamed' (ps. LXIX.4, for *erubescere*), *ascyhhan* 'to scare away, reject' (pss. L.13, for *proicere* and LXXXVII.19, for *elongare*), *geondeardian* 'to inhabit' (ps. XXXII.8, for *habitare (orbem)*), *midþeahtian* (cant. 6.27, for *consentire*),[57] *rihtgehatan* 'to pledge oneself, to swear' (ps. XIV.4, for *iurare*), *samodherian* 'to praise together' (ps. CXVI.1, for *conlaudare*),[58] and *yfelcwedolian* 'to speak evil' (ps. XXXVI.22, for *maledicere*). Several rare formations with *-lœcan* occur and are here attested for the first time: *fremedlœcan* 'to alienate' (ps. LVII.4, for *alienare*), *gesamodlœcan* 'to bring together' (ps. CXII.8, for *collocare*), *geswetlœcan* 'to batten' (ps. LXV.15, for *medullare* 'to fill with marrow'),[59] *gesyntlœcan* 'to cause to prosper' (ps. CXVII.25, for *prosperare*) and *gewundorlœcan* 'to make wonderful, magnify' (ps. XVI.7, for *mirificare*). The formation and distribution of Old English verbs in *-lœcan* have been comprehensively treated by Elmar Seebold, who imputes a Jutish dialect origin and colouring to these verbs.[60] Whatever their dialect origin may have been, for us the point of interest is simply that quite a number of the attested *-lœcan* verbs occur for the first time in the Royal gloss. Seebold[61] lists about two dozen such verbs in Old English, which would make the five

---

[56] The modern English equivalents are generally those given by CHM.

[57] The glosses to the canticles and the other liturgical texts following the psalter in Royal 2. B. V are attributable as well to the glossator of the psalms; for an examination of some points of verbal agreement between the gloss to the psalter and that to the *Quicumque uult*, see below, pp. 277–80.

[58] A rare deverbal compound noun, *samodhering* 'praising', also occurs (ps. XXXII.1, for *conlaudatio*); for verb and noun, see Gneuss, *Lehnbildungen*, p. 81.

[59] Judging from the psalm context (the quality of burnt offerings is in question) and from the first component of the verb (apparently *swete* 'sweet, fragrant'), a meaning 'to smell pleasantly, be fragrant' seems preferable for *geswetlœcan* which occurs only in the Royal Psalter and dependent glosses; cf. Gneuss, *Lehnbildungen*, p. 125. Such a meaning would, however, presume a considerably free rendering of *medullare*, here attested as a past participle *medullatus* 'full of marrow, fat'.

[60] See E. Seebold, 'Die altenglischen Verben auf *-lœcan*', in *Indogermanica Europaea. Festschrift für Wolfgang Meid*, ed. K. Heller *et al.*, Grazer Linguistische Monographien 4 (Graz, 1989), 333–57, for a morphological and etymological analysis of the type, and cf. *idem*, 'Was ist jütisch?', pp. 346–50, as well as *idem*, 'Old English Texts from Kent', pp. 419–20 and 426–8, for the assumed dialect colouring and distribution.

[61] 'Was ist jütisch?', pp. 347–8, and 'Old English Texts from Kent', pp. 420 and 427, n. 38.

rare *-læcan* formations in the Royal Psalter about one fifth of the total number of attested verbs of this type. This percentage becomes even higher if we add to the above list two more widely attested verbs occurring in the Psalter: *(to)genealæcan* 'to approach' (occurring several times, e. g. pss. XXXI.6, XXXI.9 or XC.7) and *geefenlæcan* 'to be like' (once, in ps. LXXXVIII.7, for *aequare*). In the case of *geefenlæcan* it is noteworthy that again the Royal Psalter seems to be the earliest text where the verb is recorded.[62] Furthermore, none of the five rare verbs in *-læcan* listed above occurs outside the D-type psalter glosses (which here, as elsewhere, by no means always and unanimously follow the extravagant glosses of their model).[63] All this points perhaps not so much to a Jutish dialect character of the *-læcan* verbs, but rather to an acute interest of the Royal Glossator in the potential of the suffix *-læcan* for the coinage of new verbs. Some of these, such as *geswetlæcan* or *gewundorlæcan*, seem to have a palpably recherché flavour. In view of a suspected origin of the Royal Psalter gloss in Æthelwold's circle it is worth stressing that a similar penchant for verbs with *-læcan* can be found in some Late West Saxon texts which follow Winchester usage in their vocabulary, for example in the works of Ælfric and the Lambeth Psalter.[64]

A few examples of rare adjectives in the Royal Psalter would be: *æþreclic* 'terrible' (ps. XCV.4, for *terribilis*), *bregendlic* 'terrible' (ps. XLVI.3, for *terribilis*), *hefigmod* 'oppressive' (ps. LIV.4, for *molestus*) or *manswæs* 'meek' (ps. XXIV.9, for *mansuetus*).

Nouns, however, are most conspicuous among the rare words in the Royal Psalter, notable for their number as well as for the competence and the occasional flamboyance of their word-formation. A few examples from many would be: *bleofæstnes* 'delight' (ps. CXXXVIII.11, for *deliciae*), *forecynren* and *forecynred* 'progeny, generation' (e. g. pss. XLVIII.12 and XLVIII.20, for *progenies*), *forwerennes* 'old age' (ps. LXX.18, for *senium*),

---

[62] The Vespasian Psalter has *geefenlician*, a related, but clearly distinct, formation, which, however, may have served as a model for the Royal gloss *geefenlæcan*, especially in view of the Glossator's taste for *-læcan* verbs. For a different explanation of the relationship between *geefenlician* and *geefenlæcan*, see Seebold, 'Old English Texts from Kent', pp. 426–7.

[63] For example, *gewundorlæcan* is only found in the Stowe and the Tiberius psalters; *gesyntlæcan* occurs in Vitellius and Salisbury only.

[64] Cf. Seebold, 'Was ist jütisch', p. 348, and *idem*, 'Old English Texts from Kent', pp. 420 and 427.

frumsceatt 'first-fruits' (e. g. ps. LXXVII.51, for *primitiae*), *grundweall* 'foundation' (e. g. ps. XVII.8, for *fundamentum*),[65] *ongalnes* 'song' (ps. LXX.6, for *decantatio*), *stangaderung* 'stone-wall' (ps. LXI.4, for *maceria*), *steorsprec* 'reproof' (ps. XXXVII.15, for *increpatio*), *swarcung* 'darkness (ps. XVII.29, for *tenebrae*), *trundulnes* 'circuit, surrounding space' (ps. XI.9, for *circuitus*), *wegleast* 'trackless place, wilderness' (ps. CVI.40, for *inuius*), *wiðerwengel* 'adversary' (e. g. ps. LXXIII.10, for *aduersarius*), *wylding* 'domination, rule' (ps. CII.22, for *dominatio*) and *woddream*, literally 'mad ecstasy' and hence perhaps 'madness' (ps. XCV.5, for *daemonium* 'demon, heathen god'). A short comment on this last gloss is appropriate. CHM provides as a 'translation' only the Latin lemma it glosses in the psalter: 'daemonium'. I am not as confident as Davey[66] that the Glossator's choice of the gloss *woddream* has been decisively influenced by the marginal commentary on *daemonium* in Royal 2. B. V which runs as follows: 'Quid aliter dum nihil possunt, nisi decipiunt sperantes in se' (111v).[67] As usual this derives (though not verbatim) from Cassiodorus and comments on the statement in ps. XCV.5: 'Quoniam omnes dii gentium demonia'.[68] One may rather suspect, however, that *woddream* embodies Cassiodorus's subsequent remark on *dii gentium* in the same verse: 'Haec sunt utique *dii gentium*, qui per infructuosas uaticinationes et futurorum uana praestigia festinant animas decipere consulentium'.[69] This has no reflex in the marginal commentary and would therefore suggest that the Glossator drew on a fuller version of the *Expositio psalmorum* and was not restricted to the scholia as transmitted in Royal 2. B. V. The exotic compound *woddream* (almost certainly coined by the Glossator) merits further investigation.

The following list presents a few examples culled from the words which seem to have been chosen because they belong to the register of poetry or have poetic connotations (some of these possibly coined by the Glossator himself in a poetic vein). Again, the overwhelming majority of

---

[65] On one occasion, this compound, only sporadically attested, forms the base for an extremely rare verbal derivative: *gegrundweallian* 'to establish, found' (ps. XXIII.2, for *fundare*).

[66] See Davey, 'Commentary of the Regius Psalter', p. 347.

[67] 'What else, if they can do nothing but deceive those who set their hope in them?'.

[68] 'Because all the gods of the pagans are demons'.

[69] *Expositio* II, 864: 'These are especially "the gods of the pagans" who through unfruitful prophecies and vain illusions about future events hasten to deceive the souls of those who consult them'.

such poetic words are nouns: *gedwolfær* 'a going astray' (cant. 6.36, for *abductio*), (perhaps) *fostornoþ* 'pasture' (pss. XXII.2, XCIV.7, XCIX.3, glossing all occurrences of *pascua* in the psalter), several components with poetic *frea* 'ruler, lord, king, master' as their determinant: *freamiht* 'great strength' (ps. XLII.2, for *fortitudo*), *freareccere* 'prince' (ps. CXVIII.161, for *princeps*) and *freaþancian* 'to exult' (ps. LII.7, for *exultare*),[70] *fromrinc* 'chief, prince' (cant. 4.15, for *princeps*), *gicelgebland* 'frost' (literally 'a mixture of icicles', cant. 7.70, for *pruina*), *glæterung* 'shining' (ps. XLVIII.15, for *matutinum*),[71] *hellsceaða* 'hell-foe, devil' (cant. 2.18, for *infernus*), *hroðgirela* 'crown' (ps. XX.4, for *corona*),[72] *ligræsc* 'lightning, coruscation' (compounded from *lieg* 'fire' and *ræsc* 'shower', e. g. ps. LXXVI.19, for *coruscatio*), *or* 'beginning, origin' (ps. CXVIII.160, for *principium*), *sefa* 'mind, spirit' (ps. LXXVII.72, for *sensus*),[73] (perhaps) *tohyht* 'hope, refuge, consolation' (ps. XVII.3, for *refugium*),[74] and *geðryðfullod* 'proud' (ps. CXXX.1, for *elatus*).[75]

Skeletal as such lists of examples must remain without a thorough philological, stylistic or contextual commentary, they will have created an overall impression of the striking quality of a considerable portion of the Royal gloss. We will have occasion to examine some rare or poetic words in greater detail, especially with regard to their context and possible intentions of the Glossator. For the moment a closer look at just two further examples will illustrate the ambition and sophistication with

---

[70] Note that *frea-* occurs in Old English also as an intensive prefix, often translating Latin *prae-* in the same sense. That the Glossator primarily intended an association with *frea* 'lord' for his compounds might be deduced from his glosses for the one word with *prae-* as an intensive prefix in the psalter: *praeclarus* 'very shining', hence 'brilliant, splendid'. Although the A-type gloss translates one of the three occurrences of *praeclarus* by *freabeorht* (the only *frea*-formation attested in the A-type gloss as transmitted in Vespasian A. i), the Royal gloss has the simplex *beorht* (pss. XV.6 and LXXI.14) and, once, the double gloss *beorht l mære* (ps. XXII.5).

[71] For this gloss, see below, pp. 202–3.

[72] For this gloss, see below, pp. 99–101 and 297–304.

[73] On the predominant use of this word in poetry, see Frank, 'Poetic Words in Late Old English Prose', pp. 103–4.

[74] See above, pp. 46–7.

[75] The meaning given by CHM (s. v. *þryþfullian*) 'to fill up' is not borne out by the context of this *hapax legomenon*; BTS has the more adequate translation 'to exalt, elevate'. For the poetic register to which the cognates *ðryð* and *ðryðful* belong, see Frank, 'Poetic Words in Late Old English Prose', pp. 100–1.

which the Glossator applied himself to his task. Our first example, the compound noun *breostwylm*, occurs once in *Beowulf* (line 1877) and once in the Royal Psalter (ps. XXI.10) and four dependent psalter glosses (Stowe, Tiberius, Vitellius and Eadwine). It is compounded of *breost* 'breast, heart' and *wylm* 'boiling; billow, stream; fervour'. In *Beowulf*, the context requires the sense 'strong emotion' for *breostwylm*, *wylm* being used here in an abstract, metaphorical sense. In the Psalter, however, *breostwylm* glosses *uber* 'mother's breast' ('spes mea [*scil.* Deus] ab uberibus matris'). It is clear that the compound should be understood here primarily in a literal sense; it is therefore rendered by 'breast-fountain' in CHM and 'full breast (mother's milk)' in the *DOE*. The context of the psalm verse suggests, however, that the abstract meaning 'strong emotion' (attested in the only further occurrence of the word) is implied here as well. This gives us a rather sophisticated play on the literal and the abstract sense of a gloss word which has no parallel in the two other independent psalter glosses. Vespasian has the straightforward translation *breost*, while the Lambeth Psalter in choosing *breostcofa* 'heart, affections' retains the poetic register (by employing a more frequently attested word, however) but eliminates the literal level of meaning present in the Royal Psalter.

It is interesting to note in passing that the exceedingly rare noun *frumwylm* 'new-born zeal' occurs in the first ch. of the Old English Benedictine Rule as transmitted in London, BL, Cotton Faustina A. x. The first ch. of the Rule in this manuscript translates not the *Regula* but a section from Isidore's *De ecclesiaticis officiis*. The translation of this section from Isidore can also be attributed to Æthelwold with some confidence. Here, *frumwylm* renders somewhat loosely *in primordiis suis feruore* 'with fervour in their beginning (of monastic life)'.[76]

Our second example, apart from shedding light on the Glossator's inventiveness and virtuosity, also serves to illustrate that the evidence for some such words which do not occur outside the Royal gloss is not straightforward. In this case the ingenuity of the Glossator may have defeated even the competent scribe of Royal 2. B. V.[77] A noun *ongeweorc* is

---

[76] See BR 135.5 (for the Old English word) and *ibid.*, p. 231 (for the Latin text). For the attribution of the translation to Æthelwold, see Gretsch, 'Benedictine Rule', pp. 153–7.

[77] See above, p. 28 and n. 57 for Royal 2. B. V as an excellent copy, close to the original.

listed by Schlutter[78] as one of the words from the Royal Psalter not found in BT (it is, in fact, a *hapax legomenon*). It glosses *factura* 'Creation' (ps. XCI.5). The word is admitted into BTS with a query, but it was obviously considered a ghost word (and consequently excluded) by CHM. Latin text and Old English gloss as they stand in the manuscript would let appear the existence of a noun *ongeweorc* very doubtful indeed. Text and gloss read as follows:

on ongeweorce þinum   weorcum   handa   þinra ic blissie
domine in   factura   tua   et in operibus manu{u}m tuarum exultabo

This looks suspiciously like dittography. However, the usual competence of the scribe and the unusual resourcefulness of the Glossator when coining new words should make us hesitate for a moment before endorsing this solution. Apart from that, given the Glossator's inclination towards lexical variation, we may presume that he wished to translate *factura* and *opus* by different words. He could have found translations slightly varying one from the other in the A-type gloss, which has prefixed (and therefore collective) *geweorc* for *factura* and *weorc* for *opus*; a competent, straightforward solution, a solution which may, however, not have satisfied the Royal Glossator's ambitions.[79] On the other hand, a noun *ongeweorc* would be definitely strange in terms of word-formation.[80] Could it be that the Glossator had intended a compound *orgeweorc*, formed by poetic *or* 'beginning, origin' and *geweorc* 'work' (in a collective sense through its prefix, as in the Vespasian gloss)? He would thereby have coupled a word (*geweorc*) which, in terms of morphology and semantics, closely paralleled the lemma *factura*, with a word (*or*) used by English poets to refer to God's Creation (adumbrating perhaps Cædmonian *or onstealde*). It may be significant to note that the Glossator employed poetic *or* on another occasion (ps. CXVIII.160). He may have modelled such a semipoetic coinage *orgeweorc* on the compound *ærgeweorc* 'work of olden times' (occurring in *Beowulf* and *Andreas*); compounds such as

---

[78] 'Zum Wortschatz des Regius Psalters', p. 20.
[79] The Lambeth Glossator apparently saw no need to differentiate: he has *weorc* for both lemmata.
[80] Schlutter, 'Zum Wortschatz des Regius Psalters', p. 17, explained the prefix as an intensifier, obviously not a permissible solution; cf. Meid, *Wortbildungslehre*, p. 36, and Koziol, *Wortbildungslehre*, pp. 109–10.

ærgewyrht 'deed of old', *ærgewinn* 'old warfare' or *ærgestreon* 'ancient treasure' (all of these are poetic expressions) may also have played a role.[81]

A brief look at one final example will serve to illustrate that it is not exclusively by means of rare or poetic words or by neologisms that the Glossator attempted to capture the poetic register of the psalms; sometimes he is able to achieve his goal by a plain English word. In ps. CIII.25, Latin *reptilia* refers to reptiles living in the ocean; this is rendered by *snicende* in the Vespasian and by *slicende* in the Lambeth gloss. Both *interpretamenta* are closely imitative of *reptilia*, quite possibly loan-formations.[82] The Royal Glossator, however, chose *wyrm*, thereby evoking not only the terror struck by dragons and water monsters, but also reminiscences of the serpent of Paradise.[83] That he had in mind such emotional responses (which would scarcely have been provoked by a loan or loan-formation) is revealed by the marginal commentary in Royal 2. B. V, where *reptilia* is explained: '.i. diabolicae insidiae' (120v),[84] which in turn reminds us that psalm exegesis may underlie even a (at first glance) deceptively simple gloss.

Hand in hand with this concern for choosing stylistically adequate, often recherché translation words goes the Glossator's inclination towards word-play or paronomasia (in particular *figura etymologica*) and sound effects, principally in the form of alliteration. To find such an inclination in a gloss is perhaps even more surprising than to be confronted there with a vocabulary, eccentric in parts.[85] We have

---

[81] The Glossator may perhaps also have been influenced by the phonetic similarity between *or* 'origin' and formations with the prefix *or-* such as *oreald* 'very old' or *oryldu* 'great age'. Here the prefix denotes antiquity and can be explained as an intensifier. More often, however, the prefix *or-* (< West Germanic **uz-*) denotes privation, as in *orwene* 'hopeless' or *orsorg* 'without care or anxiety', that sense being a strong argument against explaining *orgeweorc* as modelled exclusively on formations with this prefix. For the prefix *or-*, see Meid, *Wortbildungslehre*, p. 39, Koziol, *Wortbildungslehre*, p. 110, and Kastovsky, 'Semantics and Vocabulary', p. 381; the prefix is not related to the noun *ōr*, see Holthausen, *Altenglisches etymologisches Wörterbuch*, s. vv. *or-* and *ōr*.

[82] Latin *reptile* derives from *repere*, *reptare* 'to creep'; the Old English glosses are present participles from *snican* and *slican*, both meaning 'to creep'.

[83] Cf. *Genesis* (A), ed. G. P. Krapp, *The Junius Manuscript*, ASPR I, 30: 'Me nædre beswac ... fah wyrm þurh fægir word' (lines 897 and 899).

[84] This succinct remark perhaps echoes remotely a passage from Cassiodorus's lengthy exposition of the psalm verse; cf. *Expositio* II, 937.

[85] For the importance of paronomasia in Old English religious verse, see the comprehen-

seen[86] that a preoccupation with rhetorical embellishments occasionally influenced the Glossator's choice of lexical variants and that it may have played a role in his use of loanwords. Some further examples will illustrate this feature of the gloss. In ps. CXLIII.4, the days of human life are said to pass away like shadows: 'sicut umbra praetereunt', glossed in the Royal Psalter: 'swa swa scadu forðsceocon'. The verb is glossed by (Anglian) *bileoran* in the Vespasian Psalter and by *forðgewitan* in Lambeth. *Forðgewitan* for *praeterire* is employed several times in the Royal gloss as well; *forðscacan*, however, occurs here on only one further occasion (ps. LXXXIX.4), again in a highly poetic context. Therefore *forðscacan* (attested only in the Royal Psalter and dependent glosses) may possibly have had poetic connotations and its use in the present instance may in addition have been prompted by its alliteration with *scadu*.

The 'sharp sword', *machera acuta* of ps. LVI.5 is translated *scyrseax scearp* by the Glossator (Vespasian has *mece scearp*, Lambeth *scearp swurd*). It is possible that the scribe of Royal 2. B. V has spoiled part of an originally more elaborate sound pattern: a variant *scearseax* is attested in Old English and is phonologically plausible; therefore the vowels in both words may originally have been identical as well. In any case, *scyrseax* is a rare word and it means 'razor' and thus renders *machera* more freely than the translations in Vespasian and Lambeth (nevertheless, it perfectly fits its context). The collocation *scyrseax scearp* was, apparently, not invented by the Royal Glossator. It occurs once in the Vespasian Psalter (ps. LI.4, in the Anglian form *scersæx scearp*), where it translates *nouacula acuta* 'sharp razor'. For this, the Royal Psalter presents the same collocation (another pointer, perhaps, to the Glossator's consultation of an A-type exemplar). The fact that the Glossator re-employed this phrase in ps. LVI.5 for a free rendering of *machera acuta* may confirm the suspicion that he paid close attention to aural effects.

In ps. XVII.27, the *Romanum* reading 'et cum peruerso subuerteris' is translated by the Glossator 'mid f[o]rhwyrfedum ðu forhwyrfed bist' ('you will be perverted (*or* destroyed) with the perverse'). Vespasian has 'mid ðy

---

[86] sive study by Frank, 'Some Uses of Paronomasia'. For word-play in the Hebrew original of the psalms, see A. Guillaume, 'Paronomasia in the Old Testament', *Journal of Semitic Studies* 9 (1964), 282–90.

[86] See above, pp. 46–7 and 53–4.

ðweoran ðu bist forcerred'. The A-type gloss *ðweorh* is quite common also in the Royal Psalter for *peruersus* or similar lemmata. So again the suspicion is that the Glossator has chosen this present gloss with a view to creating some rhetorical effect. A look at the Lambeth gloss at this point may confirm this suspicion. Here the *Gallicanum* reading 'et cum peruerso peruerteris' is glossed 'mid wyðerwerdum ł mid þweorum 7 þu byst behwyrfed ł miswend'. In spite of the *Gallicanum* giving greater prominence to the etymological link between adjective and verb than does the *Romanum*, and in spite of two double glosses, there is no such etymologizing word-play in Lambeth.

Our next example involves the employment of an Anglian dialect word, arguably for rhetorical purposes. In ps. LXXXVIII.24, text and gloss in the Royal Psalter read as follows:

ic afylle	fynd	his	7	feogende	hine	on	fleam	ic gecyrre
concidam	*inmicos*	*eius*	... *et*	*odientes*	*eum*	*in*	*fugam*	*conuertam*

('I cut down his enemies and I put to flight those who hate him'.) The Glossator could have found the nucleus for this display of alliteration and paronomasia in the A-type gloss, where such sound effects occasionally occur, but are employed in no way as ostentatiously as in the Royal gloss. Vespasian reads as follows: 'ic forceorfu fiond his 7 figende hine in fleam ic gecerru.'[87] The Royal Glossator achieves a more intricate sound pattern by replacing *forceorfan* with *afyllan* and by retaining *feogan* 'to hate', an Anglian word, clearly unusual in his own dialect. We may not be certain whether he was actually aware that *fynd* and *feogan* (the phonological forms as attested in Royal 2. B. V) are etymologically closely related. He certainly would have known about a phonological variant of *fynd* closer to *feogan*, namely *feond*, so that for him noun and verb were probably knitted together by more than just alliteration of their initial consonant. In any event, his choice of Anglian *feogan* in ps. LXXXVIII.24 instead of West Saxon *hatian* may with some confidence be attributed to his striving for rhetorical effects. Such a presumption receives confirmation from an inspection of the Glossator's *interpretamenta* for *odisse*. The distribution of Anglian *feogan* in Old English texts has recently been studied by Franz Wenisch.[88] In the

---

[87] Note that in the Lambeth Psalter no such rhetorical embellishments occur in the passage in question.

[88] See Wenisch, *Spezifisch anglisches Wortgut*, pp. 134–7.

psalter, Wenisch counts thirty-five instances of *odisse*, always translated by *feogan* in the Vespasian gloss. The Royal Psalter has West Saxon *hatian* for *odisse* in some thirty instances, whereas *feogan* occurs five times. Wenisch did not evaluate these five occurrences of *feogan* in their contexts. Such an evaluation reveals that in two of the five occurrences *feogan* is collocated with the noun *feond/fynd* (pss. LXXXVIII.24 and CV.41); it occurs once in a doublet with its West Saxon counterpart: *hatian ł feogan* (ps. V.7; we have seen that doublets are often employed for their stylistic potential); and on one further occasion, *feogan* occurs in a doublet as well as in collocation with *feond/fynd* (ps. XVII.41). This leaves us with just one instance of Anglian *feogan* (ps. XLIII.8) where no stylistic reason for its employment can be detected.

Furthermore, *feogan* is not the only Anglian word occasionally employed in the Royal Psalter, arguably for stylistic reasons. Anglian *medmicel* 'small, unimportant' occurs four times in the Psalter as a gloss to *pusillus* and *modicus*.[89] On all occasions *medmicel* is involved in an alliterative pattern in the Old English gloss (to which it may have lent itself readily by its internal alliteration) as in *a monte modico*, glossed *fram munte medmiclum* (ps. XLI.7).[90] On one occasion, such alliteration is combined with *figura etymologica*: *animalia pusilla et magna*, glossed *nytenu medmiclu 7 miclu* (ps. CIII.25). What is interesting is that *medmicel* does not appear in the Vespasian gloss (of Anglian dialect character), neither in the four instances in question nor elsewhere; *lytel* is the word used there on all occasions. The Royal Glossator therefore cannot simply (and thoughtlessly) have lifted *medmicel* from the A-type gloss which arguably served as his model. Rather, his must have been a conscious decision in favour of an Anglian dialect word, probably with the aim of achieving a rhetorical effect. Predictably, the Lambeth Glossator with his West Saxon and specifically Winchester type of vocabulary jettisoned *medmicel* which he will have encountered in the D-type gloss to which he made recourse. He retains it on one occasion only (ps. XXXVI.16) where, however, the alliterative pattern is marred by the introduction of one of his characteristic doublets.

In this connection mention might also be made of the frequent

---

[89] Cf. pss. XXXVI.16, XLI.7, LIV.9 and CIII.25. For the Anglian dialect character of *medmicel*, see Wenisch, *Spezifisch anglisches Wortgut*, p. 117, n. 133, and *passim*.

[90] Recall that stylistic considerations may have played a role in the consistent coupling of *mons* and *munt* in the Royal gloss; see above, pp. 53–4.

occurrence of Anglian *aldor* or *aldorman* instead of West Saxon *ealdor(man)* for *princeps* 'prince, ruler' in the Royal Psalter.[91] In terms of historical phonology the occurrence of *a* before *l* plus consonant exhibits Anglian retraction, whereas *ea* is caused by West Saxon breaking.[92] However, it has been shown that *a* (instead of *ea*) in a few forms (most notably *waldend* 'ruler') in West Saxon texts, is to be attributed to the poetic connotations of these forms and should not be judged in terms of Anglian influence.[93] By the same token, one may suspect that the Glossator meant to exploit the poetic potential of the phonological variant *aldor*, a suspicion which may be confirmed by his glossing *princeps* once by a poetic compound *freareccere* (ps. CXVIII.161).

Now a taste for rhetorical and poetic adornment as found in the Royal Psalter may be unusual for an interlinear gloss, but it would certainly not be unusual for Old English prose texts. Therefore the presence of Anglian words (or word forms), arguably employed for such rhetorical and poetic purposes, in the Royal Psalter should make us aware that we must exercise caution when adjudicating items of Anglian vocabulary in Old English texts. It has become common practice, in recent research in the dialect character of the Old English lexicon, to list 'anglische Einsprengsel'[94] (a 'sprinkling of Anglian words') in West Saxon texts, with the implication that such 'Einsprengsel' were either mechanically and mindlessly copied from Anglian exemplars, or (with texts of West Saxon composition) were employed by speakers of the West Saxon dialect with no clear notion which words should be avoided when aiming to produce a West Saxon text. (The same holds true for heterodialectal words in Old English texts in general.) However, the label 'anglisches Einsprengsel', applied in a wholesale and indiscriminate fashion, scarcely does justice to possible stylistic intentions of Anglo-Saxon scholars and authors, and may hamper an adequate critical assessment of their works. In other words, aspects of style would appear to deserve more attention in modern word studies.[95] There is a further

---

[91] For example, pss. XXIII.7, XXIII.9, XXXII.10, LXXV.13 and LXXXVI.6. Note that Lambeth usually has normal West Saxon *ealdor(man)*.

[92] See SB, § 85, and Campbell, §§ 143 and 258.

[93] See A. Lutz, 'Spellings of the *waldend* Group – Again', *ASE* 13 (1984), 51–64.

[94] See, for example, Wenisch, *Spezifisch anglisches Wortgut*, p. 136 and *passim*.

[95] For experiments with Anglian words, principally for reasons of style, in which even Ælfric, that paragon of pure West Saxon and Winchester standardization, occasionally allowed himself to indulge, see Godden, 'Ælfric's Changing Vocabulary', pp. 222–3,

factor (of a historical and political nature) in the presence of Anglian dialect features in West Saxon texts which would merit consideration by philologists. We shall return to this aspect in a later chapter.[96]

Quite possibly the potential for word-play and intricate sound patterns influenced the Glossator's decision regularly to gloss *tabernaculum* by *eardung* or *eardungstow* (and in contrast to the Vespasian and Lambeth psalters, which prefer *geteld*), even though there can be little doubt that his primary reasons for this decision were of an exegetical nature. Both Old English words (meaning 'habitation') are clearly explanatory glosses and as such may well represent in a nutshell Cassiodorus's lengthy explanation of *tabernaculum* on the first occurrence of the word in the psalter.[97] In the majority of its occurrences in the psalms, *tabernaculum* signifies 'the Tabernacle of the Jews' and hence 'the abode of the Deity', but *tabernaculum* occurs as well in the general sense 'tent for living in'.[98] In allegorical psalm exegesis, *tabernaculum* is taken to refer to the Christian Church in many of its occurrences, an interpretation which is frequently found in Cassiodorus's *Expositio* and which frequently found its way into the marginal scholia in Royal 2. B. V.[99] Aside from psalm exegesis, the Glossator may have found an interpretation of that sort in Bede's work *De tabernaculo*, for example, a verse-by-verse exposition (primarily in terms of allegory) of Exod. XXIV.12–XXX.21.[100] *Ecclesia* is not the only interpretation of *tabernaculum* provided by psalm exegesis.

---

and Hofstetter, *Winchester und Sprachgebrauch*, pp. 49–50 and 51–2. For an evaluation of the occurrence of Anglian words in the Royal gloss in terms of psalter relationships, especially with regard to a possible A-type exemplar, see above, p. 35 and n. 84.

[96] See below, pp. 316–25.

[97] See *Expositio* I, 132–3. For a comprehensive survey of the *interpretamenta* for *tabernaculum* in Old English texts, see Lendinara, 'Old English Renderings of *tabernaculum* and *tentorium*'.

[98] See Hoberg, *Die Psalmen der Vulgata*, p. 38, and Gneuss, *Lehnbildungen*, pp. 84–5.

[99] Cf., for example, the scholion for *in tabernaculo tuo* (ps. XLII.3): *id est in ecclesiam catholicam* (54r) lifted verbatim from Cassiodorus (I, 389); cf. also the scholia on 53r (ps. XLI.5, Cassiodorus I, 382), 57r (ps. XLV.5, Cassiodorus I, 417) or 71r (ps. LIX.8, Cassiodorus I, 533).

[100] See, for example, *De tabernaculo* II, 1, ed. D. Hurst, CCSL 119A (Turnhout, 1969), 3–139, at 42. (For an English translation, see *Bede: on the Tabernacle*, trans. A. G. Holder (Liverpool, 1994), p. 45.) Several (eleventh-century) manuscripts from Anglo-Saxon England have survived: see, for example, Gneuss, 'Handlist', nos. 571, 578.5, 690 and 749.

Other allegorical explanations such as 'the Catholic faith' or 'heavenly life' do occur and can be found in the marginal scholia of Royal 2. B. V (almost invariably indebted to Cassiodorus),[101] side by side with more literal interpretations, such as 'in all places'.[102] This variety of meanings may have tempted the Glossator to look in the first place for a less specific term than *geteld* 'tent' (the predominant gloss in all other psalters) to render *tabernaculum*.

What must interest us here, however, is that the introduction of *eardung* and *eardungstow* into psalter glossing provided the Glossator with a convenient opportunity for employing *figurae etymologicae*, as when, in ps. XIV.1, 'quis habitabit in tabernaculo tuo' is translated: 'hwelc eardaþ on eardungstowe þinre.'[103] Among the twenty-seven occurrences of *eardung* and *eardungstow*, nine instances of such parono-masia (mostly with *eardian*) can be found. Furthermore, the Glossator frequently took the opportunity to link *eardung* and *eardungstow* with their surrounding glosses by vocalic alliteration as in ps. LXXXVI.2, where *super omnia tabernacula* is glossed *ofer ealle eardunga*.[104] In seventeen out of the twenty-seven occurrences of *eardung* and *eardungstow*, such alliteration with at least one of the adjacent glosses occurs. By comparison, in none of the eight occurrences of the A-type gloss *geteld* for *tabernaculum* in the Royal Psalter is *figura etymologica* or alliteration employed.[105]

Apart from the Royal Psalter, *eardung* and *eardungstow* for *tabernaculum* are prominent in the Benedictine Rule but in no other texts. This has been explained as an attempt at Winchester standardization, an attempt which miscarried.[106] The agreement in their resolute promotion of

---

[101] See, for example, the scholia on 72r: *id est in fide catholica* (pertaining to ps. LX.5; cf. Cassiodorus I, 539), on 19r: *quis dignus sit ad ingressum uitae supernae* (pertaining to ps. XIV.1; cf. Cassiodorus I, 133), or on 74v: *in fide catholica ł regno celeste* (pertaining to ps. LXIV.5).

[102] See, for example, the scholion on 22v: *id est in omnibus locis* (pertaining to ps. XVII.12, cf. Cassiodorus I, 156), or the gloss *Iudeorum* (81r) clarifying *tabernaculis eorum* (ps. LXVIII.26; cf. Cassiodorus I, 617).

[103] See also, for example, pss. LX.5, LXIV.5 and LXVIII.26.

[104] Cf. also pss. XXVI.6, LXXIII.7 or CXXXI.3.

[105] Ps. CVII.8 might pass as the one exception; here *geteld* could be taken as alliterating with unstressed *to-* in *todælan*.

[106] See Lendinara, 'Old English Renderings of *tabernaculum* and *tentorium*', p. 303; for lists of the occurrences of *eardung(stow)* in the Royal Psalter and the Rule, see *ibid.*,

eardung(stow) for *tabernaculum* is an important verbal link between the Psalter and the Rule, especially in view of the fact that such a strategy cannot be paralleled from any other Old English text. However, in all probability *eardung* and *eardungstow* were not advocated in the Psalter and the Rule with the aim of lexical standardization, but because they conveniently and comprehensively rendered a term with a variety of meanings and because they easily lent themselves to word-play.

The translation of *christus*

Let us consider one final and striking example of the Glossator's endeavour to emulate the poetry of the psalms, an example which once again involves a highly unusual *interpretamentum*: the glosses for *christus*. In the psalms, the Greek loan *christus* refers, in accordance with its etymology, to someone who has been ceremonially anointed[107] and hence is in a position of worldly or spiritual power.[108] On some occasions *christus* refers specifically to King David.[109] In the Vespasian Psalter *christus* is almost invariably glossed by the loanword *crist*.[110] For an Anglo-Saxon readership, this gloss will inevitably have been associated with the second person of the Trinity, an association which is reinforced by typological psalm exegesis.[111] *Crist* is also the word most frequently employed in the variety of glosses for the lemma in the Lambeth Psalter. The Royal Psalter, however, has *crist* only once; the gloss occurs, significantly perhaps, not only at the very first instance of the lemma in the psalter, but also in a context where the association with Christ comes most naturally.[112] Otherwise the Glossator's

---

pp. 300–7; for the attestations of the A-type gloss *geteld* in these texts, cf. *ibid.*, pp. 292–3; see also Pulsiano, 'Defining the A-type and D-type Traditions', p. 314.

[107] The word derives from Greek χριστός, past participle of χρίω 'anoint'.

[108] For etymological explanations of *christus* and its semantic range in the psalter and the OT to which an Anglo-Saxon author could have had easy access, see, for example, Isidore, *Etymologiae* VI. xix. 50 and VII. ii. 2–3 or, again, Cassiodorus, *Expositio* I, 247: '*Christi* enim dicebantur . . . quos aut unctio regalis, aut sacerdotalis gloria decorabat'; see also *ibid.* II, 946, as well as the references given below, nn. 116 and 117.

[109] For example in ps. XVII.51, on which see below.

[110] On one occasion only, *christos* is translated *ða gehalgedan* 'those who are consecrated' (ps. CIV.15).

[111] See, for example, Cassiodorus, *Expositio* I, 42, 179 and 247.

[112] Cf. ps. II.2: 'conuenerunt in unum aduersus dominum et aduersus christum', glossed: 'becomon tosomne ongean – – – crist' (– signals an unglossed lemma).

standard translation word is *cyning*. It occurs five times;[113] four instances of the lemma remain without an Old English gloss;[114] one of these, however, bears the Latin interlinear gloss *regis*.[115] These remarkable glosses, *cyning* and *rex*, are unquestionably indebted to comments such as the following ones by Cassiodorus: '*Christus* ante dicebatur omnis unctus in regem';[116] or '*Christum tuum* significat unctum; quoniam illo tempore principes Hebraeorum ungebantur in regem'.[117] *Cyning* and *rex* are therefore clearly interpretative glosses; and although they do not embody an etymological explanation (at least not in terms of modern etymology),[118] the Glossator will no doubt have been informed about the 'correct' etymology of *christus* from such sources as Isidore and Cassiodorus.

What, interestingly, is stressed by translating *christus* 'the anointed' by *cyning* or *rex* is that by the mid-tenth century, anointing seems to have been of crucial importance in the making of a king – at least for an Anglo-Saxon clerical glossator and his presumed clerical readers. This evidence squares with the information provided by Anglo-Saxon coronation *ordines*. Royal anointing is a prominent feature already in the so-called First English *Ordo*, apparently used for the consecration of West Saxon kings during most of the ninth century.[119] Anointing figures

---

[113] Pss. XVII.51, XIX.7, XXVII.8, CIV.15 and CXXXI.7.

[114] See pss. LXXXIII.10, LXXXVIII.39, LXXXVIII.52 and CXXXI.10.

[115] Ps. LXXXIII.10, on 100r; note that such (not infrequent) Latin interlinear glosses are not printed in Roeder's edition (cf. *ibid.*, pp. xiv–xv). The lemmata in question appear (somewhat misleadingly) as unglossed in the edition. Pulsiano, 'The Latin and Old English Glosses', pp. 83–96, prints a list of those Latin interlinear (and marginal) glosses in the Royal Psalter which were copied from there into the Blickling Psalter; for the relationship between both psalters, see above, p. 20.

[116] 'In former times every one anointed as king was called *christus*'. *Expositio* I, 168 (comment on ps. XVII.51 where *christus* refers to King David).

[117] '*Christum tuum* means "anointed"; because in those days the leaders of the Hebrews were anointed when they were consecrated kings'; *ibid.* II, 815 (comment on ps. LXXXVIII.39).

[118] Note that multiple etymologies (for biblical names, for example) apparently posed no problems for Anglo-Saxon authors; see F. C. Robinson, 'The Significance of Names in Old English Literature', in his *The Tomb of Beowulf and Other Essays on Old English* (Oxford, 1993), pp. 185–218, at 187–8 (orig. publ. 1968); cf. also the double and triple glosses for *christus* provided by the Lambeth Glossator which look suspiciously like multiple etymologies: *gecoren ł gesmired* (ps. XVII.51), and *gecoren ł crist ł kyning* (ps. XIX.7).

[119] See Nelson, 'The Earliest Royal *Ordo*', p. 360.

prominently also in the Second English *Ordo* for which persuasive arguments for an origin in connection with the consecration of King Edward the Elder (899–924) have recently been advanced.[120] The practice of royal anointing may even be considerably older than these liturgical sources suggest. Under the annal for 785 (*recte* 787) the Parker Chronicle (A) has the entry: '⁊ Ecgferþ to cyninge [wæs] gehalgod'.[121] This has often been taken as the first written testimony of the rite of royal anointing.[122] It may be significant that at precisely the time when this royal anointing was enacted, the king is repeatedly styled *Christus Domini* 'the Lord's Anointed' in an important ecclesiastical document. The document in question is the report of the legatine mission, headed by Bishop George of Ostia and Bishop Theophylact of Todi. The report was sent by Bishop George to Pope Hadrian I (772–95), and it contains the canons promulgated at two synods held in Northumbria and Mercia in 786. We shall return to this document in due course (below, pp. 307–8).[123]

Anointing was the one rite in the investiture of a king which could never have been performed by someone who was not ordained a priest.

---

[120] See Nelson, 'The Second English *Ordo*', pp. 366–7. For anointing as an integral part of the inauguration rite in the First and Second *Ordo*, see also the table, *ibid.*, p. 362.

[121] 'And Ecgferþ was consecrated king'; *ASC MS A*, ed. Bately, p. 39. It is interesting to note that King Offa of Mercia (757–96) apparently had his son Ecgfrith (who is in question here) consecrated while he still held office.

[122] For discussion, see Nelson, 'Rulers' Inauguration Rituals', p. 285.

[123] The text of the report and the canons has been printed twice: by A. W. Haddan and W. Stubbs, *Councils and Ecclesiastical Documents Relating to Great Britain and Ireland*, 3 vols. (Oxford, 1869–71) III, 447–62 (repr. here from an inferior edition); and, from the sole surviving manuscript (now Wolfenbüttel, Herzog-August-Bibliothek, Helmstadensis 454; presumably s. xi^{in}, from Hildesheim (?)), by Dümmler, *Epistolae Karolini aevi* II, 19–29 (no. 3). For a partial translation, see *EHD*, pp. 836–40 (no. 191). The royal style *Christus Domini* is employed several times in canon 12 (ed. Dümmler, p. 24; cf. also canon 11, p. 23). For the scriptural source of the style, cf., for example, ps. CIV.15 and I Reg. XXIV.7. For the legatine mission and the synods held in 786, see (briefly) Stenton, *Anglo-Saxon England*, pp. 215–17; see further, H. Vollrath, *Die Synoden Englands* (Paderborn, 1985), pp. 162–79, Cubitt, *Anglo-Saxon Church Councils*, pp. 153–90, and P. Wormald, 'In Search of King Offa's "Law Code"', in *People and Places in Northern Europe 500–1600. Essays in Honour of Peter Hayes Sawyer*, ed. I. Wood and N. Lund (Woodbridge, 1991), pp. 25–45, esp. 28–41. For an assessment of a possible link between the royal style *Christus Domini* and the anointing of King Offa's son Ecgfrith, see Stenton, *Anglo-Saxon England*, p. 217; Vollrath, *Die Synoden Englands*, pp. 169–70, and Cubitt, *Anglo-Saxon Church Councils*, pp. 153 and 188.

Therefore it is hardly surprising that, from the eighth century onwards, leading churchmen like Chrodegang, bishop of Metz (d. 776) and Hincmar, archbishop of Rheims (d. 882) should have much concerned themselves with making royal anointing an indispensable part of that ceremony, thereby securing the control of the church over royal inauguration and the succession of kings.[124] A possible link between such Frankish clerical interest in the anointing and consecration of kings and late-ninth- or early-tenth-century Winchester has been proposed in the person of Grimbald, originally a monk from Saint-Bertin in Flanders and subsequently a member of the *familia* of Archbishop Fulco of Rheims (883–900), Hincmar's successor. As is well known, Grimbald joined the group of Alfred's helpers at the king's request in 886 or shortly thereafter.[125] In England, he may have been involved in the foundation of the New Minster, Winchester,[126] and (given the strong Frankish tradition of

[124] On the subject of clerical interest and initiative in establishing royal anointing in Francia in the eighth and ninth centuries, see Nelson, 'Rulers' Inauguration Rituals', pp. 289–96. See also C. A. Bouman, *Sacring and Crowning* (Groningen, 1957), pp. 107–18, on anointing as it was practised on the Continent during the ninth century, and as it is reflected in contemporary anointing formulas preserved in liturgical books such as pontificals. For the importance of the rite of anointing in Francia in the ninth century and the role played by leading churchmen like Hincmar in this development, see also P. E. Schramm, 'Die Krönung im 9. und 10. Jahrhundert: A. Die Krönung bei den Westfranken', in his *Kaiser, Könige und Päpste* II (Stuttgart, 1968), pp. 140–68, at 142–51. In this connection it may be relevant to mention that anointing temporarily seems to have lost some of its importance under Charlemagne's successors in Germany, apparently in an attempt to break free from clerical predominance in the coronation act. However, its indispensability was unequivocally stressed again in the coronation of Otto I in 936; see Schramm, 'Die Krönung im 9. und 10. Jahrhundert: C. Salbung und Krönung bei den Ostfranken bis zur Thronbesteigung König Heinrichs I (919)', *ibid.*, pp. 287–305, at 287–304. For details of royal anointing according to various continental *ordines*, as well as parallels to, and distinctions from, baptismal unction and the consecration of priests and bishops, see Schramm, 'Der Ablauf der deutschen Königsweihe nach dem "Mainzer Ordo" (um 960)', in his *Kaiser, Könige und Päpste* III (Stuttgart, 1969), pp. 59–107, at 71–5.

[125] For Grimbald's career, see P. Grierson, 'Grimbald of St Bertin's', *English Historical Review* 55 (1940), 529–61; for the date of Grimbald's arrival in England, see Keynes and Lapidge, *Alfred the Great*, p. 27; for Grimbald's career in England, see also *ibid.*, pp. 182–6 and 331–3. For Grimbald as the agent through which West Frankish material concerning the inauguration of kings may have reached England, see Nelson, 'The Second English *Ordo*', p. 365.

[126] Note, however, that Grimbald died in 901, the year in which the New Minster

historiography, especially in the form of annals) it has been suggested that he may have played a role in the compilation of the earliest parts of the Parker Chronicle.[127]

The point of interest for us is that, under the annal of 853, the Parker Chronicle relates the somewhat mysterious incident of four-year-old Alfred's royal anointing at Rome by Pope Leo IV.[128] The Old English wording for the rite in question is closely similar to the Chronicle entry for 787: 'he hine to cyninge gehalgode'. This is translated by Bishop Asser (whose account of the incident is based on that of the Chronicle) unambiguously as 'unxit in regem'.[129] The passage in the Chronicle (written in a hand of s. ix/x)[130] obviously attracted the special interest of a tenth-century annotator (who would have been a contemporary of the Royal Glossator). This annotator highlighted the episode by inserting large crosses in red ink in both margins of the folio.[131]

presumably was founded by Edward the Elder. On Grimbald's role in the history of the New Minster, see Keynes, *Liber Vitae*, pp. 16–17 and 81.

[127] See, for example, Parkes, 'The Palaeography of the Parker Manuscript', pp. 160–3, and Keynes and Lapidge, *Alfred the Great*, pp. 40 and 217, n. 60.

[128] See *ASC MS A*, ed. Bately, p. 45. For discussion, see Nelson, 'The Problem of King Alfred's Royal Anointing', in her *Politics and Ritual*, pp. 309–27 (orig. publ. 1967), esp. 322, where a similar episode from Hincmar's writings is adduced. See also Parkes, 'The Palaeography of the Parker Manuscript', p. 163, and Keynes and Lapidge, *Alfred the Great*, p. 232, n. 19.

[129] Cf. Asser, *Life*, ed. Stevenson, p. 7 (ch. 8), transl. Keynes and Lapidge, *Alfred the Great*, p. 69.

[130] For the date of the script, see Bately, *ASC MS A*, pp. xxi and xxiv–xxv (providing a survey of scholarly opinion on that point).

[131] On 13r; see *ASC MS A*, ed. Bately, p. 45, n. 3. The only other entry highlighted in a similar fashion is the accession of Bishop Frithestan of Winchester (909–31); see *ibid.*, p. 63, nn. 2 and 3. For these crosses and their presumed date, see Parkes, 'The Palaeography of the Parker Manuscript', p. 165. It should be noted that the attribution of the Parker Chronicle (Cambridge, Corpus Christi College 173) to Winchester has recently been challenged by Dumville, 'The Anglo-Saxon Chronicle', esp. pp. 71–2 and 97–8. For our purposes, however, it is not of crucial importance whether the traditional ascription of the compilation and the production of the manuscript of the Parker Chronicle to one of the Winchester scriptoria can be upheld or not. The point simply is that the A Chronicle furnishes interesting evidence that, by the late ninth or early tenth century, anointing had come to be regarded (at least in clerical circles) as an indispensable, if not the most important, rite in the investiture of an Anglo-Saxon king.

In other words, an interlinear gloss which consistently and (one must stress) idiosyncratically renders *christus*, a word originally meaning 'the anointed', by the Old English and Latin terms for 'king', would appear to coincide perfectly with such longstanding and acute clerical interest in the control of kingship and the making of kings. We will have occasion to return to these striking glosses in connection with the presumed authorship of the Royal gloss (below, pp. 304–10). For the moment, we may return to our point of departure: the Royal Glossator's penchant for poetic diction in his gloss. His sustained concern to render *christus* by *cyning* is most effectively and intriguingly underpinned by the fact that this lemma and its gloss for once enticed him to try his hand at Old English poetry. This trial resulted in the following lines found in the margin of 25r of Royal 2. B. V:

> Wæs mid Iudeum   on geardagum
> ealra cyninga gehwelc   Cristus nemned.[132]

This poetic comment pertains to the lemma *christus* in ps. XVII.51 which in turn refers to King David. In the manuscript it accompanies as a poetic paraphrase the marginal Latin commentary to the lemma in question: 'Omnis rex in antiquis diebus aput Iudeos nominabatur Christus'. To all appearances, the Latin text and its Old English paraphrase echo explanations by Cassiodorus such as the ones quoted above. Of especial relevance is Cassiodorus's interpretation of the lemma in ps. XVII.51 (the psalm verse in question here): '*Christus* ante dicebatur omnis unctus in regem'. The close dependence of the Old English couplet on the Latin marginal commentary, and (even more important) the explanation which is provided by these Old English verses for the consistent and remarkable glosses *cyning* and *rex* for *christus*, would seem to preclude an attribution of the verses to a later scribe and not to the Glossator himself. The couplet may be no more than a poetic pen trial, but it makes correct Old English verse and, most importantly, it clearly confirms that the Glossator

---

[132] 'In former times, the Jews called every king "Christus"'. Apparently this couplet had not been noticed by Roeder who, in his edition, provided a list of Old English glosses found in the margins of the manuscript (*Der altenglische Regius-Psalter*, pp. xv–xvi). It was first printed by K. Sisam, *Salisbury Psalter*, p. 52, n. 3. It is not included among the occasional verses edited by F. C. Robinson and E. G. Stanley, *Old English Verse Texts from Many Sources. A Comprehensive Collection*, EEMF 23 (Copenhagen, 1991).

responded not only to the linguistic difficulties of the psalms but also to their poetic language.[133]

The stylistic background

We may now turn our attention to what texts there were which may have served as an inspirational force for the kind of glossing the Royal Glossator had in mind, a glossing which encompassed a vocabulary, rich and varied, often recherché, learned and poetic, as well as various sorts of rhetorical adornments. One may be surprised to meet such language and adornments in an interlinear gloss, but the Royal Glossator was certainly not the first Anglo-Saxon who felt the urge to respond to the poetic language of the psalms. More than 200 years earlier, Bede had composed Latin metrical paraphrases of three of the psalms.[134] Given the scholarly disposition of the Glossator, it is not altogether unlikely that he would have known those poems.

Naturally, another metrical paraphrase of the psalms comes to mind in this connection: the Metrical or Paris Psalter, a rendering into Old English verse of psalms LI–CL which has survived in one manuscript (now Paris, Bibliothèque Nationale, lat. 8824, s. xi^med).[135] To all appearances, a verse translation of the entire psalter must originally have been in question. This much can be deduced from fragments of a metrical translation of the first fifty psalms which are included in the so-called 'Benedictine Office' (now Oxford, Bodleian Library, Junius 121, s.

---

[133] See below, pp. 129–30 and 309–10, for the bearing which the couplet may have on the identity of the Glossator.

[134] Bede's metrical paraphrases of pss. XLI, LXXXIII and CXII are edited by J. Fraipont, *Bedae Venerabilis liber hymnorum, rhythmi, variae preces*, CCSL 122 (Turnhout, 1955), 447–50. See also the poem entitled *De die iudicii*, a substantially longer and verbose treatment of the major themes of Bede's poems on pss. XLI and LXXXIII, which in turn served as the source for the Old English poem *Judgement Day II*. Although *De die iudicii* is frequently attributed to Bede in manuscripts, it cannot be ascribed to him with absolute certainty, chiefly for reasons of style and metre. It is edited by Fraipont, CCSL 122, 439–44. For a brief discussion (with further references) of Bede's psalm poems and *De die iudicii*, see most recently M. Lapidge, *Bede the Poet*, Jarrow Lecture 1993 (Jarrow, 1994), pp. 3–5 (repr. in his *Anglo-Latin Literature, 600–899*, pp. 313–38).

[135] The Psalter is printed by G. P. Krapp, *The Paris Psalter and the Metres of Boethius*, ASPR 5 (New York, 1932), 3–150.

xi$^{3/4}$)[136] where they occur together with fragments from the later part of the psalter (pss. LI–CL) which in turn are more or less identical with the text of the Paris Psalter.[137] The Metrical Psalter has been dismissed as 'mechanical and uninspired'[138] or as 'a pedestrian and unimaginative piece of poetic translation',[139] and consequently has not attracted much scholarly attention. Its composition has been variously dated from the late ninth to the end of the first quarter of the eleventh century, although a date after the middle of the tenth century seems to be favoured – which would clearly make the Royal gloss the earlier text.[140]

Although the pedestrian character of the Metrical Psalter appears to be in striking contrast to the more flamboyant Royal gloss, it may be worth mentioning that there is at least one intriguing verbal link between the two, namely that in ps. CI.4 both use the extremely rare compound noun *cocerpanne* to translate *frixorium* 'frying-pan'.[141] Apart from the Royal and Metrical psalters the word occurs once in the glosses to Aldhelm's prose *De uirginitate* in Brussels, Bibliothèque Royale, 1650 (and dependent glosses), as an *interpretamentum* for *sartago* 'frying-pan' (G 4555), which gives us our first important verbal link between the Royal Psalter and the Aldhelm glosses. The only other attestation of *cocerpanne* is in the Harley Glossary (London, BL, Harley 3376, s. x/xi) where it evidently derives

---

[136] Printed by J. M. Ure, *The Benedictine Office* (Edinburgh, 1957).

[137] All these so-called 'Fragments of Psalms' are edited by E. van Kirk Dobbie, *The Anglo-Saxon Minor Poems*, ASPR 6 (New York, 1942), 80–6.

[138] Greenfield and Calder, *New Critical History*, p. 232.

[139] M. S. Griffith, 'Poetic Language and the Paris Psalter: the Decay of the Old English Tradition', *ASE* 20 (1991), 167–86, at 167.

[140] For a convenient summary of the various dates and the reasons which have been adduced for them, see Hofstetter, *Winchester und Sprachgebrauch*, pp. 537–9. The most recent work on the vocabulary of the Metrical Psalter assumes a composition 'at the end of the Anglo-Saxon period', without however endorsing a more specific date; cf. Griffith, 'Poetic Language', p. 167. An attractively neat ascription of the Metrical Psalter to Winchester during the reign of King Edgar and the episcopate of Bishop Æthelwold (963 × 975) has been advanced, but unfortunately has not been substantiated by any tangible evidence; cf. S. L. Keefer, *The Old English Metrical Psalter. An Annotated Set of Collation Lists with the Psalter Glosses* (New York, 1979), esp. pp. 145–59. For this ascription, see also the brief remarks by Hofstetter, *Winchester und Sprachgebrauch*, p. 538, and the review by J. Hill, *Archiv* 218 (1981), 420–2.

[141] None of the D-type psalters has this gloss. However, since they invariably are *Gallicanum* psalters and since the *Gallicanum* reading is markedly different for the variant in question, they can provide no index to the unusual character of *cocerpanne*.

either from Royal 2. B. V or a close congener.[142] The word *cōcerpanne* is not only rare; it is also highly unusual in terms of word-formation.[143] The Royal Glossator incontestably took some interest in the word (which he may have coined himself) since he employs it in an exquisite *figura etymologica*. He translates the phrase 'et ossa mea sicut in frixorio confrixa sunt' as '7 ban mina swa swa on cocerpannan gecocsoda synd'. The verb *gecocsian* is also exceedingly rare and again may well have been coined by the Glossator.[144] The only other attestation of *gecocsian* is again in the Harley Glossary, where it glosses *confringere*, and where lemma and gloss present the same inflexional form as in the psalm verse in question,[145] thereby confirming the suspicion that the compiler(s) of that glossary drew on a glossed psalter manuscript which must have been very close to Royal 2. B. V. By the same token, the link between the Royal Psalter and the Metrical Psalter provided by *cocerpanne* can scarcely be coincidental; and again the (presumably) earlier date for the Royal gloss would seem to establish that the poet of the Metrical Psalter drew on the Royal gloss and not *vice versa*. But irrespective of any presumed dates, the Metrical Psalter

---

[142] See *Harley Glossary*, ed. Oliphant, no. 5299: '*Frixorium ł sartago, cremium*: hyrstepanne uel spæc, cocorpanne'. This entry unequivocally echoes ps. CI.4, both in its *Romanum* and *Gallicanum* reading: *frixorium* 'frying-pan' is *Romanum*; the *Gallicanum* has *cremium* (as part of an altogether different variant), here glossed by *spæc* 'small branch'.

[143] The determinant of the compound noun consists of the Latin loanword *cōc* 'cook' (from Vulgar Latin *cocus*, Latin *coquus*) plus the suffix *-ere*. The suffix forms personal agentive nouns, which here results in a meaning which apparently does not differ from that of the base (*coc*). See Holthausen, *Altenglisches etymologisches Wörterbuch*, s. v. *cōcere*, M. S. Serjeantson, *A History of Foreign Words in English* (London, 1935), p. 39, and Funke, *Die gelehrten lateinischen Lehn- und Fremdwörter*, p. 48. That *cocer* should be taken as a personal agent noun 'cook' and not as a concrete object (such as Modern English *cooker* or *boiler*) seems clear from a survey of the Old English derivatives in *-ere*. Formations where the suffix denotes a tool or implement are apparently found only in deverbal nouns, for example, *sceawere* 'mirror' (from *sceawian*) or *word-samnere* 'catalogue' (from (*ge)samnian*), and they are extremely rare; see Kastovsky, 'Semantics and Vocabulary', p. 386, and esp., *idem*, 'The Old English Suffix *-er(e)*', *Anglia* 89 (1971), 285–325, at 307 and 325. However, a verb **cocian*, from which *cocer* denoting a tool could have been derived, is not attested. Nevertheless, the ingenuity and inventiveness of the Royal Glossator should caution us to accept as sacrosanct the verdict of modern authorities on word-formation where one of his coinages is in question.

[144] The verb is derived from the Old English loan *cōc* 'cook': see Holthausen, *Altenglisches etymologisches Wörterbuch*, s. v. *cōcsian*.

[145] See *Harley Glossary*, ed. Oliphant, no. 2023: *confrixa*: *gecocsade*.

with its pedestrian and (in spite of its outward appearance) prosaic approach to the psalms, in all probability would have held no attraction for the Royal Glossator.[146]

Another poetic response to the psalms in the vernacular is the so-called 'Kentish Psalm', a lengthy metrical paraphrase of ps. L, preserved in London, BL, Cotton Vespasian D. vi (first part), a manuscript of mid-tenth-century (or perhaps somewhat later) date and of possible Canterbury (St Augustine's) origin.[147] The poem, which has elicited somewhat more commendatory remarks from its critics than the Metrical Psalter, has been dated, on stylistic grounds, not much earlier than the manuscript itself.[148] This, and its clear Kentish dialect affiliations, would seem to rule it out as a major source of inspiration for the Royal Glossator.

If we are to look for a vernacular inspirational force for the Royal Glossator, perhaps the most suitable candidate would be King Alfred's prose translation of psalms I–L (preserved in the same manuscript, Paris, BN, lat. 8824, as the Metrical Psalter).[149] Here we have a fairly literal translation of the psalms, which is, however, not entirely devoid of rhetorical embellishments such as alliteration, paronomasia, balanced sentence structure and so on.[150] Most importantly, Alfred's translation

---

[146] Note that the dependence on the Royal Psalter would set a rather precisely defined *terminus post quem* for the composition of the Metrical Psalter.

[147] The psalm is printed by E. van Kirk Dobbie, *The Anglo-Saxon Minor Poems*, ASPR 6 (New York, 1942), 88–94.

[148] See Dobbie, *ibid*., pp. lxxx–lxxxiii, and Greenfield and Calder, *New Critical History*, p. 232. For an evaluation of the recent book-length study of the Kentish Psalm by S. L. Keefer, *Psalm-Poem and the Psalter-Glosses. The Latin and Old English Psalter-Text Background to 'Kentish Psalm 50'* (New York, 1991), see the review by P. Pulsiano, *Anglia* 112 (1994), 176–9.

[149] Alfred's psalms are edited by Bright and Ramsay, *The West-Saxon Psalms*. A more recent edition is by P. P. O'Neill, 'The Old English Prose Psalms of the Paris Psalter' (unpubl. PhD dissertation, Univ. of Pennsylvania, 1980). For a facsimile of the entire manuscript, see *The Paris Psalter*, ed. Colgrave *et al*. King Alfred's authorship of the prose psalms has been advocated by several modern scholars, and, on grounds of vocabulary, has been established beyond reasonable doubt by J. M. Bately, 'Lexical Evidence for the Authorship of the Prose Psalms in the Paris Psalter', *ASE* 10 (1982), 69–95.

[150] For such stylistic features, see *ibid*., *passim*; cf. also *idem*, 'Old English Prose', pp. 130–1, and *idem*, *The Literary Prose of King Alfred's Reign: Translation or Transformation?*, Inaugural Lecture, King's College, University of London (1980), pp. 14–15.

draws on patristic psalm exegesis on a hitherto unprecedented scale, both in the Old English introductions prefaced to each psalm and in the translation itself. The exegetical compilation to which Alfred chiefly had recourse[151] goes under the name *In psalmorum librum exegesis*; the whole work has traditionally but erroneously been ascribed to Bede.[152] Apparently this compilation also served as a minor exegetical source for the marginal commentary in Royal 2. B. V.[153] In other words, King Alfred's translation, providing a commentary on the psalms, as well as striving to emulate (to some extent) the diction of the psalms, would have appealed to the Royal Glossator as being strikingly close to his own scholarly and stylistic endeavours. It might be argued that the sole surviving manuscript of Alfred's translation (bearing no mark of authorship) would not seem to point to a wide circulation of the text. However, against such an argument one must weigh the evidence that as late as the twelfth century, information could be obtained that the king had translated the first part of the psalter and was only prevented by death from completing the task. For it is to William of Malmesbury (d. *c.* 1143) that we owe the earliest ascription of such a translation to King Alfred.[154] It may therefore not be fanciful to assume that a scholar who (as we have grounds to believe) had lived for many years at the court of Alfred's grandson, King Æthelstan, could have had access to a copy of Alfred's translation of the psalms and that he would have known about their author. In view of King Æthelstan's (amply attested) personal piety, we may be permitted to imagine that for him the Old English psalms were

---

[151] For a brief but admirably clear exposition of this exegetical compilation drawn on by Alfred, see Keynes and Lapidge, *Alfred the Great*, p. 302. For more detailed discussion, see J. W. Bright and R. L. Ramsay, 'Notes on the "Introduction" of the West-Saxon Psalms', *Journal of Theological Studies* 13 (1912), 520–58, and P. P. O'Neill, 'Old English Introductions to the Prose Psalms of the Paris Psalter: Sources, Structure and Composition', *Studies in Philology* 78 (1981), 20–38. See also the brief treatment and references in Wright, 'Hiberno-Latin and Irish-Influenced Commentaries', pp. 97–8, and, for the part of that compilation ultimately deriving from Theodore of Mopsuestia's psalm commentary, see Lapidge, *Biblical Commentaries*, ed. Bischoff and Lapidge, p. 248 and nn. 24–5.

[152] *CPL*, no. 1348; it is printed among the works of Bede in PL 93, 477–1098.

[153] See Davey, 'Commentary of the Regius Psalter', p. 343.

[154] See William of Malmesbury, *Gesta regum*, ed. Stubbs I, 132.

among the most treasured of his grandfather's translations and hence available to scholars in his entourage.[155]

However, we should also look outside vernacular literature for possible stylistic models for the Royal Glossator. We should do so principally for two reasons. First, the Glossator's sound knowledge of Latin would suggest that he was widely read in Latin literature. (In this connection Bede's psalm poems have already been adverted to.) Secondly, in vernacular poetry, rhetorical embellishments such as non-structural or 'artful' alliteration,[156] assonance, rhyme or paronomasia are primarily employed for their aural effects, that poetry being composed above all for oral performance. Such aural effects might also have been intended by King Alfred when he employed similar embellishments in his translations, since we know from Bishop Asser that the king was in the habit of listening to books being read out to him by his helpers (even though these appear to have been books in Latin).[157]

An interlinear gloss, however, can never have been intended for oral recital. It is therefore to Latin authors, particularly the practitioners of the hermeneutic style, that we must turn for further possible models for the Royal Glossator. By the mid-tenth century (when Royal 2. B. V was written), no sizeable corpus of Anglo-Latin writings in the hermeneutic style composed subsequent to the Viking age was as yet in existence. But Aldhelm, the great source of inspiration for the tenth- and eleventh-century hermeneutic style was available for study. In Aldhelm's prose writings as well as in his poetic works, we find a penchant for sound effects such as alliteration, rhyme and word-play, as well as an affectation of synonyms and lexical variation, of rare and obscure words (often culled from glossaries) and of poetic expressions. In short, we meet here with broadly the same stylistic features which are employed on a much more modest scale by the Royal Glossator.[158] Now the intricacies of Aldhelm's

---

[155] See below, pp. 332–70, for the intellectual climate at King Æthelstan's court and its possible influence on the Royal Glossator.

[156] For a sensitive analysis of passages containing such alliteration which is not required by the metre but used for ornamental purposes, and for its evaluation in combination with other embellishments in Old English verse (and, to some extent, prose), see Orchard, 'Artful Alliteration', pp. 429–63.

[157] See *Asser's Life of King Alfred*, ed. Stevenson, chs. 77 (p. 63) and 88 (p. 73); cf. also the remarks by Keynes and Lapidge, *Alfred the Great*, p. 239.

[158] For a discussion of Aldhelm's prose style, see Winterbottom, 'Aldhelm's Prose Style',

style could never have been perceived through oral presentation alone; they demanded devoted and intensive study of the written texts. In other words, the writings of an author like Aldhelm had to be studied in much the same fashion as the difficult Latin of the psalms. A scholar who had been trained to respond not only to a recherché vocabulary but also to more aural stylistic and rhetorical effects when studying written texts, might well have felt tempted to reproduce some such effects, as well as to try his hand at flamboyant English neologisms, when devising an Old English gloss. And he might have assumed that at least some of his fellow scholars could be relied on to detect and appreciate such features also in an Old English gloss. We should further bear in mind that Aldhelm's poetic style and metre were much influenced by vernacular poetry, as has recently been stressed.[159] In all probability such interactions between Latin and Old English did not escape a scholar of the intellectual make-up of the Royal Glossator, and they might well have ignited his own stylistic aspirations.

However, the extravagance of such an undertaking should be stressed. Neither the Lambeth Glossator nor the more closely dependent D-type psalter glosses appear to show much interest in either rhetorical ornamentation or choice vocabulary. On the contrary (as we have seen), they tend to reduce the occurrences of such embellishments and to 'neutralize' rare words by the introduction of synonyms or by jettisoning them outright. Nor do the Glossator's stylistic experiments seem to have influenced later glossators to any remarkable extent. A few poetic words have been noted among the glosses to the *Expositio hymnorum* and a few more among those to the Durham Hymnal (Durham, Cathedral Library, B. III. 32, s. xi[1]–xi[med], probably from Christ Church, Canterbury).[160] But apart

pp. 39–46; for a full study of Aldhelm's poetic style, see Orchard, *Poetic Art of Aldhelm*, *passim* and esp. pp. 8–16, where Aldhelm's poetic and prose styles are compared. The classic survey and analysis of the hermeneutic style in tenth-century England is Lapidge, 'Hermeneutic Style'.

[159] See Orchard, *Poetic Art of Aldhelm*, esp. pp. 112–25; the point was first made by Lapidge, 'Aldhelm's Latin Poetry', pp. 255–69.

[160] See Gneuss, *Hymnar und Hymnen*, pp. 188 and 177–85 *passim*. (No mention of such poetic words is made in the section on the vocabulary of the Durham Hymnal gloss in the recent edition by Milfull, *The Hymns of the Anglo-Saxon Church*, pp. 77–91.) For the manuscripts of the *Expositio hymnorum*, see below, p. 93, n. 18. For attempts to discover poetic vocabulary and stylistic *ornatus* in Old High German glosses and interlinear versions, see S. Sonderegger, 'Frühe Erscheinungsformen dichterischer Sprache im Althochdeutschen', in *Typologia litterarum. Festschrift für Max Wehrli*, ed.

from such scattered attempts, the Royal Glossator (perhaps predictably) does not appear to have found any devoted follower.

All these various pieces of evidence, which can be assembled from close inspection of the vocabulary of the gloss, combine to suggest that for the Royal Glossator the vernacular was more than an ancillary aid used solely for purposes of gaining access to the Latin text, but that, on the contrary, he had an intrinsic interest in deploying the richness and resourcefuless of English before the foil of Latin. One implication of such an attitude would be that the Glossator did not intend his gloss exclusively or even primarily for beginners in Latin. It is true that, by its very nature, a continuous interlinear gloss provides a considerable portion of basic knowledge of Latin vocabulary and morphology. It is also true that at times the Glossator included rather elementary information about Latin grammar, as when he frequently signalled the ablative case in Latin by the English preposition *of* before a noun, regardless of what preposition would have been required in idiomatic English in the context in question.[161] Such a consistently unidiomatic use (especially when compared with the often more idiomatic prepositions in the Vespasian and Lambeth psalters) feeds the suspicion that the Glossator employed *of* simply as a case marker and, for once, did not concern himself with a contextually adequate rendering of the inflexional form of the lemma in question.[162]

S. Sonderegger *et al.* (Zürich, 1969), pp. 53–81, esp. at 69–81, and *idem*, 'Frühe Übersetzungsschichten im Althochdeutschen. Ein methodischer Beitrag', in *Philologia deutsch. Festschrift zum 70. Geburtstag von Walter Henzen*, ed. W. Kohlschmidt and P. Zinsli (Bern, 1965), pp. 101–14, at 106–10. Interestingly, such vocabulary and embellishments appear to be most clearly discernible in the ninth-century interlinear versions in the 'Murbach Hymnal' and another hymn-like poem, the so-called *Carmen ad Deum* (*inc. Sancte sator suffragator, ICL*, no. 14640).

[161] See for example: *potasti nos uino: þu drænctest – of wine* (ps. LIX.5); *ore suo benedicabant: of muðe heora hy bletsodon* (ps. LXI.5) or *igne nos examinasti: of fyre þu amyredest* (ps. LXV.10); further examples would be: pss. LXIV.10, 12 and 14, LXV.17 and so on. In the above examples, as in many others, *of* is not the preposition required in idiomatic Old English prose. In most cases this would be *mid*, which is the preposition normally used on such occasions by the Vespasian and Lambeth glossators. (In ps. LXV.10 Lambeth has *on* which is even more idiomatic in the context; Vespasian sometimes lacks a preposition altogether, for example in ps. LXI.5).

[162] A similar employment of *of* alone (without an accompanying Old English noun) as a case marker has been noted in three other Old English manuscripts by F. C. Robinson,

Nonetheless, it is obvious that the Glossator also had in mind more mature students or fellow scholars as readers and users of his gloss. Apart from the lexical and stylistic features we have been discussing, there are other, more straightforward, pointers in that direction. For example, function words, such as pronouns or certain conjunctions, frequently remain without a gloss,[163] as do the words *deus* and *dominus*, either alone or as part of an unglossed phrase.[164] A few examples of other common words or phrases that stand without a gloss would be: *est super nos* (ps. IV.7); *omnes qui* (ps. V.12), *Quoniam non est* (ps. VI.6), *et secundum* (ps. VII.9) or *nomen tuum* (ps. IX.11). By the same token, there are frequent gaps in the gloss whenever words, phrases or complete verses are repeated in the Latin, even though such repetitions may come at a considerable remove from the first occurrence. For example, the phrase *et de necessitatibus eorum liberauit eos* is unglossed in ps. CVI.13, 19, 28 and 30, after it had been glossed at its first occurrence in ps. CVI.6. Or the phrase *et ostende faciem tuam et salui erimus* is glossed in ps. LXXIX.4 but unglossed in ps. LXXIX.8. By contrast, there are no extended gaps and scarcely any omissions of single words, however common, in the Vespasian Psalter. In the Lambeth gloss such omissions and gaps are considerably fewer, and normally occur only with words and phrases repeated immediately after their first occurrence. What kind of students the Glossator had in mind also emerges from the accompanying condensed, and hence often difficult, marginal commentary in Latin, which would simply have been impenetrable for beginners in Latin.

All this leaves one with the impression that the Glossator provided his gloss for students and scholars who were in a position to appreciate and relish his experiments with the wealth of synonyms and the resourcefulness of the word-formation of their native language, his awareness of stylistic registers and his confident and at times flamboyant response to the immense challenge which the difficult language of the psalms and the

---

'Old English *Awindan*, *Of* and *Sinhere*', in his *The Editing of Old English* (Oxford, 1994), pp. 154–9, at 156–7 (orig. publ. 1973).

[163] Examples would be: *tu* (ps. III.8 and 9), *meam* (ps. VI.10), *uestris* (ps. IV.5), *eius* (ps. IX.12), *quoniam* (pss. IV.10, V.13 and VI.3).

[164] For example, *Domine deus meus* (ps. VII.2 and 7), *tu domine* (ps. IV.1) or *ad dominum* (ps. III.5).

mature richness and unrivalled suppleness of Latin posed for English as a medium for sophisticated literary and religious utterances.

We may next turn to the question of what lexical and stylistic evidence can be assembled to associate this remarkable piece of scholarship with Æthelwold and his circle.

4

The Royal Psalter and the Rule: lexical and stylistic links

The *terminus ante quem* for the origin of the Royal gloss is obviously set by the manuscript in which it is preserved, which, on palaeographical grounds, must be dated no later than the mid-tenth century.[1] Textcritical and linguistic grounds would seem to preclude an origin of the gloss considerably earlier than the date of the manuscript. It is clear that the text as transmitted in Royal 2. B. V is very close to the original gloss, and, while it is true that a later manuscript may occasionally preserve a better text than an earlier one, such an assumption is ruled out for Royal 2. B. V by the language of the gloss: the language is clearly not early West Saxon,[2] nor does it preserve any traces of an earlier West Saxon layer of glosses.

To my knowledge, an ascription of the Royal gloss to Æthelwold's circle and more specifically to one or several of his Abingdon monks (or monks from Abingdon accompanying him to Winchester) has been made (tentatively) only once, namely by Karl Wildhagen.[3] His reasons for this were threefold: the presence in the manuscript of liturgical pieces, such as the *Gloria in excelsis* or the *Quicumque uult*,[4] the remarkable quality of the gloss itself and the occurrence of phonological features pertaining to the

---

[1] For palaeographical and other details which seem to connect Royal 2. B. V with Æthelwold's circle, see below, pp. 264–73.

[2] Two prominent phonological features pointing to a Late West Saxon origin would be the use of < y > (seldom < i >) in lieu of Early West Saxon < ie > (for example, *gehyrde* (ps. IX.38), *behylt* (ps. LVII.8) or *alys* (ps. CXVIII.154)), and < a > occurring normally before nasals, whereas < o > predominates in such position in Early West Saxon (for example, *fornam* (ps. LXXIX.14), *naman* (ps. CXIV.4) or *mann* (ps. CXV.11)).

[3] 'Studien zum *Psalterium Romanum*', pp. 448–553.

[4] For the evidence of these pieces, see below, pp. 273–4.

Anglian dialect.[5] As regards the first two points, for Wildhagen the Royal Psalter represented the first fruit of the intellectual revival occasioned by the Benedictine reform (the 'erste Frucht der neuen Schulung'). The Abingdon monks suggested themselves to him as possible glossators, because Abingdon was very close to the Mercian border ('Abingdon, das hart an der mercischen Grenze lag') with, for him, the implication that its inmates were either speakers of the Anglian dialect or that at least a high level of tolerance towards Anglian dialect features could be expected among them. In addition, the close dependence on the Royal Psalter of three eleventh-century glossed psalters (Tiberius, Vitellius and Arundel), all arguably originating from Winchester, did not escape Wildhagen's notice.[6] However, he did not in any way connect the authorship of the glosses with Æthelwold himself, and consequently did not enter into a comparison of the glosses with the vocabulary of the one work attributed to Æthelwold for centuries, the Old English Benedictine Rule. For us, being able to draw on the ever-widening historical, liturgical and philological research of several intervening generations, Wildhagen's work must appear limited in many respects, no doubt. However, in an age when glosses were almost universally judged solely in terms of their contribution to dictionary entries, and when textcritical and philological questions were usually discussed at a lofty distance from their cultural context, Wildhagen was one of the very few scholars who brought historical, liturgical and art historical observations to bear on an evaluation of the Old English psalter glosses. For this he deserves our respect.

LEXICAL LINKS

More recently, several verbal links between the Royal Psalter and quotations from the psalms in the Old English Benedictine Rule have been pointed out by Phillip Pulsiano.[7] He noted an agreement in the use of translation words such as *genyþrian* for *humiliare*, *bodian* for *pronuntiare*, *gewilnung* for *desiderium* or *eardung* and *eardungstow* for *tabernaculum*. He

[5] For an evaluation of such Anglian dialect features in West Saxon texts, see below, pp. 316–25.

[6] See 'Studien zum *Psalterium Romanum*', p. 451; the quotations are on pp. 448 and 451 respectively.

[7] See Pulsiano, 'Defining the A-type and D-type Traditions', pp. 314–15.

tentatively ascribed such shared renderings not to any direct link between both texts, but to 'the likelihood that a common vocabulary was developing, and that we are witnessing its influence in both the Rule and the psalter'.[8] We have seen (above, pp. 71–3) that the last-mentioned of these examples, *eardung* and *eardungstow* for *tabernaculum*, have also been given attention in the course of Patrizia Lendinara's survey of the translation words for *tabernaculum* and *tentorium* in Old English texts, and that the agreement between Rule and Royal Psalter at this point is explained there in terms of an attempt at Winchester standardization, an attempt which did not stand the test of time.[9] (We shall concern ourselves presently with the importance of Winchester usage for establishing a common origin for Psalter and Rule.) Even though exegetical and stylistic reasons would rather seem to account for these striking glosses, at all events, the link formed by them between the Psalter and the Rule decisively gains importance in view of the frequency and consistency with which they are employed in both texts, and in no other texts than the Psalter and the Rule.[10]

Many years ago, when working on the vocabulary of Bishop Æthelwold's translation of the *Regula S. Benedicti*, I came across (inadvertently as it were) a number of clear links in word usage between this text and the Royal Psalter gloss, links which appear too striking to be explained in terms of coincidence in texts originating at approximately the same time and in the same dialect area. Such links comprise the loanwords *scrudnian* 'to investigate', *mese* 'table', *cantic* 'song of praise' and *chor* 'choir'; to which we may now add *son* 'sound' (above, p. 52); they also comprise native words like *forbrytan* 'to crush', *gedeorf* 'labour', *ælþeodig* 'foreign' and *cnapa* 'boy'.[11] These findings have subsequently been adopted by Helmut Gneuss in his seminal article on the origin of the Winchester vocabulary,[12] and since that time the Royal Psalter gloss has been connected in a loose way with the texts representing Winchester usage.[13] However, now

---

[8] *Ibid.*, p. 315.

[9] See Lendinara, 'Old English Renderings of *tabernaculum and tentorium*', esp. pp. 300–7.

[10] The lemmata *tabernaculum* or *tentorium* do not occur in the Brussels Aldhelm glosses, so there is no way of verifying the suspicion that *eardung* or *eardungstow* would have been employed there as well.

[11] See Gretsch, *Regula*, pp. 318–70 *passim*, and esp. at 374.

[12] See Gneuss, 'Origin of Standard Old English', p. 79.

[13] See, for example, Hofstetter, *Winchester und Sprachgebrauch*, pp. 463–4, Pulsiano,

that Winchester usage has been defined much more precisely than it was twenty-seven years ago, it is clear that, although there are links between the Psalter and the Rule with respect to Winchester terms, the verbal ties outside the Winchester vocabulary are even more numerous. None of the aforementioned examples belongs to the Winchester vocabulary. And since such ties are often peculiar to the Psalter and the Rule only (as in the case of *eardung* and *eardungstow*) they provide more specific evidence for a common origin of both texts than the Winchester words proper, shared by a greater number of texts. By the same token, it is important to be aware that the links between the Psalter and the Rule are often much less simple and straightforward than (say) in the case of *eardung(stow)* or, as we shall see, *scrudnian*.

I have attempted elsewhere to lay out such an intricate relationship between both texts in their use of *cantic*.[14] The rather complex evidence for this verbal link need not be rehearsed here in detail: in sum this evidence would seem to suggest that *cantic* was deliberately introduced by the Royal Glossator (no occurrence of the word unambiguously predates the Royal Psalter) to translate *canticum* 'song of praise' on all occurrences of the lemma (ten in total). In the Rule *cantic* appears with similar frequency (eight times), but here it translates *canticum* in the sense 'canticle', referring either to the group of, mainly OT, songs recited daily at Lauds, Vespers and Compline or to the so-called 'monastic canticles' sung at Nocturns on Sundays and feast days.[15] So the Glossator and the translator of the Rule unquestionably shared a pronounced taste for the loanword, a taste which cannot be paralleled from any other Old English text. But *cantic* is used in a different, more specific, sense in the Rule, as a kind of technical term. *Cantic* in the more general sense 'song of praise' (in which it occurs in the Psalter) is apparently not attested in the texts of the Winchester group, whereas it occurs there occasionally in the sense 'canticle' (for example in Ælfric or the interlinear gloss to the *Regula S. Benedicti*). All this could be satisfactorily explained on the assumption that the Psalter and the Rule originated in the same circle of scholars, Æthelwold's circle. *Cantic* would have been introduced there in the

---

'Defining the A-type and D-type Traditions', pp. 312–13, and Lendinara, 'Old English Renderings of *tabernaculum* and *tentorium*', p. 301.

[14] See Gretsch, 'Der liturgische Wortschatz', pp. 330–3 and 343–8.

[15] See *DACL* II. 2 (1910), 1975–99, and Gneuss, *Hymnar und Hymnen*, pp. 252–6.

general sense 'song of praise', its meaning being subsequently narrowed down to signify more specifically 'canticle'. In Æthelwold's school such a specific meaning could well have prevented *cantic* from being employed any longer in its original and more general sense; *lofsang* 'song of praise' is the word preferred there (in the Lambeth Psalter and Ælfric, for example).

Bearing in mind the possibility that we may have to uncover further such intricate and 'hidden' links between the Rule and the Psalter, we may now turn to the evidence provided in connection with the Winchester vocabulary.

Winchester vocabulary

Building on the hypothesis propounded by Gneuss,[16] Walter Hofstetter, in a magisterial study, has established thirteen semantic fields in which the preferential use of certain words (for which synonyms would have been available) was obviously taught and encouraged in some influential centre. The centre in question where such standardization presumably took place was the school at the Old Minster, Winchester, under Bishop Æthelwold, its influence spreading perhaps to other monastic schools in the Winchester ambit. Hofstetter has also defined the group of texts in which the so-called Winchester words were employed to the (near-)exclusion of their synonyms. Principally, these texts embrace the works of Ælfric, Bishop Æthelwold's most renowned and prolific pupil in the domain of Old English prose; they further embrace the Lambeth Psalter gloss, as well as the 'modernized' parts in the otherwise predominantly D-type glosses in the Stowe, Vitellius and Arundel psalters.[17] Also included among these works is the interlinear gloss to a widely used school text, namely the *Expositio hymnorum*, a Latin prose paraphrase of the metrical hymns sung in the Divine Office.[18] Finally the anonymous Old English prose translation of the rule for canons, originally composed by

---

[16] See Gneuss, 'Origin of Standard Old English', and cf. also *idem, Hymnar und Hymnen*, pp. 167–90.

[17] For editions of these psalters and their textual affiliations, see above, pp. 18–19 and 26–7.

[18] Preserved in London, BL, Cotton Julius A. vi (Christ Church, Canterbury, s. xi[1] or xi[med]) and London, BL, Cotton Vespasian D. xii (? Christ Church, Canterbury, s. xi[med]); ed. Gneuss, *Hymnar und Hymnen*, pp. 257–413. In addition, the interlinear gloss to the monastic canticles in Vespasian D. xii reveals Winchester usage; this gloss

Bishop Chrodegang of Metz,[19] the continuous interlinear gloss to the *Regula S. Benedicti*[20] and a regrettably short fragment of a prose translation of the *Regularis concordia*[21] belong to the 'inner group' of texts showing Winchester usage.[22] In respect of Æthelwold's own translation of the *Regula S. Benedicti*, Hofstetter's studies have confirmed the suspicion[23] that this must be regarded as a kind of forerunner, where a nucleus of Winchester vocabulary can be made out.[24] This in turn underpins the hypothesis that it was indeed at Bishop Æthelwold's instigation that such a standardized vocabulary in certain semantic fields was developed. For the Royal Psalter gloss a similar but more elusive role as a forerunner with an incipient Winchester usage has emerged from Hofstetter's work.[25]

For each of his thirteen semantic fields, Hofstetter distinguishes three categories of synonyms: first, the Winchester words, second, their 'non-Winchester' synonyms, that is to say those synonyms for Winchester words which were deliberately avoided by authors and glossators employing Winchester usage; and third, those synonyms for Winchester

---

is printed by M. Korhammer, *Die monastischen Cantica im Mittelalter und ihre altenglischen Interlinearversionen*, TUEPh 6 (Munich, 1976).

[19] Preserved in Cambridge, Corpus Christi College 191 (Exeter, s. xi³/⁴), ed. A. S. Napier, *The Old English Version, with the Latin Original, of the Enlarged Rule of Chrodegang*, EETS OS 150 (London, 1916).

[20] Preserved in London, BL, Cotton Tiberius A. iii, 118r–163v (Christ Church, Canterbury, s. xi^med), ed. H. Logemann, *The Rule of S. Benet*, EETS OS 90 (London, 1888).

[21] Preserved in Cambridge, Corpus Christi College 201, pp. 1–7 (s. xi^in), ed. J. Zupitza, 'Ein weiteres Bruchstück der Regularis concordia in altenglischer Sprache', *Archiv* 84 (1890), 1–24.

[22] See Hofstetter, *Winchester und Sprachgebrauch*, pp. 4–20, for the semantic fields in which Winchester words occur, as well as for the words themselves; pp. 29–123, for the texts belonging to the Winchester group; and pp. 554–9, for a brief summary of his findings. For a convenient conspectus of his methods and findings, see also *idem*, 'Winchester and Standardization'.

[23] See Gretsch, *Regula*, pp. 371–3, and Gneuss, 'Origin of Standard Old English', pp. 78–9.

[24] The Rule is commonly held to have been written *c.* 970, perhaps in the late 960s; see, for example, Gretsch, 'Benedictine Rule', p. 150. However, substantial parts of the translation or even the complete text may have been produced considerably earlier (see below, pp. 233–60).

[25] See Hofstetter, *Winchester und Sprachgebrauch*, pp. 30–6 for the Rule, and pp. 462–4 for the Royal Psalter.

words which were occasionally employed by 'Winchester' authors (presumably for purposes of modest or 'elegant' variation), but which occur in other texts as well, texts which otherwise do not make use of Winchester words to any notable extent and hence have no affinity with that group. A word of this third category is therefore a synonym for a given Winchester word as well as for a non-Winchester word and may occur in all sorts of Old English texts, regardless of their affiliations.[26]

Now the Royal Psalter and the Rule have a number of significant links in all three categories of Hofstetter's synonyms.[27] First, the Winchester vocabulary: the evidence for the Rule unequivocally suggests that Æthelwold must have been decisively involved in the development of a vocabulary which was to become a hallmark of Winchester texts in the next generation. In no less than five of the thirteen semantic fields, he employs the eventual Winchester terms, in some cases with considerable consistency, but more often in variation with their non-Winchester synonyms. (Variation through synonyms is a stylistic feature as important for the Rule as it is for the Royal Psalter.) The following words are in question: the verbs *gedyrstlæcan* ('to dare, presume', twenty-five occurrences) and *gerihtlæcan* ('to direct, correct', three occurrences), the nouns *oga* ('terror', one instance) and *wuldorbeag* ('crown', one occurrence) and the word-family based on the adjective *modig* for the concept of *superbia* (nine occurrences).[28]

Similarly, in the Royal Psalter, five Winchester words (occurring in three of the thirteen semantic fields) are attested. It is noteworthy that all these words here make their first appearance in an Old English text: in the field 'strange, foreign' the adjective *ælfremed* is used three times and, once, the noun *ælfremedung*; for 'to crush' the two Winchester words *tobrytan* and *tocwysan* are employed (once each); and once the Winchester verb *gewuldorbeagian* appears for *coronare*. As will have been seen, none of these words occurs with any frequency. We may recall, however, that in the choice of his words, the Glossator is much given to lexical variation and experimenting, and that he has a flair for neologisms. Therefore, the way he employs these future Winchester words squares perfectly with his

---

[26] For these three groups of words, see Hofstetter, *Winchester und Sprachgebrauch*, pp. 4–5.

[27] For tables and comments on the Rule and the Psalter respectively, see *ibid.*, pp. 30–6 and 462–4.

[28] On the concept of *superbia* and its renderings in the Rule, the Psalter and the Aldhelm glosses, see below, pp. 410–23.

overall attitude towards word usage. In any case, the occurrence of no less than five Winchester words, attested for the first time in a text composed forty or so years before the Winchester vocabulary became fully established, cannot reasonably be explained in terms of coincidence, but must be taken to point to a direct link between the Royal Glossator and the later Winchester group of texts.

By the same token there are manifest parallels between the Psalter and the Rule also in the employment of such words which, at a later stage, were more or less jettisoned from Winchester texts (Hofstetter's 'non-Winchester' words). Thus for *(prae)parare*, *praebere* (and a few other lemmata with a similar meaning) the Royal Psalter and the Rule frequently and exclusively use *(ge)gearwian* (twenty-eight occurrences in the Psalter,[29] fifteen in the Rule), not the later Winchester synonym *(ge)gearcian*. The non-Winchester adjective *fremde* 'strange, foreign' and verbs derived from it are used in both texts (Psalter: *fremde* twelve times, *fremedlæcan* once; Rule: *fremde* and *fremdian* once each); recall that in this semantic field the Winchester terms *ælfremed* and *ælfremedung* occur as lexical variants in the Psalter. The 'non-Winchester' verb *forbrytan* 'to crush' occurs in the Psalter (six times) and in the Rule (once); once again the Winchester synonyms for this, namely *tobrytan* and *tocwysan* are used sporadically in the Psalter (once each).[30] For the concept of *superbia*, only the 'non-Winchester' formations with *ofermod* occur in the Psalter (twenty-three occurrences), and such are also employed twice in the Rule, which on the whole favours the Winchester formations with *modig* (nine occurrences). For the concept of 'terror' or 'fear', *ege* clearly is the word

---

[29] To these twenty-eight occurrences of *(ge)gearwian* in the Psalter must be added six instances of *(ge)gierwan* (from the same stem and with the same meaning, but a weak verb, class I) and the nouns (derived from these verbs) *gegearwung* (three instances) and *gegierwing* (once), all of these 'non-Winchester' words. This makes a total of thirty-eight occurrences of the word family in question. For the Glossator's taste for employing weak verbs, class I (showing i-mutation) for purposes of creating intricate sound patterns with cognates (without i-mutation) of the verbs in question, see below, pp. 421–2.

[30] These verbs all translate lemmata such as *conterere*, *confringere* or *collidere*. Unfortunately, for purposes of comparison, there is only one instance of such a verb in the *Regula*, which is translated by *forbrytan* (BR 121.5, *RSB* 64.13). In the psalter, the Latin lemmata are numerous, and the Royal gloss characteristically reveals a considerable variety of translation equivalents: apart from *forbrytan*, *tobrytan* and *tocwysan* mentioned above, the 'non-Winchester' verbs *gebrytan* (once) and *forgnidan* (fourteen times) occur.

preferred in both texts (twenty-three occurrences in the Psalter, nineteen in the Rule). *Ege* belongs to the 'intermediate' category of words, those which occur occasionally in Winchester texts, but also in texts outside that group. (The Winchester synonym in that case would have been *oga*, which is used three times in the Rule, but never in the Psalter.) In short, there is suggestive lexical evidence pointing to an important role for the Psalter and the Rule in the development of the Winchester vocabulary as well as indicating a more specific link between both texts in their overall shared lexical predilections.

We may briefly return for a somewhat closer look at the 'non-Winchester' word *(ge)gearwian* (and cognates), employed in the Psalter and the Rule. In the Royal Psalter, the use of this word and that of another 'non-Winchester' word, namely *(ge)reccan*, might be attributable to an exemplar of the A-type gloss on which the Glossator arguably drew. The Vespasian Psalter invariably translates *(prae)parare* (and similar lemmata) by *(ge)gearwian*, as does the Royal Psalter (and the Rule, as we have seen). Latin *corrigere* or *dirigere* are as consistently glossed by *(ge)reccan* in the Vespasian Psalter as they are in the Royal Psalter (sixteen times); in this case the Rule has three occurrences of ('Winchester') *(ge)rihtlæcan*, but none of *(ge)reccan*. It is interesting to compare the usage in respect of *(ge)gearwian* and *(ge)reccan* in three D-type psalters of Winchester origin, namely Stowe (F), Vitellius (G) and Arundel (J), all of which present a considerable amount of glosses 'modernized' on the model of Winchester usage. In the case of *(ge)reccan*, they nearly always agree with the Royal Psalter; they never use 'Winchester' *(ge)rihtlæcan*. The same is true for psalters G and J in the case of *(ge)gearwian*; here F (the psalter with the greatest amount of Winchester words, apart from Lambeth) has replaced *(ge)gearwian* by 'Winchester' *(ge)gearcian*, but only in a few instances.[31] Both 'non-Winchester' words, *(ge)gearwian* and *(ge)reccan* are also found, though not very frequently, in the Lambeth Psalter, in spite of the close affiliation of this gloss with the Winchester group.[32] When we try to evaluate this rather complex evidence, bearing in mind that *dirigere/ corrigere* and *(prae)parare* are very prominent in the psalter, then we may be permitted to suspect that in Winchester circles, in the case of these two

---

[31] See Hofstetter, *Winchester und Sprachgebrauch* for tables and comments on the word usage in general in these psalters: pp. 67–78 for F, 79–81 for G and 82–3 for J.
[32] See *ibid.*, p. 84.

verbal concepts, there may have been a tendency to preserve older renderings in psalter glossing, renderings which had been ousted by their Winchester synonyms in other texts originating in this milieu. We would then have a valuable pointer to a possible influence which the Royal Psalter (and through it the older A-type gloss) may have exercised on the formation and structure of the vocabulary of texts from the Winchester school. Once again the Rule, with its consistent and frequent use of *(ge)gearwian*, stands out in a special relationship to the Royal Psalter.

We may next turn to two of the aforementioned 'hidden' links between the Royal Psalter and the Rule, links which, when revealed, may not only confirm the assumption of a common origin of both works, but may also teach us how the Winchester terminology for two pivotal concepts of Christianity was developed.

'corona' and 'coronare'

The Winchester group of texts is distinguished by a marked tendency to express the difference between Latin *corona* used in a concrete sense ('crown worn by a sovereign') and *corona* in a metaphorical sense (in expressions such as *corona uitae aeternae, corona martyrii* or *corona uirginitatis*) by employing different words for each of the two senses. For the concrete and literal meaning, *helm* or *cynehelm* (and the verb *(ge)helmian*) are used, whereas in the metaphorical sense (attested with much greater frequency), *wuldorbeag* (and the verb *(ge)wuldorbeagian*) are preferred. *Helm, cynehelm* and *(ge)helmian* are words which are not restricted to the Winchester group. Outside this group, they occur in both concrete and metaphorical meanings. By contrast, *wuldorbeag* and *(ge)wuldorbeagian* are typical Winchester words with no currency in other texts.[33] In the psalter, the verb *coronare* occurs three times, the noun *corona* twice. In all its occurrences, the verb has the metaphorical, abstract meaning 'to surround, encircle (in order to protect or honour)'. For this the Vespasian Psalter has a concrete gloss word: *gebeagian* (from *beag* 'ring, crown'); the Lambeth Psalter (as is to be expected) uses the Winchester term

---

[33] See Hofstetter, *Winchester und Sprachgebrauch*, pp. 17–18. Prior to Hofstetter, the Old English terminology for *corona* had already been searchingly analysed in a doctoral dissertation by Josef Kirschner, *Die Bezeichnungen für Kranz und Krone im Altenglischen*; see esp. pp. 141–58 for *corona* and *coronare* in the psalter glosses.

gewuldorbeagian. The Royal gloss has *gehelmian* in two instances (pss. V.13 and VIII.6). For this verb (apart from the literal sense 'to provide with a helmet' or 'to crown') an abstract meaning 'to cover' is attested; it is therefore a contextually adequate rendering. The third occurrence of *coronare* (ps. CII.5) is glossed by Winchester *gewuldorbeagian*. It is worth pointing out that for this occurrence of *coronare*, Cassiodorus explicitly stresses the metaphorical sense in which the word is used, quoting *inter alia* the *corona iustitiae* (mentioned by the Apostle Paul) to explain the meaning of the verb in the psalm verse in question.[34] It is also worth pointing out that only for this occurrence of *coronare* (but not for the previous ones) Royal 2. B. V has a marginal scholion (on 118r) to the effect that *coronat* here means that God will give adequate reward (to the blessed): *praemia digna restituit*. This remark is lifted verbatim from Cassiodorus's lengthy exposition of ps. CII.5.[35]

Now the verb *gewuldorbeagian*, used here for the first time in an Old English text, presupposes that the Glossator knew the noun *wuldorbeag* from which that verb is derived. The first appearance of the noun is, however, in a passage in the Rule, where 'necessitas parit coronam' (*scil.* uitae aeternae; *RSB* 7.33) is translated: 'nead [hæfð] wuldorbeah gegearwað' (BR 26.9). Given the Glossator's flair for poetic neologisms, there is no difficulty in supposing that he could have coined a substantive *wuldorbeag* (compounded of *wuldor* 'splendour, glory' and *beag* 'ring, crown') to achieve what he thought was an adequate rendering for *corona* in a metaphorical or allegorical sense.[36] He would thereby flamboyantly have expressed in his gloss the non-literal meaning of the lemma stressed by psalm exegesis. That the Rule should be the text where *wuldorbeag*, the future Winchester word, arguably coined by the Royal Glossator, is first attested, is one more striking link between both texts.

But why then did the Glossator not employ the noun *wuldorbeag* in his gloss? One of the two occurrences of *corona* in the psalter is explained in

---

[34] See *Expositio* II, 915 and II Tim. IV. 8.

[35] Cf. *Expositio* II, 915: 'quando iam beatis praemia digna restituit'.

[36] Note that the determinatum of the compound is *beag*, the word which Vespasian uses for *corona* (as it has *gebeagian* for *coronare*). A compound *wuldorhelm*, for example, would have been a perfectly acceptable alternative to *wuldorbeag* (*wuldorhelm* is attested sporadically and later than the Royal Psalter). That the Glossator did not decide on *helm* (or some other word) as the determinatum of his compound, might again point to a possible influence of the A-type gloss.

terms of allegory in psalm exegesis (and is duly glossed by *wuldorbeag* in the Lambeth Psalter).[37] In the text (ps. XX.4) the psalmist adverts to a crown which in its context is real enough: 'posuisti [*scil.* Deus] in capite eius [*scil.* regis; cf. ps. XX.1] coronam de lapide pretioso'. For this *corona*, Cassiodorus, in a lengthy exposition, adduces no less than three allegorical interpretations: the circle of the apostles, the reward for earthly toil and the Church.[38] In the marginal scholia in Royal 2. B. V one of these interpretations is adopted: with a clear verbal echo of Cassiodorus, *corona* is explained there: 'id est conuentus apostolorum' (27r). There is a second marginal comment referring to *de lapide pretioso* in the same psalm verse: 'id est Christus est ille lapis'. This could also be indebted to Cassiodorus who has a remark to the effect that the royal crown in question, when worn, is not an adornment itself but is rather made resplendent by Christ, the Lord ('Haec erat corona capitis, hoc regale diadema, quod non ornaret impositum sed de Christo Domino potius ornaretur').[39] In other words, we here have an occurrence of *corona* sparkling as it were with allegorical significations. Obviously the Royal Glossator felt that he should rise to the occasion, and he cut the verbal gem *hroþgirela* to translate this crown. The determinant of the compound, *hrōþ*, probably encompasses the meanings 'fame, praise, victory, honour'. By the tenth century, the noun must have had a distinctly archaic flavour. In Old English, it is attested only in personal names, the most famous of these being *Hroþgar*.[40] The

---

[37] The second occurrence of *corona* in the psalter is not pertinent to our discussion. Here, too, the noun is not used in its concrete sense: it occurs in the phrase *corona anni* 'circle or course of the year' (ps. LXIV.12). Winchester texts normally would not have employed *wuldorbeag* in such a collocation. (Unfortunately, the folio in question has been lost from the Lambeth Psalter, so there is no way of verifying this assumption.) The Royal Psalter has *trendel* 'sphere, circle, ring, orb'; it also has a marginal comment according to which *corona anni* signifies the world populated by the faithful ('hic mundus est cum impletione fidelium', 75r). This seems to be indebted to Cassiodorus: '*Corona anni* totus hic mundus conuenienter aduertitur, per quam catholica dilatatur Ecclesia' (*Expositio* I, 569). Therefore the *interpretamentum trendel* was perhaps intended by the Glossator to mean 'circle of the earth' and not 'the course of the year'. For discussion of the collocation *corona anni* in Medieval Latin and for the exegetical comments on its occurrence in the psalter, see Kirschner, *Kranz und Krone*, pp. 146–7.

[38] Cf. *Expositio* I, 183. [39] *Ibid.*

[40] See BT, s. v. *Hrōþ-*, and Holthausen, *Altenglisches etymologisches Wörterbuch*, s. v. *hrōþ(or)*. The nearest Old English cognates of *hrōþ* are the poetic (!) words *hrēþ* 'victory, glory' and *hrōþor* 'solace, joy'.

determinatum of the compound, *girela*, means '(splendid) dress, adornment', and again, from the tenth century onwards, it is not a very common word. The Glossator uses it elsewhere for a splendid dress adorned with gold,[41] as well as in a metaphorical sense.[42] How recherché and 'hermeneutic' *hroþgirela* must have been felt to be shows clearly from the psalter glosses dependent on the Royal gloss. Of the D-type psalters, only the Tiberius Psalter copied that word from its exemplar, whereas the others all substitute various less flamboyant terms. *Hroþgirela* is attested nowhere else in Old English texts.

Even with our deplorably fragmentary knowledge of Old English word usage and registers, we could have predicted that of the two compounds – *wuldorbeag* and *hroþgirela* – both very possibly coined by the Royal Glossator for rendering *corona* in a metaphorical and allegorical sense, *wuldorbeag* was to be the one which would have stood a better chance of survival. Both components of *wuldorbeag* are common Old English nouns, and there are numerous other compounds with *wuldor*, many of them (such as *wuldorfæder* or *wuldorcyning*) pertaining to heavenly life and glory and being possessed of distinct poetic connotations.[43] However, it is important to note that both *wuldorbeag* and *hroþgirela* are coined in exactly the same way: for a determinant they have an abstract noun meaning 'glory' or 'fame', and a concrete noun designating a piece of jewellery or adornment serves as a determinatum.

In sum, the evidence of the words for *corona* and *coronare* in the Psalter and the Rule seems to suggest that the idea of distinguishing on the lexical level between a crown worn by a worldly king and a heavenly crown (or the crown of virginity), the idea which lies at the heart of the Winchester terminology for *corona*, might well have originated in the circle of the Royal Glossator and that the Rule is a product of that circle as well. (There is liturgical and art historical evidence in connection with the psalm verse in question, evidence which points in the same direction and which we shall consider in due course, below, pp. 297–304.) The lexical evidence further suggests that the use of distinct terms and the

---

[41] Cf. ps. XLIV.10: 'in uestitu deaurato', glossed 'on gegyrelan gegyldum'.

[42] Cf. ps. CVIII.18: 'Et induit se maledictione sicut uestimentum' ('And he put on a curse like a garment'); here *uestimentum* is glossed *hrægl ł gegirelan*. Cf. also ps. CIII.6.

[43] For a list of *wuldor* compounds attested in poetry, see A. Keiser, *The Influence of Christianity on the Vocabulary of Old English Poetry*, University of Illinois Studies in Language and Literature 5 (Urbana, IL, 1919), 137.

employment of words with a recherché flavour for non-literal crowns may have been inspired by patristic exegesis, in particular that of the psalms.

There may be yet another source of inspiration for the decidedly 'hermeneutic' compound *hroþgirela* and the slightly less flamboyant *wuldorbeag*, an inspirational force which brings us back to the close study of Aldhelm which we already had reason to suspect was carried on in the circle of the Glossator (above, pp. 84–5). Aldhelm not only frequently employs *corona* in a transferred sense (*corona uirginitatis*, *martyrii* and so on),[44] he also employs a plethora of synonyms for *corona* in a metaphorical sense, for example *infula*, *diadema*, *lunula*, *sertum*, *tiara*, *taenia* and *tropeum*.[45] In some cases, the original concrete meaning 'crown' or 'head-band' is scarcely palpable any longer, and in their contexts the words are best translated by 'honour', 'distinction' or the like, as in the following example from the prose *De uirginitate*: *integritatis corona et fausta uirginitatis infula*.[46] One of these terms, the Greek-based *taenia* 'headband', occurs only once, in the *Carmen de uirginitate*, and is used there in such a highly abstract sense: *uirtutum tenia fretum* 'trusting in the distinction of virtue'.[47] In the so-called Third Cleopatra Glossary (which is predominantly an Aldhelm glossary), the lemma *tenia* is glossed: *honore uel cyninggierela* (WW 518.24), thus rendering the abstract meaning which *taenia* has in its context by the Latin gloss and providing in *cyninggierela* ('royal adornment') a concrete (if not precise) *interpretamentum*. *Cyninggierela* is extremely rare[48] and may well be the Cleopatra Glossator's stylistic response to Aldhelm's idiosyncratic use of a Greek expression. The point of interest for us is of course the similarity between *cyninggierela* and *hroþgirela*. This similarity gains significance in view of the suspected links between the circle of the Royal Glossator and Aldhelm glossing in general and the Third Cleopatra Glossary in particular (below, pp. 149–54). In other words, it may not be fanciful to suspect that the Winchester terminology for *corona* and the coinage of words such as *hroþgirela* and *wuldorbeag* might be as indebted to Aldhelm as they are to psalm exegesis.

---

[44] See the glossary in *Aldhelmi Opera*, ed. Ehwald.

[45] See Kirschner, *Kranz und Krone*, p. 180, n. 138.

[46] *Aldhelmi Opera*, ed. Ehwald, p. 261.2; 'the crown of integrity . . . the blessed distinction of virginity', *Aldhelm: the Prose Works*, transl. Lapidge and Herren, p. 85.

[47] Line 249; *Aldhelmi Opera*, ed. Ehwald, p. 363; cf. *Aldhelm: the Poetic Works*, transl. Lapidge and Rosier, p. 108.

[48] See Kirschner, *Kranz und Krone*, p. 181.

However, glossators, even those of the psalms, do not entirely live in a world of books and patristic exegesis; they are part of their society as well. Therefore a third factor should be mentioned briefly – a political factor as it were – which may have exerted some influence on the formation of the Winchester terminology for *corona*. It may be significant that we first meet an attempt to differentiate between real and spiritual crowns in a gloss which must have originated somewhere in Wessex between (say) the late 930s and the early 950s. For it was in the reign of King Æthelstan (924–39) that the crown as a sign of royal power (a 'Herrschaftszeichen') began to play a prominent role for the first time in English history. Coins issued in his reign are the first to present a crowned royal portrait (as opposed to the tiara worn by King Alfred and King Offa on their pennies, but also quite often by later kings such as Æthelred).[49] In the same fashion, portraits of crowned kings became increasingly common[50] in the aftermath of the famous dedication picture in the manuscript of Bede's two Lives of St Cuthbert (now Cambridge, Corpus Christi College 183) which King Æthelstan gave to the community of St Cuthbert at Chester-le-Street. That manuscript was written, probably between 934 and 939, some-where in southern England, perhaps at Glastonbury. The dedication picture shows King Æthelstan wearing a crown and handing the book over to St Cuthbert.[51] By contrast, the Durham Cassiodorus (now Durham Cathedral, B. II. 30: see above p. 29) or the Vespasian Psalter depict an uncrowned King David. Finally, the earliest English *Ordo* for the consecration of a king which makes mention of a crown and the ritual of coronation during the inauguration is the so-called Second English *Ordo*, very possibly drafted for the consecration of Edward the Elder in 900 and certainly used for the inauguration of his son

---

[49] See Kirschner, *Kranz und Krone*, p. 82, Nelson, 'Earliest Royal *Ordo*', p. 357, and cf. particularly the thorough study by C. E. Blunt, 'The Coinage of Æthelstan', *British Numismatic Journal* 42 (1974), 35–160, at 47–8, 56–7 and 125–7. See further C. E. Blunt, B. H. I. H. Stewart and C. S. S. Lyon, *Coinage in Tenth-Century England. From Edward the Elder to Edgar's Reform* (Oxford, 1989), pp. 108 and 268.

[50] Cf. Kirschner, *Kranz und Krone*, pp. 74–7, and the manuscript evidence for such pictures assembled there, pp. 101–17. For a complete survey of the representation of crowns in Anglo-Saxon manuscripts, see now T. H. Ohlgren, *Insular and Anglo-Saxon Illuminated Manuscripts. An Iconographic Catalogue c. A. D. 625 to 1100* (New York, 1986); cf. the references given in the index, p. 343.

[51] For CCCC 183, see below, pp. 352–9.

Æthelstan in 925.[52] The so-called First English *Ordo* for the consecration of a king, which perhaps codified the ritual as it was in use for most of the ninth century, refers to a helmet (*galea*), not a crown.[53]

In short, we may be allowed to suspect the impact of contemporary political reality on the Glossator's attempt to create a new terminology for symbolical or metaphorical coronations. As we have seen in the case of his glosses for *christus* (above, pp. 74–8), the Glossator seems to have been highly conscious of what was essential in making an earthly king. Therefore, an awareness of the significance and importance of one of the royal insignia may have combined with the influence of patristic exegesis and Aldhelm studies, to inspire his attempt to introduce neologisms for the crowns of heavenly kings and queens, words like *wuldorbeag* and *hroþgirela* which in comparison with (say) *beag* or *cynehelm*, used for the crown of a worldly king, revealed already in their semantic components the infinitely greater splendour and glory of the *corona uitae aeternae*.[54]

'ecclesia'

Our second example of 'hidden' links between the Royal Psalter and the Rule concerns the Old English words for *ecclesia*. Similar to the words for *corona*, texts revealing the full-blown Winchester vocabulary distinguish between *ecclesia* referring to a church building and *ecclesia* in an abstract sense, that is the Catholic Church as an institution. This latter sense encompasses, for example, the notion of *ecclesia* as the congregation of the faithful or that of the militant or triumphant church.[55] As we shall see presently, patristic exegesis once again seems to have been of crucial

---

[52] For the manuscript evidence of the recensions of the Second *Ordo*, see D. H. Turner, *The Claudius Pontificals*, HBS 97 (1964), xxx–xxxi, and Nelson, 'The Second English *Ordo*', pp. 361 and 363; for the role of crowning in this *ordo*, see the table *ibid.*, p. 362, and cf. pp. 366–7, for the royal inauguration for which the first recension of the Second *Ordo* was possibly drafted.

[53] For the period during which royal consecration was arguably performed according to the First *Ordo*, see Nelson, 'The Earliest Royal *Ordo*', esp. p. 360. For the use of a helmet, cf. *ibid.*, pp. 356–7. Note that *cynehelm* is the word for a royal crown in Winchester terminology as elsewhere.

[54] On the possible role played by King Æthelstan's court in the intellectual formation of the Royal Glossator, see below, pp. 332–49.

[55] For a meticulous differentiation between the various meanings of *ecclesia*, see Hofstetter, *Winchester und Sprachgebauch*, pp. 10–11.

importance for the development of a verbal differentiation in Winchester usage. For the church building, Winchester texts (in accordance with other texts of whatever origin or date) employ *cirice* (usually in its Late West Saxon form *cyrce*), one of the earliest Greek loanwords in English. For *ecclesia* meaning the church as an institution, Winchester texts use *(ge)laþung*, an abstract noun, derived from the verb *(ge)laþian* 'to invite, summon' and hence meaning 'calling, invitation' as well as 'assembly, congregation'. It is this persistent use of *(ge)laþung* for the abstract meanings of *ecclesia* by which Winchester texts stand out as a group. Other texts may show attempts to distinguish between the two basic meanings of *ecclesia*, but scarcely ever with the Winchester determination and never by using the Winchester word *(ge)laþung*. (Words chosen for such purposes would, for example, be *geferræden* or *gesamnung*.)[56] At first sight, neither the Royal Psalter nor the Rule seem to have any significant links with the Winchester group, since in neither of them is *ecclesia* translated by *(ge)laþung*. Nor does there appear to be much agreement between both texts themselves, since they use different translation words for *ecclesia*. In order to form an opinion about this rather complex situation, we may best begin by looking at the meaning of *ecclesia* and the glosses for that lemma in the psalter.

It is obvious that here as elsewhere in the Old Testament, *ecclesia* is not used in its later, specifically Christian, sense. In the psalter, it is employed in its original sense 'assembly, congregation (of the people)', together with *synagoga* which serves as a synonym. Both terms, *ecclesia* and *synagoga*, are of course Latin words of Greek origin. As was to be expected (given the importance of *ecclesia* and *synagoga* in the Bible), their etymologies are explained in patristic commentaries as in works of an encyclopaedic nature such as Isidore's *Etymologiae*. For example, Cassiodorus paraphrases the expression *a synagoga multa* (ps. XXXIX.11) as follows: 'id est in populorum congregatione densissima'.[57] Isidore explains: 'Synagoga Graece congregatio dicitur' (*Etym.* VIII. i. 7), and his etymology for *ecclesia* is: 'Ecclesia Graecum est, quod in Latinum uertitur conuocatio, propter quod omnes ad se uocet'.[58] Predictably, in typological psalm

---

[56] See *ibid.*, *passim*, for tables and discussion of the translations of *ecclesia* in Old English texts in general.

[57] *Expositio* I, 368; cf. I, 83, for a similar explanation.

[58] *Etym.* VIII. i. 1, '*Ecclesia* is Greek and means in Latin a convocation, because God calls everyone to Him'.

exegesis, *ecclesia* in the psalter is seen as a prefiguration of the Christian Church, as when Cassiodorus comments on the phrase *in ecclesia magna* (ps. XXXIX.10, literally 'before a numerous assembly') as follows: '*In Ecclesia magna*, sicut saepe diximus, catholicam dicit quae toto orbe diffusa est'.[59] By the same token, in the marginal scholia in Royal 2. B. V, three comments on *ecclesia* to that effect are found; for two of these, the commentator obviously drew on Cassiodorus.[60] No scholion on *synagoga* is entered in the margins of Royal 2. B. V.

The typological interpretation of *ecclesia* and of course the meaning the word had acquired in Christian terminology may lie behind attempts to exploit the etymologies of *synagoga* and *ecclesia* for a demonstration of the moral and intellectual superiority of what *ecclesia* stands for. Such attempts are undertaken, for example, both by Cassiodorus and by Isidore. Both authors explain that *synagoga* and *ecclesia* are synonymous to a certain extent, but that *synagoga* is a word which pertains to pre-Christian customs and religions, especially those of the Jewish people, and is never used for the Christian Church. Then Cassiodorus goes on:

Synagoga est generaliter dicta congregatio, non satis exprimens hominum coetum; Ecclesia uero conuocatio nuncupatur, quae de diuersis gentibus aggregata colligitur. Conuocari enim ad illos pertinet qui ratione praecellunt.[61]

Such a distinction between the two words, inherent already in their etymologies, namely that *conuocatio* (= *ecclesia*) implies human reason whereas *congregatio* (= *synagoga*) does not, is pointed up by Isidore as well (cf. *Etym.* VIII. i. 8).

Accordingly, even in our earliest surviving psalter gloss, the Vespasian Psalter, *synagoga* and *ecclesia* are painstakingly and persistently glossed by different words. For *ecclesia* the Vespasian Psalter has the typological gloss

---

[59] *Expositio* I, 367, '*In Ecclesia magna*, as we often have said, means the Catholic Church, which has spread over the whole world'.

[60] The comments in question are: 'ecclesia interpretatur fidelium congregatio' (29v, commenting on ps. XXI.26); 'in populo christiano' (43v, commenting on ps. XXXIV.18), and 'id est in ecclesia magna catholica' (51r, commenting on ps. XXXIX.10). The last two of these scholia are lifted verbatim from Cassiodorus: cf. *Expositio* I, 313 and 367.

[61] *Expositio* II, 757: '"Synagoga" is in a general sense a congregation; it does not satisfactorily express an assembly of human beings. "Ecclesia", however, means a convocation, which is assembled and united from various peoples. To be called together is appropriate for those who are distinguished by being endowed with reason.'

cirice, whereas its translation *gesomnung* for *synagoga* is based on the etymology of that word. It may safely be assumed that the Vespasian Glossator occasionally made use of psalm exegesis.[62] The Royal Glossator agrees with the Vespasian gloss in having *gesomnung* for all six occurrences of *synagoga*. However, of the nine occurrences of *ecclesia*, only one is glossed by A-type *cyrce* (ps. LXVII.27). Three times *ecclesia* is translated by *haligu gesomnung*.[63] On two further occasions *sanctus* appears already in the Latin text of the psalter, as a qualifying apposition to *ecclesia* in the phrase *in ecclesia sanctorum*, which is glossed *on gesomnunga haligra* (pss. LXXXVIII.6 and CXLIX.1). Once (ps. XXI.23) the gloss reads *getreowful gesomnung*, and twice *gesomnung* is used without any qualifying adjective. However, in the first of these two instances (ps. XXI.26), the pair *ecclesia: gesomnung* occurs shortly after the lemma had been glossed by adjective plus noun (*getreowful gesomnung* in ps. XXI.23), so another qualifying adjective may have been deemed unnecessary within such a brief space. In the second instance, the Latin reads *in ecclesia plebis* (ps. CVI.32), glossed *on gesomnunga folces*. Here an adjective such as *halig* or *getreowful* would have been manifestly inappropriate. It is safe to say therefore that the Glossator employed a qualifying adjective on all occasions where *ecclesia* in the psalter could possibly be seen as a prefiguration of the Christian Church.

Two points emerge from these glosses for *ecclesia*: first, that (unlike the Vespasian gloss) the Glossator did not wish to employ the common word for the Christian Church, namely *cyrce*, for *ecclesia* in the psalter, even though it is clear from the marginal scholia in the manuscript that he knew and endorsed the typological interpretation lying behind this gloss; and, secondly, that (in accordance with psalm exegesis) he wished to stress the difference between *synagoga* and *ecclesia* and the superiority of *ecclesia* over *synagoga* by the choice of his gloss words. Thus for the Royal Glossator *ecclesia* is – as is *synagoga* – a *gesomnung* (after all, this is broadly what the commentators said) but it is a *getreowful* or a *haligu gesomnung*.

---

[62] See Gneuss, *Lehnbildungen*, pp. 47–8 and *passim*, and Wiesenekker, *Translation Performance*, pp. 131–2.

[63] Cf. pss. XXV.12, XXXIV.18 and XXXIX.10. In ps. XXXIV.18 a variant form of the suffix occurs: *gesomning*. In ps. XXV.12 the gloss is unquestionably defective as it stands: *in ecclesiis*, glossed *on halgum*. In view of the fact that *gesomnung* is (apart from the one occurrence of *cyrce*) the only noun to translate *ecclesia* in the Royal Psalter, the present gloss may be safely restored to *on halgum gesomnungum*.

That this translational policy of the Royal Glossator formed the germ of the eventual Winchester terminology for *ecclesia* can be seen from the glosses in the Lambeth Psalter. This psalter follows the Royal Psalter on all occasions where the *Gallicanum* (the recension to which Lambeth belongs) retains the lemma *synagoga*, and provides the gloss *gesamnung* (which, as we have seen, was an A-type word originally). All occurrences of *ecclesia*, except one, are glossed by the Winchester term *gelaþung* in Lambeth; on two occasions *gelaþung* stands in a doublet with the Royal Psalter's *gesomnung*. By his employment of *gelaþung*, the Lambeth Glossator signals that for a practitioner of Winchester terminology, almost all occurrences of *ecclesia* in the psalter should be taken as prefigurations of the Catholic Church and should accordingly be glossed by the Winchester word for *ecclesia* in that sense.

But if, as the Lambeth Psalter reveals, later Winchester texts followed the Royal Glossator's policy in never using *cyrce* for *ecclesia* as an institution, why then did they not adopt his glosses *getreowful gesomnung* or *haligu gesomnung* for *ecclesia* 'the Catholic Church'? One explanation for this could be a certain amount of polysemy in *gesomnung*: the word is used for translating quite a number of Latin lemmata (in the psalter and elsewhere). Apart from rendering *ecclesia* and *synagoga*, it occurs for lemmata such as *congregatio*, *conuentus* or *conuenticulum*. A qualifying adjective such as *halig* or *getreowful* may, in the event, have been considered insufficient for bearing the burden of distinguishing between *gesomnung* used for all sorts of congregations and *gesomnung* used for a Latin term of paramount importance: *ecclesia*, the Catholic Church. Aside from such a suspected lack of precision, a phrase consisting of adjective and noun (as *haligu gesomnung*) must, in the course of time, inevitably have come to be regarded as stylistically inferior to a single Old English noun for *ecclesia*. Furthermore, and perhaps most important, there was no clear semantic and etymological link between *haligu* or *getreowful gesomnung* and *ecclesia*. *Gesomnung* (or *gesamnung* in its Late West Saxon form) is derived from the verb *(ge)samnian* 'to assemble, meet, gather together'. The etymologies which explained *synagoga* as meaning *congregatio* but *ecclesia* as meaning *conuocatio* will have been common knowledge in Winchester circles as elsewhere. According to such etymologies, *gesamnung* makes a perfect semantic and etymologizing equivalent to *synagoga* (and is indeed retained in Winchester texts) but not to *ecclesia*. *Gelaþung*, however, does. With this abstract noun, derived from *(ge)laþian* 'to invite, summon', one gets a clear and perfect semantic chain which must have had a strong appeal to the authors of the Winchester group: *ecclesia* means *conuocatio* and should therefore be translated by *gelaþung* 'convocation' in those instances where meanings other than the church buildings are in question.

We may now ask how the Benedictine Rule fits into this line of development which seems to lead from the Royal Glossator's attempts to find a distinctive gloss word for *ecclesia* in its abstract senses to the eventual establishment of the Winchester terminology. In the *Regula S. Benedicti*, *ecclesia* occurs on two occasions only. Once it is translated by the loanword *ecclesia* which makes here its first (and, arguably, only) appearance in an Old English text:[64] 'sicut psallit ecclesia Romana' (*RSB* 13.10) is translated: 'ealswa hit romana eclesia hylt' (BR 38.5). On the second occasion, Æthelwold has resort to a phrase to render *ecclesia*: 'audiat, quid spiritus dicat ecclesiis' (*RSB* prol. 11; quoting Apoc. II.7) is translated: 'gehyre hwæt þæt haliggast to eallum þam, ðe to Gode geladede syn, cwiþ' (BR 2.11–12). Thus, in the Rule, there is evidently the same aversion as in the Royal Psalter and in the Winchester group to use *cyrce* for *ecclesia* where this does not designate the church building. But the gloss words of the Royal Psalter are not those used in the Rule. One only needs to insert *haligu gesomnung* or *getreowful gesomnung* in the above quotations to see why. What might have been, to some extent at least, adequate English equivalents in an interlinear gloss, would have made unbearably clumsy and ambiguous renderings on many occasions in prose texts. But a single standard translation word for *ecclesia* had yet to be established. Æthelwold's experiment with the loan *ecclesia* should be viewed in the context of the numerous Latin loanwords in the Rule, attested there for the first (or almost the first) time.[65] (We have seen above, pp. 51–2, that such a penchant for introducing or establishing Latin loanwords forms an important link between the Psalter and the Rule.)

However, it is clear in retrospect why *ecclesia* was not to succeed as the much sought-after translation word. In the terminology of the Winchester group, native words invariably ousted any rival synonyms of Latin origin which there may have been for key concepts of the Christian religion. Thus *martir* was ousted by *cyþere*, *corona* was not successful against *wuldorbeag*, *cantic* did not survive in a general sense 'song of praise'

---

[64] See Funke, *Die gelehrten lateinische Lehn- und Fremdwörter*, p. 165, and see below.
[65] See Funke, *ibid.*, pp. 164–5, and Gretsch, *Regula*, pp. 364–70.

(in which *lofsang* was established) and *altare* (or *alter*) had to give way to
weofod.[66] In the case of *ecclesia*, Æthelwold has not even been credited with
the introduction of a new loanword by the compilers of modern
dictionaries of Old English, since none of these has an entry for *ecclesia*.
However, that Æthelwold will have seen his employment of *ecclesia* not as
a kind of quotation from the Latin but as an integral part of the
vocabulary of his translation seems indicated by the position of the
adjective: *ecclesia Romana* in the *Regula* becomes 'anglicized' as *romana
eclesia* in his Rule.[67] Still, the loanword must definitely be regarded as an
experiment and apparently never gained any currency in Old English.[68]

Æthelwold's second attempt to translate *ecclesia* is strongly reminiscent
of the use of *gewuldorbeagian* in the Royal Psalter (above, pp. 98–9). There
we have seen that the Glossator's use of *gewuldorbeagian* presupposes a
knowledge of the noun *wuldorbeag* (coined perhaps by the Glossator
himself) for a crown in a metaphorical and spiritual sense. In a similar
fashion, the translation of *ecclesia* by *þa þe geladede syn* presupposes the
existence of *gelaþung* in the semantic chain uncovered above: *ecclesia –
conuocatio – gelaþung*. Æthelwold's preference for a verbal paraphrase
(although perfectly idiomatic in the passage in question) may indicate
some residue of uneasiness about the use of the abstract noun *gelaþung* for
ecclesia, at least in a text composed for an audience not fluent in Latin and
perhaps not fully conversant with the Old English 'technical' terminology
of Christianity.

There is some additional confirmation that Æthelwold knew the noun
gelaþung and used it in broad agreement with later Winchester usage: he
translates *euocatio diuina* (*RSB* 7.9) by *sio godcunde geladung* (BR
23.13–14). Here *gelaþung* renders a Latin phrase which immediately
recalls the etymological explanation commonly found for *ecclesia*. But why
then did it take a whole generation – from the experiments of the Royal

---

[66] For *martir*, see Hofstetter, *Winchester und Sprachgebrauch*, p. 8; for *corona*, see *ibid.*,
pp. 18–19; for *cantic*, see above, p. 92–3 and n. 14; *for altare*, see Gretsch, *Regula*,
pp. 361–2, and Gneuss, 'Origin of Standard Old English', p. 76.

[67] For this phrase no variants where the adjective is placed before the noun are found in
the *apparatus criticus* of Hanslik's edition of the *Regula*.

[68] No more than two further occurrences of *ecclesia* are recorded in the Microfiche
Concordance, one from Ælfric, the other from Wulfstan. In both cases, it is almost
impossible to decide whether *ecclesia* is used as a genuine loan or as a Latin word
quoted in an Old English text.

Glossator to the writings of Ælfric and the Lambeth Glossator or the other proponents of the Winchester school – until *gelaþung* was securely established for *ecclesia*? Unlike the flamboyant *wuldorbeag*, *gelaþung* looks like a perfectly normal and common Old English word – which, however, it is not. It is, in fact, a verbal derivative whose propagation (if not coinage) may be traced (through the evidence of the Rule) to Æthelwold himself. Of the two morphological variants, *gelaþung* and *laþung*, only the unprefixed form occurs (once) in a text prior to the Rule. This is in the Old English *Regula pastoralis* where *laþung* is employed in a Christian context not very different from those contexts which subsequently led to its use in the sense of *ecclesia*. It refers there to the 'invitation' or 'calling' mercifully extended by God even to sinners.[69] All the other numerous occurrences of *gelaþung* and *laþung* are in texts later than the Rule. Unlike the verb *(ge)laþian* (from which the noun derives), which is common in both early and late texts of whatever origin, the noun is clearly restricted in usage. It occurs frequently only in texts which either belong to the Winchester group proper or show some clear links with that group's usage as, for example, the Durham Hymnal (Durham Cathedral B. III. 32).[70] Naturally it cannot be ascertained whether Æthelwold remembered King Alfred's use of *laþung* when he himself was experimenting with various renderings of *ecclesia*. Pope Gregory's *Regula pastoralis* presumably will have been among the texts which he studied closely with, and expounded carefully to, his students. Given his well-known interest in translating Latin texts into the vernacular in classroom instruction, it is possible that he drew on King Alfred's translation for such an exposition of Gregory's text.[71] But whether Æthelwold remembered the passage in question in the Old English *Regula pastoralis* or not, it is beyond

---

[69] *Alfred's Pastoral Care*, ed. Sweet II, 405.23–4: 'Be ðære miltsunga æfter ðære laðunga is swiðe wel gesæd ðurh Essaias ðone witgan' ('Of the mercy after the invitation is very well spoken through the prophet Isaiah'). Note that in the Latin original, the lemma translated by *laþung* is *uocatio*: *Grégoire le Grand: Règle pastorale*, ed. B. Judic *et al.*, 2 vols., Sources chrétiennes 381–2 (Paris, 1992) II, 460.47.

[70] For links between the Durham hymnal and the Winchester group, see Gneuss, *Hymnar und Hymnen*, pp. 186–90, and Hofstetter, *Winchester und Sprachgebrauch*, pp. 106–8. See now also Milfull, *The Hymns of the Anglo-Saxon Church*, pp. 80–9, esp. p. 82 and n. 57.

[71] Concerning the availability of Alfredian texts in the heyday of the Benedictine reform, Ælfric's remark (in his preface to the Catholic Homilies) will be recalled which refers to the books 'ðe Ælfred cyning snoterlice awende of Ledene on Englisc, þa synd to

reasonable doubt that his teaching and authority must be sought behind the propagation of *gelaþung* as the standard term for *ecclesia* 'the Catholic Church'.

In the light of the foregoing observations the role of the Royal Psalter's glosses in this chain of experiments *en route* to a Winchester terminology for *ecclesia* emerges ever more clearly. We have seen already why the Royal Psalter must be regarded as a forerunner to eventual Winchester usage, what links there are with the usage of the Rule, and why its two-part gloss for *ecclesia* (*haligu* or *getreowful gesomnung*) was unlikely to gain acceptance in later texts. One further consideration may tip the balance in favour of the assumption that the terms for *ecclesia* are among those items of the Psalter's vocabulary which, by their combined evidence, may allow us to assign the origin of the Royal Psalter to Æthelwold and his circle. It may reasonably be asked what the grounds were for wishing to distinguish between the various senses of *ecclesia* by the use of different words. After all, Latin had only one word for all senses (as have Modern English or German for that matter). Quite possibly, for Æthelwold and his fellow scholars with their keen interest in forging and refining the English language, the need for a second word for *ecclesia* may have made itself felt when studying and glossing the psalter. There they would have met with numerous occurrences of *ecclesia* which could designate the Christian Church only through allegorical exegesis. In the literal sense, however, *ecclesia* in the psalter meant 'assembly, congregation' and was used more or less synonymously with *synagoga*. On both these grounds, *cyrce* (the long-established loanword for the Christian Church and the A-type gloss) was apparently considered an inadequate rendering in these circles.[72] We may surmise then that the ensuing verbal experiments (*haligu* or *getreowful gesomnung* and the renditions in the Rule) which eventually led to the establishment of *gelaþung* were first undertaken in search of a word which would fit the literal context of the psalms, while stressing at the same time (in accordance with the established etymologies) the difference between *synagoga* and *ecclesia*, as well as being capable of bearing the allegorical interpretation 'Catholic Church' provided by psalm exegesis.

---

habbene', 'which King Alfred wisely translated from Latin into English, which are available' (*Homilies*, ed. Thorpe I, 2).

[72] One should compare here the Glossator's strong aversion to translating *christus* in the psalter by the A-type gloss *Crist*: see above, pp. 73–4.

In due course, such a structured terminology for *ecclesia*, with a specific word for its abstract senses (a terminology arguably originating from psalter glossing) would then have been considered convenient for employment in all sorts of texts.

STYLISTIC LINKS

Thus far we have seen that in their affiliation with incipient Winchester usage as well as in the use of words outside that range, there are a number of striking verbal links between the Royal Psalter and the Old English Benedictine Rule, which feed the suspicion of a common origin for both texts. This suspicion gains further confirmation from a number of shared stylistic predilections between both texts. It is to these shared stylistic predilections that we must now turn our attention.

The Rule

We have seen (above, pp. 44–5) that lexical variation (that is a variety of glosses employed for a given lemma) is a salient feature in the Royal Psalter. In a similar fashion, the Rule is distinguished by such variation. We have considered its various renderings of *ecclesia*; we have also seen that *ofermod* occurs besides *modig* for the concept of *superbia*, *ege* besides *oga* for 'terror' or *geþristlæcan* besides *gedyrstlæcan* for 'to presume, dare'. More such examples will come to light in ch. 6 below.[73] For the moment, it will be enough to note that lexical variation is as characteristic a feature of the Rule as it is of the Psalter. By the same token, in his translation of the *Regula*, Æthelwold is as much given to the use of doublets as is the Royal Glossator. In both texts, such doublets do not result from a failure to produce an adequate single equivalent in Old English: their occurrence must rather be attributed to stylistic reasons, sometimes also to purposes of clarification. Thus doublets are employed to express different semantic components of a lemma, to couple a literal and a metaphorical translation of a lemma, for a display of English synonyms and so on; not infrequently they are joined by alliteration.[74]

[73] For variation in the Rule, see also Gretsch, *Regula*, pp. 318–77 *passim*.
[74] Cf. above, pp. 49–51, for doublets in the Psalter, and see Gretsch, *Regula*, pp. 263–8, for their use in the Rule.

Behind the predilection for doublets in the Rule and the Royal Psalter, as well as their flair for lexical variation, one may perhaps suspect the influence of Isidore's *Synonyma* and his *Differentiae*. In both works Isidore concerns himself with the accumulation of synonymous words and phrases. Quite possibly, Bede's *De orthographia*, which contains an extensive section on synonyms (and near-homonyms) may have been a further source of inspiration. All three works circulated in England in the tenth and eleventh centuries, as is witnessed by a number of surviving manuscripts, and it is interesting to add that the *Synonyma* and the *Differentiae* are included among the twenty-one books donated by Æthelwold to Peterborough.[75]

A few examples for doublets from the Rule would be: 'unalyfedlice fyliað and hyrsumiað', 'unlawfully follow and obey' (BR 9.24–10.1, *seruientes RSB* 1.11); 'ancsum and neara', 'difficult and narrow' (BR 20.10, *angusta RSB* 5.11); 'fyrðrige and weaxan læte', 'to promote and let grow' (BR 121.7, *permittat nutriri RSB* 64.14); 'rædan and racian', 'to guide and to govern' (BR 14.6, *regere RSB* 2.31); or 'frouer and fultum', 'consolation (help) and support' (BR 55.15, *solatia RSB* 31.17). The use of alliteration in the Rule is frequent and not restricted to doublets; often it is combined with word-play. It will be recalled that such stylistic adornments play an important role in the Royal gloss. As in the Psalter, paronomasia in the Rule often appears in the form of *figurae etymologicae*. Consider, for instance, the following two examples, where it will be seen that the Old English translation by far excels the Latin original (as it not infrequently does) in its employment of rhetorical embellishments. (I have indicated the words involved in word-play by the use of italics):

ðæm þe he of mynstres æhta næbbe to *syllane*, *sylle* gode andsware, forðy hit is awriten, þæt seo gode antswaru *sy* ouer ða *selestan selene*.[76]

---

[75] Isidore's *Synonyma* (*CPL*, no. 1203) are printed PL 83, 827–68, the *Differentiae* (*CPL*, no. 1187) are edited by C. Codoñer Merino, *De differentiis uerborum* (Paris, 1992). Bede's *De orthographia* (*CPL*, no. 1566) is edited by C. W. Jones, *Bedae Venerabilis Opera. Pars I: Opera didascalica*, CCSL 123A (Turnhout, 1975), 7–57. For the importance of these works for Anglo-Saxon grammatical and stylistic studies and for the surviving manuscripts from Anglo-Saxon England, see Gneuss, 'The Study of Language', pp. 25–7. For a brief evaluation of the *Synonyma* with especial regard to their possible influence on Aldhelm, see Winterbottom, 'Aldhelm's Prose Style', pp. 59–61. For the copies of the *Synonyma* and the *Differentiae* in the Peterborough booklist, see Lapidge, 'Booklists', pp. 53–5.

[76] BR 55.6–9, 'to those whom he [*scil.* the cellarer of the monastery] cannot give

Sy þam abbode seo mæste *hogu* þæs *andfenges* þearfena and elþeodigra, forþan Cristus on hy swiðost bið *onfangen*; ðara ricra manna *ege* and *oga gemyngað*, þæt him selfum *weorðlice* sy gegearwod and *wyrðmynt* genoh geboden, ac Godes *ege* ana *myndgað*, þæt mon þearfum and elþeodegum monnum geþensum sy.[77]

The second example is distinguished in addition by one of those brief, clarifying amplifications of the original which are a prominent feature of Æthelwold's translation ('ac Godes ege ... geþensum sy'). This addition (involving some repetition), coupled with the use of doublets for a single lemma (*ege and oga* and *weorðlice sy gegearwod and wyrðmynt genoh geboden*) structures the whole passage by a conspicuous series of parallelisms. From passages such as these it becomes clear that rhetorical and stylistic embellishments like alliteration, paronomasia, doublets or parallelism do not countervail the endeavour for clarity of expression which is one of the hallmarks of Æthelwold's translation.[78] On the contrary, such rhetorical devices, when allowed their proper aural effects through reading the text aloud, would have lent clarity and emotional force to the contents of the passage.

Another feature which the Rule shares to a certain extent with the Royal Psalter is a penchant for unusual vocabulary. Given the sober prose

anything of the goods of the monastery, he shall give a kind answer, because it is written that a kind answer is of greater value than the best gift'. Cf. *RSB* 31.13–14: 'et cui substantia non est, quod tribuatur, sermo responsionis porrigatur bonus, ut scriptum est: Sermo bonus super datum optimum'; 'If goods are not available to meet a request, he will offer a kind word in reply, for it is written: a kind word is better than the best gift', *RB 1980*, p. 229.

[77] BR 85.1–6 (I have emended the manuscript reading <hoga> to *oga*, since there exists no Old English word *hoga* 'terror, fear'; apparently the scribes (of all manuscripts) carried the intended word-play *hogu* 'care': *oga* 'terror' one step further by adding unetymological <h> to *oga*). 'The abbot shall take the greatest care in receiving poor people and foreigners, because it is in these in particular, that Christ is received; the awe and terror which the rich and powerful inspire, ensures that they are honourably provided for and received with sufficient honour, but the fear of God alone ensures that we are helpful to poor people and foreigners'. Cf. *RSB* 53.15: 'Pauperum et peregrinorum maxime susceptioni cura sollicite exhibeatur, quia in ipsis magis Christus suscipitur; nam diuitum terror ipse sibi exigit honorem'. 'Great care and concern are to be shown in receiving poor people and pilgrims, because in them more particularly Christ is received; our very awe of the rich guarantees them special respect', *RB 1980*, p. 259.

[78] For this feature, see Gretsch, *Regula*, pp. 237–306 *passim*, and briefly *idem*, 'Æthelwold's Translation', pp. 143–8.

style of the *Regula S. Benedicti*, such unusual words in the Rule are scarcely ever of a poetic nature as they often are in the Psalter. Furthermore, unlike the hermeneutic vocabulary prevailing in tenth-century Anglo-Latin texts, such rare or arcane words will scarcely ever have obscured the meaning of a sentence for contemporary readers. At least they will not have done so in the opinion and after the intention of the translator, Bishop Æthelwold (but see below). The following are a few examples from the many words which are rarely attested or are even *hapax legomena*: *eaphylde* (BR 29.2, 109.6 'contented'), *æfendream* (BR 43.18 'vespers'), *hefeful* (BR 49.18 'severe'), *getæsness* (BR 59.1 'advantage, convenience'), *cisness* (BR 63.12 'fastidiousness'), *undersmugan* (BR 64.19 'to surprise'), *halfæst* (BR 72.6 ?'pious, healthy'), *unweorchard* (BR 75.8 'delicate, weakly'), *hleowfæst* (BR 89.7 'protecting, consoling'), *arwesa* (BR 115.20 'respected'), *syueræte* (BR 119.25 'abstemious') or *cwiuerlice* (BR 123.2 'zealously'). In most cases, the meaning of such rare words will have been clear from their semantic components or from their contexts or from both. Thus *arwesa* (BR 115.20) 'respected' or 'Your Honour' (when used in addressing a person) is compounded of *ar* 'honour' and a derivative from *wesan* 'to be'; it occurs in the doublet *leof* and *arwesa*, *leof* being the usual noun in respectful address: 'Sir'. Or *unweorchard* (BR 75.8) 'delicate, weakly' is formed from the negative prefix *un-*, the noun *weorc* 'work' and the adjective *heard* 'hard'; it is used in the doublet *þæm mearewum and unweorchardum*, *mearu* occurring somewhat more frequently and meaning 'tender, delicate'. *Unweorchard* is further clarified by paronomasia with its noun constituent *weorc* occurring in the same phrase: *þæm mearewum and þam unweorchardum tæce heom mon sum weorc* ('to the delicate and weakly one shall assign (at least) some work'). Nevertheless, it is interesting to note that such clarifying strategies employed by Æthelwold were apparently deemed insufficient by the scribes of several surviving manuscripts of the Rule (or by the scribes of their exemplars). In two of the five complete manuscripts (London, BL, Cotton Titus A. iv, s. xi^{med} and Durham, Cathedral Library, B. IV. 24, s. xi^2) and in the so-called 'Wells fragment' (Wells, Cathedral Library, 7, s. xi^{med})[79] rarely attested words are, in varying degrees, replaced by more common synonyms. This is precisely what happened to many of the arcane words of the Royal Psalter in the later D-type psalter glosses (see above, p. 43). As with these psalter

---

[79] For the manuscripts of the Rule, see below, p. 227.

glosses, such changes seem to have been made independently, by and large, in the individual manuscripts of the Rule, thereby revealing a fairly widespread hesitance and reluctance to adopt unusual terms or neologisms in both texts.

There is one further stylistic adornment applied occasionally in the Rule, which, by its very nature, can have no counterpart in the Royal Psalter gloss: the use of rhythmical prose. I print below a passage from the prologue to the Rule by way of example and in order to show how all these various stylistic features – rhythmical prose, alliteration and paronomasia as well as doublets, parallel phrases and the use of rare words and neologisms – may combine and reinforce each other to lend dignity and intensity to a passage. Such elaborate passages are especially conspicuous in some of its most important chs., such as the prologue or the closing ch., or the second ch. which concerns the quality and regime of an ideal abbot, or ch. 4 which gives detailed instructions for a virtuous and Christian life. The passage printed below is the closing and summarizing paragraph of the prologue (BR 5.10–6.3). It comes after the aims and compass of the subsequent monastic rule have been laid out in this prologue, and is hence in a very prominent position. From the accompanying Latin text it will be seen that in order to achieve the stylistic effects in question, Æthelwold repeatedly had resort to an uncharacteristically free rendering (often a paraphrase) of the Latin. But in any case, many of the Latin syntactical constructions would have posed considerable difficulties for any attempt to combine close translation and an idiomatic English prose style.

In the passage, I have marked the rhythmical units; it will be seen that two-stress units predominate, but three-stress units also occur, notably in clusters. No doubt in some cases a sentence could be subdivided into rhythmical units in a way different from the one proposed here, and in some places the rhythm is less pronounced than in others. The implication of such vagueness and alternative options is simply that the rhythmical units of Æthelwold's prose are not as unambiguously defined as those in (say) Ælfric's second series of *Catholic Homilies*. Nevertheless, when reading carefully through the entire text of the Rule, the distinctive rhythmical structure of a passage like the following stands out in clear relief against surrounding portions not structured in such a way. However, it will equally be clear that, unlike Ælfric's rhythmical prose, Æthelwold's sentences do not normally split up into pairs of rhythmical units, each pair being linked by alliteration and thus forming a long line.[80] Rather, Æthelwold's rhythmical units are distantly reminiscent of Wulfstan's prose rhythm, which is characterized by two-stress units (very occasionally three-stress ones) that are not normally coupled strictly in pairs, but loosely arranged into larger groups.[81] I have highlighted by the use of italics paronomasia as well as alliteration occurring outside such word-play.[82] Doublets and parallelism have not been highlighted in print so as to keep the passage readable; they will readily strike the eye when reading through the text. Also on grounds of readability, aural effects involving the internal structure of words have not been marked. Examples would be: *tæcinge* (23) and *geefenlæcende* (24), or *earfeþa* (25), *ea*htness*a* (25) and *gefea*n (26).

<pre>
     Toþí þénne   ic eórnestlìce
     séttan wílle   bysega and bígengas
     þýsses dríhtenlican   þeówdòmes.
     Þéah hwet téartlìces   hwǽthwara stíðlìce
  5 on þísum régule,   þe ures fǽryldes látteow
     to Críste ís,   gesét and getæht sy,
     for gescéades ríhtinge   and for sýnna bóte
     and sóðere síbbe   gehéaldsumnèsse,
     ne beo þú þurh þí   fórht and afǽred,
 10 nè þurh ýrhþe   ðinre hǽle wég ne forlǽt;
     þæs wéges óngin,   þe to Críste lǽt,
</pre>

---

[80] For Ælfric's prose rhythm, see especially P. Clemoes, 'Ælfric', in *Continuations and Beginnings: Studies in Old English Literature*, ed. E. G. Stanley (London, 1966), pp. 176–209, at 202–6, and Pope, *Homilies of Ælfric* I, 105–36.

[81] For Wulfstan's rhythmical prose, the classic study is A. McIntosh, 'Wulfstan's Prose', *Proceedings of the British Academy* 34 (1948), 109–42, esp. 116–24. For possible models for Wulfstan's prose rhythm, see *ibid.*, p. 127. For the occasional occurrence of rhythmical prose in earlier homilies (Blickling, Vercelli), see esp. O. Funke, 'Studien zur alliterierenden und rhythmisierenden Prosa in der älteren altenglischen Homiletik', *Anglia* 80 (1962), 9–36.

[82] Since 'structural alliteration' (that is alliteration linking a pair of rhythmical units to form one long line) is not in question, the range where alliteration has been marked is not restricted to any two rhythmical units, but is extended to include repetitions of word-initial phonemes which may reasonably be assumed to have been employed for ornamentation and to have been noticeable as such when reading the text aloud. On the same grounds, alliteration on syllables bearing not a full stress has also been marked. On such ornamental alliteration and the principle by which it is governed, see most recently Orchard, 'Artful Alliteration'.

    ne meg *beon begúnnen* on frúman   *bú*tan sumre *áncsumnỳsse*,

    ác þa geþíngþa   *hálegera* mǽgena

    ánd se gewúna   þisse *hálgan* dróhtnunge,

15   þe gedeþ *léafléoht* and *éa*þe   þǽt ðe *ǽr*

    *éa*rfoðe and *áncsumlic* þúhte;

    se wég is *rúm* and fórðheald,   þe to déaðe

    and to *héllewìte lǽt*;

    se is néara and stícol,   þe to lífe

20   and to *héofona* rìce *lǽt*;

    he is us þéah to gefárenne   mid *rúmhèortum* móde

    and mid gódum and glǽdum geþánce   and mid gefýllednesse *Gó*des gebóda

    swà þæt we on mýnstre þurhwúnigen   on Crístes *l*áre and tǽcinge,

    þæt we híne geéfen*l*ǽcende   *mí*d *geþý*lde

25   *éa*rfeþa and *éa*htnesse *þólien*   þæt we his ríces gemǽnnèsse

    ánd geféan   mid him *ág*an *mó*ten.[83]

(45) Constituenda est ergo nobis dominici scola seruitii. (46) In qua institutione nihil asperum, nihil graue nos constituros speramus. (47) Sed et si quid paululum restrictius dictante aequitatis ratione propter emendationem uitiorum uel conseruationem caritatis processerit, (48) non ilico pauore perterritus refugias uiam salutis, quae non est nisi angusto initio incipienda. (49) Processu uero conuersationis et fidei dilatato corde inenarrabili dilectionis dulcedine curritur uia mandatorum dei, (50) ut ab ipsius numquam magisterio discidentes in eius doctrinam usque ad mortem in monasterio perseuerantes passionibus Christi per patientiam participemur, ut et regno eius mereamur esse consortes.[84]

---

[83] BR 5.10–6.3: 'I therefore intend indeed to establish the occupation and observance of this service of the Lord. Even though in this Rule which is the guide for our journey to Christ some rather severe stipulations are instituted and taught somewhat harshly, for the guidance of reason and the remedy of sins, and for the preservation of true peace, this should not intimidate or frighten you nor [should you] through cowardice leave the way that leads to your salvation; the way that leads to Christ may be begun at the outset only with difficulties; but the dignity of holy virtue and the practice of this holy way of life will let appear agreeably easy and smooth what before seemed difficult and painful to you; the way is broad and inclined which leads to death and the torments of hell; the way is narrow and steep which leads to life and the heavenly kingdom; nevertheless, we have to follow this way with a wide heart and good and glad thoughts and with the fulfilment of God's precepts, by living in a monastery according to Christ's instructions and teaching, so that, in imitation of Him, we may patiently suffer hardship and persecution in order to obtain the fellowship and joy of His kingdom'.

[84] *RSB prol.* 45–50: '(45) Therefore we intend to establish a school for the Lord's service. (46) In drawing up its regulations, we hope to set down nothing harsh, nothing

Among the rare or unusual words in this passage, two compounds deserve our special attention: first, the adjective *rumheort*, occurring in the phrase *mid rumheortum mode* (21), translating Latin *dilatato corde* (*prol.* 49), literally 'with enlarged heart'. Old English *rumheort* is attested only infrequently; it occurs in poetry (twice in *Beowulf*) but also occasionally in glosses and prose. Its components are *rum* 'roomy, wide' and *heort* (literally) 'possessed of, having a heart'. With the exception of the single occurrence in the Rule, the adjective always means 'generous, liberal', a range of meaning shared with the substantive *rumheortness* and cognates such as *rummod*, *rummodness* or *rumlic*. A glance at the Old English (and Latin) context, however, reveals that Æthelwold probably intended a primarily literal, and hence strikingly unusual, meaning for *rumheort*. By the insertion of a phrase not found in the *Regula* ('se weg is *rum* and forðheald, þe to deaðe and to hellewite læt' (17–18)) he brings out more explicitly the word-play inherent already in the original text, namely that the *angusta uia salutis* (cf. *prol.* 48) should be undertaken with *dilatato corde*.[85] However, it is reasonable to assume that the established meaning of *rumheort* 'liberal, generous' would also have been implicit in the present occurrence of the word. Therefore the translator should be credited with having intended and achieved a subtle interplay of the established meaning and an unwonted literal sense of *rumheort*.

The second expression of a striking character is again an adjective: *leafleoht* (15). This is a *hapax legomenon* which has been tentatively assigned the meaning 'easy to believe (?)' both in BTS and CHM. In BTS, after the quotation from the Rule, reasons are given as to how this meaning came to be assumed: 'the English version here does not follow the Latin closely, the only part of which that seems the foundation of the English is:

> burdensome. (47) The good of all concerned, however, may prompt us to a little strictness in order to amend faults and to safeguard love. (48) Do not be daunted immediately by fear and run away from the road that leads to salvation. It is bound to be narrow at the outset. (49) But as we progress in this way of life and in faith, we shall run on the path of God's commandments, our hearts overflowing with the inexpressible delight of love. (50) Never swerving from his instructions, then, but faithfully observing his teaching in the monastery until death, we shall through patience share the sufferings of Christ that we may deserve also to share in his kingdom' (*RB 1980*, pp. 166–7).

[85] Note that the translator no doubt realized that Benedict's remark on the narrow road to salvation alluded to Matt. VII.14 and that consequently he himself based his addition on Matt. VII.13.

"Processu conuersationis et fidei". In some way *fidei* seems to have occasioned *lēaflēoht*'. This explanation and the meaning deduced from it for *leafleoht* seem unlikely on two grounds: first, the Latin phrase (= *prol.* 49) quoted by BTS and taken to underlie the formation of *leafleoht*, is more likely to be reflected in the Old English phrase: 'ac þa geþingþa halegera mægena and se gewuna þisse halgan drohtnunge' (13–14, with *fidei* being somehow echoed by *halegera mægena* rather than by *leafleoht*); and second, the meaning 'easy to believe' does not fit the context particularly well and would moreover destroy the apparently deliberate juxtaposition of the four adjectives *leafleoht and eaþe* and *earfoðe and ancsumlic*. These appear to be strong grounds for ruling out the possibility that *leafleoht* is compounded of *(ge)lēafa* 'belief' and *lēoht* 'easy' (as BTS assumed).

What we have here is perhaps a garbled version of an original compound *lēoflēoht*, composed of *lēof* 'dear, pleasant, agreeable' and *lēoht* 'easy'. Such a compound (rather unusual in terms of word-formation) would also be a *hapax legomenon* (as the attested form is) and its meaning would probably be 'agreeably or pleasantly easy'. It would perfectly fit the context which requires a near-synonym for *eaþe*, and it would echo the Latin phrase *(inenarrabili) dilectionis dulcedine* (*prol.* 49), flamboyantly surpassing the Latin, inasmuch as *leofleoht* not only has alliteration of the initial consonants of its components, but also an identical vowel in both parts. In other words, it would be a coinage very much in the vein of the Royal Glossator's neologisms.[86] Textual corruption must accordingly have taken place at an early stage in the transmissional history of the Rule, since all manuscripts attest the form *leafleoht*. Such corruption could be easily explained by the unusual character of the compound itself and by the diphthong *ea* occurring in two words in close proximity (*eaþe* and *earfoðe*).

The preface to the Rule

Except for passages with a pronounced prose rhythm, all stylistic embellishments and lexical predilections occurring in the Rule are found

---

[86] For a different explanation of the adjective, attempting to rescue the attested form *leafleoht*, see H. D. Meritt, *Some of the Hardest Glosses in Old English* (Stanford, CA, 1968), pp. 98–9.

(with increased frequency) in the short text which passes under the name *Edgar's Establishment of Monasteries*, the authorship of which may safely be ascribed to Æthelwold[87] and which was almost certainly composed by him to serve as a preface to his translation of the *Regula S. Benedicti*.[88] The text of the Preface is transmitted uniquely in the latest manuscript of the Rule (BL, Faustina A.x (s. xii[1]), 148v–151v) where it immediately follows the text of the Rule.[89] We will have occasion to return to the Preface as a historical witness of some importance in ch. 7, below. For the moment and for considerations of vocabulary and style which concern us here, a brief survey of the principal contents of the tract will be appropriate.

The Preface begins with an account of the coming of Christianity to England (heavily drawing on Bede's *Historia ecclesiastica*).[90] After a lacuna in the manuscript of either one or three folios,[91] the text goes on extolling the accomplishments of young King Edgar as a ruler, as well as praising his virtuous lifestyle, and dwelling on his expulsion of the secular canons (said to have been utterly debauched) from the Old and New Minsters at Winchester and from other places in England. The monks and nuns whom Edgar is reported to have installed in their place in minsters all over the country were (according to the text) given the privilege of his and his queen Ælfthryth's especial care and protection. Impelled by his pious cast of mind, Edgar is said to have commissioned a translation of the *Regula S. Benedicti* into the vernacular. The production of such a translation is defended on the grounds that it is a desideratum for the more simple-minded natives as well as for those only recently converted to the monastic life and as yet ignorant of Latin. The tract concludes with an urgent admonition to the author's successors in office and to abbesses, prohibiting them from any alienation of church property. By the same token, worldly authorities are warned against confiscating church

---

[87] For Æthelwold as the author of the tract, see the important article by Whitelock, 'Authorship', and see below, pp. 230–3.

[88] For the function of the text, see Gretsch, 'Benedictine Rule', pp. 146–52, and below, pp. 232–3.

[89] The Preface has been printed (with facing English translation) most recently by Whitelock, *CS*, pp. 142–54. For an English translation, see also *EHD*, pp. 920–3 (no. 238).

[90] Especially *HE* I. 23–6 and 33, and II. 1.

[91] Cf. *CS*, p. 145, and Ker, *Catalogue*, p. 195 (no. 154).

property, in case any ecclesiastic in charge of church possessions should be found guilty in any respect.

Even from such a skeletal summary it will be clear that the prefatory tract was aimed at an audience rather different from that for which the Old English Rule was intended in the first place. In this it might be compared with King Alfred's famous prefatory letter accompanying the individual copies of his translation of Pope Gregory's *Regula pastoralis* and addressed to the king's bishops who (presumably) would not have needed the translation. No doubt much in the preface to the Rule could have been read with profit also by those monks and nuns who were in need of a translation of the *Regula*, as for example the account of St Augustine's mission or the statement to the effect that the translation was made for those with no Latin, so that they should not have occasion to plead ignorance, should they infringe any precept of the Rule.[92] However, a number of passages point to a more educated audience in higher ecclesiastical or worldly ranks. The most conspicuous of such passages is of course the lengthy final section concerning the inviolability of church property and directed at Æthelwold's successors in office, at abbesses and secular magnates.[93] But mention should also be made of the lengthy apologia for translating religious texts into the vernacular.[94] While such an apologia *per se* would seem to be aimed at those with a solid knowledge of Latin, the passage contains an additional reference to a threefold exegesis of scriptural texts, applicable both to the literal and the spiritual level of meaning.[95] This remark possibly draws on Bede's distinction between *allegoria in factis* and *allegoria in uerbis* in his *De schematibus et tropis*.[96] The reference is not prompted by the context of the passage. Apart from revealing the author's concern with allegorical exegesis, it

---

[92] 'Hæbben forþi þa ungelæreden inlendisce þæs halgan regules cyþþe þurh agenes gereordes anwrigenesse, þæt hy þe geornlicor Gode þeowien and nane tale næbben þæt hy þurh nytennesse misfon þurfen'. 'Therefore let the unlearned natives have the knowledge of this holy rule by the exposition of their own language, that they may the more zealously serve God and have no excuse that they were driven by ignorance to err', *CS*, p. 152; throughout, translations from the Preface are those provided by Professor Whitelock.

[93] See Whitelock, *CS*, pp. 152–4.   [94] *Ibid.*, pp. 150–2.

[95] *Ibid.*, p. 151; the passage is quoted above, p. 10.

[96] Cf. *De schematibus et tropis*, ed. Kendall, pp. 164–6. For Bede's distinction between the two forms of allegory, see *idem*, *Bede, libri ii*, pp. 26–8.

rather looks like a deliberate and ostentatious display of knowledge paraded for those who were in a position to relish it.

In view of this putative audience it is perhaps not surprising that lexical and rhetorical embellishments are even more pronounced in the prefatory tract than they are in the Rule itself. But such ornamentation is of the same kind as we have met with in the Rule: doublets (note that the following examples are all found within one sentence, *CS*, pp. 144–5): *manode and lærde* 'admonished and instructed', *lofe and weorþunge* 'praise and honour', *tæhte and gesette* 'taught and established', *an heorte and an saul* 'one heart and one soul'; word-play, especially in the form of *figurae etymologicae* (again, the following examples are all contained within one brief passage, *CS*, pp. 147–8): *gewita – wat – wiste* 'wise man – he knows – he knew', *toweard – towearde* 'approaching – towards', *fremful – fremfullice* 'beneficial', *rihtwisa – rihtlice* 'righteous – rightly', *leangyfa – to leanes* 'rewarder – as a recompense', *friþast and fyrþrast* (occurring twice) 'protect and advance'; and alliteration, often combined with paronomasia (see above) but also occurring outside that rhetorical figure, for example: *þyses lænan lifes* 'of this transitory life' (p. 146), *mid gastlicum gode* 'with spiritual benefits' (p. 147), *to his cynedome gecoren* 'elected to his kingdom' (p. 147), *mærlic mynster* 'glorious minster' (p. 148) or *welm awlacige* 'the zeal may become lukewarm' (p. 152). A considerable number of rarely attested words occur: *earfoðwylde* 'hard to subdue' (p. 146), *leangyfa* 'rewarder' (p. 147), *scearpþancol* 'quick-witted' (p. 151), *earmful* 'wretched' (p. 151) or *inhold* 'loyal at heart' (p. 153) would be a few examples of *hapax legomena* or exceedingly rare expressions.

Since the preface to the Rule is a piece of original Old English prose, not a translation, such unusual words cannot have been chosen or coined in imitation of difficult Latin lemmata. Thus they serve to confirm the suspicion raised by the occurrence of numerous rare expressions in the Rule, namely that Æthelwold had a predilection for such words. The same consideration applies in respect of the frequent doublets, of paronomasia and alliteration in the preface, none of which can have been occasioned by a Latin model. We have seen, that these stylistic features are also very prominent in the Royal Psalter gloss. Within the constraints of a comparison between a prose text and an interlinear gloss, therefore, there are clear parallels between the Rule and its preface and the Royal Psalter.

ÆTHELWOLD AND ALDHELM

Concerning the Royal Psalter, we have seen that the frequent occurrence of stylistic and rhetorical ornamenation, so manifestly unusual in an interlinear gloss, may have resulted from a careful study of Latin hermeneutic texts, in particular the works of Aldhelm. As Michael Lapidge has shown, Bishop Æthelwold was one of the most ardent adherents of the hermeneutic style in Latin, and the influence of Aldhelm is pervasive in his own Latin writings. Unfortunately, the corpus of such Latin writings as can be attributed to Æthelwold with any confidence is not large, and as with the Old English Rule and its preface, none of the Latin texts in question bears an attribution of authorship.[97] The corpus of Æthelwold's writings comprises a few charters, the most notable of these being the New Minster Foundation Charter, which records the instalment of Benedictine monks in the New Minster, Winchester in 964.[98] The corpus further includes a letter written by an unnamed English bishop (very probably Æthelwold) to a likewise unnamed foreign duke or count, asking him to restore a gospelbook which had previously been stolen from the bishop's church by two clerics.[99] Finally, the *Regularis concordia* is the one substantial work which is now generally believed to have been composed by Æthelwold. This monastic consuetudinary was drafted after a synod convened at Winchester in 973 or thereabouts with the aim of standardizing liturgical practice and other aspects of monastic life in the

---

[97] For Æthelwold and his school at Winchester as practitioners of the hermeneutic style, see Lapidge, 'Hermeneutic Style', pp. 123–8. For the criteria for establishing the corpus of Æthelwold's Latin writings, for that corpus itself, for the style affected in those writings and the pervasive influence of Aldhelm revealed in them, see Lapidge, 'Æthelwold as Scholar and Teacher', pp. 187–95, and *idem*, *Wulfstan: Life*, pp. lxxxvii–xci. In addition to the texts discussed there, and listed briefly here, Æthelwold may well have composed a number of Latin prayers for liturgical and private use: see Lapidge, *Wulfstan: Life*, pp. lxx–lxxv, lxxxi–lxxxiii and lxxxiv–lxxxv.

[98] This charter (dated 966) is preserved in a *de luxe* manuscript, now London, BL, Cotton Vespasian A. viii (S 745, BCS 1190); it is most recently printed in *CS*, pp. 119–33 (no. 31). For verbal links between this charter and the preface to the Old English Rule, see Whitelock, 'Authorship', pp. 130–2. For this charter, see also below, pp. 129, 236–7 and n. 30, and 309–10. The other charters in question are S 687 (BCS 1055), dated 960, and S 739 (BCS 1175 and Sawyer, *Charters of Burton Abbey*, no. 21), dated 966.

[99] The letter is preserved in a late-tenth-century Anglo-Latin letter-collection, now London, BL, Cotton Tiberius A. xv; it is printed by Stubbs, *Memorials*, pp. 361–2.

reformed English monasteries.[100] However, since the *Regularis concordia* is a compilation which draws heavily on continental (principally Fleury) sources, its main text may be counted among Æthelwold's own writings only with due caution.[101] But the *Regularis concordia* is provided with a *prohemium* for which no written source has been identified, nor is there any need to assume such a source. Consequently, this *prohemium* may be regarded as a piece of original Latin prose composed by Æthelwold. Here, as in the other works listed above, the influence of Aldhelm is preeminent. Such influence is not limited to a substantial amount of words and phrases lifted verbatim from Aldhelm's writings;[102] it makes itself also felt in Æthelwold's pronounced taste for flamboyant and recherché vocabulary and the employment of alliteration for ornamental purposes,[103] stylistic features which also play a role in the Old English Rule and its preface as well as in the Royal Psalter gloss. By the same token, the occurrence of rhyming prose in the New Minster charter,[104] and the employment of words and phrases 'which naturally pertain to verse'[105] in the *prohemium* to the *Regularis concordia* may be indebted to Aldhelm, and they again recall the display of aural effects in the Psalter and the Rule, and the Royal Glossator's penchant for poetic expressions.[106] That such

---

[100] For the date of the Winchester synod, see most recently and most authoritatively, Symons, 'History and Derivation', pp. 40–2. For the editions and a translation of the *Regularis concordia*, see above p. 15, n. 30.

[101] For recent views on the indebtedness of the stipulations of the *Regularis concordia* to continental customs, see conveniently Lapidge, 'Æthelwold as Scholar and Teacher', p. 193, and *idem, Wulfstan: Life*, pp. lvi–lx. For earlier scholarly opinions, see Symons, *Regularis Concordia*, pp. xlv–lii, and *idem*, 'History and Derivation', pp. 43–59.

[102] For such verbal links with Aldhelm, see Lapidge, 'Æthelwold as Scholar and Teacher', pp. 191 and n. 60, and 193 and n. 71.

[103] See *ibid.*, pp. 191–2 and 194. For an analysis of Aldhelm's style in general, see Winterbottom, 'Aldhelm's Prose Style', pp. 39–46, and Orchard, *Poetic Art of Aldhelm*, pp. 8–16.

[104] Cf. Lapidge, 'Æthelwold as Scholar and Teacher', p. 189.

[105] *Ibid.*, p. 193.

[106] Even though in the *prohemium* to the *Regularis concordia* doublets (a hallmark of the Rule and the Royal Psalter) are not a prominent feature, the occurrence of a very similar stylistic mannerism should be noted, namely the numerous pleonastic phrases combining near-synonyms, as for example *dissentiendo discordarent* (ch. 4, p. 3) or *nausiae tedio* (ch. 5, p. 4); cf. Kornexl, *Die 'Regularis Concordia' und ihre altenglische Interlinearversion*, p. clxxv and n. 18. Such tautologies are also a characteristic feature

Aldhelmian features should occur in the Rule, a vernacular text composed by an author demonstrably influenced by Aldhelm, may confirm our earlier presumption concerning the stylistic influence at work in the Royal Psalter and may provide us with a significant clue as to the intellectual milieu where the Royal Psalter gloss may have originated. Furthermore, that such Aldhelmian features should be traceable in the Rule, an English text composed with a primarily didactic and practical aim, goes to show how deeply Æthelwold's sense of style had been imbued with Aldhelmian diction.

Interlaced word-order

There is a further intriguing stylistic link between Aldhelm, the *prohemium* to the *Regularis concordia* and the Rule: a shared predilection for hyperbaton or interlaced word-order, whereby an adjective is separated from its governing noun through the insertion of an appositional genitive (or genitive phrase) governed by the same noun as the adjective. (It is obvious that such a mannerism could not be imitated in an interlinear gloss.) A few examples from the beginning of the *Regularis concordia* would be: *ab ineunte suae pueritiae aetate* (ch. 1, p. 1) 'from the earliest beginning of his childhood', *regiam catholicae fidei uiam* (ch. 1, p. 1) 'the royal way of the Catholic faith', *cum magna animi alacritate* (ch. 2, p. 2) 'with great alacrity of mind' or *eiectisque neglegentium clericorum spurcitiis* (ch. 2, p. 2) 'and having driven out the negligent clerks with their abominations'. Even though Aldhelmian frequency and sophistication of interlaced word-order (such as *melliflua diuinarum studia scripturarum* 'the mellifluous study of the Holy Scriptures')[107] go unchallenged, it is clear nonetheless that Æthelwold took great pains to follow Aldhelm's lead. That Æthelwold consciously adopted this Aldhelmian mannerism can be seen further from the fact that he apparently attempted to imitate such interlaced word-order in the Rule. A few examples from that text would be: *mid ... þam beorhtestum hyrsumnesse wæpnum* (BR 1.8 'with the most shining weapons of obedience', cf. *RSB prol.* 3: *oboedientiae ... praeclara*

---

of Aldhelm's style; cf. Winterbottom, 'Aldhelm's Prose Style', pp. 41–6 *passim*, and Lapidge and Herren, *Aldhelm: the Prose Works*, pp. 20–1.

[107] Cf. *Aldhelmi Opera*, ed. Ehwald, p. 229.11–12. For the overall importance of hyperbaton in its various forms in Aldhelm's prose, see Winterbottom, 'Aldhelm's Prose Style', pp. 40–1 and 50–1, and Orchard, *Poetic Art of Aldhelm*, p. 10.

arma), *þeos laþiende Godes stefn* (BR 3.4 'this inviting voice of God', cf. *RSB prol.* 19 *uoce domini inuitantis nos*), *on lancsumere mynsteres drohtnunge* (BR 9.6 'during a long sojourn in a monastery', cf. *RSB* 1.3 *monasterii probatione diuturna*), *to þæm stræcstum mynstermonna cynne* (BR 10.4–5 'to the strongest kind of monks', cf. *RSB* 1.13 *ad coenobitarum fortissimum genus*) or *on þæm egefullum Godes dome* (BR 10.20 'at God's terrible judgement', cf. *RSB* 2.6 *in tremendo iudicio dei*). The frequency with which such phrases occur is decidedly unusual. It should also be noted that the foregoing examples are characteristic inasmuch as in none of them could the Old English word-order have been prompted by the Latin *Regula*. Moreover, interlacing of the same sort occurs also in the preface to the Rule (that is to say, in Æthelwold's original English prose), as can be seen from the following examples: *þære þancweorþan Cristes gyfe* (*CS*, p. 144 'of the thankworthy grace of Christ'), *þære halgan Godes gyfe* (*CS*, p. 144 'of the holy grace of Christ'), *þæt gastlice munyca angin* (*CS*, p. 149 'that spiritual beginning with monks') or *þa fultumigendan Godes gife* (*CS*, p. 149 'the supporting grace of God'). It is therefore a mannerism which must have held much attraction for Æthelwold and which provides tangible and valuable evidence that Æthelwold aimed to imitate a characteristic feature of Aldhelm's prose style in his own Old English prose.

The couplets

Let us consider briefly one final link, this time between Aldhelm's style, Æthelwold's Latin writings and the Royal Psalter. For Aldhelm it has been stated that 'a deep love of poetry' is one of his most important and distinctive stylistic traits, a love which resulted in his affectation in prose of many features pertaining to poetry.[108] We have noted that the Royal Glossator and Æthelwold in his Latin writings share a predilection not only for flamboyant vocabulary in general but in particular for poetic expressions. We are informed by Wulfstan that his master was deeply concerned with the system of Latin metrics, and that he took great care to pass on its rules to his students in classroom teaching. We know of two of Æthelwold's pupils, Wulfstan himself and Godeman (the scribe of

---

[108] See Orchard, *Poetic Art of Aldhelm*, p. 8. For Aldhelm's indebtedness to vernacular poetry, see above p. 85 and n. 159.

Æthelwold's lavish Benedictional, now London, BL, Add. 49598, and author of a Latin poem which serves as a preface to this Benedictional) that they were proficient poets and metricians, and they presumably learned their skill from Æthelwold.[109] If Æthelwold himself composed any Latin verse, almost nothing has survived.[110] However, at the beginning of the New Minster Foundation Charter an elegiac couplet occurs (on 3r, where it accompanies the frontispiece showing King Edgar, flanked by the Virgin and St Peter and offering the charter to Christ seated in majesty). The couplet is as follows:

> Sic celso residet solio qui condidit astra;
> rex uenerans Eadgar pronus adorat eum.

This is not much to go on, but the verses appear in a prominent position, they scan correctly and their author seems to have been familiar with Vergil and Latin Christian poets such as Prudentius.[111] Since the couplet was presumably composed by the draftsman of the charter, it represents 'arguably the sole surviving specimen of Æthelwold's Latin verse'.[112]

In the Royal Psalter we have encountered (above, p. 78) two lines of Old English verse, occurring rather unexpectedly among the Latin scholia in the margin of 25r:

---

[109] Wulfstan's statement that, at Glastonbury, Æthelwold studied the 'honey-sweet system of metrics' ('mellifluam metricae rationis dulcedinem') is found in ch. 9 of his *Vita S. Æthelwoldi* (*Wulfstan: Life*, pp. 14–15). For Wulfstan's remark that Æthelwold concerned himself to pass on the rules of metrics to his students ('regulas ... metricae rationis tradere'), see ch. 31 of his *Vita* (*ibid.*, pp. 48–9). For Godeman's and Wulfstan's metrical skill, see Lapidge, *Wulfstan: Life*, pp. lxxxvii–lxxxviii and xcv–xcix, as well as xiii–xxxix (for Wulfstan's proficiency as a poet). For Godeman, see also Lapidge, 'Hermeneutic Style', pp. 123–4 and 143–4.

[110] It may not be fanciful to surmise that Æthelwold did compose at least some Latin poetry; cf. Lapidge, *Aldhelm: the Prose Works*, ed. Lapidge and Herren, p. 12, where for example the composition of dedicatory verses for churches or altars is reckoned among the normal functions of Anglo-Saxon ecclesiastics. Such a suspicion may further be fed by the survival of some three distichs (dedicating various items of church furniture) from the pen of Dunstan, Æthelwold's friend and colleague; for these distichs, see Lapidge, 'Dunstan's Latin Poetry', pp. 153–5.

[111] For the couplet and the possible allusions therein to Vergil and Christian Latin poets, see Lapidge, 'Æthelwold as Scholar and Teacher', p. 190 and n. 53; see also *idem*, *Wulfstan: Life*, p. lxxxix.

[112] Lapidge, *Wulfstan: Life*, p. lxxxix.

Wæs mid Iudeum   on geardagum
ealra cyninga gehwelc   Cristus nemned.

Like the Latin couplet, these lines are not spectacular *per se*, but like the Latin verses again, they are metrically correct and occur in a prominent position, inasmuch as they explain in poetic language one of the most remarkable and idiosyncratic of the Royal Psalter's glosses, namely *cyning* for *christus*. This and their indebtedness to the Latin scholia are strong grounds for ascribing the composition of the verses to the Royal Glossator himself. Therefore, if the connection of the Royal Psalter with Æthelwold can be accepted, these lines would arguably be the only specimen of Old English verse which so far can be traced back to Æthelwold with some plausibility, and they would provide palpable evidence that Æthelwold's concern with metrical composition comprised Old English poetry as well as Latin. We shall return to these Old English and Latin verses in a later ch. (below, pp. 309–10) in order to uncover with the help of art historical evidence a subtle link between them, a link which may further confirm their suspected authorship.

CONCLUSIONS

In sum, the various evidence which we have canvassed in this ch. points suggestively (though not yet decisively) to an origin of the Royal Psalter in Æthelwold's circle and to an active and leading role played by Æthelwold in the composition of that gloss. No doubt Æthelwold's deep love of Aldhelm, revealed in the exiguous corpus of his own Latin writings (and in the works of his pupils), his consistent endeavour to reproduce lexical and stylistic features of Aldhelm's prose in his vernacular writings, and the Royal Glossator's equally pronounced taste for flamboyant vocabulary and stylistic embellishments – all this forms an intriguing and suggestive triangle. This triangle becomes even more intriguing and suggestive when we reflect how striking and unusual it is to encounter such traces of an imitation of the most difficult Anglo-Latin author in an Old English prose text, let alone in an Old English interlinear gloss – a gloss, moreover, which must have been in existence by *c.* 950 at the latest, that is to say well before the apogee of Aldhelm's influence in the post-Viking age had been reached. By the same token, the lexical links which so far have been established between the Psalter and the Rule are strong pointers to a shared origin of both works. Of especial interest and importance in this connection are the verbal ties with regard to a nascent Winchester vocabulary. Such ties are often not straightforward and the lexical evidence can sometimes be evaluated only with difficulty. However, the attempt to uncover such 'hidden links' is worthwhile, for it is through them that we may gain a fascinating glimpse of what the motives may have been behind the creation of a vocabulary distinctive of the most influential school in late Anglo-Saxon England. Lexical and stylistic evidence such as has come to light in this and the preceding chapter may be difficult, occasionally even impossible, to evaluate, but it may remind philologists that the vocabulary of Old English prose texts and even of glosses is more than a database of lexical items, from which lists of dialect words, Winchester words or loan formations can be compiled.

It now remains to be seen what further verbal ties between the Psalter and the Rule can be established. In this we shall have to bear in mind, however, that a lexical comparison between the Royal Psalter and the Old English Rule (that is, an interlinear gloss and a prose text) is in principle much hampered by the fact that they are texts of an utterly different character. We shall return to the nature of such difficulties at a later point. But before we may proceed with our philological detective work, we must turn our attention to a third text whose origin seems to be bound up with that of the Rule and the Royal Psalter: the thousands of interlinear and marginal Old English glosses to Aldhelm's major work, the prose *De uirginitate*, as they are transmitted in Brussels, Bibliothèque Royale, 1650.

5

The Aldhelm glosses

In the course of an analysis of words or word families shared by the Psalter and the Rule, remarkable parallels in usage have come to light between those texts and the Old English glosses to Aldhelm's prose *De uirginitate* as they are transmitted in Brussels, Bibliothèque Royale, 1650. It is necessary therefore to examine the genesis and the textual affiliations of the Brussels corpus of Aldhelm glosses and to see what can be ascertained concerning the nature of the glosses themselves.

THE GLOSSES IN BRUSSELS 1650

The main text of that manuscript was written at the beginning of the eleventh century. Several thousands of Old English glosses (alongside a substantial number of Latin ones) were entered between the lines and in the margins by several scribes during the first half of the eleventh century, perhaps at Abingdon.[1] Almost all these glosses of the Brussels manuscript are also found in another manuscript of Aldhelm's prose *De uirginitate*, now Oxford, Bodleian Library, Digby 146 (s. x^ex), into which they were copied from Brussels 1650 around the middle of the eleventh century, again perhaps at Abingdon.[2] The number of entries in Goossens's edition

---

[1] See Ker, *Catalogue*, pp. 6–7 (no. 8). The Old English glosses are edited by Goossens, *Old English Glosses*; in each case where a lemma is glossed in English, any Latin glosses to that lemma are printed there as well; cf. *ibid.*, p. 143.

[2] For Digby 146 and the date and origin of the glosses, see Ker, *Catalogue*, pp. 381–3 (no. 320). The Digby glosses are printed by Napier, *OEG*, pp. 1–138 (no. 1). For the dependence of the Digby Old English glosses on Brussels 1650 (not yet realized by Napier), see R. Derolez, 'De Oudengelse Aldhelmglossen in HS. 1650 van de Koninklijke Bibliotheek te Brussel', *Handelingen IX der Zuidnederlandse Maatschappij*

of the Brussels glosses is 5380, that in Napier's edition of the Digby glosses is 5504, but actually the number of glosses is higher in Brussels 1650, since in both editions multiple glossing of a single Latin lemma is not counted separately, and since such multiple glossing occurs more frequently in Brussels 1650.[3] Goossens gives no exact figures for the Old English or the Latin glosses in his edition of the Brussels manuscript, but the Old English glosses alone would seem to amount to approximately 6000. Parts of this vast corpus of glosses appear also in other manuscripts of Aldhelm's prose *De uirginitate*, as well as in glossaries containing Aldhelm material. We shall return shortly to the textual affiliations of the extant Old English Aldhelm glosses inasmuch as they are of importance for our purpose of tracing the origin of at least one branch of Aldhelm glossing.

The linguistic (and stylistic) links between the three texts (the Rule, the Psalter and the Brussels glosses) are too numerous and striking to be wholly coincidental or to be explained away by positing an origin in the same dialect area and thus presuming a shared dialect vocabulary. On the assumption that Aldhelm had a profound and pervasive influence on Æthelwold's sense of style and that it is entirely possible that it was Æthelwold who was responsible 'for placing Aldhelm's Latin prose at the centre of the late Anglo-Saxon curriculum',[4] there would *a priori* be no difficulty in the hypothesis that Æthelwold and his circle and (later on) his school played a pivotal role in providing Aldhelm's principal work with a substantial amount of Old English glosses. However, for various reasons, a comparison of vocabulary and usage in the Aldhelm glosses, the Royal Psalter and the Benedictine Rule is not simple and straightforward. It is obvious that the same structural differences which hamper a comparison between the Psalter and the Rule, that is to say between an interlinear gloss and a prose translation, also obtain in the case of a comparison between the Aldhelm glosses and the Rule. But there is also a fundamental difference between the two gloss texts, the Psalter and the

---

voor Taal- en Letterkunde en Geschiedenis (1955), 37–50, at 45, as well as Ker, *Catalogue*, pp. 382–3, and Goossens, *Old English Glosses*, pp. 25–6.

[3] See Goossens, *Old English Glosses*, p. 17 and n. 3.

[4] Cf. Lapidge, *Wulfstan: Life*, p. xci. For Aldhelm as the principal author of the Anglo-Saxon curriculum after the mid-tenth century, see also *idem*, 'Hermeneutic Style', pp. 112–13, and see below, ch. 9, for the presumed origins of tenth-century Aldhelm studies.

Rule. The Latinity of the psalter, even though it is fraught with many difficulties (as we have seen), is quite distinct from Aldhelm's difficult and flamboyantly hermeneutic prose. The implication of such differences in wording is not only that the lexical material for a comparison between both glosses is much reduced; the implication is also that we may have to reckon with the possibility that the distinct stylistic registers in both texts may have prompted the choice of different *interpretamenta* for a given lemma, even if both gloss corpora, the Psalter and the Aldhelm glosses, should have originated within the same group of scholars. Furthermore, the Royal Psalter is a full interlinear version providing an Old English gloss for almost every Latin word. By contrast, the Aldhelm glosses, even in the most densely glossed Brussels manuscript, and even in the most densely glossed parts of that manuscript, do not amount to anything like such a continuous interlinear version.[5] The lexical material available for comparison is thereby narrowed down once again.

Such different methods of glossing may perhaps be attributed to the specific needs arising at different stages in a student's career at which both texts were first studied. Although the Royal Glossator does not seem to have been content with catering just for the necessities of novices, the psalter was foremost among the texts first studied by those entering the monastic life and aspiring to learn the language of religion and scholarship. The study of Aldhelm's prose, on the other hand, must have been reserved for the intellectual exercises of the more advanced students.[6] At

---

[5] The glossing grows markedly less dense towards the end of the text. At a rough estimate, approximately one third of the text appears to have been glossed on average, ranging from 43.5 per cent in a sample passage drawn from the beginning of the text to 6.38 per cent in a sample passage from the end. In order to form some notion of the overall density of glossing in Brussels 1650, see the facsimile edition by G. van Langenhove, *Aldhelm's De Laudibus Virginitatis with Latin and Old English Glosses. Manuscript 1650 of the Royal Library in Brussels* (Bruges, 1941).

[6] It should be noted, however, that not all glossing found in Aldhelm manuscripts testifies to an advanced knowledge of Latin by the readers of these manuscripts. This much can be seen, for example, from the approximately 160 dry-point glosses in Old English entered (probably s. x^2) in what is now arguably the oldest surviving manuscript of the prose *De uirginitate* (New Haven, Yale University, Beinecke Library, 401, s. ix^{in}). By their rather elementary nature these glosses seem to point to the study of Aldhelm by students with no great grasp of Latin: see P. G. Rusche, 'Dry-Point Glosses to Aldhelm's *De Laudibus Virginitatis* in Beinecke 401', *ASE* 23 (1994), 195–213, at 199–203.

this stage, the students would, perhaps, be in need not so much of a complete interlinear version but they would want help in construing Aldhelm's tortuous sentences, and they would want Latin synonyms and Old English equivalents for clarifying Aldhelm's recherché vocabulary. All this is provided between the lines and in the margins of Brussels 1650, as well as in most of the other manuscripts of the prose *De uirginitate* from Anglo-Saxon England, although usually on a much more reduced scale there.[7] Help with the Latin syntax could be obtained from the construe marks or syntactical glosses (not reproduced in Goossens's edition).[8] Help with the syntax could also be gleaned from a substantial number of merographs, that is glosses which give only part of the Old English *interpretamentum* for the Latin lemma, as for example, *ce*, probably for *{woruldli}ce* glossing *mundi* (G 678) or *cere*, probably for *{werli}cere* glossing *uirili* (G 3602). Reducing Old English words in such a way to a bare indication of word class, case and gender was clearly undertaken to facilitate construing the sentence (the lexeme, that is the semantic information in the word in question, being taken for granted).[9] The same

---

[7] For a survey of the English manuscripts of the prose *De uirginitate* with glosses (Old English and Latin), see Goossens, *Old English Glosses*, pp. 17–20, and see below, pp. 143–4. There are thirteen glossed manuscripts as against only two without any glosses. Note that Goossens (*ibid.*, p. 16) refers to three unglossed manuscripts, but one of these (his fragment A[1]) is part of his no. 9 (p. 16); see Ker, *Catalogue*, pp. 10–11 (no. 12), and B. Shailor, *Catalogue of Medieval and Renaissance Manuscripts in the Beinecke Rare Book and Manuscript Library, Yale University, II: MSS 250–500* (Binghamton, NY, 1987), pp. 280–4. For the amount of glossing (in Latin and Old English) in English manuscripts of the prose *De uirginitate*, see also Gwara, 'Manuscripts of Aldhelm's *Prosa de Virginitate*', pp. 106–7.

[8] Such diacritical marks or letters aiming to clarify the structure of a Latin sentence by linking the various constituents (often far apart) of the subject, object, etc. of that sentence are not infrequently found in Latin manuscripts from Anglo-Saxon England (and from the Continent); see F. C. Robinson, 'Syntactical Glosses in Latin Manuscripts of Anglo-Saxon Provenance', *Speculum* 48 (1973), 443–75, and M. Korhammer, 'Mittelalterliche Konstruktionshilfen und altenglische Wortstellung', *Scriptorium* 34 (1980), 18–58. In the case of Brussels 1650, the syntactical glosses were already noted and commented on by Ehwald, *Aldhelmi Opera*, p. 215.

[9] On merographs among Old English glosses, see for example Meritt, *Old English Glosses*, p. ix. It should be noted that in Brussels 1650 (as elsewhere) merographs are employed as well to convey semantic information. In such cases, the inflexional ending of an Old English word or its suffix are omitted, as for example, *dælni*, for *dælni{mendysse}* or *dælni{munge}* glossing *participio* (G 773). It should also be noted that in Brussels 1650 the number of Old English merograph glosses is considerably lower than in other

---

objective lies behind those cases where no more than an Old English preposition is given to indicate a Latin ablative, as when the lemma *rumore* is glossed by the Latin equivalents *opinione* and *fama* and, in addition, by the Old English preposition *of* (G 12).[10]

However, decidedly more prominent than such syntactical aids is the lexical glossing in Brussels 1650 as well as in most other manuscripts of the prose *De uirginitate*, which in turn reminds us that it was principally Aldhelm's vocabulary which intrigued and bewildered his tenth-century students. Lexical help is therefore provided copiously. Lexical merographs form only a small part of this type of glossing; in innumerable instances we are provided not only with one or two Latin synonyms for the lemma in question as in the example just cited (G 12), but in addition with one or more Old English renderings. Consider, for example, the expression *celesti numine* which bears the following glosses: *uirtute, superni claritate* ł *dignitas, cum, heofenlicere mihte* (G 1582); or the lemma *confutati*, glossed *conuicti* ł *redarguti, superati, oferstælede* (G 2839); or *scin{t}illantibus*, glossed *spyrcendum, brastliendum, splendentibus* (G 3851); or (our final example) *praeconia*, glossed *laudes, fauores, lofu* ł *herunga* (G 3870). Usually, but not invariably, such multiple glosses are entered by different hands (on which see below).

In a word, reading through the Brussels glosses, one can scarcely escape the impression that the glossators somehow had been ignited by Aldhelm's verbal exuberance, and in their turn strove to display in their glosses the range of Latin and Old English synonyms at their disposal. It is evident that such multiple glossing adds to the difficulties in assessing verbal links between the Aldhelm glosses and the Royal Psalter or the Rule. On the other hand, we should recall that a penchant for variation in the translation of a given lemma and, to some extent, for verbal

---

manuscripts of the prose *De uirginitate* such as London, BL, Royal 5. E. XI (text s. x/xi, glosses s. xi[in-med], both from Christ Church, Canterbury) where the overwhelming majority of glosses are merographs. The inked glosses from this manuscript are printed *OEG*, pp. 164–71 (no. 8); the scratched glosses from the same manuscript are printed (in part) by Meritt, *Old English Glosses*, pp. 1–6 (no. 2). For some further dry-point glosses from Royal 5. E. XI, see F. Robinson, 'Old English Lexicographical Notes', in his *The Editing of Old English* (Oxford, 1994), pp. 149–54, at 151, n. 18 (orig. publ. 1965).

[10] For such help with Aldhelmian syntax provided in Brussels 1650, see briefly Goossens, *Old English Glosses*, pp. 28–9.

playfulness are among the hallmarks of the Royal Psalter gloss as well as the Rule.

THE TRANSMISSION OF THE OLD ENGLISH ALDHELM GLOSSES

The most formidable obstacles, however, to a comparison between the three texts are caused by the transmissional history of the Brussels glosses and their affiliations with other surviving vernacular glosses to the prose *De uirginitate*. The details of this textual history and affiliation are exceedingly complex and have not as yet been unravelled. Apart from the glossed psalters the Old English *interpretamenta* to Aldhelm's prose *De uirginitate* constitute the largest corpus of Old English glosses. As Arthur Napier noted,[11] about seven eighths of the materials he printed in his *OEG* are Aldhelm glosses and the overwhelming majority of these are glosses to the prose *De uirginitate*.[12]

A brief comparison with the glossed psalters may highlight how well-defined and transparent the textual history of the psalter glosses is in relation to the Aldhelm glosses, and where the principal problems for the textual criticism of the Aldhelm glosses must be sought. As we have seen, there are three distinct interlinear versions to the Latin psalter, transmitted in their purest form in the Vespasian (A), the Royal (D) and the Lambeth (I) psalters. These three versions originated at various points between the ninth and the late tenth or early eleventh centuries, and all of them have been preserved in at least one manuscript which is fairly close to the original gloss. Scholars may disagree, for example, about the indebtedness of D to A, but the distinctiveness of D and its role as the progenitor of the later D-type psalters have never been seriously in question. By the same token, the complete version as it is transmitted in D (or in A or I for that matter) may be attributed with some confidence either to a single glossator or to a group of scholars working in close contact.

---

[11] See *OEG*, p. xi.

[12] For a convenient survey of the manuscripts containing glosses to the prose *De uirginitate* and for editions of these glosses, see Goossens, *Old English Glosses*, pp. 17–20, and see below, pp. 143–4. Since Goossens's edition appeared, a considerable number of dry-point or scratched glosses has come to light and is gradually being printed; see, for example, R. I. Page, 'More Aldhelm Glosses from CCCC 326', *English Studies* 56 (1975), 481–90, and Rusche (as in n. 6 above).

No such basic understanding and broad agreement obtain in the case of the Aldhelm glosses. The manuscript evidence for the Old English glosses to the prose *De uirginitate* (on which we have to base our reconstruction of their textual history) is not unlike a hypothetical situation in psalter glossing, where we would have neither the Vespasian, nor the Royal or the Lambeth psalters in the flesh, but (except for a number of eleventh-century psalter manuscripts glossed only haphazardly) no more than the Stowe Psalter (F), its gloss dating from the second half of the eleventh century. We have seen (above, p. 26 and n. 53) that F is a psalter which is predominantly D-type, but which contains A-type material as well as glosses which are characteristic of I only. Fortunately, such a scenario for the textual history of the glossed psalters needs to be depicted only by way of trying to give some more vivid notion of what the textual situation of the Aldhelm glosses is like.

It is commonly assumed that the interlinear Old English (and Latin) glosses to the prose *De uirginitate* are the product of a revival of Aldhelm studies in the course of the tenth century and that they are intimately connected with various centres of the Benedictine reform.[13] However, in spite of the considerable number of glossed manuscripts of the *De uirginitate*, the bulk of the Old English glosses, and with some 6000 *interpretamenta* the only really vast corpus of Old English Aldhelm glosses which has been preserved, is in effect found in one manuscript, namely Brussels 1650. If we disregard the more than 5500 Old English glosses in Digby 146 as having no independent textual value, since they were copied directly from the Brussels manuscript,[14] the number of Old English glosses in other Aldhelm manuscripts is dramatically lower than in Brussels 1650: it ranges between 436 (in Royal 5. E. XI) and six (in BL, Harley 3013). Furthermore, the great majority of these glosses was entered in the manuscripts in question not before the eleventh century. In Brussels 1650, for example, the glosses were entered during the first half of the eleventh century; and they were copied into that manuscript by several scribes. Are we then to assume that these various scribes made use of different sources for their portions and that therefore the glosses in Brussels 1650 can by no means be considered a single

---

[13] See, for example, Goossens, *Old English Glosses*, p. 14, and Gwara, 'Manuscripts of Aldhelm's *Prosa de Virginitate*', pp. 154–9.

[14] See above, p. 132.

corpus? We shall return to the problem of the various scribes in Brussels 1650 and their layers of glosses presently. For the moment, it is important to note that since the glosses to the *De uirginitate* do not amount to a continuous interlinear version, we may have to reckon with accretions each time a manuscript and its glosses was copied. Such accretions could either have been supplied by the individual scribe himself (from his understanding of the text) or they could stem from a different written source which the scribe had conflated with the glosses he was copying. In other words, the Aldhelm glosses as they are transmitted in a certain manuscript and especially in Brussels 1650 are likely to represent the intellectual activities, not of an individual or a group of scholars closely collaborating (as in the case of the Vespasian, Royal and Lambeth psalters) but of various glossators, working at different times and at different centres.

A further obstacle in assessing the textual history and relationship of the surviving Aldhelm glosses is that we have to reckon with a substantial loss of manuscripts (perhaps more than is usual with Anglo-Saxon texts in general). Later generations of scholars will have seen no particular reason to preserve manuscripts which were encrusted with hundreds and thousands of uncalligraphic glosses – Old English glosses, moreover, which were soon to become cryptic; and once the enthusiasm for Aldhelm had ebbed away, some time after the Norman Conquest, the text itself was not of the nature to guarantee interest in or respectful handling of a manuscript of the prose *De uirginitate* by post-Conquest scholars.

A LOST MANUSCRIPT AND ITS AFFILIATIONS

By a fortunate coincidence we have knowledge of one such lost manuscript and what its textual affiliation and its contents (in addition to the prose *De uirginitate*) must have been. At one point in his *Vita S. Ecgwini*, Byrhtferth of Ramsey inserts almost verbatim a brief passage from the prose *De uirginitate* into his own text and in this quotation he supplies Old English glosses to four lemmata.[15] These four glosses are closely

---

[15] The *Vita S. Ecgwini* is transmitted uniquely in London, BL, Cotton Nero E. i, 24r–34v (s. xi^med, from Worcester). It was composed sometime after the year 1000, possibly shortly after 1016 (see *Enchiridion*, ed. Baker and Lapidge, pp. xxix–xxx and xxxiv). Most of the glosses and scholia which accompany the text in the manuscript are in Latin. It seems clear that the glosses were added by Byrhtferth himself: see

related to the corresponding ones in Brussels 1650 (G 1110–15), but they are linked even more closely to the glosses for these Aldhelm lemmata in the third glossary in London, BL, Cotton Cleopatra A. iii, 92r–117r (on which see below).[16] Since Cleopatra A. iii is of mid-tenth-century date, it cannot be entirely ruled out that Byrhtferth drew on that glossary itself (either in Cleopatra A. iii or a closely related manuscript), but in view of the fact that in the passage in question he has inserted a quotation from the prose *De uirginitate* into his own text, it seems decidedly more likely that for this quotation Byrhtferth drew on a glossed manuscript of the prose *De uirginitate* and that he copied out the Latin text together with its Old English glosses. Before it came into Byrht-ferth's hands, this same manuscript (or a very close congener) would have been used by the compiler of the Third Cleopatra Glossary, sometime before the mid-tenth century; it has subsequently perished.[17] Again, at one point in the Old English portion of his *Enchiridion*, where he alludes to classical mythology, drawing jointly on the prose *De uirginitate* and the *Carmen de uirginitate*, Byrhtferth not only translated Aldhelm's wording, but also incorporated into his Old English prose the English (and Latin) glosses which must have accompanied Aldhelm's lemmata in the manu-script he used.[18] It would appear, therefore, that this glossed manuscript which was laid under contribution by Byrhtferth and (several decades previously) by the compiler of the Third Cleopatra Glossary contained both the prose and the *Carmen de uirginitate*.[19]

M. Lapidge, 'Byrhtferth and the *Vita S. Ecgwini*', in his *Anglo-Latin Literature 900–1066*, pp. 293–315, at 313–15 (orig. publ. 1979). So far, the *Vita S. Ecgwini* is available in print only in the edition by Giles, *Vita quorundum Anglo-Saxonum*; the glosses in question are found in II. 1 (p. 361).

[16] See WW I, 491.7–10.

[17] See Baker, 'The Old English Canon of Byrhtferth of Ramsey', pp. 29–30, for a discussion of these four glosses in the *Vita S. Ecgwini*. For a fifth Old English gloss in the *Vita* to a lemma which Byrhtferth again lifted from the prose *De uirginitate* in a near-verbatim quotation, see below, p. 176. Here, once again, the Old English gloss adopted by Byrhtferth is somewhat closer to the Third Cleopatra Glossary than to Brussels 1650. All five Old English glosses from the *Vita* have been printed *OEG*, no. 35 (p. 201).

[18] See *Enchiridion*, ed. Baker and Lapidge, III. 1.205–8; the quotation from the prose *De uirginitate* corresponds to p. 292.17, that from the *Carmen*, to p. 353 (lines 24–7) in Ehwald's edition.

[19] See *Enchiridion*, ed. Baker and Lapidge, pp. lxxxiii–lxxxiv, cix–cx and 318–19.

It is a great pity that this manuscript has not survived, for apart from its apparently close relationship to the most important vernacular gloss corpus for the prose *De uirginitate*, namely that in Brussels 1650, whose origin we need to trace here, this early glossed manuscript, which must have been in existence by the mid-tenth century at the latest, was remarkable in at least two further respects. First, among the manuscripts of Aldhelm's *opus geminatum* which have survived from Anglo-Saxon England, there is none in which both texts, the prose and the metrical version, are transmitted together. (There is none either among the continental manuscripts collated in Ehwald's edition.) Secondly, the manuscript laid under contribution by the compiler of the Third Cleopatra Glossary (and later by Byrhtferth) must have contained far more Old English glosses to the *Carmen de uirginitate* than any of the surviving manuscripts of that text. The edition of the Third Cleopatra Glossary by Wright and Wülker comprises more than 650 glossed lemmata from the *Carmen*,[20] whereas the number of lemmata with Old English glosses in the five surviving manuscripts of the *Carmen* ranges between seventy-three and two.[21] Regrettable as the loss of this manuscript is, the compilation made from it for the Third Cleopatra Glossary, and the fact that Byrhtferth was arguably still in a position to draw on the manuscript, allow us to form some notion of how the loss of important witnesses must affect our understanding of the textual history and the relationships of the Old English glosses to Aldhelm's prose *De uirginitate*.

---

[20] Cf. WW I, 516.17–535.11.

[21] All surviving manuscripts of the *Carmen de uirginitate* have some Old English glosses, but in most of these such glosses are extremely scarce. The following manuscripts are in question: Cambridge, University Library, Gg. 5. 35 (s. xi[med], provenance Canterbury, St Augustine's, Ker, *Catalogue*, no. 16, Gneuss, 'Handlist', no. 12), two glosses (ptd *OEG*, no. 16); Cambridge, Corpus Christi College 285 (s. xi[in], Ker no. 54, Gneuss, no. 82), forty-seven glosses (ptd *OEG*, nos. 18 and 22); Oxford, Bodleian Library, Bodley 49 (s. x[med], prov. Winchester, Old Minster, Ker, no. 299, Gneuss, no. 542), ten glosses (ptd *OEG*, nos. 15 and 20); Oxford, Bodleian Library, Bodley 577 (Canterbury, Christ Church, s. x/xi, Ker, no. 314, Gneuss, no. 584), eight glosses (ptd *OEG*, nos. 14 and 19); and Oxford, Bodleian Library, Rawlinson C. 697 (text northeast Francia, s. ix[3/4], Ker, no. 349, Gneuss, no. 661), seventy-three glosses (s. x[2]; ptd *OEG*, nos. 17 and 21). From these figures it will be clear that the lost manuscripts on which the compiler of the Cleopatra Glossary (and Byrhtferth) drew must have been of prime importance for the Old English gloss corpora to the *Carmen de uirginitate*.

THE TEXTUAL CRITICISM OF THE GLOSSES TO THE
PROSE *DE VIRGINITATE*

Serious research in the domain of the textual affiliations of the Old English interlinear glosses to the prose *De uirginitate* was instituted by Arthur Napier in his introduction to *OEG*.[22] However, to the astonishment of later scholars, Napier misunderstood the relationship of the glosses in Digby 146 (which he printed as *OEG*, no. 1) and those in Brussels 1650, inasmuch as he failed to realize that the Digby glosses were copied from the Brussels manuscript but assumed instead that both the Digby and the Brussels glosses derived independently from a common original (now lost). Nonetheless, in addition to making available most of the extant glosses to the prose *De uirginitate* for the first time in a reliable form, his lasting contribution to the disentanglement of the textual affiliations of these glosses consisted in establishing three broad branches of transmission which he called the 'Digby', the 'Salisbury' and the 'independent' group respectively.[23] (The rationale for the inclusion of a manuscript in the third group being no other than that it does not belong to either of the first groups.) Louis Goossens, in his discussion of the textual relationships prefaced to his edition of the Brussels glosses, builds on Napier's findings, revising and supplementing them in the light of more recent scholarship, notably that of René Derolez and Neil Ker.[24] Goossens distinguishes the same three groups of manuscripts established by Napier, except that Napier's 'Digby' group is renamed the 'Abingdon' group, on the grounds that Ker's research appears to have revealed a close connection with Abingdon for all the manuscripts in question.[25] The manuscripts belonging to the Salisbury group originated at Canterbury and Goossens (in accordance with earlier scholarship) assumes that their glosses represent the Canterbury tradition of Aldhelm glossing.[26]

The following are the manuscripts in question and their respective affiliations. Note that the dates given for glosses refer to Old English glosses only (disregarding any Latin gloss corpora in a manuscript) and,

---

[22] See *OEG*, pp. xxiii–xxvi.   [23] See *ibid*.
[24] See Goossens, *Old English Glosses*, pp. 7 and 16–27.   [25] See *ibid*., pp. 16 and 22.
[26] See *ibid*., p. 20.

in cases of glosses entered at various dates, only to the most important of these layers. Also note that the figures given for the glosses refer to the editions as quoted and do not include any scratched glosses which may occur in a manuscript.

Abingdon group

Brussels, Bibliothèque Royale, 1650, text s. xi^{in}, glosses s. xi^1, Abingdon (?) (Ker, *Catalogue*, no. 8, Gneuss, 'Handlist', no. 806; *c.* 6000 glosses, ptd Goossens, *Old English Glosses*).

Oxford, Bodleian Library, Digby 146, text s. x^{ex}, glosses s. xi^{med}, Abingdon (?) (Ker, no. 320, Gneuss, no. 613; *c.* 5500 glosses, ptd *OEG*, no. 1).

London, British Library, Royal 6. B. VII, s. xi^{ex}, probably Exeter (Ker, no. 255, Gneuss, no. 466; 502 glosses, ptd *OEG*, no. 2 and M. Richter, *Die altenglischen Glossen zu Aldhelms 'De laudibus virginitatis' in der Handschrift BL, Royal 6 B. VII* (Munich, 1996)).

London, British Library, Royal 7. D. XXIV, text s. x$^{2/4}$, glosses s. x, southwest England (Glastonbury?) (Ker, no. 259, Gneuss, no. 473; 43 glosses, ptd *OEG*, no. 5).

Hereford, Cathedral Library, P. I. 17, s. xii/xiii, provenance Cirencester (Ker, no. 120; 57 glosses, ptd *OEG*, no. 3).

Salisbury group

Salisbury, Cathedral Library, 38, s. x^{ex}, Canterbury, Christ Church or St Augustine's (Ker, no. 378, Gneuss, no. 707; *c.* 350 glosses, ptd H. Logeman, 'New Aldhelm Glosses', *Anglia* 13 (1891), 27–41; corrections and additions by A. S. Napier, 'Collation der altenglischen Aldhelmglossen des Codex 38 der Kathedralbibliothek zu Salisbury', *Anglia* 15 (1893), 204–9).

London, British Library, Royal 5. E. XI, text s. x/xi, glosses s. xi^{in-med}, Canterbury, Christ Church (Ker, no. 252, Gneuss, no. 458; 436 inked glosses, ptd *OEG*, nos. 8 and 8B; for details and for scratched glosses, see Ker, p. 321; see also above, p. 136, n. 9).

London, British Library, Royal 6. A. VI, s. x^{ex}, Canterbury, Christ Church (Ker, no. 254, Gneuss, no. 464; 396 glosses, ptd *OEG*, no. 7).

Manuscripts belonging neither to the Abingdon nor to the Salisbury group

Membra disiecta, now located at various places. The most substantial portion of the text (twenty-eight leaves) is now shelved as New Haven, Yale University, Beinecke Rare Book and Manuscript Library 401 and 401A, text s. ix^{in}, glosses s. x^2 (Ker no. 12, Gneuss, no. 857; for details, see Ker, pp. 10–11, and *idem*, 'Supplement', p. 122. See also B. Shailor, *Catalogue of Medieval and Renaissance Manuscripts in the Beinecke Rare Book and Manuscript Library, Yale University, II: MSS 250–500* (Binghamton, NY, 1987), pp. 280–4. Over 200 inked glosses, ptd *OEG*, 11 and 12 and H. D. Meritt, 'Old English Aldhelm Glosses', *Modern Language Notes*, 67 (1952), 553).

Cambridge, Corpus Christi College 326, s. x/xi, Canterbury, Christ Church (Ker, no. 61, Gneuss, no. 93; 93 inked glosses, ptd *OEG*, no. 4).

London, British Library, Harley 3013, s. xii^2, Newminster, Northumberland (Ker, no. 238, 6 glosses, ptd *OEG*, no. 10).

London, British Library, Royal 5. F. III, text s. ix^{ex} or ix/x, glosses s. xi^{in}, Mercia (Worcester?) (Ker, no. 253, Gneuss, no. 462; 19 glosses, ptd *OEG*, no. 9).

Oxford, Bodleian Library, Bodley 97, s. xi^{in}, provenance Canterbury, Christ Church (Ker, no. 300, Gneuss, no. 545; 30 glosses, ptd *OEG*, no. 6).

As Napier and Goossens noted, a certain amount of glosses shared by manuscripts which otherwise belong to different groups points to extensive contamination between all three groups.[27] But, as Goossens hastens to stress, the details of the relationships between the groups and even within the groups have never been thoroughly explored.[28] If we

---

[27] See Goossens, *Old English Glosses*, pp. 20–1, and Napier, *OEG*, p. xxiv and n. 1, and pp. xxv–xxvi. Of especial interest in this respect is a common core of about one hundred glosses shared by manuscripts from the Abingdon and the Salisbury group, which may point to a common archetype for both branches; see Napier, *OEG*, p. xxii.

[28] For example, it should be noted that even in the case of the textual affiliations within the Abingdon group, a group where, according to Goossens (*Old English Glosses*, p. 22), direct links between manuscripts can be established (apart from the connection between Brussels 1650 and Digby 146), Goossens himself saw the need to revise (in a later article) a hypothesis (advanced in his edition) concerning the relationship of Brussels 1650 and Royal 6. B. VII; see his *Old English Glosses*, pp. 22–5, and cf. *idem*,

recall the reasons for our interest in the Aldhelm glosses, namely their links with words and usage in the Royal Psalter gloss and the Benedictine Rule, it is important to note that such links appear to exist to any remarkable degree only with manuscripts belonging to the Abingdon group, in particular with Brussels 1650. (Digby 146 and Royal 6. B. VII, being dependent in various ways on the Brussels corpus, cannot, for our purposes, be counted as textual witnesses in their own right.) However, it should be borne in mind that, in comparison with the 6000 or so glosses in Brussels 1650, the manuscripts of the two other groups are only sparsely glossed. There are, for example, no more than 436 Old English glosses in Royal 5. E. XI, the most densely annotated manuscript of the Salisbury group.

A comprehensive scrutiny of the textual affiliations of the Latin and Old English glosses to the prose *De uirginitate* is currently being undertaken by Scott Gwara in a series of articles.[29] So far, Gwara's publications have confirmed the immense intricacies of these affiliations and the widespread contamination of the manuscripts. Gwara has, however, challenged a number of commonly held assumptions; for example, he rejects the Abingdon origin of Brussels 1650 and Digby 146 (assumed by Ker and others), positing a Canterbury origin instead.[30] In view of the possibility (mentioned above) that the glosses might have attracted accretions each time they were copied, it would no doubt be of interest to have secure knowledge of the centre in which the text of Brussels 1650 or Digby 146 was written and where their glosses were entered. However, since not only the Digby glosses, but (as we shall see presently) those in Brussels 1650 as well, were clearly copied from one or several exemplars, the origin of both manuscripts need not give us any clue as to where, in the tenth century, the core of the corpus ultimately originated. By the eleventh century, when the glosses were entered in the manuscripts in

---

'Latin and Old English Aldhelm Glosses: a Direct Link in the Abingdon Group', in *Anglo-Saxon Glossography*, ed. Derolez, pp. 139–49, at 141–9. Goossens's original and his revised positions have come under vehement attack from S. Gwara, who offers a third, completely different explanation for the identical glosses in Brussels 1650 and Royal 6. B. VII; see Gwara, 'The Transmission of the "Digby" Corpus', pp. 152–64.

[29] See, for example, Gwara, 'Manuscripts of Aldhelm's *Prosa de Virginitate*', and *idem*, 'The Transmission of the "Digby" Corpus'; much of Gwara's argument is based on his unpublished Toronto dissertation.

[30] See 'The Transmission of the "Digby" Corpus', p. 143 and n. 21, and p. 167 (for Brussels 1650); but cf. below, p. 377, n. 157.

question, scholars in any of the intellectual centres of late Anglo-Saxon England may be credited with a keen interest in producing a copy of a densely glossed exemplar of the prose *De uirginitate*, irrespective of whether the glosses had their origin in that centre or had been obtained from elsewhere.

BRUSSELS 1650: THE LAYERS OF GLOSSES

If we now attempt to get somewhere near the presumed tenth-century origin of the Brussels corpus of glosses, we shall first have to consider the problem that the glosses were entered in the manuscript by several, though roughly contemporary, scribes during the first part of the eleventh century. Following Ker, Goossens distinguished five glossing hands in Brussels 1650, called by him A, B, C, CD and R respectively.[31] The alphabetical order indicates the assumed chronological sequence of these scribes. However, it is important to note that the scribes are not responsible each in turn for the glosses in successive portions of the text, but that they generally overlap in their work, that is to say that, for example, scribe CD went through and glossed the entire text of the prose *De uirginitate* after it had been glossed by scribes A and C, who, in their turn, had each gone through the whole text, providing glosses prior to CD. The last of the scribes (R) is negligible, since only a very few glosses were entered by him, and since moreover he does not seem to be readily distinguishable from scribe CD. Similarly, the amount of Old English glosses entered by scribes A and B is not high, scribe B occurring, moreover, only between 33r and 45r. The amount of Old English glosses entered by scribe C is higher, but in this case there is the serious problem of distinguishing his hand clearly from that of scribe CD. It is for this reason that Goossens named this scribe CD and not D, as would have been expected in an alphabetical sequence. CD entered the bulk of the Old English glosses (some 65 per cent).

In the discussion of verbal links between the Brussels glosses, the Royal Psalter and the Benedictine Rule in the following ch., I have not

---

[31] For discussion of the dates and relative chronology of these hands (building on Ker, *Catalogue*, pp. 6–7), their approximate share in the total of glosses and of the difficulties in distinguishing between them, see Goossens, *Old English Glosses*, pp. 42–52.

normally listed which hand entered the glosses in question. One of my reasons for this was the obvious difficulty in distinguishing between some of these hands. But there are other, more urgent grounds for considering the vast Brussels corpus of glosses as an entity, at least for the present discussion. All glossing hands in Brussels 1650 worked from an exemplar.[32] Evidence for this is furnished by the fact that the scribes of the glosses occasionally altered or corrected the text of the *De uirginitate* in Brussels 1650. For example, on 44r *secundos* had been originally left out and was supplied by scribe C. Or in the original reading *ab (s)celestissimi* (34v) *celestissimi* was underlined and the reading *ecclesiastico* (found in most other manuscripts) was written above it by scribe CD.[33] Evidence for the scribes entering their glosses into Brussels 1650 from a glossed exemplar of the *De uirginitate* is further furnished by numerous mistakes which could have arisen only in the process of copying from an exemplar, as well as by a mixture of forms from different dialects discernible in each of the glossing hands.[34] Furthermore, it is clear that the scribes of the Brussels glosses checked the glosses in their exemplars against those which they found already in Brussels 1650. This much emerges, for example, from corrections and additions made by them to glosses entered by their predecessors.[35] It is obvious therefore that, say, scribe C had in his exemplar glosses which had also been in the exemplar of the somewhat earlier scribes A and B (and which had already been entered by them). By the same token, scribe CD (the latest and most important of the four main hands) may well have had in his exemplar a substantial amount (or even most) of the materials contained in the exemplars of all his predecessors. It is reasonable then to assume that a scribe would have

---

[32] See Goossens, *Old English Glosses*, p. 32, n. 3, and pp. 42, 45–50, 134–6 and *passim*; cf. also Gwara, 'The Transmission of the "Digby" Corpus', pp. 161–3.

[33] Such corrections and additions by the scribes of the glosses are pointed out in the *apparatus criticus* of Goossens's edition. The examples quoted above occur on pp. 303.1 and 286.17 respectively in Ehwald's edition.

[34] For this mixture of dialect forms, see the comprehensive treatment of the phonology and morphology of the Brussels glosses by Goossens, *Old English Glosses*, pp. 54–139. The earlier work on the language of the Aldhelm glosses by K. Schiebel, *Die Sprache der altenglischen Glossen zu Aldhelms Schrift 'De Laude Virginitatis'* (Halle, 1907) has been completely superseded, since it treats the gloss material in an utterly uncritical fashion and since the Brussels glosses were by then not available in a reliable edition.

[35] See Gwara, 'The Transmission of the "Digby" Corpus', pp. 161–3, and Goossens, *Old English Glosses*, p. 45 and n. 5, and p. 51.

avoided duplicating a gloss which he had in his exemplar, but which he found already in Brussels 1650 when he entered his glosses there.[36] Such an assumption is of course most pertinent in the case of scribe CD. We simply cannot say that a gloss entered in hand C (or A or B) would not have been extant also in the exemplar of scribe CD, and would have been entered by him, had he not found it already in Brussels 1650 when he worked through that manuscript. On the other hand, we may be reasonably certain that scribes A, B and C did not have at their disposal the whole impressive range of CD's material.

Therefore, if verbal links between the Brussels glosses, the Royal Psalter and the Rule could be detected only among glosses entered by scribes A, B or C, it would be crucial to identify the gloss layer with which such verbal links existed, since in that case the vast CD corpus would have to be ruled out for a comparison. It is, however, just the gloss material entered by scribe CD which supplies the bulk of the verbal links between the three texts in question. The clear implication of this situation is that for the present discussion we will have to consider the evidence of *all* the Old English glosses in Brussels 1650. That the overwhelming majority of verbal ties which connect the Brussels glosses with the Psalter and the Rule are provided by the CD corpus, may be largely attributable to the fact that some 65 per cent of the Brussels glosses were entered by scribe CD. However, there is a further feature of the CD corpus which may explain the links between that corpus and the Psalter and the Rule. Walter Hofstetter has identified a high percentage of Winchester words among the Brussels glosses. These Winchester words were almost exclusively entered by scribe CD.[37] The implication is that the source on which CD drew (and which contained material extant also in the sources of scribes A, B and C) at some point must have undergone revision at a centre where Winchester usage was taught. Apparently, the sources on which scribes A, B and C drew had no such contacts with a centre practising Winchester usage, or, if they had, this must have been before that usage had been developed to any remarkable degree. The employment of numerous Winchester words obviously enhances the

---

[36] In a number of cases, however, duplication of a gloss stemming from different scribes does occur (see Goossens, *Old English Glosses*, pp. 30–1), which in turn serves to strengthen our argument.

[37] See Hofstetter, *Winchester und Sprachgebrauch*, pp. 129–39.

possibility that the origin of at least part of the CD glosses in Brussels 1650 should be sought in Bishop Æthelwold's school. But this conformity to Winchester usage also creates a problem. It is clear that the employment of a fully-fledged Winchester vocabulary (as it occurs in the CD glosses) is a phenomenon of the second generation of the Benedictine reform, that of Ælfric or the glossator of the Lambeth Psalter, for example. It is found neither in the Benedictine Rule nor in the Royal Psalter, although we have seen that both texts show unmistakable signs of a nascent Winchester usage. In other words, how confident may we be that at least part of the Brussels CD glosses originated as early as the mid-tenth century and might therefore be attributable to Æthelwold himself and scholars of his circle while, not yet burdened with the duties of his episcopate, he studied with them ('studiose legebat') 'catholicos quoque et nominatos ... auctores', the best-known Christian writers, as his pupil and biographer Wulfstan recorded many years later?[38] This question gains importance when we consider that the CD corpus does not appear in any glossed manuscript of the prose *De uirginitate* anterior to Brussels 1650 (where, we have seen, the glosses were entered only during the first half of the eleventh century).[39]

THE CLEOPATRA GLOSSARIES

Naturally, the verbal links which can be detected between the Rule, the Royal Psalter and the Brussels glosses are a strong pointer to an origin of all three texts in the same circle. There is, however, further material and irrefutable evidence for the existence of substantial portions of the CD glosses by the middle of the tenth century. Such evidence is provided by a text we have already had occasion to consider briefly, namely the third of the glossaries in Cleopatra A. iii, a manuscript written in the mid-tenth century, possibly at St Augustine's, Canterbury.[40] The Third Cleopatra

---

[38] See *Wulfstan: Life*, ch. 9 (p. 14).

[39] See, for example, Gwara ('The Transmission of the "Digby" Corpus', p. 152), who concludes his discussion of the CD glosses by stating: 'the CD corpus ostensibly copied from an exemplar, has no extant source'. He draws attention (*ibid.*) to scratched glosses (as yet unprinted) in three manuscripts which seem to be connected with the CD glosses. It should be noted, however, that scratched glosses (apart from many other difficulties involved in them) are notoriously difficult to date.

[40] See Ker, *Catalogue*, pp. 180–2 (no. 143); for the possible St Augustine's origin of

Glossary (Cleo III: 92r–117r) is a compilation of glosses (mainly Latin–Old English, but including some Latin–Latin entries as well) of Aldhelm's *De uirginitate*, both the prose and the metrical versions.[41] It consists of *glossae collectae*, that is, the glosses are copied out in the order in which they occur in the text. It is, therefore, a first-stage glossary, a compilation where the *lemmata* and their *interpretamenta* were drawn directly from a manuscript with interlinear glosses. We have seen (above, p. 140) that the very manuscript from which the compiler of Cleo III collected his glossed lemmata (or a very close congener of that manuscript) was laid under contribution by Byrhtferth for his *Vita S. Ecgwini* and his *Enchiridion*, at the turn of the millennium, and was subsequently lost.

Interestingly, a substantial portion of the glosses of Cleo III is also found in the first glossary in the same manuscript (Cleo I: 5r–75v). Here the material from Cleo III has been recast to form part of an a-glossary. In an a-glossary, all the lemmata beginning with the same letter are grouped together, but no sorting according to their second letters has been done.[42] In Cleo I (as in other a-order glossaries), under each letter in the alphabet, the lemmata drawn from a single source are copied out together in a group or batch in the order in which they occur in that source. This procedure permits us to conclude that the compiler of Cleo I worked systematically through the exemplar of *glossae collectae* from which Cleo

---

Cleopatra A. iii, see most recently Dumville, 'Square Minuscule' [*ASE* 23], pp. 137–9. On this manuscript and its third glossary, see also above, p. 140 and below, pp. 367–8.

[41] Cleo III is printed WW I, 485.21–535.11 (part of no. 12). The glosses to the prose version are WW I, 485.21–516.16; those to the metrical version, WW I, 516.19–535.11. There is also an edition of Cleo III in an unpublished dissertation by Quinn, 'The Minor Latin–Old English Glossaries'.

[42] Cleo I comprises the letters A to P. Although its entries are predominantly arranged in a-order, batches sorted according to the first two letters of the lemma do occur (ab-order); see Ker, *Catalogue*, pp. 180–1 (no. 143), and Goossens, *Old English Glosses*, pp. 14–15. The ab-order batches correspond to substantial parts of the Corpus Glossary (Cambridge, Corpus Christi College 144, s. ix$^{2/4}$, perhaps from St Augustine's Canterbury). Approximately half of the Old English glosses in Corpus occur also in Cleo I; see, for example, Lübke, 'Über verwandtschaftliche Beziehungen', pp. 393–6, and Pheifer, *Épinal–Erfurt Glossary*, pp. xxxi–xxxii. Cleo I is printed WW I, 338.1–473.2 (no. 11). There is also an edition in an unpublished dissertation by Stryker, 'Latin–Old English Glossary'.

III was copied,[43] sorting its lemmata into alphabetical order (after their first letter only) and incorporating them in batches into his larger compilation, which comprised material drawn from other sources as well.[44] Apart from these Aldhelm batches taken from Cleo III, under each letter of the alphabet there are two further substantial batches from Aldhelm's works (principally the prose *De uirginitate*) which do not seem to correspond to any surviving Aldhelm glosses.[45] (It is reasonable to assume that these batches, like the ones deriving from Cleo III, were ultimately drawn from glossed manuscripts of Aldhelm's works, manuscripts which have since been lost.) As a result, Cleo I is to a large extent an Aldhelm glossary; some 2100 of its approximately 5000 lemmata are drawn from his works.[46] Further research on the Cleopatra glossaries and their relationships with extant glossed manuscripts of Aldhelm's works is an urgent desideratum. But even from a very cursory assessment of their evidence it becomes clear that by the mid-tenth century, a number of distinct sets of vernacular glosses must have been in existence and were drawn on by the compilers of the Cleopatra glossaries. Whether such sets were available in the form of glossed manuscripts of the *De uirginitate* or of *glossae collectae* or of a-order glossaries we cannot say.

We may now return to the question of what evidence concerning the origin of the CD corpus in Brussels 1650 is provided by Cleo III. Arthur Napier drew attention already to a number of lemmata and *interpretamenta* which the glosses in Digby 146 (which he printed as *OEG*, no. 1) and those in Brussels 1650 (from which the Digby glosses were copied) have in common with the Cleopatra glossaries.[47] (Napier did not distinguish in any way between the two glossaries, Cleo I and III.) Since the Old

---

[43] We probably should rule out the possibility that it was Cleo III as transmitted in Cotton Cleopatra A. iii itself which served as the source for the compiler of Cleo I, since Cleo I comes first in the manuscript. This implies that at least one further copy of the *glossae collectae* represented in Cleo III must have existed.

[44] Cleo I contains some 5000 lemmata. Apart from the works of Aldhelm, these are drawn principally from the Bible, Isidore's *Etymologiae*, Orosius and Gildas (*De excidio Britanniae*); cf. Stryker, 'Latin–Old English Glossary', pp. 11–13. Many of these glosses occur also in the Corpus Glossary (see above, n. 42).

[45] See Lübke, 'Über verwandtschaftliche Beziehungen', pp. 399–401, and Stryker, 'Latin–Old English Glossary', pp. 11–12. There are additional small batches and isolated Aldhelm glosses appearing randomly among material drawn from other sources.

[46] See Stryker, 'Latin–Old English Glossary', p. 11.   [47] See *OEG*, p. xxvi.

English Digby glosses were almost all copied from the Brussels manuscript by a single scribe,[48] and since at that time no reliable edition of the Brussels glosses existed, it follows that Napier had no information concerning the different strata of glosses in Brussels 1650, and hence could not pronounce on the question in which of these strata the correspondences with the Cleopatra glossaries were to be found. Napier did not give his estimate of the overall number of glosses common to Brussels 1650 (and Digby 146) and the Cleopatra glossaries. He adduced seven examples, six of which pertain to glosses in Cleo III (which subsequently were copied from there into Cleo I).[49] Goossens, referring to Napier, speaks of 'a few' glosses which Brussels 1650 has in common with the Cleopatra glossaries.[50] Hofstetter has one further gloss shared by Cleo III and Brussels 1650.[51] All this creates the impression that the identical glosses common to Cleo III and Brussels 1650 are few and far between.

It should be stressed again that the details of the links between Cleo III and Brussels 1650 await closer scrutiny; but even a random collation of fifty glosses in Cleo III against their counterparts in Brussels 1650 reveals affinities which hitherto do not seem to have been suspected. The following figures result from a collation from the first fifty entries in Cleo III (WW 485.21–487.2) with the corresponding glosses in Brussels 1650 (G 42–218). The glosses translate or explain lemmata from a passage of the *De uirginitate* spanning p. 229.15 to p. 232.2 in Ehwald's edition. Such a comparison immediately reveals that the text in the Brussels manuscript is much more densely glossed: 176 lemmata in Brussels 1650 against 50 in Cleo III are provided with *interpretamenta*. If we recall that in Brussels 1650 a lemma is frequently glossed by several Old English or Latin words, whereas such multiple glossing only occurs very sporadically in Cleo III, the difference in the density of glossing becomes even more apparent. Such a difference in the density of glossing in the passage under inspection here is borne out by the total number of glosses in both texts: 974 lemmata from the *De uirginitate* are glossed in Cleo III (the number of *interpretamenta* being only slightly higher through multiple glossing), whereas some 6000 glosses occur in Brussels 1650.

The details from the sample collation are as follows: five of the fifty

---

[48] See Ker, *Catalogue*, pp. 382–3 (no. 320).   [49] See *OEG*, p. xxvi.

[50] See Goossens, *Old English Glosses*, p. 31.

[51] See Hofstetter, *Winchester und Sprachgebrauch*, p. 133.

glosses in Cleo III correspond to glosses in Brussels 1650 entered by scribe A; cf., for example, WW 486.11: *striden{t}e*: *breht{m}ende*, G 92: *bearhtmiendum* (for *breahtmiendum*) A; or WW 486.26: *algosis*: *ðæm warihtum*, G 128: *warihtum* A.

Fourteen of the fifty glosses in Cleo III are identical with glosses in Brussels 1650 entered by scribe CD; cf., for example, WW 485.30: *strenua*: *þa strangan oððe foremihtiglice*, G 69: *þa stra{n}gan ł foremihti* CD; or WW 486.34: *caltarum*: *clafrena*, G 193: *clæfre* CD. With these shared glosses, the CD *interpretamentum* is often fuller, providing additional glosses, as in WW 485.23: *gimnosophistas*: *plegmen*, G 54: *leorneres ł plegmen* CD.

For nine of the fifty lemmata, Cleo III has a gloss which is similar to (though not identical with) the corresponding Brussels gloss entered by scribe CD; cf., for example, WW 486.2: *cum emulo*: *mid wiðerweardum*, G 70: *mid wiþerwurdnessa* CD, or WW 486.19: *classicis*: *ðæm sciplicum*, G 114: *sciplicum herium* CD.

For eighteen of the fifty lemmata, the glosses in Cleo III are completely different from those in Brussels 1650; cf., for example, WW 485.28: *nauiter*: *hrædlice*, G 66: *agiliter, uelociter* A; *alacriter, sprindlice ł caflice* CD, or WW 486.17: *facetus*: *linguosus*, G 106: *facundus, getincge* CD.

In four of the fifty cases under inspection, a lemma bears a gloss in Cleo III, but is not glossed in Brussels 1650; cf., for example, WW 486.1: *anthletarum* [*sic*]: *cempena*, or WW 486.15: *calcaribus*: *spurum*.

In sum, even from a sample collation such as the foregoing, it can be established beyond reasonable doubt that Cleo III and the interlinear glosses in Brussels 1650 are intimately related: more than half of the glosses in Cleo III are identical with, or at least similar to, glosses in Brussels 1650. What is of utmost importance for our purposes is that through the glosses in Cleo III we have incontestable manuscript evidence that a substantial portion of the massive corpus of vernacular glosses entered in Brussels 1650 by scribe CD must have been in existence by no later than the middle of the tenth century, when Cleopatra A. iii was written. We should also note, however, that more than one third of our sample glosses in Cleo III have no links whatsoever with the Brussels glosses. This could (but need not) confirm the possibility considered in connection with the three distinct Aldhelm batches in Cleo I, namely that several sets of interlinear or marginal glosses to the prose *De uirginitate* might have circulated as early as *c.* 950. One would accordingly have to assume that by that time two (or more) of such sets were already conflated in the interlinear glosses in one manuscript, and that it was from such a conflated manuscript that Cleo III was compiled. Alternatively, one might venture the hypothesis that the glosses in Cleo III not now found in Brussels 1650 once belonged to the same corpus as those shared by Cleo III and Brussels 1650, but that they were lost or jettisoned in the course of transmission and revision of that corpus.

For the purposes of establishing the age and ancestry of individual components of the Brussels glosses, it is important to note that they also contain *interpretamenta* which correspond to glosses found in Cleo I only (but not in Cleo III), where they occur in Aldhelm batches which were not drawn from Cleo III. A few examples would be: G 3469/70: *callositas*: *wearrihtnys* C, *wærihtnys* CD = WW 372.3: *wearrihtnes*; G 4241: *adolesceret*: *wlancude* C, *ic wlancige* CD (glossing the same lemma, which is repeated by CD in the margin as *adolesco*) = WW 343.9: *wlancode*; or G 764: *ambronibus*: *gifrum* A = WW 339.11: *gifrum*.[52]

In short, it will have emerged even from these few and preliminary remarks that the relationship of both Cleopatra glossaries with the vernacular glosses in Brussels 1650 would merit close attention by Old English philologists.

THE CORPUS GLOSSARY

Of equal interest as regards the ancestry of the glosses in Brussels 1650 are a number of *interpretamenta* which the Brussels glosses share with the Corpus Glossary (Cambridge, Corpus Christi College 144, s. x$^{2/4}$, perhaps from St Augustine's, Canterbury).[53] However, so far, no examples seem to have been detected where the gloss in question occurs in the Corpus Glossary only, and not in either Cleo I or Cleo III (or both) as well, a situation which does not appear to have been taken into account whenever

---

[52] For *wearrihtnes*, see Napier, *OEG*, p. xxvi; for *wlancude*, see Hofstetter, *Winchester und Sprachgebrauch*, p. 133. Note in passing that in G 3469/70 and 4241, scribe CD repeats (in a somewhat modified form) the *interpretamentum* entered already by scribe C, thereby confirming the suspicion that CD's exemplar contained material which was extant also in the exemplar of scribe C.

[53] The Corpus Glossary is printed by Hessels, *An Eighth-Century Latin–Anglo-Saxon Glossary*, as well as by W. M. Lindsay, *The Corpus Glossary* (Cambridge, 1921); there is a facsimile edition by Bischoff *et al.*, *The Épinal, Erfurt, Werden and Corpus Glossaries*.

scholars have referred to such links between the Brussels glosses and the Corpus Glossary.[54] (It will be recalled that Cleo I corresponds in substantial batches to the Corpus Glossary.)[55] The Corpus Glossary comprises a considerable amount of material which can be traced to Aldhelm's works.[56] A few examples of such glosses shared between Brussels 1650, Corpus and one (or both) of the Cleopatra glossaries would be:

G 3817: *armonia: swinsung* CD; WW 342.39 (Cleo I): *swinsunge* (Cleo III (WW 520.13) has *armonia: swinsunge* as a gloss to a lemma in the *Carmen de uirginitate*); Corpus (A 720):[57] *armonia: suinsung*.

G 5121 *redimiculum: cynewiððan*, 'head-band', C; WW 513.25 (Cleo III): *cy{n}ewiððan* (for [n], the manuscript reads *r*); Corpus (R 186): *ridimiculae: cynewiððan*.

G 1128: *dracontia: gimroder*, 'precious stone', A; WW 385.40 (Cleo I) and WW 491.16 (Cleo III): *gimroder*; Corpus (D 364): *dracontia: gimro dicitur*.

G 2280: *pro rostris: heahseldum*, 'throne', A; WW 470.10 (Cleo I): *hehseldum*; Corpus (P 741): *prorostris: haehsedlum*.[58]

There can be little doubt that more such correspondences would come to light through a systematic comparison of the Brussels glosses and the Corpus Glossary. As long as no glosses have been detected which are shared by Brussels 1650 and the Corpus Glossary alone – to the exclusion of Cleo I or Cleo III – it is not altogether clear how such correspondences should be explained. The most economical explanation would be that the Corpus glosses found their way into Brussels 1650 via older glossed manuscripts of the prose *De uirginitate*. (Note, however, that such an explanation would imply the survival of glossed Aldhelm manuscripts from the pre-Viking age into the tenth century.) But naturally it cannot be ruled out that at some point in the tenth century the compilers of the

---

[54] See, for example, Napier, *OEG*, p. xxvi, Goossens, *Old English Glosses*, p. 13, n. 4, and p. 31, and Hofstetter, *Winchester und Sprachgebrauch*, pp. 134–5.

[55] See above, p. 150, n. 42.

[56] See W. M. Lindsay, *The Corpus, Épinal, Erfurt and Leyden Glossaries* (Oxford, 1921), pp. 97–105, and Pheifer, *Épinal–Erfurt Glossary*, pp. lv–lvii. See below, n. 64, for the possibility (propounded by Lindsay for many of the 'Aldhelm lemmata' in Corpus) that Aldhelm himself may have been indebted to glossaries.

[57] Corpus is quoted after the numbering in Hessel's edition.

[58] For *heahseldum*, see Napier, *OEG*, p. xxvi; for *cynewiððan*, see Hofstetter, *Winchester und Sprachgebrauch*, pp. 134–5.

core of the Brussels glosses occasionally drew on a glossary in a- (or ab-) order, closely related to the Corpus Glossary.[59] In any event, it is clear that among the components of the Brussels glosses there is material which can be traced back to the study and glossing of Aldhelm in the pre-Viking age.

The likelihood is that the compilers of the Brussels glosses had specific reasons whenever they adopted these older glosses from wherever they may have found them. Of the examples quoted above, *heahseld*, *gimrodor* and *cynewiðð* are exceedingly rare words: they are in fact recherché terms with a distinctly archaic and poetic flair. In short, they had everything to recommend them to the practitioners of the hermeneutic style. Of special interest are *gimrodor* and *cynewiðð*. *Cynewiðð* (compounded of *cyne-* 'royal' and *wiðð* 'cord, band') is an extremely old *interpretamentum* for Latin lemmata denoting a precious head-band (*redimiculum* and *murenula*). Its earliest occurrence is in an epitome of Isidore's *Etymologiae*. This epitome was excerpted from a manuscript (now lost) of the *Etymologiae* which must have been provided with a certain amount of interlinear or marginal glosses and some of these glosses were copied into the epitome together with their Latin lemmata (in our case *murenulae*).[60] As Michael Lapidge has shown, the Old English glosses copied from the lost manuscript of the *Etymologiae* can be dated to *c.* 700 for various reasons, notably on philological grounds and because the compiler of the Épinal–Erfurt glossary also drew occasionally on this same lost manuscript of the *Etymologiae*.[61] (The earlier of the two surviving manuscripts of the Épinal–Erfurt glossary, now Épinal, Bibliothèque Municipale, 72, was written in England *c.* 700.)

As we have seen (above, pp. 98–104) in our examination of the terms *hropgierela* and *wuldorbeag*, there are grounds for suspecting that, between them, the Royal Psalter and the Benedictine Rule account for the origin of the Winchester words for *corona* and *coronare* in a metaphorical sense.

---

[59] The Corpus Glossary itself cannot have been drawn on by the compilers of the Brussels glosses as is clear from the erroneous or truncated forms *hæhsedlum* and *gimro* in Corpus (see above).

[60] For the intellectual milieu in which the epitome was presumably produced, see below, p. 173, n. 95.

[61] See Lapidge, 'Old English Glossography', pp. 173–4, and *idem*, 'An Isidorian Epitome', pp. 188–93; see also Hofstetter, *Winchester und Sprachgebrauch*, pp. 134–5, for the few (and interdependent) occurrences of *cynewiðð* in later glosses.

We have further noted that the exceedingly rare word *cyninggierela*, occurring for a metaphorical tiara in Cleo III (WW 518.24), may have served as a source of inspiration for the coinage of the new terms, particularly for the formation of *hropgierela*. This inference gains plausibility now that we have uncovered close links between Cleo III and the Brussels glosses, which in their turn show striking similarities in usage with the Royal Psalter and the Rule. With *cynewippe* in the Brussels glosses, an exceptionally rare word which ultimately derives from one of the oldest layers of vernacular glosses, and which is used in the Brussels glosses in a distinctly poetic context,[62] we have perhaps another cornerstone for the formation of the Winchester terminology for *corona*. In this connection it may be relevant to note that, aside from the single occurrence of *cynewippe*, the Brussels glosses employ Winchester's *wuldorbeag* for a metaphorical *corona* on four occasions.[63]

In a similar fashion, the adoption of *gimroder* in the Brussels glosses from older gloss material may also be related to the nascent Winchester terminology for *corona*. *Gimroder* (*gimrodor* in the Cleopatra glossaries) glosses *dracontia*, a lemma occurring only once in the prose *De uirginitate* (Ehwald, p. 244.22) and denoting there 'a precious stone' in a general sense, not, as is usual, 'dracontites' (a stone from the head of a dragon). Arguably, all eight occurrences of Old English *gimrodor* are related to this Aldhelmian lemma, either directly as glosses for that lemma or indirectly by way of occurring in a glossary from which Aldhelm himself may have culled some items of his vocabulary.[64] In terms of word-formation *gimrodor* is not entirely clear. Its second element could be (as the spelling suggests) *rodor* 'sky, heaven'. In that case, one of the semantic components of *rodor*, either 'brightness' or 'exquisiteness', would have led to its use as

---

[62] In the *De uirginitate* the lemma (*redimiculum*) occurs in a quotation from Vergil (*Aen.* IX. 614); cf. *Aldhelmi Opera*, ed. Ehwald, p. 316.22.

[63] See Hofstetter, *Winchester und Sprachgebrauch*, p. 129.

[64] Such a relation might obtain for the entry *dracontia: gimrodr* in the Erfurt Glossary (Erfurt I, spelled there <grimrodr>); see Pheifer, *Épinal–Erfurt Glossary*, no. 345a. It is thought that in the case of Aldhelmian lemmata occurring in the Épinal-Erfurt Glossary, it was Aldhelm who borrowed from the archetype of that glossary (and not *vice versa*). This archetype was, perhaps, compiled in his school at Malmesbury; cf. Pheifer, *ibid.*, pp. lvi–lvii. One wonders whether the unusual sense in which Aldhelm employs *dracontia* (namely as a generic term and not as a designation for a specific gem) and the Old English *interpretamentum* for *dracontia* in Erfurt I (namely *gimrodor* meaning 'splendid gem') might somehow be connected.

157

a determinatum in a compound, and *gimrodor* would accordingly mean 'bright gem' or 'exquisite gem'.

An attractive alternative explanation has been suggested by H. D. Meritt.[65] In his view, *rodor* is an idiosyncratic spelling for *hroðor*, a poetic word denoting 'joy', but also 'glory, splendour'; an original *gimhroðor* would accordingly mean 'gem splendour'. In that case, there would be a clear semantic and etymological link between *gimroder* in the Brussels glosses, a rare and exotic word, culled from earlier gloss material, and *hroþgierela*, the recherché *hapax legomenon* coined by the Royal Glossator, since *hroþ* 'fame, praise, victory' is a close and rare cognate of poetic *hroþor*. The case for such a link becomes even more pressing if we recall that the *corona* in ps. XX.4 which is translated by *hroþgierela* is made *de lapide pretioso*. But even if the second element of *gimrodor* is, after all, *rodor* 'heaven' (as the various scribes apparently took it to be) that compound denoting a resplendent gem is incontestably of a similar flamboyant type as the Royal Glossator's *hroþgierela*.

From examples such as *gimrodor* and *cynewiððe* it will have become clear that it would be worthwhile assembling the material in the Brussels glosses which was demonstrably drawn from older sources, and assessing it in terms of word-formation and stylistic register. A careful study of such older gloss material may reveal what attracted the tenth-century compilers in the work of their predecessors, thereby allowing us an intriguing glimpse of their stylistic predilections.

THE VOCABULARY OF THE BRUSSELS GLOSSES

There is some further confirmation for the suspicion that glosses such as *gimroder*, *cynewiððe* or *heahseld* in Brussels 1650 were adopted from older gloss material, because, by their eccentricity and archaic flavour, they captured the interest of the original compilers of the Brussels corpus, and that therefore these compilers reveal the same flair for recherché vocabulary in the vernacular which we have encountered in the Royal Psalter and to some extent in the Rule. Such confirmation is furnished by the very nature of many of the Brussels glosses themselves. Characteristically, aspects of the textual affiliations of the Brussels glosses, as well as of their phonology and morphology, have been treated in some detail, but so far

---

[65] See Meritt, *Fact and Lore*, pp. 72–3 (no. 3 A 17).

scarcely any attention has been given to the performance of the glossators, to their intellectual milieu and to the question of whether they were attempting to imitate Aldhelm's exuberantly rich and eccentric vocabulary.[66] After all, Aldhelm is not an easy author to gloss in any language, let alone in one still in its intellectual infancy. The following brief explorations of a few examples will enable us to form some picture of the glossators' scholarly methods, their creativity and versatility when applying the resources of their native language to Aldhelm's vocabulary. The examples were singled out almost at random from among the large number of glosses which catch the eye of even the cursory reader, either by their perfection and elegance in rendering a difficult lemma, or by their striking and 'hermeneutic' character as items of the Old English vocabulary. Practically all the examples turned out to be exceedingly rare words, often occurring only in the Brussels corpus and dependent glosses.

It will be seen that all the scribes contributed to our sample glosses, CD's contribution being of course the most important one. As opposed to my practice in the following ch., I have recorded in each case which of the glosses were entered by which scribe. I have done so principally with the aim of demonstrating that it is not difficult to find examples where it is reasonable to assume that a scribe had in the exemplar from which he was copying a gloss which he found already entered in Brussels 1650 by one of his predecessors and that therefore he refrained from duplicating the gloss in question. Such interfaces between the layers of glosses will serve to bear out the hypothesis advanced above (p. 148) that we would get a distorted picture of the Brussels glosses by completely taking apart the

[66] See above, pp. 142–6, for textual criticism and p. 147, n. 34, for work on the phonology and morphology of the glosses. This situation has not been decisively remedied in the most recent edition of the Old English glosses in a manuscript closely dependent on Brussels 1650 by M. Richter, *Die altenglischen Glossen zu Aldhelms 'De laudibus virginitatis' in der Handschrift BL, Royal 6 B. VII* (Munich, 1996). This edition (aside from the traditional concerns of Old English Aldhelm philology) meticulously tabulates and briefly comments on what is called the 'function of the glosses', that is whether they elucidate the grammar or the meaning of a lemma, whether they make an accurate translation of the lemma or are at least contextually adequate and so on (see pp. liv–lxi and *apparatus criticus, passim*), but scarcely a word is said about the nature and quality of these glosses and their position within the Old English lexicon. In a recent 'philological commentary' on a few Old English Aldhelm glosses (*Neuphilologische Mitteilungen* 95 (1994), 267–71) even traditional philology has reached a nadir comparable to the standard of Latin at Canterbury in the early 870s.

different layers and examining the glosses layer by layer, concentrating on one stratum at a time. Notwithstanding their long transmissional history, for an assessment of their Old English vocabulary, the Brussels glosses (with due caution and circumspection) must be treated as a single and coherent corpus.

Historiographus: wyrdwritere ('a writer of fate or destiny')
Chronographus: tidwritere ('a writer about times')

Wyrdwritere is unique among our examples in that it must have gained some currency after it had arguably been coined by the glossators of the Brussels corpus. Interestingly, it captured the interest of two authors stylistically as far apart as Ælfric (seven occurrences) and Byrhtferth (one occurrence). Otherwise, aside from glosses dependent on Brussels 1650, the word is not attested in Old English literature.[67] *Historiographus* 'historiographer' occurs as a lemma three times; each time it is glossed by *wyrdwritere* (G 287, 1941 and 2586, twice spelled *wurdwritere*; all glosses by CD, but in 287, in addition to CD's *wyrdwritere*, there is a second gloss *wyrdwritere*, probably by A, which has partly been erased). The degree of deliberateness which went into the choice (and probably coinage) of *wyrdwritere* as an *interpretamentum* emerges not only from the consistency with which it is employed to gloss *historiographus*; the deliberateness can also be gleaned from the fact that the one occurrence each of the adjective *historicus* and the adverb *historialiter* (both meaning 'historical') are glossed by *gewyrdelic* (G 2929, spelled *gewurdelic*; CD) and *gewyrdelice* (G 4141 C) respectively, that is, by derivatives of the noun *wyrd*, the determinant in *wyrdwritere*.[68] On the other hand, for the four occurrences of *historia* in

---

[67] Note that I have on no occasion counted such dependent glosses as separate occurrences of an Old English word.

[68] Note that in 4141 scribe C repeated lemma and gloss in the margin. Such repetitions of lemmata and *interpretamenta* (in the case of nouns often in the nom. sg., in that of verbs in the infinitive) are made frequently by scribe C. They were, presumably, preparatory to an eventual extraction of lemmata and *interpretamenta* from the manuscript for a compilation of *glossae collectae*. These marginal glosses were first printed and discussed by R. Derolez, 'Zu den Brüsseler Aldhelmglossen', *Anglia* 74 (1956), 153–80; see also Goossens, *Old English Glosses*, pp. 30–1 and 47–8. In 4141, C's repetition shows that C attached enough importance and authority to the highly unusual *interpretamentum gewyrdelic* for *historialiter* to prepare its incorporation in a first-stage glossary.

the *De uirginitate* which are glossed in Brussels 1650, the common noun *gerecenes* 'narrative' is used (G 281, 1784, 2234 and 2802; once (2234) in a doublet together with *racu* 'account, narrative'; all glosses entered by CD). What at first sight seems to invalidate a hypothesis of a deliberate and consistent employment of formations with *wyrd* for the Latin word-family *historia*, becomes wholly consonant with the evidence revealed thus far, when we consider these four occurrences of *historia* in their context. They all refer, not to 'history' in any abstract sense such as the history of a certain race, but rather to a 'story', a narrative account, a written source. Thus on two occasions (G 2234 and 2802) the reference is to passages from Rufinus's Latin translation of Eusebius's *Ecclesiastical History*. Such an attempt to distinguish the principal senses of a Latin word by the choice of different Old English lexemes is distinctly reminiscent of a similar tendency in the Winchester terminology for *corona* and *ecclesia*.[69]

Old English *wyrd* 'fate, destiny' is a perfect gloss for *historia* in an abstract sense, though it is in no way an exact semantic or morphological translation of *historia* (Greek ἱστορία originally meaning 'knowledge, lore'). *Wyrd* denotes an important mental concept in the Anglo-Saxon thoughtworld, and the fact that it frequently occurs in poetry and in King Alfred's translation of Boethius, will have recommended its use in a freshly coined compound to translate *historiographus*. Furthermore, the internal alliteration in *wyrdwritere* will not have gone unnoticed by the glossators. On the assumption that the glossators not infrequently appear to have had resort to Isidore's *Etymologiae* (see below), one wonders whether the equation of *historia* and *wyrd* and hence the compound *wyrdwritere* might not have been prompted by a sentence in Isidore's lengthy explanation of what *historia* is: 'Nam historiae sunt res uerae quae factae sunt'.[70] It is the verb in this sentence which could have inspired the coinage *wyrdwritere*. *Factae sunt* would best be translated here by a form of Old English *weorþan*, and *wyrd* is a derivative of this Old English verb.[71] Against such an assumption one might argue that the glossators did not have at their disposal the research tools of modern philologists, and might therefore not have been aware of the etymological link

---

[69] See above, pp. 98–104 and 104–13.

[70] 'For *historiae* are true events which happened'. For Isidore's explanation of *historia*, see *Etymologiae* I. xli–xliv; the quotation is at I. xliv. 5.

[71] See Holthausen, *Altenglisches etymologisches Wörterbuch*, s. v. *(ge)wyrd*.

between *weorþan* and *wyrd*. But, as we have seen in the case of the Royal Glossator, the practitioners of the hermeneutic style were exceedingly responsive to sound patterns relating different words, and a similarity between *wyrd* and *wurdon* etc. (the preterite forms of *weorþan*) would have been easily recognizable. (Note that in the Aldhelm glosses, *wyrd* is spelled <wurd> several times. Judging from the Middle English evidence, this is no mere orthographic variant; it rather represents an Old English (esp. West Saxon) sound change /wyr/ > /wur/, dated *c.* 1000. Note also that /weor/, as in *weorþan*, seems to have developed to /wur/ as early as *c.* 900.)[72]

In close proximity to *historiographus* in G 287, and used by way of lexical variation, is the unique occurrence in the *De uirginitate* of *chronographus* 'chronicler' (G 289), a word not widely current in Anglo-Latin literature.[73] The lemma *chronographorum* is first paraphrased in Latin as *temporum scriptorum* (A) and then translated into Old English as *tydwritera* (CD), a compound not perhaps as striking as *wyrdwritere*, but an adequate and idiomatic loan translation. It was apparently coined for this rare Aldhelmian lemma; it occurs nowhere else in Old English literature. (Its four attestations are all interdependent glosses to the same lemma.) Its existence by the mid-tenth century is guaranteed by its occurrence in both Cleopatra glossaries.[74] The close similarity between *tydwritere* and *wyrdwritere* might suggest that *wyrdwritere*, too, was coined at some point early on in the development of the Brussels corpus. By the same token, *tydwritere* occurring side by side with *wyrdwritere* may indicate that the glossators somehow aimed to emulate in their Old English glosses Aldhelm's penchant for lexical variation.

Several points emerge from a consideration of our first two examples for striking coinages in the Brussels glosses: first, the glossators did not set about their work in a haphazard or incompetent way. They would therefore deserve a systematic and competent assessment by modern scholars. For such a serious assessment, all occurrences of a lemma and its

---

[72] See Luick, *Historische Grammatik*, § 286, SB, §§ 113 and 118, and Campbell, §§ 320–2. For the Middle English evidence, see Luick, § 286, n. 3, and Campbell § 324.

[73] *Chronographus* captured the interest of Byrhtferth, once again. He employs it on one occasion, in a passage with verbal echoes of the Aldhelmian sentence in question; see *Enchiridion*, ed. Baker and Lapidge, p. 375, and cf. the glossary of rare Latin words, *ibid.*, p. 474. The Aldhelmian passage is p. 232.21–3 in Ehwald's edition.

[74] See WW 487.13 (Cleo III) and WW 370.40 (Cleo I).

glosses would have to be considered. Second, it will often be necessary to consider as well the specific context in which a lemma and its gloss occur. Third, the glossators' predilection for translating members of a Latin word-family by words which are cognates in Old English would merit attention, as would the possibility that standard reference works such as the *Etymologiae* were laid under contribution by the glossators. And fourth, the fact that in the copying of the *wyrd* glosses (so closely interlinked) no less than three scribes were involved points unmistakably to an amount of overlapping material (awaiting more precise definition) in the exemplars from which these scribes were copying.

Urbanitatis disertudo: burhspæc ('elegant speech, courtly speech', *lit.*
'speech which is used in a *burh*')

Like *tidwritere*, this remarkable coinage (G 42, entered by CD) belongs to the stratum of the Brussels glosses which was demonstrably in existence by the mid-tenth century: *burhspræc*, too, occurs in the Third Cleopatra Glossary (WW 485.22). Otherwise, the word is not attested in Old English. Because *burhsp(r)æc*[75] is so unusual and because the Latin lemmata it translates are clearly discernible in the compound, a first superficial glance at the word might prompt one to group it with those numerous still-born loan renditions which no Anglo-Saxon would ever have been able to understand without a sound knowledge of Latin (and many of which were coined, perhaps, for no other purpose than that of clarifying the morphological and semantic structure of the lemma they translated). But *burh* 'fort, castle, walled town' is no exact translation of *urbanitas* 'urbanity' and *spræc* 'speech' renders *disertudo* 'eloquence' only in a very general way. Furthermore, a host of additional glosses (Latin and Old English) which surround the Latin lemmata shows clearly that the glossators had understood the Latin correctly and that much attention had been lavished on its interpretation and hence, presumably, on the coinage of this specific gloss, *burhspræc*. Apart from *burhspræc*, the two Latin words bear the following glosses:[76] *urbanitatis: eloquentiae* (A),

[75] Loss of *r* in *sprecan* 'to speak' or *spræc* 'speech' is generally considered a feature of Late Old English, but there are grounds for believing that such forms were current in spoken English much earlier; see Gretsch, 'The Language of the "Fonthill Letter"', pp. 67–8.

[76] Because of the numerous glosses accompanying the two lemmata (*urbanitatis dissertu-*

loquela (CD), *gleawnysse* ('prudence, skill', CD); *dissertudinem*: *enarrationem* (A), *gleawnesse* (A; note that, positioned over *urbanitatis*, CD repeats this gloss, entered here by A), *prudentiam* (CD), *getincnesse* ('eloquence, skill', CD).

All this gives us reason to believe that *burhspræc* furnishes valuable evidence that some notion of what is called 'register' by modern linguists must have existed by the mid-tenth century with regard to the English language. A notion of stylistic register must have been well-established in Anglo-Saxon England as can be clearly seen from the diction of Old English verse, so utterly distinct from that of prose. But there must have been an awareness of social register as well. An Old English compound *burhspræc* makes sense only if the glossators could rely on a fairly widespread understanding among educated speakers of English that there is a noticeable difference between the speech of (educated) inhabitants of a *burh* and (say) the utterances of the peasant population or the discourse of members of clerical and monastic communities. This notion of social register in language enabled the glossators to coin a compound more powerful than Aldhelm's *urbanitatis disertudo*. For a determinant of this compound they chose, not an abstract noun to render *urbanitas* 'urbanity',[77] but the concrete substantive *burh*, thereby enhancing the metaphorical quality of the Old English *interpretamentum* as well as making it less redundant than the Latin phrase (both *disertudo* and *urbanitas* can denote 'eloquence' or 'elegant, sophisticated speech'). Interestingly, among the Old English words which would have been eligible to translate *urbs*, it was *burh* on which the glossators' choice fell, and not *ceaster* nor *tun*. It is tempting to think that they had in mind the inhabitants of, say, a royal vill conversing in the elegant and sophisticated language to which Aldhelm makes reference.

---

dinem), and because both lemmata are linked in a compound-like relation, it is not always certain, from the position of a gloss, which lemma that gloss was meant to interpret. However, from the position of *burhspæce* in the manuscript it becomes fairly clear that it was meant to gloss both words: it is entered above the line, between the two lemmata.

[77] For example *getyngness*, appearing as one of the supplementary glosses (see above), would have been a potential choice.

The influence of Isidore's 'Etymologiae'

We have already had reason to suspect that an etymological explanation provided by Isidore may have influenced the formation of *wyrdwritere* to render *historiographus*. There can be little doubt that, on closer inspection, a substantial amount of the Brussels glosses would reveal such Isidorian influence. In any event, from our (randomly chosen) examples it would appear that the glossators frequently resorted to the *Etymologiae*.

Dialectica: flitcræft

Dialectica (as part of the *trivium*) occurs once as a lemma in the Brussels corpus. It is glossed by *flitcræft* (G 3015, by C); this is a *hapax legomenon* compounded of *flit* 'dispute' and *cræft* 'art, science'. Its formation may well have been inspired by Isidore's explanation according to which *dialectica* through '*most subtle disputations* distinguishes between the things which are true and those which are not' ('disputationibus subtilissimis uera secernit a falsis', *Etym.* I. ii. 1). *Flitcræft* may be a *hapax legomenon*, but the compound is not an isolated *ad hoc* formation in the Brussels corpus. The three occurrences of the adjective *dialecticus* (all referring to the academic discipline) are translated by compounds with *flit*, on two occasions by *flitful* (G 3116 and 3247, both by CD) and once by *flitcræftlic* (G 3101, by CD). Of these, *flitcræftlic* is of special interest for two reasons: first, being a derivative of the noun *flitcræft*, it presupposes that an equation of *dialectica* and *flitcræft* had been established in some measure (in spite of *flitcræft* being attested only once). Secondly, *flitcræftlic*, the derivative, is entered by CD, *flitcræft* by C, which permits us, once again, to suspect that *flitcræft* was extant as well in the exemplar from which CD copied out his glosses, but that he refrained from duplicating a gloss which he found already entered in Brussels 1650 by one of his predecessors.

Both adjectives, *flitcræftlic* and *flitful*, occur only here, and (*flitful* only) in dependent glosses. Since Old English *flit* normally occurs in a prefixed form as *geflit*, it is, presumably, significant that the glossators coined all their *flit* compounds from the unprefixed form. However, precisely what significance should be attached to such omission of the prefix is impossible to say. It may have been to distinguish these coinages from established Old English words (*geflit* and derivatives) denoting 'strife, quarrel' in a negative sense, but given the vague semantic range and force of *ge-*, there is no way of attaining certainty.[78] What is clear, however, is that, as in the case of formations with *wyrd* employed for derivatives of *historia*, we have here, once again, a deliberate translation of Latin cognates by Old English words which are closely related as well, and which, moreover, are all exceedingly rare and were very probably coined by the glossators themselves or in the circle where they were active.

In view of the rarity of the Old English words and the coherent glossing provided for *dialectica* and *dialecticus*, it is worth remarking that the noun *dialectica* is, in fact, not part of Aldhelm's text in the passage in question. Aldhelm here enumerates *septem species* of grammatical and philosophical disciplines which, he says, comprise 'arithmetica, geometrica, musica, astronomia, astrologia, mechanica, medicina' (Ehwald, p. 277.4–5). This is clearly not the 'classical' system of the *septem artes*. The system presented by Aldhelm apparently took its origin from Isidore's *De differentiis rerum*[79] where *physica* is subdivided into the seven disciplines in question. The system occurs principally in Hiberno-Latin grammatical treatises such as the *Anonymus ad Cuimnanum*, and Aldhelm's adoption of the system should probably be ascribed to the influence of this Irish tradition.[80] In Brussels 1650 all the seven Aldhelmian disciplines bear Old English glosses (G 3016–22). In addition, the Latin names of the three disciplines of the 'classical' system which do not appear among Aldhelm's *species* are recorded in the margin: *grammatica*, *dialectica* and *rhetorica*. Two of these are glossed in Old English, namely *dialectica*, our *flitcræft* (G 3015) and *rhetorica* as *þelcræft*.[81] In other words, we have here a lemma, *dialectica*, which is *not* part of the text of the *De uirginitate*, glossed by *flitcræft* and three occurrences of *dialecticus in* the text, glossed by close cognates of *flitcræft*. The implication of all this apparently is that

---

[78] In view of the fact that *flit*, a word which (at least in its prefixed form) had clear negative connotations, has been chosen to translate *dialectica*, it may be worth noting that rhetoric and dialectic were regarded as the most dangerous disciplines within the system of the liberal arts by Anglo-Saxon scholars such as Aldhelm, Bede or Bonifatius; see P. Riché, *Education and Culture in the Barbarian West. Sixth through Eighth Centuries*, transl. J. J. Contreni (Columbia, SC, 1976), pp. 388–90.

[79] *CPL*, no. 1202, ptd PL 83, 69–98, at 93–4.

[80] See B. Bischoff, 'Eine verschollene Einteilung der Wissenschaften', in his *Mittelalterliche Studien* I, 273–88, esp. 276–8.

[81] G 3014, by C; from *þyle* 'orator', with Kentish dialect phonology.

an Old English terminology for *dialectica* and derivatives from it (presumably based on Isidore) had already been established in the circle of the glossators and was not devised specifically for the purposes of glossing the *De uirginitate*, but that it was applied here in a systematic fashion. Aldhelm enumerates six of his seven disciplines on a second occasion in the *De uirginitate* (Ehwald, p. 320.13–14). On this occasion, only five of the disciplines are glossed (G 5315–19), and the 'missing' classical disciplines have not been supplied. All these Old English glosses to terms for the liberal arts would merit close scrutiny with regard to their semantic components, word-formation, frequency and distribution in the Old English lexicon.[82]

Geometrica: eorðcræft, eorðgemet

Let us consider briefly one further discipline and its Old English glosses. On its first occurrence as a lemma (G 3017), *geometrica* bears two Old English glosses: *eorðcræft* (A) and *eorðgemet* (C, *gemet* 'act of measuring'). On its second occurrence (G 5316) it is glossed by C, both in Old English and Latin: *eorðgemet, terrae mensuram*. Of the two Old English glosses, *eorðcræft* occurs only here; *eorðgemet* is attested twice outside the Aldhelm glosses.[83] Both Old English words may well be coinages based on Isidore's explanation that *geometry* is concerned with measuring and surveying the earth ('mensuras terrae dimensionesque conplectitur': *Etym*. I. ii. 3). Obviously, *eorðgemet* is very close to Isidore's explanation, whereas *eorðcræft*, through its second component, *cræft*, links the Old English term for

---

[82] As regards the possibility of an incipient standardization of the Old English terminology for the *artes*, it may be of interest to note that in a tenth-century manuscript, probably from St Augustine's, Canterbury (now London, BL, Cotton Domitian i, fols. 2–55), which contains *inter alia* Isidore's *De natura rerum* (*CPL*, no. 1188), a series of Latin lemmata and Old English glosses for the *artes* occurs. These lemmata refer to Isidore's system of the *artes* as it is found in his *De differentiis rerum* (and Aldhelm). Interestingly, Domitian i does not contain a copy of this text, and the lemmata were entered on the originally blank first leaf (now 2r) of the manuscript (immediately preceding the text of Isidore's *De natura rerum*) by a hand dated s. x/xi (see Ker, *Catalogue*, pp. 185–6, no. 146 c). The Old English glosses are closely related to the Brussels *interpretamenta* for the *artes* in Aldhelm; they are printed *OEG*, p. 221 (no. 55).

[83] Once in the Old English Martyrology and once in the Isidore glosses mentioned above, n. 82.

geometrica to the English names given to some of the other disciplines which are mentioned in the passage in question (such as *tungelcræft* for *astronomia* (G 3019) or *lǣcecræft* for *medicina* (G 3022)).

Leuiathan, palatum, Europa, Alpes, pelta

By the same token, the gloss for the unique occurrence of *leuiathan* (G 832) may be indebted to Isidore. The lemma has first been provided with a Latin explanation by scribe C: '.i. serpens aquaticus' (cf. 'id est serpens de aquis', *Etym.* VIII. xi. 27) and is then translated as *sǣdraca* ('seadragon', by CD). Aside from this gloss, *sǣdraca* occurs only once, namely in *Beowulf* (1426). It is therefore a first indication that we should be prepared to meet in the Brussels glosses not only a predilection for rare words but also a taste for terms which are employed in poetry, a combination which, it will be recalled, is a salient feature of the Royal Psalter gloss.

Three further glosses behind which Isidore's influence might be sought would be the *interpretamenta* for *palatum, Europa* and *Alpes*. The lemma *palatum* 'palate' (G 425) is glossed in Latin by *os* (C) and in Old English by *muþhrof* (CD; *hrof* 'roof, ceiling, top', also 'sky, heaven'). This compound, attested only in Brussels 1650 and dependent glosses, seems to echo Isidore's: 'Palatum nostrum sicut caelum est positum' (*Etym.* XI. i. 55). *Europa* is explained on one occasion as *middaneardes norðdæl* (G 4447, CD), an *interpretamentum* which may have been drawn from Isidore's description of the location of the continents (cf. *Etym.* XIV. ii. 2–3).[84] *Alpes* (G 2004) is glossed in Latin and Old English: *montes* (A), *heahtorras* (R; compounded of *heah* 'high' and *torr* 'rock'). The Old English gloss is, once again, a *hapax legomenon*, presumably coined after the pattern of *heahcliff* 'high cliff' or *heahbeorg* 'mountain', and it could be indebted to Isidore's etymology: 'Gallorum lingua "alpes" monti alti vocantur' (*Etym.* XIV. viii. 18).

Our final example, the lemma *pelta* 'a small shield', is glossed once by *plegscyld* (G 825, CD; from *plega* 'play, games, exercise' and *scyld* 'shield'). In addition, the Latin glosses *clipeus* (A) and *parma* (C) have been provided. *Plegscyld* is exceedingly rare and was presumably coined for this

---

[84] A second occurrence of the lemma is provided with what is probably a merograph gloss: *norð*, perhaps for *norð[dæles middaneardes]* (G 2001, scribe R, who is, perhaps, identical with CD; cf. Goossens, *Old English Glosses*, p. 50).

Aldhelmian lemma. Its existence by the mid-tenth century is guaranteed by its occurrence in the First Cleopatra Glossary (WW 464.21). *Pelta* occurs as a lemma on two further occasions (G 2861 and 3684); on both occasions it is provided with a variety of Latin and Old English glosses. Clearly, the glossators took an active interest in Latin *pelta*, but did not decide on a standard translation for it. Such an interest on the glossators' part comprised other Latin terms for 'shield' as well. This much can be seen from the wealth and variety of *interpretamenta* they employed for such terms and from the fact that on two occasions (glossing *scutum* and *parma*) they even used a French loanword, *tudenard*, which is not attested elsewhere (see below, p. 406). It would be consonant with this interest if, for information about *pelta*, the glossators should have consulted Isidore, where (for *pelta* and for *parma*, the word they used as a Latin gloss for *pelta*) they would have found explanations as follows: 'Peltum [*sic*] scutum breuissimum in modum lunae mediae',[85] and 'Parma leuia arma, quasi parua, non clypeum'.[86] Explanations such as these may very possibly lie behind the coinage of the rare compound *plegscyld*.

The *Etymologiae*, glossaries and Isidorian scholia

As has been mentioned, the likelihood is that a systematic search would bring to light many more glosses which owe their existence to information drawn from Isidore. In the course of such a search, the question would have to be addressed whether in each case the glossators' resort was to the *Etymologiae* themselves or whether they possibly culled their information about the etymology and meaning of a lemma from an *interpretamentum* in some glossary, which in turn might (but need not) have been derived from an explanation given by Isidore. For example, the etymological explanation of *geometrica* which led to the formation of *eorðgemet* might have been derived from the Leiden-Family of glosses.[87] Similarly, *interpretamenta* for *Alpes* and *pelta* which are consonant with the

---

[85] '*Pelta*, a very short shield, like the half moon': *Etym.* XVIII. xii. 4.

[86] '*Parma*, light armament, as if small (*parua*), not a *clipeus*' (that is, a heavy round shield, which is explained in the same section: XVIII. xii. 1): *Etym.* XVIII. xii. 6.

[87] Cf. *Geometrica: terrae mensura* in the Leiden Glossary (ed. Hessels, xxx. 48), and see the similar *interpretamenta* in the Corpus Glossary (ed. Hessels, G 39) and the Épinal and Erfurt (I) glossaries (ed. Goetz, *Corpus Glossariorum* V, 362.42).

explanations provided by Isidore are found among the glossaries printed by Goetz.[88]

However, the possibility of an additional resort to glossaries on the part of the Brussels glossators need in no way invalidate the overall importance of the *Etymologiae* themselves for the formation of the vernacular gloss corpus in Brussels 1650. The importance of the *Etymologiae* is confirmed by a different piece of evidence: a substantial corpus of Isidorian scholia in Latin which has been preserved in three manuscripts of the prose *De uirginitate*, where these scholia are entered between the lines and in the margins. The manuscripts in question are: BL, Royal 7. D. XXIV (scholia from s. x^med), Digby 146 (scholia from s. xi^1) and BL, Royal 6. A. VI (scholia from s. xi^1). The scholia are unprinted so far.[89] Of these manuscripts, Royal 7. D. XXIV is of paramount importance for tracing the origin of Aldhelm glossing in the tenth century (see below, pp. 360–2). The glossators who first entered these scholia in a manuscript of the prose *De uirginitate* either knew their way around the *Etymologiae* extremely well, or they were in a position to draw on a vast compendium of Isidore scholia,[90] arranged perhaps in alphabetical order. Whatever the case, the pivotal role which the *Etymologiae*, from an early point onwards, played in the (Latin and Old English) exegesis of the prose *De uirginitate* seems to be established beyond reasonable doubt.

The Isidore scholia are noteworthy also in connection with a possible link between the Brussels glosses and the circle in which the Royal Psalter gloss originated. As we have seen, Royal 2. B. V is unique among glossed psalter manuscripts in that it contains throughout a large number of marginal Latin scholia on the psalms, drawn principally from Cassiodorus's *Expositio psalmorum*. As we have also seen, not infrequently these scholia provided the stimulus for the choice or coinage of an Old English gloss. In other words, the Royal Glossator and the early glossators of

---

[88] Cf. *Corpus Glossariorum* V, 560.32 and V, 39.2.

[89] See Gwara, 'Manuscripts of Aldhelm's *Prosa de Virginitate*', pp. 150–3, who quotes a number of examples from these scholia. The dates for the scholia recorded above are those given by Gwara; cf. also Ker, *Catalogue*, nos. 254, 259 and 320. Apparently the Isidore scholia in the three manuscripts are closely related but not directly dependent on each other.

[90] As has been suggested by Gwara, 'Manuscripts of Aldhelm's *Prosa de Virginitate*', p. 153.

Aldhelm's prose *De uirginitate* set about their task in a similar scholarly way. Not only did they constantly resort for their vernacular glosses to some standard encyclopaedic or exegetical handbook, but they provided as well future generations of students with a large amount of helpful Latin scholia drawn from these handbooks. Naturally, the picture is much clearer in the case of the Royal Psalter: a continuous interlinear version, presumably the work of principally one scholar, transmitted in an early manuscript (written throughout by a single scribe) which also contains the Latin scholia and which must be very close to the original version of the Old English glosses. By contrast, Brussels 1650, the most important (though regrettably late) manuscript for the Old English gloss corpus, contains no Isidore scholia; at least no scholia of the scope of Royal 7. D. XXIV or Digby 146. But there are incontestably Isidore scholia among the Latin glosses intermingled with the Old English glosses such as the explanation *serpens aquaticus* for *leuiathan* (above, p. 168). The degree to which the Latin glosses in the Brussels corpus represent Isidore scholia also awaits scrutiny.[91]

Gymnosophistae

On the assumption that the glossators regularly consulted Isidore's *Etymologiae* whenever they had to translate a lemma of some encyclopaedic character, we may suspect that in those cases where their Old English *interpretamenta* disagree with an explanation provided by Isidore, the glossators deliberately chose to ignore that explanation for one reason or another. Their Old English renderings of *gymnosophistae* will serve to illustrate that point. *Gymnosophistae* 'gymnosophists' (literally 'naked philosophers') were a sect of Indian ascetics who, spurning the adornment and protection of clothes, were living in the woods.[92] An explanation to that effect is given by Isidore (cf. *Etym.* VIII. vi. 17). A reference to the nakedness of the gymnosophists, if not to their status as philosophers, is

---

[91] Note also that in Digby 146 the Brussels corpus is transmitted together with a substantial corpus of Isidore scholia, though entered by different scribes; cf. Ker, *Catalogue*, p. 382 (no. 320), and Gwara, 'Manuscripts of Aldhelm's *Prosa de Virginitate*', pp. 153 and 137.

[92] See *Der kleine Pauly. Lexikon der Antike*, ed. K. Ziegler *et al.*, 5 vols. (Stuttgart, 1964–75) II, 892–3.

also provided by the Second Erfurt Glossary, a compilation of English origin: 'qui nudi per eremum ambulant'.[93]

Gymnosophistae appears three times as a lemma in the Brussels glosses. On the first two occasions, Aldhelm clearly intended the word to denote 'athletes'; on the third occasion, he employed it unambiguously in the sense of 'philosophers'. *Gymnosophistae* meaning 'athletes' occurs in a tortuous and heavily ornate passage where Aldhelm likens the nuns of Barking, the dedicatees of his *De uirginitate*, striving industriously for erudition in divine doctrine ('diuinis dogmatibus erudiri'), to *gymnosophistas*,[94] that is (as the context clarifies) antique athletes performing in a contest of various Olympic disciplines. In Brussels 1650, in the left margin, glossing the phrase *uelut sagaces gymnisophistas* ([*sic*] Ehwald, p. 230.5) the following *interpretamenta* are found: *swilce wittige ł gleawe* [ł *gleawe* above the line] *leorneres ł plegmen* (G 54 and 55, entered by CD; *leornere* 'student, scholar', *wittig* and *gleaw* 'wise, prudent; skilful', *plegman* 'athlete, sportsman', from *plega* 'play, game, exercise'). In an interlinear position above the lemma *gymnisophistas* itself, as a third gloss for that lemma, Old English *upwitu* occurs (G 56, also entered by CD; erroneous for *upwitan* 'wise men, philosophers', from *up-* intensive prefix and *wita* 'wise man').

On its second occurrence in the passage in question, *per gymnisophistas* (Ehwald, p. 230.24) is glossed (above the line), again by CD, as follows: *þurh plegemen ł gligmen* (G 132, *gligman* 'player', from *gliw* 'play, pleasure').

On the third occurrence of the lemma, Aldhelm records how Chrysanthus (one of his male virgins) had been handed over to 'gymnosofistis et rhetoribus' (Ehwald, p. 276.24) in order to be instructed by them in the liberal arts. Here *gymnosophistae* clearly signifies 'philosophers'. The gloss for the lemma on this occasion is *upwita*, one of the three *interpretamenta* used on the first occurrence of *gymnosophista*. Again, the adjective *gleaw* is added in the margin. (G 2996, *upwita* is probably by

---

[93] See Goetz, *Corpus Glossariorum* V, 298.35. For the English origin of Erfurt II (transmitted in Erfurt, Wissenschaftliche Bibliothek, Amplonianus 2° 42, 14v–34v, written at Cologne, *c.* 830), see now Pheifer, in *Épinal, Erfurt, Werden and Corpus Glossaries*, ed. Bischoff *et al.*, pp. 49–63. Erfurt II has been printed by Goetz, *Corpus Glossariorum* V, 259–337; it provides the only instance of the lemma *gymnosophista* among the glossaries in his *Corpus*.

[94] *Aldhelmi Opera*, ed. Ehwald, p. 230.5 and 230.24.

scribe A; this gloss in interlinear position is repeated in the right margin by scribe C, who (presumably) also added the adjective *gleaw*.)

All this gives rise to the suspicion that the glossators, who will have known Isidore's explanation of *gymnosophistae*, realized that this explanation would not have suited Aldhelm's text, and therefore refrained from utilizing it for their glosses. If Aldhelm himself had known Isidore's exegesis, he too, had deliberately chosen to ignore it.[95] Instead of drawing on Isidore, the glossators apparently based their Old English *interpretamenta* on scholia widely current in explanation of the two words which they obviously perceived as the constituent parts for the formation of *gymnosophistae*, namely *gymnasium* and *sophistae*. The meaning 'wise men, philosophers' for *sophistae* is guaranteed by Isidore (cf. 'sophistas, id est sapientes, aut doctores', *Etym*. VIII. vi. 2). It is also found in the glossaries;[96] and accordingly, the only occurrence of *sophistae* as a lemma in Brussels 1650 is glossed by *uþwitan* (G 1813, by scribe A), the very word used twice to gloss *gymnosophistae* (G 56 and 2996).

Gymnasium in the sense of a 'place for intellectual activities' is also guaranteed by Isidore ('Gymnasium generalis est exercitiorum locus. Tamen apud Athenas locus erat ubi discebatur philosophia et sapientiae exercebatur studium').[97] However, the etymology of *gymnasium* and its original meaning, namely a group of buildings and courts, principally (but not exclusively) for physical exercise and training,[98] are also referred to by Isidore on several occasions.[99] By the same token, both meanings

---

[95] It is assumed that Aldhelm (639/40–709/10) had been a student of Theodore (d. 690) and Hadrian (d. 710) at Canterbury; see (most recently) Lapidge, *Biblical Commentaries*, ed. Bischoff and Lapidge, pp. 2, 268–9 and *passim*. Isidore's *Etymologiae* (published soon after his death in 636) was certainly one of the most recent scholarly handbooks, which was drawn on for the purposes of classroom instruction in that school; see *ibid.*, pp. 204–5. In fact, an epitome of the *Etymologiae* was compiled by an anonymous Anglo-Saxon scholar who presumably belonged to the Canterbury ambit, and who may even have worked on his compilation at Malmesbury: see *ibid.*, and Lapidge, 'An Isidorian Epitome', p. 193.

[96] See, for example, Goetz, *Corpus Glossariorum* IV, 173.7, 568.43 and V, 151.5.

[97] *Etym*. XV. ii. 30, '*Gymnasium* is a place for exercise in a general sense. However, at Athens it was a place where philosophy was taught and the study of wisdom pursued.'

[98] See, for example, *Reallexikon für Antike und Christentum*, ed. F. Dölger, H. Lietzmann *et al.* (Stuttgart, 1950–) XIII (1986), 155–76.

[99] In the passage quoted above, for example, he continues: 'Sed et balnea et loca cursorum et athletarum gymnasia sunt' (*Etym*. XV. ii. 30), 'but baths and places for runners and

are assigned to *gymnasium* in the glossaries, where the word frequently occurs as a lemma (and where the *interpretamenta* often seem to be drawn from Isidore).[100] It would appear that the Brussels glossators chose to interpret *gymnasium* as a place for intellectual studies, although, given their intimate knowledge of the *Etymologiae*, there can be little doubt that they will have been informed about the original meaning of the word as well. On its two occurrences as a lemma, *gymnasium* is translated by *leornunghus* (G 3117, A) and *leorning{hus}* ł *larhus* (G 61, CD; *lar* 'learning, study' being the determinant in *larhus*). Both words, *leorninghus* and *larhus*, were very probably coined for this Aldhelmian lemma. *Larhus* occurs only here; *leorninghus* appears also in the Third and First Cleopatra Glossaries (WW 485.25 and 424.20)[101] which guarantees its existence as an *interpretamentum* for this lemma in the *De uirginitate* by the mid-tenth century. In a similar fashion, the adjective *gymnicus* 'gymnastic' (occurring twice as a lemma in the Brussels glosses) is interpreted as referring to intellectual exercise. It is glossed *lareowlic* 'belonging to a teacher' (G 60, CD) and *larlic* 'instructive' (G 2241, CD). On two further occasions, however, *gymnicus* is used as a substantive in the sense of 'athlete', and is therefore linked directly to the employment of *gymnosophista* in that sense. Furthermore, these two occurrences of *gymnicus* 'athlete' (Ehwald, p. 231.7–8) are found in the very same passage where *gymnosophistae* 'athletes' appears. The Old English glosses for *gymnicus* in these instances – *plegman* (G 159, CD) and *leornere* (G 156, CD) – closely parallel those provided for *gymnosophistae*.

This rather complex evidence permits us to conclude that the glossators aimed to make it clear by their Old English *interpretamenta* for *gymnosophista* (and *gymnicus*) that, according to their understanding (and in

athletes are also *gymnasia*'; cf. also *Etym.* XV. ii. 40. For the etymological information, revealing *gymnasium* as being derived from γυμνός 'naked', see, for example, *Etym.* XVIII. xvii. 1–2.

[100] See, for example, Leiden (ed. Hessels, xlv. 1): 'Gymnasium: locus exercitationis ubi diuerse arte[s] discantur', and the related entries in Corpus (ed. Hessels, G 192) and Épinal–Erfurt I (ed. Goetz, *Corpus Glossariorum* V, 363.3). For *gymnasium* as a place of study, cf. further the *interpretamenta* in Goetz, *Corpus Glossariorum* IV, 412.18, 522.47, 589.2, 599.31, V, 205.22 and 448.52.

[101] Otherwise, *leorninghus* is attested only once (also for *gymnasium*) in the Antwerp–London Glossary (ed. L. Kindschi, 'The Latin–Old English Glossaries in Plantin-Moretus MS 32 and British Museum MS Additional 32, 246' (unpubl. PhD dissertation, Stanford Univ., 1955), no. 587 (WW 184.10).

accordance with the two meanings widely attributed to *gymnasium*) *gymnosphista* (and *gymnicus*) could carry two senses, namely 'student, scholar' and 'sportsman, athlete'. Of the *interpretamenta* which they chose for *gymnosophista* (and *gymnicus*), two are attested rather frequently in Old English: *uþwita* 'wise man, philosopher' and *leornere* 'student, scholar'. The two other terms, those which they provided for the sense 'sportsman, athlete', are striking. (For a proper assessment of the glossators' choice it is important to bear in mind that, to our knowledge, nothing comparable to a performance of athletic disciplines in a Greek *gymnasium* existed in Anglo-Saxon England.) One of the glosses is an established term for a kind of professional entertainer: *gliwman*. 'Minstrel, player, jester' are the meanings attributed to that word in the dictionaries. It clearly has positive connotations (as, for example, in *Beowulf* 1160), but it may also refer to more notorious entertainers (such as the *yfele gligmen* occurring in the *Regula pastoralis* (ed. Sweet, p. 327.7). The employment of *gliwman* for *gymnosophista* 'athlete' may, perhaps, have been provoked by Latin scholia such as the following one (referring to *gymnasia*): 'Sunt loca . . . in quibus iuuenes coram potentibus iocabant'.[102] In view of the negative connotations which are unmistakably attested for *gliwman*, but which clearly were not intended when used to gloss *gymnosophista* on the present occasion, it may be worth mentioning that the Royal Glossator coined the compound *gliwmæden* 'female musician', a word also wholly positive in its connotations (as is clear from the context).[103] In the Brussels glosses, *gliwman* occurs on two further occasions, as one of several glosses for *parasitus* (G 3202 and 4047). Here again, *gliwman* does not appear to have any negative connotations, since *parasiti* refers to 'guests' (Ehwald, p. 279.19) and 'household attendants' (Ehwald, p. 297.1) respectively.

The second gloss for *gymnosophista* 'athlete', namely *plegman*, is exceedingly rare and was very probably coined to translate this Aldhelmian lemma (as well as *gymnicus* in G 156). That *plegman* belongs to the tenth-century layer of glosses is certain from its occurrence in the Third Cleopatra Glossary (WW 485.23). Apart from the glosses to the prose *De uirginitate*, *plegman* occurs only once, again to gloss *gymnosophista*. In his

---

[102] Goetz, *Corpus Glossariorum* IV, 589.2, '[gymnasia] are places where young men jested before influential persons'.

[103] Ps. LXVII.26, see below, p. 192. The exotic character of *gliwmæden* emerges from the fact that only two D-type psalters (Tiberius and Eadwine) adopt the Glossator's coinage.

Vita S. Ecgwini, Byrhtferth provided *gymnosophistae* with the Old English gloss *plegmen* in a sentence which is heavily indebted in its wording to the relevant passage in the prose *De uirginitate* (Ehwald, p. 230.5–6). We have seen that on several occasions in his *Vita S. Ecgwini* and his *Enchiridion*, Byrhtferth apparently had resort to a glossed manuscript of both versions of the *De uirginitate*, and that he incorporated glosses he found in this manuscript (together with quotations from Aldhelm) into his own texts. Here again the implication is that Byrhtferth simply lifted *plegmen* together with the lemma *gymnosophistae* from this glossed manuscript of the *De uirginitate*.[104]

Some clearer notion of the meaning of *plegman* and of its connotations may perhaps be gained when we link that neologism with another compound, namely *plegscyld*, which very possibly was also coined for a lemma (*pelta*) in the *De uirginitate*. As we have seen (above, pp. 168–9), this denotes a small shield which (as the glossators understood it) was used for training or sporting competitions, not in warfare. Such a link between *plegman* and *plegscyld* would, at least, prevent us from seeing in *plegman* an Anglo-Saxon forerunner of a twentieth-century playboy.

In sum, the details surrounding the glossing of *gymnosophistae* are extraordinarily intricate. We are presented with glosses denoting a philosopher (*upwita*) and a student or scholar (*leornere*) alongside a word denoting an entertainer of somewhat doubtful standing (*gliwman*) and a freshly coined compound (*plegman*) whose meaning and connotations can only be established tentatively, since it never appears in an unambiguous prose context. All this conflicting and baffling evidence becomes much clearer when we consider (as we have done) the situation with which the glossators were confronted. They had to translate three occurrences of the lemma for which the context revealed unequivocally that the explanation provided by Isidore for *gymnosophistae* (and which the glossators probably knew) was clearly not pertinent. Furthermore, as might also have been

---

[104] See *Vita S. Ecgwini*, *epil.* (ed. Giles, p. 349), and M. Lapidge, 'Byrhtferth at Work', in *Words and Works: Studies in Medieval English Language and Literature in Honour of Fred C. Robinson*, ed. N. Howe and P. Baker (Toronto, 1998), pp. 25–43, at 34–7. As with the glosses considered above, pp. 139–40, the Aldhelm manuscript on which Byrhtferth drew must have been closer to the lost manuscript from which Cleo III was compiled than to Brussels 1650. In Cleo III (as in the *Vita*) *plegmen* is the only gloss to *gymnosophistae* (WW 485.23), whereas in Brussels 1650 the *interpretamenta* are *leorneres ł plegmen* (G 54).

gleaned from the context, Aldhelm's use of the word was ambiguous itself: he employed it to mean 'athlete' as well as 'philosopher'. Of these two meanings, the classical concept of an athlete was certainly not a familiar one in Anglo-Saxon circles. The glossators responded to all these difficulties by providing various glosses for both meanings. (That they understood both meanings correctly shows from the nature of their glosses.) The glosses for 'philosopher' posed no serious problem: it was the sense 'athlete' which provided the challenge. The glossators met this challenge by way of substituting (through a semantic loan) a somewhat related term from Anglo-Saxon civilization (*gliwman*). Apparently, they were not wholly satisfied by such an equation (because *gliwman* belonged to a different cultural sphere? because of its latent negative connotations?) and they therefore had resort to a fresh formation, *plegman*. That, in spite of all their efforts to provide suitable glosses for the sense 'athlete', the glossators still perceived 'philosopher, scholar' to be the principal meaning of *gymnosophista*, emerges from the fact that in the Aldhelmian passage which requires the sense 'philosopher' (Ehwald, p. 276.24, G 2996) only *upwita* appears as a gloss, whereas the two occasions where the context requires the sense 'athlete' (Ehwald 230.5 and 230.24, G 54–6 and 132) *plegman* and *gliwman* are qualified by the adjective *gleaw* 'prudent', and *leornere* and *upwita* are provided as additional glosses.[105] In other words, what at first sight looks like helpless and amateurish groping around for a suitable gloss for *gymnosphista*, on closer scrutiny allows us an intriguing glimpse of scholars at work who had thoroughly studied the text they were glossing, who knew how to obtain information about a difficult Latin lemma and how to convey their knowledge in English glosses. (It should be noted that, once again, the glosses in question, although they are all intimately linked, were entered by no fewer than three scribes.)

Sophisma

A further coinage for a Greek word from the intellectual sphere, striking by its aptness and exquisiteness, is *wordsnoterung* for *sophisma*. This is an abstract noun derived from the adjective *wordsnotor* 'wise', literally 'wise

---

[105] Such a procedure squares well with the glosses *leorninghus* and *larhus* stressing the meaning of *gymnasium* as a place for intellectual training.

in words', hence meaning 'wisdom in words' and (presumably) 'wisdom, learning'. The noun occurs only in Brussels 1650 (and related glosses), where it is used twice to gloss *sophisma* (G 2229 and 4028, both glosses entered by CD).[106] Similarly, the adjective *wordsnotor*, from which the noun is derived, is very rare. It is interesting therefore that *wordsnotor* occurs at two points in the Brussels glosses, and that these are arguably the earliest occurrences of the adjective.[107] Here *wordsnotor* is employed (used as a noun) to gloss the name of the poet Homer (G 2379, CD) and the lemma *oratores* (G 3106, CD; this lemma bears the additional Latin glosses *grammatici*, A, and *rhetores*, C). Finally, the adjective *wordsnoterlic* is used once to gloss *philosophicus* (G 2231, CD). Like the noun *wordsnoterung*, apart from dependent glosses, *wordsnoterlic* occurs nowhere else.[108]

In other words, we once again have a predilection for a word-family which is extremely rare, has some exotic flair, and which presumably owes its existence to the glossators of the *De uirginitate*. From the lemmata they gloss, it is clear that the adjectives *wordsnotor* and *wordsnotorlic* carry no negative connotations. This in turn strongly suggests an unequivocally positive range of meaning 'wisdom, learning, philosophy' for the noun *wordsnoterung* as well, which is noteworthy, since the lemma it glosses, *sophisma*, normally denotes 'a false conclusion, sophism, sophistry'.[109] It is employed by Aldhelm in this negative sense on the first occasion (Ehwald, p. 262.10) whereas it seems to have more positive shades of meaning on its second occurrence (Ehwald, p. 296.18). The presumption of a positive range of meaning for *wordsnoterung* is confirmed further by the Latin scholion which accompanies *wordsnoterung* on its first occurrence (G 2229, interestingly the point where Aldhelm seems to have had

---

[106] It is not absolutely certain whether, in G 4028, the gloss for the lemma *sophismatum* really is *wordsnoterung*. The entry reads *wordsnoterū*, for *wordsnoterungum*? or rather for *wordsnoterum* (the adjective used as a substantive 'wise man')? However, if *ū* is to be expanded to *um*, the inflexional ending (dative plural) would not be correct in either case; the lemma requires a genitive plural.

[107] It is impossible to attain certainty at what stage *wordsnotor* became part of the Brussels corpus, since it is not attested in the Cleopatra glossaries. *Wordsnotor* occurs sporadically in other texts such as homilies by Ælfric and Wulfstan.

[108] In the manuscript *word* has been erased, but is still partly legible; cf. Goossens's note on 2231. However, *wordsnoterlic* occurs at the same point in Digby 146, where it was copied from Brussels 1650.

[109] The plural *sophismata* occurs once in a positive sense in a glossary printed by Goetz: 'graece generalis philosophia', *Corpus Glossariorum* V, 333.35 (Erfurt I).

'sophistry' in mind): here *sophismata* (the lemma for *wordsnoterung*) is explained as *sapientiae argumenta* (by scribe C).

It is not possible to produce irrefutable proof that the compound *wordsnoterung* itself was part of the tenth-century layer of Aldhelm glosses, since the word does not occur in the Cleopatra glossaries. However, a wholly positive interpretation of *sophisma* already in that early layer of glosses, is guaranteed by the Latin gloss *scientia* in Cleo III (WW 495.6) for *sophisma* at that very point in the text (Ehwald, p. 262.10, G 2229) in spite of the negative connotations implied here by Aldhelm. It may also be noteworthy that *sophisma* in such a positive sense 'learning, knowledge' (otherwise poorly attested) occurs in one of the Latin poems which have convincingly been ascribed to Bishop Æthelwold's school at Winchester.[110]

Poetic words

The gloss *sædraca* (for *leuiathan*, above, p. 168), a word which otherwise occurs only in *Beowulf*, gives us reason to suspect that on occasion the glossators' choice of their *interpretamenta* was guided by a taste for poetic words. Another such word would be the adjective *wittig* which in its sense 'wise, sagacious' belongs to the register of poetry. It occurs in that sense among the various glosses surrounding *gymnosophistae* (G 54, see above, p. 172). Our suspicion that the glossators had some penchant for poetry is further confirmed by their use of *mece* and *hilting*. The lemmata for various kinds of swords, *machera* (G 823 and 2654), *framea* (G 948) and *romphea* (G 1205), are all glossed by the universal Latin term *gladius* (by scribe A); *machera* in 2654 has the additional Latin gloss *mucro* (by C). All these lemmata are glossed in Old English by *mece* (by CD); *machera* in 823 has the additional Old English gloss *hilting* (by CD). Old English *mece* has been dealt with several times, most notably by Kenneth Sisam.[111] It is an old poetic word which even in poetry of demonstrably West Saxon origin (like *Brunanburh* or *Maldon*) appears in its Anglian (and Kentish) form *mēce* (as opposed to West Saxon *mǣce*). The word does not occur in ordinary

---

[110] See Lapidge, 'Three Latin Poems', p. 252.

[111] See K. Sisam, *Studies in Old English Literature* (Oxford, 1953), pp. 126–8; cf. also Wenisch, *Spezifisch anglisches Wortgut*, p. 211 and n. 829, with full references to further literature on the word.

prose, and is attested only infrequently in glosses and glossaries. The bulk of such attestations in glosses stems from Aldhelm *interpretamenta* (Brussels 1650 and related glosses; twice in Cleo I).

In this connection it may be worth noting how the Royal Glossator responded to the one occurrence of *mece* which he would have found in the A-type gloss to which he presumably resorted regularly. The Vespasian Psalter (and other A-type psalters) employ *mece* once for *machera* (ps. LVI.5). The gloss has been replaced in the Royal Psalter by *scyrseax* 'razor' (from *scieran* 'to shear' and *seax* 'knife'), probably not with the intention of jettisoning an originally Anglian dialect word, but in order to achieve, through the collocation *scyrseax scearp*, an intriguing stylistic effect (see above, p. 67). Otherwise, the Royal Glossator translates all sixteen occurrences of *gladius* in the psalter by the common word *sweord*, as well as *framea* on one occasion (ps. IX.7).[112] These unconspicuous glosses render it even more likely that he was prompted by the poetic character of *mece* in his A-type exemplar to employ an extremely rare word which in the form *scearseax* (which he probably had in mind when devising his gloss, instead of the transmitted form *scyrseax*) would yield an intricate sound pattern with its accompanying adjective: *scearseax scearp*.

Since it is beyond reasonable doubt that *mece* should be allocated to the poetic register, the predilection shown by the Aldhelm glossators for this word may help in evaluating the alternative gloss which has been added to *mece* on one occasion: *hilting* (G 823, by CD). This word occurs only here and in the copy of the Brussels glosses in Digby 146. Note that the Digby scribe restored (as he often did) the correct form of the suffix: he wrote *hilting* (*OEG*, 1.758), whereas Brussels reads *hiltinc*. There can be no uncertainty about *hilting* meaning 'sword', since it is used together with *mece* and the Latin gloss *gladius* to render *machera*. What is not certain,

---

[112] The Glossator's glosses for *framea* are interesting with a view to the presumed persistent recourse which he had to Cassiodorus's exegesis. In the Royal Psalter, the remaining three instances of *framea* are glossed by *flan* 'javelin', which is the original meaning of *framea*. The Royal Psalter here disagrees with the Vespasian Psalter which has *sweord* for *framea* on all occasions. It is entirely possible that for his gloss *flan* the Royal Glossator consulted Cassiodorus, who states at various points that *framea* may denote 'javelin' as well as 'sword' (cf. e. g. *Expositio* I, 148, 202 and 305–6). However, in his commentary to ps. IX.7, Cassiodorus attributes only the meaning '*gladius*' to *framea* (*Expositio* I, 99), and this is the one occasion where the Royal Glossator has *sweord*. (There are no scholia pertaining to the literal meanings of *framea* in the margin of Royal 2. B. V.)

however, is the etymology of *hilting*. Goossens (in his note to 823) endorses the explanation provided by Napier (note to *OEG*, 1.758) to the effect that *hilting* is derived from the Old English *hilt(e)* 'handle, hilt' by means of the suffix *-ing*.[113] Consequently, *hilting* (literally 'having a handle') would denote 'sword' by way of *pars pro toto*. Meanings to be explained by metonymy or synecdoche are not infrequently found in Old English poetry (where this feature passes under the Old Norse technical term *heiti*), as, for example, *rand* 'border' or *lind* 'lime tree' for 'shield', and *ord* 'point' or *æsc* 'ash tree' for 'spear'. However, according to the pattern in the examples just cited (and in numerous further instances) we would expect *hilt(e)* not *hilting*, a suffixed form, as a *heiti* for 'sword'. We may be permitted therefore to look for a different etymology.

There would be no morphological difficulty in deriving *hilting* from the poetic noun *hild* 'war, combat'. Such a derivative, *hilding*, would then signify 'someone or something pertaining to war', a perfect coinage to denote a sword. In this connection we should recall that the suffix *-ing* occurs several times in Old English names given to swords, such as *Hrunting*, the sword which Unferth lent to Beowulf, or *Nægling*, Beowulf's own sword which snapped in his fight with the dragon.[114] That in our case the attested spellings are <hiltinc> in Brussels 1650 and <hilting> in Digby 146 need not invalidate our etymology when we consider the vast number of scribal errors and idiosyncrasies in Brussels 1650.[115] Particularly, <t> instead of etymologically correct <d> is not uncommon, especially in glosses entered by scribe CD (as *hiltinc* is),[116] and final <ing> frequently appears as <inc>.[117] Accordingly, the scribe of

---

[113] The suffix has a fairly wide (and vague) range of meaning: 'belonging to', 'of the kind of', 'possessed of the quality of', see *OED*, s. v. *-ing*[3], and Kluge, *Nominale Stammbildungslehre*, pp. 11–16.

[114] See *Beowulf* 1457, 1490, 1659 and 1807 for *Hrunting*, and 2680 for *Nægling*. For the etymology of *Hrunting* and *Nægling*, see *Beowulf and the Fight at Finnsburh*, ed. F. Klaeber, 3rd ed. (Lexington, MA, 1950), p. 438, and Holthausen, *Altenglisches etymologisches Wörterbuch*, p. 176 and the references given in these. For a possible third name for a sword with the suffix *-ing* in *Beowulf* (*Hunlafing*, 1143), see discussion by C. Brady, 'Weapons in *Beowulf*: an Analysis of the Nominal Compounds and an Evaluation of the Poet's Use of them', *ASE* 8 (1979), 79–141, at 96–101. See also Kluge, *Nominale Stammbildungslehre*, pp. 54–5, for *-ing* as a suffix frequently occurring in the names of swords in various Germanic languages.

[115] See Goossens, *Old English Glosses*, p. 42, and his notes *passim*.

[116] See *ibid*., p. 106.   [117] See *ibid*., p. 118.

the Old English glosses in Digby 146 (who wrote <hilting>) would have corrected CD's idiosyncrasy with regard to the spelling <inc>, but he presumably did not realize that the first element of the word should be *hild*, a further pointer to the unusual character of *hilding*.

If the derivation from *hild* 'war' can be accepted, there is one further interesting aspect to be considered. *Hilding* may have been coined by the glossators as a poetic synonym to accompany the old poetic word *mece*. Alternatively, it may be a Scandinavian loanword. Old Norse *hildingr*, meaning 'war king' (denoting a man, not a sword), is attested several times in Scandinavian poetry.[118] In that case it would follow that the glossators had at least some knowledge of Old Norse poetry.

At all events, it emerges from *interpretamenta* such as *sædraca, wittig, mece* or *hilding* that occasionally the glossators chose their glosses from the poetic register or else introduced neologisms in a poetic vein.

Summary: the vocabulary

Our exploration of a handful of glosses can be no more than a first step towards an overall and thorough evaluation of the vast Brussels corpus. We have focused our attention here on a few *interpretamenta* which spring to the eye by their unusual, often eccentric, character, and there is little doubt that many more such glosses could be found. We have not considered in any detail the competent manner in which the glossators dealt with less difficult Aldhelmian lemmata, for example, if and how consistently they coupled a lemma with one and the same Old English gloss or which from several existing Old English synonyms they chose for their *interpretamentum*, and so on. By the same token, it would be worthwhile to examine which Aldhelmian lemmata they chose to gloss, and which not, and which principles possibly guided their selection. Or to find out if and to what extent the Latin and Old English glosses complement each other by stressing different semantic aspects of their lemma. Questions such as these await close attention. Nevertheless, even our handful of examples will have enabled us to form some impression of

---

[118] See R. Cleasby, G. Vigfusson and W. A. Craigie, *An Icelandic–English Dictionary*, 2nd ed. (Oxford, 1957), s. v. *hildingr*. Apparently the word is not attested as the name for a sword; see the comprehensive list of names for swords in Old Norse literature compiled by H. Falk, *Altnordische Waffenkunde*, Videnskapsselskapets Skrifter II, Hist.-Filos. Klasse 1914, no. 6 (Kristiania [Oslo], 1914), pp. 47–64.

the men who provided Aldhelm's most influential work with a massive corpus of Latin and Old English glosses. They were not beginners in Latin but first-rate scholars who had thoroughly studied and understood the difficult text they were explaining. In their attempt to clarify and interpret this text, they frequently had repair to scholarly handbooks (such as Isidore's *Etymologiae* or glossaries) and they were able to draw consistently on their own ample resources of Latin synonyms and their creative versatility in their native language.

CONCLUSIONS

It is clear that the corpus of Latin and Old English glosses which is transmitted in Brussels 1650 is the work of several generations of scholars. This much is obvious from the fact that various scribes (all working from exemplars) entered various layers of glosses in that manuscript. As regards the Old English glosses and potential links with other Old English texts revealed by these glosses, the most important of the scribes is CD, the latest hand. There will probably never be a way of knowing to what degree precisely the Old English glosses entered by scribes A, B or C were extant also in the exemplar from which CD copied his glosses into Brussels 1650 (and which he consequently refrained from duplicating). It is, however, reasonably certain that CD's exemplar did contain a considerable number of the glosses entered by the earlier scribes. With respect to the history of the CD corpus, it can be demonstrated that what on palaeographical grounds is the youngest layer of glosses in Brussels 1650 was in existence in substantial portions as early as the mid-tenth century. Such an early date is guaranteed by the occurrence of a large number of CD glosses in the Third (and First) Cleopatra Glossary. However, what the exact relationship is between the CD glosses (and others of the Brussels glosses) occurring in Cleo III and the *original* CD corpus cannot as yet be determined. Furthermore, the CD corpus (and the other layers in Brussels 1650) contain material culled from older glossaries such as Corpus or Épinal–Erfurt. The full amount of such material and the precise relationship of the Brussels glosses to the pre-Viking glossaries has yet to be established. A comparison of the number of glosses entered by scribe CD in the Brussels manuscript with those glosses which are attested already in Cleo III suggests that the CD corpus was considerably augmented in the course of transmission. Such augmentation comprises the number of lemmata from Aldhelm's text which bear glosses, as well as an increase in double or even triple glosses. At some stage, the CD corpus must have undergone a certain amount of revision to bring it into better conformity with later and fully developed Winchester usage. But already in its earliest attested stage (in the Cleopatra glossaries), the CD corpus provides ample evidence of *interpretamenta*, striking by their competence, inventiveness and learning.

For these various reasons, it would be a matter of great interest and importance to possess secure information as regards the scholarly circle in which the Brussels vernacular glosses originated. The localities where the glosses were entered into Brussels 1650 (and Digby 146) cannot provide such secure information, since the glosses in these manuscripts are demonstrably at several removes from the original core of glosses and since by the time the Brussels and Digby glosses were copied, Aldhelm had been established as the most important curriculum author for several decades. If therefore verbal links could be detected between the Brussels glosses and works which may be associated with Æthelwold and his circle, such links might furnish valuable information on the origin and first stages of this impressive and ambitious scholarly undertaking. So far, our evaluation of the nature of some of the Brussels glosses has suggested that the Aldhelm glossators, the Royal Glossator and the translator of the Rule shared some stylistic predilections (such as a flair for striking and brilliant neologisms) and a similar scholarly disposition (in their constant resort to standard reference works). It will also be recalled that we singled out Aldhelm's prose as an important stylistic force in the shaping of the attitude towards the vernacular which is revealed in the Royal Psalter gloss and (to some extent) in the Rule. It is to the examination of manifest verbal links and shared common usage between the Brussels glosses, the Royal Psalter and the Old English Rule that we now must turn.

6

Word usage in the Royal Psalter, the Rule and the Aldhelm glosses

For various reasons a comparison of word usage between the three texts, the Rule, the Psalter and the Aldhelm glosses, for which a common origin may be suspected, is hampered by serious difficulties. We have noted (above, pp. 133–7) that the two glosses do not lend themselves easily to such a comparison. Thus an evaluation of the lexical evidence which they present is fraught with problems resulting from the different character (in terms of style and register) of the glossed texts, the psalter and the prose *De uirginitate*. Similar problems arise from the considerable difference in the method of glossing which exists between a continuous interlinear version (where every Latin word is provided with an English *interpretamentum*, usually no more than a single word), and a text which, although encrusted with thousands of glosses, offers no full interlinear version and where instead very frequently a lemma bears several Old English and Latin glosses which may or may not have originated at various stages in the transmissional history.

Such difficulties are aggravated if we attempt to evaluate the lexical evidence offered by an interlinear gloss and a prose work with a view to establishing a common origin in the same circle for the texts in question. The principal problem here is that in an interlinear gloss in each case lemma and *interpretamentum* are immediately adjacent, with the implication that we may have to reckon with an impact of the morphological and semantic components of the lemma on the Old English *interpretamentum* to a much larger extent than would be expected in a prose translation (especially an idiomatic one) which was made to be read and understood in its own right without any recourse to the Latin original. Thus it is entirely conceivable that, for a gloss, a scholar might have used (or coined) a word which he would not have employed for the same lemma in a prose translation. He might have done so because in the gloss his primary aim was to make transparent the morphological and semantic structure of the lemma, whereas in a prose translation (where the lemma would not have been physically present) his lexical choice might have been influenced much more by considerations of Old English style. For example, it may be asked whether the glossator of the Vespasian Psalter would have employed coinages such as *efenherian* (for *conlaudare*) or *ymbeardian* (for *circumhabitare*) if he had translated the psalms into Old English prose.[1] The point worth stressing here is that such a close imitation of a Latin lemma in no way implies (as it has been taken to do)[2] that a glossator was incapable of providing a more idiomatic translation. Rather, such coinages should be judged in the light of an injunction found in a catalogue poem of medical terms (preserved in Cambridge, University Library, Gg. 5. 35, s. xi^med, provenance St Augustine's, Canterbury): 'omnia dic que sunt uerbi, que sillaba signet' ('tell me all things about each word, what every syllable signifies').[3] In any event, *interpretamenta*, closely modelled on the Latin lemma, when found in a gloss, permit no inference as to what word the glossator would have employed in prose. A further difficulty involved in an evaluation of the verbal links between the Rule and the gloss texts is that the evidence of these links cannot be tested and corroborated in the light of syntactic and stylistic features such as a predilection for certain types of word-order, for certain phrases, adverbs or conjunctions, or for stable collocations of words. Features such as these may often be of minor importance for an estimation of an author's stylistic aspirations and performance, but they may be immensely helpful for establishing a common authorship for any two texts.[4]

Apart from the problems inherent specifically in a lexical comparison of our three texts, we have to face the difficulties encountered by anyone

---

[1] For these loan-translations, see Gneuss, *Lehnbildungen*, pp. 81 and 140. Note that in the employment of the (extremely rare) verb *ymbeardian* (ps. XXX.14) the Royal Psalter agrees with Vespasian: a further pointer to the Glossator's recourse to an A-type gloss.

[2] See H. Sweet, *A Student's Dictionary of Anglo-Saxon* (Oxford, 1896), p. viii.

[3] In the poem this line has been lifted verbatim from one of Alcuin's *enigmata*. The poem has been printed by Lapidge, 'Hermeneutic Style', pp. 141–2; for a discussion, cf. *ibid.*, pp. 122–3 and 478–9.

[4] For the importance of these features where a common authorship for Old English texts is in question, see Baker, 'The Old English Canon of Byrhtferth of Ramsey', pp. 25–8 and 32–4.

setting about to work on the Old English lexicon. Such difficulties are primarily attributable to our deplorably fragmentary knowledge of the Old English vocabulary, which in turn results from the very limited range of texts which have survived from the more than six hundred years during which this variety of the English language was spoken. For example, in many cases where a word is attested only rarely or is even a *hapax legomenon*, we may not be certain what its status in the language really was. In some cases (as with *hroþgirela*, above pp. 100–1) we may, for various reasons, infer that the word in question will indeed have been rare or even unique; in others we may safely deduce (for example, from the type of text in which such a word occurs) that it must have been fairly frequent, in spite of its being attested only sparsely.[5] But in many more cases we simply do not know. Furthermore, aside from the language of poetry, we know regrettably little about registers in Old English. Then we are confronted with the problem of dialect vocabulary and its acceptability in other regions in a language in which only one dialect (West Saxon) is amply attested but where, during most of the centuries when this language was spoken and written, no standard variety existed. Or we have to consider that almost the entire corpus of Old English poetry, a substantial amount of Old English prose and (with a very few exceptions) all Latin–English interlinear glosses and glossaries, are transmitted anonymously and often without a safe date for their composition or compilation. This implies that the style and lexicon of individual authors, compilers, schools or periods can be ascertained only to a limited extent. For our purposes the point of this enumeration (by no means exhaustive) of problems pertaining to the study of Old English vocabulary is simply that in a bare list recording verbal ties, the items will seldom speak for themselves. As we have seen with the 'hidden links' between the Rule and the Psalter in respect of the Winchester vocabulary (above, p. 93) and as will emerge from the discussion in this ch. and elsewhere in the present book, a certain amount of exegesis is often required to uncover and estimate agreements in usage between the Rule, the Royal Psalter and the Aldhelm glosses.

Note that in the following discussion I usually do not provide lists

---

[5] For such a text containing numerous *hapax legomena* or rare words which, nevertheless, must once have been quite common, see Gretsch, 'The Language of the "Fonthill Letter"', pp. 78–90.

recording all attestations for the lemmata and *interpretamenta* in question. The inclusion of all occurrences would have involved the presentation of a huge amount of material which in turn would not have been conducive to a clear and succinct evaluation of the often immensely complex evidence. Information about the attestations of the Old English words is easily accessible in the *Microfiche Concordance*. The attestations of the Latin lemmata in the three texts under inspection here may be controlled with equal facility via the word indexes in Weber's edition of the *Psalterium Romanum*, Hanslik's edition of the *Regula S. Benedicti* and Goossens's edition of the glosses in Brussels 1650.

WYNDREAM, DREAM, DRYMAN AND MUSICAL TERMINOLOGY

The Vespasian Psalter glosses both *iubilatio* and *exaltatio* invariably by *wynsumnis*, a word primarily meaning 'loveliness, pleasantness'; most of the instances where *wynsumnis* means 'joyousness, rejoicing' seem to come from psalter glosses. *Iubilatio* occurs five times in the psalter. The Royal Psalter glosses its first occurrence by *lof* 'praise', the second by the doublet *wyndream ł lof*, and the remaining three instances by *wyndream* alone, a compound occurring only in the Royal Psalter and dependent glosses. All occurrences of *iubilatio* in the psalter could be assigned the sense 'joyful song of praise', 'music in honour of God'; cf. for example: 'Cantate ei canticum nouum, bene psallite ei in iubilatione' (ps. XXXII.3) or 'laudate eum in cymbalis iubilationis' (ps. CL.5). There are several clues which may indicate that the Royal Glossator used (and perhaps coined) *wyndream* to denote some kind of joyous musical performance as well, and not just unspecified jubilation. Such a wider sense 'jubilation, rejoicing' would have been natural enough for *wyndream* which is compounded from *wynn* 'joy, pleasure' and *dream* with the (presumably) original meaning 'joy, bliss'.[6] The pointers to a more specialized meaning of *wyndream* are as follows:

1. It is obvious that the Royal Glossator was in search of an adequate rendering of *exultatio* as well: for none of the fifteen occurrences of that lemma does he use the A-type gloss *wynsumnis*; nor did he decide on a single *interpretamentum*. Among his Old English glosses for *exultatio* we

---

[6] See *DOE*, s. v. *dream* 1. In BT and CHM, *wyndream* is in fact translated by 'jubilation, joyful sound'.

find: *gefægnung* (most frequently) 'rejoicing', *bliss* 'bliss, merriment', *blissung* 'exultation' (possibly again one of his coinages) or *upahefednes* 'exultation'.[7] However, in spite of its original meaning 'joy, bliss', *dream* is never employed to gloss *exultatio*, either alone or as part of a compound. As regards *wyndream*, the consistent gloss for *iubilatio*: if for the Glossator this had possessed the general sense 'rejoicing', it would have been a perfect gloss for *exultatio* as well.

2. OE *dream* in the sense 'music, musical instrument' occurs in the Royal Psalter on several occasions (but not in the Vespasian gloss). Thus *organum*[8] 'organ, musical instrument' or 'music produced by this instrument' is glossed *dream* in ps. CXXXVI.2 and *orgeldream* in ps. CL.4; this compound occurs only here and in one dependent gloss (Blickling) and is a coinage of great interest to which we must return in due course (below, p. 394–7). Given the approximately 225 occurrences of *dream* (not counting the compounds formed therefrom), it is difficult to estimate precisely when and in what texts the meaning 'music, musical instrument' is first attested. However, from the numerous quotations adduced in the *DOE*, it would appear that it was in the Royal Psalter (together with the Aldhelm glosses and the Rule) where such a specialized sense for *dream* (and for the derivative *dryman* as we shall see presently) was first vigorously fostered.

3. The Vespasian gloss for the verb *iubilare* is always *wynsumian* 'to rejoice, exult', which, again, is never used by the Royal Glossator. His preferred gloss is *dryman* (five occurrences) a verb to which the *DOE* assigns the meanings 'to rejoice' and 'to sing, make music'. All the instances in the psalter where *iubilare* is glossed by *dryman* could be translated 'to sing, make music'. The suspicion that the Glossator interpreted *iubilare* in that sense, and hence had in mind the meaning 'to sing, make music' for *dryman* as well, is confirmed by one instance where *iubilare* is glossed *singan* (ps. LXXX.2).[9] By the same token, *psallere*, which is usually glossed *singan*, is on one occasion translated by *dryman* (ps. XX.14).[10] *Prima facie* OE *dryman* is a *jan*-derivative from the

---

[7] This is clearly a lexical experiment since *upahefednes* usually means 'presumption, arrogance, pride'.

[8] For a brief survey of the development of the various senses of Latin *organum*, see Holschneider, *Die Organa von Winchester*, pp. 135–9, esp. 138.

[9] The remaining two occurrences of *iubilare* in the psalter are glossed in a more general sense (cf. Vespasian's *wynsumian*) by *gefeon* 'to rejoice' and *herian* 'to praise'.

[10] Given the Glossator's interest in loanwords (above, pp. 51–4), it may be worth noting

Primitive Germanic stem of OE *dream* and as such should have been inherited from Primitive Germanic. However, the verb does not occur in demonstrably early texts. The occasional occurrence in poetic texts, is – given the increasing uncertainty about the dating of Old English poetry – no irrefutable proof for an early currency of *dryman*.[11] In any event (as is noted by the *DOE*), the bulk of the approximately sixty occurrences of *dryman* is found in psalter glosses. Its use as a gloss word starts with the Royal Psalter, and the result of this situation is that the sense of *dryman* which is best attested in Old English is 'to sing, make music'. Whether the Royal Glossator turned to an inherited but – at least to us – not well attested word for a verbal expression of the concept of 'jubilant musical performance', or whether he even coined such a verb himself (to match *dream*) in imitation of pairs such as *geleafa* 'belief' and *gelyfan* 'to believe', we simply do not know. What is clear, however, is that the three texts under inspection here reveal a pronounced and peculiar penchant for pairs (of a more exotic type) where a substantive is coupled with a verbal derivative, the vowel of the verb being altered by i-mutation. (We shall return to this predilection in a later ch., below, pp. 421–2.) What is also clear is that the unambiguous sense 'to sing, make music' which *dryman* bears in the Royal Psalter may further confirm the suspected meaning 'singing, music' for *(wyn)dream* in that text.

4. It emerges unequivocally from psalm exegesis that although throughout the psalter *iubilatio* and *iubilare* may imply exuberant noise and jubilant joyfulness, too rapturous to be expressed by words, the terms should by no means be taken as referring to unrestrained, clamorous rejoicing and revelry, but that rather they denote the sound of joyous voices and instruments giving praise and thanks to God. Consider, for example, the following passage from Cassiodorus:

immolare se dicit *in tabernaculo eius hostiam iubilationis*, id est in Ecclesia eius offerre sacrificium laudis. *Iubilationem* quippe dicimus ex eo quod nos iuuat laudare, quando delectantes cum summa iucunditate gratias referre contendimus. Diximus superius aliud esse *cantare*, aliud *psalmum dicere*. *Cantare* est sola uoce

---

that on two occasions (pss. XCVII.4 and CIV.2) the gloss for *psallere* is *sealmian*, a derivative from *sealm* 'psalm', which apparently occurs here for the first time in an Old English text.

[11] Thus *dryman* occurs once each in *Guthlac* A and in *Genesis* A in the general sense 'to rejoice'.

laudes canere; *psalmum dicere*, bonis operibus gloriam Domini praedicare. *Cantare* enim *et psalmum dicere*, ipsa est hostia iubilationis.

he says that he is offering *up in his tabernacle a victim* [sacrifice] *of jubilation*, in other words, he is offering in His Church the sacrifice of praise. We speak of *jubilation* because we take delight in praise when in our joy we hasten to give thanks with the utmost pleasure. Earlier we said that it was one thing to sing, another to recite a psalm. Singing means uttering praises with the voice alone, whereas reciting a psalm means proclaiming the Lord's glory by good works. Singing and reciting a psalm are themselves *the victim* [sacrifice] *of jubilation*.[12]

5. On one occasion (ps. XLVI.6), the *Psalterium Gallicanum* replaces the *Romanum* reading *iubilatio* by *iubilum*, a word occurring elsewhere in the Bible (Job VIII.21, XXXIII.26) and meaning 'a sound or cry of joy'. Interestingly, Wulfstan, the precentor of the Old Minster and Æthelwold's student, twice employs this word in the sense of 'joyful music in praise of God', in the phrase *feriunt iubilum*. That Wulfstan in fact understood *iubilum* as a kind of musicological term emerges from the way he uses it in his description of the famous Old Minster organ in the *Epistola specialis*, prefaced to his *Narratio metrica de S. Swithuno* and dedicated to Bishop Ælfheah of Winchester (984–1005), Æthelwold's successor:

> Et feriunt iubilum septem discrimina uocum,
> permixto lyrici carmine semitoni.

And the seven distinct notes, with the 'lyric' semitone added, strike the *iubilum*.[13]

This various evidence combines to establish beyond reasonable doubt the sense 'joyful song of praise', 'music in honour of God' for *wyndream*, the gloss for *iubilatio* in the Royal Psalter. It is worth noting that here again

---

[12] *Expositio* I, 238–9 (ps. XXVI.6); trans. Walsh, *Cassiodorus* I, 266 (my alternatives in square brackets); cf. also *Expositio* I, 285 or II, 856.

[13] *Epistola specialis*, lines 165–6. For an edition and translation of the text (with full commentary), see Lapidge, *The Cult of St Swithun* (forthcoming). I am deeply indebted to Michael Lapidge for placing at my disposal his edition of the *Epistola*. The second occurrence of the phrase *feriunt iubilum* is in an epanaleptic poem on All Saints (*inc.* 'Aula superna poli', *ICL*, no. 1409a), ptd and transl. P. Dronke, M. Lapidge and P. Stotz, 'Die unveröffentlichten Gedichte der Cambridger Liederhandschrift (CUL Gg. 5. 35)', *Mittellateinisches Jahrbuch* 17 (1982), 54–95, at 62–5; for Wulfstan as its probable author, see *ibid.*, pp. 61–2, and Lapidge, *Wulfstan: Life*, pp. xxix–xxx. Here *iubilum* (line 6) refers to the sound of cymbals, and in the Cambridge manuscript bears the gloss *in cimbalis iubilationis* (echoing ps. CL.5).

the Glossator chose and possibly coined a recherché compound with a pronounced poetic tinge. It is also worth noting (in terms of his possible resort to the A-type gloss) that the determinant of his compound is identical with the nucleus of Vespasian's gloss for *iubilatio* (and *exultatio*): *wynsumnis*. Surely *wyndream* will not have been the only choice open to the Royal Glossator. He will have seen no difficulty in selecting other *dream* compounds; for example, *gleodream* (occurring in *Beowulf* 3021 in the sense of 'mirth, merriment') would have been a suitable candidate, since he employs several other compounds with *gliw*, *gleo* 'pleasure' with reference to musical instruments and their players, such as *sealmglig* for *psalterium* 'psaltery', *gligbeam* for *tympanum* 'timbrel', or (to the delight of his German readers) *gliwmæden* for *tympanistria* 'female timbrel-player'. Therefore it is possible but not provable that the Glossator's choice of *wyndream* was influenced by an A-type gloss.

We may now turn to the other two texts: in the Rule, we find the simplex *dream* denoting some kind of music on one occasion: *sealma dreame* (BR 43.8) 'the singing of psalms' for *psalmorum modulatione* (*RSB* 18.12). Also once, the compound *æfendream* 'evensong, vespers' is attested in the Rule – and in no other text (BR 43.18, *RSB* 18.15); it is employed here to vary the Rule's usual *æfensang* for Latin *uespera*. As was to be expected, *dream* or *dream* compounds meaning 'bliss, rejoicing' do not occur in the Rule.

This is true also for the Aldhelm glosses where the *dream* family is amply attested, the noun occurring nine times, the adjectives *dreamlic* 'musical' and *dryme* 'melodious, harmonious' once each, the adjective *gedryme* 'melodious, harmonious' four times and the verb *dryman* twice. Latin *iubilatio* occurs twice as a lemma in the Aldhelm glosses, on both occasions meaning, however, 'jubilation' in a general sense. Here the Old English glosses are the very same as used for *exultatio* in the Royal Psalter: *bliss*, *fægnung* and (perhaps) *ahefenung*.[14] In the Aldhelm glosses, the

---

[14] For the glosses for *exultatio* in the Psalter, see above, pp. 188–9. In the case of *ahefenung*, I take the spelling in the manuscript, *heofunge* (G 1376), to be an error for OE *ahefenung* (or *ahefednung* or *ahafenung*). Even though such nouns are not attested in Old English texts, there is no difficulty in explaining them as morphological variants of *(up)ahefennes*, *-hafennes* and *-hefednes*, all of which are attested in Old English. The Royal Psalter has, *inter alia*, the gloss *upahefednes* for *exultatio* (see above). The meaning of OE *heofung* (the form in the manuscript) 'lamentation, moaning' would be contrary to the required sense. We should, perhaps, not completely rule out the possibility that

lemmata for the *dream* words invariably and unambiguously denote musical terms. For the substantive *dream*, for example, the lemmata are: *concentus*, *harmonia*, *melodia* and *psalmodia*. These lemmata are glossed predominantly by *dream* (on nine occasions out of fourteen). If glossed otherwise, it is primarily the general term *sang* which is employed, and in most of such cases *dream* (or one of its derivatives) is the gloss for an adjacent lemma, as in *concentibus : sangum* (G 485), *melodiae : dreames* (G 486). Very often, the Latin lemmata for the musical terms are explained by Latin glosses as well, thus revealing the glossators' active interest in musical terminology, Latin and English. For example, the aforementioned *concentibus* (G 485) has the additional Latin glosses *melodiis* and *cantibus*. A keen interest in providing an adequate terminology in Old English emerges further from the fact that most of the musical terms which occur in Aldhelm's *De uirginitate* bear at least one Old English gloss. For example, out of all occurrences of *concentus* (5 ×), *harmonia* (4 ×), *melodia* (3 ×) and *psalmodia* (2 ×) in the *De uirginitate*,[15] only one occurrence each of *harmonia* and *psalmodia* is not glossed in Old English.

It would appear then that the highest frequency of *dream* and its derivatives referring unequivocally to the sphere of music in any single text is found in the Brussels glosses to the prose *De uirginitate*. In their remarkable preference for the *dream* family, the Aldhelm glosses obviously agree with the Royal Psalter and its innovative and frequent employment of the family in the same sense. In both glosses, as well as in the Rule, we find rare compounds and derivatives: *æfendream*, *wyndream*, *orgeldream*, *dreamlic* and the somewhat enigmatic *dryman*. In all three texts, *dream* is never used in the sense 'joy, bliss'. As 'singing' and 'music' in the three texts always refers to a performance in honour and praise of God, we witness here a Christian redefinition of an old term which in its original meaning 'joy, bliss, revelry' expresses one of the key concepts of Old English heroic poetry. It may be significant to note that such a sense development in *dream* forms an intriguing parallel to the shift of meaning in another key term of poetry, namely *modig*, shifting from 'spirited,

---

the present gloss in its restored form, as well as *upahefednes* in the Royal Psalter, had their origin as glosses to an erroneous lemma *exaltatio*. For a different explanation of *heofung*, see Napier, *OEG* 1.1345, followed by Goossens (note to G 1376).

[15] The figures are taken from Ehwald's *index uerborum*. Recall that no more than approximately one third of the text's total vocabulary is glossed; see above, p. 134 and n. 5.

brave, bold' to '*superbus*' (in an entirely negative sense) in the usage of the Winchester group of texts (on which see below, pp. 417–18).

Concerning musical terminology, mention should be made of a further link of a more general nature which connects the Aldhelm glosses, the Royal Psalter and (to some extent) the Rule. For the Aldhelm glosses we have noted a pervasive interest in such terminology by the amount of glossing in Latin and English which the lemmata in question receive. A similar interest can be observed in the Royal Psalter, apart from its deliberate and innovative use of the *dream* words. It is in this gloss that a number of Latin loanwords pertaining to music and musicology make their first or their first prominent appearance. Among these are *chor* 'choir (singers)' from Latin *chorus*, a Latin loan which the psalter shares with the Rule,[16] *cantic* 'song of praise' which (eleven times) glosses *canticum* and which is also prominent in the Rule (denoting here the monastic and daily canticles),[17] *saltere* 'psaltery' for *psalterium* and *sealmian* 'to sing psalms' for *psallere*, a verbal derivative for the earlier loan *sealm*. Next, the Royal Glossator's predilection for recherché and poetic compounds makes itself felt pronouncedly in respect of musical terminology. We already have encountered *wyndream* for *iubilatio*, *orgeldream* for *organum* and the compounds with *gliw, glig, gleo* 'pleasure', namely *sealmglig* (*psalterium*), *gligbeam* (*tympanum*) and *gliwmæden* (*tympanistria*). To these we may add *wynwerod* 'joyous band' for *chorus* and *hearpsweg* 'sound of the harp' for *cythara*. With the exception of *gligbeam* (to which we shall return presently) all these compounds may well have been coined by the Glossator, since they are attested only here and in dependent psalter glosses. That such coinages are not indebted exclusively to the native poetic tradition or to Aldhelmian diction, but may reveal as well the Glossator's scholarly inclination, emerges from a closer look at *wynwerod* (ps. CL.4). Latin *chorus* in this psalm verse is explained by Cassiodorus: '*Chorus* est plurimarum uocum ad suauitatis modum temperata collectio.'[18] Very possibly, *wynwerod* reflects *suauitas* and *collectio* from this or a similar scholion.

---

[16] See Funke, *Die gelehrten lateinischen Lehn- und Fremdwörter*, pp. 152, 160 and 164; and cf. above, p. 52.

[17] See Gretsch, 'Der liturgische Wortschatz', pp. 329–33 and 342–8, and, above, pp. 51 and 92–3.

[18] 'A *chorus* is a gathering of several voices ordered to achieve a pleasant harmony', *Expositio* II, 1328, transl. Walsh, *Cassiodorus* III, 464.

Furthermore, a comparison with the Vespasian Psalter reveals that, strikingly, the Royal Glossator has assigned different names to all the musical instruments occurring in the psalter: Latin *tuba* is always glossed *byme*; the corresponding Anglian–Kentish form *beme* occurs only once in the Vespasian Psalter; the remaining four occurrences are glossed there by *horn. Psalterium* 'psaltery' is glossed six times by the new loan *saltere*[19] in the Royal Psalter, once by the neologism *sealmglig*,[20] and once only by *hearpe* 'harp', the word which is invariably used in the Vespasian gloss. It may be worth noting that the unique instance of *hearpe* in the Royal gloss is found for the first occurrence of *psalterium* in the psalms (ps. XXXII.2), which again may point to the Glossator's resort to an A-type gloss. Latin *cythara* 'cithara' is translated as *hearpe* 'harp' on nine occasions in the Royal Psalter and once (through metonymy) as *hearpsweg* 'sound of the harp', whereas the Vespasian Psalter always employs the loan *citre*.[21] For *cymbalum* 'cymbal' we find *belle* (two occurrences); Vespasian again presents a loan: *cimbala. Organum*, which may refer to any kind of musical instrument as well as to an organ,[22] is glossed (as we have noted) once by *dream* and once by *orgeldream*; the Vespasian Psalter uses the loan *organe*. And for *tympanum* 'timbrel' (three occurrences) the Royal Psalter has the native compound *gligbeam*, Vespasian the loan *timpana*. Apart from the Royal Psalter and dependent glosses, *gligbeam* (*gleobeam*) occurs three times in poetry (for example *Beowulf* 2262) where it is used in variation for *hearpe* 'harp'. The noun must, however, have retained enough of the

---

[19] Revealing its learned character by the retention of the Latin initial consonant cluster on one occasion (*psaltere*, ps. LXXX.3), a word-initial cluster, then as now, not normally permissible in English.

[20] As is clear from the context, this refers unambiguously to the musical instrument, not the music produced by this instrument, or the chant of psalms: 'in psalterio decem chordarum psallam tibi : on sealmglige tyn strenga ic singe ðe' (ps. CXLIII.9); cf., however, ps. LVI.9, where by metonymy *sealmleoð* lit. 'psalm-song' is employed for *psalterium*.

[21] See Isidore, *Etymologiae* III. xxii. 7, for a concise description of the difference between *cythara* and *psalterium*; some such explanation may have exerted an influence on the glosses for these two instruments in the Royal Psalter. See above, pp. 169–71, for Isidorian influence on the vernacular Aldhelm glosses.

[22] See Holschneider, *Die Organa von Winchester*, pp. 135–9. For example, Isidore (*Etymologiae* III. xxi. 2) uses *organum* as a general term to include all wind instruments, whereas Cassiodorus explains it as an organ (*Expositio* II, 1382).

meaning of its components ('pleasure' and 'wood') to be transferred to an entirely different musical instrument in the Royal Psalter.

In short, it is clear that the Vespasian Psalter presents a greater number of loanwords used consistently for musical instruments: *citre*, *cimbala*, *organe* and *timpana*, whereas apart from the newly introduced *saltere*, the Royal Psalter has only one further loan: *orgeldream* (on one occasion, and in a compound with a native determinatum).[23] Since there is no question of the Vespasian Psalter generally preferring loanwords against a preference for native gloss words in the Royal Psalter, two interrelated considerations arise from such a situation. The first of these concerns the origin of Vespasian's terms. Is it possible that these may reflect a terminology in use at Canterbury (where the Vespasian gloss presumably originated) in the earlier ninth century, having been established there through the teaching of Archbishop Theodore and Abbot Hadrian more than a century earlier? These masters will have explained to their students the forms and sounds of musical instruments from biblical sources. Such

---

[23] Terms for musical instruments in Old English texts are listed by F. M. Padelford, *Old English Musical Terms* (Bonn, 1899), pp. 63–107. In connection with the names for the musical instruments in the two psalter glosses, mention must be made of a recent article on the Anglo-Saxon harp and related instruments by R. Boenig, 'The Anglo-Saxon Harp', *Speculum* 71 (1996), 290–320. Regrettably, the section on musical terminology in the psalter glosses (pp. 305–16) is crawling with inaccuracies, errors and absurdities. For example, both the Latin text of the Vespasian Psalter and its Old English gloss are dated to the eighth century (p. 310). Similarly, the prose and the metrical psalms in the Paris Psalter are treated indiscriminately, and for both an origin in the late ninth century is considered (pp. 308–9). In the 'Kentish Psalm' (ps. L), the introductory identification of King David as the author of this psalm is said to be probably derived from 'some Latin manuscript's prefatory material' (p. 310). Even more appalling are philological absurdities, as when *earpung* in the Eadwine Psalter bears the following comment: 'the *h* of the harp occasionally disappears, regularly surfacing as a phonologically suspect *æ*' (p. 308). Or when in a ridiculous line of philological argument *chorus* is said to have been understood by some Old English glossators as denoting the musical instrument *crwth* (p. 307). Furthermore, the author is sublimely unconcerned with relationships between psalter glosses. Thus the Vitellius, the Stowe and the Salisbury psalters are all analysed and commented on as independent witnesses, whereas their common ancestor, the Royal Psalter, is not so much as mentioned (pp. 306–8). Or a towering argument concerning a 'growing confusion in the early Middle Ages between harps and citoles' (p. 306) is built on the double gloss *on hearpan 7 on citran* for *in cythara* (ps. XCI.4) occurring in the Vitellius Psalter, when in fact *on citran* is no more than one of the occasional additions of an A-type gloss to the overall D-type Vitellius Psalter; and so on.

explanations will have been in Latin and may thus have paved the way for the introduction and establishment of Latin loans for musical instruments at their Canterbury school. At least one of their explanations (involving two instruments which also occur in the psalter) has survived in the Leiden Glossary[24] (and one further manuscript belonging to the 'Leiden-Family'). Here *cynaris* 'harps' in Ecclesiasticus XXXIX.20 is explained as follows:

Cyneris. nabl[a]. idest citharis longiores quam psalterium. Nam psalterium triangulum fit. Theodorus dixit.

Harps: are *nabla*, that is, citharas longer than a psaltery, for a psaltery is triangular. Theodore said so.[25]

If we reflect that the Corpus Glossary (Cambridge, Corpus Christi College 144), which also contains a large amount of material from the 'Leiden-Family' (and hence of Theodore's and Hadrian's classroom instruction),[26] was written, like the Vespasian gloss, in the first part of the ninth century, possibly at Canterbury (St Augustine's), then it may not be fanciful to think that the Vespasian glosses for musical instruments could

---

[24] This glossary (now Leiden, Bibliotheek der Rijksuniversiteit, Voss. lat. Q. 69, 20r–36r) was written at St Gallen, *c.* 800, but was clearly copied from an Anglo-Saxon exemplar. It is the principal witness of a group of glossaries (the 'Leiden-Family') all ultimately deriving from the activities of the Canterbury school of Theodore and Hadrian. See Lapidge, 'The School of Theodore and Hadrian', pp. 149–62, *idem* in *Biblical Commentaries*, ed. Bischoff and Lapidge, pp. 173–9, and below, pp. 244–5.

[25] Cf. *A Late Eighth-Century Latin–Anglo-Saxon Glossary*, ed. Hessels, xii.40 (p. 13). The translation is taken from Lapidge, *Biblical Commentaries*, p. 177. Note that the description of the *psalterium* as triangular also occurs in Isidore (*Etymologiae* III. xxii. 7) with the additional information that the psaltery is similar in shape to the *cithara barbarica*. An explanation such as this may underlie the equation of *psalterium* with a native term, *hearpe*, in the Vespasian Psalter (so unusual for this gloss). For possible implications of Isidore's expression *cithara barbarica* and the suggestion that this may refer to a type of stringed instrument in use, above all, in the British Isles, see A. M. Luiselli Fadda, 'Cithara barbarica, cythara teutonica, cythara anglica', *Romanobarbarica* 10 (1988–9), 217–39.

[26] For the relationships of the Corpus Glossary and the 'Leiden-Family', see J. D. Pheifer, 'Early Anglo-Saxon Glossaries and the School of Canterbury', *ASE* 16 (1987), 17–44, at 34–7, and *idem*, 'The Relationship of the Second Erfurt Glossary to the Épinal–Erfurt and Corpus Glossaries', in *Anglo-Saxon Glossography*, ed. Derolez, pp. 189–205, at 195–205. For links between the Corpus Glossary and the Brussels Aldhelm glosses, see above, pp. 154–8.

be indebted to the noted Canterbury school. There is, however, no way of verifying such a suspicion.

The second consideration concerns the attitude of the Royal Glossator. On the assumption that he had knowledge of the A-type gloss, his terms for the musical instruments must be judged to be a repudiation of Vespasian's terminology wherever that terminology was derived from. The consistency of such a repudiation, and the consistency with which the new terminology is applied, as well as the predilection for native equivalents for the Latin terms and the striking character of some of these native equivalents – all combine to reveal the Glossator's intrinsic interest in music and musicology. There is some confirmation that the Glossator's terms were no idiosyncrasies but enjoyed some currency, at least in later Winchester circles. Such confirmation is provided by the Lambeth Psalter, whose glossator, highly competent and independent, nevertheless drew on both a D-type and an A-type exemplar. Therefore, this glossator's adherence (with only minor divergences) to the terms of the Royal Psalter is strong evidence for their general acceptability in early-eleventh-century Winchester. A further piece of evidence for the currency of at least one of the terms chosen by the Royal Glossator is worth mentioning, since it occurs outside the psalter glosses. That *hearpe* (and not the loanword *citre*) was the common name for *cythara* in Wessex in the 940s and 950s emerges from a remark in B's *Vita S. Dunstani*: 'Sumpsit ... cytharam suam quam lingua paterna hearpam uocamus'.[27]

We have seen that the glossators of the Brussels corpus took great pains to provide *interpretamenta* for musical terms in the prose *De uirginitate*. It is therefore a great pity that – with the exception of one instance of the adjective *organica* – none of the Latin terms for musical instruments in the psalter occur in the *De uirginitate*. However, on this one occasion, the adjective (in the phrase *organica armonia* 'music of the organ') bears the gloss *dreamlic* which squares with *dream* and *orgeldream* for *organum* in the Royal Psalter. The Rule shares the common interest of the Psalter and the Aldhelm glosses in musical terminology in the wider context of its endeavour to establish a standard liturgical nomenclature. We have already noted the occurrence of the loans *chor* and *cantic* in the Rule and

---

[27] *Sancti Dunstani Vita Auctore B.*, ed. Stubbs, p. 21 (ch. 12). In all probability B was an Englishman (with an origin in the vicinity of Glastonbury) who left England for Liège in *c.* 960: see Lapidge, 'B. and the *Vita S. Dunstani*', esp. pp. 280–2.

the Psalter (above, p. 194). Further liturgical and musical terms from the Rule which prove Æthelwold's concern with a standardized terminology would be *halsung* (for the *Kyrie*), *ymen* (for liturgical hymns) and *lofsang* (for 'canticle').[28]

It is well known that Winchester during Æthelwold's episcopacy and thereafter was noted for its music. The bishop's most brilliant pupil was Wulfstan, the *cantor* or precentor of the Old Minster, who, in addition to his many other accomplishments, was one of the most proficient and renowned musicians of his age.[29] He may have played a crucial part in the development of the famous Winchester organa (an early form of polyphonic chant), as they are transmitted in two music manuscripts, the so-called 'Winchester Tropers',[30] and he may even have been one of the two scribes (Scribe II) of the older manuscript (Cambridge, Corpus Christi College 473).[31] But Wulfstan was not only a practitioner and (in all probability) a composer: he was also interested in musical theory, as emerges from a treatise on music, entitled *Breuiloquium super musicam*, now lost but still extant in the fifteenth century. This treatise is the only theoretical work on music written in Anglo-Saxon England of which we have knowledge.[32] We have no information as to who was responsible for Wulfstan's musical education. While it is true that none of our sources indicate that his master Æthelwold distinguished himself in musical theory or practice, there is ample evidence for Æthelwold's enthusiasm for liturgical music. The *Regularis concordia* and the (presumed) instalment of an organ in his rebuilt cathedral church are just two witnesses to such an enthusiasm.[33]

[28] See Gretsch, 'Der liturgische Wortschatz', pp. 323–8, 330–3 and 334–7.

[29] For a comprehensive survey and evaluation of Wulfstan's work, see Lapidge, *Wulfstan: Life*, pp. xiii–xxxix.

[30] See Holschneider, *Die Organa von Winchester*, pp. 76–80.

[31] For the two manuscripts (CCCC 473 and Bodley 775) and their Winchester connections, see below, p. 301. For the possibility that Wulfstan may have been one of the scribes, see Lapidge, *Wulfstan: Life*, p. xxxvi (with further references). There are, however, palaeographical difficulties involved in such a hypothesis: see Lapidge, 'Autographs of Insular Latin Authors', pp. 134–5.

[32] See Lapidge, *Wulfstan: Life*, pp. xvi–xvii.

[33] See above, pp. 14–16, and below, pp. 272–3, for the pervasive role played by an elaborate liturgy in the stipulations of the *Regularis concordia*. The Old Minster organ, as it was enlarged by Æthelwold's successor Ælfheah, is described by Wulfstan himself in the dedicatory verses (lines 145–76) of his *Narratio metrica de S. Swithuno*. For an evaluation of his description, see Holschneider, *Die Organa von Winchester*, pp. 139–43,

If not only the Rule, with its concern with liturgical vocabulary, but also the Royal Psalter and the Aldhelm glosses were to be connected with Æthelwold, these texts would attest to his active interest in musical terminology from an early date onwards. If some of these terms such as *gligbeam*, *sealmglig*, *wynwerod*, *wyndream* or *orgeldream* appear to be somewhat vague and of an emotional quality not now considered appropriate in technical vocabulary, we should compare the epithets, not precisely technical, by which the musical expert, Scribe II, of CCCC 473 (the Winchester Troper) describes the organa: 'melliflua organorum modulamina', 'laus amoenissima ... dulciter reboanda', 'laus iocunda Christi gloriae digna', 'electus concentus', and so on.[34] We should further bear in mind that *wynwerod* which, to modern eyes, looks much less expert and appropriate than the loan *chor* (which also occurs in the Psalter and the Rule) almost certainly owes its origin to patristic exegesis, a background which applies to *wyndream* for *iubilatio* as well.

DÆGRED, DÆGREDSANG, GLÆTERUNG, GLÆTERIAN

In the Vespasian Psalter, the adjective *matutinus* 'morning-' (one occurrence) and the noun derived therefrom, *matutinum* 'morning' (six occurrences) are always glossed by *margentid* 'morning-time', whereas for the noun the Royal Psalter has the compound *dægred* (*dæg* + *read* 'red') five times and once the *hapax legomenon glæterung* 'glitter(ing), brilliance'. The Latin adjective is glossed here by an English adjective: *dægredlic*. There are three occurrences of *diluculum* 'dawn' in the psalter, which are glossed by *ærmargen* in Vespasian, and again by *dægred* in the Royal Psalter. According to the *DOE*, approximately 110 occurrences of *dægred* are found in Old English texts, a substantial amount of these in psalter glosses dependent on the Royal Psalter, where no doubt *dægred* and *dægredlic* were first introduced into psalter glossing in a deliberate and consistent fashion.[35] None of the dependent glosses shows the Royal

---

and Lapidge, *The Cult of St Swithun* (forthcoming); for further evidence for Æthelwold's interest in organs, see below, p. 395.

[34] Cf. *The Winchester Troper*, ed. Frere, p. 85, and Holschneider, *Die Organa von Winchester*, pp. 41–3.

[35] There are three occurrences of *dægred* in Vespasian A. i, not in the psalter glosses but in the gloss to one of the three hymns contained in the manuscript. The lemmata are

Glossator's consistency, nor does the Lambeth Glossator unreservedly follow his lead: he employs the A-type glosses *morgentid* and *ærmorgen* side by side with (predominating) *dægred*. *Glæterung* does not occur in any of the dependent glosses.

Two principal reasons seem to account for the Royal Glossator's choice of *dægred*: the compound is of a somewhat poetic nature (and according to the *Microfiche Concordance* it does occur frequently in poetry), and it describes with greater precision than *morgentid* a limited and well-defined period within the longer span of the entire morning. Such a desire for a more precise rendering very possibly may have been stimulated by explanations of the various subdivisions of the morning such as those provided by Isidore's *Etymologiae* or Bede's *De temporum ratione*.[36] A 'scientific' use of *dægred* is well attested in Ælfric's *De temporibus anni* or Byrhtferth's *Enchiridion* (who based himself largely on Ælfric in the passage in question).[37] The poetic nature of *dægred* not only squares well with the Glossator's delight in poeticisms: it is also consonant with patristic exegesis, according to which *matutinum* is the hour of Christ's resurrection (and hence of the Last Judgement). Such an explanation is given by Cassiodorus on several occasions.[38] Characteristically, in ps. XLVIII.15, where Cassiodorus's exegesis describes in particularly glowing terms the glory of the Resurrection at daybreak ('*In matutino*, ac si diceret, in albescente die cum gloria resurrectionis illuxerit, quando iam beatitudinis claritas aperitur et incohat esse dies qui nulla nocte finitur'),[39] not

---

aurora 'dawn' (twice) and *crepusculum* 'twilight'; cf. *Vespasian Psalter*, ed. Kuhn, p. 158 (no. 11, *inc.* 'Splendor paternae gloriae'). For the hymns in Vespasian A. i and the relationships of their glosses, see Gneuss, *Hymnar und Hymnen*, pp. 17–19 and 123–5.

[36] Cf., for example, *Etymologiae* V. xxxi. 12–13: 'Matutinum est inter abscessum tenebrarum et aurorae aduentum; et dictum matutinum quod hoc tempus inchoante mane sit. Diluculum quasi iam incipiens parua diei lux.' This explanation is echoed almost verbatim by Bede, *De temporum ratione*, ch. 7 (ed. C. W. Jones, *Bedae Opera de Temporibus* (Cambridge, MA, 1943), p. 195). See also Cassiodorus: '*Matutinum* uero dicimus, quando discendentibus tenebris crepusculum coeperit elucere', *Expositio* I, 257.

[37] See *Enchiridion*, ed. Baker and Lapidge, p. 308 (commentary to II.3.133–43). For Byrhtferth's employment of words favoured by Æthelwold, see below, pp. 216–18 and ch. 10, *passim*.

[38] For example, *Expositio* I, 257 and 437.

[39] *Expositio* I, 437; '*In the morning* is the equivalent of saying, "At the first light of day when the glory of the resurrection dawns"; for then the brightness of blessedness is

only do we find Cassiodorus's remarks (in an abbreviated and modified form) in the margin of Royal 2. B. V (60v), but we also observe the Glossator resorting to an even more recherché *interpretamentum* for *matutinum*: the *hapax legomenon glæterung*.[40] *Glæterung* 'brilliance' is certainly not a very appropriate gloss for *matutinum* in the sense of 'early morning hour(s)', but it is an *interpretamentum* which successfully aims to convey the allegorical dimension of the lemma by a single Old English word.

In the *Regula S. Benedicti, matutini* (occurring invariably as the masc. pl. form of the adjective, used as a noun) always means 'Lauds', the first of the day hours in the monastic Office following after Nocturns. (Note that now, confusingly, the office of Nocturns is often referred to as 'Matins'.) On all occasions, *matutini* is translated by *dægredsang* in the Old English Rule.[41] The Rule is the earliest Old English text where this designation for Lauds occurs. The parallel between the consistent use of *dægredsang* in the Rule and *dægred* in the Royal Psalter is all the more striking when we reflect that in later texts[42] *dægredsang* has been replaced to a large extent by the more precise but less poetic *æftersang*.[43]

---

revealed, and that day begins which is ended by no night'; transl. Walsh, *Cassiodorus* I, 476.

[40] See below, p. 203, for the derivation of *glæterung*.

[41] The one occurrence of *dægred* for *matutini* (BR 40.13) should be seen as a form of what is called 'clipping' in Modern English word-formation, the full form *dægredsang* having been used shortly before; cf. the similar short form *æfen* (occurring twice) for normal *æfensang* (*uespera*).

[42] Of the thirty occurrences of *dægredsang* counted by the *DOE*, some eleven come from the Rule, with an additional six occurrences in the Winteney Version of the Rule. (For statistical purposes, and purposes of quotation, the *DOE* treats the Winteney Version as a separate text, which is not entirely justified, since Winteney is no more than an early-thirteenth-century redaction of the Old English Rule, retaining most of its vocabulary.)

[43] Unlike *dægredsang*, the term *æftersang* indicates that (especially from Easter until the beginning of November) Lauds should follow immediately after Nocturns: cf. *RSB* 8.4 *paruissimo interuallo*, an injunction being repeated verbatim in the *Regularis concordia* (ed. Symons, chs. 19 (p. 14) and 54 (p. 53)). During the summer months, Nocturns should be ended at daybreak; cf. *Regularis concordia* (ed. Symons, chs. 19 (p. 15) and 54 (p. 53)), again in agreement with the *Regula* (*incipiente luce*, *RSB* 8.4), whence the special appropriateness of the term *dægredsang*. Since *uhtsang* for Nocturns had been established in Old English from an early date onwards (*uht* meaning 'early morning, dawn'), the desire for unambiguous terms for the two monastic hours – Nocturns and

The lemmata *matutinus*, *matutinum* or *matutini* do not occur in the Brussels glosses. There is, however, one striking agreement between these glosses and the rendering of *matutinum* in the Royal Psalter: the Aldhelm glosses present one occurrence of the extremely rare word *glæterian* 'to glitter, shine', the very verb from which the *hapax legomenon glæterung* in the Psalter is derived by way of a suffix forming abstract nouns. Apart from Brussels 1650, *glæterian* occurs only in the Aldhelm glosses in Digby 146, where it has been copied from Brussels 1650, and in an entry in the huge glossary preserved in BL, Harley 3376 (west England, ?Worcester, s. x/xi); this entry again is clearly derived from the Brussels corpus.[44] In the Brussels glosses (and in the attestations derived therefrom) the verb occurs as a present participle (*glæteriend*, G 615) and the lemma is *flauus* 'all shades of yellow', here describing the colour of gold ('flaua auri specie splendescit').[45] The lemma occurs in a highly poetical context which may corroborate the suspicion that *glæterung* in the Royal Psalter was chosen because of its poetic connotations.[46]

THE GLOSSES FOR LATIN *HONOR*

The plethora of synonyms employed by the Royal Glossator in rendering Latin *honor* has been noted already by Wildhagen.[47] Whereas the Vespasian Psalter glosses *honor* invariably by *ar*, the Royal Psalter presents *arweorþung* (5 ×), *arweorþnesse* (1 ×), *weorþung* (2 ×), *weorþscipe* (1 ×) and *wyrðmynt* (1 ×). A search through the relevant entries in the *Microfiche Concordance* reveals that *arweorþung*, the word obviously favoured by the Royal Glossator, was introduced by him into psalter glossing and may, in fact, be one of his many neologisms. With one exception (the gospel of

---

Lauds — may also have played a part in the ousting of *dægredsang* in later texts. For a brief discussion of the Old English terms for the *horae* of the monastic Office, see H. Gneuss in *Anglia* 77 (1959), 226–31, at 227–8 (review of J. M. Ure, ed., *The Benedictine Office*).

[44] Cf. WW 239.35, Oliphant, *Harley Glossary*, no. 4956. A number of entries in the Harley Glossary represent *lemmata* and their *interpretamenta* from the prose *De uirginitate*; cf. Goossens, *Old English Glosses*, pp. 15–16.

[45] *Aldhelmi Opera*, ed. Ehwald, p. 237.14: 'glows with the tawny glint of gold' (*Aldhelm: the Prose Works*, ed. Lapidge and Herren, p. 66).

[46] See above, pp. 179–82, for *interpretamenta* with poetic connotations in the Brussels glosses.

[47] 'Studien zum *Psalterium Romanum*', p. 449.

Nicodemus), *arweorþung* occurs only in glosses dependent on the Royal Psalter. Here, as elsewhere, the Glossator may have been influenced in his choice of a gloss by the A-type *interpretamentum*: *ar*. The second compound with *ar* (*arweorþness*) is very common, particularly in Late Old English (Ælfric), but there are quite a number of occurrences in early texts as well (such as the Old English Bede). By the same token, the three derivatives of the adjective *weorþ* (*weorþung, weorþscipe* and *wyrþmynt*) are all well attested.

This variety of *interpretamenta* for Latin *honor* is wholly consonant with the penchant for lexical variation so characteristic of the Glossator. Since *honor* is not a very difficult lemma to translate, in this case such lexical variation may have been inspired, to some extent, by the Anglo-Saxon inclination to employ a multitude of synonyms for the key concepts of their vernacular poetry. A closer inspection of how the various glosses for *honor* are used reveals that the Glossator's lexical choice was apparently prompted by yet another consideration: he seems to have aimed at a lexical distinction between the instances where *honor* refers to God and those where it refers to secular persons. Whenever *honor* refers to God, the *ar*-compounds (*arweorþung* and *arweorþness*) are preferred: of the six occurrences of these compounds, four refer to God. Whenever *honor* refers to secular persons, the *weorþ*-derivatives (*weorþung, weorþscipe* and *wyrðmynt*) predominate: of the four occurrences of these derivatives, three refer to secular persons.[48] Such an attempted distinction in usage, which can be discerned in the Psalter, stands out in even clearer relief in the Rule. Here, three of the Psalter's synonyms appear: *arweorþness, wyrþmynt* and *weorþscipe*.[49] Of these, *arweorþness* occurs eleven times, always referring to God, whereas *wyrþmynt* (2 ×) and *weorþscipe* (1 ×) are used exclusively with reference to secular persons.

In the Brussels glosses the lemma *honor* does not occur; a single instance of *reuerentia* (used as a synonym for *honor* and referring to God) is glossed (in accordance with the Psalter and Rule) by *arweorþnesse* (G 379).

---

[48] Among these three occurrences, ps. XCVIII.4 may be revealing: although *honor* in the phrase *honor regis* refers to God in the wider context of the psalm, the collocation with *rex* in which it occurs (in a difficult passage) may have prompted the use of *wyrðmynt* in this instance.

[49] As *reuerentia* in the *Regula* is used as a synonym for *honor*, the Old English renderings of both lemmata have been considered for the Rule. For the psalter glosses *reuerentia* has not been taken into account, since on its two occurrences in the psalms it means 'shame'.

The *weorþ*-derivatives are represented by the same items as in the Rule: *wyrþmynt* (6 ×) and *weorþscipe* (3 ×). (That is to say both texts do not employ the third of the three derivatives found in the Psalter: *weorþung*.) They occur primarily for two lemmata: *priuilegium* and *praerogatiua* 'privilege' and never refer to God. An example would be: 'purae uirginitatis priuilegium' (Ehwald, p. 319.6) where *priuilegium* is glossed by *weorþmynt* (G 5270).

In other words, all three texts reveal a tendency to differentiate lexically (and by the choice of identical synonyms) between the honour which is due to God and the reverence due to secular persons. This is not a universal tendency in Late Old English usage, as emerges, for example, from the later psalter glosses: the Salisbury Psalter (otherwise closely dependent on the Royal gloss) invariably has *wyrþmynt* for all occurrences of *honor*.[50] This same *interpretamentum* is also used, almost exclusively, by the Lambeth Glossator (renowned for his voluminous vocabulary). It is interesting to note that the single occurrence of *arweorþung* in the Lambeth Psalter (ps. XLVIII.21) refers to *homo*, not to God; for this, the Royal gloss has *weorþscipe*.

WORDS FOR 'SACRIFICE'

The concept of 'offering, sacrifice (to God)' is expressed by a considerable number of (near-) synonyms in the psalter and the lemmata of the Aldhelm glosses: *sacrificium, holocaustum, holocaustoma, oblatio, libamen* and *hostia*. Of these, only *oblatio* occurs in the *Regula S. Benedicti* in the sense of 'oblation', that is the ceremony of presenting to God young children destined for a monastic life. The Royal Psalter, the Rule and the Brussels glosses agree in clearly preferring *offrung* as an Old English equivalent for the Latin words. *Offrung* is the only rendition employed in the Rule and, with two exceptions (one of these probably contextually conditioned), in the Aldhelm glosses.[51] *Offrung* does not occur in the Vespasian Psalter and was introduced into psalter glossing by the Royal Glossator. Less frequent synonyms in the Royal Psalter are: *onsægdness* (the most

---

[50] See Sisam, *Salisbury Psalter*, p. 44.
[51] In G 4949 *sacrificium* is glossed by *þenung* 'church service'; it is immediately followed by *holocaustoma*, glossed by *offrung* (G 4950). In G 2912 *hostia* is translated by *ansægdness*.

important A-type gloss for the lemmata for 'sacrifice'), the early loan *oflǽte* (from *oblatio*, also occurring in the Vespasian gloss), and (once, ps. L.21) the extremely rare *bring* (occurring only here and in dependent glosses and most peculiar in terms of word-formation). Except for *bring*, all these words from the Royal gloss also appear in the Lambeth Psalter, but note that here (as in the A-type gloss) *onsǽgdness*, not *offrung*, is the predominant *interpretamentum*.

Even more obvious are the links between the Royal Psalter, the Rule and the Aldhelm glosses in respect of the verbs expressing the concept of 'sacrifice': *offerre*, *sacrificare* and *immolare*. In the Royal Psalter, all occurrences of *offerre* are glossed by *bringan*, whereas Vespasian and – most interestingly – Lambeth use the loanword *offrian*. Now *offerre* in the psalms regularly means 'to offer (in a general sense), to give as a gift'. The verbs employed there for denoting a ritual or liturgical sacrifice are *sacrificare* and *immolare*. With one exception these are always translated by *offrian* in the Royal Psalter.[52] The Lambeth Psalter follows the Royal gloss in most of its *interpretamenta* for *sacrificare* and *immolare*, whereas Vespasian has *onsecgan* for *sacrificare* and *(a)geldan* for *immolare*. Thus in the Royal Psalter, as opposed to Vespasian and Lambeth, *offrian* is restricted to the meaning 'to sacrifice in a ritual or liturgical ceremony'. It may be worth noting that for such a restricted and specific meaning of *offrian*, the Glossator for once had to sacrifice his taste for equating a Latin etymon (*offerre* in this case) with its Old English loanword.[53] However, restricting *offrian* to the sense 'to sacrifice, offer up' enabled him to link the verb in a clear etymological relationship with his preferred noun for 'sacrifice': *offrung* – a rhetorical device for which he also had a pronounced taste.

Of the three verbs (*offerre*, *sacrificare* and *immolare*) only *offerre* occurs in the *Regula* and among the lemmata of the Brussels glosses. The Rule (in accordance with the Royal Psalter) never uses *offrian* for *offerre* where this has the general meaning 'to offer, give'. The verbs employed for *offerre* in this sense are *gebeodan*, *syllan* and *bringan*. There are three occurrences of *(ge)offrian* for *offerre* in the ch. dealing with the oblation of children (ch.

---

[52] Note that this exception (not unexpectedly) is found at the first occurrence of *sacrificare* in the psalter (ps. IV.6); it is glossed by the A-type word *onsecgan* (again not unexpectedly). Also note that by using *onsecgan* on this occasion, the Glossator preserves the paronomasia of the Latin psalm verse: *sacrificate sacrificium* is glossed *onsecgaþ onsǽgdnesse* (*onsǽgdnesse* as well being the A-type gloss).

[53] For this predilection, see above, pp. 52–4.

59). Since such an oblation is seen in terms of a ritual sacrifice (ch. 59 providing the details for the ceremony), these occurrences of *(ge)offrian* again square exactly with the usage in the Royal Psalter. When we recall that *offrung* is the only word employed to translate *oblatio* in the Rule, we find that here noun and verb are linked in precisely the same way as in the Psalter.

The Brussels glosses tie in with the usage presented by the Psalter and the Rule. We have noted already the agreement concerning the preference of *offrung*. As regards the verb, among the Aldhelm lemmata *offerre* always has the general sense 'to offer, give'. Accordingly it is never glossed by *offrian* in Brussels 1650, but by *beodan*, *beodan ł ongean beran* and *forgifan ł bringan*. There are two occurrences of *offrian* among the *interpretamenta*, both glossing *litare* 'to sacrifice, offer up' in a religious sense. Such parallels in usage between the three texts in question concerning the preferred words for the concept of 'sacrifice' and the specialized sense of *offrian* stand in view even more prominently when we reflect that such usage is by no means widespread in Old English texts and that, for example, the Lambeth Psalter prefers a different noun (*onsægdness*) and employs *offrian* without any semantic restrictions.

HOSP 'SCORN, OPPROBRIUM, INSULT' AND *HYSPAN* 'TO MOCK, SCORN, DERIDE, REVILE'

Both *hosp* (noun) and *hyspan* (verb) occur with great frequency in the Royal Psalter, thus allowing us to form a clear notion of the Glossator's usage. Practically all occurrences of Latin *opprobrium* and *inproperium* (used as synonyms meaning 'scorn, insult, disgrace, opprobrium') are translated by *hosp* (on twenty-one occasions).[54] All occurrences (eleven in total) of the verbs pertaining to the Latin nouns, namely *inproperare* and *exprobrare*, are glossed by *hyspan*. For these Latin lemmata the Vespasian Psalter invariably has the pair *edwit* (noun) and *edwitan* (verb). Thus the Royal Glossator, with (for him) exceptional consistency, not only employs staple *interpretamenta* for the Latin nouns and verbs, he also introduces these *interpretamenta* into psalter glossing. By and large his lexical choice has

---

[54] *Inproperium* is left unglossed on one occasion (ps. LXVIII.21), where it is a repetition of the same lemma in the preceding verse.

been adopted by the directly dependent D-type glosses as well as by the critical and innovative Lambeth Glossator.

In the Royal Psalter, *hyspan* is employed on a number of further occasions for *deridere*, *subsannare* 'to mock' and *inritare* 'to irritate', not consistently though for these lemmata.[55] The single occurrences each of *calumnia* and *calumniator* in the psalter are glossed by *hosp* and *hyspend* respectively. On one occasion the exceedingly rare adjective *hospul* is used (ps. LXXXVIII.35), coined, perhaps, by the Glossator himself. It glosses Latin *inritus* 'void, of no effect', which the Glossator presumably and mistakenly associated with *inritare* 'to irritate'. In all these cases, the Lambeth Glossator does not follow the Royal Psalter's lead, which may suggest that *hosp* and *hyspan* had gained recognition as *interpretamenta* only for *opprobrium*, *inproperium* and *inproperare*, *exprobrare* respectively. In any event, the evidence of the Royal Psalter attests to the Glossator's intrinsic interest in the word-family and enables us (once again) to observe him experimenting with an etymologically connected group of words.

In comparison with the psalter, the *Regula* and the Aldhelm lemmata contain a much smaller amount of relevant material. Nevertheless, definite links in usage between the three texts can be detected. In the *Regula*, of the psalter's principal lemmata for *hosp* and *hyspan* only *opprobrium* occurs (three times). It is translated by *hosp* once, and twice by the doublet *hosp and edwit*. There is one further occurrence of that doublet in the Rule, this time for *iniuria*, used here (*RSB* 58.3) in the sense of *opprobrium*. Although doublets are one of the characteristic traits of the Rule, such a threefold repetition of a doublet is a rarity and points to the translator's concern with an adequate rendering of the lemma. Further-more, this specific doublet, *hosp and edwit*, occurs, apart from the Rule, only (occasionally) in later psalter glosses (where it is an amalgam of the A-type and D-type *interpretamenta*), and once in the Brussels Aldhelm glosses (translating *inproperium*, G 4089). When we recall that *edwit* is Vespasian's consistent *interpretamentum* for *opprobrium/inproperium*, and when we consider that *edwit* would not have been the only lexical choice open to the translator if he wished to couple *hosp* and a (near-)synonym in a doublet (for example *bysmer* or *teona* might very suitably have been

---

[55] Note that Vespasian presents two occurrences of *hyspan* (for *subsannare* and *susurrare* 'to calumniate'). It is doubtful, however, that such sporadic occurrences should have triggered the massive use of *hosp* and *hyspan* in the Royal Psalter.

employed instead), then the unusually frequent repetition of the uncommon doublet *hosp and edwit* may permit us to surmise that the
translator of the *Regula* was thoroughly familiar with vernacular psalter
glossing.

The Brussels glosses present eight instances of *hosp*, but only two of
edwit, one of these (as we have just noted) in the rare doublet *hosp* ł
edwit.[56] The lemmata for *hosp* are principally *opprobrium* and *inproperium*,
but also *calumnia*, *contumelia* 'contumely' or *cauallatio* 'mockery'. Such a
wider range of Latin lemmata glossed by *hosp* links the Aldhelm glosses
with the Royal Psalter, whereas the occasional occurrence of *edwit* forms a
link with the Rule. There are two occurrences of *(ge)hyspan* in the
Aldhelm glosses, for *insultare* and *subsannare*. (The verbs *inproperare* and
exprobrare, consistently glossed by *hyspan* in the Psalter, do not occur
among the lemmata of the Aldhelm glosses.)

We may now consider briefly the question of why the Royal Glossator
so consistently rejected the A-type glosses *edwit* and *edwitan*, why he
chose *hosp* and *hyspan* as substitutes, and how we are to evaluate the
parallels in usage between the Psalter, the Rule and the Aldhelm glosses
when set against the occurrence of *hosp* and *hyspan* in other Old English
texts. The verb *edwitan* has been classified as Anglian by Franz Wenisch
(in accordance with earlier literature).[57] However, apart from the A-type
psalter glosses, a few scattered instances in D-type glosses and a number
of attestations in the Eadwine Psalter (in that part which apparently has
no connection with surviving psalter glosses), the verb occurs only twice
in the Lindisfarne Gospel gloss (whence on one occasion it has been
copied into the Rushworth gloss) – somewhat slender evidence for a
convincing dialectal classification. Moreover, Wenisch does not pronounce
on a potential dialectal restriction of the noun *edwit*. Not only would the
occurrences in the Rule and the Aldhelm glosses seem to speak against
any such restriction; *edwit* appears occasionally also in the works of
Ælfric, in King Alfred's translation of the *Regula pastoralis* and of the
psalms, in the Old English Orosius and so on. Now positing a verb
edwitan, restricted to the Anglian dialect, alongside a noun *edwit* in
general currency, would be a hypothesis which has not much to
recommend it. Apparently the surviving Old English texts give us only

---

[56] There are two occurrences of the adjective *edwitful* for *probrosus* 'disgraceful'.
[57] Cf. Wenisch, *Spezifisch anglisches Wortgut*, pp. 122–4.

an incomplete picture of the dialectal distribution and currency of both words, as emerges from a glance at the relevant entries in the *Middle English Dictionary*.[58] Both words seem to occur with moderate frequency in Middle English and as late as the fifteenth (noun) and even sixteenth (verb) centuries. Nonetheless, it is a fact that outside psalter glosses, for whatever reason, the verb *edwitan* is attested only very rarely in Old English texts. The sparse attestations may partly account for the Royal Glossator's rejection of the A-type verb. However, by taking the decision to jettison *edwitan*, he would have lost the potential for paronomasia inherent in A-type *edwit* and *edwitan*, a rhetorical embellishment for which (as we have seen) he had a great predilection. But by rejecting *edwit* as well and choosing the pair *hosp* and *hyspan* instead, he would have gained a new and more sophisticated etymological link between a noun and a verb representing a prominent concept in the psalter. In *hosp* and *hyspan* the difference in vowels results from i-mutation in the verb, a relationship between substantive and verb which attracted the Glossator on several other occasions (as it did the translator of the Rule and the Aldhelm glossators: see below, pp. 421–2). There will have been other reasons for the Royal Glossator's lexical choice and his rejection of *edwit* and *edwitan*, reasons such as undesirable phonological resemblance between *edwit* and the noun *edwist* bearing a positive sense ('being, substance' and 'sustenance, food'). Given the Glossator's awareness of, and interest in, sound relationships he no doubt will have noticed such a resemblance and cannot have been too pleased with it.[59]

How current were *hosp* and *hyspan* in Old English, and what may be inferred from their currency concerning the relationship between our three texts? The frequency with which both words are listed in the *Microfiche Concordance* is deceptive, as the bulk of these attestations comes from the numerous psalter glosses (from the Royal Psalter and dependent glosses, as well as from the Lambeth Psalter). Apart from these glosses (augmented by the material from the Brussels and dependent glosses), *hosp* is found frequently only in Ælfric (approximately fifty occurrences); however, Ælfric does not use the verb. The other occurrences of *hosp* and *hyspan* are, on the whole, inconspicuously and haphazardly scattered over

---

[58] See *MED* s. vv. *edwit*, *edwiten*.

[59] For the possibility that the Glossator abandoned *interpretamenta* because of undesirable phonological similarities, see above, p. 47.

a variety of texts (*hyspan* being clearly less frequently attested than *hosp*). In the light of this evidence, the similarities in usage in respect of *hosp* and *hyspan* in the Royal Psalter, the Rule and the Brussels glosses gain importance. If the Royal Psalter gloss were to be connected with Æthelwold (who in his Rule incontestably promoted the use of *hosp*), the Psalter's deliberate and consistent employment of *hosp* and *hyspan* might suggest that these words were among the translation equivalents taught (at some later stage) by Æthelwold or in his school. The frequent use of *hosp* by Æthelwold's pupil Ælfric, and the agreement of the Lambeth Psalter with the usage of the Royal Psalter, might corroborate such a presumption. On the other hand, it is evident that the word pair did not gain a wide currency, not even in Winchester circles. Why this was so, our archaeology of words does not permit us to say.

SCRUDNIAN 'TO EXAMINE, INVESTIGATE, SCRUTINIZE, MEDITATE ON', *ASCRUDNIAN* 'TO SEARCH (THROUGH)', *SCRUDNUNG* 'INVESTIGATION, SCRUTINY'

These loans ultimately derive from Latin *scrutari* 'to examine, investigate, scrutinize'. Their appearance in the Royal Psalter, the Rule and the Aldhelm glosses is of utmost importance in our search for a shared origin of the three texts, since they represent one of the most remarkable verbal links between them. Eight out of nine occurrences of *scrutari* in the psalter are translated by the simplex *scrudnian* in the Royal gloss. In the remaining instance, *scrutari* is used in a concrete sense: 'to search through someone's possessions' (ps. CVIII.11); this is glossed by the prefixed form *ascrudnian*. The Latin noun *scrutinium* (one occurrence) is translated by *scrudnung*, an abstract noun derived from *scrudnian*. *Scrudnian* or a derivative never gloss any other lemmata than forms of *scrutari*. In a word, the Latin etyma and the Old English loans derived therefrom are coupled on all their occurrences in the psalter. That the Royal Glossator took delight in employing the loanwords is suggested by his exquisite paronomasia in ps. LXIII.7: 'hy scrudnodon unryhtwisnesse hy geteorodon scrudniende scrudnunge',[60] which perfectly parallels Latin 'scrutati sunt iniquitatem defecerunt scrutantes scrutinium'. Such a predilection for the loans has no equivalent in the other psalter glosses: Vespasian

---

[60] 'They plotted iniquity, they exhausted themselves by excessive plotting'.

invariably has *smeagan* and *smeang* for *scrutari* and *scrutinium*, *interpretamenta* which are also definitely preferred by the Lambeth Glossator who, apart from following the Royal gloss on the one occurrence of *ascrudnian*, uses *scrudnian* only once and in a doublet only (*scrudnian* ⁊ *smeagan*, ps. CXVIII.115). A similar reluctance to follow the Royal Glossator's lead can be observed in the directly dependent D-type glosses. The verb *smeagan* 'to think, meditate on, scrutinize', and the noun *smeaung* or *smeang*[61] derived therefrom, occur very frequently also in the Royal Psalter but only as translations for *meditari* and *meditatio*. For these lemmata, *smeagan* and *smeang* (*smeaung*) are the usual *interpretamenta* in the Vespasian and Lambeth psalters as well, which as a result do not distinguish in their glosses between *meditari* and *scrutari* or *meditatio* and *scrutinium*. By contrast, the principal rationale behind the Royal Glossator's lexical choice seems to have been the achievement of such a distinction between the lemmata, probably because they were not full synonyms and perhaps in a further attempt to emulate the lexical opulence of the Latin language.

Although the Royal Psalter is the earliest text where *(a)scrudnian* and *scrudnung* are attested, there is reason to suspect that these loans had belonged to the Glossator's active English vocabulary for some time and were not first introduced into the language by him while he occupied himself with glossing the psalter. Some such reason may be found in the forms with a native prefix or suffix: *ascrudnian* and *scrudnung*. Although it is possible that such hybrid forms were introduced simultaneously with the primary loanword, it is perhaps more natural to assume that *scrudnian* had been in existence for some time before it underwent processes of vernacular word-formation. Furthermore, in the Royal Psalter, *scrudnian* and *ascrudnian* bear somewhat different meanings, the simplex denoting a mental process, the prefixed verb being used for a literal search. Such a distinction between shades of meaning by the employment of different morphological forms may suggest a certain familiarity with the loanword, the more so since nothing like it is found in the lexis of the psalter. Finally we have to note that in all its attestations in the Royal Psalter, *scrudnian* (and its derivatives) is consistently spelled with <d>, whereas

---

[61] See above, p. 38, for the important link which is established by the occurrence in the Royal Psalter of Vespasian's exceedingly rare form *smeang*. Lambeth and the other glosses use *smeaung* or *smeagung*.

the Latin lemmata in Royal 2. B. V invariably offer normal Latin <t>: *scrutari*. We shall return to the potential significance of this spelling shortly; for the moment, it is sufficient to stress that it would have been distinctly odd if a glossator, having decided to introduce a fresh loanword as one of his *interpretamenta*, had adopted a spelling (and hence a pronunciation) which differed markedly from that of the etymon. Since he was producing an interlinear gloss, such an oddity would have been immediately apparent to any future user of his gloss. If, however, the loanword in question had already been incorporated into his vocabulary and that of at least part of his readers, and if, in fact, they pronounced the medial plosive in *scrudnian* as represented by the spelling, namely /d/, then there would be no particular peculiarity in the divergent spellings of the Latin and Old English words, coupled as lemmata and glosses.

If we now turn to the Rule and its preface, we find clear evidence that Æthelwold was familiar with the loanwords *scrudnian* and *scrudnung* and that he did not depend on *scrutari* or *scrutinium* in his Latin exemplar for a stimulus to use both words. On the contrary, the two occurrences of *scrutari* in the *Regula*[62] are translated by *asmeagan*, whereas *scrudnian* occurs once in a doublet, *smeað and scrutnoð* for Latin *quaerere*, used here in the sense of 'to meditate on'.[63] In the preface to the Rule (that is in Æthelwold's original English prose), the exceedingly rare noun *scrudnung* occurs once, again in collocation with *smeagan*: 'He [*scil.* King Edgar] began mid geornfulre scrudnunge smeagan 7 ahsian be þam gebodum þæs halgan regules'.[64]

Two points are important here. First, the spelling: like the Psalter, the Preface offers medial <d>.[65] In the Rule, two manuscripts (Oxford, Corpus Christi College 197 and Durham Cathedral B. IV. 24) write

---

[62] *RSB* 7.14 and 55.16; note that in 55.16, *scrutari* is the reading of the *textus receptus* and hence that of Æthelwold's exemplar. The *textus purus* has here the later derivative *scrutinare*; see Hanslik's *apparatus criticus* for the variants (*Benedicti Regula*, p. 143). For the textual recensions of the *Regula* and Æthelwold's exemplar, see below, pp. 241–51.

[63] See *RSB* prol. 14 and BR 2.16.

[64] 'With earnest scrutiny he began to investigate and inquire about the precepts of the holy rule', *CS*, p. 150.

[65] As we have seen, the preface to the Rule is preserved uniquely in a twelfth-century manuscript (BL, Cotton Faustina A. x, s. xii[1]). However, the scribe does not appear to have tampered much with the orthography of his exemplar. In any event, if he had tampered with the noun in question, one would expect <scrutnunge>, <t> being the usual spelling for the family outside Æthelwold's circle.

<scrutnoð>, two further manuscripts (London, BL, Cotton Titus A. iv and the 'Winteney Version', London, BL, Cotton Claudius D. iii) have <scrudnaþ>, Cambridge, Corpus Christi College 178 lacks the prologue (where *scrudnian* occurs), and in BL, Faustina A. x, a word has been erased, presumably *scrudnaþ* or *scrutnaþ* (to judge from the still legible traces).[66] In short, we have no unambiguous evidence whether in this instance Æthelwold originally spelled the verb with <d> or <t>, but it may well have been *scrudnaþ*. The second point worth noting concerns the (presumably) unusual character of the word-family. As we have just seen, *scrudnian* has probably been erased in Faustina A. x. This may indicate that the scribe (or a corrector) felt some uneasiness about the word. Such a suspicion that the word was of a somewhat exotic nature could be confirmed by the fact that *scrudnian* occurs only once in the Rule and then in a doublet with the extremely frequent verb *smeagan*, which leaves its meaning in no doubt. We should recall that utter clarity of diction was one of Æthelwold's principal stylistic aims when translating the *Regula*. On the other hand the preface to the Rule is addressed (at least in part) to a more learned audience and parades a somewhat more flamboyant vocabulary and phraseology.[67] It is suggestive therefore to see Æthelwold here employing *scrudnung* in his original English prose in an elaborate sentence and without feeling the need to add an explanatory synonym. In any event, it is clear that *scrudnung* was of an even more recondite character than the verb *scrudnian*. Apart from the two occurrences we have been discussing, one in the preface to the Rule, the other in the Royal Psalter, there is only one further attestation, namely in Byrhtferth's *Enchiridion* (on which see below).

In the Brussels glosses, *scrutnian* appears once for Latin *scrutari* (G 270); regrettably, *scrutari* occurs no more than three times as a lemma. What has been said about the original spelling of *scrudnian* in the Rule applies here to an even larger extent: since these glosses are at several removes from the original glossed manuscript, their original orthography is irrecoverably lost.[68] In the Aldhelm glosses, *scrutnian* means 'to meditate on, scrutinize'; it has therefore the same abstract sense found almost

---

[66] See Schröer's *apparatus criticus* (*Benediktinerregel*, p. 2). For the manuscripts of the Rule and their dates, see below, p. 227.

[67] For the style of the Preface in comparison to that of the Rule, see above, pp. 121–4, and for the historical context in which both texts may have originated, see below, pp. 233–60.

[68] For the textual history of the Brussels glosses, see above, pp. 142–58.

exclusively in the Psalter and the Rule. A further point of agreement with the Rule is that *scrutnian* is not invariably the translation equivalent for the lemma *scrutari*.[69]

As a result of a search for further occurrences of *scrudnian* or its derivatives, the verbal links between the Psalter, the Rule and the Aldhelm glosses stand out even more clearly. The words are attested only sporadically, and several of the texts where they are attested show some influence of Winchester vocabulary or are even members of the Winchester group. In this last category belongs the Old English translation of the Rule of Chrodegang, where an agent noun *scrudnere* (for Latin *exactor* in the sense of 'investigator, judge') is attested as a *hapax legomenon*. (Note the spelling with <d>, and that again the Latin lemma is not a derivative of *scrutari*.) The verb *scrutnian* in the sense 'to meditate on, consider' is used twice by Ælfric. (Note again the spelling, this time with <t> which might be explained on the grounds of Ælfric's ideal of linguistic correctness.) Most interestingly, on both occasions the verb has been jettisoned in several manuscripts. In the first instance, of the eight manuscripts containing the homily in question, only five attest *scrutnian* in an unadulterated form; it is replaced by other verbs (*geðencan, smeagan*) in two manuscripts, and one manuscript adds an explanatory Old English gloss (*gecnawan*).[70] The verb has been substituted even more drastically on its second occurrence: of the nine manuscripts containing the homily in question, *scrutnian* is preserved unadulterated only in two; it is replaced by other verbs in six manuscripts ((*a-/on-)scunian, truwian*), and in one manuscript again, it is provided with an explanatory gloss (*smeagan*).[71] In both cases it is clear, *inter alia* from the nature of the variants, that *scrutnian* was the original reading. What is not clear altogether is whether

---

[69] It may be noteworthy that among the alternative glosses for *scrutari*, we meet *gecneordlæcan* 'to be diligent, study' (G 1138). This verb belongs to a word-family (consisting further of the noun *gecneordness* and the adjective *gecneord*) which is very prominent in the Royal Psalter, the Rule and its preface and the Brussels glosses themselves, but which otherwise is not very common in Old English texts.

[70] See *Catholic Homilies*, ed. Thorpe I, 582.25. I am deeply grateful to the late Professor Peter Clemoes for kindly letting me have the relevant manuscript variants from the *apparatus criticus* of his forthcoming edition of the first series of the *Catholic Homilies*. (This edition has now been published: *Ælfric's Catholic Homilies. The First Series. Text*, ed. P. Clemoes, EETS SS 17 (Oxford, 1997); cf. *ibid.*, p. 510.18.).

[71] See *Catholic Homilies* II, ed. Godden, p. 48.205; cf. Godden's critical apparatus for the variants.

at least one or two of the variant readings are attributable to Ælfric himself or whether they are all due to later scribes.[72] We do not know for certain, therefore, whether only those scribes took offence at *scrutnian* or whether Ælfric himself replaced it when revising his homilies, thus eliminating from his own works a word with which he will have been familiar through his teacher Æthelwold, or through the course of his Winchester education, but which he himself had scarcely used in his voluminous writings. It may be worthwhile to recall here that another prominent member of the Winchester group of texts, the Lambeth Psalter, retains only two of the Royal Psalter's numerous occurrences of *scrudnian*.

One further occurrence of *scrutnian* is found in the anonymous homily on the Seven Sleepers, which although it does not belong to the Winchester group proper, has some clear verbal links with this group.[73] Note, however, that *scrutnian* is used here in the concrete sense (otherwise only poorly attested) 'to search, look for'. Among the few and random Old English glosses to Isidore's *Synonyma* in London, BL, Harley 110 appears a further instance of *scrudnian* (spelled with <d>); again, interestingly, the Latin lemma is not *scrutari* but *inuestigare*. The manuscript (containing Prosper's *Epigrammata* and *Versus ad coniugem* in addition to the *Synonyma*) is dated s. x^ex and was written at Christ Church, Canterbury. The Old English glosses are nearly contemporary with the text.[74] They are too sparse (fifteen in total, with a further three from the *Epigrammata*) to permit speculation on the intellectual milieu in which they originated.[75] Nevertheless, the occurrence of the rare verb *scrudnian* in so small a set of glosses is remarkable and tantalizing.

There is, however, one author who shows an infatuation with *scrudnian* and its derivatives comparable to the Royal Glossator's: Byrhtferth of

---

[72] For a general discussion of the possibility that variant readings in the manuscript of the *Catholic Homilies* may be traced to Ælfric, see Godden, *Catholic Homilies*, pp. lxxviii–lxxxvi.

[73] See Hofstetter, *Winchester und Sprachgebrauch*, pp. 154–5; the homily is printed in *Lives of Saints*, ed. Skeat I, 488–541.

[74] See Ker, *Catalogue*, p. 304 (no. 228). The Old English glosses have been printed by Meritt, *Old English Glosses*, pp. 24–5 (no. 21).

[75] Nor (as it would appear) could the more frequent Latin glosses in the manuscript offer much help in this respect, since it seems likely that they travelled with the text in the exemplar from some continental centre; see Lapidge, 'Study of Latin Texts', pp. 465–70 and 494–5.

Ramsey (b. *c.* 970; d., perhaps, after 1016).[76] The verb occurs eight times in his *Enchiridion*, always in the prefixed form, *ascrutnian*, and always meaning 'to investigate, examine, work through'. Moreover, Byrhtferth uses members of the word-family in precisely the same kind of parono-masia as the Royal Glossator (*mid scrutniendre scrutnunge*, *Enchiridion* I. 2. 114), a paronomasia in which he also parades the Latin etyma in the Latin portions of his *Enchiridion* on several occasions.[77] Walter Hofstetter has shown the remarkable affinity of Byrhtferth's vocabulary with the usage of the Winchester group of texts.[78] We have already had occasion to note Byrhtferth's keen interest in glosses and glossed manuscripts, and we shall consider his penchant for unusual words and some of his verbal links with the Royal Psalter, the Rule and the Aldhelm glosses in a later ch..[79] For now it is sufficient to remark that, when compared with the precarious state *scutnian* has in the works of Ælfric, Byrhtferth's taste for the word-family may reveal somewhat further the connotations carried by these loans and their stylistic register. Whereas Ælfric promoted his ideal of clarity and simplicity of diction with a kind of rigorist determination throughout his works,[80] Byrhtferth has a pronounced propensity for an arcane, 'hermeneutic' vocabulary in his English as well as in his Latin writings.[81] In other words, Ælfric's and Byrhtferth's attitude towards the *scrudnian* words may confirm our earlier suspicion concerning the exotic flair of that word-family.

Is it possible to get even closer to an appreciation of what precisely made up the exotic character of *scrudnian* and its derivatives? An answer to this question may be found in the spelling *scrudnian* with medial <d> occurring in the Royal Psalter and the Rule (as well as in the Rule of

---

[76] For an evaluation of the evidence for Byrhtferth's life and career, see *Enchiridion*, ed. Baker and Lapidge, pp. xxv–xxxiv.

[77] For Byrhtferth's use of the *scrudnian* family, see also below, pp. 407–10.

[78] See Hofstetter, *Winchester und Sprachgebrauch*, pp. 268–72 and 412–15, esp. 414.

[79] See above, pp. 139–41 and 176, and below, pp. 396–420, *passim*. For Byrhtferth's interest in the vocabulary of glosses, see *Enchiridion*, ed. Baker and Lapidge, pp. cvi–cxi. On the arcane quality of much of his diction, see also (briefly) M. R. Godden, 'Literary Language', in *The Cambridge History of the English Language* I, ed. R. M. Hogg (Cambridge, 1992), pp. 490–535, at 533–4.

[80] For a classic study of Ælfric's prose style, see P. Clemoes, 'Ælfric', in *Continuations and Beginnings*, ed. E. G. Stanley (London, 1966), pp. 176–209, esp. 196–202.

[81] For the hermeneutic vocabulary of Byrhtferth's Latin works, see Lapidge, 'Hermeneutic Style', pp. 128–32; see also below, p. 399, n. 40.

Chrodegang and the gloss to the *Synonyma* in Harley 110). This spelling very possibly reflects a pronunciation of Latin *scrutari* with Romance lenition of the plosive in intervocalic position. A development from *t* to *d* in this position cannot be accounted for by any native sound change, which lends even greater plausibility to this explanation.[82] Now given the historical background in mid-tenth-century England, 'Romance' influence can only mean the pronunciation of *scrutari* by West Frankish speakers. Accordingly, *scrudnian* would have to be connected with the small group of French loanwords which can be identified among the Brussels glosses. We shall return to these loans later (below, ch. 10). For the moment, it is important to note that, in all probability, the Royal Glossator had adopted *scrutari* as a loanword in a form presumably influenced by Romance (Old French) pronunciation, some time before he glossed all occurrences of *scrutari* in the psalter by *scrudnian*. Æthelwold's use of *scrudnian* and *scrudnung* in an identical form and for a lemma other than *scrutari*, or even without being prompted by a Latin lemma at all, points in the same direction. At some stage in their ephemeral career, the Romanized forms were re-Latinized to *scrutnian* and *scrutnung*, the form in which they appear in the Brussels glosses.

In a word, the phonological evidence combines with the evidence of the meaning of the words and that of their infrequent attestations to suggest that the loans were adopted by a small circle of scholars in learned discussions with their West Frankish colleagues, and that they therefore belonged to the sphere of scholarly and clerical jargon. Such a presumption would help to explain why they apparently never gained a wider currency, why they would not have appealed to Ælfric and why they would have been so attractive to Byrhtferth. In Byrhtferth's case the two-years' contact (985–7) with his master Abbo of Fleury may additionally have encouraged his use of these loanwords (which he probably had encountered in the course of his extensive reading). This in turn serves to confirm the presumed recondite and scholarly nature of *scrudnian* and its derivatives.

---

[82] Campbell's explanation (§546, n. 1) that *d* in *scrudnian* reflects 'native voicing of *t* before *n*', is unsatisfactory, *inter alia* because none of our Old English grammars, not even Campbell himself, adduces any further examples for such a presumed voicing. See also Funke, *Die gelehrten lateinischen Lehn- und Fremdwörter*, p. 130, who considered Romance influence in the phonological form of *scrudnian* as possible. We shall examine the phonological evidence in greater detail in a later ch., below, pp. 408–10.

FURTHER AGREEMENTS BETWEEN THE PSALTER,
THE RULE AND THE ALDHELM GLOSSES

Having examined closely some of the interesting and suggestive verbal ties linking the Royal Psalter, the Rule and the Brussels glosses, we may now consider very briefly a number of further agreements in usage between the three texts (or between any two of them).

In the Vespasian Psalter, *epulari* 'to dine, feast' (two occurrences) is glossed by *symblian* 'to feast, carouse'. For nouns meaning 'festival, holy day' (*dies solemnis*, *festus* etc.) *symbel* and words derived therefrom (such as *symbeldæg*) are used there. The Royal Psalter, the Aldhelm glosses and the Rule seem to agree in a gradual and successive replacement of the *symbel* family. In the Psalter, the verb *symblian* is replaced by *gewistfullian* 'to feast' (perhaps in order to avoid an unambiguously secular, hedonistic use of the stem *symbel-*), but *symbel* as a simplex or part of a compound noun is retained (perhaps under the influence of the A-type gloss). The Aldhelm glosses seem to square with the Psalter: they offer *(ge)wistfullung* for (hedonistic) *deliciae* and *opulentiae* (the last lemma (G 1906) has *epulae* as an additional Latin gloss; cf. *epulari*, glossed *gewistfullian* in the Royal Psalter), but they use *symbelness* for *solemnitas* 'solemnity'. In the Rule, the noun *symbel(-)* does not occur; lemmata such as *dies festus* or *solemnitas* (referring of course to Christian feastdays) are translated by *freolsdæg* and *freolstid* (*solemnitas* once (BR 37.5) by *weorþung*, which points to verbal experimentation). *Freolstid* (for *solemnitas*, G 2526) occurs once in the Aldhelm glosses as well. (Regrettably, the lemma *epulari* (or a synonym) occurs neither in the Brussels corpus nor in the *Regula*; as in the Psalter, *symblian* is not used in the glosses and the Rule.) When we recall that *symblian* is the A-type gloss for *epulari*, and in view of the various compounds with *symbel* (attested in other texts) which unequivocally refer to feasting (such as *symbelgal* 'drunk'), we may suspect that the *symbel* words may have borne too many connotations of feasting and carousal to let them appear satisfactory terms for a Christian (or religious) feastday – at least to translators deeply concerned with the meanings and registers of words. On this hypothesis, the Royal Glossator's attempt to dissociate *epulari* and *symblian* (by substituting *gewistfullian*) and to restrict *symbel(-)* to the religious sphere (an attempt also discernible in the Aldhelm glosses), in the event, would have been abandoned in favour of a fresh terminology for Christian feastdays, nascent in the Aldhelm glosses and the Rule.[83]

The Royal Psalter and the Rule agree in using a compound (*galsmere*, Rule) and a derivative (*agælan*, Psalter) of *gal*, not with the clear sexual overtones ('wanton(ness), lust') which this word-family usually has in Old English, but in a sense which presupposes the extremely rare meaning 'gay (in the old sense), light, cheerful' for the adjective *gal* which underlies both formations.[84] This sense of *gal* may very possibly be attributable to Old Saxon influence, and we shall consider *galsmere* and *agælan* in this context in a later ch. (below, pp. 390–1). *Galsmere* (BR 30.9)[85] 'frivolous, facetious, jocose' is a *hapax legomenon* and translates *facilis ac promptus in risu* (*RSB* 7.59). The Royal Psalter twice has *agælan* for *profanare* 'to profane' (ps. LXXXVIII.32 and 35). As a causative verb, derived from *gal* (in its 'Old Saxon' sense), *agælan* would mean 'to make light of' and is therefore a perfect translation for *profanare* in contexts such as: 'neque profanabo testamentum meum' (ps. LXXXVIII.35). However, the Glossator did not settle on a single *interpretamentum* for *profanare*: (*ge*)*wemman* (closer in meaning to the A-type gloss for *profanare*, namely *besmitan* 'to soil, defile') is used as an alternative, once (ps. LXXXVIII.40) alone, and once (ps. LXXXVIII.32) in a doublet with *agælan*. Although the Brussels glosses offer no instance of *agælan*, it is interesting to note that they reveal a similar indecision in respect of the lemma *profanare* (occurring once, G 2658): four Latin glosses are followed by the extremely rare Old English verb *awidlian*.

The links between our three texts in their translations of *furor* 'furor, wrath' and *zelus* 'zeal', also 'rivalry, jealousy', are intricate. To put it briefly, both lemmata are glossed indiscriminately by *hatheortness* in the Vespasian Psalter. While offering the A-type gloss for *furor*, the Royal Glossator obviously aimed at a different *interpretamentum* for *zelus*. For this he employs once (ps. LXXVIII.5) *eorre* and once (ps. LXVIII.10) the extremely rare noun *tyrging*, which is derived from the verb *tyrgan* 'to

---

[83] According to Wenisch, *Spezifisch anglisches Wortgut*, pp. 230–1, the noun *symbel* is Anglian, a labelling which is questionable at least, since it does not take into account the distribution of the verb and of the numerous compounds.

[84] For the numerous attestations of a sexual meaning for members of the *gal* family, see B. v. Lindheim, 'Traces of Colloquial Speech in Old English', *Anglia* 70 (1951), 22–42, at 40–2.

[85] The determinatum of the compound belongs to *smerian* 'to laugh, scorn'.

exasperate, provoke' (not very frequent itself). This verb occurs both in the Royal Psalter and in the Aldhelm glosses as a translation for *exacerbare*. The Aldhelm glosses agree further in the *interpretamentum hatheort* for *furibundus* (once, G 2921; *furor* itself, glossed by *hatheortness* in the Psalter, does not occur among the lemmata of the Brussels glosses, nor is it employed in the *Regula*). For reasons which space forbids to be discussed here, both glosses for *zelus* in the Royal Psalter (*eorre* and *tyrging*) do not seem to have turned out as satisfactory equivalents for *zelus*. The lemma is translated by *anda* and *æfest* in the Rule; *æfest* and derivatives of *anda* (*andig* and *andian*) in that same sense (though for other lemmata) occur also in the Aldhelm glosses.

All three texts stand out by the great frequency with which the adjective *geþwære* 'concordant, compliant, gentle' and its derivatives (*geþwærness*, *geþwærian*, also with the negation prefix *un-* : *ungeþwære* etc.) occur. In the Rule, these words are employed also in passages which are translated freely or which have been added to the original, which reveals the word-family as belonging to Æthelwold's active and preferred vocabulary.

Another adjective well attested in the three texts is *þæslic* 'suitable, congruous'. It is especially frequent in the Rule (including its preface) and the Aldhelm glosses. Both these texts also feature the uncommon formations *þæslæcan* 'to agree with', *unþæslic* 'inappropriate' and *unþæslicu* 'incongruity', which points to the vitality of the word-family in these texts. The three texts agree further in that they employ the (not very common) adjective *gehyþe(lic)* 'suitable, proper, convenient' as a synonym for *þæslic*.

Similarly, all three texts show a predilection for the noun *gymen* 'care, heed, diligence' and related words. In the Royal Psalter, *begyman* (for *intendere*, *obseruare* and *attendere*) and *(be)gyming* (for *obseruatio*) are introduced into psalter glossing as opposed to A-type *(be)haldan* and *gehæld*. Other words of that family which occur are: *ofergyman*, *gymeleas*, *forgymeleast* and *forgymeleasian*.

Between them, the Royal Psalter and the Aldhelm glosses offer three occurrences of the exceptionally rare noun *gehwædness* 'insignificance' (ps. CI.24, G 20 and 2521) which is attested only twice elsewhere. The Aldhelm glosses and the Rule agree in using the (not very common) adjective *gehwæde* 'slight, insignificant' several times (for example BR 12.3 and 89.13; G 3637 and 5297).

The three texts reveal a sustained and judicious effort to distinguish, by their lexical choice, between *disciplina* meaning 'teaching instruction, training' and *disciplina* in the sense of 'discipline' (that is either the ability to control your own behaviour or punishment for not obeying the rules). For *disciplina* in the first sense they tend to employ *lar*, whereas *disciplina* in the second sense is rendered by *steor*, *þeawfæstness* or *þreal*. Such a distinction is by no means to be expected in Old English translations, let alone in interlinear glosses (where often no attention is paid to any contextual meanings).[86]

As far as can be reconstructed from the lexical material, the three texts seem to aim to distinguish between the various senses of the Latin prefix *con-*, inasmuch as the Old English prefix *samod-* is used for *con-* meaning 'together', but *efen-* for *con-* meaning 'equal'. Examples would be: *gesamodlæcan* (*collocare*), *samodhering* and *samodherian* (*collaudatio, collaudare*) in the Psalter,[87] *samodcuman* (*confluere*), *samodefestan* (*concurrere*) and *efen-hlytta* (*consors* 'companion') in the Aldhelm glosses, and *efenþeow* (*conseruus*) in the Rule. By the same token, *efen-* invariably means 'equal, like' in words translating other lemmata than those prefixed with *con-*, for example in *efenlæcan* 'to imitate' (*imitari*, Rule) and its derivatives *efenlæcung* (Aldhelm glosses, Rule) and *efenlæcere* (Aldhelm); or in *efen-modlice* (*aequanimiter*, Aldhelm), *efenness* (*aequitas*, Psalter) and *efenfela* 'just so many' (*totidem*, Aldhelm). By contrast, the Vespasian Psalter presents no such restricted use of *efen-*, employing the prefix for *con-* 'together' (for example in *efenhergan* and *efenherenis* for *collaudare, collaudatio*), as well as in the sense 'equal, like' (for example in regular and frequent *efenness* for *aequitas*; this in accordance with the Royal Psalter).[88] The Royal Psalter seems to have been one of the earliest texts where *samod-* for *con-* 'together' was used.[89]

---

[86] For *lar* as an *interpretamentum* for *disciplina* in the second sense in some interlinear glosses, see Kornexl, *Die 'Regularis Concordia' und ihre altenglische Interlinearversion*, p. 169.

[87] For these loan formations, see Gneuss, *Lehnbildungen*, p. 81.

[88] See *ibid.*, p. 110.

[89] It is interesting to note here again some lexical experimentation in the Royal Psalter: for *con-* 'together' in *comparare* (ps. XLVIII.13 and 21), glossed by *efen(a)metan* in Vespasian (cf. Gneuss, *Lehnbildungen*, p. 130), the Royal Psalter presents *wiðmetan*. The use of *wið* (having the primary sense 'against, opposite, beside') may suggest that for the Royal Glossator the prefix in *comparare* had a (slightly) different meaning from that in, say, *collaudare* (which he translated by *samodherian*).

In all three texts (otherwise rarely attested) prefix formations with *þurh-* can be found. The Psalter offers *þurhbitter* for *peramarus*, the Rule *þurhwunung* for *perseuerantia* and the Aldhelm glosses *þurhhalig* for *sacrosanctus*, *þurhwerod* for *praedulcis* and *þurhwacol* for *peruigil*.

Aside from such agreements in vocabulary and usage involving all three texts, there are a number of verbal links between any two of them. For example, the Royal Psalter and the Aldhelm glosses employ the following rare words: *cocerpanne* 'cooking-pan', *fyrþolle* and *þolle* 'implement for roasting (martyrs)',[90] three compounds with *firen* 'crime, sin' used with a sexual meaning (*firenligrian* 'to fornicate', *firenhycge* and *firenhycgend* 'fornicator'), *haligern* 'sanctuary', *onal* 'burning', *onælan* 'to burn', *orceapungum*, *orceapes* 'gratis', *þeosterful* 'dark, dusky', *metsian* in the sense 'to feed', and *ypplen* 'top, height'.[91]

Striking agreements between the Rule and the Aldhelm glosses comprise the use of *(ge)widmærsian* 'to spread about', *leohtbrædness* 'levity, frivolity' and *onhnigan* 'to bend down, bow'. A most suggestive link between these two texts is provided by the phrase *þæt gastlice andgit*, referring to allegorical exegesis of the Bible in general or, specifically, to one of the four levels of biblical exegesis. Among the several hundreds of attestations for *gastlic* recorded in the *Microfiche Concordance*, the collocation *gastlic andgit* is exceedingly rare – apart from Ælfric, where it occurs frequently. *Gastlic andgit* is found once for *allegoria* in the Brussels glosses (and in related glosses, G 282). Note that *gastlic andgit* glosses *anagogen* (one of the four levels of exegesis) already in the First Cleopatra Glossary (WW 338.10). This attestation and the occurrence in the Rule (BR 66.19) are the earliest recorded instances of the phrase, and there is reason to think that Æthelwold may have coined the expression (see above, pp. 8–11). Apart from the Rule and the Aldhelm glosses (and the numerous instances in Ælfric), I have counted only four other attestations of *gastlic andgit*, one of these in the Rule of Chrodegang, a text clearly belonging to the Winchester ambit.

A further important link between the Rule and the Aldhelm glosses has recently been uncovered by Walter Hofstetter in the course of his

---

[90] On *(fyr)þolle*, see Meritt, *Fact and Lore*, pp. 82–3.

[91] As regards *ypplen* as well as *cocerpanne* (and a few other glosses) there are interesting links with the voluminous glossary in Harley 3376 (?Worcester, s. x/xi) which would merit closer study; on *cocerpanne*, see also above, pp. 80–1.

study of the stylistic range and the chronological and dialectal distribution of the Old English compound adjectives with *-cund* as their second component (*woruldcund, eorþcund, godcund* etc.). Hofstetter's study has revealed that the Rule and the Brussels glosses share a predilection for such adjectives which are otherwise rare in later West Saxon texts.[92]

Among the noteworthy lexical agreements between the Rule and the Royal Psalter, their use of *nytennes* should be counted, which is employed here in the sense of 'ignorance', a meaning not very common in Old English texts but one which (apart from the Psalter and the body of the Rule) occurs three times in the preface to the Rule, that is to say without being prompted by any Latin lemma. Note further the exclusive use of *becypan* for *uendere* and *uenundare* in both texts (as opposed to more frequent *beceapian* or *(ge)sellan*). A most important link between the Royal Psalter and the Rule consists in their shared attempt to distinguish between *humiliare* used transitively 'to humiliate someone' and *humiliare* in the sense 'to humiliate oneself, be humble'. For the first sense, both texts tend to use *geniþrian*, for the second, *geeaþmedan*. This common usage shared between the Rule and the Royal Psalter gains importance when we consider that neither the Vespasian nor the Lambeth Psalter nor even the directly dependent D-type glosses seem to aim at such a lexical distinction. (*Humiliare* does not occur as a lemma in the Aldhelm glosses, which leaves us without a means of comparing these glosses with the usage in the Royal Psalter and the Rule.)

CONCLUSION

At the end of our survey of verbal agreements between the Rule, the Royal Psalter and the Aldhelm glosses, it should be stressed that this survey does not aim at completeness. There can be little doubt that closer inspection of the lexis of the three texts would reveal a sizeable number of further links. It should also be stressed – and it will have become clear in the course of our explorations – that a considerable amount of philological archaeology is needed to recover the common usage shared between three texts of so different a nature. Traditional philological labels such as 'dialect vocabulary' or 'loan formations' can offer little help in our

---

[92] See Hofstetter, 'The Old English Adjectival Suffix *-cund*', in *Words, Texts and Manuscripts*, ed. Korhammer, pp. 325–47, esp. 344–6.

archaeological work. In spite of the limited range of the foregoing survey, the evidence which we have been able to unearth is suggestive. If we add to this evidence the links between the Psalter and the Rule which we have encountered in the course of our examination of the Psalter's vocabulary (above chs. 3 and 4), and if we recall that the Brussels gloss corpus (so obviously composite) at some point in its textual history received revision at a centre where Winchester usage was practised (above, pp. 148–9), and that its method of glossing is similar in many ways to that of the Royal Glossator (above, pp. 148–83), then the hypothesis of a common origin for all three texts gains probability. We will have occasion to consider further lexical links between the three texts in our examination of the small group of Old French and Old Saxon loans which they present (below, ch. 10). But it is time now to ask whether there is any evidence, other than that offered by philology, which may suggest an origin of the Royal Psalter and the Aldhelm glosses with Æthelwold and his circle.

7

Æthelwold and the Old English Rule

In our attempt to trace the intellectual home of the Royal Psalter and of the core of the Brussels Aldhelm glosses, our attention has focused thus far on verbal and to some extent on stylistic links between the Old English Benedictine Rule, the Psalter and the Aldhelm glosses. It has also focused on some general principles which seem to have been crucial in the choice or coinage of Old English *interpretamenta* (such as a taste for words with a 'hermeneutic' flavour) and which are shared between the three texts. In a philological study concerned with the origin and authorship of texts, such verbal and stylistic links and shared common principles must be the cornerstones and the *conditio sine qua non* for any hypothesis assuming for the texts in question an origin either with a single author or within a distinct intellectual group or school. However, philology is not an island. Therefore, philological arguments for a common authorship of any two or more works must bear scrutiny in the light of various kinds of external evidence and must seek confirmation and supplementation by such evidence as may be gleaned from (say) history, liturgiology, palaeography or art history. We may best begin this task by briefly reviewing and reassessing what is known about the authorship and the date of the Old English prose translation of the *Regula S. Benedicti*, since this is the one text which has been assigned to Bishop Æthelwold for centuries.

THE AUTHORSHIP OF THE OLD ENGLISH RULE

None of the five complete copies of the Old English Rule and none of the three fragments which have survived from Anglo-Saxon England bears an attribution of authorship. The following eight manuscripts are in question:[1]

Complete texts:

Oxford, Corpus Christi College 197, 1r–105r (x); s. $x^{3/4}$, provenance: Bury St Edmunds.[2]

Cambridge, Corpus Christi College 178, pp. 287–457 (w); s. xi^1, provenance after 1100: Worcester.

London, British Library, Cotton Titus A. iv, 2r–107r (j); ?Winchester, ?Canterbury, St Augustine's, s. xi^{med}.

Durham, Cathedral Library, B. IV. 24, 98v–123v (s); s. xi^2, provenance: Durham.

London, British Library, Cotton Faustina A. x, 102r–148r (F); s. xii^1.

Fragments:

Wells, Cathedral Library, 7, 1r–23v (u); s. xi^{med} (chs. 50–64).

London, British Library, Cotton Tiberius A. iii, 103r–105r (i*); Canterbury, Christ Church, s. xi^{med} (ch. 4).

Gloucester, Cathedral Library, 35, 6v (G); s. xi^2, provenance after 1100: Gloucester (part of ch. 4).

In addition, an early Middle English redaction of the Old English Rule (presenting a text adapted for nuns) has survived as London, British Library, Cotton Claudius D. iii, 50r–138v; s. xiii^{in}, from the Cistercian nunnery at Wintney in Hampshire (the so-called 'Winteney Version' (WV)).[3]

The Old English text follows the Latin text chapter by chapter in manuscripts x, w, j, u, i* (and WV); in s, the Latin text in its

---

[1] The sigla are those given in Gretsch, *Regula*; they are as far as possible identical with those assigned to the respective manuscripts in Hanslik, *Benedicti Regula*. For descriptions of the manuscripts, see Ker, *Catalogue*, and Gretsch, *Regula*, pp. 20–44. Cf. also *ibid.*, for a listing and brief description of the surviving pre-Conquest manuscripts of the Latin *Regula* (twelve in total). The date and place of origin and provenance for the manuscripts of the Old English Rule are as given by Gneuss, 'Handlist'.

[2] On the importance of this manuscript as evidence for the dissemination of Anglo-Caroline minuscule, see Dumville, *English Caroline Script*, pp. 7–85.

[3] WV is printed by A. Schröer, *Die Winteney-Version der Regula S. Benedicti* (Halle, 1888; repr. with a supplement by M. Gretsch, Tübingen, 1978); see also M. Gretsch, 'Die Winteney-Version der *Regula Sancti Benedicti*: Eine frühmittelenglische Bearbeitung der altenglischen Prosaübersetzung der Benediktinerregel', *Anglia* 96 (1978), 310–48.

entirety precedes (on 74v–95v) the Old English text; F and G present the Old English translation only.

Not only do the surviving manuscripts of the Rule fail to mention Æthelwold as its author, he is not credited either with such a translation in the two *Vitae* composed by his pupils, Wulfstan, the precentor at the Old Minster, and Ælfric the homilist. However, the silence of Æthelwold's biographers on this point is less remarkable than might appear at first sight, since they make no mention either of any of the writings which have reasonably been attributed to Æthelwold such as the *Regularis concordia* by modern scholars. Moreover, Ælfric's *Vita* is not an independent witness but an epitome of the much longer Life by Wulfstan to which it adds only a few insignificant details. However, both Wulfstan and Ælfric state that their master much enjoyed translating Latin texts for his students.[4]

Nonetheless, in spite of the absence of such straightforward pre-Conquest evidence, Æthelwold has been unanimously recognized as the author of the Old English Rule ever since Thomas Wharton in his *Anglia Sacra* (1691) first made available in print the late-twelfth-century *Liber Eliensis* (the chronicle of Ely) which has a remark to the effect that Æthelwold translated the *Regula S. Benedicti* into the vernacular.[5] On the face of the evidence, the ascription of the Old English Rule to Æthelwold would therefore seem to rest on a late-twelfth-century source. However, it can be shown that at this point (as in many other places) the *Liber Eliensis*

---

[4] Wulfstan's *Vita* is ed. and transl. in *Wulfstan: Life*, pp. 4–69; Ælfric's epitome is printed *ibid.*, pp. 70–80. For the dependence of Ælfric on Wulfstan, see *ibid.*, pp. cxlvi–clv; for Æthelwold's Latin writings, see *ibid.*, pp. lxxxviii–xci, and cf. above, pp. 125–6. For Wulfstan's (ch. 31, pp. 46–8) and Ælfric's (ch. 20, p. 77) remarks concerning the translations Æthelwold did in classroom instruction, see below, p. 262.

[5] Cf. T. Wharton, *Anglia Sacra*, 2 vols. (London, 1691) I, 591–688, at 604. Wharton printed a much abbreviated version of the *Liber Eliensis* (from London, Lambeth Palace Library, 448; for this version, cf. Blake's edition of the *Liber* (below), pp. xxv–xxvii). The passage concerning Æthelwold's authorship of the Rule as found in Wharton is quoted by Schröer in the introduction to his edition of the Rule (*Benediktinerregel*, pp. xiii–xiv). The first to refer to Æthelwold's authorship quoting the full version of the *Liber Eliensis* was Humfrey Wanley in his *Librorum Vett. Septentrionalium Catalogus* (Oxford, 1705), pp. 122–3. The *Liber Eliensis* in its full, late-twelfth-century form is edited by Blake, *Liber Eliensis* (1962). For the reference to Æthelwold's authorship, see *ibid.* II, ch. 37 (p. 111). For a short list of scholarly works anterior to Schröer's edition of the Rule (i. e. 1885) which refer to Æthelwold as the translator of the *Regula*, see Gretsch, *Regula*, pp. 10–11.

faithfully reproduced material from an earlier text, the so-called *Libellus Æthelwoldi episcopi*. This *Libellus* is a Latin account, principally of the acquisition of the Ely endowments after the abbey's refoundation by Bishop Æthelwold in (presumably) 970,[6] as well as of the defence of these endowments during the time of the anti-monastic reaction following King Edgar's death in 975.[7] The *Libellus Æthelwoldi* was compiled in the earlier twelfth century by an Ely monk and at the instigation of Hervey, bishop of Ely (1108–31). It is based to a large extent on (now lost) material in Old English pertaining to the Ely estates and originating in the late tenth century. Most of the *Libellus Æthelwoldi* was subsequently incorporated into the comprehensive late-twelfth-century cartulary-chronicle of Ely abbey, the *Liber Eliensis*. It is principally in this late and Latin form that the original Old English material has been accessible to modern scholarship (in the edition by Blake). The Old English source material is now irrecoverably lost. The early-twelfth-century *Libellus Æthelwoldi*, however, survives in two twelfth-century manuscripts (Cambridge, Trinity College O. 2. 41 and London, BL, Cotton Vespasian A. xix). It has been printed separately only once;[8] a new edition by Simon Keynes and Alan Kennedy is in preparation.[9] The passage in the *Libellus*

---

[6] For the presumed date (970) for the refoundation of Ely, see Blake, *Liber Eliensis*, p. 74, n. 3, and Lapidge, *Wulfstan: Life*, p. 39, nn. 5 and 6. The evidence for that date turns principally on four royal charters (S 776, 779, 780 and 781) in favour of Ely, all of which are dated 970. Wulfstan does not give a precise date in his account of the refoundation (ch. 23).

[7] For these events, see D. J. V. Fisher, 'The Anti-Monastic Reaction in the Times of Edward the Martyr', *Cambridge Historical Journal* 10 (1950–2), 254–70, Keynes, *Diplomas*, pp. 169–72, *idem*, 'England 900–1016', and A. Williams, 'Princeps Merciorum gentis: the Family, Career and Connections of Ælfhere, Ealdorman of Mercia 956–83', *ASE* 10 (1982), 143–72, esp. at 167–70. The principal sources are printed in *CS*, pp. 155–65.

[8] By T. Gale, *Rerum Anglicarum Scriptorum Veterum II: Historiae Britannicae, Saxonicae, Anglo-Danicae Scriptores XV* (Oxford, 1691), pp. 463–88.

[9] S. Keynes and A. Kennedy, *Anglo-Saxon Ely: Records of Ely Abbey and its Benefactors in the Tenth and Eleventh Centuries* (Woodbridge, forthcoming). Meanwhile, see A. Kennedy, 'Law and Litigation in the *Libellus Æthelwoldi episcopi*', *ASE* 24 (1995), 131–83, esp. at 131–3, for some preliminary remarks on the tenth-century Old English sources available to the compiler and translator of the *Libellus*. On Gregory, an Ely monk, and possibly the author of the *Libellus*, see Lapidge, *Wulfstan: Life*, pp. 81–3. See also the valuable remarks on the *Libellus* by D. Whitelock in her 'Foreword' to Blake's edition of the *Liber Eliensis*, pp. ix–xviii, as well as Blake, *ibid.*, p. xxxiv.

concerning Æthelwold's authorship of the Rule is identical with the text of the *Liber Eliensis* as printed by Blake and is as follows:

Æadgarus rex et Alftreð dederunt sancto Æðelwoldo manerium, quod dicitur Suðburn, et cyrographum quod pertinebat, quod comes, qui dicebatur Scule, dudum possederat, eo pacto ut ille regulam sancti Benedicti in Anglicum idioma de Latino transferret. Qui sic fecit. Deinde vero beatus Æðelwoldus dedit eandem terram sancte Æðeldreðe cum cyrographo eiusdem terre.[10]

The point which needs stressing in this intricate history of the ascription of the Old English Rule to Æthelwold is that such an ascription ultimately rests on Old English material dating from the late tenth century and extant in one of Bishop Æthelwold's principal foundations. Furthermore, in this Old English source (chiefly concerned with the Ely endowments) the translation of the *Regula S. Benedicti* was intimately tied up with one of Ely's estates (Sudbourne). We must therefore assign the highest authority to the Ely witnesses.

There is yet another text which testifies to Æthelwold's authorship of the Old English Rule, a witness which thus far has not been adduced as evidence in this matter. The text in question is one we have already concerned ourselves with from a stylistic point of view: the short treatise which passes under the name 'Edgar's Establishment of Monasteries' (EEM). This treatise survives anonymously in but a single (late) manuscript, now BL, Cotton Faustina A. x, 148r–151v (s. xii[1], of unknown origin and provenance), where it is appended to the text of the Rule (102r–148r).[11] Dorothy Whitelock has convincingly demonstrated that EEM was composed by Æthelwold himself, thereby bringing to a conclusion earlier debates over its authorship.[12] Her principal argument for Æthelwold's authorship was the existence of clear and striking links in

---

[10] *Liber Eliensis*, ed. Blake, p. 111. 'King Edgar and Ælfthryth gave to the holy Æthelwold the estate called Sudbourne (which once had belonged to a certain *comes* named Scule) and the chirograph pertaining to that estate on the condition that he translate the *Regula S. Benedicti* from Latin into English; which he did. Subsequently, however, the blessed Æthelwold donated the estate in question (together with the chirograph) to Ely'. I am very grateful to Simon Keynes for information on the text as transmitted in the *Libellus Æthelwoldi*.

[11] The text has been printed and transl. most recently by Whitelock in *CS*, pp. 142–54 (no. 33). For a brief summary of the contents of EEM, see above, pp. 122–3. For an assessment of some of its stylistic features, see above, p. 124.

[12] See Whitelock, 'Authorship', pp. 125–36; for earlier views concerning the authorship

vocabulary and phraseology between the treatise and the Old English
Rule.[13] In this she went on the assumption that Æthelwold's authorship
of the Rule was beyond doubt and that therefore verbal links between the
Rule and EEM would reveal Æthelwold as author of EEM as well.
However, the evidence of the verbal ties can be used *vice versa*. If it could
be shown (as I think it can) on grounds other than common lexical and
stylistic predilections shared between the Rule and EEM, that there are
indubitable reasons for believing that EEM was composed by Æthelwold,
then the close links in style and vocabulary between EEM and the Rule
would add further confirmation to the assumption that Æthelwold was
indeed the author of the Old English translation of the *Regula*. Such
reasons pointing to Æthelwold as the author of EEM are as follows:

1. Dorothy Whitelock herself adduced parallels in wording and line of
   argument between EEM and two Latin charters (S 745 and 782) the
   composition of which she tentatively assigned to Æthelwold.[14] The
   earlier of these charters, the famous and lavish New Minster
   Foundation Charter (S 745) has since been shown beyond reasonable
   doubt to have been drafted by Æthelwold himself.[15]
2. Similarly, there are close links both in terms of argument and
   phraseology between EEM and the *prohemium* and the epilogue to the
   Regularis concordia almost certainly composed by Æthelwold.[16]
3. The author of EEM reveals an intimate knowledge of the early stages of
   the Benedictine reform in England and a vehement detestation of
   the secular clerics whose expulsion from various churches is justified
   on the grounds that they abounded in all kinds of sins.[17]
4. More important still is the conspicuous absence of any commendatory
   epithet for the first abbot of reformed Abingdon. He is not even
   named but simply referred to as *se abbod* (*CS*, p. 148) and *se foresprecena
   abbud* (p. 149). This is in stark contrast to what the author has to say
   about other contemporaries; for example, he lavishes profuse praise on

of EEM, cf. *ibid.*, pp. 125–30; see also the brief summary of scholarly opinions by
Gneuss, 'Benediktinerregel', pp. 271–2.

[13] See Whitelock, 'Authorship', pp. 133–5.   [14] Cf. *ibid.*, pp. 131–3.

[15] See below, pp. 236–7 and n. 30.

[16] For such links, see Gretsch, 'Benedictine Rule', pp. 146–9; for Æthelwold as author of the
Regularis concordia (and in particular of the *prohemium*), see Lapidge, 'Æthelwold as Scholar
and Teacher', pp. 192–4, *idem, Wulfstan: Life*, p. lxxxviii, and see above, pp. 125–6.

[17] See *CS*, pp. 149–50.

King Edgar (pp. 146–51) or he has an appreciative remark on Archbishop Dunstan as the king's chief adviser (p. 149).

5. The author admonishes in an urgent and mandatory tone his successors in office (*mine æftergengan*, p. 152), abbesses (p. 153), secular magnates (p. 153) and kings (p. 154), strictly prohibiting the alienation of any church property. Such admonitions unequivocally point to an ecclesiastic with episcopal power and authority.

6. EEM was almost certainly composed to accompany the Old English translation of the *Regula* from the start, that is from the time its first copies were distributed to the reformed monasteries.[18] The tract contains a passage (pp. 151–2) defending translations of religious texts written in Latin on the grounds of their usefulness, and it specifically refers to the translation of the *Regula* as '*þisse* engliscan geþeodnesse' ('*this* English translation', p. 151), thereby implying that both EEM and the Rule were destined for transmission in one manuscript. What is striking in this connection is the chance survival of the preface (in no more than one out of five complete manuscripts of the Rule, and even here not as a preface but as a kind of postscript). Such a low survival rate may perhaps be explained by the fact that much of EEM is taken up with a glowing account of the early stages of the Benedictine reform and a long panegyric on the pivotal role played by King Edgar in the success story of that reform (pp. 145–51), a panegyric which in many ways would meet

---

[18] See Gretsch, 'Benedictine Rule', pp. 149–50; Whitelock ('Authorship', p. 136 and *CS*, pp. 142–3) opted for a date of composition of EEM considerably later than the translation of the *Regula*, sometime after 975, and she would connect its composition with the anti-monastic reaction after King Edgar's death (on the anti-monastic reaction, see above, p. 229, n. 7). However, several points in the text itself seem to preclude such a late origin. For example, the author fails to mention King Edgar's death and his burial at Glastonbury, an omission which would seem odd after 975, given the importance attached to Edgar and Glastonbury in the text. Next, King Edgar is portrayed at some length as the moving force behind the Benedictine reform, but the author is silent on the existence of the *Regularis Concordia* (*c.* 973) and Edgar's decisive role in its promulgation (see *Regularis Concordia*, ed. Symons, ch. 4 (pp. 2–3) for this role, and see below, pp. 238–9). Rather, the king is depicted as an extremely youthful, yet immensely sagacious and virtuous ruler. In a word, the text as it has been preserved would seem best to suit a point in the mid-sixties. For the significance which EEM (as the preface to the Old English Rule) might have for establishing the date of the Rule itself, see below, pp. 238 and 240–1.

the standards of a late-twentieth-century product-placing campaign. As a result much of the contents of EEM will inevitably have looked dated in the historical context of the eleventh century, when most of the surviving copies of the Old English Rule were written.[19] Furthermore, since EEM bears no attribution of authorship, the lengthy (and in some ways very personal) diatribe against the alienation of church property (pp. 152–4) will have lost much of its cogency, once the text was no longer associated with the redoubtable bishop of Winchester.

In sum, the first five of the aforementioned arguments unequivocally point to Æthelwold as the author of EEM, while the sixth establishes an intimate textual relationship between EEM and the Rule. Therefore the close verbal and stylistic ties between the tract and the Rule (which were pointed out by Whitelock) provide us with valuable additional evidence that Bishop Æthelwold translated the *Regula S. Benedicti* into Old English prose.

THE DATE OF THE OLD ENGLISH RULE

What is less clear is at which point during his long career Æthelwold composed his translation of the *Regula*. A date 964 × 975, with a focus on the years around 970, which is usually assigned to the translation,[20] hinges on the testimony of the *Liber Eliensis* in combination with the probable dates (*c.* 970) for Æthelwold's (re)foundation of the great fenland monasteries Ely, Peterborough and Thorney.[21] Since the *Liber*

---

[19] Only one of the surviving manuscripts was written in the tenth century: CCCO 197 (s. $x^{3/4}$). It is interesting to add that William of Malmesbury (*c.* 1095–*c.* 1143) refers to a copy (now lost) of the Old English Rule with a preface which seems to have been identical with EEM; cf. his *Vita S. Dunstani*, printed in *Memorials of St Dunstan*, ed. Stubbs, pp. 250–324, at 290.

[20] See, for example, Gneuss, 'Benediktinerregel', p. 273, Lapidge, 'Æthelwold as Scholar and Teacher', p. 195, Gretsch, 'Benedictine Rule', p. 150, and Dumville, *English Caroline Script*, pp. 13–14.

[21] The (re)foundation of Ely, Peterborough and Thorney is related by Wulfstan in his *Vita S. Æthelwoldi* in chs. 23 (Ely) and 24 (Peterborough and Thorney), but no exact dates for these events are provided there. For the evidence pointing to 970 for Ely's refoundation, see Lapidge, *Wulfstan: Life*, p. 39, nn. 5 and 6, and cf. above, n. 6; for '*c.* 970' for Peterborough and Thorney, see Lapidge, *Wulfstan: Life*, p. 40, n. 6, and p. 41,

Eliensis states that both Edgar and Ælfthryth gave the *manerium* of Sudbourne to Æthelwold in return for his translation, the outside limits for the Rule seem to be established by their marriage in 964 (or 965)[22] and Edgar's death in 975. As we have seen, the *Liber Eliensis* bases itself in this statement on a late-tenth-century account in the vernacular and is therefore a witness of prime importance. However, on close inspection this witness does not validate the assumption (commonly made) that Æthelwold did not set about his translation until after Edgar and Ælfthryth had commissioned him to do so. The *Liber* says no more than that Edgar and Ælfthryth gave Sudbourne to Æthelwold in return for a translation of the *Regula S. Benedicti* which he duly produced.

The Latin phrase 'eo pacto ut ille regulam sancti Benedicti in Anglicum idioma de Latino transferret'[23] may well echo some Old English wording such as: 'wiþ þæm þe (*or* for þæm þe) he brohte (*or* wende) ... of Ledene on ure gereorde'. The meanings assigned by the dictionaries to the conjunction *wiþ þæm þe* are 'provided that, on the condition that, in return for, because';[24] it thus implies, even less than does *eo pacto ut*, a sequence of instigation and subsequent execution. Therefore the Sudbourne estate should probably be taken as a fee which Æthelwold received for the 'publication' of his translation, and as a result we are left without any approximate date for its actual composition and have to turn our attention to a fresh search for whatever clues for its origin there may be.

---

nn. 7 and 8. Recall that Æthelwold donated to Ely the *manerium* of Sudbourne which he received for his translation; however, we have no information for how long Sudbourne had been in his possession and when precisely the donation was made.

[22] 964, according to John of Worcester (cf. *The Chronicle of John of Worcester*, ed. Darlington and McGurk II, 416); 965 according to the ASC (D and F). On charter evidence (S 725, possibly genuine) indicating that the marriage took place no later than 964, see Dumville, *English Caroline Script*, p. 13 and n. 31.

[23] *Liber Eliensis*, ed. Blake, p. 111.

[24] Cf. for example the entry in BT, s. v. *se* V: '*wið ðam ðe* "in return for, on condition (that)", connecting two clauses containing mutual concession.' On the somewhat vague meaning of the formula *wiþ þæm þe/þæt*, see also Mitchell, *Old English Syntax* II, §§ 2917 and 3659.

The evidence of Æthelwold's career

The idea of translating the *Regula S. Benedicti* into Old English to cater for the needs of novices and newly professed monks and nuns (one of the principal reasons for the translation, according to its preface) could have arisen with Æthelwold as early as the Glastonbury stage of his career (that is from *c*. 940 onwards). While there, he himself was professed a Benedictine monk and lived in a monastery, the only one then in existence in England, as he remarked in the Preface.[25] We shall have occasion to consider more closely the evidence provided by Æthelwold's biography and in favour of a Glastonbury origin of at least a draft of the translation at some later point (below, pp. 251–9). For the moment, let us turn our attention to the subsequent stages of his career.

The need for a translation of the *Regula* will have made itself felt even more urgently when, as abbot of Abingdon (*c*. 954–63), Æthelwold was in charge of an ever-increasing *grex monachorum*.[26] There are grounds for suspecting that Æthelwold during this period did not envisage terminating his career as abbot of Abingdon. In any event, when in 963 he was finally promoted to the bishopric of Winchester (the town where he was born and where he had embarked on his career during the reign of King Æthelstan (924–39)), the energy and determination with which he proceeded to convert the principal churches at Winchester into Benedictine communities within a few months after his consecration have every appearance of having been premeditated for some time. Æthelwold was consecrated bishop on 29 November 963, the secular clerics were expelled from the Old Minster on 19 February 964; the ejection of the secular clergy from the New Minster took place in the same year, as did presumably the conversion of the Nunnaminster into a house of Benedictine nuns. (Here, apparently, no expulsion of canonesses was necessary.)[27] In order to ensure the success and the permanence of his expulsion

---

[25] See *Wulfstan: Life*, ch. 9 (p. 14), and *CS*, p. 149. See below, Appendix I, for a tabular presentation of major events in Æthelwold's life.

[26] See *Wulfstan: Life*, ch. 11 (p. 20). For the date of Æthelwold's ordination as abbot (which cannot be established with precision), see Lapidge, *ibid.*, pp. xliv and 21, n. 8; for an estimate of the size of the Abingdon community, see *ibid.*, p. 21, n. 7.

[27] See *Wulfstan: Life*, ch. 16 (p. 30), for the date of Æthelwold's consecration as bishop; chs. 16 and 17 (pp. 30–2), for the expulsion of the clerics from the Old Minster; ch. 20 (p. 36), for the expulsion of the New Minster clerics (in this case the precise date is

of the secular clergy from the Old Minster, Æthelwold had not only secured royal support in the person of the powerful and influential thegn Wulfstan of Dalham who, as a delegate sent by King Edgar, was present on the occasion; he had also sought and obtained papal permission for his actions. Such permission survives in the form of an apparently genuine letter from Pope John XII (955–64) to King Edgar; the letter appears to have been written before November 963 and hence before Æthelwold's consecration as bishop on 29 November of that year.[28]

On the assumption that Æthelwold's procedure in 963–4 had been plotted for some time, it cannot have escaped his consideration how effectively his projected eruptive establishment of Benedictine monasticism at Winchester would have been aided by a vernacular version of the *Regula S. Benedicti*. We may suspect therefore that together with the monks he brought from Abingdon to assist him in the rapid enactment and realization of his reform programme,[29] he also brought a translation of the monastic rule which henceforth was to regulate the lives of the inmates of the three minsters. In this connection it is interesting to remark that the lavishly written and decorated New Minster Foundation Charter, issued to commemorate the installation of Benedictine monks in the New Minster and presumably drafted by Æthelwold himself, contains a lengthy section explaining how the monks' lives shall be governed by the *Regula*, a rather unusual feature in a text which otherwise follows (if only in very broad outline) the structure of a tenth-century royal diploma, and a feature which unequivocally reveals the urgency with which Æthelwold enjoined a strict observation of the stipulations of the *Regula*.[30]

---

provided by the ASC (A) only); and ch. 22 (pp. 36–8), for the reformation of the Nunnaminster. For discussion of these events (with references to further contemporary sources and to relevant literature), see Lapidge, *ibid.*, pp. xlv–xlviii, and notes to chs. 16, 17, 20 and 22.

[28] The letter has been printed and discussed most recently by Whitelock, *CS*, pp. 109–13 (no. 29).

[29] For these Abingdon monks, see *Wulfstan: Life*, chs. 16 and 17 (pp. 30–2).

[30] The charter (S 745, BCS 1190), now BL, Vespasian A. viii, is printed most recently in *CS*, pp. 119–33 (no. 31); the section concerning the *Regula* is *ibid.*, at 127–8 (chs. 12 and 13). For the manuscript, see Wormald, 'Late Anglo-Saxon Art', in his *Collected Writings* I, 105–10, at 108–10 and pls. 96–8, Temple, *Anglo-Saxon Manuscripts*, p. 44 (no. 16); see also the description of the lay-out of the manuscript and the convenient summary of the contents of the Charter by Keynes, *Liber Vitae*, pp. 26–8, and cf. *ibid.*,

The New Minster Charter is composed in Æthelwold's difficult and ostentatious Latin. We do not know how many of the New Minster clerics in 964 opted for the new way of life and how good their Latin was. In any case, the Charter is not a text for daily use in the monastery but a sumptuous official document, and it is dated 966, that is two years after the tumultuous events of 964, when in the meantime the newly established monastic schools will have gone some way towards improving the level of Latin literacy at Winchester.[31] As regards the Old Minster, Wulfstan tells us (ch. 18) that all the debauched canons chose to leave because they detested the monastic life ('uitam execrantes monasticam', p. 32), only three of them returning at some unspecified point in the future. Therefore the likelihood is that (apart from some Abingdon monks) many of the first inmates of the reformed Old Minster (and presumably many of those in the New Minster and the Nunnaminster as well) will have been men and women attracted by the new bishop's monastic ideals, but not yet conversant with Benedictinism nor very proficient Latinists; in a word, they will have been in acute need of a translation of the *Regula*. Characteristically, Æthelwold expressly states in the Preface that his translation should deprive uneducated monolingual speakers of English of their excuses for not obeying the precepts of the *Regula* on account of their deficient knowledge of Latin:

Hæbben forþi þa ungelæreden inlendisce þæs halgan regules cyþþe þurh agenes gereordes anwrigenesse, þæt hy þe geornlicor Gode þeowien and nane tale næbben þæt hy þurh nytennesse misfon þurfen.[32]

---

pls. I-IV. For Æthelwold as author of the text, see Lapidge, 'Æthelwold as Scholar and Teacher', pp. 189–90, and *idem*, *Wulfstan: Life*, pp. lxxxix–xc, and cf. above, pp. 125 and 129, and below, pp. 309–10.

[31] Regrettably little is known about the New Minster community in the 960s and 970s; for an evaluation of what evidence there is, cf. Keynes, *Liber Vitae*, pp. 24–6 and 28–30.

[32] CS, p. 152: 'Therefore let the unlearned natives have the knowledge of this holy rule by the exposition of their own language, that they may the more zealously serve God and have no excuse that they were driven by ignorance to err.' Cf. also *ibid.*, p. 151: 'þisse engliscan geþeodnesse ... is þeah niedbehefe ungelæredum woroldmonnum þe ... þone halgan þeowdom þises regules geceosaþ; þy læs þe ænig ungecyrred woroldman mid nytnesse 7 ungewitte regules geboda abræce 7 þære tale bruce þæt he þy dæge misfenge þy he hit selre nyste.' The expression *ungecyrred woroldman* here obviously refers to novices not yet professed as monks or nuns.

237

A different piece of evidence which similarly may suggest that a vernacular version of the *Regula* was in existence by the 950s at the latest, is provided by King Edgar's interest in monasticism. The Preface relates how he became deeply concerned with the ideas and precepts of the *Regula* ('He began mid geornfulre scrudnunge smeagan 7 ahsian be þam gebodum þæs halgan regules, 7 witan wolde þas sylfan regules lare').[33] In order fully to understand the whole range of Benedict's teaching, he commissioned a translation of the *Regula* ('þurh þises wisdomes lust he het þisne regul of læden gereorde on englisc geþeodan', *CS*, p. 151). No date for these events is given in the text, but although Edgar is styled king,[34] and although the translation is attributed to his instigation, the suspicion must be that it was Æthelwold himself who had kindled this desire for a thorough knowledge of Benedictine monasticism already in the young ætheling. We know from the *prohemium* of the *Regularis concordia* and from Byrhtferth's *Vita S. Oswaldi* that Æthelwold acted as Edgar's tutor, perhaps at Abingdon.[35] In any event, by declaring the translation to have been commissioned by the king himself, Æthelwold effectively enhanced the authority of the Old English Rule, and this was what he probably had in mind when relating these events. In other words, Edgar's alleged commission of the translation, as reported in EEM, is no more a reliable testimony for a date for the origin of the translation after 959 (Edgar's accession to the throne) than is the remark in the *Libellus Æthelwoldi* for a date after 964/5 (the marriage of Edgar and Ælfthryth).

In this connection it may be relevant to mention that Æthelwold took pains to present King Edgar's close involvement in another of his own works, namely the *Regularis concordia*. In the *prohemium* to that work, the king is credited with having convened the synodal council at Winchester whose decrees were laid down in the *Regularis concordia* ('synodale concilium Wintoniae fieri decreuit', ch. 4 (p.2)). He is further reported to have encouraged this synod by sending a beautifully written exhortatory letter ('illucque uerba exhortatoria ac pacifica pitacio luculentissime

---

[33] *CS*, p. 150: 'With earnest scrutiny he began to investigate and inquire about the precepts of the holy rule, and wished to know the teaching of that same rule'.

[34] Edgar became king of the Mercians in 957 (ASC (B and C)) and succeeded his brother Eadwig as king of the West Saxons in 959 (ASC (all versions)).

[35] Cf. *Regularis Concordia*, ed. Symons, ch. 1 (p. 1), and Byrhtferth, *Vita S. Oswaldi*, ed. Raine, *Historians* I, 426–7. For a discussion (with further references) of where and when this tutelage would have taken place, see Lapidge, *Wulfstan: Life*, p. xlv, n. 20.

caraxata humillimus destinauit', *ibid*.). Most important in this respect is, however, the full-page line drawing which precedes the text of the *Regularis concordia* in BL, Cotton Tiberius A. iii (2v). Here, King Edgar, wearing a crown, is seated in the centre of the composition, flanked by Archbishop Dunstan and Bishop Æthelwold, the three men holding a scroll, presumably representing the *Regularis concordia*. As Robert Deshman has pointed out, their joint possession of the scroll should be interpreted in terms of a joint authorship of the text.[36] As Deshman has also shown, there is every likelihood that this mid-eleventh-century drawing in a manuscript of Christ Church origin is derived from a Winchester original devised by Æthelwold himself and intended to accompany the *de luxe* dedication copies of the *Regularis concordia*.[37]

During the long years of study when (under Edgar's predecessors) Æthelwold had to await promotion to an office where he could get his reform programme under way, he must have become almost painfully aware that the kind of monastic renewal which he had in mind could successfully be carried through only if assisted by generous and un-swerving royal support. Therefore, when young Edgar came under Æthelwold's tutelage, at a time when the future bishop was aged almost fifty, Æthelwold will have availed himself immediately and as best he could of this singular opportunity of instilling a zeal for monasticism into an ætheling who stood a chance of being elected king at some point during the following years.[38] What better way for instilling such a zeal would there have been for Æthelwold (whom we know to have been a

---

[36] See Deshman, '*Benedictus Monarcha*', pp. 205–6.

[37] See *ibid*., pp. 210 and 227. The suggestion made by Higgitt ('Glastonbury', p. 286) that the drawing in Tiberius A. iii derives from a Glastonbury or Canterbury exemplar (rather than from a Winchester one) has less to recommend it for various reasons: it was evidently Æthelwold who was the driving force behind the Winchester synod of *c*. 973, he was the author of the *Regularis concordia*, and its earliest copies will therefore presumably have been produced in the Winchester scriptoria.

[38] Edgar was born in 943 (ASC (B), s. a. 959); he would have been about ten when Æthelwold taught him ('ab ineunte suae pueritiae aetate', as the *Regularis concordia* states (ch. 1 (p. 1))); he was fourteen when he became king of the Mercians in 957. The years subsequent to King Eadred's death in 955, and especially the events in 957, when the kingdom was divided between Eadwig, Edgar's elder brother, and Edgar himself, are in many respects a dark period in tenth-century history. See Keynes, 'England 900–1016', for a brief evaluation of the evidence (with further references).

highly expert teacher) than to expound St Benedict's text to his pupil from a vernacular version?

In sum, such evidence as may be gleaned from Æthelwold's career would seem to suggest a date between *c.* 940 and the mid-950s as most likely for the composition of the Old English Rule. By contrast, 970 or thereabouts, the date which has previously been suggested, in connection with the (re)foundation of Ely, Peterborough and Thorney, would appear rather late in view of the urgency with which Æthelwold went about his reforms, and given the fact that the *Regula* was the principal text of the reform. Furthermore, the early 970s were apparently the period when the need for the *Regularis concordia* was acutely felt, because of the great number of reformed monasteries by then already in existence. In the *prohemium* to the *Concordia*, Æthelwold himself remarks that the Bene-dictine Rule was universally and fervently adhered to in the new monasteries ('Regulari itaque sancti patris Benedicti norma honestissime suscepta', ch. 4 (p. 2)). The problem with which he saw himself confronted now was that the monasteries, though united in a common faithful adherence to the *Regula*, still followed different monastic customs ('una fide, non tamen uno consuetudinis usu', *ibid.*) in the innumerable details of monastic life and liturgical practice for which Benedict had made no provisions in his *Regula*. Æthelwold addressed this problem by producing a monastic customary (his *Regularis concordia*) based decisively on early-ninth-century Carolingian legislation and the practice of Fleury, while incorporating many details from other continental monasteries (such as Ghent) as well as native English customs.[39] Therefore the likelihood is that by the time the *Concordia* was promulgated (*c.* 973), the text of the *Regula* (in Latin *and* Old English) had been carefully studied for some years in the reformed monasteries throughout England.

However, several passages in EEM seem to preclude an origin of the Old English Rule as early as the Glastonbury or Abingdon periods in Æthelwold's career, that is, if we proceed on the assumption that the tract

---

[39] For the date of the *Regularis concordia* (*c.* 973), see Symons, 'History and Derivation', pp. 40–2; for the standard editions by Symons (1953, quoted here throughout) and Symons and Spath (1984), see above, p. 15, n. 30. Dom Symons's introduction to his (1953) edition is still valuable for the structure and the sources of the *Concordia* (pp. xxix–lii). For the sources, see also the *apparatus fontium* in both editions; for the sources and Æthelwold's authorship of the text, see Lapidge, 'Æthelwold as Scholar and Teacher', pp. 192–4, and *idem, Wulfstan: Life*, pp. lviii–lx.

accompanied the Rule as a preface from the earliest stages of its transmissional history. We have seen for example that in the concluding section of EEM, Æthelwold clearly speaks with the authority of a bishop, pronouncing *inter alia* an anathema on any prospective alienators of church property. Similarly, the expulsion of secular clerics from holy places (*haliga stowa*, *CS*, p. 149) in Wessex is mentioned, Queen Ælfthryth is styled the patroness of nuns (p. 150), and the remark about the expulsion of clerics from churches in Mercia (p. 150) may even refer to a date in the late 960s.[40] There are two ways open for an explanation of such an apparent incompatibility between events and persons mentioned in EEM and an early date for the Old English Rule. One would be that Æthelwold substantially revised and updated an original preface (which would have contained, for example, the lengthy apologia for translations into the vernacular) when his reform programme was finally set in motion. The length and heterogeneity of the text (which cannot here be argued in any detail) might suggest one or more stages of revision. Thus, in its context, the remark concerning the expulsion of the secular clergy from Mercian churches looks suspiciously like a later interpolation which, in this case, need not even have been made by Æthelwold himself.

On the second hypothesis, the Preface would have been drafted *in toto* in 964 or thereabouts, when the first copies of the Old English Rule were being distributed to the reformed minsters, Æthelwold availing himself at that point of the opportunity of promulgating some of his views on monastic reform together with his vernacular version of the principal document of Benedictine monasticism. In any event, the point which needs stressing is that an origin in the 960s either for the complete preface to the Old English Rule or for any parts of it, would in no way entail an identical date for the composition of the Rule itself.

The textual recensions of the 'Regula'

We must now consider briefly in which of its textual forms the *Regula* served as the exemplar for Æthelwold's translation and what evidence for

---

[40] The principal witnesses for the events in Mercia here apparently alluded to are Byrhtferth's *Vita S. Oswaldi*, ed. Raine, *Historians* I, 424–7 and 433–5, and John of Worcester, *Chronicle*, ed. Darlington and McGurk, s. a. 969 (p. 419). For an evaluation of the evidence of these sources, see *ibid.*, p. 149 and *CS*, pp. 114–15.

a date of that translation may possibly be gleaned therefrom. As was shown a hundred years ago by Ludwig Traube in his classic study of the textual history of the *Regula*, the Latin text survives in three principal recensions which since have come to be known as the *textus purus*, *textus interpolatus* and *textus receptus* respectively.[41] Although some modifications of Traube's three categories have been suggested by subsequent scholarship,[42] they still have to be regarded as valid in broad outline, and in his critical edition of the *Regula*, Rudolf Hanslik based his discussion of the manuscripts on Traube's categories,[43] as did Adalbert de Vogüé and Jean Neufville in their multi-volume edition with a massive commentary.[44]

The *textus purus* recension has its origin in a copy made at the instigation of Charlemagne from a manuscript at Monte Cassino, then thought to be Benedict's autograph.[45] The Monte Cassino manuscript

---

[41] See L. Traube, *Textgeschichte der Regula S. Benedicti*, Abhandlungen der königlich bayerischen Akademie der Wissenschaften, philosophisch-philologische und historische Klasse 21 (Munich, 1898), 599–731; this has been revised in some points in a second edition, ed. H. Plenkers, *ibid.*, 25 (1910). Note that Traube himself does not employ the term *textus receptus*; he speaks instead of 'contaminated' ('kontaminierte') manuscripts (*ibid.*, pp. 61–3).

[42] See, for example, R. Hanslik, 'Textkritisch-sprachliche Bemerkungen zur *Regula Benedicti*', in *ΜΝΗΜΗΣ ΧΑΡΙΝ. Gedenkschrift Paul Kretschmer* (Wien, 1956), pp. 146–53, at 146–8, and especially the important study by P. Meyvaert, 'Towards a History', at p. 105 and n. 86; see also below, p. 246 and n. 58.

[43] See R. Hanslik, ed., *Benedicti Regula* (2nd ed., 1977), pp. xxii–lxiv. In the second edition, Hanslik's discussion of the manuscripts of the *Regula* does not differ substantially from that in the first edition (1960), especially in respect of the *receptus*-family. Interestingly, however, his elaborate *stemma codicum* has disappeared from the second edition. For a critical discussion of this stemma, see especially Meyvaert, 'Towards a History', pp. 83–110. For the inadequacy of Hanslik's stemma where the English manuscripts of the *Regula* are concerned, see also Gretsch, *Regula*, pp. 88–121. Hanslik reported to have collated *c.* 300 manuscripts, the variant readings of some sixty-three of which appear in his *apparatus criticus*; cf. p. ix in his *Benedicti Regula* (first ed. only), and *idem*, 'Die Benediktinerregel im Wiener Kirchenvätercorpus', *Commentationes in Regulam S. Benedicti*, ed. B. Steidle, Studia Anselmiana 42 (Rome, 1957), pp. 159–69, at 168. Regrettably, Hanslik never published a list of the manuscripts which he collated.

[44] See *La Règle de Saint Benoît*, ed. de Vogüé and Neufville I, 319–51.

[45] It has since been shown conclusively that the Monte Cassino manuscript, though close to Benedict's original, was no autograph: see P. Meyvaert, 'Problems Concerning the Autograph Manuscript of Saint Benedict's Rule', *Revue Bénédictine* 69 (1959), 3–21, esp. 3–9, and Hanslik, *Benedicti Regula*, pp. xxi–xxii.

was subsequently destroyed by fire; its copy was brought to Aachen and is now also lost. What survives is a copy at two removes from the Aachen manuscript, written by two monks from Reichenau in 817 or thereabouts and preserved as St Gallen, Stiftsbibliothek, 914. Ever since Traube, in 1898, established the close relationship of the St Gallen manuscript to St Benedict's original, editions of the *Regula* have been based on this manuscript.[46] Presumably, and for reasons which will become clear presently, the *textus purus* did not enjoy a wide circulation and apparently never reached England during the Middle Ages.

The *textus interpolatus* was the recension in almost universal use in Europe during the seventh and eighth centuries. It probably originated at Rome around the year 600 and, apart from a considerable number of alterations made for no apparent reason, it is distinguished by numerous corrections aimed to bring St Benedict's Vulgar Latin word forms and constructions into conformity with standard Medieval Latin.[47] This recension was firmly rooted in England. The oldest surviving manuscript of the *Regula* from anywhere belongs to the *interpolatus* tradition, and it is of English origin: Oxford, Bodleian Library, Hatton 48. It was written in an unidentified centre, probably in Southumbria, *c.* 700 (or s. viii[1], possibly even s. viii[med]). It is clear from numerous variant readings (of contemporary date), entered between the lines or in the margins, that the text was corrected against a second exemplar which also belonged to the *interpolatus* recension.[48] This second exemplar (now lost) against which

---

[46] For a facsimile edition, see *Regula Benedicti de codice 914 in bibliotheca monasterii S. Galli seruato quam simillime expressa*, ed. B. Probst (with a palaeographical introduction by B. Bischoff) (St Ottilien, 1982).

[47] For some of the problems connected with the origin and dissemination of the *interpolatus*, see Engelbert, 'Regeltext und Romverehrung', esp. pp. 44–7. Attempts to establish (against Traube) the textual superiority of the *interpolatus* have not gained wide acceptance. See, for example, (briefly) E. Manning, 'À propos de la tradition manuscrite de la Règle Bénédictine', *Regulae Benedicti Studia* 10–11 ([1981–2] Hildesheim, 1984), 47–9, and the rejoinder by K. Zelzer, 'Nochmals à propos de la tradition manuscrite de la Règle Bénédictine', *Regulae Benedicti Studia* 12 ([1983] Hildesheim, 1985), 203–7. For references to further participants in this debate, see Engelbert, 'Regeltext und Romverehrung', pp. 56–7, n. 32.

[48] Cf. Lowe, *Codices Latini Antiquiores* II, no. 240 (pp. 34, 53 and 59), and D. Wright, 'Some Notes on English Uncial', *Traditio* 17 (1961), 441–56, at 449–50. For a facsimile edition, see D. H. Farmer, *The Rule of St Benedict. Oxford Bodleian Library, Hatton 48*, EEMF 15 (Copenhagen, 1968).

Hatton 48 was corrected had close textual affiliations with Würzburg, Universitätsbibliothek, M. p. th. q. 22, a manuscript copied from an Anglo-Saxon exemplar, probably at Fulda, *c.* 800.[49] Furthermore, an *interpolatus* text of the *Regula* was carefully studied in the school of Archbishop Theodore and Abbot Hadrian at Canterbury at the end of the seventh century. This much can be seen from the so-called Leiden-Family of glossaries. This family is represented by some twenty-five manuscripts (principally of continental origin) which have been shown to derive ultimately from a corpus of *glossae collectae* (primarily Latin–Latin, but containing a considerable number of Old English *interpretamenta* as well) which originated in the Canterbury school of Theodore (d. 690) and Hadrian (d. 709).[50] The most voluminous of these glossaries is the Leiden Glossary, now Leiden, Bibliotheek der Rijksuniversiteit, Voss. lat. Q. 69, 20r–36r, written *c.* 800 at St Gallen, but clearly copied from an Anglo-Saxon exemplar.[51] The Leiden Glossary (and two further manuscripts from the group) contains a batch of lemmata drawn from the *Regula S. Benedicti*,[52] and various of these lemmata unmistakably present *inter-*

---

[49] See B. Bischoff and J. Hofmann, *Libri Sancti Kyliani. Die Würzburger Schreibschule und die Dombibliothek im VIII. und IX. Jahrhundert*, Quellen und Forschungen zur Geschichte des Bistums und Hochstifts Würzburg 6 (Würzburg, 1952), 54 and 110, and Meyvaert, 'Towards a History', pp. 97–100.

[50] See Lapidge, 'The School of Theodore and Hadrian', pp. 149–60; and Appendix, pp. 163–8, for a list of the continental manuscripts of the Leiden-Family; see also *idem, Biblical Commentaries*, ed. Bischoff and Lapidge, pp. 173–9. For material drawn from the Canterbury corpus of *glossae collectae* in English manuscripts, see Pheifer, *Épinal–Erfurt Glossary*, pp. xxviii–li. On glosses to books of the Bible in the Leiden-Family, see *idem*, 'The Canterbury Bible Glosses: Facts and Problems', in *Archbishop Theodore: Commemorative Studies on his Life and Influence*, ed. M. Lapidge, CSASE 11 (Cambridge, 1995), 281–333.

[51] On the manuscript, see E. A. Lowe, *Codices Latini Antiquiores* IX (Oxford, 1959), no. 1585, and Bischoff, *Mittelalterliche Studien* II, 26 and III, 289. The Leiden Glossary is edited by Hessels, *A Late Eighth-Century Glossary*; there is a further edition by P. Glogger, *Das Leidener Glossar*, 3 vols. (Augsburg, 1901–7). See Lapidge, *Biblical Commentaries*, ed. Bischoff and Lapidge, pp. 545–6, for a brief description of the contents of the originally separate part (fols. 7–47) of the (now composite) manuscript, Voss. lat. Q. 69, where the Leiden Glossary occurs.

[52] Printed (from the Leiden Glossary) by Hessels, *A Late Eighth-Century Glossary*, pp. 3–7 (ch. ii, 1–193). For a convenient table of the full contents of the Leiden Glossary, see Lapidge, 'The School of Theodore and Hadrian', pp. 150–1, and *Biblical Commentaries*, ed. Bischoff and Lapidge, pp. 174–5.

polatus readings. Interestingly, the manuscript of the *Regula* from which the Leiden lemmata were drawn appears to have had closer affiliations with the *interpolatus* text as it is transmitted in some continental manuscripts (in particular St Gallen, Stiftsbibliothek, 916)[53] than with the English Hatton 48.[54] Distinct traces of the *textus interpolatus* have survived in English manuscripts long after the third recension, the *textus receptus*, had become universally established in England. This much emerges from the remarkable admixture of typical *interpolatus* readings (closely related to Hatton 48) in two English manuscripts belonging to the *receptus* tradition, namely Cambridge, Corpus Christi College 57, written *c.* 1000, possibly at Abingdon, and Durham Cathedral B. IV. 24, written in the second half of the eleventh century, perhaps at Christ Church, Canterbury.[55]

The *textus receptus* was the recension prevailing in the Carolingian empire from the mid-ninth century onwards and in due course in Benedictine monasteries all over Europe, until Traube's research revealed the superiority of the *textus purus* as preserved in St Gallen 914. The *receptus* is not a homogenous recension. According to Traube, it originated in the wake of the ecclesiastic and monastic reforms introduced in the Carolingian church by Benedict of Aniane (*c.* 750–821) under the emperor Louis the Pious (814–40), Charlemagne's successor.[56] These reforms were launched at two synods held at Aachen in 816 and 817 and embraced *inter alia* the universal and exclusive observance in all monasteries of the *Regula S. Benedicti* in its *textus purus* recension, made available (as we have seen) in the Carolingian empire by Charlemagne himself.[57] Promulgation of the text-form recently obtained from Monte

---

[53] St Gallen 916 was written at St Gallen at the beginning of the ninth century; see Bischoff, *Mittelalterliche Studien* III, 81–2.

[54] Cf. Lapidge, 'The School of Theodore and Hadrian', pp. 158–60.

[55] For the *interpolatus* affiliations of these manuscripts, see Gretsch, *Regula*, pp. 91, 102, 104, 106–7, 120, and *idem*, 'Æthelwold's Translation', p. 134; for CCCC 57, see also Meyvaert, 'Towards a History', p. 100.

[56] On Benedict of Aniane and his reforms, see *LkMA* I (1980), 1864–7, *Theologische Realenzyklopädie*, ed. G. Krause and G. Müller (Berlin, 1977–) V, 535–8, P. Schmitz, 'L'influence de saint Benoît d'Aniane dans l'histoire de l'ordre de Saint-Benoît', *Settimane di studio del Centro italiano di studi sull'alto medioevo* 4 (1957), 401–15, and R. Grégoire, 'Benedetto di Aniane nella riforma monastica carolingia', *Studi medievali* 26 (1985), 573–610.

[57] The *acta* of these synods are printed by J. Semmler, in *Initia Consuetudinis Benedictinae*,

Cassino rapidly led to extensive and multifarious contamination between this 'pure' text and the 'interpolated' recension, the text which had been in use up to this point. The result of such contamination (as Traube saw it) was the *textus receptus*, originating therefore not from a single centre but from individual monasteries all over the Carolingian empire and beyond and embracing in various degrees *purus*, *interpolatus* as well as idiosyncratic readings.

However, it would appear that Traube's analysis of the origin of the *textus receptus* is somewhat in need of modification in the light of more recent research. The nub of the problem is in the vast number of 'idiosyncratic' readings in the *receptus* tradition (especially in French manuscripts), that is, readings which cannot be assigned either to the *interpolatus* or the *purus* text-forms. Apparently these must be explained as originating (at least in part) in Francia as early as the seventh and eighth centuries and resulting primarily from the widespread tendency to correct Benedict's Vulgar Latin forms. Therefore the *textus purus* (presumably because of its vulgarisms as they are preserved in St Gallen 914) seems to have been less influential in the Carolingian *receptus* tradition than Traube had assumed.[58] Whatever the case, the question of the continental origin of the *receptus* version does not bear significantly on its dissemination in England. What is important to note, however, is that, given the heterogenous and highly intricate genesis of the *textus receptus*, the suspicion must be that regional groupings will play a pre-eminent role in this recension, and such a

---

ed. Hallinger, CCM 1 (Siegburg, 1963), 433–6 (*Synodi primae Aquisgranensis acta praeliminaria* [816]), pp. 451–68 (*Synodi primae Aquisgranensis decreta authentica* [816]), and pp. 469–81 (*Synodi secundae Aquisgranensis decreta authentica* [817]). The *Regula Sancti Benedicti abbatis Anianensis siue collectio capitularis* (*ibid.*, pp. 501–36) dates from *c.* 818/19 and was compiled from the decrees of the aforementioned Aachen synods. See the brief introduction to these texts by Semmler, *ibid.*, pp. 423–32, as well as *idem*, 'Zur Überlieferung der monastischen Gesetzgebung Ludwigs des Frommen', *Deutsches Archiv zur Erforschung des Mittelalters* 16 (1960), 310–88, and *idem*, 'Die Beschlüsse des Aachener Konzils im Jahre 816', *Zeitschrift für Kirchengeschichte* 74 (1963), 15–82.

[58] See K. Zelzer, 'Zur Stellung des Textus Receptus und des interpolierten Textes in der Textgeschichte der Regula S. Benedicti', *Revue Bénédictine* 88 (1978), 205–46, esp. 205–18 and 228, and *idem*, 'Von Benedikt zu Hildemar. Zu Textgestalt und Textgeschichte der Regula Benedicti auf ihrem Weg zur Alleingeltung', *Frühmittelalterliche Studien* 23 (1989), 112–30, at 117–22. For Traube's view on the origin of the *receptus*, see *Textgeschichte*, pp. 61–3.

suspicion is confirmed, for example, by Hanslik's discussion of the *receptus* manuscripts which he collated for his *apparatus criticus*.[59]

It is not clear at which point the *receptus* reached England to establish in due course a distinctive English tradition. Apart from Hatton 48, all surviving manuscripts written in England before 1100 (some eleven, including one substantial fragment) belong to the *receptus* recension.[60] Since none of these manuscripts was written before the mid-tenth century, it is possible that the *receptus* did not travel to England prior to the early stages of the Benedictine reform. However, it is entirely conceivable (and indeed probable) that copies of the *receptus* were available in England as early as the ninth century.[61] A pointer in that direction might be that several documents of the aforementioned Aachen synods of 816–17 (that is of texts originating well before the tenth-century Cluniac reforms) are preserved in English (eleventh-century) manuscripts. In question are the *Acta praeliminaria* and the *Collectio capitularis*, as well as the so-called *Memoriale qualiter*, a supplement to the *Regula S. Benedicti*, perhaps compiled by Benedict of Aniane himself.[62] Interestingly, in five of these Anglo-Saxon manuscripts (Cambridge, University Library, Ll.1. 14, CCCC 57, Tiberius A. iii, Titus A. iv and London, BL, Harley 5431), the texts in question follow the Latin or bilingual text of the *Regula S. Benedicti*, thereby pointing up the pivotal role played by the *Regula* in Benedict of Aniane's reforms and in the Aachen decrees.[63] Furthermore, it

---

[59] See Hanslik, *Benedicti Regula*, pp. lv–lxiii.

[60] For a list of these manuscripts, see Gretsch, 'Æthelwold's Translation', p. 126; for a discussion of their textual affiliations, cf. *ibid.*, pp. 130–4, and *idem*, *Regula*, pp. 61–176; see also Meyvaert, 'Towards a History', pp. 100–3, for valuable observations on the affiliations of some of these manuscripts.

[61] Meyvaert, 'Towards a History', p. 103, already suggested this much but did not pursue the matter further.

[62] For the *Acta* and the *Collectio*, see above, n. 57. The *Memoriale qualiter* is printed by D. C. Morgand and S. Wandrille, in CCM 1 (ed. Hallinger), 177–282.

[63] For a brief discussion of these manuscripts and of the influence which the texts of the Aachen legislation and the *Memoriale qualiter* exerted on the English reform, see Lapidge, *Wulfstan: Life*, pp. lvi–lviii. For the selection and arrangement (of especial significance) of the texts in Tiberius A. iii, see Deshman, '*Benedictus Monarcha*', pp. 228–30. For a brief description of the English manuscripts and their (often prominent) place in the transmissional history of the Aachen texts (with further references), see now also H. Mordek, *Bibliotheca capitularium regum Francorum manuscripta. Überlieferung und Traditionszusammenhang der fränkischen Herrschererlasse*, MGH, Hilfsmittel 15 (Munich, 1995), 94–5, 97–8, 223–6, 231–2, 642–3 and 416.

is clear now that the version of the Old English Rule adapted for the use in nunneries (and very possibly prepared by Æthelwold himself) draws heavily on another text of this early-ninth-century Carolingian legislation, namely the rule for canonesses as laid down in the *Institutiones Aquisgranenses* (promulgated in 816).[64] In other words, the transmission of the *receptus* text of the *Regula* in Anglo-Saxon England – and indeed the Old English Rule itself – seems closely tied up with the early reforms of the Carolingian church.

For an agency through which the Aachen texts, together with the *textus receptus* recension of the *Regula*, might have travelled to England, one thinks perhaps most naturally of Grimbald and John, two continental scholars invited by King Alfred to help him with his revitalizing programme for English scholarship. Both are styled 'priest and monk' by Asser, Alfred's biographer.[65] Grimbald (d. 901) originally had been a monk of Saint-Bertin in the town of Saint-Omer in Flanders, whereas John ('the Old Saxon'), of continental Saxon extraction, may have been recruited from some monastery in the northern or central parts of Germany.[66] Both will therefore have been thoroughly familiar with the *receptus* recension of the *Regula*, and both presumably brought books with them to England. In fact, the arrival in England of a number of manuscripts written on the Continent (prior to s. x) but owned in England before 1100 has been tentatively associated with King Alfred's

---

[64] See R. Torkar, 'Zur weiblichen Fassung der Benediktinerregel in angelsächsischer Zeit und der Aachener Kanonissenregel', *Anglia* (forthcoming). The Aachen rule for canonesses is printed by A. Werminghoff, *Concilia aeui Karolini* I, MGH, Leges (Berlin, 1906), 422–56; cf. esp. p. 455 for parallels with ch. 62 of the 'feminine' version of the Old English Rule. For the context of the Aachen rule, see (briefly) *LkMA* V (1990), 451–2. For the version of the Old English Rule adapted for nuns and Æthelwold as its probable author, see Gretsch, 'The Benedictine Rule', pp. 143–6 and 150–3.

[65] See Asser, *Life* (ed. Stevenson) ch. 78 (p. 63; transl. Keynes and Lapidge, *Alfred the Great*, p. 93) and ch. 94 (p. 81; Keynes and Lapidge, p. 103).

[66] For Grimbald and John, see conveniently Keynes and Lapidge, *Alfred the Great*, p. 260, nn. 168 and 169; on Grimbald's career, see also P. Grierson, 'Grimbald of St Bertin's', *English Historical Review* 55 (1940), 529–61, and J. Bately, 'Grimbald of St Bertin's', *Medium Aevum* 35 (1966), 1–10; see also above, pp. 76–7. For John's continental origins, see Lapidge, 'Poems as Evidence', p. 66 and nn. 81 and 82. See also below, pp. 342–7, for the role John may have played in the rise of the tenth-century hermeneutic style.

continental helpers.[67] As was to be expected, among these continental books, there are two psalters and a (now lost) collectar, in other words, texts which will have been needed for the performance of the daily liturgy in mass and Office.[68] By the same token, copies of a monastic rule (which at this point – several decades after the Aachen reforms had been instituted – can have meant only the *Regula S. Benedicti* in its *receptus* form), will have been needed for King Alfred's newly established monastic foundations at Shaftesbury and Athelney (where he appointed John abbot).[69] In short, we have reason to think that copies of the *Regula S. Benedicti* in its *receptus* recension were available in England by the late ninth century, even though no such copies have survived.

Now Æthelwold can unequivocally be shown to have composed his translation after an exemplar of the *receptus* recension, although (perhaps not unsurprisingly) none of the surviving Latin manuscripts of the *Regula* can be identified as his exemplar.[70] However, since the likelihood is that the *receptus* text would have been available (if in a few copies only) in England from the times of King Alfred onwards, the fact that this recension underlies the Old English Rule does not force us to conclude that the translation was undertaken at a time when the English reform movement was well under way and when books from continental reformed monasteries were brought to England on a large scale. Furthermore, additional copies of the *receptus* text of the *Regula* may have been brought to England during the first half of the tenth

---

[67] For the books in question, see Keynes and Lapidge, *Alfred the Great*, pp. 26–7 and 214, n. 26, Gneuss, 'Anglo-Saxon Libraries', pp. 678–9, and Lapidge, 'Prolegomena to an Edition of Bede's Metrical *Vita Sancti Cuthberti*', pp. 155–7.

[68] The psalters in question are CCCC 272 and Utrecht, Universiteitsbibliotheek, 32 (on both manuscripts, see below, pp. 275–7). The *Commune sanctorum* in the now lost collectar arguably served as an exemplar for the Durham Collectar (now Durham, Cathedral Library, A. IV. 19, s. ix/x, written somewhere in south England) and Ælfwine's prayer book (now London, BL, Cotton Titus D. xxvi and xxvii, 1023–31, written at the New Minster, Winchester); see A. Corrêa, *The Durham Collectar*, HBS 107 (London, 1992), 121–2.

[69] See Asser, *Life*, chs. 93–7 (ed. Stevenson, pp. 80–5, transl. Keynes and Lapidge, *Alfred the Great*, pp. 103–5) on Athelney, and ch. 98 (ed. Stevenson, p. 85, transl. Keynes and Lapidge, p. 105) on Shaftesbury. It is worth noting that (according to Asser) a number of the Athelney monks came from Francia.

[70] See Gneuss, 'Benediktinerregel', pp. 280–2, Gretsch, *Regula*, pp. 123–76, and *idem*, 'Æthelwold's Translation', pp. 129–30 and 134–7.

century[71] by influential ecclesiastics such as Oda, archbishop of Canterbury (941–58)[72] or Ælfheah, bishop of Winchester (934–51)[73] who themselves had been professed monks but apparently had not the zeal (or the opportunity) to convert their *familiae* into monastic communities.

As regards Æthelwold and the first monastic community over which he presided, we have the testimony of the late-twelfth- or early-thirteenth-century supplement to the Abingdon chronicle (*De abbatibus Abbendoniae*) that he sent for a copy of the *Regula* from Fleury while he was abbot of Abingdon: 'Fecit etiam uenire regulam sancti Benedicti a Floriaco monasterio.'[74] The hypothesis that Æthelwold may already have been

---

[71] The possibility that a Benedictine community (of some sort) resided at Bath during the reign of Æthelstan (924–39) cannot be completely ruled out; see Keynes, 'Æthelstan's Books', pp. 161–2. For the suggestion that among this community there may have been monks from Fleury who went into exile because they did not wish to submit to the reforms instituted at Fleury by Odo of Cluny in the 930s, see J. Nightingale, 'Oswald, Fleury and Continental Reform', in *St Oswald of Worcester*, ed. Brooks and Cubitt, pp. 23–45, at 26–7.

[72] We know from Byrhtferth's *Vita S. Oswaldi* (ed. Raine, *Historians* I, 413) that Oda was a Benedictine monk, professed at Fleury, but we have no information as to when his profession occurred. On Oda's career, see J. A. Robinson, *St Oswald and the Church of Worcester*, British Academy Supplemental Papers 5 (London, 1919), 38–51, and Brooks, *The Early History*, pp. 222–37; see also below, pp. 339–41 and 370–2.

[73] Bishop Ælfheah is commonly assumed to have been a monk: see, for example, Robinson, *Times of Saint Dunstan*, Stenton, *Anglo-Saxon England*, p. 445, Symons, *Regularis Concordia*, pp. xi and xiii, Brooks, 'The Career of St Dunstan', p. 5, and (with a note of caution) Knowles, *Monastic Order*, pp. 35–6. This would be of special interest in view of Æthelwold's sojourn in the bishop's *familia* at some point between 934 and 939; cf. *Wulfstan: Life*, ch. 9 (p. 14). The presumption of Ælfheah's Benedictinism rests principally on two (not altogether clear or reliable) testimonies: a charter, issued by King Æthelstan in 925, which is attested by one Ælfheah 'sacerdos et monachus' (S 394, BCS 641, *Charters of St Augustine's Abbey, Canterbury*, ed. S. E. Kelly, Anglo-Saxon Charters 4 (Oxford, 1995), no. 26; see *ibid.*, p. 101, for this Ælfheah's identity), and B (Dunstan's earliest biographer), who tells us that Dunstan received the monastic habit from his kinsman, Bishop Ælfheah, thereby implying that the latter was a monk himself; cf. *Sancti Dunstani Vita Auctore B*, ed. Stubbs, pp. 13–14. However, Wulfstan, *Life*, chs. 7 and 8 (pp. 10–12) relates how Dunstan and Æthelwold were ordained priests (not professed monks) by Bishop Ælfheah on the same day, and he goes on to say (ch. 9, p. 14) that Æthelwold was professed as monk only under Dunstan's abbacy at Glastonbury.

[74] *Chronicon Monasterii de Abingdon*, ed. Stevenson II, 278.

familiar with the *receptus* version, or even the presumption that he had finished his translation by the time he sent for the Fleury copy, in no way implies that we have to dismiss this Abingdon testimony as late and unreliable. Even if Æthelwold had been acquainted with the *receptus* and its predominant role on the Continent for many years, he will have had a keen interest in obtaining a copy of the *Regula* from Fleury, the centre on whose customs he drew most extensively when compiling his own consuetudinary, the *Regularis concordia* for the English reformed monasteries.[75] On the other hand, in the light of the foregoing considerations, the remark in the Abingdon chronicle clearly cannot be taken to indicate that the Fleury copy was the first *textus receptus* which came to Æthelwold's notice.

The early Glastonbury years and the evidence of CCCC 57

When we now ask at what stage of his career Æthelwold will have occupied himself most diligently with a close and verbatim study of the *Regula* (a study which perhaps included a translation into the vernacular), there is but one answer: the early Glastonbury years. When Æthelwold left Winchester, presumably late in 939 or in 940,[76] to join Dunstan at Glastonbury, he obviously went there in order to become a Benedictine monk. Dunstan's biographer, B, reports that upon being installed as abbot of Glastonbury (*c.* 940), Dunstan immediately introduced there the *Regula S. Benedicti*.[77] We know from Æthelwold's own testimony, as well as from Wulfstan, that at that time Glastonbury was the only regular monastery anywhere in England.[78] Since there must have been a monastic

---

[75] Symons ('Some Notes on English Monastic Origins', *Downside Review* 80 (1962), 55–69, at 61–5) was even of the opinion that the manuscript in question was a copy not of the *Regula*, but of the Fleury customs. For the importance of the Fleury observance on the compilation of the *Regularis concordia*, see conveniently Lapidge, 'Æthelwold as Scholar and Teacher', p. 193, and *idem, Wulfstan: Life*, pp. lix–lx.

[76] For the date, see *Wulfstan: Life*, ch. 9 (p. 14 and n. 3).

[77] Cf. *Sancti Dunstani Vita Auctore B*, ed. Stubbs, ch. 15 (p. 25). The beginning of Dunstan's abbacy cannot be established with absolute precision; for a brief evaluation of the evidence, see Lapidge, *Wulfstan: Life*, p. 14, n. 4.

[78] See Æthelwold's remark in the preface to the Rule: 'Næs þæt [*scil.* monastic life] na fealdre þonne on anre stowe, seo is Glæstingabyrig gehaten', 'This was in no more places than one, which is called Glastonbury', *CS*, p. 149, and cf. *Wulfstan: Life*, ch. 18 (p. 32).

community of some sort at least at St Augustine's, Canterbury,[79] Æthelwold's and Wulfstan's assertions can only be taken to mean that Glastonbury in the 940s was the only place where life was regulated in accordance with Benedictine observance and in a way similar to continental monasteries. Wulfstan goes on to say that Æthelwold was 'eventually' (*tandem*, ch. 9, p. 14) professed a monk. According to the provisions laid down in the *Regula* (ch. 58.9–14), the minimum time required for a novitiate before monastic vows could be taken would have been twelve months. Such stipulation in the *Regula* was confirmed by the *acta* of the Aachen synods of 816 and 817.[80] During that time (again according to the *Regula*) a careful study of St Benedict's text was to be the novice's chief occupation. The decrees of the Aachen synods elaborate on this stipulation: they not only demand that the *Regula* be discussed word for word ('singula uerba discutientes'); they require that the entire text be committed to memory where possible ('ut monachi omnes qui possunt memoriter regulam discant').[81]

We do not know in which recension, the *interpolatus* or the *receptus*, Æthelwold will have studied the *Regula* at Glastonbury. We have seen already that it could well have been a *receptus* text, especially in a place such as Glastonbury, which heralded a new era in English monasticism. On the other hand, the occurrence of distinctively *interpolatus* readings in later *receptus* copies of the *Regula* (see above, p. 245) suggests that the *interpolatus* tradition still played a role in tenth-century England and that therefore Æthelwold may well have been familiar with this text-form. Interestingly, the English *receptus* manuscript which has the most obvious links with Hatton 48 (*interpolatus*) may point to Æthelwold himself. The manuscript in question is CCCC 57, written *c.* 1000, possibly at Abingdon.[82] That a copy amalgamating the older and newer textual traditions of the *Regula* could arguably be produced in Æthelwold's own monastery at a time when the reform movement had already passed its peak may suggest that here, as in matters of liturgical

---

[79] For the monastic community at St Augustine's, see Knowles, *Monastic Order*, pp. 34–5; see also Dumville, *English Caroline Script*, p. 87.

[80] See, for example, the *Collectio capitularis*, CCM 1, 523 (no. xxviii).

[81] *Ibid.*, p. 516 (nos. i and ii).

[82] The text of the *Regula* from CCCC 57 is printed by Chamberlin, *The Abingdon Copy*. On its textual affiliations, see Meyvaert, 'Towards a History', p. 100, and Gretsch, *Regula*, pp. 95, 104 and 120.

practice,[83] Æthelwold did not reject outright older English traditions, in spite of his clear orientation towards continental models.

As regards CCCC 57, it is important to add that in spite of its links with the older *interpolatus* tradition, it is by no means an old-fashioned book. On the contrary, its contents clearly reveal a continental outlook, and they equally unambiguously indicate that the manuscript was intended for daily use in the monastery. Thus the *Regula* (2r–32v) is followed by two of the texts connected with the reforms of Benedict of Aniane, namely the *Memorale qualiter* (33r–37r) and the *Collectio capitularis* (37v–40v). These in turn are followed by a Latin Martyrology (41r–94r) and the *Diadema monachorum* (95r–162r) by the early-ninth-century author Smaragdus of Saint-Mihiel, who belongs in the Carolingian reform circles. The presence of these two works has a bearing on the use of the *Regula* in the manuscript. In the wake of Benedict of Aniane's reforms, it became established practice to read aloud portions of the martyrology and the *Regula* every day in Chapter after the morning mass.[84] Similarly, the *Diadema monachorum* (surviving in a vast number of manuscripts) was composed by Smaragdus for recital during the period of communal reading before Compline, as prescribed by the *Regula* (cf. *RSB* 42.3–7).[85] Further evidence that this copy of the *Regula* (in spite of its links with the older textual tradition) was designated for daily use in the monastery is offered by a number of insertions into its text pertaining to monastic customs and the liturgy, nearly all of these unique among the English

---

[83] For the English elements in the liturgical customs of the *Regularis concordia*, see Symons, *Regularis Concordia*, p. xlvi, *idem*, 'History and Derivation', pp. 44–5, and Lapidge, *Wulfstan: Life*, p. lx.

[84] See, for example, the stipulation in the *Collectio capitularis*: 'Ut ad capitulum primitius martyrilogium legatur et dicatur uersus, deinde regula aut omelia quaelibet legatur' (CCM 1, 532 (no. lxvi); cf. also *ibid.*, p. 480 (no. xxxvi); and see *Regularis Concordia*, ed. Symons, ch. 21 (p. 17): 'ad Capitulum ... legatur martyrologium ... legatur regula'.

[85] The *Diadema* is printed PL 102, 593–690; for the purpose of the work, see Smaragdus's preface: 'Et quia mos est monachorum, ut regulam beati Benedicti ad capitulum legant quotidie matutinum, uolumus ut iste libellus ad eorum capitulum quotidie legatur uespertinum' (*ibid.*, 593). On the *Diadema*, see Rädle, *Studien zu Smaragd*, pp. 68–78, who (p. 78) notes more than a hundred manuscripts of the work (no more than three or four of these are of English pre-Conquest origin). On Smaragdus, see also below, p. 255.

manuscripts of the *Regula*.[86] Interestingly, one of these accretions, which makes mention of the liturgical use of the 'Athanasian Creed', may again point to Æthelwold (see below, pp. 273–4).

There is no irrefutable proof that CCCC 57 was written at Abingdon; but the manuscript was certainly there by the mid-eleventh century.[87] Irrespective of an Abingdon origin of CCCC 57, however, the English tradition of the *interpolatus* version and Æthelwold's keen interest in the text of the *Regula*[88] strongly suggest that he will have been acquainted with the *interpolatus*, and that therefore the decision to base his translation on the *receptus* will have been made deliberately, and in all probability will have been guided by the information he had concerning the status of the *receptus* in continental monasteries. The evidence of Æthelwold's biography as a Benedictine monk points to the early Glastonbury years as the period when he will have concerned himself most deeply with the text of the *Regula* and its recensions.

---

[86] These insertions are conveniently listed by Chamberlin, *The Abingdon Copy*, pp. 78–9. For their distinctive character, see (with due caution) Hanslik's (*Benedicti Regula*) *apparatus criticus*.

[87] The eleventh-century Abingdon provenance of CCCC 57 emerges from numerous obits entered in the martyrologium and two formulae for announcing a death in the community, all pertaining to Abingdon. These are printed by James, *Catalogue* I, 115–18; see also Keynes, *Diplomas*, p. 239, n. 22, and J. Gerchow, *Die Gedenküber-lieferung der Angelsachsen*, Arbeiten zur Frühmittelalterforschung 20 (Berlin, 1988), 245–52 and 335–8. For the eleventh-century date of the entries, see Ker, *Catalogue*, pp. 46–7 (no. 34), and Dumville, *English Caroline Script*, p. 136, n. 106. An insertion in ch. 7 of the *Regula* which CCCC 57 shares with Tiberius A. iii (s. xi^med, from Christ Church, Canterbury) can scarcely be taken to point to a Canterbury origin for CCCC 57 as has been tentatively suggested by R. Gameson ('The Origin of the Exeter Book of Old English Poetry', *ASE* 25 (1996), 135–85, at 176), since a considerable number of texts in Tiberius A. iii derive from Winchester exemplars, for example, the Old English interlinear version to the *Regula*. For these Winchester exemplars of Tiberius A. iii, see Gneuss, 'Origin and Provenance of Anglo-Saxon Manuscripts', p. 17; for the origin of the Old English gloss to the *Regula*, see especially Hofstetter, *Winchester und Sprachgebrauch*, pp. 117–23. CCCC 57 is discussed most recently by T. Graham, 'Cambridge Corpus Christi College 57 and its Anglo-Saxon Users', in *Anglo-Saxon Manuscripts and their Heritage*, ed. P. Pulsiano and E. M. Treharne (Aldershot, 1998), pp. 21–69; for a discussion of the origin of the manuscript, cf. *ibid.*, pp. 31–4.

[88] In this connection, see below, pp. 285–7, for Æthelwold's demonstrable interest in textual variants between the *Romanum* and the *Gallicanum* versions of the psalter.

The 'Expositio in Regulam S. Benedicti'

There is a further piece of evidence which may suggest an origin of the Old English Rule (or at least a draft version of the translation) during Æthelwold's Glastonbury years. For his translation Æthelwold drew occasionally on the commentary on the *Regula* by Smaragdus, whose exegesis he incorporated into his English version, chiefly in the form of brief additions to the Latin text of the *Regula*. Smaragdus (*c.* 760 – *c.* 830), abbot of Saint-Mihiel in northern France, composed his *Expositio in Regulam S. Benedicti* in 820 or so. It is the earliest surviving commentary on the *Regula* and was written in the train of Benedict of Aniane's reforms of the Carolingian church.[89] Smaragdus's commentary is cast as a series of brief passages from the *Regula*, each followed in turn by an exposition (usually lengthy). The work *per se* would therefore not lend itself easily to use in a verbatim translation of the *Regula*, where additions to the text would have to be restricted in size and number.[90] That Æthelwold drew occasionally, and in points of minute detail, on this commentary nonetheless reveals that he was thoroughly familiar with Smaragdus's exegesis of the *Regula*.

Two manuscripts of the *Expositio* have survived from Anglo-Saxon England. The earlier of these, which concerns us here, now Cambridge, University Library, Ee. 2. 4, is of mid-tenth-century date and was written somewhere in southwest England, possibly at Glastonbury. The manuscript is one of the earliest examples of Anglo-Caroline script. Interestingly, it contains corrections and additions which seem to suggest collation with a second manuscript. It has been conjectured that most of these corrections were made by Dunstan himself.[91] We have Wulfstan's

---

[89] The critical edition is by Spannagel and Engelbert, *Smaragdi Abbatis Expositio in Regulam S. Benedicti* (1974). On Smaragdus in general, see Rädle, *Studien zu Smaragd*; the *Expositio*, however, is not treated in any detail in this study. For this, see the brief introduction by Engelbert in the Spannagel–Engelbert edition, pp. xxii–xxxiv.

[90] It is, in fact, often difficult to decide whether an addition is derived from Smaragdus and may not have suggested itself independently to the translator. For a discussion of Æthelwold's recourse to the *Expositio*, see Gretsch, *Regula*, pp. 257–62, and *idem*, 'Æthelwold's Translation', pp. 144–6. See also above, pp. 9–10, for the resort which Æthelwold possibly had to the *Expositio* when translating a crucial passage in the *Regula*.

[91] CUL Ee. 2. 4 is now mutilated: quires 1–6 and 23 are missing; several folios have been torn out; *membra disiecta* are preserved as Oxford, Bodleian Library, lat. theol. c. 3, fols.

testimony that upon his arrival at Glastonbury (in 940 or thereabouts), Æthelwold became Dunstan's disciple ('ac postmodum Glastoniam peruieniens magnifici uiri Dunstani, abbatis eiusdem monasterii, discipulatui se tradidit') and that he profited greatly from Dunstan's teaching ('cuius magisterio multum proficiens').[92] However, in the light of Dunstan's and Æthelwold's respective scholarly achievements, there may be grounds for thinking that these remarks should not be interpreted too narrowly, but that they should rather be seen as a reflection of the great love and veneration which Æthelwold clearly felt for his lifelong friend and colleague,[93] especially so, when we consider that they must have been more or less coeval,[94] that during the 930s they had attended King

1, 1* and 2. For the script and localization and for the suggestion that Dunstan himself could have been the corrector, see Bishop, 'An Early Example of Insular-Caroline', pp. 396–400, and *idem, English Caroline Minuscule*, p. 2 (no. 3). Dunstan's hand (hand 'D') has, more or less tentatively, been identified in the glosses, additions and corrections in several other manuscripts. For lists of the manuscripts in question, see for example, Lapidge, 'Schools, Learning and Literature', p. 27, n. 82, and Budny, 'St Dunstan's Classbook', pp. 137–8 (adding two further manuscripts to the list, one of these, Oxford, Bodleian Library, Hatton 30, since rejected by Dumville, 'Square Minuscule' [*ASE* 23], p. 148). See also below, p. 351 and n. 61, for one of the manuscripts arguably containing annotations by Dunstan. For the possible connection of CUL Ee. 2. 4 with Glastonbury, Dunstan and Æthelwold, see also Lapidge, *Wulfstan: Life*, pp. liii–liv. Note that Dumville, *English Caroline Script*, p. 97, doubts the Glastonbury origin of CUL Ee. 2. 4.

[92] See *Wulfstan: Life*, ch. 9 (p. 14). It may be presumed that most of the events in Æthelwold's biography which Wulfstan reports but cannot have witnessed himself he will have learned from his former abbot and master by way of personal communication; see Lapidge, *Wulfstan: Life*, pp. c–ci. Such communication may particularly be suspected in matters of a more personal concern as in this case.

[93] In his own writings, Æthelwold refers with affection to Dunstan several times. See for example: 'Dunstanus, egregius huius patriae archiepiscopus, praesago afflatus spiritu ... prouide ac sapienter addidit', 'Dunstan, the noble archbishop of our country, moved by the spirit of prophecy, providently and wisely added these further instructions' (*Regularis Concordia*, ed. Symons, ch. 7 (p. 4)). Similarly, in his preface to the Rule, Æthelwold links (rather unexpectedly) King Edgar's successful programme of monastic renewal with Dunstan's councillorship: 'breac þa gesinlice Dunstanes his ercebisceopes rædes; þurh his myndgunge he wæs smeagende embe his saule hæle, 7 no þæt an, ac eacswylce be ealre æfestnesse 7 gesundfulnesse his andweardes', 'he availed himself continually of the counsel of his archbishop, Dunstan; through his admonition he constantly inquired about the salvation of his soul, and not that alone, but likewise about all the religion and the welfare of his dominion' (*CS*, pp. 149–50).

[94] B (unique among Dunstan's biographers in that he had known him personally) placed

Æthelstan's court in what must have been similar positions as secular retainers,[95] and that both had been ordained priests by Bishop Ælfheah of Winchester on the same day.[96]

Whatever may have been the case, there can be little doubt that, at Glastonbury, Dunstan and Æthelwold immediately embarked on an intense and ambitious programme of study. Æthelwold (through Wulfstan's record) even supplies us with an outline sketch of the scope of such studies: 'Didicit namque inibi [*scil.* at Glastonbury] liberalem grammaticae artis peritiam atque mellifluam metricae rationis dulcedinem, et more apis prudentissimae ... diuinorum carpebat flores uoluminum. Catholicos quoque et nominatos studiose legebat auctores'.[97] We may be certain that the *Regula S. Benedicti* was among the *diuina uolumina* which Æthelwold studied at Glastonbury. Was Smaragdus among the *catholicos quoque et nominatos auctores*? It is not unreasonable to think that Æthelwold acquired his intimate familiarity with the *Expositio* (and the text of the *Regula* which it presented) during the early 940s, when he will have occupied himself most intensely with the *Regula*. Close study of the

Dunstan's birth in the reign of King Æthelstan (924–39) (*Vita S. Dunstani*, ed. Stubbs, ch. 3 (p. 6)), which would make him some twenty years younger than Æthelwold (born in the reign of King Edward the Elder (899–924), probably 904/5 × 909: see *Wulfstan: Life*, ch. 1 (pp. 2–4), and cf. Lapidge, *ibid.*, p. xlii. However, such a late date for Dunstan's birth has been rejected by most historians, and a date 909/10 has been proposed instead; see, for example, Robinson, *The Saxon Bishops of Wells*, pp. 28–40. The assumption of Dunstan's birth not before 924, would make him about sixteen when he was appointed abbot of Glastonbury (*c.* 940; cf. *Vita S. Dunstani*, ed. Stubbs, ch. 13 (p. 25) and *Wulfstan: Life*, ch. 9 (p. 14)) and about ten to fifteen when he was ordained priest by Bishop Ælfheah of Winchester (934–51), and in the reign of Æthelstan (i. e. *ante* 939). For an attempt to rescue B's chronology in spite of these difficulties, see Brooks 'The Career of St Dunstan', pp. 3–5. For a possible explanation of B's confusion about Dunstan's birth, see Lapidge, 'B. and the *Vita S. Dunstani*', p. 282.

[95] For Dunstan at King Æthelstan's court, see *Vita S. Dunstani*, ed. Stubbs, ch. 6 (pp. 11–12), and *Wulfstan: Life*, ch. 7 (p. 10); see also below, pp. 354–5.

[96] For the ordination of Dunstan and Æthelwold, see *Wulfstan: Life*, chs. 7 and 8 (pp. 10–12); for the date and place of the ordination, see Lapidge, *ibid.*, p. 11, n. 11, and p. 13, n. 3.

[97] 'At Glastonbury he learned skill in the liberal art of grammar and the honey-sweet system of metrics; like a provident bee ... he laid toll on the flowers of religious books. He was eager to read the best-known Christian writers', *Wulfstan: Life*, ch. 9 (pp. 14–15).

Expositio (in CUL Ee. 2. 4, or any other manuscript) would have made Æthelwold aware that different recensions of the *Regula* were in circulation. Not only does Smaragdus discuss variant readings for a number of passages in the *Regula* and their respective merits;[98] the recension of the *Regula* on which he based his commentary has been shown to have been the *textus purus*.[99] This seems only natural in the light of the aforementioned close links between Smaragdus's *Expositio* and Benedict of Aniane's promulgation of the *textus purus* in Carolingian monasteries. However, the text of the *Regula* in CUL Ee. 2. 4 appears to have been contaminated to some degree by readings from the more recent *receptus* tradition.[100] This also seems natural, since the *purus* (to judge from the very few surviving manuscripts) never enjoyed a wide circulation, and since by the mid-tenth century, the *receptus* had long reached its predominant position. In any event, the text of the *Regula* as it is contained in CUL Ee. 2. 4 (and presumably in any other manuscript of the *Expositio* available in Anglo-Saxon England) is distinctly different from the earlier *interpolatus* tradition, a difference which will have been immediately perceptible upon close study.

The evidence of CUL Ee. 2. 4 cannot provide proof for an early date of the Old English Rule. Nevertheless, the evidence of a manuscript written (in an innovative type of script) in the mid-tenth century in a centre in

---

[98] See Engelbert, *Smaragdi Abbatis Expositio*, ed. Spannagel and Engelbert, p. xxxii.

[99] See *ibid.*, pp. xxxii–xxxiv, and Hanslik, *Benedicti Regula*, p. xxxi; that Smaragdus drew on the *purus* had already been realized by Traube, *Textgeschichte*, pp. 46–7 and 114.

[100] See Gretsch, *Regula*, pp. 101–2 and 114–16. My findings there resulted from a textcritical assessment of some 210 selected variant readings. The hope expressed there (p. 116) that a forthcoming critical edition of the *Expositio* might clarify the position of CUL Ee. 2. 4 within the manuscript transmission of that text has not been fulfilled. The aim of this new edition (by Spannagel and Engelbert), as stated by the editors (pp. lxxx–lxxxii), has been a reconstruction of the archetype of the text. Variant readings have been admitted to the *apparatus criticus* only in those cases where the reading of the archetype is in doubt or where a reading is of special importance for an individual branch of transmission. The variant readings for Smaragdus's text of the *Regula* listed in Hanslik's *apparatus criticus* are culled from the Spannagel–Engelbert text; cf. Hanslik, *Benedicti Regula*, p. xxxi (first ed. (1960), p. xxxiii). From Engelbert's discussion of the manuscript affiliations (*Smaragdi Abbatis Expositio*, pp. lii–liii) it is clear, however, that the exemplar for CUL Ee. 2. 4 must have come from Francia (as was to be expected): two of its closest relatives originated at Fécamp and Cluny respectively.

southwest England (Glastonbury?), and containing a text which *per se* points to a Benedictine monastery and which, by its contemporary annotations, incontestably indicates careful study of Smaragdus's commentary – the evidence of such a manuscript helps to confirm our suspicion that Æthelwold may have known some form of the *receptus* text during his Glastonbury years and that questions of textual criticism and exegesis of the *Regula S. Benedicti* may well have exercised him during those years.

Winchester vocabulary

Finally, a different class of evidence suggesting an early date in Æthelwold's career for the Old English Rule is worth mentioning briefly. This is of a lexical nature and concerns the employment of Winchester vocabulary. We have seen (above, pp. 93–113, and see below, pp. 410–23) that a strong link between the Rule and the Royal Psalter is forged by the presence in both texts of an incipient Winchester usage, and that they often reveal the same kind of lexical experimentation *en route* to the eventual Winchester terminology. This agreement could be explained most naturally on the assumption that the Rule and the Royal Psalter gloss originated at approximately the same time, that is to say by the 950s at the latest, the outside limit being set by the manuscript of the gloss, Royal 2. B. V. The lexical ties concerning an incipient and experimental stage of Winchester usage would be rather more difficult to explain if we had to assume a point in the early 970s for the composition of the Rule, that is after a lapse of more than twenty years since the Royal gloss was compiled. Furthermore, the 970s would have been the time when, at his Old Minster school, Bishop Æthelwold taught young Ælfric or the future glossator of the Lambeth Psalter, both of whom in due course became pre-eminent proponents of the fully-developed Winchester usage. The discrepancy between pupils employing consistently the fully-fledged Winchester vocabulary and their master revealing no more than an experimental stage of that usage in a work presumed to have been composed during the very time he acted as their teacher, has always been passed over in silence in discussions of Æthelwold's school and Winchester vocabulary. An early date for the Old English Rule would help to explain the difference between Æthelwold's and Ælfric's usage, just as it would aid in our understanding the common features of vocabulary shared by the Rule and the Psalter. By the same token, an early date for the Rule would carry with it the implication that we need not assume that Winchester usage in its late-tenth- and early-eleventh-century form resulted from a concerted effort by Æthelwold's students after their master's death. On the hypothesis of an origin of the Rule in the 940s or 950s, Winchester usage might well have been developed from an experimental stage to its final form at Æthelwold's instigation and under his supervision during his latter years at the Old Minster school.

The matter must be left there. We have no further ways of ascertaining the date of origin for the Rule. If we assume a date in the 940s or early 950s, as some of the evidence seems to suggest, this would imply that Æthelwold provided his translation with its preface (the tract known as 'Edgar's Establishment of Monasteries') in the form in which this has survived, at some point after King Edgar's marriage to Ælfthryth (who is mentioned therein) in 964 × 965. He would presumably either have drafted the Preface or revised it to its final form on the occasion of the 'publication' of the Rule, when the translation first left his immediate entourage, that is his Glastonbury and Abingdon circles, to be studied in the newly established Benedictine communities, first at Winchester and soon all over the country.

8

Æthelwold and the Royal Psalter

At first glance, the evidence (other than that provided by lexical and stylistic links) for ascribing the Royal Psalter gloss to Æthelwold and his circle is less straightforward than one might wish, since we have no source, contemporary or later, in which Æthelwold is connected with that gloss or with psalter glossing at large. Furthermore, it is notoriously difficult to ascertain whether glosses, as they have been transmitted in a manuscript, are the work of a single author or of a group of scholars closely collaborating, or even of several generations of scholars. Even if we rule out this last possibility, since (unlike the Aldhelm glosses), the Royal Psalter is a continous interlinear version, revealing (in spite of its rich and varied vocabulary) much homogeneity and pronounced lexical and stylistic predilections, and since the manuscript in which it is transmitted must be fairly close to the original gloss, the question of single or multiple authorship remains nonetheless to be considered. However, if the various reasons for assuming an origin of the Royal Psalter gloss in a circle where Æthelwold was active can be accepted, we may be certain that his influence on the compilation of this gloss was paramount and pervasive. Not only do we have knowledge of Æthelwold's active interest in translating into the vernacular (an interest attested by his own remarks in the preface to the Rule, and of course by the Rule itself), we also have ample testimony from Æthelwold's pupils concerning their master's competence, brilliance, vigour and enthusiasm as a teacher, and this testimony again includes several references to the importance which Æthelwold attached to the translation of Latin texts into Old English.

ÆTHELWOLD AS TEACHER

The *locus classicus* among these testimonies to Æthelwold's concern with classroom instruction is the remark in ch. 31 of Wulfstan of Winchester's biography of his master (presumably composed soon after Æthelwold's *translatio* on 10 September 996):

Dulce namque erat ei adolescentes et iuuenes semper docere, et Latinos libros Anglice eis soluere, et regulas grammaticae artis ac metricae rationis tradere, et iocundis alloquiis ad meliora hortari.[1]

This remark is repeated almost *verbatim* in the much abbreviated epitome of Wulfstan's *Life* which Ælfric produced between 1004 and 1006.[2] Ælfric commented on his tutelage by Æthelwold on several other occasions; most interestingly, in the preface to his *Grammar*, he refers to the problem that a given Latin lemma can be translated into English in various ways ('scio multimodis uerba posse interpretari'), and he concludes his brief discussion by stating that he will be content to do it after the fashion which he, and many others, have been taught at Æthelwold's school ('nos contenti sumus, sicut didicimus in scola Aðelwoldi, uenerabilis praesulis, qui multos ad bonum imbuit').[3] Further references to Æthelwold as a brilliant and renowned teacher are found in a hymn for Vespers for one of Æthelwold's feastdays (composed almost certainly by Wulfstan),[4] and in the *Responsio discipuli*, one of three anonymous Latin poems from Æthelwold's school (preserved in Cambridge, University Library, Kk. 5. 34, 74v–75r). Here, in buoyant adonics (a rare and eccentric metre in Anglo-Latin poetry) the schoolmaster Ioruert is derided for having questioned his Old Minster students' competence in composing Latin poetry. The ultimate argument to silence Ioruert's criticism is that it is preposterous to think that anyone who has had the

---

[1] 'It was always agreeable to him to teach young men and the more mature students, translating Latin texts into English for them, passing on the rules of grammar and metric, and encouraging them to do better by cheerful words', *Wulfstan: Life*, pp. 46–9.

[2] Printed *ibid.*, pp. 70–80, at 77.

[3] See *Ælfrics Grammatik und Glossar*, ed. H. Zupitza, 2nd ed. with foreword by H. Gneuss (Berlin, 1966), p. 1; see also Ælfric's Latin preface to his *Catholic Homilies*, ed. Thorpe I, 1, and his 'Letter to the Monks of Eynsham', ed. Nocent, p. 155.

[4] See above, p. 1.

privilege of the bishop's (that is Æthelwold's) teaching, should not be capable of writing Latin verses which make correct metre and sense:

> atqui
> credere ni uis
> quod pueri sic
> edere metrum
> (improbe!) possunt
> hic resident qui
> dogmate docti
> pontificali,
> ut neque sensum
> prodere murcum
> siue poema
> non fore rectum:
> indice quibus
> rite loquel*is*
> temet adhortor (54–68)[5]

From such remarks it is obvious that Æthelwold's students throughout their careers felt the distinction of having been taught by such a master, and it should be noted that no comparable interest in the vernacular and in teaching is attested for any other scholar among Æthelwold's contemporaries.

The date we have to assume for the origin of the Royal gloss may underpin the pivotal role which would have been played by Æthelwold in any such scholarly undertaking by his circle. The gloss must have been compiled during his Glastonbury or Abingdon years, that is before he was burdened with the duties and responsibilities of being bishop of a large and important diocese, and before much of his enormous energy will have been channelled into the urgent realizations of his monastic ideals. A date before 963 (Æthelwold's elevation to Winchester) is indicated by the sole surviving manuscript of the gloss in a pure, uncontaminated form, namely Royal 2. B. V. We must, therefore, next turn our attention to

---

[5] 'And unless you wish to believe (you scoundrel!) that we boys who live here and are taught by the bishop's teaching can compose verse in such a way as neither to give a mutilated sense or an incorrect poem, show us properly by what words [we err], I urge you.' The poem has been printed and translated by Lapidge, 'Three Latin Poems', pp. 262–7.

ascertaining what precisely is known about the date and origin of this unique testimony of the original gloss.

THE MANUSCRIPT EVIDENCE

Royal 2. B. V

Royal 2. B. V is a copy, though not at many removes from the original. The manuscript is written in Anglo-Saxon Square minuscule (Phase III, see below) and is dated unanimously to the mid-tenth century; its place of origin has been tentatively assigned either to Winchester or to Worcester.[6] However, such attributions rest on evidence other and later than the text of the psalter, the Old English interlinear gloss and the marginal Latin scholia (all written by the same scribe). Royal 2. B. V has been assigned to Worcester on the grounds that a manuscript which has been called its companion volume, namely Royal 4. A. XIV, can be shown to have been at Worcester in the twelfth century.[7] Royal 4. A. XIV is a companion volume to the Royal Psalter for two reasons: first, its principal contents (3r–105v) are a psalm commentary, namely a (now fragmentary) copy of Jerome's *Tractatus .lix. in psalmos*.[8] This commentary is interpolated with portions from the anonymous ('pseudo-Jerome') *Breuiarium in psalmos*.[9] Royal 4. A. XIV therefore attests to an active interest and expertise in psalm exegesis similar to that revealed in the Royal Psalter. Second, Royal 4. A. XIV is palaeographically closely related to Royal 2. B. V, so that an origin within the same scriptorium, perhaps with the same scribe, may be assumed.[10]

---

[6] See Ker, *Catalogue*, p. 320 (no. 249), and Sisam, *Salisbury Psalter*, pp. 53–4; for the date, see also Dumville, as cited below, n. 14. For Royal 2. B. V as a close copy of the original gloss, see Sisam, *Salisbury Psalter*, pp. 54–5 and 71–2.

[7] Cf. Ker, *Catalogue*, p. 320 (no. 250), and Sisam, *Salisbury Psalter*, p. 53.

[8] *CPL*, no. 592; see above, p. 28, n. 59, for an edition and for the probable loss of quires at the beginning of the manuscript. In Royal 4. A. XIV only the *tractatus* on pss. CIX–CXLIX have survived.

[9] *CPL*, no. 629, ptd PL 26, 871–1346. The anonymous *Breuiarium* is possibly of seventh-century Irish origin: cf. above, p. 28, n. 59, and see Wright, 'Hiberno-Latin Commentaries', pp. 98–9 (no. 15). For a survey of the various places and authors to which the *Breuiarium* has been ascribed, see also Machielsen, *Clavis Patristica Pseudoepigraphorum* IIA (1994), pp. 541–2 (no. 2357).

[10] K. Sisam (*Salisbury Psalter*, pp. 52–3) was of the opinion that both manuscripts were

Royal 2. B. V (and accordingly Royal 4. A. XIV) has been assigned to Winchester on account of a quire (fols. 1–7) added at the beginning of the manuscript and containing an Office for the Virgin Mary (1v–6r). The saints (SS Machutus and Eadburg) invoked in a prefatory prayer to the Office (1r–v) point to liturgical use of the Office in Winchester. The script of Office and prayer has been variously dated either to the first or to the second half of the eleventh century, and the texts have been attributed either to the New Minster or the Nunnaminster.[11] In any event, it is clear that the additional quire must have been bound up with the psalter as early as the eleventh century, since 7r–v contains (in an eleventh-century hand) a Latin preface to the psalter.[12] All this additional material obviously has some bearing on the question of where the Royal Psalter was in the eleventh century, and it is a matter of great interest that, at some point in the eleventh century, this place should have been Winchester.[13] It is clear, nonetheless, that the added quire is no more proof of a Winchester origin of Royal 2. B. V (and Royal 4. A. XIV) than is the twelfth-century Worcester home of Royal 4. A. XIV for a Worcester origin of both manuscripts.

Recently, David Dumville has categorically excluded a Winchester origin for Royal 2. B. V (and for Royal 4. A. XIV), since its type of script (Anglo-Saxon Square Minuscule, Phase III) was, in his view, practised there (as elsewhere) only during the period 939/40 × 959. At the

written by the same scribe. Ker similarly noted the close relationship of the script (of the type now called Anglo-Saxon Square minuscule, Phase III) in both manuscripts, and assigned them to the same scriptorium (cf. *Catalogue*, p. 320, nos. 249 and 250). Dumville speaks of a 'scribally related pair' ('Square Minuscule' [*ASE* 23], p. 149; cf. also his *English Caroline Script*, p. 14, n. 33).

[11] The Office and prefatory prayer are edited by E. S. Dewick, *Facsimiles of Horae de Beata Maria Virgine from English Manuscripts of the Eleventh Century*, HBS 21 (London, 1902), cols. 1–18; the prayer (with English translation) is printed by M. Clayton, *The Cult of the Virgin Mary in Anglo-Saxon England*, CSASE 2 (Cambridge, 1990), 74–5. For the date of the script and the ascription to one of the Winchester minsters, see Dewick, *Facsimiles*, pp. x–xii, Warner and Gilson, *Catalogue* I, 40 (arts. 1 and 2), Sisam, *Salisbury Psalter*, p. 53 and n. 3, Ker, *Catalogue*, pp. 319 and 320 (no. 249, arts. b and c), *idem*, *Medieval Libraries of Great Britain*, 2nd ed. (London, 1964), pp. 104 and 202, Gneuss, *Hymnar und Hymnen*, p. 112, Clayton, *The Cult of the Virgin Mary*, pp. 70–7, and Dumville, *Liturgy and Ecclesiastical History*, p. 102, n. 35.

[12] Cf. Warner and Gilson, *Catalogue* I, 40 (art. 5).

[13] For the sojourn of Royal 2. B. V at Canterbury (Christ Church) at some later point in the eleventh century, see below, Appendix II.

beginning of Æthelwold's episcopate (963), a rather different type of Square minuscule (Phase IV) was in use at Winchester.[14] Even if one does not wish to endorse unreservedly Dumville's assertion that Phase III of Anglo-Saxon Square minuscule was practised only during the reigns of Kings Edmund, Eadred and Eadwig,[15] in the case of Royal 2. B. V, Dumville's outer limits for the origin of the book, namely 939/40 × 959 (limits which rest on a thorough scrutiny of all the manuscripts exhibiting this type of script) square well with the date assigned to Royal 2. B. V by earlier scholars.[16]

From a palaeographical point of view, Dumville sees no difficulty in assigning Royal 2. B. V (and Royal 4. A. XIV) either to Glastonbury or Abingdon. However, Dumville's denial of Winchester (before 959) as a place of origin (and his suggestion of a Glastonbury or Abingdon origin instead) turns on a connection of the Royal Psalter with Æthelwold, a connection which had been vaguely suspected for some time (see above, pp. 82–92). On purely palaeographical grounds, Royal 2. B. V and its sister volume, Royal 4. A. XIV, could evidently have been written, at some point in the 940s or 950s, at Winchester, as they could have been at Worcester, or, for that matter, at any other of the centres where Anglo-Saxon Square minuscule, Phase III, was practised. Therefore, palaeography alone does not provide us with clear, irrefutable proof of a place of origin. It does provide us, however, with a span of some twenty years during which the manuscripts very probably were written. This span would coincide with Æthelwold's Glastonbury and Abingdon years, a period during which his scholarly pursuits are well attested and during which his translation of the *Regula S. Benedicti* was possibly produced.

The contents and layout of Royal 2. B. V are further pointers in the direction of Glastonbury or Abingdon. The Royal Psalter was not intended primarily (if at all) for liturgical use, but rather for the close scholarly study of the psalms. The text of the psalter lacks the typical large initials for certain psalms, as well as the subdivisions of some longer psalms, features which normally occur in psalters intended for liturgical use. The Royal Psalter has no more than the threefold division in so-called fifties (with large initials at pss. I, LI and CI), a division which has

---

[14] See Dumville, 'Square Minuscule', [*ASE* 23], pp. 149–50, and *idem, English Caroline Script*, p. 14, n. 3; cf. also *idem*, 'On the Dating', p. 48.

[15] Cf. Dumville, 'Square Minuscule', [*ASE* 23], p. 144.   [16] See above, p. 264, n. 6.

no bearing on the use of the psalter in the liturgy.[17] Interestingly, for his *Expositio psalmorum* (the commentary heavily laid under contribution for the marginal scholia in Royal 2. B. V) Cassiodorus adopts the threefold division and expressly refers to it in his *praefatio*: 'Quem tamen codicem etiam per quinquagenos psalmos cum praefationibus suis trina sum diuisione partitus'.[18] By the same token, the vast corpus of Latin scholia (principally drawn from one of the leading psalm commentaries and unprecedented among Anglo-Saxon psalters) points to a scholarly use for Royal 2. B. V, as does the Old English gloss, which shows a strong scholarly bias in that, for its *interpretamenta*, it frequently resorts to psalm exegesis.

This various evidence, in combination with the paramount role played by the psalter in reformed Benedictinism (on which see below), would render the assumption of an origin of Royal 2. B. V (and, consequently of Royal 4. A. XIV) at a place other than a centre connected with the earliest stages of the Benedictine reform, an unlikely hypothesis. Moreover, given the outer limits for the production of the manuscripts, given the lexical and stylistic reasons we have seen for connecting the original gloss with Æthelwold and his interests, and given the textual proximity of Royal 2. B. V to that original gloss, a Glastonbury or Abingdon origin for Royal 2. B. V seems very probable indeed.

The evidence of the eleventh-century Winchester psalters

What is known of the Royal Psalter's subsequent whereabouts may confirm the suspected link between Æthelwold, the gloss and the manuscript in which the gloss has survived. We have seen that Royal 2. B. V very probably was at Winchester in the eleventh century. There, it was evidently held in great esteem. This much is clear from the fact that its gloss served as the exemplar for the four surviving glossed psalters which

---

[17] For the various divisions of the psalter, see Wildhagen, 'Studien zum *Psalterium Romanum*', pp. 423–5 and 452, Sisam, *Salisbury Psalter*, p. 4 and n. 1, and Hughes, *Medieval Manuscripts for Mass and Office*, pp. 225–9. For the divisions in Royal 2. B. V, see also Roeder, *Der altenglische Regius-Psalter*, p. xiv. For the widespread use of the threefold division (very often combined with some kind of liturgical division) in English and continental psalters of the eighth and ninth centuries, see Wright, *Vespasian Psalter*, pp. 47–8. On liturgical divisions, see also below, p. 272 and n. 34.

[18] See *Expositio* I, 3–4.

originated at Winchester in the eleventh century, namely, BL, London, Cotton Vitellius E. xviii, 18r–140v (s. xi^{med}), BL, Cotton Tiberius C. vi, 31r–129v (s. xi^{med} or xi$^{3/4}$), BL, Stowe 2, 1r–180v (s. xi^{med} or xi$^{3/4}$), and BL, Arundel 60, 13r–46v (s. xi^2).[19] By the same token, the Royal gloss pervasively influenced the Lambeth Psalter, the sole surviving witness of a fresh interlinear version of the psalms undertaken in the eleventh century. The manuscript of the Lambeth Psalter (London, Lambeth Palace Library, 427, 5r–182v, s. xi^1) was possibly written at Winchester.[20] In any event, the Lambeth gloss has clear Winchester connections inasmuch as it is one of the principal testimonies to Winchester usage.[21] We may therefore permit ourselves to imagine that Royal 2. B. V was among the books brought by Æthelwold to Winchester in 963.

Interestingly, of these eleventh-century Winchester psalters, only the Tiberius Psalter (probably from the Old Minster) is a fairly close copy of the Royal gloss. Vitellius, Stowe and Arundel all incorporate in varying degrees and at different points A-type gloss material, as well as some (apparently) original glossing.[22] As regards these original glosses, it is of especial interest that the influence of Winchester vocabulary is clearly exhibited in them, most manifestly so in the Stowe Psalter.[23] Thus a free and flexible use of the Royal Psalter gloss is revealed in the surviving psalters from eleventh-century Winchester. (It will be recalled that less extensive but basically similar lexical and syntactical revisions and updatings are found in eleventh-century manuscripts of the Old English Rule, see above, p. 116.) Such an attitude is carried a step further by the Lambeth Glossator, for whom the Royal Psalter was the point of departure and a cornerstone on which to base a fresh and monumental psalter gloss.

It may therefore not be unreasonable to assume that these Winchester psalters provide us with a window on psalter scholarship as it was conducted in Bishop Æthelwold's school at Winchester and carried on there in the generation of his pupils. Such scholarship will have embraced

---

[19] It should be noted that this does not imply that Royal 2. B. V itself was the manuscript from which the later Winchester psalters were copied; the implication is only that the gloss in this manuscript initiated the Winchester D-type tradition.

[20] O'Neill, 'Latin Learning at Winchester', esp. pp. 158–66.

[21] Cf. Hofstetter, *Winchester und Sprachgebrauch*, pp. 84–8, and see above, p. 93.

[22] For details, see above, pp. 26–7.

[23] See Hofstetter, *Winchester und Sprachgebrauch*, pp. 67–83.

psalm exegesis as well as a persistent concern with vernacular psalm glossing. Psalm exegesis (aside from the Royal Psalter itself) is most prominent in the Latin scholia (drawn from various commentaries) in the Lambeth Psalter.[24] Concerning the vernacular glosses, two points are especially noteworthy: first, the time-honoured A-type gloss, the gloss of the Vespasian Psalter, apparently still had some currency in Æthelwold's Winchester and later, and was regularly laid under contribution for the eleventh-century psalter glosses originating there. This in turn may corroborate our earlier hypothesis that the Royal Glossator himself devised his gloss by having resort to an A-type psalter.[25] Second, the Royal Glossator's flair for flamboyant coinages evidently met with some reservation by his followers who often replaced such neologisms with more common, more sober (and more pedestrian) Old English *interpretamenta*. By such substitutions, these redactors of the Royal gloss confirm our earlier suspicions about the highly unusual, even exotic character of many of the glosses in the Royal Psalter.[26]

From this brief conspectus of the influence which the Royal gloss had in eleventh- (and presumably tenth-) century Winchester, let us now return to the original compilation of this gloss.

THE LITURGICAL EVIDENCE

A *fresh translation of the Book of Psalms*

Why do it? Why should a young priest, who upon King Æthelstan's death, in 939, left Winchester for Glastonbury in order to follow there his vocation to Benedictine monasticism, as well as to study Latin grammar, metrics and patristic literature in a circle of scholars[27] (all of whom presumably enjoyed a reasonable command of Latin) – why should such a priest apply his diligence and ingenuity to compiling a vernacular psalter gloss? The psalter was an important yet elementary text in the Anglo-Saxon curriculum (as elsewhere). Moreover, a vernacular gloss (the A-type gloss) had been in existence for more than a century and presumably was available in Æthelstan's Winchester in a manuscript still

---

[24] See O'Neill, 'Latin Learning at Winchester', pp. 151–61.
[25] See above, pp. 33–41 and *passim*.
[26] See above, pp. 58–73 and *passim*.   [27] Cf. *Wulfstan: Life*, p. 14 (ch. 9).

extant, now Oxford, Bodleian Library, Junius 27, 10r–149v, the Junius Psalter, written in the 920s, arguably at Winchester.[28]

There are several answers to such a question. To begin with, the Vespasian gloss would have been considered dated by the young intelligentsia assembled at Glastonbury in the 940s. It exhibited phonological features and employed the vocabulary of a dialect which was unmistakably not that of the Royal Glossator. More important perhaps, although the Vespasian gloss was a competent scholarly performance, it aimed to be no more than an ancillary aid for a better understanding of the Latin text. The Royal Glossator was more ambitious. As we have seen, he strove to convey as much as possible of the dignity and exquisiteness of the poetic language of the psalms in his native idiom. Such an ambition presupposes a keen interest in the vernacular, its resourcefulness and its potential for intellectual refinement; in other words, an interest which is well-attested for Æthelwold, both by the testimony of his students and by the style and diction of his Rule, which strikingly combines clarity of expression with stylistic pretensions (see above, p. 113–21). However, the refinement of the English language as a means for sophisticated expression is only one facet of Æthelwold's interest in the vernacular. It is in the promotion of his urgent lifelong concern, namely the promulgation of Benedictine monasticism, that he made use of the vernacular in a strategic way. A fresh translation of the psalter would be wholly consonant with Æthelwold's pedagogical (and disciplinary) intentions when translating the *Regula*.

After all, the psalter was not only an elementary text in the Anglo-Saxon curriculum, not only an anthology of fascinating and challenging poetry: it was (after the *Regula*) the most important book for a Benedictine monk or nun. Even a cursory reading of the liturgical chs. (8–18) in the *Regula* rapidly reveals that psalmody is the core of Benedict's Divine Office. In these chs., Benedict sets out with great care which psalms in which order are to be chanted during the daily Offices over the week, and in what way longer psalms should be subdivided or shorter ones be joined together. In addition to such meticulous stipulations, the importance Benedict attached to the chant of psalms emerges from several of his remarks, as when he prescribes, for example, that the

---

[28] See above, p. 26, for the A-type affiliations of Junius; for the manuscript, its gloss and Æthelwold's response to both, see below, pp. 315–31.

number of lessons should be reduced at Nocturns during the summer months (because the nights are so short) while stressing at the same time that the number of psalms (twelve) sung during that Office may under no circumstances be reduced: 'ut numquam minus a duodecim psalmorum quantitate ad uigilias nocturnas dicantur' (*RSB* 10.3).[29] And even though Benedict was not dogmatic about the way he had distributed the psalms over the daily Offices and expressly allowed for some variation from his scheme, he repeatedly insisted that the entire psalter, complete and unabridged, be recited once within a week and that the cycle of the 150 psalms should be begun afresh each Sunday at Nocturns ('omnimodis id adtendat, ut omni ebdomada psalterium ex integro numero centum quinquaginta psalmorum psallatur et dominico die semper a caput reprendatur ad uigilias', *RSB* 18.23).[30] The psalm which Benedict himself thought most suitable for a fresh start of the *cursus* was ps. XX (cf. *RSB* 18.6). His suggestion is of potential significance for the Royal gloss and its connection with Æthelwold, and we shall return to it in due course (see below, pp. 297–304). Aside from recital at the Offices, Benedict prescribed the study of psalms during the periods he had assigned for private reading; cf., for example: 'Post refectionem autem uacent lectionibus suis aut psalmis' (*RSB* 48.13; see also *RSB* 8.3).

In his stipulations for psalmody (as in much else of his liturgy), Benedict based himself in broad outline, but not in all the details of its distribution, on the Roman secular Office as it was performed in his time, according to the so-called *Ordo Romanus Primus*.[31] He himself acknowledges this source at one point in his *Regula*: 'sicut psallit ecclesia Romana'.[32] This secular Roman Office of the sixth century in its turn had been influenced by earlier monastic and ascetic rules, and, in due course, developed into the secular Office of the medieval church.[33] Therefore the

---

[29] Cf. also ch. 19 ('De disciplina psallendi'), where it is stressed that the disposition and outward appearance of the monk should be consonant with his psalmody; and see ch. 50, which stipulates that monks who, for various reasons, cannot attend the *opus Dei* in their monastery church should perform the entire *cursus* on their own as best they can.

[30] Cf. also *RSB* 18.24, for insistence on a weekly *cursus*; and see *RSB* 18.20–2, for Benedict's tolerance towards other arrangements of the psalms in the weekly *cursus*.

[31] The *Ordo* is printed by M. Andrieu, *Les Ordines Romani du haut Moyen Age*, 5 vols. (Louvain, 1931–61) II, 1–108; see also *DACL* XII (1935), 2406–24.

[32] *RSB* 13.10, with regard to the daily canticles at Lauds.

[33] See de Vogüé, *La Règle de Saint Benoît* V, 545–54, for Benedict's weekly recital of the psalter, its sources and parallels and its difference from other modes of psalmody. See

recital of the psalter once a week, as instituted by St Benedict, was not a novel feature *per se*, and such recital will (presumably) have been regular practice also among the secular Anglo-Saxon clergy since the days of St Augustine. (Several of the surviving psalters from Anglo-Saxon England, such as the Junius Psalter, bear decorated or upgraded initials pointing to liturgical use in the secular Office.)[34] Nevertheless, by the emphasis placed on the chant of psalms in the *Regula*, and by the way the psalms were apportioned among the daily Hours, the Benedictine *cursus* was from its beginning clearly and unmistakably distinct from that of the secular clergy. Moreover, after the reforms of Benedict of Aniane, and especially during the tenth century, Benedictinism was characterized by ever-increasing psalmody. As we have seen (above, pp. 14–16), psalms were added to the normal *cursus*, either as part of the daily supplementary Offices (such as the Office for the Virgin Mary or the Office for the Dead), or as self-contained groups (such as the fifteen gradual psalms (CXIX–CXXXIII), to be recited every night before Nocturns), or for performance together with additional prayers (such as the psalms said for

also *ibid.* I, 102–3 for tables comparing the distribution of the psalms over the week according to the Roman Office and to Benedict's *opus Dei*. Similar tables comparing the medieval secular and monastic (Benedictine) usage are widely available; see, for example, Hughes, *Medieval Manuscripts for Mass and Office*, pp. 52 and 230 (and cf. the brief remarks, *ibid.*, pp. 50–1), and Harper, *Forms and Order*, pp. 258–9 and 243–50. For a tabular presentation of the Benedictine *cursus* of psalms, see also Tolhurst, *Monastic Breviaries*, pp. 11–13. For the pre-Benedictine development of the secular and monastic Office, see A. G. Martimort, in *The Church at Prayer*, ed. A. G. Martimort *et al.*, rev. ed., 4 vols. (Collegeville, MS, 1985–7) IV, esp. 170–5. For this and the medieval development of the Divine Office, cf. also *DACL* II.i (1910), 1262–1316, and *LThK* II (1958), 679–81. See also P. F. Bradshaw, *Daily Prayer in the Early Church. A Study of the Origin and Early Development of the Divine Office* (New York, 1982), pp. 111–49, and P. Salmon, *L'Office divin au Moyen Age*, Lex Orandi 43 (Paris, 1967), 21–43.

[34] In the Junius Psalter (Bodleian, Junius 27) such initials mark, for example, the beginnings of pss. XXVI, XXXVIII, LII, LXVIII, LXXX, XCVII and CIX (two of these initials are now cut out; there are further initials highlighting, for various reasons, other psalms). The initials indicate the first of the psalms sung at Nocturns from Monday to Saturday (the first psalm sung at Nocturns on Sundays was ps. I which would have had an especially decorated initial in any case); they also indicate the first of the psalms (CIX) for Vespers on Sundays, all according to the secular Office (which in the case of the psalms for Nocturns is markedly different from the Benedictine Office). For a similar liturgical division in the Vespasian Psalter, see Wright, *The Vespasian Psalter*, p. 47.

the king, queen and benefactors). As we have also seen, for late-tenth-century England such elaboration of the original Benedictine *cursus* is most fully in evidence in Bishop Æthelwold's own *Regularis concordia*.[35] In short, a fresh vernacular gloss to the psalter, which aimed to help the newly converted monks and nuns in their study of the difficult Latin texts, while attempting at the same time to match the diction of the psalms, would square well with the enhanced role played by psalmody in the liturgy of the tenth-century Benedictine *renovatio*.

The Athanasian Creed and its gloss

The Creed

That the Royal Glossator's mind was indeed keyed to the new forms of the liturgy emerges from one further item in Royal 2. B. V. This manuscript (apart from being provided with a full set of the daily canticles) is the oldest surviving psalter written in England to contain the so-called 'Athanasian Creed' or *Quicumque uult* (after its *incipit*), complete with Old English interlinear gloss and marginal Latin scholia,[36] all written in the same hand as the psalter. Karl Wildhagen, again, was the only scholar to sense the potential significance of the presence of this text in Royal 2. B. V.[37] The Athanasian Creed was introduced into the Office in England not before the tenth century. The *Regularis concordia* prescribes its recitation for Prime at Easter,[38] a specification which is confirmed by Ælfric in his 'Letter to the Monks of

---

[35] For a general survey of the monastic *horarium* according to the *Regularis concordia* and the place which additional psalmody occupies therein, see Knowles, *Monastic Order*, Appendix xviii (pp. 714–15), and *Regularis Concordia*, ed. Symons, pp. xliii–xliv. For convenient tables with specifications (drawn from the *Regularis concordia*) which additional psalms are in question, see now S. E. Roper, *Medieval English Benedictine Liturgy. Studies in the Formation, Structure and Content of the Monastic Votive Office c. 950–1540* (New York, 1993), pp. 197–205. Unfortunately, the *Regularis concordia* is quoted there only from the (inferior) edition in CCM (for this edition, see above, p. 15, n. 30).

[36] 184r–186v; text and Old English gloss are printed by Roeder, *Der altenglische Regius-Psalter*, pp. 297–301; the Latin scholia are unprinted.

[37] See Wildhagen, 'Studien zum *Psalterium Romanum*', pp. 426 and 452–3, and above, p. 89.

[38] Cf. *Regularis Concordia*, ed. Symons, p. 51 (ch. 53) and n. 9.

Eynsham'.[39] From there, its use spread to Prime on Sundays and other feastdays (precisely when is unclear) and, in some places apparently, to Prime on other days as well.[40]

Interestingly, a manuscript of the *Regula S. Benedicti*, written (possibly) at Abingdon *c*. 1000, somewhat unexpectedly has a specification for the use of the *Quicumque uult*. The manuscript in question is CCCC 57. We have seen (above, p. 253) that the contents of this manuscript (apart from the *Regula*), namely a martyrology and Smaragdus of Saint-Mihiel's *Diadema monachorum*, reveal that the book was compiled for daily use in the monastery. We have also seen that its text of the *Regula* has strong links with the older English *interpolatus* tradition. This, and the fact that the manuscript contains in addition two of the texts connected with the Aachen legislation of 816/17 (the *Collectio capitularis* and the *Memoriale qualiter*; cf. above, pp. 245 and 247) seem to indicate that CCCC 57 has ties with the origins of the English reform movement. As regards the Athanasian Creed, the interesting point is that at various places in CCCC 57, additions to the text of the *Regula* are inserted. For the most part, such additions consist of short non-liturgical prayers to be said on specific occasions such as the departure of a monk for a journey on behalf of the monastery. The only accretion peculiar to CCCC 57 and pertaining to the liturgy, is the stipulation that at Prime on Sundays, after the chant of four sections from ps. CXVIII, should follow 'hymnus "De fide catholica"', that is the Athanasian Creed. This unique interpolation (well buried both in Hanslik's *apparatus criticus* and in Chamberlin's edition of CCCC 57)[41] occurring in a manuscript of the *Regula* arguably written at Abingdon, a book, moreover, having clear affiliations with early English reform manuscripts, may thus possibly be a reflection of Æthelwold's concern with the introduction of the Athanasian Creed into the monastic Office some fifty years earlier.

The continental psalters

It may not be unreasonable to think that the Royal Glossator's decision to supplement the psalms by a glossed text of the Athanasian Creed

---

[39] Ed. Nocent, p. 174.

[40] See Tolhurst, *Monastic Breviaries*, pp. 50 and 199, Hughes, *Medieval Manuscripts for Mass and Office*, pp. 38 and 76, and Harper, *Forms and Orders*, pp. 99–100.

[41] See Hanslik, *Benedicti Regula*, *app. crit.* to *RSB* 18.2 (p. 75), and Chamberlin, *The Abingdon Copy*, p. 38.

(together with the canticles, also glossed) was influenced by one or more of the ninth- or tenth-century psalters written on the Continent but demonstrably or arguably in England by the mid-tenth century. There are five psalters in question:

1 London, BL, Cotton Galba A. xviii, the 'Æthelstan Psalter', written somewhere in northeastern Francia in the first part of the ninth century. From two quires added at the beginning of the manuscript (now fols. 1–19) and containing computus material and a metrical calendar, it is clear that the psalter was in England by the first decade of the tenth century. Three further quires (now fols. 178–200) were added in the second quarter of the tenth century. Their contents, especially a Greek litany of the saints and a Greek *Sanctus* (both in Roman characters) strongly suggest that, by the time these additions were made, the psalter was at Winchester, very possibly in the household of King Æthelstan (924–39).[42]

2 Utrecht, Universiteitsbibliotheek, 32, the Utrecht Psalter, famous for its miniatures and influence on late Anglo-Saxon art. The manuscript was written and lavishly illustrated at Rheims (or its vicinity) sometime during the first half of the ninth century.[43]

3 Cambridge, Corpus Christi College 272, a psalter written (on palaeographical grounds) at Rheims in the last quarter of the ninth century. From petitions in the litany of saints the date can be narrowed down to 883 or 884.[44]

4 Salisbury, Cathedral Library 180, written in Brittany *c*. 900.[45]

5 Cambridge, Corpus Christi College 411, a psalter written on the Continent, perhaps in the Loire valley (Tours?) in the earlier tenth century. The psalter was in England by *c*. 1000 at the latest, as can be seen from various additions to the manuscript such as a litany of the

---

[42] For this manuscript, see below, pp. 310–15.

[43] For full facsimiles, see *Utrecht Psalter. A Collotype Facsimile*, 2 vols., The Palaeographical Society (1874), and *Utrecht Psalter*, 2 vols., Codices Selecti Phototypice Impressi 75 (Graz, 1982–4; vol. I contains the facsimile, vol. II, by K. van der Horst and J. H. A. Engelbregt, is a commentary volume).

[44] See James, *Catalogue* II, 27–32, and Lapidge, *Litanies of the Saints*, pp. 64 and 114.

[45] See E. Maunde Thompson, 'Catalogue of Manuscripts in the Cathedral Library of Salisbury', in *Catalogue of the Library of the Cathedral Church of Salisbury* (London, 1880), pp. 3–44, at 35.

saints. The manuscript has occasionally been thought to be of English origin, but on no convincing grounds, as it would appear.[46]

All these psalters are *Gallicanum* texts (we shall return to this point shortly) and they all include the Athanasian Creed among the liturgical pieces appended to the psalms. On the presumption of a Winchester origin for the Royal Glossator and his connection with King Æthelstan's court, we may suspect that he had access to at least one of these psalters, namely Galba A. xviii, the 'Æthelstan Psalter'. This suspicion may be confirmed by the momentous impact which the Æthelstan Psalter seems to have exerted on the iconography of Æthelwold's own Benedictional (see below, pp. 310–11).

Three of the remaining four psalters may also have been available at Winchester during the reign of King Æthelstan. First, the Utrecht Psalter. The circumstances of its arrival in England are not now known. Both Grimbald of Saint-Bertin (who came from Rheims: note the Rheims origin of the psalter) and the exchange of books during King Æthelstan's reign have been suggested as possible vehicles for the importation of this manuscript.[47] The Utrecht Psalter was certainly at Canterbury in the twelfth century and presumably as early as *c.* 1000.[48] However, Robert Deshman has shown that the Utrecht Psalter or a close copy must have been available to the artists of Bishop Æthelwold's Benedictional at Winchester in the early 970s.[49]

The next psalter with an arguable Winchester connection is CCCC 272. It is not known when the manuscript came to England, but, again,

---

[46] See James, *Catalogue* II, 296–8, Temple, *Anglo-Saxon Manuscripts*, pp. 63–4 (no. 40), and Lapidge, *Litanies of the Saints*, pp. 65–6.

[47] See Keynes and Lapidge, *Alfred the Great*, p. 214, n. 26, and Deshman, *Benedictional*, pp. 167–8.

[48] At Christ Church, the Utrecht Psalter served as a model for the Eadwine Psalter (*c.* 1155–60, now Cambridge, Trinity College R. 17. 1). For the Eadwine Psalter and its relation to the Utrecht Psalter, see Gibson *et al.*, *The Eadwine Psalter, passim*, and esp. p. 209 for the eleventh- and twelfth-century Canterbury home of the Utrecht Psalter. Presumably in the same (Christ Church) community, work on the psalter now preserved as BL, Harley 603 (the earliest of the surviving copies of Utrecht) was begun in the first decades of the eleventh century. For the Harley Psalter and its connection with the Utrecht Psalter, see Noel, *The Harley Psalter*, esp. pp. 140–9, and 189–96 for the Canterbury sojourn of the Utrecht Psalter.

[49] See Deshman, *Benedictional*, esp. pp. 36–7, 86, 167–8, 229 and 253.

it may have been among the books brought by Grimbald of Saint-Bertin to King Alfred's court, since this psalter was also written at Rheims, in 883 or 884, and Grimbald came to England *c.* 886 from the household of Archbishop Fulco of Rheims, who is mentioned in the litany contained in the manuscript.[50] Winchester connections have also been tentatively suggested for Salisbury Cathedral 180. Once again, we have no certain knowledge of when the manuscript reached England, but its origin in Brittany *c.* 900 might suggest its arrival in England in the context of the numerous Bretons seeking refuge at King Æthelstan's court.[51]

Interestingly, the fifth of the continental psalters, CCCC 411, may have links with Abingdon on the evidence of a litany added in England *c.* 1000 or slightly later. In this litany, SS Vincent, Eustace and Benedict are invoked (in capital letters). The invocation of St Benedict points to a Benedictine monastery, and SS Vincent and Eustace were especially culted at Abingdon.[52] One or several of these surviving continental psalters (and there may well have been others) could have provided the Royal Glossator with a notion of which texts were usually appended to the psalms in psalters on the Continent. Among these texts, the Athanasian Creed was an addition to the Benedictine Office of some importance, its recitation being restricted at first either to a very prominent Christian feast (Easter) or to the Office of Prime on Sundays only.

The gloss

That the need for a vernacular gloss to this new item in the liturgy was acutely felt is revealingly illustrated by the Salisbury Psalter (Salisbury, Cathedral Library, 150). The Latin text of this psalter was written somewhere in southwestern England, perhaps Shaftesbury, in the second half of the tenth century. The interlinear Old English gloss to the psalms was entered *c.* 1100; it is a D-type gloss and very closely dependent on Royal 2. B. V (see above, p. 26). But the Old English interlinear gloss to

---

[50] See Lapidge, *Litanies of the Saints*, pp. 64–5 and 144, and Keynes and Lapidge, *Alfred the Great*, pp. 182–6 and 214, n. 26. Cf. also above, p. 31 and n. 72, for the Latin commentary entered in the margins of this psalter, somewhere in England in the eleventh century.

[51] See Lapidge, *Litanies of the Saints*, p. 84.

[52] See Lapidge, *Litanies of the Saints*, pp. 66 and 123, and *idem*, 'Æthelwold and the *Vita S. Eustachii*', p. 218.

the *Quicumque uult* was entered by a tenth-century hand (s. x^2), perhaps identical with the scribe of the psalter, and originally this was the only glossed item in the manuscript.[53] In contrast to the psalter gloss, the gloss to the Athanasian Creed is entirely independent of the gloss in Royal 2. B. V. It is not a very competent translation, and the glossator makes some egregious mistakes.[54]

Further evidence for a particular need for a gloss to the Athanasian Creed comes from another psalter, London, BL, Harley 863, written at Exeter in the third quarter of the eleventh century. The Athanasian Creed (107r–108r) is the only text in this manuscript to be glossed in Old English. The gloss is in a hand contemporary with that which wrote the psalter, canticles and litany in this manuscript. Only about two thirds of the text of the Creed are glossed (up to verse 31 in Roeder's edition of the Royal Psalter). This gloss is very closely dependent on Royal 2. B. V.[55] Harley 863 is therefore a late witness to the influence of the Royal gloss, as is the gloss to the *Quicumque uult* in the Vespasian Psalter. In Vespasian A. i, Latin text and Old English gloss were entered in the eleventh century, presumably copied from Royal 2. B. V itself or a very close congener (see below, Appendix II).

It is beyond reasonable doubt that the gloss to the *Quicumque uult*, as transmitted in Royal 2. B. V, was produced by the Royal Glossator himself and was part of the original translation programme comprising the psalter, the canticles, the *Quicumque uult* and the *Gloria in excelsis Deo*.[56] The verbal and stylistic links between the psalter gloss and the gloss to the Athanasian Creed are clear and unmistakable (in spite of the

---

[53] See Ker, *Catalogue*, p. 450 (no. 379), and Sisam, *Salisbury Psalter*, p. 12. Text and gloss of the Athanasian Creed are printed *ibid.*, pp. 305–8.

[54] Cf., for example, the following blunders: *Salisbury Psalter* (ed. Sisam), p. 307, verse 32: *subsistens: wiðstandende*; p. 308, verse 40: *reddituri sunt ... rationem: alysede beoð ... gebedum* or p. 308, verse 42: *poterit: awacað*, and see Sisam, *ibid.*, p. 13.

[55] Latin text and Old English gloss are printed by F. Holthausen, 'Eine altenglische Interlinearversion des Athanasianischen Glaubensbekenntnisses', *Englische Studien* 75 (1942–3), 6–8. For the manuscript, see Ker, *Catalogue*, pp. 306–7 (no. 232), and Lapidge, *Litanies of the Saints*, p. 74.

[56] The *Gloria* (186v–187r in Royal 2. B. V) was used in both Office and mass; see Hughes, *Medieval Manuscripts for Mass and Office*, pp. 37–8, and Harper, *Forms and Orders*, p. 116. It is a chant prescribed on several occasions by the *Regularis concordia*; cf. pp. 29–30 (ch. 32), p. 48 (ch. 48) and p. 57 (ch. 58) in Symons's edition; and it is interesting to note that on one occasion the solemnity of this chant is stressed by the stipulation that all the bells shall peal while it is being sung (*ibid.*, p. 48 (ch. 49)).

brevity of the Creed). For example, *procedere* is translated by *forðgewitan* (v. 23), the Old English word which is used invariably for *procedere* in the Royal Psalter gloss (pss. XVIII.6; XLIV.5; LXXXVIII.35), but not in the Vespasian or Lambeth psalters. For Latin *uiuus*, the double gloss *cwic* ł *lifende* is used in the *Quicumque uult* (v. 39) and in the Psalter (ps. CXIV.9), again in contrast to the Vespasian and Lambeth glosses.[57] Furthermore, a total of three double glosses in so short a text reveals the same penchant for the type of glossing found in the Psalter.[58] The intriguing and somewhat obscure coinage *limgesihþ* for *corpus* (v. 40) is further evidence for the delight in ostentatious neologisms so pervasive in the psalter gloss. By the same token, the gloss to the Athanasian Creed has links with the Brussels Aldhelm glosses and with the Old English Benedictine Rule. For example, *integer* (v. 2) is glossed *anwalh* (but *ansund* in the Lambeth Creed). In the Aldhelm glosses, the adjective once translates *integer* (G 5162), and the noun *anwealhnyss* is found seven times as a gloss to *integritas* (G 696, 2381 etc.). *Onwealh* and *onwealhnes* occur in texts with Alfredian connections (especially the Old English Bede) but are much rarer in later texts. Latin *necessarius* is glossed *niedbehefe* (v. 29; Lambeth: *neodþearf*), an adjective found once for *necessarius* in the Brussels Aldhelm glosses (G 5106) and frequently in the Old English Rule (e. g. BR 92.2, 127.5, 137.20). It occurs also in Æthelwold's preface to the Rule (*CS*, p. 151). Apart from Ælfric the word is not very common. Latin *conuersio* is glossed by *gecyrredness* (v. 35; Lambeth: *awendednyss*), a word which frequently occurs in the Old English Rule (e. g. BR 12.20, 13.1, 107.10 and 11), and here, interestingly, often in additions to, or free renderings of, the *Regula*. In the Rule, *gecyrredness* always signifies the entrance of a secular person into the monastery and hence the 'conversion' of a secular person into a monk or a nun (cf. also the expression *ungecyrred woroldman* for (presumably) a novice in the preface to the Rule, *CS*, p. 151). Again, the substantive is not common in other texts, apart from Ælfric. The Latin expression *reddere rationem* is translated *agyldan gescead* (v. 40; Lambeth: *agyfan* ł *agyldan gescead*). The same translation often

---

[57] Since text and gloss to the Athanasian Creed in Vespasian A. i. are closely tied up with Royal 2. B. V (see above), the Vespasian Psalter is no independent witness for the Creed. It is therefore especially noteworthy that in v. 39 Vespasian has a single gloss (*cwic*) only.

[58] The remaining doublets are *credat: he hyhte* ł *gelyfe* (v. 29) and *omnipotentis: ælmihtiges* ł *eallwaldendes* (v. 39).

occurs in the Rule (e. g. BR 54.21, 115.1, 126.10); here, Lambeth's alternative gloss, *agyfan*, is never used in this phrase. In short, it is clear from examples such as these that one glossator (or team of glossators) was responsible for the psalter gloss and the gloss to the Athanasian Creed.[59] Furthermore, by its manifest verbal links (astonishing, given its brevity) with the Old English Rule and the glosses to Aldhelm's prose *De uirginitate*, the gloss to the Athanasian Creed may confirm our supposition of a shared common origin for the Rule, the Aldhelm glosses and the interlinear versions in Royal 2. B. V.

The assumption of an origin of the Royal gloss in a centre intimately connected with the nascent Benedictine reform gains further confirmation from a striking and idiosyncratic textual variant in the Royal Psalter which we must now consider.

THE TEXTCRITICAL EVIDENCE

The 'Benedictine' reading

There is a curious point of agreement between the Royal Psalter (Latin text and gloss) and the *Regula S. Benedicti*; an agreement concerning a variant reading in a psalm verse, to which, in passing, Karl Wildhagen first drew attention.[60] His detection of this shared variant is all the more striking, since he did not have at his disposal a critical edition of either the *Psalterium Romanum* or of the *Regula S. Benedicti*.

In ch. 7 of the *Regula*, Benedict, having mentioned evil thoughts in human beings, goes on to say:

Nam ut sollicitus sit circa cogitationes suas peruersas, dicat semper utilis frater in corde suo: *Tunc ero inmaculatus coram eo, si obseruauero me ab iniquitate mea* (RSB 7.18).[61]

The last sentence (*Tunc ... mea*) is a quotation from ps. XVII.24, slightly adapted; the psalm verse is as follows: 'et ero inmaculatus coram

---

59 Such shared authorship extends to the gloss to the canticles and the *Gloria* in Royal 2. B. V, which space forbids to be discussed here in any detail.

60 Cf. Wildhagen, 'Studien zum *Psalterium Romanum*', p. 452.

61 'That he must take care to avoid sinful thoughts, the virtuous brother must always say to himself: *I shall be blameless in his sight if I guard myself from my own wickedness*' (RB 1980, p. 195).

eo et obseruabo me ab iniquitate mea'. The small alterations in the *Regula* (first *et* changed to *tunc*, second *et* to *si* and *obseruabo* to *obseruauero*) were apparently made on grounds that a hypotactic construction with a conditional clause would fit the immediate context better than the two parallel *et*-clauses in the original psalm verse. By contrast, the two *et*-clauses in ps. XVII.24, in their context, are fully consonant with a considerable number of adjacent verses, all containing two statements, each of which being introduced by *et*.[62] It is clear, therefore, that Benedict's version of the verse in question is not a variant reading of that verse, simply lifted from some psalter manuscript, but a deliberate adaptation;[63] and predictably (with the exceptions discussed below) Weber's *apparatus criticus* of his edition of the *Psalterium Romanum* does not list any psalter text which has the Benedictine *Tunc . . . si* version of ps. XVII.24. Neither is such a variant reading listed in the critical editions of the *Gallicanum* or *Hebraicum* versions of the psalter.[64] On the other hand, according to Hanslik's *apparatus criticus*, the 'Benedictine' reading of this psalm verse seems to have been preserved distinct and fairly uncontaminated. It occurs in all three recensions of the *Regula*, and only a few manuscripts are listed in the *apparatus* which show some kind of contamination with the psalm reading proper.[65]

Latin text and Old English gloss of ps. XVII.24 in Royal 2. B. V read as follows:

Et ero inmaculatus coram eo, *si obseruauero* me ab iniquitate mea: 7 ic beo unwemme beforan – *gif* ic healde ł warnie – fram unryhtwisnesse minre.

It will be seen that in the Latin the first *et* is preserved in accordance with the original psalm text, but that the second *et* and the verb tense have been changed according to the variant in the *Regula S. Benedicti*, which results in a reading less appropriate in the immediate context than the

---

[62] Cf., for example, ps. XVII.25–7.

[63] Such an adjustment of a quotation from the Scriptures to its immediate context in the *Regula* is not without parallels: cf., for example, *RSB, prol.* 18: '[Et cum haec feceritis,] oculi mei super uos et aures meae ad preces uestras'; here the wording of ps. XXXIII.16 ('oculi Domini super iustos et aures eius ad preces eorum') is altered so as to fit the direct speech attributed to God the Father at this point in the *Regula*.

[64] See Weber, *Le Psautier Romain*, p. 32, *Biblia Sacra iuxta Latinam Vulgatam Versionem*, ed. Quentin *et al.* X, 71 (for the *Gallicanum*), and de Sainte-Marie, *Sancti Hieronymi Psalterium iuxta Hebraeos*, p. 26.

[65] Cf. Hanslik, *Benedicti Regula*, p. 47.

original *Romanum* wording. It will also be seen that this 'Benedictine' reading was the one which the Royal Glossator had in his exemplar. It is fairly clear that such contamination of a psalm verse with a variant presumably introduced from the *Regula S. Benedicti* could have occurred only with someone thoroughly familiar with the *Regula*, someone, in fact, who knew its text more or less by heart (as was stipulated for Benedictine monks by the Aachen legislation of 816/17; see above, p. 252).

It may be significant to note that the 'Benedictine' reading for ps. XVII.24 occurs in two further glossed psalters from Anglo-Saxon England as well as in the *Romanum* text in the mid-twelfth-century Eadwine Psalter (Cambridge, Trinity College R. 17. 1). The textual affiliations of this post-Conquest *Romanum* from Christ Church, Canterbury have not been systematically investigated but (not surprisingly) seem to lie with tenth- and eleventh-century English *Romanum* versions.[66] The two psalters from pre-Conquest England which are in question are: first, the Bosworth Psalter (London, BL, Add. 37517, 4r–95r). The origin of this *Romanum* psalter (written, on palaeographical grounds, in the last third of the tenth century) has been assigned to various places, most often to Christ Church, Canterbury under Dunstan's archiepiscopate (959–88). The manuscript was clearly intended for liturgical use by a Benedictine community, as can be seen from the Benedictine psalm divisions,[67] and from further items such as the monastic canticles (129r–135r) or the Benedictine hymnal (105r–128r). In fact, Add. 37517 is the earliest manuscript surviving from Anglo-Saxon England to contain a complete version of the so-called New Hymnal.[68] Interestingly, in ps. XVII.24, the

---

[66] On the *Romanum* in the Eadwine Psalter, see most recently O'Neill, 'The English Version', pp. 137–8. Eadwine's text is collated in Weber's edition of the *Psalterium Romanum* (siglum D). For the relation of its Old English gloss to Royal 2. B. V, see also briefly above, p. 27.

[67] For the various psalm divisions, see above, p. 267, n. 17 and p. 272, n. 34. The question of precisely when the cathedral clergy at Christ Church was fully turned into a Benedictine community is a vexed one. Apparently, this process occurred only gradually and does not seem to have continued apace (if at all) under Dunstan's archiepiscopate. For a brief discussion of the problems involved in an evaluation of the available evidence, see Brooks, *Early History*, pp. 255–61. However, such considerations need not invalidate an association of the Bosworth Psalter with Canterbury and Dunstan, for which other (liturgical and palaeographical) evidence can be adduced; see the references cited below, n. 68.

[68] For Add. 37517, see especially F. A. Gasquet and E. Bishop, *The Bosworth Psalter*

'Benedictine' reading (which was originally the same as that presented by Royal 2. B. V) has been altered by a later hand from *si obseruauero* to *si obseruabo*, and *et* has been added before *si*. The Old English gloss (added at the beginning of the eleventh century) does not include all the psalms;[69] ps. XVII.24 bears no gloss.

The second psalter from Anglo-Saxon England to contain the 'Benedictine' reading is the Cambridge Psalter (Cambridge, University Library, Ff. 1. 23, 5r–250v), again a *Romanum*. The Latin text of ps. XVII.24 in the Cambridge Psalter is identical with Royal 2. B. V ('Et ero inmaculatus coram eo si obseruauero me ab iniquitate mea'). The Old English gloss (written by the same scribe as the Latin text) is as follows: '7 ic beom unwemme beforan hym – ic healde me from unrihtwisnysse minre'.[70] Since the Cambridge Psalter presents an A-type gloss, closely dependent on Vespasian A. i, Latin *si* in the 'Benedictine' reading of its psalter text is left unglossed. (The difference between *obseruabo* (*Romanum*) and *oberuauero* (*Regula*) could not have been expressed in the Old English tense system.) CUL Ff. 1. 23 has traditionally been dated to *c.* 1050, and its origin has been assigned to Winchcombe (Glos.) on account of the prominence given to the boy martyr St Kenelm in the litany (274r–276v).[71] Recently, however, the manuscript has been shown to have been written as early as *c.* 1000, and it has been ascribed to either Ramsey or St Augustine's, Canterbury.[72] At whichever place CUL Ff. 1. 23 was

(London, 1908), Gneuss, *Hymnar und Hymnen*, pp. 104–5, M. Korhammer, 'The Origin of the Bosworth Psalter', *ASE* 2 (1973), 173–87, and Dumville, 'On the Dating', p. 45. The Bosworth Psalter is collated by Weber, *Le Psautier Romain* (siglum B).

[69] For details, see above, p. 20. The gloss has been edited by Lindelöf, 'Die altenglischen Glossen im Bosworth-Psalter.'

[70] The Cambridge Psalter has been edited by Wildhagen, *Der Cambridger Psalter*. For the textual affiliation of the gloss, see briefly above, p. 26.

[71] See, for example, Ker, *Catalogue*, pp. 11–12 (no. 13).

[72] See Lapidge, 'Abbot Germanus', esp. pp. 414–17, for the association with Ramsey, principally on grounds of manuscript affiliations and of liturgical evidence drawn from the litany; and cf. Dumville, 'On the Dating', pp. 40–1, and *idem*, *English Caroline Script*, pp. 75–85, for an association with St Augustine's, principally on grounds of palaeographical evidence and of the textual affiliation of the Old English psalter gloss. It should be noted, however, that the palaeographical evidence pointing to Canterbury is restricted to the hand which added some private Offices on 4r. This hand wrote a type of Anglo-Caroline script (Style II) practised at St Augustine's in the late tenth and early eleventh century (cf. Dumville, 'On the Dating', p. 41). It should also be noted that the close dependence of the Cambridge Psalter's gloss on that in Vespasian A. i (a

written, it seems clear that its origin is intimately connected with Germanus, first abbot of Winchcombe (refounded by Bishop Oswald, *c.* 969) until the suppression of that monastery in the course of the anti-monastic reaction in 975, then domiciled with his Winchcombe community at Ramsey for the following seventeen years, and from 992 until his death, in 1013 or thereabouts, abbot of Cholsey (Berks.).[73]

In other words, these two manuscripts, the Bosworth and the Cambridge psalters and their respective affiliations with Dunstan's Canterbury and one of Bishop Oswald's principal followers may strengthen the supposition that the variant reading of ps. XVII.24, first found in Royal 2. B. V, must indeed have been closely tied up with the English Benedictine reform. It may conceivably have been an established reading in the early reform circles. As regards such a potential link specifically with the *early* stages of the reform, it may be worthwhile to add that the ungainly and highly idiosyncratic script of the Latin text and its Old English gloss in CUL Ff. 1. 23 has been thought of in terms of an old man who could only with difficulty adjust his hand to the Anglo-Caroline script, which by *c.* 1000 had been practised in the better scriptoria for some decades.[74]

By the same token, it should be noted that the Cambridge Psalter appears to be somewhat in a cultural backwater in two further respects: it is a *Romanum* text, even though, by *c.* 1000, this version had been replaced almost universally by the *Gallicanum* (see below, p. 288), and it preserves a pure A-type gloss, closely dependent on Vespasian A. i, thereby revealing that its compiler was not abreast of more recent developments in vernacular psalter glossing. From the layout of the manuscript (where equal space is assigned to the Latin text and the Old English gloss) it is clear that CUL Ff. 1. 23 was planned as a glossed psalter from the beginning. There is no question therefore of haphazardly copying out some vernacular psalter gloss which conveniently had come to hand at some subsequent stage. In short, the evidence of the script, the *Romanum* version and the A-type gloss in CUL Ff. 1. 23 combine to suggest that the 'Benedictine' reading in ps. XVII.24 may have been a variant of some

Canterbury book) by no means implies a Canterbury origin for CUL Ff. 1. 23, since the A-type gloss was available outside Canterbury, as we have had occasion to observe several times (see for example above, pp. 39–40).

[73] For the career of Germanus, see Lapidge, 'Abbot Germanus', pp. 405–14.

[74] See *ibid.*, p. 415.

currency specifically during the early stages of the reform. The scribe of the Cambridge Psalter may either have copied out this reading from his somewhat dated exemplar or else he may have supplied it from memory as the variant he had learned in his youth. Such a presumption of an early currency only for the variant may gain further confirmation from the later corrections made to the 'Benedictine' reading in the Bosworth Psalter.

The situation, however, is different in respect of the Royal Psalter. Its manuscript is incontestably and markedly older than the Bosworth and especially the Cambridge Psalter, and in its case there can be no question of simply copying an old-fashioned reading. Moreover, Royal 2. B. V is not only the earliest surviving psalter to attest the striking variant of ps. XVII.24, it is also unique among glossed psalters in providing an Old English gloss which matches the Latin text. As we have seen, the most plausible explanation for the peculiar variant of ps. XVII.24 is that it was introduced into the psalter from the *Regula S. Benedicti* where it fits its context in a way it does not in the psalm. We have also seen that for such a contamination to have occurred between the two texts one must assume an intimate knowledge of the *Regula*. Therefore this contamination cannot reasonably have originated considerably anterior to the exemplar of Royal 2. B. V; in fact, one may suspect that it originated with the Royal Glossator himself. In any event, the Royal Glossator undoubtedly approved of this reading and based his gloss on it, in spite of the slight oddity of the variant in the psalm context, and although he presumably worked with a psalter containing the A-type gloss beside him, a psalter which is unlikely to have exhibited the reading in question.[75] All this strongly suggests that the 'Benedictine' variant must have been natural to the Royal Glossator and that consequently, he must have had an intimate knowledge of the *Regula S. Benedicti*. There can be no doubt that during the 940s or early 950s, when the Royal Psalter gloss was produced, the number of English scholars in whom such an intimate knowledge of the *Regula* may be presumed was very restricted.

For Æthelwold himself we have unmistakable evidence from his Winchester period that he paid close attention to variant readings in

---

[75] Recall that the scribe of the Cambridge Psalter has the 'Benedictine' variant in his Latin text, but that he evidently did not find it in the gloss of his A-type exemplar which he was following closely, and that consequently he left the conjunction *si* without a gloss.

psalms and that occasionally he employed one of two variants to explain the other. Such evidence comes from the prologue to the *Regularis concordia*. Having invoked there for the last time the authority of the *Regula S. Benedicti* (*inter alia* by quoting verbatim from its text) which he considered the cornerstone on which to build his consuetudinary, Æthelwold draws the *prohemium* to a conclusion as follows:

ut ab ipso aeternae uitae remunerationem cuncti concorditer et gratulabunde conseruantes recipiant, *qui facit unanimes*, id est *unius moris, habitare in domo*, ubi est rex Deus, Dei et uirginis filius, qui cum Patre et Spiritu Sancto uiuit et regnat Deus in saecula saeculorum. Amen.[76]

Here a psalm verse (ps. LXVII.7) is employed to sum up a leitmotif of the prologue to the *Regularis concordia*: the necessity of, and reward for, unanimity and uniformity in daily monastic observance. In the quotation from the psalm, the variant *unanimes* comes from the *Psalterium Romanum*, whereas *unius moris* (given as an explanatory gloss for it) is the *Gallicanum* reading.

What must interest us here is not only a ready familiarity with the psalter which allows Bishop Æthelwold to produce a minute but highly pertinent quotation from the psalms at a very strategic point in his *prohemium*; even more striking are his interest in the textual criticism of the psalms and his command of variant readings in psalm verses revealed in the above quotation. If Æthelwold is to be associated with the Royal Psalter gloss, it may be permissible to surmise that the 'Benedictine' reading in ps. XVII.24 is more than just an intrusion of a variant from the *Regula* into the psalter inadvertently occasioned by someone intimately familiar with both texts. Perhaps it should rather be judged in terms of the authority which the *Regula* enjoyed in the Glossator's circle. Such a hypothesis may gain some confirmation from the consideration that the Royal Glossator and his circle must have been fully aware of the existence of different recensions of the psalter text, none of these (by the 940s) carrying ultimate authority. As regards the two principal recensions

---

[76] '[and we pray] that all who observe these customs in peace and thanksgiving may receive the reward of eternal life from Him *Who maketh those of one mind*, that is, *of one way of life, to dwell in that house* where God is King, even the Son of God, born of a Virgin, Who with the Father and the Holy Ghost liveth and reigneth God for ever and ever. Amen': *Regularis Concordia*, ed. Symons, ch. 12 (p. 9). The italicized words are quotations from ps. LXVII.7.

(the *Romanum* and the *Gallicanum*) it may be significant to observe that the text of the brief quotation in the *Regularis concordia* is basically that of the *Romanum*. Not only is the *Romanum* variant *unanimes* cited first, *habitare* is *Romanum* for *Gallicanum inhabitare*, and the *Romanum* only has a relative clause, introduced by *qui*, whereas the *Gallicanum* omits the *qui* and has an independent sentence instead ('Deus inhabitare facit unius moris in domo').

We may therefore deduce that the psalter text which came to Bishop Æthelwold most naturally (even as late as in the 970s) was the *Psalterium Romanum*. This would square perfectly with the fact that the Royal Psalter, too, is a *Romanum* text. But given the continental orientation of the English reform in general and Æthelwold in particular, the Royal Glossator's adherence to the older (*Romanum*) version of the psalter is somewhat in need of explanation. It is a question to which we must turn next.

The 'Psalterium Romanum' as the exemplar for the Royal gloss

As we have seen (above, p. 22), two versions of the psalter were in liturgical use in medieval Europe, the *Romanum* and the *Gallicanum*.[77] By *c.* 940, the *Gallicanum* had ousted the *Romanum* almost everywhere on the Continent, and certainly in Germany and Francia, for more than a century. English scholars must have been aware of this situation well before the Benedictine reform movement invigorated their contacts with continental monastic houses and increased the import of books from such centres. For example, knowledge about the version prevailing on the Continent may be assumed for the reign of King Æthelstan (924–39) and even as early as the reign of King Alfred the Great (871–99). A number of noted continental scholars were active at the courts of both kings, and all surviving psalter manuscripts which were imported from the Continent to Anglo-Saxon England (and which we have reviewed briefly in connection with the Athanasian Creed, above, pp. 274–7) contain the *Gallicanum*. (Salisbury Cathedral 180 even has the text of the *Hebraicum* in addition.) We have seen reason to suspect that at least some

---

[77] The *Psalterium iuxta Hebraeos*, the last of St Jerome's translations, made directly from the Hebrew psalter, was never used in the liturgy; it was, however, transmitted in Bibles and in psalter manuscripts presenting parallel texts of the various recensions.

of these psalters will have been brought to England by the aforementioned scholars.

In England too, the *Romanum* was eventually ousted, no doubt in the wake of the Benedictine reform and its orientation towards the Continent. The earliest surviving English *Gallicanum* was written not long after Royal 2. B. V: the Salisbury Psalter (Salisbury Cathedral 150), dated to the second half of the tenth century.[78] It received an English gloss *c.* 1100, closely dependent on Royal 2. B. V. All the five psalters which were demonstrably or arguably written and glossed in eleventh-century Winchester and which reveal the Royal Psalter's paramount influence in Æthelwold's episcopal see are *Gallicanum* texts (see above, pp. 267–8).

We must ask, therefore, why the Royal Glossator should have turned to the *Romanum* version of the psalter. We have come to know the Glossator as a man who set out to create a fresh vernacular gloss to the psalter, which in many ways differed radically from the existing Vespasian-type of gloss, which made use of psalm exegesis on a hitherto unprecedented scale and which even incorporated such exegesis into the manuscript in the form of marginal scholia. We have seen him further including and glossing, for the first time in an English psalter manuscript, liturgical pieces such as the Athanasian Creed which presumably had reached England from the Continent by the vehicle of the ninth- and early-tenth-century Gallican psalters imported from there. By the same token, we have seen that the Royal Glossator was fully conversant with the text of the *Regula S. Benedicti*, which by the 940s unmistakably suggests orientation towards the Continent. On the hypothesis of an involvement of Æthelwold in the origin of the Royal gloss, we have to note that he probably had an early and thorough acquaintance with at least one of the imported psalters, namely the Æthelstan Psalter (Galba A. xviii, see below). On such a hypothesis again, we are forced to consider that Æthelwold chose the pre-eminent continental recension of the *Regula* (the *textus receptus*) as the exemplar on which to base his translation of that text, composed, possibly, during the period when he was involved in the production of the Royal gloss. Considerations such as these inevitably lead to the conclusion that the Glossator's choice of the *Romanum* is not to be explained simply as the result of the (by then) wide currency of that

---

[78] For a single leaf (Worcester, Cathedral Library, F. 173, fol. 1) surviving from a Gallican psalter written in England and dated s. x^2, see above, p. 31, n. 72.

version in England, but that, on the contrary, his decision must have been made deliberately. But what were his reasons for such a decision?

There are several answers to this question, and they all turn on the authority attached to the *Romanum* and *Gallicanum* respectively. To begin with, for an Anglo-Saxon scholar in the 940s, the *Gallicanum* would have been the version which he probably knew to be in almost universal use on the Continent, but apparently not on grounds of any promulgation by (say) an imperial edict or a church synod. Moreover, such a scholar would have been aware that yet a third recension, that *iuxta Hebraeos*, was in circulation on the Continent. Matters were quite different in respect of the textual recensions of the *Regula S. Benedicti*. It was obviously understood among the new Benedictines in England that the *textus receptus* was linked with the reforms of Benedict of Aniane and Emperor Louis the Pious, as emerges, for example, from the inclusion of important texts of the Aachen synods of 816/17 in Anglo-Saxon manuscripts of the *Regula* (see above, p. 247).[79] Given the absence of any such institutionally approved superiority for the *Gallicanum*, the venerable tradition of the *Romanum* in England would inevitably have come into play.

Ever since the days of St Augustine, the *Romanum* had been the psalter of the English church. It was (as we have seen) the version habitually quoted by Bede, and young Wilfrid, the future bishop of York, who had been taught the *Gallicanum* by his Irish masters, had to learn the Roman version when staying at St Augustine's in 650 or thereabouts (and this will have been known through his *Vita*).[80] All surviving Anglo-Saxon psalters earlier than Salisbury Cathedral 150 and London, BL, Harley 2904 (dated s. x^2 (969 × 987) and s. $x.^{ex}$ (? before 992) respectively) have *Romanum* texts. It will also have been known in England that the *Psalterium Romanum* was still in use in the churches at Rome,[81] which no doubt will have contributed to the authority attached to the *Romanum*. Evidence for such knowledge is found, for example, in an entry in the inventory of some sixty books donated by Bishop Leofric to his cathedral church at Exeter (1069 × 1072). Among these books, three psalters are listed and referred to as follows: 'ii salteras 7 se þriddan saltere swa man

---

[79] For a mid-tenth-century Anglo-Saxon scholar to recognize the textual priority of the *textus purus* or to obtain a copy of that recension would have been next to impossible, since the *purus* never established a distinct tradition; see above, p. 243.

[80] See above, p. 24.   [81] For this continued use of the *Romanum*, see above, p. 22.

singð on Rome'.[82] Confirmation that the use of the *Romanum* was maintained at Rome will have come each time a newly appointed archbishop of Canterbury and his entourage made their trip there to collect the pallium. A special relationship between the English metropolitan see and Rome is indicated by the fact that at Christ Church the *Romanum* seems to have been in official use long after other Anglo-Saxon centres had adopted the *Gallicanum* in their liturgy.[83] Two eleventh-century Roman psalters of Christ Church origin are of interest here: Harley 603, which is a copy of the famous Utrecht Psalter, which in turn was at Christ Church by *c.* 1000.[84] But while the artists strove to imitate closely the lavish illustrations of the Utrecht Psalter, the *Gallicanum* text of that psalter was replaced by the *Romanum*, written by three scribes (one of them the renowned Eadwig Basan) during the first two decades of the eleventh century.[85] The second Roman psalter in question is Arundel 155 written (and decorated) by Eadwig Basan, 1012 × 1023 (on the testimony of its calendar). Various evidence, such as a set of canticles following the psalms, indicates that this psalter was intended for official liturgical use.[86]

The notion that the English church in general (not only the see of Canterbury) had enjoyed an especial and intimate relationship with Rome

---

[82] The 'ii salteras' are presumably *Gallicanum* texts. The Leofric list has most recently been printed and discussed by Lapidge, 'Booklists', pp. 64–9; for the entry in question, see p. 65 (nos. 9 and 10).

[83] For the continued use of the *Romanum* at Christ Church, see Brooks, *Early History*, pp. 261–5. Of course, the contacts between the English church and Rome were numerous throughout Anglo-Saxon times and not restricted to the metropolitan see; cf., for example, Ortenberg, *The English Church and the Continent*, pp. 127–96 (esp. for the tenth and eleventh centuries), and Keynes, 'Entries in the *Liber Vitae* of Brescia', esp. pp. 99–103 and 116–19 (for earlier such contacts).

[84] For the Utrecht Psalter (and its relationship to Harley 603), see above, p. 275 and n. 43, and p. 276 and n. 48.

[85] For the text in Harley 603, see Noel, *The Harley Psalter*, pp. 23–4. The *Gallicanum* version of the exemplar is retained only in pss. C–CV.24 and coincides with the work of one of the scribes. For Eadwig Basan as one of the scribes, see *ibid.*, *passim* and esp. p. 19; cf. also Bishop, *English Caroline Minuscule*, p. 22 (no. 24) who had first identified Eadwig as the scribe of Harley 603, 28r–49v.

[86] For the psalter text, see Ker, *Catalogue*, p. 171 (no. 135), and Sisam, *Salisbury Psalter*, p. 49, n. 1; for Eadwig Basan as the scribe of Arundel 155, see Bishop, *English Caroline Minuscule*, p. 22 (no. 24), and most recently Dumville, *English Caroline Script*, esp. pp. 122–3 and 139–40.

from its very beginnings was an idea close to Æthelwold's heart. Clear proof of this comes from his preface to the Old English Rule. As we have seen, this text is introduced by a lengthy passage (based on Bede's *Historia ecclesiastica*) which extols the part played by Pope Gregory the Great in the conversion of the English race. No mention is made of missionaries of Irish extraction such as Aidan, but Æthelwold took great care to point out that Pope Gregory, having been prevented from coming to England himself, remained, nevertheless, closely involved in the progress of the English mission, being continually in touch with, and giving instructions to, Augustine, a most holy and orthodox man whom he himself had chosen as his representative ('He þeah sanctum Agustinum, þæt getreoweste bearn þæs halgan geleafan, him to gespelian funde, 7 hine hider asende ... He georne þone his gespelian þurh ærendracan manode 7 lærde...').[87] It squares well with Æthelwold's notion of such long-standing and close ties between the English church and Rome that, on the occasion of his expulsion of the secular clergy from the Old Minster, he produced a letter from Pope John XII, sanctioning his drastic actions through *auctoritate apostolica* (see above, p. 236).

By the same token, in spite of his pervasive adoption of continental monastic customs, Æthelwold had an ingrained penchant for the traditions of the English church (at least the ones he approved of). Thus, several stipulations in the *Regularis concordia* such as the frequent prayers for the Royal House or the three prayers for the veneration of the Cross on Good Friday are thought to represent native customs. In fact, Æthelwold occasionally points out that a certain custom should be observed *usu patrum* (ch. 8, p. 5) or that such customs should be followed, 'nam honestos huius patriae mores ad Deum pertinentes, quos ueterum usu didicimus, nullo modo abicere sed undique, uti diximus, corroborare decreuimus'.[88]

Even in the case of the text of the *Regula S. Benedicti*, the native

---

[87] *CS*, p. 144. The chs. in Bede's *Historia ecclesiastica* from which Æthelwold's account of the Gregorian mission is drawn are I. 23–7, 33 and II. 1.

[88] *Regularis Concordia*, ed. Symons, ch. 23 (p. 30). 'For we have ordained that the goodly religious customs of this land, which we have learned from our fathers before us, be in no wise cast off, but confirmed on all hands.' For such stipulations in the *Regularis concordia* referring to native traditions, see *Regularis Concordia*, ed. Symons, p. lxvi, and *idem*, 'History and Derivation', pp. 44–5, as well as Lapidge, *Wulfstan: Life*, p. lx; cf. also Gretsch, 'Der liturgische Wortschatz', pp. 351–2.

tradition was apparently not jettisoned wholesale within Æthelwold's sphere of influence. We have seen (above, p. 252) that, in spite of Æthelwold's unequivocal preference for the *textus receptus*, one manuscript, CCCC 57 written (possibly) at Abingdon *c.* 1000, has remarkable links with the *interpolatus* tradition, that is with the textual recension which had circulated in England in the seventh and eighth centuries. In short, the authority of Rome and the venerable traditions of the English church were factors which unquestionably exerted an important influence on Æthelwold, and both these factors were bound up with the *Psalterium Romanum* in a way they were not with the *Gallicanum*.

Given the Royal Glossator's orientation towards Benedictine monasticism, and his scholarly disposition as revealed by his consistent recourse to psalm exegesis, there are two further reasons why he should have decided to base his gloss on a *Romanum* psalter rather than on a *Gallicanum*. The *Psalterium Romanum* was the text habitually quoted by Cassiodorus in his *Expositio psalmorum*, the commentary principally drawn on by the Royal Glossator.[89] And the *Romanum* was the version followed by St Benedict in his numerous quotations from the psalms.[90] For example, in the aforementioned 'Benedictine' reading of ps. XVII.24 (= *RSB* 7.18) the variant 'ero inmaculatus *coram* eo' is *Romanum*, the *Gallicanum* has 'ero inmaculatus *cum* eo.'[91]

---

[89] For Cassiodorus's version of the psalter, see *Expositio Psalmorum*, ed. Adriaen, p. xix, and G. A. Löffler, 'Der Psalmenkommentar des M. Aur. Cassiodorus Senator. Die exegetische Bildung des Verfassers und sein Psalmentext' (unpubl. dissertation, Freiburg Univ., 1920); for a brief summary of Löffler's results, see P. Volk, *Die Schriftzitate* (see below, n. 90), pp. 24–5.

[90] For Benedict's version of the psalter, cf. (briefly) Vogüé, *La Règle de Saint Benoît* I, 139–40, and (with an annotated list of all the readings in question) P. Volk, *Die Schriftzitate der Regula S. Benedicti*; printed as an appendix in E. Munding and A. Dold, *Palimpsesttexte des Codex Latin. Monacensis 6333* (Beuron, 1930), pp. 1–35, at 15–25. Volk's work on Benedict's psalter was done before critical editions of the *Romanum* and *Gallicanum* were available. His findings, however, are confirmed when compared with these critical editions.

[91] Further examples would be: *RSB* 7.23 and *Romanum* text of ps. XXXVII.10: 'Ante te *est* omne desiderium meum', *est* being omitted in the *Gallicanum*; *RSB* 7.38 and *Romanum* text of ps. XLIII.22: 'Propter te *morte adficimur tota* die, aestimati sumus *ut* oues occisionis', *Gallicanum*: 'Propter te *morificamur omni* die aestimati sumus *sicut* oues occisionis'; and *RSB* 7.40 and *Romanum* text of ps. LXV.10: 'Probasti nos, deus, igne nos examinasti, sicut *igne* examinatur argentum'; the second *igne* being omitted by the *Gallicanum*.

In sum, these various considerations lead one to the impression that it was predictable in some ways that a scholar of the intellectual and spiritual make-up and backdrop of the Royal Glossator should have chosen the *Psalterium Romanum* as the version on which to base his vernacular gloss. In the event, it turned out that his choice would not stand the test of time. With the massive importation of customs (liturgical and otherwise) from the continental centres of reformed Benedictinism (in which Æthelwold himself had been instrumental) the *Psalterium Gallicanum* ultimately emerged victorious. It is a matter of interest that the Royal gloss itself survived the replacement of the *Romanum*. All extant glossed psalters with a D-type gloss are *Gallicanum* texts. In cases of divergence between the two versions, the scribes of these D-type psalters either copied mindlessly the original glosses for the *Romanum* readings over their *Gallicanum* counterparts, or the *Gallicanum* variants were left unglossed, or they were glossed afresh (more or less intelligently) by some later glossator.[92] We may be allowed to regard this adherence to the Royal gloss, shown almost unanimously by the eleventh-century psalters, as a strong pointer to the authority which was attached to this mid-tenth-century gloss and the high esteem in which it was held by later generations.

For an estimation of the role played by Æthelwold in the Royal gloss, it is relevant to bear in mind that there is textual evidence as well which reveals Æthelwold's personal attachment to the *Romanum*, even as late as the 970s. We already had occasion to observe (above, pp. 285–7) that his quotation from ps. LXVII.7 in the *prohemium* to the *Regularis concordia* ('qui facit unanimes, id est unius moris, habitare in domo', ch. 12, p. 9) is unequivocally *Romanum*, interpreted in the light of a *Gallicanum* variant. In the body of the *Regularis concordia* there are numerous further

---

[92] See, for example, Sisam, *Salisbury Psalter*, pp. 17–19, for the not very intelligent methods by which the glossator of the Salisbury Psalter tried to cope with the difficulties involved in copying a *Romanum* gloss to accompany a *Gallicanum* text. A special case is presented by the mid-twelfth-century gloss to the Eadwine Psalter (Cambridge, Trinity College R. 17. 1). Extensive corrections to this gloss were made after a D-type exemplar (see above, p. 27), and the Old English gloss is entered in a *Romanum* text. However, the Eadwine Psalter is a *psalterium triplex*, its *Gallicanum* text bearing a Latin commentary, while its *Hebraicum* is provided with an Anglo-Norman interlinear version. (On the Latin commentary, see M. Gibson, 'The Latin Apparatus', in *The Eadwine Psalter*, ed. Gibson *et al.*, pp. 108–22; on the Anglo-Norman gloss, see D. Markey, 'The Anglo-Norman Version', *ibid.*, pp. 139–56.)

quotations from the psalter, principally in the form of brief psalm *incipits*, given in lieu of psalm numbers (presumably to facilitate recognition), and specifying which psalms are to be sung on which occasion. On account of the brevity of the *incipits*, there are not many cases in which a variant reading between the two versions would show up; interestingly, such as can be found invariably seem to present the *Gallicanum* reading.[93] Such evidence carries no necessary contradiction. In the *prohemium*, Æthelwold's quotation from the psalter, woven into his line of argument, reveals his ready familiarity with both versions as well as his ingrained predilection for the *Romanum*. On the other hand, the use of the *Gallicanum* in the *Regularis concordia*'s official stipulations concerning psalmody may indicate the adoption of the *Gallicanum* as the official text for mass and Office by the 970s, at least at Winchester and the monasteries in its orbit. This last point may be noteworthy, since we otherwise have no means of establishing whether the change to the *Gallicanum* took place at Winchester already during Æthelwold's episcopate, as all the *Gallicanum* psalters linked with Winchester date from the eleventh century,[94] and as no other

---

[93] Cf., for example, 'Domine ne in furore tuo', *Regularis concordia*, ch. 35 (p. 34) and *Gallicanum*, ps. XXXVII.2; *furore tuo] ira tua: Romanum.* 'Deus misereatur nostri', *Reg. con.*, ch. 27 (p. 24) and *Gallic.*, ps. LXVI.2; *nostri] nobis: Rom.* 'Nisi quia Dominus', *Reg. con.*, ch. 35 (p. 34) and *Gallic.*, ps. CXXIII.1; *quia] quod: Rom.* 'In pace in idipsum dormiam', *Reg. con.*, ch. 39 (p. 38) and *Gallic.*, ps. IV.9, *dormiam] obdormiam: Rom.*

[94] The sole surviving Gallican psalters written in England (though not at Winchester), possibly during Æthelwold's episcopate are the Salisbury Psalter and Harley 2904. The Salisbury Psalter (Salisbury Cathedral 150) was written in the second half of the tenth century (a period 969 × 987 may be deduced from computus material contained in the manuscript) in southwestern England, perhaps at Shaftesbury; see Ker, *Catalogue*, pp. 449–51 (no. 379), Sisam, *Salisbury Psalter*, pp. 11–12, and D. Stroud, 'The Provenance of the Salisbury Psalter', *The Library* 6th ser. 1 (1979), 225–35. Harley 2904 was (on palaeographical grounds) written in the last quarter of the tenth century. Its origin has been assigned to Winchester, but it is now thought to have originated at Ramsey, written, perhaps, for the personal use of Bishop Oswald (961–92); see C. Niver, 'The Psalter in the British Museum, Harley 2904', in *Medieval Studies in Memory of A. Kingsley Porter*, ed. W. R. W. Koehler, 2 vols. (Cambridge, MA, 1939) II, 667–87, Lapidge, 'Abbot Germanus', pp. 398–403, Dumville, *English Caroline Script*, pp. 58–65, R. Gameson, 'Book Production and Decoration at Worcester in the Tenth and Eleventh Centuries', in *St Oswald of Worcester*, ed. Brooks and Cubitt, pp. 194–243, at 200–4, and A. Corrêa, 'The Liturgical Manuscripts of Oswald's Houses', *ibid.*, pp. 285–324, at 292–6. (Cf. above, p. 3, n. 72 for a leaf from a Gallican psalter, written in England, perhaps s. x².)

service books for mass or Office in which psalm *incipits* would be expected (such as graduals or plenary missals, antiphoners or breviaries) with a demonstrably Winchester origin before 984 have survived.[95]

Such *incipits* of psalms are also found in the Old English Rule. Here they occur (as additions to the bare numbers of psalms referred to in the original) in the liturgical chs. (8–18) where Benedict apportions the psalter for recital at the Divine Office over the week. As in the *Regularis concordia*, the *incipits* are quoted for reasons of easy reference, and (again as in the *Regularis concordia*) because of their brevity not many variants would show up. On the hypothesis that Æthelwold occupied himself with the Royal gloss and the translation of the *Regula S. Benedicti* at approximately the same time, we should expect the *incipits* in the Old English Rule to be quoted from the *Romanum* version. In effect, the evidence appears confusing at first sight. Both the *Romanum* and the *Gallicanum* versions are quoted. For example, the *Gallicanum* text is found in BR 37.7 (= ps. LXVI.2): 'Deus misereatur *nostri*' (*Romanum: nobis*) or BR 42.10 (= ps. VI.2): 'in furore tuo' (*Romanum: in ira tua*); the *Romanum* is quoted, for example, in BR 44.7–8 (= ps. IV.2): 'cum inuocarem *te*' (*Gallicanum: te* omitted) or BR 37.17 (= ps. LXIII.2): 'Exaudi deus orationem meam cum *tribulor*' (*Gallicanum: deprecor*).

When we reflect, however, that all surviving manuscripts of the Old English Rule were written at least several decades after the presumed date of its composition and at a time when the *Gallicanum* must have been firmly established in liturgical use, when we further reflect that, in some manuscripts, alterations to the wording of the Rule are not infrequently made (characteristically to substitute old-fashioned or rare words),[96] then it will no longer occasion much surprise to find *Gallicanum* readings in

---

[95] For the date, origin or provenance of the surviving books for mass and Office, see Gneuss, 'Liturgical Books', pp. 91–141. For an evaluation of what fragmentary evidence there is, pertaining to the liturgy in Æthelwold's Winchester, see Lapidge, *Wulfstan: Life*, pp. lx–lxxxv.

[96] Cf., for example, BR 17.12 *aræfnian* (= *suffere*): *forberan*, Titus A. iv and Durham Cathedral B. IV. 24; BR 18.9 *ræde* (= *lectio*): *ræding*, Titus A. iv and Durham B. IV. 24; BR 121.12 *drefre* (= *turbulentus*): *gedrefed*, Titus A. iv, *drefend*, Durham B. IV. 24, *dræfend*, BL Faustina A. x, *drefende*, Wells Cathedral 7. In this connection it may be worth noting that in the 'Benedictine' reading of ps. XVII.24 (= *RSB* 7.18), the *Romanum* variant *coram* has been altered to *Gallicanum cum* by a later hand in the Latin text of Titus A. iv (s. xi^med, possibly from Winchester). The typical 'Benedictine' variant (*si obseruauero*), however, is left untouched.

the psalm *incipits* in the Old English Rule. Since the *Gallicanum* variants are found in all surviving manuscripts of the Rule, they probably date from a rather early stage in the transmissional history of the text, say, from the 960s or 970s.

Conversely, the *Romanum* readings in the psalm *incipits* are not likely to represent later substitutions. They will, therefore, preserve the *incipits* in the form in which they were originally quoted by Æthelwold in his translation of the *Regula*. Thus the *Romanum* variants in the Old English Rule, occurring in quotations added to Benedict's text, may corroborate the supposition of an early date for the translation. By the same token, the *Romanum* variants in the Rule and the *prohemium* to the *Regularis concordia* may confirm our suspicion that Æthelwold personally was firmly attached to the *Psalterium Romanum* and during the early stages of his career actively propagated its use in the liturgy, even though he will have known Gallican psalters such as Galba A. xviii and even though he will have been aware of the role which this version played in the liturgy on the Continent.

THE ART HISTORICAL EVIDENCE

Let us now turn to yet a different class of evidence which most suggestively points to a close involvement of Æthelwold in the Royal gloss. Such evidence is of an art historical nature and it is provided by Æthelwold's own Benedictional (London, BL, Add. 49598), one of the most lavish manuscripts produced in Anglo-Saxon England. A benedictional is a bishop's book; it contains benedictions, that is tripartite prayers, said during mass on Sundays and feastdays, after the *Pater noster* and immediately before communion; such benedictions could be pronounced by a bishop only.[97]

Robert Deshman has advanced compelling reasons for thinking that Æthelwold himself played a decisive role in devising the immensely complex and interrelated iconography of his Benedictional.[98] Similarly,

---

[97] For manuscripts containing benedictionals from Anglo-Saxon England, cf. Gneuss, 'Liturgical books', pp. 133–4; for the structure and contents of benedictionals, see the articles by A. Prescott (below, n. 99). For an edition of the text of Æthelwold's Benedictional and a black and white facsimile, see Warner and Wilson, *The Benedictional of St Æthelwold*.

[98] The notion of Æthelwold's pivotal role in the production of the Benedictional

and in confirmation of Deshman's findings, the text of the Benedictional reflects Æthelwold's personal liturgical and scholarly interests, inasmuch as it is a scholarly compilation systematically providing for each Sunday and each feast the text of the two principal traditions, namely of the 'Gallican' and of the 'Gregorian' benedictions, as well as adding a substantial number of benedictions not found in any source and therefore presumably composed either by Æthelwold himself or under his supervision.[99] As Deshman has also shown, some of the iconographic motifs (such as the emphasis on coronation scenes or the link which is forged between baptism and coronation) strongly suggest that the Benedictional was produced for King Edgar's coronation at Bath in 973.[100]

Posuisti in capite eius coronam de lapide pretioso

As we have seen (above, p. 100), the lemma *corona* in this psalm verse (ps. XX.4) is rendered by *hroþgirela*, a compound almost certainly coined by the Royal Glossator. It is a flamboyant, recherché coinage carrying a distinctly archaic flavour, and (with the exception of the Tiberius Psalter) it was not accepted by the dependent psalter glosses. Such an exquisite coinage would be wholly consonant with the pronounced predilection for this type of poetic and 'hermeneutic' vocabulary revealed by the Royal Glossator throughout his work.

We must recall that further important lexicological evidence is provided by this rendering of *corona*, evidence which clearly points to Æthelwold. *Corona* in a metaphorical sense 'crown of life' etc. belongs to the groups of Latin words for which Winchester usage developed a standardized and distinctive terminology. In this case, the Winchester

permeates Deshman's magisterial study, *The Benedictional of Æthelwold*, but see esp. pp. 252–4. This book includes full-size colour plates of all the miniatures and of a selection of the initial pages of the Benedictional. A deep concern with the make-up of his Benedictional is assumed for Æthelwold also by Gameson, *The Role of Art in the Late Anglo-Saxon Church*, pp. 32, 58 and 125.

[99] The text of the Benedictional has been searchingly studied by A. Prescott, 'The Structure of English Pre-Conquest Benedictionals', *British Library Journal* 13 (1987), 118–58, at 119–21, and *idem*, 'The Text of the Benedictional of St Æthelwold', in *Bishop Æthelwold*, ed. Yorke, pp. 119–47; cf. esp. pp. 128–32 (table 1) where the sources for each of the benedictions are listed. For the 'English' benedictions, see also Lapidge, *Wulfstan: Life*, pp. lxxix–lxxxiii.

[100] Cf. Deshman, *Benedictional*, pp. 192–214, esp. 212–14, and 260–1.

word would have been *wuldorbeag*. We have seen that the Royal Glossator employed the verb *gewuldorbeagian* for *coronare*, here attested for the first time. Since the verb is derived from the noun, its use implies that the Glossator also knew *wuldorbeag*. This noun makes its first appearance in the Old English Rule, which gives us an important verbal link between the Rule and the Psalter, and the suspicion must be that Æthelwold, who (it would appear) initiated the Winchester usage, coined both noun and verb. Such a suspicion gains confirmation when we consider that, for various reasons, both texts seem to have been composed at about the same time (see above, pp. 233–60).

But why then is *hroþgierela*, not *wuldorbeag*, employed to translate *corona* in ps. XX.4? So far, our answer to this question has been twofold: both texts, the Psalter and the Rule, represent an incipient, experimental stage in the development of Winchester usage, and the Glossator may have felt the urge to respond to the challenge posed by the various layers of meanings which psalm exegesis assigned to *corona* in the verse in question by the coinage of an expression even more flamboyant than *wuldorbeag*. The evidence of Bishop Æthelwold's own Benedictional may provide yet a further explanation for the employment of *hroþgierela*, in this specific verse, thereby strengthening the case for Æthelwold's involvement in the Royal gloss. Such evidence is, however, of a somewhat intricate nature.

To begin with, crowns play an important role in the iconography of the Benedictional. Crowns occur in eight of the Benedictional's thirty miniatures, where they are often depicted in an innovative way,[101] as for example in the image of the crowned Magi,[102] the miniatures of the choirs of saints,[103] or the feast picture for the Assumption of the Virgin.[104] It is fairly obvious that such a keen interest in crowns and crown symbolism in the Benedictional closely parallels the Winchester preoccupation with the terminology for *corona* and *coronare*. This parallel may be pursued a step further: Latin, a language more sophisticated and refined than Old English in almost every respect, does not distinguish by the use of different words between *corona* according to whether it carries a literal or a metaphorical sense. Winchester usage does. Similarly, the iconography of the Benedictional distinguishes between two types of crowns: a trefoiled crown worn by worldly rulers (as in the case of the

---

[101] Cf. *ibid.*, p. 192.   [102] Cf. *ibid.*, pl. 18 and pp. 26–7.
[103] *Cf. ibid.*, pls. 1–3 and p. 149.   [104] Cf. *ibid.*, pl. 34 and pp. 136–7 and 204.

Magi, pl. 18),[105] or saints (as in the choirs of saints, pls. 1–3, or in the miniature of the coronation of the Virgin, pl. 34), and a diadem, worn by, or offered to, Christ (in the inital for the Octave of Pentecost, pl. 27, and in the miniatures of the Adoration of the Magi, pl. 18, and of the Baptism of Christ, pl. 19).

It is in the feast picture for the translation of St Benedict (pl. 33) that the symbolism of the two types of crowns is exploited in an extremely subtle manner. Benedict wears a jewelled diadem and he holds a trefoil crown in his left hand, that is, he is represented as *imago Christi*, having been empowered to bestow on his followers the crown of eternal life and glory.[106] Benedict is the only saint in the Benedictional to be represented with the diadem of the Deity, and he is so only in his feast picture. By contrast, in the choir of saints (pl. 1) he is depicted as one of them, wearing the same trefoiled crown of eternal life as they do.[107]

As Deshman has pointed out, the representations of Benedict are remarkable in several respects.[108] Thus they are the earliest extant portraits of the 'father of monks' north of the Alps, and apparently only four miniatures have survived where Benedict is depicted as wearing a crown or diadem,[109] and these are all closely connected with Æthelwold. Apart from the two miniatures in his own Benedictional, the two others are the portrait following the psalter in Arundel 155 (133r), produced at Canterbury (Christ Church) 1012 × 1023,[110] and the picture in Tiberius A. iii (117v), of mid-eleventh-century date and again, presumably Christ Church origin.[111] Here, the portrait precedes the only surviving copy of the *Regula S. Benedicti* with a continuous interlinear gloss in Old

---

[105] All plate numbers referring to the miniatures of the Benedictional are those given by Deshman, *Benedictional*.

[106] Cf. Deshman, *Benedictional*, pp. 117–21, and *idem*, 'Benedictus Monarcha', pp. 217–18.

[107] Cf. Deshman, *Benedictional*, pp. 119 and 150.   [108] *Ibid.*, p. 117.

[109] For further innovative features in Benedict's portraits, see Deshman, *Benedictional*, pp. 172–3.

[110] For reproductions, see Deshman, *Benedictional*, fig. 136, and Temple, *Anglo-Saxon Manuscripts*, no. 66, fig. 213; colour reproduction in *The Golden Age of Anglo-Saxon Art. 966–1066*, ed. J. Backhouse, D. H. Turner and L. Webster (London, 1984), pl. xviii.

[111] For reproductions, see Deshman, *Benedictional*, fig. 137, and Temple, *Anglo-Saxon Manuscripts*, no. 100, fig. 314.

English.[112] The pictures in Arundel 155 and Tiberius A. iii are closely related, presumably deriving from the same exemplar. Deshman has mounted a compelling argument that (in spite of the Canterbury origin of the surviving copies) the lost archetype was devised by Æthelwold himself to accompany, as a frontispiece, the dedication copies of his translation of the *Regula S. Benedicti*.[113]

As in the feast picture in the Benedictional, in the miniatures in Arundel 155 and Tiberius A. iii, Benedict is portrayed wearing a diadem, whereby again he is elevated above the status of an ordinary saint and functions as *imago Christi*. In other words, the evidence of these four portraits, coupled with the pervasive role played by crowns elsewhere in the Benedictional, unequivocally indicates that Æthelwold was deeply concerned with the symbolism of crowns, and particularly so with regard to the portraiture of St Benedict.

For a potential source of inspiration behind the feast picture of the crowned Benedict, Deshman has drawn attention to the psalm verse which the New Minster Missal has as proper for the mass offertory on the

---

[112] Printed by Logeman, *The Rule of S. Benet*.

[113] See *Benedictional*, pp. 117 and 119–20, and *'Benedictus Monarcha'*, esp. pp. 206–7 and 211–19. For a different view concerning the origin of the archetype of the pictures, see Higgitt, 'Glastonbury', pp. 283–5, who would see the origin of this archetype intimately linked with Dunstan, either at Glastonbury or Canterbury. Higgitt's arguments for associating the archetype of the portraits with Dunstan appear to have less to recommend them than an association with Æthelwold, not least because this archetype most plausibly will have served as a frontispiece to the Benedictine Rule and because of its close links with the iconography of St Benedict's feast picture in the Benedictional; cf. also Deshman, *'Benedictus Monarcha'*, pp. 210 and 216 and n. 55. Even so, it is interesting to note that the portrait of Christ in Oxford, Bodleian Library, Auct. F. 4. 32 (1r), which incontestably is associated with Dunstan, stresses the kingship of Christ; see Higgitt, 'Glastonbury', pp. 278–80; for the drawing, see Temple, *Anglo-Saxon Manuscripts*, no. 11 (p. 41); for the drawing as a stylistic antecedent of the Benedictional, see Deshman, *Benedictional*, pp. 224–5; see also Budny, 'St Dunstan's Classbook', pp. 127–35, for a technical description of the picture and a brief survey of interpretations. The kingship of Christ (not exclusively represented by means of crown symbolism) is a feature of utmost importance also in the iconography of the Benedictional – and in the lexicography of the Royal Psalter gloss. Such shared iconographic motifs and predilections raise the tantalizing question whether, and to what extent, Dunstan may have been involved in the initial stages of what was to become the Winchester vocabulary; cf. also below, pp. 372–6.

feast of the translation of St Benedict (11 July).[114] This verse is ps. XX.4 ('Posuisti in capite eius coronam de lapide pretioso'), the very verse where *corona* is glossed *hroþgierela* by the Royal Glossator. In the New Minster Missal, the same offertory chant recurs in the mass on the day of the deposition of St Benedict (21 March, a feast not commemorated in the Benedictional).[115] However, the New Minster Missal (Le Havre, Bibl. mun., 330) dates from the second half of the eleventh century, that is, about a century after Æthelwold's episcopacy, and hence offers no secure and direct evidence for the performance of mass in Æthelwold's Winchester, let alone at Glastonbury during the 940s. No plenary missals or graduals (which would have contained the mass chants) from tenth-century Winchester have survived.[116]

We are somewhat nearer to Æthelwold's days with the evidence of the so-called 'Winchester Tropers', two musical manuscripts which (apart from sequences and the famous organa) preserve the trope repertory of late-tenth-century Winchester.[117] One of these two books, now Oxford, Bodleian Library, Bodley 775, dates from the mid-eleventh century but was apparently copied from a lost Winchester exemplar written *c.* 978 × *c.* 985. The other, now Cambridge, Corpus Christi College 473, was written at Winchester *c.* 1000; it may have been the copy that was owned (and partly written in) by Wulfstan, the precentor of the Old Minster and one of Æthelwold's students.[118] Both tropers agree in giving the chant cue *Posuisti* (the *incipit* of ps. XX.4) for one of the offertory tropes in the mass on the day of St Benedict's deposition. (No tropes are provided for the feast of the translation.)[119]

---

[114] *Benedictional*, p. 118.

[115] See Turner, *The Missal of the New Minster*, p. 124 (*translatio*) and p. 82 (*natale*).

[116] For what fragmentary evidence there is for the shape of the mass in Æthelwold's Winchester, see Lapidge, *Wulfstan: Life*, pp. lxii–lxvii.

[117] *The Winchester Troper*, ed. Frere, pp. 3–68. For a full inventory of the tropes in the two manuscripts, see Planchart, *The Repertory of Tropes at Winchester*, vol. II.

[118] Cf. Planchart, *Repertory* I, 26–33, for the date and provenance of CCCC 473, and I, 40–3, for the date and provenance of Bodley 775, and see Lapidge, *Wulfstan: Life*, pp. xxxi, xxxvi and lxxxiii–iv. For CCCC 473, see, however, Lapidge, 'Autographs of Insular Latin Authors', pp. 134–5, who finds the closest parallels to the script of Scribe II (= Wulfstan?) in the type of Anglo-Caroline minuscule written in the second quarter of the eleventh century, which would rule out Wulfstan as an owner and scribe of CCCC 473.

[119] See Planchart, *Repertory* II, no. 269 ('Gloriosus es deus'); the trope with its chant cue is

Ps. XX.4 is also one of the mass chants proper for the *Depositio S. Benedicti* in the earlier, continental, part of the so-called Leofric Missal.[120] The core of this manuscript (now Oxford, Bodleian Library, Bodley 579; a sacramentary, not a plenary missal) was written in northeast Francia or Flanders in the second half of the ninth century (= Leofric A). That this part was in England, perhaps at Glastonbury, in the later tenth century is clear from various additions which it received there, possibly around *c.* 980 (= Leofric B). (The still later accretions made at Exeter (s. xi[2] = Leofric C) need not concern us here.) The assumption of a Glastonbury sojourn in the later tenth century of the continental sacramentary (Leofric A) rests primarily on the evidence of a liturgical calendar in Leofric B and has recently been called into question.[121] In any event, on the evidence of an initial added to Leofric A (154r) and various additions made by English scribes, the continental sacramentary must have been in England as early as *c.* 930.[122]

Psalm XX.4, together with the preceding verse, *Desiderium animae eius*, are the mass-chants proper for offertory and/or gradual on St Benedict's deposition and translation in post-Conquest mass books such as the Sarum Missal, the Sarum Gradual or the Westminster Missal.[123] It cannot be established if and to what extent such later and apparently universal

on 24r of CCCC 473 and 41v of Bodley 775; cf. Planchart, *Repertory* II, 3 and 14. Trope and chant cue are printed by Frere, *Winchester Troper*, p. 14 (§ 69).

[120] Temple, *Anglo-Saxon Manuscripts*, pp. 44–5 (no. 17). The entire manuscript is edited by F. E. Warren, *The Leofric Missal* (Oxford, 1883); the chant cue in question is at p. 139; for the continental origin of the *incipits* for the mass chants, cf. *ibid.*, p. xxxvii.

[121] See D. N. Dumville, 'The Liturgical Kalendar of Anglo-Saxon Glastonbury: a Chimaera?', in his *Liturgy and Ecclesiastical History*, pp. 39–65, and *idem*, *English Caroline Script*, pp. 94–6. For the art historical evidence pointing to Glastonbury, see R. E. Deshman, 'The Leofric Missal and Tenth-Century English Art', *ASE* 6 (1977), 145–73, and Higgitt, 'Glastonbury', pp. 277–8.

[122] See Deshman, 'The Leofric Missal', p. 148, Dumville, *English Caroline Script*, pp. 94–5, and *idem*, 'Square Minuscule' [*ASE* 16], p. 176.

[123] See *The Sarum Missal*, ed. J. Wickham Legg (Oxford, 1916), pp. 258 and 290, *Graduale Sarisburiense*, ed. W. H. Frere (London, 1894), pp. 204 and 222, and *Missale Westmonasteriense*, ed. J. Wickham Legg, 3 vols., HBS 1, 5 and 12 (1891–7) II, 865 and 783. Neither the deposition nor the translation of St Benedict are among the feasts represented in the comprehensive yet selective edition of the Roman gradual by the monks of Solesmes, *Le Graduel romain: Édition critique*, 4 vols. (Solesmes, 1957–62; vols. I and III have not yet been published).

adoption of ps. XX.4 as proper for the feasts of St Benedict may be traced to Æthelwold's influence. The likelihood is, however, that *Posuisti in capite* was indeed one of the mass-chants sung at Winchester during his episcopacy, and perhaps at Glastonbury in the 940s (irrespective of a possible Glastonbury sojourn of the Leofric Missal). Interestingly, this psalm verse seems to have been lifted from the mass-chants proper for martyrs, not confessors. For example, in the New Minster Missal, it occurs almost invariably in masses for martyrs (cf. masses for SS Felix (p. 59), Vincent (p. 64), Tiburtius (p. 142), John the Baptist (p. 152), mass for one martyr (p. 198), and so on). Apart from St Benedict, the only masses for confessors where this chant is proper are SS Martin (p. 152) and (characteristically) Dunstan (p. 96).[124]

One may speculate therefore whether the universal employment of ps. XX.4 (and other verses from this psalm) in St Benedict's mass may be associated with the important role which this specific psalm played in the Benedictine *cursus*. We have seen (above, p. 271) that St Benedict insisted that the weekly recital of the entire psalter should start afresh each Sunday at Nocturns (*RSB* 18.23), and that he himself had instituted ps. XX as the psalm with which to begin the weekly *cursus* (*RSB* 18.6), an institution which was followed in Benedictine monasteries throughout the Middle Ages. Therefore, *Posuisti in capite* (and other verses from this psalm) will have been particularly well-placed in the sung parts of the mass for St Benedict's feasts. Whatever the case, there is little doubt that the miniature of Benedict in Æthelwold's Benedictional as well as the lost archetype for the portraits of St Benedict in Arundel 155 and Tiberius A. iii were inspired, to some extent at least, by the verse 'Posuisti in capite eius coronam de lapide pretioso.' In this connection it is also noteworthy that precious stones are set in the diadems worn by St Benedict (and Christ) in the Benedictional.[125]

To return to the Royal Glossator and his verbal gem *hroþgierela* for *corona* in ps. XX.4: in view of the immensely intricate symbolism carried

---

[124] In the New Minster Missal no chant cues are given for the feasts of St Æthelwold, cf. pp. 132–3 and 159–60 of Turner's edition.

[125] This feature does not show readily in the plates reproduced from St Benedict's miniature (cf., e. g., Deshman, *Benedictional*, pl. 11); however, in the reproduction of the miniature of Christ in the Octave of Pentecost (pl. 27), it can be clearly seen that the diadem has been 'tooled with markings indicating settings of precious stones'; *ibid.*, p. 92; cf. also p. 118, and Deshman, *'Benedictus Monarcha'*, p. 218.

by the two crowns associated with St Benedict in his feast picture, it may be legitimate to ask whether the Glossator's lexical choice might not be more than just experimenting with synonyms *en route* towards Winchester terminology. It is conceivable that the Glossator might have deliberately coined the highly ornate compound *hroþgierela* and given it preference over the less flamboyant *wuldorbeag* (also probably coined by him) as a gloss for *corona* in a psalm and psalm verse closely associated with Benedict. He would have done so in order to stress the especial splendour of the diadem with which he ordered Benedict to be depicted in a manuscript some thirty years later. It is striking in this connection that the marginal Latin scholia in Royal 2. B. V cut down Cassiodorus's lengthy exposition of how *corona* is to be understood in the verse in question (namely as a reward for earthly toils, as the church or as the apostles, cf. above, p. 100) to the laconic explanation: 'Id est conuentus apostolorum' (27r). Similarly, in respect of *de lapide pretioso*, we find the verbose exegesis by Cassiodorus distilled to 'Id est Christus est ille lapis' (*ibid.*).

All this is not a matter of simple and straightforward relationships. The marginal scholia in Royal 2. B. V, the Winchester desire for a distinctive terminology for *corona* in a metaphorical sense, the Royal Glossator's predilection for precious 'hermeneutic' words, the importance attached to ps. XX in the Benedictine *cursus*, and to ps. XX.4 for the feastdays of St Benedict, the pervasive role played by crowns in the iconography of Æthelwold's Benedictional, the elaborate symbolism of the two crowns in St Benedict's feast picture with its Christological overtones – all seem to be woven together in an exquisite fabric designed for the glorification of Benedictine monasticism.

Christus – rex – cyning

The iconography of Æthelwold's Benedictional plays a crucial role also in an attempt to explain a further striking rendering of a Latin lemma in the Royal Psalter and in associating this rendering with Æthelwold and his circle. The glosses in question are among the most idiosyncratic ones in the Royal Psalter, and they are striking as well, by the consistency with which they occur: the lemma *christus* is almost invariably glossed *cyning* or *rex*. We have considered a number of aspects of such an idiosyncratic translation in an earlier ch.[126] There we have seen that this translation is utterly distinctive of the Royal Glossator. He could not have found the equation *christus: cyning* in an A-type gloss to which he presumably had resort, and the glossator of the Lambeth Psalter (who in the eleventh century provided a fresh interlinear version of the psalms, while drawing heavily on D-type gloss material) adopted the Royal Glossator's *interpretamentum* only very sporadically. We have also seen that the glosses *cyning* and *rex* for *christus* are explanatory but not etymologizing (*christus* meaning 'the anointed', and hence someone with temporal or spiritual power), that psalm exegesis exerted some influence on the choice of these *interpretamenta* and that *cyning* or *rex* employed for a lemma meaning 'the anointed' was in agreement with contemporary emphasis on unction as the most important ceremony in the coronation *ordo* for an Anglo-Saxon king as it was in use during the tenth century. Finally, we have considered the coupling of *christus* and *cyning* in the context of the Royal Glossator's desire to emulate the poetic language of the psalms, since this gloss gave rise to two lines of Old English verse found in the margin of Royal 2. B. V (verses which, for various reasons, must be attributed to the Glossator himself, not to a later scribe). From all this it has emerged that the Glossator attached a special significance to the glosses in question and that he had a keen interest in what constituted the essence of kingship.

Now one of the most persistent motifs in Æthelwold's Benedictional is that of Christ being represented as king, either wearing a crown or being crowned or invested with other royal insignia such as a sceptre.[127] Such iconographic emphasis on Christ's royalty must in part be attributed to the Carolingian and Byzantine models of the Benedictional, but, as Robert Deshman has shown, the depiction in the miniatures is often innovative, revealing a deep concern with the kingship of Christ and (by implication) a Christological interpretation of temporal rulership.[128] It may be worth noting that a similar concern is revealed in the prefatory poem to the Benedictional. This poem was composed in ostentatious Latin by Godeman, the scribe of the Benedictional and one of Æthel-

---

[126] See above, pp. 73–9.

[127] Apart from the initial to the Octave of Pentecost (Deshman, *Benedictional*, pl. 27) which we have considered above, the miniatures in question are: the Second Coming (pl. 10), the Adoration of the Magi (pl. 18) and Christ's Baptism (pl. 19).

[128] See Deshman, *Benedictional*, esp. pp. 26–7, 45–8, 62–8, 92–9, 192–5 and 209–14.

wold's students, who eventually became abbot of Æthelwold's foundation at Thorney. Within the brief compass of thirty-eight hexameters (some of which, interestingly, testify to Æthelwold's close involvement in the making of his Benedictional), Christ is twice styled king and sovereign: 'cum principe summo' (line 24) and 'rex bonus orbis' (line 33).[129]

Of special interest for our purposes is the close link which the iconography of the Benedictional forges between Christ's baptism, the baptismal unction with chrism and a king's coronation. Thus, in the miniature of Christ's baptism (pl. 19), His baptism is represented as an imperial coronation. Such iconography implies that, conversely, the coronation of a temporal ruler is seen in terms of baptism and baptismal unction.[130] We have seen that there are grounds for thinking that the Benedictional was produced for King Edgar's coronation at Bath in 973.[131] The decisive factor for staging this coronation in 973 may have been Edgar's age: he then was in his thirtieth year, as was Christ when He was baptized.[132] For an important source of inspiration for such a close link between coronation and baptism as revealed in the date of Edgar's coronation and in the iconography of the Benedictional (presumably produced for this ceremony), Deshman has pointed to the *Via regia*, a mirror for princes composed by Smaragdus of Saint-Mihiel for the Emperor Louis the Pious (814–40).[133] (We should recall here that Smaragdus belongs within the ambit of the monastic reforms launched by Benedict of Aniane and that these reforms were decisively influential on the nascent English reform Benedictinism, and on Æthelwold in particular, not least through Smaragdus's commentary on the *Regula S. Benedicti*.)[134] In the prologue to the *Via regia*, Smaragdus stresses that the

---

[129] The poem is printed by Lapidge, 'Hermeneutic Style', pp. 143–4, and previously only in the facsimile edition by Warner and Wilson, *The Benedictional of St Æthelwold*, p. 1. There are several translations: cf. most recently Deshman, *Benedictional*, p. 148 (reprinting the translation by F. Wormald, *The Benedictional of St Ethelwold* (London, 1959), pp. 7–8). On Godeman and his ostentatious style, see Lapidge, 'Hermeneutic Style', pp. 123–4, and *idem*, 'Æthelwold as Scholar and Teacher', pp. 200–1, as well as *Wulfstan: Life*, ch. 24 (p. 41 and n. 9).

[130] See Deshman, *Benedictional*, pp. 45–8 and 193–4, and *idem*, 'Benedictus Monarcha', pp. 233–6.

[131] Above, p. 297 and n. 100.

[132] Cf. Deshman, *Benedictional*, pp. 212–13, and *idem*, 'Benedictus Monarcha', p. 235.

[133] Deshman, *Benedictional*, esp. p. 212; the *Via regia* is printed PL 102, 931–70.

[134] See above, 245, 247–8 and 255.

king wears his crown because at his baptism God has anointed him with chrism.[135]

When we now return to the Royal Psalter and its consistent coupling of *christus* (literally 'the anointed', 'Christ' in psalm exegesis) and *cyning*, two points are thrown into clear focus in the light of the iconography of the Benedictional. The first point concerns an important ideological concept of the reform (as it is revealed in the images of Æthelwold's book), namely the emphasis on the kingship of Christ, with its implication of a Christological perception of temporal rulership: this concept was tangibly present as early as the 940s, when it occurs in a gloss which, on other grounds, can be shown to be rooted in the nascent reform movement. Of course, Æthelwold was not alone in developing this concept. We have seen, for example, that anointing played a crucial role in the 'Second English *Ordo*' which was drawn up several decades before Æthelwold could have exerted any influence.[136] Yet, the pervasiveness of the concept, and the multiple iconographic innovations employed in its depiction in the miniatures in Æthelwold's personal book on the one hand, and the idiosyncratic, unprecedented insistence on the translations *cyning* or *rex* for *christus* by the Royal Glossator on the other, are striking in their similarity.

In addition to the Carolingian models which have been adduced as sources for Æthelwold's perception of kingship (as revealed in his Benedictional), it may be rewarding to look for English sources as well in which he could have found similar notions. We have seen (above, p. 75) that the perception of the king as *Christus Domini*, 'the Lord's Anointed' (cf. ps. CIV.15), was of some importance as early as 786, in the canons promulgated by the legatine synods held in Northumbria and Mercia that year. These canons have survived in the report sent by George, bishop of Ostia and one of the papal legates, to Pope Hadrian. There is no way of knowing for certain whether Æthelwold was familiar with the twenty canons of the legatine synods. (The only surviving manuscript is of continental origin; see above, p. 75, n. 123.) However, from the stipulations of the *Regularis concordia* it is clear that he had closely studied the decrees of the Aachen synods of 816/17 (above, p. 245); and he will have given equally close attention to the decrees of English church councils, since the traditional customs of the English church are invoked

---

[135] PL 102, 933.   [136] Cf. above, p. 75.

with reverence several times in Æthelwold's own customary (see above, p. 291). The preface to the Old English Rule would be another of Æthelwold's works to reveal his interest in the history of the English church (see above, p. 291). In any case, it is noteworthy that Archbishop Oda's *Constitutiones*, drafted 942 × 946 (that is, during Æthelwold's Glastonbury years) drew extensively on the decrees of the legatine synods;[137] and it is of especial interest that the stipulations of the *Regularis concordia* concerning the election of abbots and abbesses may base themselves on canon 5 of these synods.[138] If Æthelwold had studied the decrees of the legatine synods, there can be no doubt that (aside from the royal style *Christus Domini* and the stipulation for the election of abbots and abbesses) they would have contained much else to attract his interest, and that for him they would have ranked as a document of primary importance in the history of the English church.[139]

---

[137] Oda's *Constitutiones* have been printed several times, most recently by Whitelock, *CS*, pp. 67–74. For their indebtedness to the canons of the legatine synods, cf. *ibid.*, pp. 67–8.

[138] Cf. *Alcuini Epistolae*, ed. Dümmler, p. 22, and *Regularis Concordia*, ed. Symons, ch. 9 (p. 6 and n. 4); cf. also *idem*, 'History and Derivation', p. 44.

[139] Examples of such points of interest for Æthelwold would have been the decrees which pronounce on the lifestyle desirable for monks or canons (c. 4, in *Alcuini Epistolae*, ed. Dümmler, p. 22), on the close links between Rome and the English church (c. 8, p. 22), on the relations between the king and the church (c. 11–12, pp. 23–4), on excessive tributes imposed on churches (c. 14, p. 25) and so on. Furthermore, the overall goal of the document is a moral reform of Anglo-Saxon society, clerics and laymen, the decrees providing for both groups of society; cf. Cubitt, *Anglo-Saxon Church Councils*, pp. 158–9, and P. Wormald, 'In Search of King Offa's Law-Code', in *People and Places in Northern Europe 500–1600. Essays in Honour of Peter Hayes Sawyer*, ed. I. Wood and N. Lund (Woodbridge, 1991), pp. 25–45. From a stylistic point of view, it is interesting to note that the canons are steeped in quotations and allusions, mainly from the Scriptures, but occasionally also from patristic authors and even the *Regula S. Benedicti*, a feature which would have much recommended them to Æthelwold's taste for a flamboyant display of learning. The verbal link between the canons and the *Regula* is *RSB* 64.5: '[prohibeant] prauorum praeualere consensum' (concerning the election of an abbot) and c. 12 (p. 23): '[nullus permittat] prauorum praeualere assensum' (concerning the election of a king); cf. also c. 5 (p. 22): 'pastores, qui sollicite animarum sibi commissarum [curam] gerant', and the similar wording in *RSB* 2.31, 34, 37 and 38. For the biblical and patristic quotations and allusions, see the references in Dümmler's edition. Similarly, the remark that the legatine canons had been read and expounded in Latin and the vernacular ('tam latine quam theodisce', p. 28) would not have been lost on Æthelwold, given his lifelong

The second point where the Benedictional sheds new light on the Royal Psalter concerns the couplet of Old English verse found among the *scholia* in the margin of Royal 2. B. V (25r), and explaining, as it were, the *cyning* and *rex* glosses:

> Wæs mid Iudeum   on geardagum
> ealra cyninga gehwelc   Cristus nemned.[140]

What, at first sight, appeared to be little more than a poetic pen trial should now (in the light of the Benedictional) rather be seen as an attempt to couch in succinct poetic language one of the most pivotal tenets of the Benedictine reform in England: that Christ is *rex regum*,[141] and that, from the days of the patriarchs onwards, the earthly ruler was conceived of as *Christus Domini*, the Lord's Anointed.

Similarly and interestingly, the iconography of the Benedictional also sheds new light on two further lines of verse, again very possibly composed by Æthelwold. In question is the elegiac couplet in Latin which precedes the text of the New Minster Foundation Charter:

> Sic celso residet solio qui condidit astra
> rex uenerans Eadgar pronus adorat eum

Unlike the Old English couplet, the Latin verses occupy a very prominent position in this *de luxe* manuscript: they occur on the first opening of the book (3r) facing the famous frontispiece on 2v which shows King Edgar (flanked by the Virgin Mary and St Peter) genuflecting and offering the charter to Christ seated in majesty. The elegiac couplet (written in gold display uncial) is the sole content of 3r, its two lines matching in their layout the upper (Christ in majesty) and lower (Edgar genuflecting) registers of the picture. The first word of the second line (*rex*) has usually been taken to refer to King Edgar: 'Thus he who established the stars sits

---

preoccupation with the vernacular. If, as has been assumed by several modern historians (cf. most recently Cubitt, *Anglo-Saxon Church Councils*, pp. 165–90), the canons of the legatine synods had been drafted by Alcuin (who had been a member of the legatine mission), his authorship conceivably might have been known in tenth-century England and would no doubt have enhanced the importance of the document in the eyes of contemporary readers.

[140] For this couplet viewed in the context of the Glossator's taste for poetic diction, see above, pp. 78–9.

[141] As is the inscription on Christ's mantle in the Second Coming (quoting Apoc. XIX.16); see Deshman, *Benedictional*, pl. 10.

on a lofty throne/ King Edgar, prostrate, venerates and adores him'.[142] However, *rex* could be taken here to refer (by a kind of ἀπὸ κοινοῦ construction) to both: Christ (or the Deity) in the first line, and Edgar in the second line. Such deliberate ambiguity would again point up in a subtle way the dual notion of Christ as king and of the king as *imago Christi*.[143] Such striking similarity with regard to their underlying basic idea between the Latin couplet (probably by Æthelwold) and the Old English verses in the Royal Psalter may of course strengthen the case for Æthelwold's authorship, not only of the Old English verses, but of the Royal gloss as a whole, since both gloss and verses are inextricably intertwined.

ÆTHELWOLD, GALBA A. XVIII AND JUNIUS 27

The Galba Psalter

Art historians are agreed that a psalter which presumably was available at Winchester in the first half of the tenth century exerted a considerable influence on the iconography of Æthelwold's Benedictional: Galba A. xviii, the so-called 'Æthelstan Psalter'.[144] This Gallican psalter, written in northeastern Francia (possibly in the area of Liège or of Rheims) in the first part of the ninth century, was demonstrably in England by the first

---

[142] See Gameson, *The Role of Art in the Late Anglo-Saxon Church*, p. 7; for a description of the contents and layout of 2v and 3r see *ibid.*, pp. 6–7; for a similar translation and a description of the folios, cf. also Keynes, *Liber Vitae*, pp. 26–7, and see *ibid.*, pls. I and II, for facsimiles. For the language of the couplet and its probable attribution to Æthelwold, see Lapidge, 'Æthelwold as Scholar and Teacher', p. 190, and *idem*, *Wulfstan: Life*, pp. lxxxix–xc, and see above, pp. 128–9. For the New Minster Charter, see also above, pp. 236–7 and n. 30.

[143] I am very grateful to Michael Lapidge for confirming my parsing of the couplet (pers. comm.).

[144] On the art historical aspects of Galba A. xviii, see Temple, *Anglo-Saxon Manuscripts*, pp. 36–7 (no. 5), Wormald, 'The "Winchester School" before St Ethelwold' in his *Collected Writings* I, 76–84, at 79, R. Deshman, 'Anglo-Saxon Art after Alfred', *Art Bulletin* 56 (1974), 176–200, esp. 178–90, 193 and 197–8, and particularly Deshman, 'The Galba Psalter'. On the influence of the Galba Psalter on the Benedictional, see for example Alexander, 'The Benedictional of St Æthelwold', pp. 176, 178–9 and *passim*, Temple, *Anglo-Saxon Manuscripts*, p. 49 (no. 23), and Deshman, *Benedictional*, pp. 20–4, 84–6, 146–58, 166–7, 259–60 and *passim*.

decade of the tenth century, when it received (in two quires added at the beginning of the manuscript), the first of several accretions produced in England in the course of the tenth century (see above, p. 275).[145] Four full-page miniatures have survived, painted by English artists (also perhaps as early as the first decade of the tenth century) and inserted at various points in the manuscript.[146] Some notion of the impact which these miniatures had on the pictures of Æthelwold's Benedictional may be formed from the fact that the choirs of angels, prophets and saints (2v and 21r) in the Galba Psalter have been used for reconstructing the contents of the lost miniatures at the beginning of the Benedictional.[147]

It has traditionally been assumed that Galba A. xviii was a book which King Æthelstan (924–39) gave to the Old Minster, Winchester. There is, however, no conclusive contemporary evidence for such an assumption,[148] and, as a result, the association with Æthelstan and Winchester has

---

[145] For the date and continental origin of Galba A. xviii, see Gneuss, 'Handlist', no. 334, which is based in turn on B. Bischoff's forthcoming catalogue of ninth-century continental manuscripts. See Keynes, 'Anglo-Saxon Entries in the *Liber Vitae* of Brescia', pp. 117–19, for a recent description (with bibliography) of the manuscript, drawing attention to a possible Italian sojourn of Galba A. xviii prior to its arrival in England, and for the suggestion that the manuscript may already have travelled to England at some point in the latter part of the ninth century.

[146] The surviving miniatures are Christ in majesty with choirs of angels and prophets (2v), Christ enthroned with choirs of martyrs, confessors and virgins (21r), the Ascension (120v) and the Nativity (now detached as Oxford, Bodleian Library, Rawlinson B. 484, fol. 85); for reproductions, see, for example, Temple, *Anglo-Saxon Manuscripts*, pls. 30–3. A fifth miniature (probably the Crucifixion) originally placed before ps. LI is now lost. See Deshman, 'The Galba Psalter', esp. pp. 111–28, for a searching interpretation of the iconography of these pictures. Deshman (*ibid.*, pp. 128–35) makes a strong case for assuming a close link between the message conveyed by the Galba miniatures and the reform programme initiated by King Alfred.

[147] See Temple, *Anglo-Saxon Manuscripts*, p. 49 (no. 23), Warner and Wilson, *The Benedictional of St Æthelwold*, p. xv, Wormald, *Collected Writings* I, 92–3, and Deshman, *Benedictional*, pp. 259–60.

[148] The assumption rests principally on an inscription (on 1r) entered by Thomas Dackomb, the sixteenth-century owner of Galba A. xviii, and recording that the manuscript was the 'psaltirium Regis Ethelstani'. Dackomb (a canon of Winchester Cathedral) had assembled a small collection of manuscripts, several of which came from the religious houses at Winchester. For a judicious assessment of the evidence for associating Galba A. xviii with King Æthelstan, see Keynes, 'Æthelstan's Books', pp. 193–6.

recently been called into question.[149] Nonetheless, the strong influence which the miniatures of the Galba Psalter exerted not only on Æthelwold's Benedictional but on other (eleventh-century) Winchester manuscripts as well, would seem to establish a Winchester home for Galba A. xviii beyond reasonable doubt, at least from the second half of the tenth century onwards,[150] and there are grounds for thinking that the psalter was at Winchester already during King Æthelstan's reign. Such grounds may be found in the contents of the three quires added at the end of the manuscript (now fols. 178–200). These quires have some bearing also on the question as to when Æthelwold may first have come into contact with the 'Æthelstan Psalter'. Galba A. xviii is a small book, not a lavish manuscript which by its outward appearance would inevitably attract attention. Nonetheless, we may suspect that the Galba Psalter had captured Æthelwold's interest considerably earlier than 963, when he returned to his native city as the bishop of Winchester.

The prinicipal contents of the three quires added at the end of Galba A. xviii in England and datable to the second quarter of the tenth century by the type of script (Anglo-Saxon Square minuscule, Phase II)[151] are the so-called 'Romana' series of psalter collects (178r–199v).[152] Psalter collects are short prayers based on one or several themes of a psalm and intended to be said privately after the recital (in the Divine Office) of the psalm in question. Wilmart and Brou distinguished three series of psalter collects, known to psalter scholars as the 'Africana', the 'Hispana' and the 'Romana' series respectively.[153] Only four psalter manuscripts from Anglo-Saxon England contain such psalter collects.[154] In addition to the Galba Psalter, the 'Romana' series is found in CCCC 272, where the collects are part of the original ninth-century continental psalter.[155] The 'Hispana' series is found in Tiberius C. vi (s. xi^med or

---

[149] See Dumville, 'The Anglo-Saxon Chronicle', pp. 73–7 and 87–8.

[150] See Keynes, 'Æthelstan's Books', p. 195, and Deshman, *Benedictional*, p. 20, n. 70. See now also Deshman, 'The Galba Psalter', esp. pp. 137–8, for a (probable) Winchester origin of the Psalter's early-tenth-century additions (including the miniatures).

[151] Cf. Dumville, 'Square Minuscule' [*ASE* 16], p. 176.

[152] Printed by Wilmart and Brou, *The Psalter Collects*, pp. 174–227.

[153] The 'Africana' and 'Hispana' series are printed by Wilmart and Brou, *ibid.*, pp. 2–111 and 112–73 respectively.

[154] Cf. Gneuss, 'Liturgical Books', p. 138.

[155] See James, *Catalogue* II, 28; for the manuscript, see also above, pp. 275–7. Note,

xi$^{3/4}$, probably from the Old Minster, Winchester) and in BL Stowe 2 (s. xi^{med} or xi$^{3/4}$, probably from the New Minster, Winchester).[156] The origin and subsequent transmission of the psalter collects still await comprehensive examination. In any event, the addition of these collects to the original ninth-century continental psalter in Galba A. xviii, made in England presumably at some point during Æthelstan's reign, attests to a deep concern with the spirituality of the psalms and their role in private devotion. It may also be of interest to note that among the three series of collects, from a stylistic point of view, the 'Romana' is the most ambitious and ornate, at times trying to match the poetic language of the psalms.[157]

It cannot be established for certain who was responsible for adding the collects in the Galba Psalter. However, as regards the group of texts which immediately follow the collects on the same folio and on the last folio of the added quires (199v–200v), we have good grounds for associating these texts with the interests and activities of a certain scholar at King Æthelstan's court. In question are four Greek prayers, transliterated in Roman characters, namely a litany of the saints, the Lord's prayer, a creed in a form known as the 'Old Roman Version', and a *Sanctus* or *Trisagion*. (Since the *Trisagion* breaks off incomplete, the suspicion is that one or several leaves have been lost at the end of the psalter.) As Michael Lapidge has shown, these prayers can be traced back to a book or booklet of Greek prayers which very probably Archbishop Theodore brought with him when he arrived in England in 669.[158] As Lapidge has also shown, there are strong reasons for thinking that Israel

---

however, that the text in this manuscript was not considered reliable by Wilmart and Brou, and hence excluded from their *apparatus criticus*.

[156] The collects (principally the 'Hispana' series) are contained also in the twelfth-century Eadwine Psalter (Cambridge, Trinity College R. 17. 1). For the collects in this manuscript and their relationship with the texts transmitted in the pre-Conquest manuscripts, see R. W. Pfaff, 'The *Tituli*, Collects, Canticles, and Creeds', in *Eadwine Psalter*, ed. Gibson *et al.*, pp. 88–107, at 94–103.

[157] Cf. Wilmart and Brou, *The Psalter Collects*, pp. 64–7, esp. 67: 'Je dis seulement ici que, de nos trois séries de collectes, si la romaine n'est pas la plus originale, c'est du moins celle qui est le mieux équilibrée, la plus digne, la plus sobre des trois – surtout quant à l'usage du symbolisme – la plus belle, enfin.'

[158] See Lapidge, *Litanies of the Saints*, pp. 13–25, and *idem*, *Biblical Commentaries*, ed. Bischoff and Lapidge, pp. 168–72.

the Grammarian was the scholar who had these four Greek prayers copied into the Galba Psalter.[159]

Israel (d. *c.* 970) was apparently a Breton by birth who, during the 930s, very probably spent some time at the court of King Æthelstan where, together with many other Bretons, he would have been seeking refuge from the political turmoils in his homeland.[160] In his time, Israel was one of the most learned men in Europe; he was a noted Greek scholar with a taste for a Greek-based, hermeneutic vocabulary also in Latin composition. This much emerges from a small dossier of texts associated with his name and transmitted in several English and continental manuscripts.[161] (The Greek prayers copied into Galba A. xviii are part of this dossier.) Israel may have exerted some influence on the Latinity of King Æthelstan's charters, the earliest prose texts composed in tenth-century England to affect the hermeneutic style which was to become the hallmark of Anglo-Latin composition in the course of the century.[162] Furthermore, Israel seems to have had some interest in glossing, both in Latin and in the vernacular;[163] he apparently took an interest also in Latin

---

[159] Cf. Lapidge, 'Israel the Grammarian in Anglo-Saxon England', pp. 101–3.

[160] On Israel's career and scholarly achievements, see Lapidge, 'Israel the Grammarian'; on the sojourn of Bretons at King Æthelstan's court, see Brett, 'A Breton Pilgrim in England in the Reign of King Æthelstan', pp. 43–50.

[161] For the texts of Israel's dossier and the manuscripts in which it is transmitted, see Lapidge, 'Israel the Grammarian', pp. 92–9.

[162] The charters composed in hermeneutic style are particularly those drafted by the royal scribe 'Æthelstan A'. On this scribe and the Latinity of his charters, see below, pp. 334–5. It is striking that the adverb *tanaliter* (?'in a deadly manner') is attested only in one of the charters drafted by 'Æthelstan A' (S 425, BCS 702) and in the so-called Saint-Omer hymn, a poem transmitted with Israel's dossier, composed perhaps by Israel himself; cf. Lapidge, 'Schools, Learning and Literature', p. 21, and *idem*, 'Israel the Grammarian', p. 95.

[163] There are several Breton glosses in two of the poems of the Israel dossier (Lapidge, 'Israel the Grammarian', pp. 94 and 97), and there are indubitable links, as yet largely unexplored, between the dossier and the Harley Glossary, now Harley 3376, a massive compilation (containing primarily Latin–Latin, but also extensive Latin–Old English and a few Latin–Celtic entries as well) of apparently English origin; the manuscript was written *c.* 1000 in some unidentified English centre (perhaps Worcester); ptd Oliphant, *Harley Glossary*. For the links with Israel's dossier, see Lapidge, 'Israel the Grammarian', p. 93, and M. Herren, 'Hiberno-Latin Lexical Sources of Harley 3376, a Latin–Old English Glossary', in *Words, Texts and Manuscripts*, ed. Korhammer, pp. 371–9, at 377–8.

metrics, as is revealed by his *De arte metrica*, one of the poems of his dossier;[164] and he was responsible for a redaction of the commentary on Donatus's *Ars minor* by Remigius of Auxerre.[165] Finally, given the 'style fleuri' which has been claimed for the Romana series of psalter collects,[166] we may perhaps be permitted to surmise that these prayers as well were copied into Galba A. xviii along with the Greek texts at Israel's instigation.

In other words, it is not difficult to imagine how much attraction Israel's scholarly interests will have held for young Æthelwold who during the 930s (the time of Israel's presumed sojourn at King Æthelstan's court) was a member of the royal household where (according to Wulfstan's testimony) he 'plura a sapientibus regis utilia ac proficua sibi didicit'.[167] If therefore Galba A. xviii may be associated not only with King Æthelstan's household, but (as the Greek prayers and, possibly, the psalter collects seem to suggest) also with the intellectual concerns of the pre-eminent scholar Israel the Grammarian, it is difficult to escape the conclusion that the Galba Psalter in its entirety should be reckoned among the books held in great veneration by Æthelwold, long before he returned to its miniatures as a source of inspiration for his own Benedictional.

The Junius Psalter

The Galba Psalter may be crucial for our understanding of the origin and development of Æthelwold's iconographic, stylistic and scholarly preoccupations; however, it contains no Old English glosses and can, therefore, shed no light on this facet of his later activities. Junius 27, the Junius Psalter, has a continuous Old English interlinear gloss. Latin text and Old English gloss were written (possibly by the same scribe)[168] in Anglo-Saxon Square minuscule (Phase I), presumably during the 920s or

---

[164] *ICL*, no. 14392; see Lapidge, 'Israel the Grammarian', p. 92 and n. 39.

[165] See C. Jeudy, 'Israël le grammairien et la tradition manuscrite du commentaire de Remi d'Auxerre à l' "Ars Minor" de Donat', *Studi medievali*, 3rd ser. 18 (1977), 751–71.

[166] Cf. Wilmart and Brou, *The Psalter Collects*, p. 65, and see above, p. 313, n. 157.

[167] *Wulfstan: Life*, ch. 7 (p. 10); 'learning much from the king's *witan* that was useful and profitable to him.'

[168] Cf. Ker, *Catalogue*, p. 409 (no. 335).

shortly before.[169] On palaeographical and art historical grounds, the manuscript has traditionally been assigned to Winchester.[170] Such an ascription has recently been challenged by David Dumville, who argues a Canterbury (Christ Church) origin for Junius 27 instead.[171] However, quite apart from the palaeographical and art historical links which Junius 27 has with other (presumably) Winchester manuscripts, one of Dumville's chief arguments for a Canterbury origin, namely that the psalter gloss in Junius 27 is a direct copy of Vespasian A. i[172] (for which a Canterbury, probably St Augustine's origin and medieval provenance is generally assumed) does not bear scrutiny, as we shall see presently; and (as we shall also see) a Canterbury origin for the Junius gloss seems to be excluded on philological grounds as well.

The Junius gloss and the evidence of dialect features in the tenth century

First, the relationship with Vespasian A. i. It is clear that Junius 27 is an A-type psalter, very closely related to Vespasian A. i. But its gloss can scarcely have been copied directly from the Vespasian Psalter. This much has recently been demonstrated by Phillip Pulsiano on the basis of an extensive collation of both manuscripts.[173] However, the material most relevant for demonstrating that Junius 27 cannot be a faithful copy (and, in effect, no copy at all) has been available for some ninety years. Ironically, it was assembled by two psalter scholars who, in spite of their material, were convinced that Junius 27 had been copied directly from

---

[169] Cf. Dumville, 'The Anglo-Saxon Chronicle', pp. 92–3 and 104–6, and *idem*, 'Square Minuscule' [*ASE 16*], p. 171.

[170] See Ker, *Catalogue*, pp. 408–9 (no. 335), Bishop, 'An Early Example of the Square Minuscule', p. 247, Parkes, 'The Palaeography of the Parker Manuscript', pp. 150 and 154–60, Temple, *Anglo-Saxon Manuscripts*, pp. 38–9 (no. 7), Sisam, *Salisbury Psalter*, p. 48, and Lapidge, 'Tenth-Century Metrical Calendar from Ramsey', pp. 361–2.

[171] See Dumville, 'The Anglo-Saxon Chronicle', pp. 73–5, 77–8, 87–8, 92–3 and 104–6, *idem*, 'Square Minuscule' [*ASE 16*], pp. 169–73, and *idem*, *Liturgy and Ecclesiastical History*, pp. 1 and 37–8.

[172] See Dumville, 'The Anglo-Saxon Chronicle', pp. 77–8, and *idem*, *Liturgy and Ecclesiastical History*, pp. 1 and 38.

[173] See Pulsiano, 'The Originality of the *Vespasian Psalter*', pp. 48–62; for a brief summary of scholarly opinion on the matter, cf. *ibid.*, pp. 37–8 and 48–9.

Vespasian A. i, a conviction which still has an impact on scholarly opinion on the origin of the manuscript. Both Uno Lindelöf (in a preliminary but extensive collation of Junius 27 with Vespasian A. i) and Eduard Brenner (in his edition of the Junius Psalter) formed their view of a direct dependence on the evidence of the overall close agreement between both psalters and a considerable number of striking shared variants.[174]

Nevertheless, Brenner in an appendix to his introduction (pp. xxxvi–xlii, basing himself heavily on Lindelöf's previous collations) printed a list of more than 200 *interpretamenta* where the Junius gloss disagrees with the Vespasian Psalter. Since most of the *interpretamenta* which have been substituted in Junius occur more than once in the psalter, the number of lexical disagreements contained in this ninety-year-old list would at least be tripled on a count by token not by type. It is clear therefore, that (in spite of its intimate links with the Vespasian Psalter), the gloss in Junius 27 transmits some kind of revision of the A-prototype gloss as represented in Vespasian A. i. It is a point of minor interest whether this revision was undertaken in the course of copying out the gloss (from its A-prototype exemplar) into Junius 27, or whether the Junius scribe already had on his desk such a revised exemplar. It is perhaps reasonable to assume that a revision of a model gloss involving hundreds of lexical substitutions (many of these made with great consistency) would not have been carried out in the process of entering the gloss in question in a handsome psalter manuscript such as Junius 27, but that the revised gloss would rather have been copied out from at least some kind of trial version.

What is important for our purpose is the philological aspect, more precisely the dialect of the gloss. The meticulous analysis of the phonology of the Junius gloss (including some morphological peculiarities) which was undertaken by Lindelöf and Brenner[175] may shed important light on the origin of that gloss, if the findings of these scholars are interpreted in terms of what is now known about dialect

---

[174] Cf. U. Lindelöf, *Die Handschrift Junius 27 der Bibliotheca Bodleiana*, Mémoires de la Société Néophilologique à Helsingfors 3 (Helsingfors, 1901), 3–73, esp. 43–8, and Brenner, *Junius-Psalter*, esp. pp. xiii–xv.

[175] See Lindelöf, *Die Handschrift Junius 27*, pp. 48–73, and Brenner, *Junius-Psalter*, pp. xv–xxxiii.

features and the prestige attached to individual dialects in the 920s, when Junius 27 was written.

First, there are no Kenticisms in the glosses. A comprehensive assessment of Kenticisms in manuscripts produced at Canterbury is still a desideratum.[176] However, if, as seems probable, most manuscripts containing Old English and written at Canterbury after *c.* 1000 (when West Saxon had attained the status of a standard) reveal at least some traces of Kentish forms, then the absence of any Kenticisms in a manuscript written at a time when West Saxon was still far from being the most prestigious dialect would seem to preclude for the manuscript in question an origin at Canterbury, the more so, since (as we shall see in a moment) the dialect of the Junius gloss is mixed.[177]

Second, the gloss has been thoroughly and pervasively 'Saxonized', that is, glosses adopted from the Anglian A-prototype, as well as substituted *interpretamenta*, reveal predominantly West Saxon dialect features. Such West Saxon dialect features are broadly consonant with what we know to have been the state of West Saxon in the 920s (for example, the result of palatal diphthongization of *e*, as well as of i-mutation of *ea*, is *ie* or *i*, rarely *y*). Since in the 920s West Saxon had not yet attained its later prestige, the presumption must be that the transformation of an Anglian exemplar into a broadly West Saxon text was made somewhere in Wessex, by a West Saxon and principally for speakers of the West Saxon dialect. The presumption of an origin of Junius 27 in a West Saxon scriptorium with West Saxon readers in mind obtains equally if the Junius Psalter is a copy of the original West Saxon redaction.

Third, there is a distinct admixture of Anglian (Mercian) forms

---

[176] Such an inventory and assessment is in preparation by Ursula Kalbhen as part of her study of southeastern dialect features in Old English manuscripts. For a preliminary list of manuscripts containing Kentish dialect features, see Gneuss, 'Origin and Provenance of Anglo-Saxon Manuscripts', pp. 47–8.

[177] It is true that the Vespasian Psalter gloss (written at Canterbury) is also (apparently) free from Kenticisms. This may, however, be a reflex rather of the political (as opposed to the dialectal) situation obtaining in ninth-century Canterbury; and it should be borne in mind that our knowledge of the early (ninth-century) Kentish dialect is tenous, and that one of the most characteristic Kentish features (namely *e* from *y* which in turn had resulted from i-mutation of *u*) had not been established before *c.* 900; cf. SB, § 31, n. 1, and Campbell, §§ 288–90. The historical context for the Vespasian gloss still awaits investigation; for the dialect of the gloss, cf. Campbell, 'The Glosses', pp. 85–90.

throughout the gloss, exhibited not only in the *interpretamenta* adopted from the A-prototype exemplar, but occasionally also in Junius's lexical substitutes (for example, i-mutation of *ea* results not infrequently in *e*, and *a* before *l*+consonant shows no diphthongization to *ea*). Judged from a historical perspective, such tolerance towards Anglian forms is precisely what we would expect in Wessex in the first half of the tenth century, and particularly at the royal court and the Winchester minsters.

It is well known that Anglian features occur with some frequency in King Alfred's writings (and in the texts associated with his translation programme) where they are usually attributed to the influence of the king's Mercian helpers. The only manuscripts of a text composed during Alfred's reign which were written while the king was still alive are the two oldest copies of Alfred's own translation of Pope Gregory's *Regula pastoralis*: Oxford, Bodleian Library, Hatton 20, and the fragments now London, BL, Cotton Tiberius B. xi (together with Kassel, Landesbibliothek, 4° Ms. theol. 131).[178] Both manuscripts exhibit a substantial admixture of Anglian forms.[179] However, Mercian influence or, at least, a tolerance towards Anglian dialect features in West Saxon texts, must still have been an important factor in the first half of the tenth century. The remaining two of our principal manuscript witnesses for the early West Saxon dialect are well sprinkled with Anglian dialect forms. The manuscripts in question are: Cambridge, Corpus Christi College 173, 1r–25v, the Parker Chronicle (or A-Chronicle) in its earlier parts, up to and including the annal for 920,[180]

---

[178] See Ker, *Catalogue*, pp. 257–9 (no. 195) and 384–6 (no. 324), and Dumville, 'Square Minuscule' [*ASE* 16], pp. 162–3. Both manuscripts are written in pointed Anglo-Saxon minuscule and are datable on the evidence of a (now lost) note, once prefixed to the Tiberius manuscript, to the last decade of the ninth century.

[179] For the most comprehensive listing of the non-West Saxon dialect features in the two manuscripts, one has still to rely on P. J. Cosijn, *Altwestsächsische Grammatik*, 2 vols. (The Hague, 1883–6). Unfortunately, this book is difficult to use for the non-specialist, and, because of its largely unstructured presentation of the material and the absence of any summaries or conclusions, the consultation of its many lists of phonological and morphological forms usually is very time-consuming for the specialist as well.

[180] Cf. Ker, *Catalogue*, pp. 57–9 (no. 39). There are two distinct portions in question: 1r–16v, written in Anglo-Saxon proto-Square minuscule at some point after 891 (the latest annal in this portion): cf. most recently Dumville, 'Square Minuscule' [*ASE* 16], pp. 163–4; and 16v–25v, written in Anglo-Saxon Square minuscule Phase I, datable (presumably) to the 920s: cf. Dumville, *ibid.*, p. 170 and p. 148, n. 2. The

and the so-called Lauderdale manuscript of the Old English translation of Orosius's *Historiae aduersus paganos*, now London, BL, Add. 47967.[181] (It is worth mentioning that the principal scribe of the Lauderdale Orosius and that of the Parker Chronicle, 16v–25v, are thought to be identical, and that this scribe may have been responsible also for most of the text in Junius 27.)[182]

Such a widespread and frequent occurrence of Anglian forms in the principal witnesses for early West Saxon (as well as the more occasional – yet noticeable – occurrence of such forms even in later West Saxon texts) have been duly noted, and examples have been recorded in our standard grammars of Old English.[183] The most recent editor of the Orosius and the Parker Chronicle has discussed them in great detail on the basis of the full evidence provided by the two manuscripts.[184] It is interesting to see that the conspicuous and somewhat baffling presence of Anglian forms in tenth- (or early-eleventh-) century manuscripts of otherwise West Saxon texts even encouraged a brilliant historical phonologist such as Karl Luick

script, date and localization of these early portions have been discussed comprehensively (and controversially) by Dumville, 'The Anglo-Saxon Chronicle', pp. 55–96.

[181] Cf. Ker, *Catalogue*, pp. 164–6 (no. 133). This manuscript is also written in Anglo-Saxon Square minuscule Phase I and hence, presumably, during the 920s: cf. Dumville, 'Square Minuscule' [*ASE* 16], p. 171.

[182] See Ker, *Catalogue*, pp. 58, 166 and 409 (nos. 39, 133 and 335), Parkes, 'The Palaeography of the Parker Manuscript', p. 154, n. 1, and Dumville, 'The Anglo-Saxon Chronicle', pp. 72–3.

[183] See, for example, the general remarks on the dialect situation in early West Saxon by Campbell, § 17. Both Campbell and Sievers–Brunner record such Anglian forms in West Saxon texts in the course of their discussion of the individual phonemes; cf., for example, SB, § 8, n. 1 and Campbell, § 143: for *a* (instead of *ea*) before *l*+consonant; SB § 101, n. 1 and Campbell § 198: for *oe* (instead of *e*) as a result of i-mutation of *o*; SB, § 104 and Campbell, § 200: for *e* (instead of *ie, i, y*) as a result of i-mutation of *ea*. For a convenient listing of the most conspicuous Anglian dialect features found in West Saxon texts, see also *The Life of St. Chad*, ed. R. Vleeskruyer (Amsterdam, 1953), p. 42, n. 4.

[184] See *The Old English Orosius*, ed. J. Bately, EETS SS 6 (1980), xl–xliv; see also *ibid.*, pp. xlix–li, for non-West Saxon features in the later (s. xi[1]) manuscript, London, BL, Cotton Tiberius B. i, otherwise written in standard Late West Saxon. For the Parker Chronicle, see *The Anglo-Saxon Chronicle MS A*, ed. Bately, pp. cxxxiv and cxxxviii–cxxxix; see also *ibid.*, pp. cxliv–cxlv for non-West Saxon features in the later annals. Non-West Saxon dialect features in the various portions of the Parker Chronicle are also listed by C. Sprockel, *The Language of the Parker Chronicle*, 2 vols. (The Hague, 1965–73).

to the point of suggesting that certain distinctively Anglian sound changes were indigenous as well to some West Saxon dialects.[185]

It would appear, however, that in their attempts to explain Anglicisms in tenth-century West Saxon texts, philologists have not been sufficiently aware of the fact that the 'making of England' under Alfred's successors, Kings Edward the Elder (899–924) and Æthelstan (924–39), opened up a number of fresh avenues for Mercian influence on the affairs of the newly forged kingdom of the Anglo-Saxons. Written evidence for King Edward's reign is comparatively scarce, not least through the absence of any charters for the last fifteen years of his reign (the period between 910 and 924). Nonetheless, there are reasons for thinking that already during the first years of Edward's reign, Mercia was a part of the state ruled over by the king of Wessex;[186] and it is a matter of great interest that a distinctively 'Mercian' style has been detected in some of the (Latin) charters issued during the early years of Edward's reign.[187]

The impact of Mercia and the Mercians is even more manifest in King Æthelstan's reign. According to William of Malmesbury, Æthelstan had been raised at the Mercian court of Æthelred and Æthelflæd.[188] On Edward's death, in 924, he seems to have been elected first king of the Mercians, and with some delay only appears to have succeeded his father as king of the Anglo-Saxons (that is of the Mercians and the West Saxons). During the first years of his reign, Æthelstan's relationship with the West Saxon establishment at Winchester appears to have been rather

---

[185] See Luick, *Historische Grammatik der englischen Sprache*, for example § 146.2 (with respect to *a+l+*consonant), or § 194 (for *e* as a result of i-mutation of *ea*).

[186] For an evaluation of the evidence for King Edward's reign, see Keynes, 'England 900–1016'. That Mercia had been part of the 'kingdom of the Anglo-Saxons' (consisting of 'English' Mercia, Wessex, Kent and Sussex) already during the greater part of King Alfred's reign (from the early 880s onwards) has been demonstrated in an important study by Simon Keynes, which estimates the evidence provided by the Anglo-Saxon Chronicle, charters and ninth-century coinage: 'King Alfred and the Mercians', in *Kings, Currency and Alliances: The History and Coinage of Southern England*, ed. M. A. S. Blackburn and D. N. Dumville (Woodbridge, 1998), pp. 1–45. The article includes a stimulating discussion of the Mercian element in Alfred's court culture which merits close attention by philologists.

[187] See S. Keynes, 'The West Saxon Charters of King Æthelwulf and his Sons', *English Historical Review*, 109 (1994), 1109–49, at 1141–3 and 1145.

[188] Cf. William of Malmesbury, *Gesta regum*, ed. Stubbs I, 145; transl. *EHD*, p. 305 (no. 8).

strained;[189] and one of his most distinctive clerks, the draftsman known as 'Æthelstan A' (who was responsible for drafting the royal diplomas between 928 and 934) seems to have had a recognizable Mercian background.[190] However, it is not only in royal circles and not only in the reigns of Æthelstan and Edward that we should look for close contacts between inhabitants of Wessex and Mercia. For example, Ælfhere, ealdorman of Mercia (956–83), belonged to a family whose members owned estates both in Mercia and Wessex and as a result will have had close ties with both regions.[191]

In short, it is difficult not to think that Mercian influence on the polity of the Anglo-Saxon state in the first decades of the tenth century and beyond should have made itself felt, in one way or another, in contemporary spoken and written English, even if the precise limits of this impact cannot now be defined in every detail. It seems natural that such impact should have resulted in the increased acceptability of Anglian dialect features in West Saxon circles. Presumably such tolerance towards Anglian features would not have been restricted to phonological or morphological peculiarities, but would have included (to some extent at least) the acceptance of Anglian dialect words. In the Junius Psalter, for example (in spite of its 'Saxonized' language), Anglian dialect words have by no means been eliminated in a systematic and consistent fashion.[192] It might be argued that the Junius Psalter by its close affiliation with a

---

[189] On the Mercian component in Æthelstan's reign and the political situation which may have obtained between Edward's death on 17 July 924 and Æthelstan's coronation at Kingston-upon-Thames on 4 September 925, see M. Wood, *In Search of the Dark Ages*, rev. ed. (London, 1987, repr. Harmondsworth, 1994), pp. 125–6, Keynes, 'Æthelstan's Books', pp. 186–7, Yorke, 'Æthelwold and the Politics of the Tenth Century', pp. 69–73, Keynes, *Liber Vitae*, pp. 19–22, *idem*, 'England 900–1016', and see below, n. 190.

[190] On 'Æthelstan A', see above, p. 314, n. 162, and below, pp. 334–5. There will be a comprehensive discussion of the Mercian background of 'Æthelstan A' and the Mercian component in King Æthelstan's reign in a forthcoming publication by S. Keynes (*The Charters of King Æthelstan*). On 'Æthelstan A', see meanwhile Keynes, *Liber Vitae*, p. 22, and *idem*, 'England 900–1016'.

[191] See A. Williams, '*Princeps Merciorum gentis*: the Family, Career and Connections of Ælfhere, Ealdorman of Mercia, 956–83', *ASE* 10 (1982), 143–72, esp. 144–5.

[192] For the treatment of Anglian words in the Junius Psalter, see Wenisch, *Spezifisch anglisches Wortgut*. The retention or substitution in the psalter of the Anglian words discussed by Wenisch in his book may best be traced through the references he gives in his index for 'PsB' (p. 349).

Mercian exemplar is a special case, but it is clear nonetheless that a number of words (such as *dieglan* 'to hide', *blinnan* 'to cease', *feogan* 'to hate', or *snytru* 'wisdom') which occur (occasionally) in early West Saxon texts are, later on, restricted to texts of an Anglian dialect character. This marked difference as regards the distribution of such words in earlier and in later Old English texts has been explained in terms of their development from common Old English words to Anglian dialect words in the course of the tenth century.[193] However, if we give due consideration to the historical context, it seems more reasonable to see here a reflex of the political and social situation which obtained in the first half of the tenth century, and therefore much can be said for assuming that the words in question were Anglian dialect words for the entire span of their existence, and that they were admitted into West Saxon texts more freely anterior to the rise of a West Saxon literary standard, that is up to (say) the 970s.

In any event, for the Junius Psalter the sum of the philological evidence incontestably establishes that its gloss reflects the linguistic situation pertaining to earlier West Saxon texts (and, to some extent perhaps, to spoken West Saxon as well) in the first half of the tenth century. In this connection it is important to add that some tolerance towards Anglian forms can still be detected in the Royal Psalter gloss made two decades or so after the Junius gloss.[194] Phonological Anglicisms were pointed out long ago by Karl Wildhagen, who attributed them to two factors: a lost Anglian exemplar from which (in his view) the Royal gloss was partly derived, and an origin of the gloss at Abingdon, that is, close to Mercian territory.[195] In our discussion of the vocabulary of the Royal gloss, we have noted the occasional occurrence of Anglian

---

[193] See, for example, Wenisch's summary of his findings, pp. 325–6, and cf. *passim*, for the discussion (with further literature) of the individual words listed in the summary as 'Anglian' only from the tenth century onwards.

[194] For example *a* is sometimes retained before *l*+consonant, as in *aldorlicum* (ps. L.14) or *salde* (ps. XV.7); West Germanic *ā* occasionally appears as *ē* (instead of WS.˙ *ǣ*), as in *tobreddest* (ps. IV.2), *spreca* (ps. XI.7) or *geledde* (ps. XVII.20); i-mutation of *ea* sporadically appears as *e* (not *ie*, *i*, or *y*), as in *hehsta* (pss. XLV.5 and XLIX.14), or *eo* appears in lieu of i-mutation of *io* (which would have resulted in *ie*, *i* or *y*), as in *eorre* (ps. LIV.4).

[195] See Wildhagen, 'Studien zum *Psalterium Romanum*', pp. 449–51. For Wildhagen's suggestion of Abingdon as the home of the Royal gloss, see above, pp. 89–90. For the sprinkling of Anglian dialect features in the gloss, see also Sisam, *Salisbury Psalter*, p. 54.

dialect words (see above, pp. 68–71); we also noted that such lexical Anglicisms almost always occur at points where the words in question are also found in the Vespasian Psalter and that, interestingly, they usually can be shown to have been employed for some stylistic reason.

Given the strong Mercian component which prevailed in the affairs of the state during King Æthelstan's reign, what is striking (at first sight) about such Anglian features in the Royal Psalter is not their appearance in a gloss dating from the 940s but that they should occur in a text which seems to be closely connected with Æthelwold, the scholar who is thought to have played a decisive role in the rise of the West Saxon literary standard.[196] However, on account of the political situation it would seem highly unlikely that the deliberate and vigorous propagation of the West Saxon dialect (in a regularized form) as a literary standard all over England could have occurred prior to a date in the 970s without having met resentment in the non-West-Saxon regions of the kingdom; and, even more important, in the 940s the idea of the dominance of a standardized West Saxon over other dialects (Mercian in particular) would, in all probability, have appeared strange to a young scholar raised in the intellectual climate of King Æthelstan's court.[197]

Full discussion of the rise and spread of the Late Old English standard is beyond the scope of the present book, though the question merits fresh and comprehensive consideration. What is clear, however (and what has been thrown into stronger relief in our evaluation of Winchester words in the Royal Psalter), is that the origin of Winchester vocabulary should be seen as quite distinct from the rise of Standard Old English.[198] Winchester vocabulary is not primarily (if at all) concerned with standardization and dialect promotion, but is rather bound up with Benedictine spirituality and a taste for flamboyant experiments with Old English words and the resourcefulness of Old English word-formation;[199]

---

[196] See Gneuss, 'Origin of Standard Old English'.

[197] See below, pp. 332–49, for an evaluation of this intellectual climate and its presumed impact on Æthelwold.

[198] Gneuss made this point clearly in his much-quoted article (above, n. 196), pp. 74–5, 79 and 82, and see his *aggiornamenti* to the article in the reprint, but standard Old English and Winchester vocabulary have been lumped together, more often than not, by scholars referring to this article.

[199] See above, the discussion of the *interpretamenta* for *ecclesia* (pp. 104–13) and *corona* (pp. 98–104 and 297–304), and see below, pp. 410–23, on the Winchester termi-

and (unlike the literary standard) its origin can unequivocally be traced back to the Royal Psalter gloss.

The Junius gloss and the Royal Psalter

What must interest us next is the question of whether the Junius gloss exerted any influence on the gloss in the Royal Psalter. As we have seen, the gloss in Junius 27 is a moderate lexical revision and comprehensive Saxonization of the A-prototype gloss (as represented in Vespasian A. i). It was in existence by *c.* 925 (and presumably not much earlier); and on palaeographical, art historical and philological grounds it is possible that Junius 27 originated at Winchester. By the same token, we have seen that, although the Royal Psalter is a fresh interlinear version of the psalms, there are indisputable indications that the Royal Glossator (of undoubted West Saxon extraction) frequently resorted to an A-type gloss before deciding on his own *interpretamenta*. Since there are reasons for attributing the Royal gloss to Æthelwold and since Æthelwold had been trained at Winchester and had been ordained a priest there (in the 930s), it would be natural to assume that the Junius gloss rather than the Vespasian prototype was the version on which he drew when compiling the Royal gloss.

Unfortunately, the lexical alterations in the Junius Psalter have never been adequately studied. An adequate study would embrace more than mere word-lists compiled for the purpose of assessing textual relationships among psalter glosses. For example, more rewarding (but also much more intractable) questions would be: what were the reviser's aims in substituting lexical items? Why did he substitute some words fairly consistently, and others (apparently) only haphazardly? Was his choice influenced by the immediate context in the psalm or by psalm exegesis? How did he deal with rare words, neologisms, archaisms, or dialect words in his source gloss? How consistent and successful was he in achieving his ends? Do we know of any other Old English texts which show his verbal predilections?[200]

nology for *superbia*. There is little doubt that similar motifs should be sought behind other items of the Winchester vocabulary such as the terms for *terror, timor* or for *uirtus*.

[200] Apart from some useful comments given by Brenner in his word-list (*Junius-Psalter*, pp. xxxvi–xlii), the only attempt at a more thorough study of the lexical alterations in Junius 27 has recently been undertaken by E. Wiesenekker, 'The *Vespasian* and

Pending a thorough investigation of these problems, even a cursory look through Brenner's word-list reveals that the lexical changes in Junius 27 were made by a competent reviser, but that they are in no way striking. Thus it becomes immediately clear that the Royal Glossator could not have found here any models for the poetic or flamboyant coinages for which he had such a great predilection. Furthermore, in the overwhelming majority of instances, the lexical choice of the Royal Glossator (D) differs from the substitutes in the Junius Psalter (B). A few examples would be: ps. XVI.10: *gelynde* B: *fætnys* ł *rysl* D (*adeps*); ps. XXXIV.12: *unwæstmbærnes* B: *stedignis* D (*sterilitas*); pss. L.9 and LXVII.15: *ablæcean* B: *ablican* D (*dealbare*); ps. LI.3: *wea* B: *yfelnesse* D (*malitia*); ps. LXXXII.4: *geswiporlice* B: *gleawlice* D (*astute*); ps. CXIII.1: *elreordig* B: *elþeodig* D (*barbarus*); ps. CXIII.8: *stanclif* B: *clud* D (*rupes*); ps. CXIV.9: *ðeodland* B: *rice* D (*regio*); ps. CXVIII.107: *welgelicwyrðe* B: *gecweme* D; ps. CXL.5: *welgelicwyrðnes* B: *gecwemnes* D (*beneplacitus, -um*); and so on.

It is interesting to note that in certain cases of disagreement, the Royal gloss has (?preserves) the word of the Vespasian Psalter (A). Examples would be: ps. XI.4: *facenful* B: *fæcen* DA (*dolosus*); pss. CIV.29, CXXXIV.11 and CXXXV.18: *cwellan* B: *ofslean* DA (*occidere*); ps. CXV.16:

Junius Psalters Compared: Glossing or Translation?', *Amsterdamer Beiträge zur älteren Germanistik* 40 (1994), 21–39. Unfortunately, this work is severely flawed. Apart from applying an absurdly complex and rigid scheme for evaluating the performance of the Junius reviser (cf. pp. 24–7), an evaluation, moreover, where all the praise goes to a successful 'struggle for greater freedom from the constraints of Latin word structure', and 'a movement towards greater "naturalness"' (p. 27; cf. also p. 23), the article betrays its author's exuberant ignorance in almost every field of Anglo-Saxon studies. The Junius gloss is said to be written 'in uninterrupted, small Anglo-Saxon minuscule' (p. 23). It is stated (p. 23) that the manuscript contains 'no hymns' (that is canticles). The interesting preterite form *slypton* in the Vespasian Psalter is said to derive from *slupan* (p. 36; impossible not only on phonological grounds but for semantic reasons as well; in any case *slypton* is an eleventh-century (!) addition to the text, not part of the original Vespasian gloss). The composite psalter commentary in PL 93, 483–1098 (*CPL*, no. 1384) is attributed wholly and unreservedly to Bede's authorship (e. g. p. 36), and Augustine's *Enarrationes in psalmos* are still quoted from Migne (e. g. p. 36; the CCSL edition (nos. 38–40) being in print since 1956!) And the author duly reports that his search for any influence of Æthelwold's Winchester school has been in vain (p. 35) – in a gloss which must have been in existence by *c.* 925! This list is by no means exhaustive, and many of the blunders found here have survived from Wiesenekker's more comprehensive study on the glosses in the Vespasian, Royal and Lambeth psalters (*Translation Performance*).

tobrecan B: *toslitan* DA (*disrumpere*); pss. CXVIII.131 and CXXXIV.17: *oroð* B: *gast* DA (*spiritus*). In this connection it may be worth mentioning that in Junius 27 the Anglian dialect word *dieglan* 'occultare' is replaced by its West Saxon equivalent *bedieglan* in three of its five occurrences in Vespasian A. i, but in only two of these occurrences in Royal 2. B. V, and that the Old English Rule as well reveals some tolerance towards Anglian *dieglan*: here the term occurs once (BR 28.13).[201]

In those instances where the Royal *interpretamenta* agree with the lexical substitutes in Junius 27, it is always difficult and often impossible to determine whether the Royal Glossator independently chose the word in question or whether he might possibly have consulted the Junius gloss (or a congener), especially when one recalls that he and the Junius reviser were speakers of the same dialect and were approximately coeval. The following are examples where (judged from the distribution and frequency of the shared *interpretamenta* in other texts) it would seem more likely than not that an agreement between the Junius and the Royal psalters does not so much point to a dependence of the Royal Glossator on Junius 27, but rather to a common West Saxon origin and background for both: pss. XVII.7, LIII.9 etc.: *geswinc* BD (*tribulatio*; *geswencednis* A); pss. LXXVII.46, CIV.34 and CVIII.23: *gærstapa* BD (*locusta*; *gershoppe* A); ps. XLII.1: *unryhtwis* BD (*iniquus*; *unreht* A); ps. LXXXVIII.10: *(g)eliðgan* BD (*mitigare*; *gemildgan* A); ps. CVIII.18: *awergednes* B, *awyrgednis* D (*maledictio*; *wergcweodulnis* A) and pss. LXI.5 and CVIII.28: *wergean* B, *wyrian* D (*maledicere*; *wergcweoðan* A); pss. LXXXIX.9, CVI.5 and CXVIII.123: *ateorian* B, *geteorian* D (*deficere*; *aspringan* A) and ps. CXLI.4 *ateorung* B, *geteorung* D (*deficiendum*; *aspringung* A); pss. CI.6 and CXXXVI.6 *ætclifian* B, *ætclifian, geclifian* D (*adherere*; *ætfeolan* A).

Examples where it is just conceivable that the Royal Glossator drew on the Junius gloss (because the agreement between them is of a slightly more striking nature) would be: pss. LVI.9, CVII.3 and CXVIII.148: *dægred* BD (*diluculum*; *ærmargen* A); pss. LXIV.6, LXVI.5 etc. *efnes* B, *efennis* D (*aequitas*; *rehtwisnis* A); ps. LXXVIII.6: *cunnan* BD (*cognoscere*; *oncnawan* A), or ps. LXXXIX.14: *gelustfullian* BD (*delectare*; *geblissian* A). In order to form a more precise notion of the nature of such possible verbal links between Junius 27 and Royal 2. B. V, it would be necessary

---

[201] On the distribution of *dieglan* in Old English texts, see Wenisch, *Spezifisch anglisches Wortgut*, pp. 276–8.

to adjudicate all lexical agreements between Royal 2. B. V and the revised portions of Junius 27 in terms of the frequency and distribution of the words in question in other Old English texts and in terms of their relationship to their Latin lemma, a task which obviously cannot be undertaken here, and which, presumably, would not yield a picture much clearer realized in outline than the one obtained from our preliminary evaluation of the evidence.

To sum up: although it cannot altogether be ruled out that the Royal Glossator, on occasion, drew on the revised A-type psalter gloss as transmitted in Junius 27, it is reasonable to assume that the A-type gloss which he seems to have consulted regularly in the course of his work did not contain the Junius revisions, and was, perhaps, more closely related to Vespasian A. i.[202] Such a result is striking in view of the probable Winchester connections of both psalters and because the revised A-type gloss in Junius 27 did have some impact on later psalter glosses, as is clearly revealed by the glosses in the Bosworth Psalter (BL Add. 37517). The glosses in this psalter exhibit A-type as well as D-type affiliations.[203] As regards the A-type affiliations, the Bosworth glosses are strikingly dependent on specifically Junius readings. This much had been demonstrated already by the editor of the Bosworth glosses, Uno Lindelöf,[204] and has been confirmed by subsequent investigations of psalter relationships.

What is especially remarkable about the Royal Psalter's failure to show any noticeable influence of the Junius gloss, is that such failure squares precisely with the total absence of any influence of the Junius Psalter's illuminations on Æthelwold's Benedictional. The numerous initials in Junius 27, decorated with interlaced acanthus scrolls, animals and animals' heads exerted considerable influence on the initials in later manuscripts (the Bosworth Psalter among them).[205] Though the influence of the Junius Psalter on later Anglo-Saxon manuscript illumination may

---

[202] In this connection, the striking orthographic agreement between Vespasian A. i and Royal 2. B. V concerning the noun should be recalled; see above, p. 38.

[203] See above, pp. 26–7.

[204] See Lindelöf, 'Die altenglischen Glossen im Bosworth-Psalter', pp. 206–24.

[205] For a description of the initials, see Wormald, 'Decorated Initials in English Manuscripts from A. D. 900 to 1100', repr. in his *Collected Writings* I, 47–75 at 55–6. For lists of later manuscripts with initials deriving from the Junius types, see *ibid.*, pp. 72–5. See also Temple, *Anglo-Saxon Manuscripts*, pp. 38–9 (no. 7).

have been considerable, art historians are agreed that zoomorphic interlace initials are conspicuously and deliberately absent from the Benedictional of Æthelwold.[206] It is difficult therefore to escape the conclusion that, for some reason, Bishop Æthelwold ordered the interlace motifs to be suppressed in his Benedictional, just as, at an earlier point in his career, he decided not to incorporate the Junius revisions into his own psalter gloss. But what were his reasons? This question cannot be satisfactorily answered as yet. Art history provides no explanation, nor does the lexicological evidence of the psalter gloss.

At this point, it will be helpful to recall that during the first years of his reign, King Æthelstan apparently met with strong and active resistance from the political and clerical establishment at Winchester (a situation which may well have strengthened the aforementioned Mercian component of his reign).[207] Such dissension becomes palpable, for example, in the conspicuous absence of Frithestan, bishop of Winchester (909–31), not only from the king's coronation at Kingston-upon-Thames in 925, but also from the witness lists of all the charters issued by King Æthelstan, up to 928.[208] It is not now entirely clear what the grounds were for the opposition to Æthelstan, but a memory of faction seems to have lingered on for a surprisingly long time: an account of the early history of the New Minster (composed 988 × 990 and subsequently incorporated, as an introduction, into the *Liber Vitae* of the New Minster (now London, BL, Stowe 944), written in 1031) makes no mention at all of King Æthelstan.[209] This historical evidence may allow us to infer that Æthelwold, whose loyalties during his early Winchester years will have lain with the royal court rather than with one of the

---

[206] See Temple, *Anglo-Saxon Manuscripts*, p. 52 (no. 23), Alexander, 'The Benedictional of St Æthelwold', pp. 174 and 181–2, and Deshman, *Benedictional*, pp. 248–9 and 252. It is interesting to note that zoomorphic interlace motifs are conspicuously absent also from the donor portrait in the New Minster Foundation Charter (Vespasian A. viii, 2v: see Deshman, *Benedictional*, p. 233; for reproductions of 2v see, for example, *ibid.*, figs. 135 and 143. For Æthelwold as the probable author of this charter, see above, pp. 125, 236–7 and 309–10.

[207] For this opposition, see above, pp. 321–2 and n. 189, and cf. Keynes, 'England 900–1016', *idem*, *Liber Vitae*, pp. 19–21, and Yorke, 'Æthelwold and the Politics of the Tenth Century', pp. 71–3.

[208] Cf. Keynes, *Liber Vitae*, pp. 20–1.

[209] See *ibid.*, p. 21; for the date of the historical account, see *ibid.*, pp. 82 and 31–2. For the date of the *Liber Vitae*, see *ibid.*, pp. 66–7.

minsters,[210] might have rejected the Junius Psalter in its entirety because of this manuscript's association with the one minster or the other.

If we pursue this hypothesis a step further, Æthelwold's presumed rejection of the Junius Psalter and his apparently lifelong fascination with the Galba Psalter (both revealed in his Benedictional) might in effect be closely connected. If Galba A. xviii did belong to the royal household (and we have seen that there are grounds for this supposition), for young Æthelwold this must have implied a great respect and deep veneration for the manuscript. Such respect and veneration will even have been increased, if (as seems plausible) the manuscript came to the notice of the renowned continental scholar Israel the Grammarian who (while temporarily domiciled at Æthelstan's court) had entered in it some material in Greek, the language which will have held an immense attraction for a young scholar who was to become one of the principal proponents of the hermeneutic style in tenth-century Anglo-Latin.

If these inferences can be accepted, they would not only shed light on the political and intellectual influences which Æthelwold underwent in his formative years; they would also enable certain deductions to be made concerning the manuscripts themselves and the authorship of the Royal Psalter gloss. As regards the manuscripts, the ascription of Junius 27 and Galba A. xviii to Winchester (for which much can be said on palaeographical and art historical grounds) could be confirmed by the response which these manuscripts elicited from Winchester's pre-eminent bishop in the tenth century, a man who had lived through his childhood and adolescence in this city. What we may suspect about the political situation obtaining at Winchester in the 920s, in combination with what knowledge we have of the early stages of Æthelwold's career, could explain why he responded in such different ways to both manuscripts. This in turn could corroborate the association of Galba A. xviii with Æthelstan's household and of Junius 27

---

[210] Æthelwold cannot have been ordained priest before 934, the year of Bishop Ælfheah's accession. Before his consecration, Æthelwold will have belonged to King Æthelstan's immediate entourage, where his standing seems to have been somewhat more than that of an obscure youth, since he apparently enjoyed some kind of political training by the king's powerbrokers, and since Æthelstan himself twice interfered in young Æthelwold's career (see *Wulfstan: Life*, chs. 7 (p. 10) and 9 (p. 14)).

with Bishop Frithestan[211] and, perhaps, the Old Minster.[212] As regards the Royal Psalter gloss, Æthelwold's involvement in that gloss would help to explain the circumstance, otherwise exceedingly curious, that a highly competent and scholarly West Saxon glossator, who apparently had frequent recourse to an A-type gloss, did not (to any noticeable extent) make use of a revised and Saxonized version of the A-type gloss antedating his own by only fifteen years or so, and transmitted in an otherwise influential manuscript.

In cases of suspected authorship, certainty drawn from external evidence is not obtainable where a text of such paramount and universal importance as the psalter is in question. Nonetheless, our exploration of such evidence has enabled us to uncover a number of suggestive possibilities and links of various kinds: historical, art historical, liturgical, textcritical and palaeographical. This various evidence combines to reinforce and extend the hypothesis suggested by the verbal and stylistic links of the Royal Psalter gloss. On grounds of these distinctive verbal links, judged in combination with the various kinds of external evidence, Æthelwold has strong claims to be considered the principal author of the Royal Psalter gloss. It is time now to turn to what external evidence there may be, which points to an involvement of Æthelwold and his circle in vernacular Aldhelm glossing.

[211] For grounds of associating Junius 27 with Frithestan, see Parkes, 'The Palaeography of the Parker Manuscript', pp. 159–60, and Wormald, '"The Winchester School" before St Ethelwold', in his *Collected Writings* I, 77–8.

[212] Concerning a dissension between the royal court and the Winchester establishment, manifest in Bishop Frithestan's conspicuous absence from the royal entourage, we should bear in mind that this holds true only for the years 924–7. Bishop Frithestan appears to have established good relations between the clergy of the minsters and the royal court during King Edward's reign (899–924); cf. Keynes, *Liber Vitae*, pp. 18–19. And eventually matters seem to have been straightened out also in Æthelstan's reign, since Frithestan reappears among the king's councillors from 928 until his retirement in 931; cf. Keynes, *Liber Vitae*, pp. 21–2. By the same token, it should be borne in mind that links between Galba A. xviii and Junius 27 do exist. Such links are of an art historical and textual nature; cf., for example, Temple, *Anglo-Saxon Manuscripts*, p. 39 (no. 7) for the art historical links. The textual links concern the so-called 'Metrical Calendar of Hampson', contained in the earliest (s. x^in) English additions to Galba A. xviii, and (in fragmentary form) in Junius 27; see Lapidge, 'Tenth-Century Metrical Calendar', pp. 360–2, and P. McGurk, 'The Metrical Calendar of Hampson', *Analecta Bollandiana* 104 (1986), 79–125, at 84–5.

9

Æthelwold and the Aldhelm glosses

In our search for non-linguistic evidence which could confirm the suspicion (grounded on lexical and stylistic considerations) that Æthelwold played a leading part in vernacular Aldhelm glossing, we must first address a question which thus far has not been satisfactorily answered, namely in what historical and intellectual context the origins of the late Anglo-Saxon fascination with Aldhelm and the hermeneutic style may be sought.

KING ÆTHELSTAN'S COURT

The resuscitation of the hermeneutic style first becomes tangible during the reign of Æthelstan (924–39), the first monarch to rule over a unified England and the first to extend the territory of a southern king beyond the Humber. From Æthelstan's charters and his coinage, where, from 927 onwards (after the annexation of Northumbria), he is referred to by the royal style *rex totius Britanniae*, or by some similar formula, it is abundantly clear that the king and his entourage were well aware and proud of what had been achieved.[1] It may not be out of question,

---

[1] For an overview and an evaluation of the evidence for Æthelstan's reign, see Stenton, *Anglo-Saxon England*, pp. 339–57, Keynes 'England 900–1016', and Dumville, *Wessex and England*, pp. 141–71. For Æthelstan's imperial aspirations, see esp. Wood, 'The Making of King Æthelstan's Empire'. For the coinage, see C. E. Blunt, B. H. I. H. Stewart and C. S. S. Lyon, *Coinage in Tenth-Century England from Edward the Elder to Edgar's Reform* (Oxford, 1989), pp. 108–12 and 266–8, and C. E. Blunt, 'The Coinage of Æthelstan, King of England, 924–39', *British Numismatic Journal*, 42 (1974), 35–160, esp. 55–6. Æthelstan's charters are listed in Sawyer, *Anglo-Saxon Charters*, nos. 386–438; for the distinctive character of some of these, see below. For the revival of

therefore, to suspect that, from its beginnings, there was a strong political and national component in the tenth-century revival of the hermeneutic style. After all, Aldhelm (*c.* 640–709 × 710), the principal source of inspiration for tenth-century Anglo-Latinity,[2] was an author who had been held in great esteem and had been much imitated by Anglo-Saxon (and continental) writers[3] before the production of Latin literature seems to have come to a complete standstill in England in the wake of the Viking depredations in the ninth century. And it is interesting to note that, apparently, Aldhelm's works were among the earliest books which were re-imported from the Continent for the restocking of English libraries from the times of King Alfred onwards,[4] and that King Alfred

Latin scholarship during Æthelstan's reign, see Lapidge, 'Schools, Learning and Literature', pp. 18–24. A still valuable introduction to the intellectual attainments of Æthelstan's reign is Robinson, *The Times of Saint Dunstan*, pp. 25–80. For the intellectual atmosphere at Æthelstan's court as revealed by his donations of books to various institutions in his kingdom, see Keynes, 'Æthelstan's Books', pp. 143–201. See also below, pp. 384–5 and n. 3.

[2] For the principal sources of the tenth-century hermeneutic style in England, see Lapidge 'Hermeneutic Style', pp. 107–15 and 139. In brief, apart from Aldhelm's writings, the most important are the third book of Abbo of St Germain-des-Prés, *Bella Parisiacae urbis*, and lexical material drawn from Latin–Latin and Latin–Greek glossaries, as printed by Goetz, *Corpus Glossariorum*; many more such glossaries still await publication.

[3] For Aldhelm's influence on eighth- and ninth-century Anglo-Saxon (and continental) authors, see Lapidge, *Aldhelm: the Prose Works*, transl. Lapidge and Herren, pp. 1–3, and *idem*, *Aldhelm: the Poetic Works*, transl. Lapidge and Rosier, pp. 1–4. The influence of Aldhelm's poetic works on pre-tenth-century Anglo-Latin literature has been comprehensively treated by Orchard, *Poetic Art of Aldhelm*, pp. 242–68 and 274–80.

[4] Two such manuscripts containing works by Aldhelm are still extant: Oxford, Bodleian Library, Rawlinson C. 697, containing the *Carmen de uirginitate* and the *Enigmata*, written somewhere in northeastern Francia in the third quarter of the ninth century (the earliest copy of the *Carmen* surviving from Anglo-Saxon England; for this manuscript, see below, pp. 350–1); and London, BL, Royal 15. A. XVI; containing, *inter alia*, the *Enigmata*, written in the last quarter of the ninth century or *c.* 900 in northwestern Francia ('Kanalküste' or, possibly, England according to Bernhard Bischoff); my information is drawn from materials for Gneuss, 'Handlist'. For these manuscripts, cf. also Lapidge, *Aldhelm: the Prose Works*, pp. 2 and 180, n. 15. For the state of the Anglo-Saxon libraries in the ninth century, see H. Gneuss, 'King Alfred and the History of Anglo-Saxon Libraries' in his *Books and Libraries*, no. III, 29–49 (orig. publ. 1986), as well as M. Lapidge, 'Latin Learning in Ninth-Century England', in his *Anglo-Latin Literature 600–899*, pp. 409–54; for an assessment of the textual transmission of Anglo-Latin works written before the ninth century, see *ibid.*, pp. 417–25.

himself (according to William of Malmesbury)[5] venerated Aldhelm as the greatest of all poets in vernacular Old English. No Old English poetry by Aldhelm has survived or has been identified. It has, however, incontestably been demonstrated that Aldhelm's Latin poetry was profoundly influenced by the principles of Old English metrical composition.[6]

'*Æthelstan A*'

The flair which Æthelstan and his circle had for the hermeneutic, 'Aldhelmian' style, makes itself felt most impressively in his diplomatic. A substantial portion of the charters issued in the king's name (more than half of these) are composed in almost impenetrable Latin. Their proems consist of long convoluted sentences, parading an ostentatious display of Greek and glossary-based vocabulary and containing numerous unmistakable verbal reminiscences of Aldhelm's writings. Nothing similar had previously been attempted in Anglo-Saxon diplomatic and although, later in the tenth century, other charters affecting the hermeneutic style were composed, the ferocious lexical and syntactic difficulties of these Æthelstan charters were never to be surpassed. All the charters in question were drafted by a single royal scribe, known to students of Anglo-Saxon diplomatic as 'Æthelstan A'. It is, perhaps, significant that 'Æthelstan A' can be first seen at work in 928, that is within a few months after the 'making of England' had been achieved. He is subsequently responsible for the drafting of all surviving charters up to 934 (eighteen in total, two of these preserved as original single sheet charters). In 935 he was joined by one or several colleagues; in this year he drafted three more charters, and thereafter his career came to an end.[7]

---

[5] *Gesta pontificum*, ed. Hamilton V, § 190 (p. 336).

[6] See Lapidge, 'Aldhelm's Latin Poetry', esp. pp. 261–9, and Orchard, *Poetic Art of Aldhelm*, esp. chs. 2 and 3.

[7] The term 'Æthelstan A' was coined by Drögereit, who made the first detailed analysis of this scribe's charters; see 'Angelsächsische Königskanzlei', esp. pp. 345–8, 361–9, 410–13, 418–22, 428 and 431. A fresh and comprehensive study of 'Æthelstan A's' activities (and of the entire corpus of King Æthelstan's diplomas) by S. Keynes is in preparation: *The Charters of King Æthelstan* (forthcoming). I am immensely grateful to Simon Keynes for letting me have a draft version of his monograph. For a brief evaluation of 'Æthelstan A's', work, see meanwhile Keynes, 'England 900–1016'; see also *idem*, *Diplomas*, pp. 16 and 43–4, and *idem*, *Atlas of Attestations*, table xxvii. The surviving original single sheet charters drafted by 'Æthelstan A' are S 416 (BCS 677)

In view of the fact that Æthelwold, the future glossator of the Royal Psalter, presumably lived at Æthelstan's court while 'Æthelstan A' was active, it is perhaps interesting to remark that, on the evidence of the 'Æthelstan A' charters, the king seems to have attached special importance to psalmody (or that 'Æthelstan A' let the king appear to have done so). Whatever the case, it is noteworthy that in three charters drafted by 'Æthelstan A' in favour of a religious community, the members of that community are required regularly to sing a certain number of psalms for the king in return for the land they had received.[8] Such a request for special psalmody for the king occurs only in the 'Æthelstan A' charters. In charters of Æthelstan other than those drafted by 'Æthelstan A', and in favour of a religious community, that community is sometimes required to say unspecified prayers for the king, but no mention is made of any special psalmody.[9] In any event, these stipulations concerning the recital of the psalter in return for a grant of land should by all means be included among the 'English sources' of the *Regularis concordia*. Bishop Æthelwold no doubt will have recalled such stipulations when he himself instituted the numerous additional psalms to be chanted daily for the king, queen and benefactors of the house.

To return to the sources of the hermeneutic revival in the tenth century: important as the 'national' component may have been, that is, the affection of a style associated with a glorious intellectual past in order to boost what was conceived as a glorious military and political achievement, the continental component in the revival should not be overlooked.

---

and S 425 (BCS 702). For the Latinity of the charters, see Drögereit, 'Angelsächsische Königskanzlei', pp. 361–9, and Lapidge, 'Schools, Learning and Literature', pp. 20–1. For the hermeneutic style in these and other tenth-century diplomas, see *idem*, 'Hermeneutic Style', pp. 137–9, and Bullough, 'The Educational Tradition', pp. 302–8. Much of value concerning the style of the tenth-century diplomatic is still to be found in Drögereit, 'Angelsächsische Königskanzlei'. There will be a comprehensive analysis of the style and structure of Æthelstan's charters in Keynes, *The Charters of King Æthelstan*.

[8] The charters in question are S 419 (dated 932: the nuns of Shaftesbury are requested to sing fifty psalms and say mass for the king every day), S 422 and S 423 (both dated 933 and both in favour of Sherborne abbey: the community is requested to sing the entire psalter for the king once a year, on All Saints' Day).

[9] Cf., for example, S 429 (dated 935, to Shaftesbury abbey), S 438 (dated 937, to Wilton abbey) or S 432 (dated 937, to the church at Athelney).

The continental background

On several occasions, Michael Lapidge has drawn attention to the continental background and impetus for tenth-century Anglo-Latinity, thereby pointing out that, for example, the cultivation of the hermeneutic style in northern Francia in the early tenth century is noteworthy.[10] It may also be noteworthy that Aldhelm himself appears to have been indebted primarily to continental (rather than Irish) models for the peculiarities of his style.[11] This continental background and impetus is tangible as well at King Æthelstan's court. We do not know for certain who 'Æthelstan A' was, whether of English or foreign extraction, although the boundary clauses in his two surviving single sheet charters, written in impeccable Old English, would seem to indicate an Englishman; but we do have knowledge of the presence of a substantial number of foreigners at Æthelstan's court, some of them scholars who demonstrably were practitioners of the hermeneutic style. In connection with Galba A. xviii (the Æthelstan Psalter), we already have had occasion briefly to discuss the activities of one of these continental scholars, namely Israel the Grammarian (above, pp. 313–15). We have seen there that Israel (presumably a Breton by birth) had a clear penchant for the hermeneutic style. This penchant is revealed in a small dossier of texts which may reasonably be associated with his name; some of these texts (liturgical material in Greek) were probably entered in the Æthelstan Psalter at some point during his presumed stay at the king's court. We have further seen that Israel may have been responsible for copying into this manuscript the Romana series of psalter collects, notable for their *style fleuri*, and that there is a tantalizing verbal link (the adverb *tanaliter*) between one of the poems in Israel's dossier and one of 'Æthelstan A's' charters. In other words, there can be little doubt that Israel should be reckoned among the progenitors of the hermeneutic style at Æthelstan's court.

And there were others, even though their personalities and association with Æthelstan's court circles as yet remain more shadowy than Israel's.

---

[10] See Lapidge, 'Hermeneutic Style', p. 111; see further *idem*, 'Latin Poems as Evidence', pp. 85–6, and *idem*, 'L'influence stylistique de la poésie de Jean Scot', in *Jean Scot Érigène et l'histoire de la philosophie*, Colloques internationaux du Centre National de la Recherche Scientifique 561 (Paris, 1977), 441–52.

[11] See Winterbottom, 'Aldhelm's Prose Style', esp. pp. 46–70.

The continental scribe (coming probably from north or northeast Francia) who copied and, one may suspect, also composed the poem to commemorate Æthelstan's donation of a lavish gospelbook (now London, BL, Cotton Tiberius A. ii) to Christ Church, Canterbury, would presumably be one of these scholars. The poem (*Rex pius Æðelstan*) is written in hermeneutic Latin; it is preserved on what is now 15r of Tiberius A. ii. However, since 15v bears a prose dedication for the gospelbook, this folio was evidently once a flyleaf to the volume, presumably added at the time of Æthelstan's donation. Tiberius A. ii. is a continental manuscript (written in the late ninth or early tenth century, possibly at Lobbes (Belgium)). It probably came into Æthelstan's possession as a gift from the German emperor Otto I (936–73) in the context of Otto's marriage proceedings with Æthelstan's half-sister Eadgyth in 929 or thereabouts.[12] Æthelstan's donation of the manuscript, and hence the date of the poem (which commends his donation and refers to Æthelstan as still living) can therefore be established between 929 and 939, the king's death. On internal evidence from the poem, this date may perhaps be narrowed down to 937 × 939, that is after the battle of Brunanburh.[13] There are reasons for assuming that *Rex pius Æðelstan* was composed at Canterbury, and hence outside Æthelstan's immediate court circle.[14] This does not preclude, however, that the poet, at one stage of his career, did belong to Æthelstan's entourage. In the context of tenth-century England, we have constantly to be aware that a scribe or scholar could be active at various places. This much can, for example, be demonstrated unequivocally in the case of the scribe who (on 15v of Tiberius A. ii) recorded Æthelstan's donation in prose, and who (on the evidence of the poem) at this point of his career was working at Christ Church. However, this scribe also wrote

---

[12] For a comprehensive discussion of the circumstances in which Tiberius A. ii may have come to Æthelstan and in which it was subsequently given by him to the Christ Church community, see Keynes, 'Æthelstan's Books', pp. 147–53. The poem *Rex pius Æðelstan* is printed (with translation) most recently, and fully discussed, by Lapidge, 'Latin Poems as Evidence', pp. 81–5; see also *idem*, 'Schools, Learning and Literature', p. 22. For a facsimile of the poem, see Keynes, 'Æthelstan's Books', pl. iv.

[13] Cf. Lapidge, 'Latin Poems as Evidence', p. 85, n. 158. On palaeographical grounds, the prose dedication (written by an English scribe in Anglo-Saxon Square minuscule, Phase II) can also be dated to Æthelstan's reign: see Dumville, 'Square Minuscule' [*ASE* 16], p. 175.

[14] See Lapidge, *Anglo-Latin Literature 900–1066*, p. 472 (*aggiornamento* to 'Latin Poems as Evidence').

several charters issued in the names of kings Edmund and Eadred between
944 and 949, when presumably he was one of the royal scribes, attached
to the king's court.[15] By the same token, the foreign scholar who very
possibly composed *Rex pius Æðelstan* may be identical with a continental
scholar named Petrus who almost certainly belonged to King Æthelstan's
entourage on his campaign to Northumbria in 927, an expedition which
resulted in Æthelstan gaining supremacy over all England, after a
meeting with the northern leaders *æt Eamotum* on 12 July.[16] This Peter
probably composed the poem *Carta dirige gressus*, commemorating Æthelstan's achievement of the political unity of England. *Carta dirige gressus* is
modelled on a poem addressed to Charlemagne and gives us therefore an
intriguing glimpse of Æthelstan's imperial aspirations.[17] Whether or not
this Peter was also the author of *Rex pius Æðelstan*, there can be little
doubt that this recherché and difficult poem, abounding in praise not
only of Æthelstan's generosity to Christ Church, but also of his achievements as a Christian king and military leader, will have been known and
approved of in court circles. The following quotation of the opening lines
of the poem will give an impression of its style and nature:

> Rex pius Æðelstan, patulo famosus in orbe,
>> cuius ubique uiget gloria lausque manet,
> quem Deus Angligenis solii fundamine nixum
>> constituit regem terrigenisque ducem,
> scilicet ut ualeat reges rex ipse feroces
>> uincere bellipotens, colla superba terens.
>
> (Holy king Athelstan, renowned through the wide world,
> whose esteem flourishes and whose honour endures everywhere,
> whom God set as king over the English, sustained by the foundation

---

[15] See Keynes, 'Æthelstan's Books', pp. 149–50.

[16] The meeting *æt Eamotum* (a place not securely identified) is recorded by the *Anglo-Saxon Chronicle* (D), s. a. 926; for possible locations, see Lapidge, 'Latin Poems as Evidence', p. 79, n. 140; see also below, p. 365.

[17] The poem *Carta dirige gressus* is discussed, printed, translated and tentatively restored from the two rather garbled copies which have survived (London, BL, Cotton Nero A. ii, 10v–11v, and Durham, Cathedral Library, A. II. 17, pt. i, 31v) by Lapidge, 'Latin Poems as Evidence', pp. 71–81 and 86. It had previously been printed on several occasions, see *ibid.*, p. 71, nn. 104 and 105. For Petrus and his identity, see *ibid.*, pp. 80–1; for a tentative attribution of *Rex pius Æðelstan* to this Petrus, cf. *ibid.*, p. 85, and Lapidge, 'Schools, Learning and Literature', p. 18.

of the throne, and as leader of [His] earthly forces,
plainly so that this king himself, mighty in war, might be able
to conquer other fierce kings, treading down their proud necks)[18]

A further witness to the enthusiasm for the hermeneutic style at
Æthelstan's court could be the poem in praise of Æthelstan which
William of Malmesbury reports to have seen 'in quodam sane uolumine
uetusto' ('in a certain obviously ancient book').[19] Concerning this poem
many questions are now unanswerable. What is clear, however, is that the
'ancient' poem which William adverts to, and the one from which he
quotes extensively in his account of King Æthelstan, are not identical.[20]
What is also clear from William's remarks about the 'ancient' poem, and
what must concern us here, is that this poem was composed in
hermeneutic Latin and that King Æthelstan is referred to as still living.[21]
We do not know who the author of William's 'ancient' poem was,
whether one of the foreign scholars in Æthelstan's entourage or some
Englishman in his service, or someone else. Michael Lapidge has
conjectured that William's 'ancient' poem might be identical with the
acrostic on Æthelstan composed probably by John the Old Saxon (on
which see below).[22] It might be identical with this acrostic, but it need
not be so, in which case William of Malmesbury's 'ancient' poem – even
though now irrecoverably lost – would nonetheless furnish additional
evidence that the hermeneutic style was practised at Æthelstan's court.

Oda

In connection with the hermeneutic revival in Æthelstan's entourage, a
further scholar, this time of English (or rather Anglo-Danish) extraction,

---

[18] Text (lines 1–6) and translation quoted from Lapidge, 'Latin Poems as Evidence',
pp. 83–4.

[19] See William of Malmesbury, *Gesta regum*, ed. Stubbs I, 144. William's account of King
Æthelstan is translated *EHD*, pp. 303–10 (no. 8); the quotation is *ibid.*, p. 305.

[20] The poem from which William quotes *in extenso* (*Gesta regum* I, 145–6 and 151–2) no
doubt is more or less contemporary with William himself and hence of early-twelfth-
century date, as M. Lapidge has demonstrated, thereby depriving historians of their
long-cherished notion that William's quotations supply important tenth-century
evidence (not found elsewhere) for Æthelstan's reign; see Lapidge, 'Latin Poems as
Evidence', pp. 50–9; see also Keynes, 'Æthelstan's Books', pp. 144–5, n. 15.

[21] *Gesta regum*, ed. Stubbs I, 144.   [22] See Lapidge, 'Latin Poems as Evidence', p. 52.

should be mentioned: Oda, bishop of Ramsbury in Wiltshire (*c.* 909 × 927–941) and archbishop of Canterbury (941–58).[23] Our principal source for pre-Conquest information on Oda is the lengthy account given by Byrhtferth of Ramsey in the first part of his *Vita S. Oswaldi*.[24] Unfortunately, Byrhtferth's chief aim in this work was clearly not historical accuracy and, consequently, many details of Oda's life and career can now be only dimly perceived.[25] Concerning his relationship with King Æthelstan, it seems probable that Oda was promoted to the see of Ramsbury at some point early in Æthelstan's reign (*c.* 926).[26] We have a late-tenth-century record that, while bishop of Ramsbury, Oda was sent by the king to Francia on a diplomatic mission on at least one occasion, perhaps in 936.[27] Whatever the precise nature of his relationship to the

---

[23] On Oda's career, see Brooks, *Early History*, pp. 222–7, and J. A. Robinson, *St Oswald and the Church of Worcester*, British Academy Supplemental Papers 5 (London, 1919), 38–51.

[24] The *Vita S. Oswaldi* is edited by Raine, *Historians* I, 399–475; the section on Oda is at pp. 401–10. A new edition of the *Vita* by M. Lapidge is forthcoming: *Byrhtferth of Ramsey: the Lives of Oswald and Ecgwine*, Oxford Medieval Texts.

[25] For an account of what were Byrhtferth's principal aims when writing the *Vita S. Oswaldi*, and for evidence of his disregard for historical veracity, see Lapidge, 'Byrhtferth and Oswald', pp. 64–83; regarding Oda, cf. esp. pp. 66–8.

[26] See Brooks, *Early History*, p. 222, and Lapidge, 'Byrhtferth and Oswald', pp. 67–8. The dates for Oda's promotion to Ramsbury (*c.* 909 × 927) given by Keynes, 'Episcopal Succession', p. 220 rest on (scarce) charter evidence (cf. S 400) and our information concerning the establishment of the diocese of Ramsbury at some point during the reign of Edward the Elder (899–924).

[27] The presumption is that this embassy should negotiate the terms for a return of Louis d'Outremer (Æthelstan's nephew) to Francia from his temporary exile at his uncle's court. The source for Oda's mission is Richer of Rheims, *Historiae* II, 4 (ed. R. Latouche, *Histoire de France, 888–995*, 2 vols. (Paris 1930–7) I, 130), written in the 990s. The information has generally been accepted as authentic; see, for example, Brooks, *Early History*, p. 222 and p. 371, n. 47, and Lapidge, 'Schools, Learning and Literature', pp. 28–9. Recently, however, Oda's mission has been questioned on grounds of its being recorded solely in a source which is not considered very reliable; see D. Bullough, 'St Oswald: Monk, Bishop and Archbishop', in *St Oswald of Worcester*, ed. Brooks and Cubitt, pp. 1–22, at 5, n. 20. That Richer was not above 'embellishing' historical facts with materials drawn, *inter alia*, from epic or other narrative sources has been pointed out in some detail already by Manitius, *Geschichte der lateinischen Literatur des Mittelalters* II, 214–19; see also the brief but judicious evaluation of Richer's work by M. Bur, *LkMA* VII (1994), 830–1. It should be noted, however, that Richer reports his father to have been a *miles* (of some standing,

king and his circle may have been, there can be no doubt that Oda was a fervent admirer and practitioner of the hermeneutic style. This much is revealed by the fact that, as archbishop of Canterbury, he commissioned Frithegod, a West Frankish scholar temporarily staying in his household, to compose a metrical contrafactum to Stephen of Ripon's early-eighth-century prose *Vita S. Wilfridi*. This *Breuiloquium uitae Wilfridi* of some 1400 hexameters, which Frithegod duly produced (948 × 958), has been called 'one of the most brilliantly ingenious – but also damnably difficult – Latin products of Anglo-Saxon England.'[28] Archbishop Oda composed a short prose preface to Frithegod's poem, which shows that he was in a position fully to match his protégé's stylistic aspirations. Like Frithegod's, Oda's hermeneutic style is characterized by an extremely recondite vocabulary, bristling with Greek-based arcane words, many of them neologisms.[29] No Latin writings by Oda before his Canterbury period (that is, after Æthelstan's death) have survived, but it may not be unreasonable to suspect that his profound predilection for the hermeneutic style originated in the flamboyant and cosmopolitan days of King Æthelstan.

The Alfredian roots

Astonishing as this burgeoning of hermeneutic writings during Æthelstan's reign may appear, there were harbingers, and the roots of the movement must be sought out two generations earlier, among the foreign scholars assembled at the court of Alfred the Great (871–99). We have

---

apparently) in the personal retinue of King Louis IV, d'Outremer, the very king with whose return to Francia Oda's mission is assumed to have been concerned (cf. *Historiae* II, 87, ed. Latouche I, 274).

[28] The poem has been edited most recently by Campbell, *Frithegodi monachi Breuiloquium*, pp. 1–62. For the style and transmission of the poem and a reconstruction of Frithegod's career, see Lapidge, 'A Frankish Scholar', pp. 157–81; the above quotation is found *ibid.*, p. 158. For Frithegod's style, see also Lapidge, 'Hermeneutic Style', pp. 116–19, and *idem*, 'Schools, Learning and Literature', pp. 29–30.

[29] The preface has been printed by Campbell, *Frithegodi monachi Breuiloquium*, pp. 1–3; for Oda's style, see Lapidge, 'Hermeneutic Style', pp. 115–16. The close stylistic agreement between Oda's preface and the *Breuiloquium* may suggest that Frithegod also composed the preface; in which case it would still be significant that the preface is written in Oda's name and that Oda commissioned Frithegod's poem; see also below, pp. 371–2.

seen (above, p. 334) that King Alfred felt a great veneration for Aldhelm, and it is possible therefore that the Latin texts to which the more advanced students in his palace school had to apply their ingenuity included works by Aldhelm.[30] As regards any literary activities of Alfred's helpers in which an Aldhelmian and hermeneutic flavour might be detected, one thinks, perhaps, first of Bishop Asser's biography of the king. There are verbal echoes of Aldhelm's writings in Asser's *Life of King Alfred*, and the hermeneutic features in Asser's style have recently deluded a modern historian to the point of declaring this work a product of the late tenth or early eleventh century and attributing it to Byrhtferth of Ramsey.[31] One might further mention that among the charters issued in King Alfred's name, there is, perhaps, one which by its ambitious vocabulary adumbrates the diction of the Æthelstan charters.[32] Of especial interest, however, for a link between Alfred's reign and Æthelstan's court circles are three acrostic poems, probably composed by John the Old Saxon, the continental scholar who helped Alfred with his translations and whom the king, at some unspecified point, installed as abbot of Athelney.[33] Two of these acrostic poems are on King Alfred himself, while the third, written in hermeneutic Latin, is addressed to his grandson Æthelstan.[34] The Æthelstan acrostic perhaps commemorates an

[30] For instruction in Latin in Alfred's school, see the king's own preface to his translation of the *Regula pastoralis*, ed. Sweet I, 7; see also Bishop Asser's *Life of King Alfred* (ed. Stevenson), ch. 75 (p. 58); transl. Keynes and Lapidge, *Alfred the Great*, p. 90.

[31] For an edition of Asser's *Life*, see n. 30 above. On Asser's Latin style and 'hermeneutic' flair, see most recently, Keynes and Lapidge, *Alfred the Great*, pp. 54–5 and 221–2. The absurd attribution of Asser's *Life* to Byrhtferth is found in A. P. Smyth, *King Alfred the Great* (Oxford, 1995), pp. 271–367.

[32] S 346; the charter is preserved only in the late-eleventh-century Worcester cartulary; for its Latinity, see Lapidge, 'Schools, Learning and Literature', p. 10, n. 25.

[33] Asser (*Life* (ed. Stevenson), ch. 94 (p. 81); transl. Keynes and Lapidge, *Alfred the Great*, p. 103) says that John was of 'Eald-Saxonum genere', that is, his native language would presumably have been Old Saxon. It is not known from where on the Continent, whether from Saxon territory or from somewhere else, John came to England. On John as the king's assistant, see Alfred's preface to his translation of the *Regula pastoralis* (ed. Sweet I, 7). On his somewhat tumultuous and, perhaps, only brief abbacy, see Asser, *Life*, chs. 94–7.

[34] The three acrostics are printed, translated and discussed by Lapidge, 'Latin Poems as Evidence', pp. 60–71. The ascription to John (which is suggested there) is entirely plausible, *inter alia*, because the right-hand legend of the third acrostic spells out the name Iohannes (extremely rare in Insular sources), and because their contents give

event from the future king's childhood, while Alfred was still alive, and it would accordingly have been composed between *c.* 894 and 899.[35] In any event, it is clear from the wording of the poem that the addressee is of tender age. The poem is as follows:

> 'Archalis' clamare, triumuir, nomine 'saxI'.
> Diue tuo fors prognossim feliciter aeuO
> 'August*a*' Samu- cernentis 'rupis' eris -elH,
> Laruales forti beliales robure contrA.
> Saepe seges messem fecunda prenotat altam; iN
> Tutis solandum petrinum solibus agmeN.
> Amplius amplificare sacra sophismatis arcE.
> Nomina orto- petas donet, precor, inclita -doxuS.

> (You, prince, are called by the name of 'sovereign stone'.
> Look happily on this prophecy for your age:
> You shall be the 'noble rock' of Samuel the Seer,
> [Standing] with mighty strength against devilish demons.
> Often an abundant cornfield foretells a great harvest; in
> Peaceful days your stony mass is to be softened.
> You are more abundantly endowed with the holy eminence of learning.
> I pray that you may seek, and the Glorious One may grant, the [fulfilment implied in your] noble names.)[36]

This eight-line acrostic is the earliest poem written in hermeneutic Latin which has survived from the period after the Viking incursions, and it is addressed to a child, then perhaps no more than five years old, who, in due course, was to become the first patron of hermeneutic literature in tenth-century England.

This link between King Alfred's court and that of his grandson stands even more prominently in view when we consider the manuscript transmission of John's three acrostics. The two Alfred acrostics are uniquely preserved in a pocket-size gospelbook, now Bern, Burger-bibliothek, 671 (74v). The gospels in this manuscript were written at

---

reason to think they were composed by a foreigner. (The Alfred acrostics are translated and briefly discussed also in Keynes and Lapidge, *Alfred the Great*, pp. 192–3 and 338.)

[35] See Lapidge, 'Latin Poems as Evidence', pp. 67–9.

[36] Text and translation as given by Lapidge, 'Latin Poems as Evidence', pp. 60–1; cf. *ibid.* for a philological commentary.

some unidentified Celtic centre in Britain (perhaps Cornwall).[37] The manuscript had probably travelled to England by the time of King Alfred's reign, where the acrostics were entered at some point during this reign.[38] The subsequent whereabouts of the manuscript suggests that the Alfred acrostics were copied into the gospelbook at a place associated with the royal household: in the first decades of the tenth century the book was at Bedwyn (Wiltshire), a royal estate of some importance, where a few entries pertaining to that estate were copied onto 75v–76v by various hands.[39] The most economical explanation would therefore be that the Celtic gospelbook, which was possibly among the books brought to England by Alfred's helpers, was in (private) use[40] in the royal household, and that, sometime during Alfred's reign, the acrostics, composed by one of these helpers, were entered, perhaps at the king's instigation, but perhaps without such commission, as a token of the gratitude and devotion felt by his clerical assistants.

The Æthelstan acrostic

We may now ask whether the preservation of the Alfred acrostics can be paralleled by similar circumstances in the transmission of the Æthelstan acrostic. Like the Alfred acrostics, the Æthelstan poem is preserved in but a single manuscript, Oxford, Bodleian Library, Rawlinson C. 697. Like Bern, Burgerbibliothek, 671, this is a foreign manuscript, imported into

---

[37] See W. M. Lindsay, *Early Welsh Script* (Oxford, 1912), pp. 10–16; pl. V is a facsimile of the acrostics.

[38] For the date and English origin of the texts of the acrostics, see Morrish, 'Dated and Datable Manuscripts', p. 531; cf., however, Dumville, 'The Anglo-Saxon Chronicle', p. 79, n. 110, who (following Lindsay, above, n. 37) thinks it possible that the script could be Celtic.

[39] For the entries in question, see Ker, *Catalogue*, pp. 4–5 (no. 6a and c). On these entries, their script (Anglo-Saxon Square minuscule Phase I) and their scribal connections, see also Dumville, 'Anglo-Saxon Chronicle', pp. 79–82, and *idem*, 'Square Minuscule' [*ASE* 16], p. 170. On the royal estate of Bedwyn, see Keynes and Lapidge, *Alfred the Great*, p. 318, n. 28; see also Dumville, 'Anglo-Saxon Chronicle', pp. 107–12.

[40] The pocket size of Burgerbibliothek 671 and the absence of any indications of pericopes suggest that this gospelbook was not intended for liturgical use. On pericopes in Anglo-Saxon gospels, see now U. Lenker, *Die westsächsische Evangelienversion und die Perikopenordnungen im angelsächsischen England*, TUEPh 20 (Munich, 1997).

England. According to Bernhard Bischoff, Rawlinson C. 697 was written in northeastern Francia in the third quarter of the ninth century.[41] Its principal contents are as follows: Aldhelm's *Enigmata* (1r–16r), his *Carmen de uirginitate* (17v–61r), and Prudentius, *Psychomachia* (64r–78v).[42] Rawlinson C. 697 is the earliest surviving manuscript of the *Carmen de uirginitate* from Anglo-Saxon England, and, excepting a fragment dated s. viii, the earliest text of the *Enigmata* from Anglo-Saxon England; the manuscript has therefore been adduced as evidence that the works of Aldhelm had to be re-imported to England after the Viking catastrophe.[43] As is clear from various glosses and annotations (on which see below), Rawlinson C. 697 was in England by the first part of the tenth century and, in fact, may have been among the books which King Alfred's helpers brought with them.[44] The earliest of the additions to Rawlinson C. 697 made in England in the tenth century is the Æthelstan acrostic, copied onto the last page (78v) of the manuscript – on palaeographical grounds, it would seem, during the reign of King Æthelstan.[45]

We have, therefore, a striking parallel: the three poems (presumably by one author) being entered in manuscripts which were imported into England in what was arguably the same context. In both cases, the poems stand out in being clearly the earliest accretions to the manuscripts in question. Here, however, the parallel ends; but the difference

[41] See B. Bischoff, 'Bannita: 1. Syllaba, 2. Littera', in his *Mittelalterliche Studien* III, 243–7, at 247 (orig. publ. 1976).

[42] For the text of the *Psychomachia* in Rawlinson C. 697 and its relationship with other manuscripts of this work of Anglo-Saxon provenance, see G. R. Wieland, 'The Anglo-Saxon Manuscripts of Prudentius's *Psychomachia*', *ASE* 16 (1987), 213–31. Rawlinson C. 697 is the earliest surviving copy of the *Psychomachia* from Anglo-Saxon England.

[43] See above, p. 333, n. 4. For the eighth-century fragment of the *Enigmata*, see O'Keeffe, 'The Text of Aldhelm's *Enigma* no. C', p. 66; see also below, p. 350.

[44] For a tentative list of such manuscripts (Rawlinson C. 697 among them), see Keynes and Lapidge, *Alfred the Great*, p. 214, n. 26; for the possible arrival of Rawlinson C. 697 in an Alfredian context, see also Lapidge, 'Schools, Learning and Literature', p. 9.

[45] See Dumville, 'Square Minuscule' [*ASE* 16], p. 175. The acrostic is written in Anglo-Saxon Square minuscule Phase II, which marks the highpoint in the development of this script, and which Dumville associates with the reign of Æthelstan (924–39), *ibid.*, esp. pp. 173 and 178. For a facsimile of the Æthelstan acrostic, see M. Lapidge, 'The Revival of Latin Learning in Late Anglo-Saxon England', in *Manuscripts at Oxford*, ed. A. C. de la Mare and B. C. Barker-Benfield (Oxford, 1980), pp. 19–22, at 20, and Keynes, 'Æthelstan's Books', pl. I.

in their transmission may be significant as well. Unlike the Alfred poems, the Æthelstan acrostic was copied out about twenty-five years or more after its composition, and John (its presumed author) or his colleagues could have had no hand in this. John appears to have survived into the reign of Edward the Elder (899–924); he apparently attests a charter dated 901,[46] but this is the last we ever hear of him, and he can hardly have been active in the reign of Æthelstan, if indeed he was still alive by 924.[47]

The transmission of the Æthelstan acrostic permits certain deductions to be made: first the fact that the little poem was entered into a manuscript after the lapse of a considerable number of years since its assumed composition suggests that it was preserved and cherished in Æthelstan's circle (and – one is inclined to think – scarcely outside his circle) during the intervening years, perhaps as a prophecy of young Æthelstan's future greatness. Second, the hermeneutic style in Latin literature (in which this poem is written) was familiar to Æthelstan in one way or another ever since his childhood days, and, for him, was associated not only with Aldhelm, the great spiritual and literary authority (of West Saxon extraction) in the pre-Viking age, but also with the revival of learning and literature initiated by his grandfather, Alfred the Great. Third, we do not know in which centre, or centres, Rawlinson C. 697 was owned in Anglo-Saxon times. The fact that it preserves the unique copy of a difficult Latin poem, entered *c.* 924 × 939 and intimately connected with King Æthelstan's early childhood (a poem, in other words, which is unlikely to have circulated widely), raises the possibility that Rawlinson C. 697 was at some time in the king's household. (The transmission of the Alfred acrostics in a manuscript associated with the

---

[46] S 364; see Keynes and Lapidge, *Alfred the Great*, p. 260, n. 169.

[47] Asser says that John was a 'priest and monk' when he came to England: *Life*, ed. Stevenson, ch. 78 (p. 63; Keynes and Lapidge, *Alfred the Great*, p. 93) and ch. 94 (p. 81; Keynes and Lapidge, p. 103). Since the canonical age for priesthood was thirty, and since he presumably arrived in England in 886 or thereabouts (see Keynes and Lapidge, *Alfred the Great*, pp. 27 and 213, n. 23, and p. 260, nn. 168 and 169), this would make him at least sixty-eight by 924; we may suspect, however, that he was considerably older, since it is likely that King Alfred would have looked out for experienced scholars of some standing. Asser says that upon his arrival John indeed was 'in omnibus disciplinis literatoriae artis eruditissimus' (ch. 78 (p. 63); Keynes and Lapidge, p. 93), and in his poem to young Æthelstan, John casts himself in the role of an elderly prophet ('Samuel, the Seer', line 3).

royal household could corroborate such a supposition.) In this case
Rawlinson C. 697 would furnish material proof of the existence of at least
one copy of Aldhelm's works in that household. And since it is unlikely
that this panegyric, and in some ways very private, poem dedicated to
Æthelstan would have been copied out into any manuscript which
happened to be nearest at hand, the presence of the Æthelstan acrostic in
a manuscript of Aldhelm's *Carmen de uirginitate* and *Enigmata* points in an
oblique way to the veneration in which Aldhelm was held in King
Æthelstan's circle.

Æthelstan and Malmesbury

There is converging evidence of a different kind which tends to confirm
Æthelstan's love for Aldhelm: the king's attachment to Malmesbury.
According to William of Malmesbury, King Æthelstan made many
donations to Malmesbury abbey.[48] Two charters in favour of Malmesbury
abbey and issued in the name of Æthelstan have survived.[49] However,
since the king seems to have been extremely generous with movable
possessions and estates at his disposal, freely giving them away to a great
number of institutions and individuals,[50] more significant, perhaps, is the
fact that Æthelstan should have chosen Malmesbury abbey as the burial
place for his two cousins, Ælfwine and Æthelwine (sons of King Alfred's
youngest son, Æthelweard) who were killed at the battle of Brunanburh
in 937,[51] and that when the king died, two years later, on 27 October
939, he too was buried at Malmesbury in fulfilment of instructions he
had given during his lifetime.[52] Even if the reasons why Æthelstan
'discriminated against Winchester as a place of burial for members of the

---

[48] See *Gesta pontificum*, ed. Hamilton, pp. 397–9 and 401–3 and *Gesta regum*, ed. Stubbs
I, 151.

[49] S 434 (BCS 716) and S 435 (BCS 718); although these charters are not authentic in
their received form, they are apparently based on genuine Æthelstan charters; see
Keynes, *Diplomas*, p. 44, n. 78, and *idem*, *The Charters of King Æthelstan* (forthcoming).

[50] See Keynes, 'Æthelstan's Books'; for donations, other than books, made by Æthelstan,
see *ibid.*, pp. 143–4.

[51] According to William of Malmesbury, *Gesta regum*, ed. Stubbs I, 151 and *Gesta
pontificum*, ed. Hamilton, pp. 396–7.

[52] Again, according to William of Malmesbury, *Gesta regum*, ed. Stubbs I, 157 and 151,
and *Gesta pontificum*, ed. Hamilton, p. 397. See also John of Worcester, *Chronicon*, ed.
Darlington and McGurk II, 394 (s. a. 940).

royal family'[53] were to be sought in a dissension with the Winchester establishment during the earlier years of his reign (see above, p. 329), the fact that Æthelstan's choice fell upon Malmesbury for creating a new royal mausoleum still seems remarkable. It is also worth noting that there may be grounds for believing that John the Old Saxon, too, was buried at Malmesbury.[54]

Conclusions

In William of Malmesbury's testimony, concerning King Æthelstan, there was a strong belief current among his (early-twelfth-century) contemporaries that 'nemo legalius uel litteratius rempublicam adminis-trauerit'.[55] Unlike his renowned grandfather, Æthelstan left no writings of his own, and he found no Asser, and it is only with difficulties and only in part that his thought-world and the intellectual milieu of his court can be recreated. Nevertheless, if we now ask what impress Æthelstan's court culture with its flair and enthusiasm for hermeneutic composition will have made upon Æthelwold and Dunstan, two young men with a strong scholarly disposition, born into leading West Saxon families and receiving their education at that court, in spite of the scarcity of written evidence there is not much difficulty in imagining what this impress will have been. Young Æthelwold and Dunstan,[56] in King Æthelstan's entourage, will have witnessed a splendour and grandeur unthinkable only a generation previously. They will have witnessed the unification of England (under the rule of a West Saxon king) achieved with apparent ease,[57] witnessed the triumphant assertion of southern supremacy in 934

---

[53] Keynes, *Liber Vitae*, p. 22.

[54] This much may be inferred from a remark by William of Malmesbury (*Gesta regum*, ed. Stubbs I, 132) and from an early-eleventh-century compilation, *þa halgan on Angelcynne* (ed. F. Liebermann, *Die Heiligen Englands* (Hanover, 1889), p. 18); see Lapidge, 'Latin Poems as Evidence', p. 67.

[55] *Gesta regum*, ed. Stubbs I, 144; 'No one more just or learned administered the state', *EHD*, p. 305.

[56] For Dunstan's attendance at court, presumably only intermittent, see below, pp. 354–5.

[57] The unity of England was of primary importance to Æthelwold, as is clear from his own preface to the Old English Rule. Here, his principal criticism of King Eadwig's short reign (955–9) is that this king divided the unity of the kingdom, thereby bringing it to the brink of ruin ('se ... þis rice tostencte 7 his annesse todælde', *CS*, p. 146). I intend to return to this point on another occasion.

and 937 against a powerful northern alliance, witnessed the foreign embassies come to Æthelstan's court to negotiate the marriages of continental princes to the king's half-sisters (bringing and receiving costly and luxurious gifts), witnessed the influx of foreign noblemen and scholars seeking the haven of Æthelstan's court in order to escape from the threats and turmoils in their homelands.[58] For Æthelwold and Dunstan (as for other scholars in Æthelstan's entourage) the hermeneutic 'Aldhelmian' style, increasingly practised in court circles and apparently encouraged by royal patronage, must have represented a fitting literary equivalent to the political and military splendour of the royal court. Furthermore, the venerable figure of Aldhelm the scholar, man of letters, and bishop, will have furnished the future leaders of the Benedictine reform movement with a brilliant example of how a love for lavish display could be reconciled with a deep and orthodox piety. It may, therefore, not be hazardous to assume that a close study of Aldhelm's writings will have formed an essential part of Æthelwold's and Dunstan's curriculum during their stay at Æthelstan's court, and that it was through such careful study in the royal ambit that the seeds were sown for the placement of Aldhelm in a central position in the late Anglo-Saxon curriculum.

THE MANUSCRIPT EVIDENCE

We may next turn to the question of what clues are provided by manuscripts copied (or written in) during the reign of King Æthelstan or shortly thereafter, clues which may further confirm the presumption that the enthusiasm for the hermeneutic style, and the devotion to Aldhelm and careful study of his works, originated in the intellectual milieu of Æthelstan's court, and that such predilections were thence brought by Æthelwold and Dunstan to their subsequent place of study and activity at Glastonbury. Given the comparative paucity of surviving manuscripts from the decades in question, and given our usually deficient knowledge of the origin and subsequent whereabouts of these manuscripts, we can scarcely expect our exploration of this sort of evidence to yield clear, irrefutable proof. Such exploration is necessary and rewarding, never-

---

[58] For the contemporary evidence for, and evaluation of, these historical events, see the references given above, p. 332, n. 1.

theless, even if the following remarks will result in no more than the uncovering of a number of suggestive and tantalizing links between the manuscripts, persons and places in question, and between the manuscripts themselves.

Oxford, Bodleian Library, Rawlinson C. 697

We may best begin by looking at the traces of study subsequent to Æthelstan's reign which can be detected in this Aldhelm manuscript, a book we already have come to know (above, pp. 344–7) as a witness of utmost importance for the ascendancy of the hermeneutic style in the king's immediate entourage and for the adumbration of such stylistic predilections in an Alfredian context. That this manuscript was carefully studied over several decades is clear from the glosses and annotations (such as variant readings or corrections) in Latin and Old English entered in the text of the *Carmen de uirginitate* and the *Enigmata* by various hands from about the mid-tenth century onwards.[59] By the same token, it has been demonstrated beyond reasonable doubt that the version of Aldhelm's *Enigma* no. C (*De creatura*) which is transmitted in Rawlinson C. 697 served as the exemplar from which Riddle 40 in the Exeter Book was translated.[60] Such a verse translation reveals an eager interest in the vernacular *per se* and suggests that the study of Aldhelm embraced not only a concern with clarifying his Latin (by means of more common synonyms for his choice terms or through explanatory scholia) but that, at least occasionally, such study prompted the urge to convey part of Aldhelm's flamboyance through the Old English poetic register, an urge which may have been further stimulated by Aldhelm's own, now lost, poetry in Old English. (Recall that a similar tendency towards recreating the stylistic register of Aldhelm's diction in the vernacular occasionally makes itself felt in the Old English glosses in the Brussels corpus; see above, pp. 158–9.)

[59] For the principal contents of Rawlinson C. 697, see above, p. 345. For the dates of the glossing hands, see Ker, *Catalogue*, p. 427 (no. 349); for the glosses to the *Enigmata*, see, briefly, N. Porter Stork, *Through a Gloss Darkly: Aldhelm's Riddles in the British Library MS Royal 12. C. xxiii* (Toronto, 1990), p. 22. The Old English glosses to the *Carmen* (seventy-three) and to the *Enigmata* (five) are printed *OEG*, pp. 182–3 (no. 17), p. 190 (no. 21) and p. 193 (no. 24). The Latin glosses and annotations are not available in print.

[60] See O'Keeffe, 'The Text of Aldhelm's *Enigma* no. C', pp. 61–73.

With regard to the various annotations in Rawlinson C. 697, several points concerning a relationship with some other manuscripts and a suggested identification of one of the annotators are noteworthy for our purposes. First, T. A. M. Bishop attributed some of the interlinear and marginal glosses (beginning on 17r) to the *Carmen de uirginitate* to Dunstan (Hand D), an attribution which has been followed almost universally by other scholars.[61] Second, Bishop also pointed out that some corrections in black ink in Rawlinson C. 697 have some resemblance to the hand of scribe 2 in Cleopatra A. iii, a manuscript which was possibly written at St Augustine's, Canterbury (and on which see below).[62] Third, corrections and alternative readings to the *Enigmata* also point to Canterbury: they were probably taken from a (lost) manuscript which also served as the exemplar for the *Enigmata* in CUL Gg. 5. 35 (s. xi^med, prob. St Augustine's) and BL, Royal 12. C. XXIII (s. x^2 or x/xi Christ Church).[63] Fourth, Scott Gwara has proposed the identity of one of the annotating hands in the *Carmen de uirginitate* in Rawlinson C. 697 with one of the glossing hands in Royal 7. D. XXIV (on which see below).[64] He further points out that Rawlinson C. 697 and Royal 7. D. XXIV often agree in introducing glosses or variant readings by employing *pro* (instead of the more common *.i.* or *.s.*).[65]

In sum, we are left with the important information that Rawlinson C. 697 was instrumental in the poetic rendition of one of Aldhelm's *Enigmata*; we are further left with the tantalizing possibility that Dunstan annotated this manuscript, and with some tentative links with two other manuscripts under discussion here (Cleopatra A. iii and Royal 7. D. XXIV). But before we may turn to these two books, we have to consider a further manuscript of crucial importance.

---

[61] See Bishop, 'An Early Example of Insular-Caroline', p. 399, and *idem*, *English Caroline Minuscule*, p. 2 (no. 3). For other manuscripts in which Dunstan's hand (Hand D) can arguably be identified, see above, p. 255 and n. 91; but cf. Lapidge, 'Autographs of Insular Latin Authors', pp. 128–31, as well as Dumville, *English Caroline Script*, pp. 50–2, for some reservations about such identification.

[62] See Bishop, 'Notes on Cambridge Manuscripts', p. 93.

[63] See O'Keeffe, 'The Text of Aldhelm's *Enigma* no. C', pp. 64–8.

[64] See Gwara, 'Manuscripts of Aldhelm's *Prosa de Virginitate*', p. 130.

[65] See *ibid.*, pp. 130–1; for example: 'condat *pro* abscondidit' (Rawlinson C. 697, 52r).

Cambridge, Corpus Christi College 183

This manuscript, containing Bede's prose and metrical Lives of St Cuthbert, is one of the numerous books which King Æthelstan donated to religious foundations. It is one of the two volumes which he gave to the community of St Cuthbert at Chester-le-Street.[66] Its famous frontispiece (1v) shows the king handing over the book to St Cuthbert himself.[67] CCCC 183 is unique among the books known to have been donated by Æthelstan in that it was written in England during his reign. One may suspect that one of Æthelstan's reasons for presenting this volume and its almost perished companion, as well as many other valuable gifts, to St Cuthbert's community would have been to secure the good will of one of the most powerful institutions north of the Humber (a region where southern supremacy had been established only as recently as 927). CCCC 183 is therefore a precious document, testifying to the king's piety, his patronage of learning and his political instincts. Since CCCC 183 is of such crucial importance as a witness to the intellectual climate at Æthelstan's court and because of its ties with other manuscripts under discussion here, we must inspect its contents somewhat more closely.

The texts contained in the manuscript when it was given to St Cuthbert's community are as follows:

1 Bede's prose *Vita* of St Cuthbert, 2r–56r.[68]
2 Book IV, chs. 31 and 32 of Bede's *Historia ecclesiastica*, 56r–58r, pertaining to posthumous miracles of St Cuthbert.[69]

---

[66] For a detailed description of the manuscript, see James, *Catalogue* I, 426–41. For a discussion of its contents, date and place of origin (with full bibliographical references) and an assessment of CCCC 183 in the context of Æthelstan's other donations, see Keynes, 'Æthelstan's Books', pp. 180–5. The other manuscript which Æthelstan gave to the community of St Cuthbert is a continental gospelbook of late-ninth- or early-tenth-century origin, now London, BL, Cotton Otho B. ix, of which only a few charred fragments survived the fire at Ashburnham House in 1731; for this manuscript, see *ibid.*, pp. 170–9.

[67] There are numerous reproductions; see, for example, Keynes, 'Æthelstan's Books', pl. IX and Temple, *Anglo-Saxon Manuscripts*, pl. 29. For a different interpretation of the miniature's iconography, see D. Rollason, 'St Cuthbert and Wessex: the Evidence of Cambridge, Corpus Christi College MS. 183', in *St Cuthbert, his Cult and his Community to AD 1200*, ed. G. Bonner *et al.* (Woodbridge, 1989), pp. 413–24, at 420–2.

[68] Printed Colgrave, *Two Lives of Saint Cuthbert*, pp. 141–307 and 341–59.

[69] Printed Colgrave and Mynors, *Bede's Ecclesiastical History*, pp. 444–9.

3 Lists of popes, Christ's disciples and English bishops, 59r–64v.[70]
4 Royal genealogies and regnal lists, 65r–67r.[71]
5 Miscellaneous useful information, principally pertaining to chronology and metrology (such as the measurements of the Tabernacle), 67r–69v.[72]
6 A glossary of difficult words in Bede's metrical *Vita* of St Cuthbert, 70r–v. It comprises fifty-one *lemmata*, nineteen of these with English *interpretamenta*.[73]
7 Bede's metrical *Vita* of St Cuthbert, 71r–92v.[74]
8 A mass and Office for St Cuthbert, 92v–95v.[75]

The type of script throughout is Anglo-Saxon Square minuscule Phase II, and the production of the manuscript has therefore been assigned to King Æthelstan's reign, on palaeographical grounds alone.[76] CCCC 183 was presumably written between the summer of 934 and 939 at the outside, these dates being established by the appointment of Ælfheah (the last name in the Winchester episcopal list in the manuscript; above art. 3) as bishop of Winchester in 934 and Æthelstan's death in 939. The book must therefore have been sent north subsequent to the king's visit to St Cuthbert's shrine earlier in 934, during his expedition to Scotland.[77] The episcopal lists also furnish important information regarding the scriptorium where CCCC 183 was produced. Only the lists for the metropolitan see of Canterbury and for the West Saxon sees have been updated to

---

[70] Printed James, *Catalogue* I, 428–35, and (the episcopal lists) R. I. Page, 'Anglo-Saxon Episcopal Lists', *Nottingham Medieval Studies* 10 (1966), 2–24, at 8–12.

[71] Printed James, *Catalogue* I, 435–8, and Dumville, 'The Anglian Collection', pp. 32–4.

[72] Printed James, *Catalogue* I, 439–40; cf. Bischoff and Lapidge, *Biblical Commentaries*, p. 210. Interestingly, a number of these entries also occur in Royal 2. B. V, 187r–190v, where they were added in a late-tenth-century hand; cf. Warner and Gilson, *Catalogue* I, 41, art. 8.

[73] See Ker, *Catalogue*, pp. 64–5 (no. 42). The Old English glosses are printed by Meritt, *Old English Glosses*, p. 16 (no. 8). The Latin glosses are unprinted.

[74] Printed Jaager, *Bedas metrische Vita Sancti Cuthberti*.

[75] Printed C. Hohler, 'The Durham Services in Honour of St Cuthbert', in *The Relics of St Cuthbert*, ed. C. F. Battiscombe (Oxford, 1956), pp. 155–91. These liturgical pieces were apparently composed in Wessex; see *ibid.*, pp. 156–7.

[76] See Dumville, 'Square Minuscule' [ASE 16], pp. 174–5.

[77] For an evaluation of the historical evidence for the dating of the manuscript, see Keynes, 'Æthelstan's Books', pp. 181–4.

the time when the manuscript was written. The lists of the North-umbrian, Mercian and other southern dioceses come to an end around the mid-ninth century. This points to an origin of the manuscript somewhere in Wessex.[78] A Winchester scriptorium seems to be excluded because the scribe's knowledge with regard to the succession of the bishops of Winchester is curiously defective.[79] Glastonbury or nearby Wells have been suggested instead.[80] The attribution to Wells rests primarily on the evidence that a post-Conquest parish church there was dedicated to St Cuthbert.[81] We have no knowledge of what intellectual activities were going on at Wells Cathedral or whether a skilled and practised scriptorium, prerequisite for the production of a manuscript of such high quality, was in existence there during the years in question. Glastonbury, on the other hand, must have held some attraction as a place for prolonged and intensive study for Dunstan at some point in the 930s and for Æthelwold after 939.[82]

As regards the question of precisely when these future leaders of the Benedictine reform arrived at Glastonbury, it seems clear from Wulfstan's account that Æthelwold remained at Winchester throughout King Æthelstan's reign, first as a member of the royal household (cf. *Wulfstan: Life*, ch. 7), and then, 'at the king's wish' (*praecipiente rege*, *Life*, ch. 9, p. 14) for some time in the household of Bishop Ælfheah (which cannot have been prior to 934, the year of Ælfheah's elevation). It was only after Æthelstan's death in 939 that he was free to follow his scholarly interests and monastic vocation and go to Glastonbury (*Life*, ch. 9). Unfortunately, B, Dunstan's earliest biographer (probably a younger contemporary and a member of Dunstan's personal retinue until *c*. 960), is no match for Wulfstan where the chronology of events and the accuracy of historical details are concerned.[83] From B's rather muddled account of Dunstan's

---

[78] An origin at Canterbury seems to be excluded on grounds that only the West Saxon (but no other southern) sees are updated; see Keynes, 'Æthelstan's Books', pp. 181–2.

[79] See *ibid.*, p. 184.

[80] See Robinson, *The Saxon Bishops of Wells*, p. 14, Keynes, 'Æthelstan's Books', pp. 184–5, and Dumville, 'Square Minuscule' [*ASE* 16], pp. 177–8.

[81] Cf. Keynes, 'Æthelstan's Books', p. 185.

[82] Apart from Glastonbury's longstanding association with the West Saxon royal family, art historical evidence has also been advanced in favour of a Glastonbury origin of CCCC 183; see Higgitt, 'Glastonbury', p. 278.

[83] B's *Vita S. Dunstani* is printed by Stubbs, *Memorials of St Dunstan*, pp. 3–52. For a tentative reconstruction of B's career and an assessment of what impact B's own

early career up to the end of Æthelstan's reign (chs. 2–12) one gets the impression that Dunstan was in and out of court (and Bishop Ælfheah's household?) a good deal, at one time even being expelled from court through the plotting of his colleagues (ch. 6). Nevertheless, reading B's narrative, it seems clear that, during Æthelstan's reign, Dunstan spent considerable time studying at Glastonbury. It also seems clear from Wulfstan's infinitely more precise and reliable *Vita* of Æthelwold that by 939 Dunstan was indeed at Glastonbury, where he was then joined by Æthelwold (*Wulfstan: Life*, ch. 9). In other words, if CCCC 183 was written and decorated at Glastonbury, it is entirely possible that it was produced during a period while Dunstan was pursuing his studies there, at a place where he had presumably been tutored from infancy.

Wherever in Wessex CCCC 183 was written, there can be little doubt that royal circles took an immediate interest in its compilation and production. This much emerges from the fact that it was produced on royal commission, and further evidence for such an assumption may be found in the texts copied into the manuscript. CCCC 183 is the earliest manuscript which contains the full set of what has been called the 'Anglian collection of royal genealogies and regnal lists' (art. 4 above).[84] This collection as it is transmitted in CCCC 183 comprises genealogies for the royal families of Deira, Bernicia, Mercia, Lindsey, Kent, East Anglia and Wessex and regnal lists for Northumbria and Mercia. The collection perhaps originated in Mercia *c.* 796; the lists in CCCC 183 were evidently copied from a (now lost) exemplar written in Mercia *c.* 840.[85] It is interesting to remark that, as opposed to the aforementioned episcopal lists in the manuscript (updated for the West Saxon sees), no attempt has been made to provide a regnal list for the West Saxon kings.[86] While the appropriateness of such a predominantly Anglian

---

biography had on his account of Dunstan's life, see Lapidge, 'B. and the *Vita S. Dunstani*'. For a survey of the early stages of Dunstan's career, based on B's *Life* and other available sources, see Brooks, 'The Career of St Dunstan', pp. 1–11; see also below, pp. 372–6.

[84] See Dumville, 'The Anglian Collection'.

[85] Cf. *ibid.*, esp. at pp. 42 and 46. For the place of origin of the compilation itself (which may have been either Mercia or Northumbria), see *ibid.*, pp. 45–50.

[86] Such a list and similar material pertaining to the West Saxon royal house have indeed been added to the original lists in a later manuscript which preserves this collection (and which is closely related to CCCC 183 and by some of its contents may give some confirmation of a supposed Glastonbury connection of CCCC 183): London, BL,

collection (omitting of course any Viking rulers of York or the Danelaw) in a manuscript destined for Chester-le-Street is obvious, it may be asked whether Glastonbury, or any other scriptorium in the southwest, would have been a likely place where the Mercian exemplar for the lists would have been extant. Perhaps a more economical explanation would be to associate this exemplar with the 'Mercian component'[87] of Æthelstan's reign and to suspect that it was provided by someone in the royal household.

Of greater interest still are the principal items in CCCC 183: the two Cuthbert *Vitae*. CCCC 183 contains the earliest surviving copy of Bede's prose Life (above, art. 1), so there may be no way of telling whether it was copied from a continental or an English exemplar.[88] The prose Life is followed by two chs. from Bede's *Historia ecclesiastica* (IV. 31 and 32, above, art. 2). These relate miracles worked by St Cuthbert which are not contained in the prose Life (nor in the metrical *Vita*) and are usually appended to the prose Life in later manuscripts.[89] Again, we cannot say whether the chs. were first combined with the prose Life in CCCC 183 or whether the compiler of that manuscript found them together already in his exemplar. Whatever the case, supplementing Bede's prose Life with two chs. drawn from his chief work reveals the compiler's scholarly disposition and the provision of further posthumous miracles in these chs. is wholly consonant with King Æthelstan's obsession with relics and (one may assume) the miracles worked by them.[90]

Since CCCC 183 is the earliest surviving text of the prose Life, it follows that it is also the first manuscript to contain jointly the prose and the metrical Lives (above, art. 7), and again we do not know whether the

---

Cotton Tiberius B. v (s. xi[2/4], ?Christ Church, Canterbury, ?Winchester); see D. N. Dumville, 'The Catalogue Texts', in *An Eleventh-Century Anglo-Saxon Illustrated Miscellany. British Library, Cotton Tiberius B. v. Part I*, ed. P. McGurk *et al.*, EEMF 21 (Copenhagen, 1983), 55–8, at 56–8.

[87] See above, pp. 321–2. It should be noted that the names in the lists have not been thoroughly Saxonized, thereby testifying again to a tolerance towards Anglian dialect forms during Æthelstan's reign, cf. e. g. *Coenred, Coenwulf, Cuþwalh, Cenwalh, Weoþolgiot* (Dumville, 'The Anglian Collection', p. 33).

[88] See the (rather sparse) remarks on the manuscripts and their relationships by Colgrave, *Two Lives of Saint Cuthbert*, pp. 20–42 and 45–50.

[89] Cf. *ibid*, pp. 20–37.

[90] For a brief survey of the evidence for Æthelstan's renown as a collector of relics, see Keynes, 'Æthelstan's Books', pp. 143–4.

compiler found both Lives combined in one exemplar. The fact that the prose Life and the metrical version are separated by eleven intervening folios containing the regnal and episcopal lists might suggest that the *Vitae* were copied from different exemplars. As opposed to the prose, two earlier manuscripts of the metrical Life from Anglo-Saxon England have survived, and both are books imported from the Continent: London, BL, Harley 526 (written in the second half, probably last quarter of the ninth century) and Paris, Bibliothèque Nationale, lat. 2825 (written probably *c.* 900). On palaeographical grounds, Harley 526 was presumably written in the same scriptorium in northeast Francia where Rawlinson C. 697 (containing the *Carmen de uirginitate* etc.) originated, and both books were arguably imported to England in the same Alfredian context.[91] Again on palaeographical grounds, and on grounds of textual relationship, it is possible that BN lat. 2825 was written in the same scriptorium as Harley 526 (and hence Rawlinson C. 697). Both Harley 526 and BN lat. 2825 were in England by no later than the mid-tenth century, as is clear from a few Old English glosses and other additions entered by that time.[92] Like the Aldhelm texts in Rawlinson C. 697, Bede's metrical Life of St Cuthbert apparently had to be re-imported, because it was no longer available (or not widely available) in England in the late ninth and early tenth century. Since (as we have seen) there are reasons to suspect that Rawlinson C. 697 was associated with King Æthelstan's circle and since Rawlinson C. 697 and Harley 526 may have reached England by the same agency, it is possible that Harley 526 (and perhaps BN lat. 2825) were in the royal household by the time CCCC 183 was commissioned. It should be noted, however, that CCCC 183 does not seem to be derived in direct line from either of these texts.[93] This should serve as a reminder that even in the case of works which arguably had to be re-imported after the Viking age, the textual affiliation of the surviving English manuscripts is not always one of direct descent from these continental texts. This in turn suggests that, even at an early stage, the transmissional

---

[91] See above, p. 345.

[92] For the origin, arrival in England and textual affiliation of Harley 526 and BN lat. 2825, see Lapidge, 'Prolegomena to an Edition of Bede's Metrical *Vita Sancti Cuthberti*', pp. 155–7.

[93] Jaager (*Bedas metrische Vita Sancti Cuthberti*, pp. 33–44, esp. at 34) assigns CCCC 183 on the one hand and Harley 526 and BN 2825 on the other to different manuscript groups.

history of the texts in question was more complex than the surviving manuscripts seem to indicate.

In any event, since Harley 526 (and BN lat. 2825), at one point, may have belonged to the royal household, it may not be unreasonable to presume that a copy of Bede's prose Life (wherever it came from) would have been available in court circles as well. By the same token, we may suspect that the close parallel between Bede's prose and metrical Lives of St Cuthbert and Aldhelm's prose and verse *De uirginitate* would not have escaped the scholars engaged in the compilation of CCCC 183. In this connection it may be significant to recall that the Aldhelm manuscript from which the third glossary in Cleopatra A. iii was culled seems to have contained both versions of the *De uirginitate*.[94] (The Third Cleopatra Glossary offers decisive manuscript evidence for a tenth-century predecessor of the vast corpus of vernacular glosses in Brussels 1650 and is therefore of great importance for establishing a link between the eleventh-century Brussels glosses and Æthelwold's circle; cf. above, pp. 151–4.) It is further noteworthy that such combined transmission and study of Bede's and Aldhelm's *opera geminata* in some way adumbrates the burgeoning of verse contrafacta of prose saints' lives later in the tenth century, a burgeoning which has been associated with Bishop Æthelwold's school and sphere of influence.[95] That at Canterbury, within a decade or so after CCCC 183 had been written, Frithegod should compose his metrical contrafactum of Stephen of Ripon's Life of St Wilfrid, at the instigation of Archbishop Oda (who at an earlier stage of his career had been associated with Æthelstan's entourage, above, pp. 339–41), may confirm the suspicion that the combined study of prose and verse *Vitae* was one of the scholarly concerns during Æthelstan's reign and in his circle.

One final point in the transmission of Bede's *Vitae* deserves our notice: the small glossary of arcane words prefaced to the metrical version (above, art. 6). It is introduced as follows: 'Haec sunt quae in libello sequenti caraxata sunt atque archana'.[96] While the glossary *per se* testifies to an incipient interest in what may be called hermeneutic

---

[94] See above, pp. 139–41, for the recourse which Byrhtferth of Ramsey apparently could still make to this manuscript.

[95] See M. Lapidge, 'Tenth-Century Anglo-Latin Verse Hagiography', *Mittellateinisches Jahrbuch* 24–5 (1991), 249–60, esp. 259–60.

[96] Cf. James, *Catalogue* I, 440.

philology,[97] the grecism *caraxare*, used in the sense of *scribere*, in the superscription provides a clear link with King Æthelstan's charters. The word occurs frequently in later hermeneutic compositions, and in charters it is common from the reign of Æthelstan onwards.[98]

In short, wherever CCCC 183 was written, its contents not only cater in an obvious way for its Chester-le-Street recipients, but its assemblage of texts also seems to reflect in various ways the intellectual activities of the court circles, activities which were brought to full fruition in the decades subsequent to Æthelstan's reign. We may now turn to the links which CCCC 183 has with another manuscript, namely Royal 7. D. XXIV. These links will bring us back to Aldhelm studies during Æthelstan's reign and to the glossing done on Aldhelm's works in the following decades.

BL, Royal 7. D. XXIV, part ii, fols. 82–168[99]

This manuscript contains Aldhelm's prose *De uirginitate* (82r–162r) followed by Aldhelm's letter to Ehfrid (162v–168r).[100] The manuscript is written and decorated with some pretension, but has never been fully completed, a point to which we shall return in due course. Royal 7. D. XXIV is the earliest copy of the prose *De uirginitate* surviving from the time after the Viking incursions. Its date is established by its type of script and its scribal and art historical links. The text is written in Anglo-

---

[97] Although Bede's work is in no way 'hermeneutic', it is a difficult poem to read, its diction being so terse in many places.

[98] See M. Herren, 'Insular Latin *c(h)araxare (craxare)* and its Derivatives', *Peritia* 1 (1982), 273–80, at 279. It may be noteworthy that Æthelwold apparently took a fancy to this word: he once attests a charter of King Edgar (arguably composed by himself) with a seemingly unique form of the word, *karessi*: 'ego Æþelwold episcopus karessi' (S 739, BCS 1175; Sawyer, *Charters of Burton Abbey*, no. 21). This is a pretentious, grecizing but spurious form: see Lapidge, 'Æthelwold as Scholar and Teacher', p. 184.

[99] The manuscript is now composite. Its first part (fols. 2–81) contains Guitmundus, *De corpore et sanguine Domini*, written in the twelfth century; cf. Warner and Gilson, *Catalogue* I, 192.

[100] Fols. 163–5 are paper leaves, inserted in the seventeenth century; cf. Warner and Gilson, *Catalogue* I, 192. The letter is printed by Ehwald, *Aldhelmi Opera*, pp. 486–94 (no. 5); it is translated by Herren, in Lapidge and Herren, *Aldhelm: the Prose Works*, pp. 143–6 (no. V).

Saxon Square minuscule Phase II, which *per se* would point to King Æthelstan's reign.[101] Such a date receives confirmation by the circumstance that its main scribe (fols. 82–127 and 136–62) is identical with the main scribe in CCCC 183.[102] In addition, there are close art historical links between Royal 7. D. XXIV and CCCC 183: the decorated initals in both manuscripts were almost certainly executed in the same scriptorium, probably by the same artist.[103] Concerning the relative chronology of the two manuscripts, it is generally agreed that, both in script and decoration, CCCC 183 is the superior and more mature work, and was therefore probably produced after its companion volume.[104]

As opposed to Bede's prose Life of St Cuthbert (of which CCCC 183 is the first extant copy), a fragmentary copy of the prose *De uirginitate* from the pre-Viking age and of English origin has survived. This manuscript is now preserved as a number of *membra disiecta*, the most substantial of these being New Haven, Yale University, Beinecke Library 401 (see above, p. 144). The fragments have been dated on palaeographical grounds to the first half of the ninth century, probably to its earlier part.[105] It has been shown that Royal 7. D. XXIV is textually closely related to the Yale fragments, presumably deriving in direct line from this manuscript, albeit through at least one intermediary copy.[106] The textual and transmissional history of the prose *De uirginitate* therefore appears to have in its English branch a continuity which bridges the gap of the Viking age. Royal 7. D. XXIV has been much written in during the decades following its production.[107] There are a number of Old English glosses

---

[101] The manuscript is dated accordingly by Dumville, 'Square Minuscule' [*ASE* 16], pp. 174–5.

[102] This was first noted by Bishop. 'An Early Example of the Square Minuscule', p. 247, and has since been confirmed by Dumville, 'Square Minuscule' [*ASE* 16], pp. 174–5.

[103] See Temple, *Anglo-Saxon Manuscripts*, p. 38 (no. 6) and p. 36 (no. 4), and the references given there.

[104] See *ibid.*, p. 38 (no. 6), Bishop, 'An Early Example of the Square Minuscule', p. 247, and Dumville, 'Square Minuscule' [*ASE* 16], p. 174.

[105] See Morrish, 'Dated and Datable Manuscripts', p. 527.

[106] See Gwara, 'Manuscripts of Aldhelm's *Prosa de Virginitate*', pp. 120–5, and his stemma on p. 111. For example, Royal 7. D. XXIV preserves many idiosyncratic word-divisions characteristic of the Yale fragments, and both manuscripts agree in the conspicuous omission of one line of text.

[107] See Warner and Gilson, *Catalogue* IV, pl. 54a (showing 124r), to form an impression of the manuscript itself and the density of the glossing.

(forty-three), appearing sporadically throughout the text, and being entered by several scribes.[108] These glosses are in no way distinguished nor do they reveal any stylistic pretensions. They are no more than cribs, as can be seen from the fact that they are often merographs, spelling out only a few letters of the Old English word, just enough to remind the reader of the usual translation for the lemma in question.[109] Textually the Old English glosses are affiliated with the so-called 'Abingdon group', that is, the family to which the glosses in Brussels 1650 belong.[110]

Of greater interest than the sparse Old English glosses are the thousands of Latin glosses and scholia entered in multiple layers and by several scribes. These glosses are still unprinted. Concerning their date, the only scholar who so far has studied them thoroughly holds that they span a period from the 930s (which would be contemporary with the text itself) to the mid-tenth century.[111] It will be recalled that one of the glossing hands in Royal 7. D. XXIV may be identical with one of the glossators in Rawlinson C. 697 (the manuscript containing the *Carmen de uirginitate* etc., the Æthelstan acrostic and, among its annotations, possibly the hand of Dunstan), and that both Royal 7. D. XXIV and Rawlinson C. 697 often introduce *interpretamenta* in the same unusual

---

[108] These glosses are printed *OEG*, pp. 153–4 (no. 5); they are dated by Ker to s. x, without any further specification (*Catalogue*, p. 330 (no. 259)).

[109] Cf., for example, *sollertiam*: *emb{hydignesse}* (*OEG*, no. 5.10) or *colonus*: *bu{gend}* (*OEG*, no. 5.17).

[110] For the 'Abingdon group' see above, pp. 142–3. Cf., for example, *municipes*: *burgleode* (*OEG* no. 5.40); *burhleodan* (G 4733 [CD]); *scintillante*: *spircendre* (*OEG*, no. 5.22 = G 1029 [CD]). In view of the fact that the Latin text in Digby 146 (s. x^ex) is closely related to Royal 7. D. XXIV (cf. Ehwald, ed., *Aldhelmi Opera*, p. 222, and Gwara, 'Manuscripts of Aldhelm's *Prosa de Virginitate*', pp. 137–42) it may be noteworthy that the Old English glosses in Royal 7. D. XXIV as well have a special affinity to the glosses in Digby 146, and there to the earliest stratum of (some thirty) glosses, that is to the layer of glosses which was already extant in Digby 146 before the bulk of the vernacular glosses was copied into it from Brussels 1650 by the mid-eleventh century. (For the relationship between Brussels 1650 and Digby 146, see above, p. 132; cf. also below, p. 377.) Eleven glosses in Royal 7. D. XXIV are identical with glosses in this early stratum in Digby 146 (a stratum not contained in Brussels 1650); cf. Ker, *Catalogue*, pp. 381–2 (no. 320) and p. 330 (no. 259).

[111] See Gwara, 'Manuscripts of Aldhelm's *Prosa de Virginitate*', pp. 127–9, where the various glossing hands are described briefly. Note, however, that no precise dates are indicated for the individual hands themselves. For numerous examples from the Latin glosses and scholia in Royal 7. D. XXIV, cf. *ibid.*, pp. 142–53.

fashion.[112] A link in the glossing method between the Latin scholia in Royal 7. D. XXIV and the Brussels corpus of vernacular glosses is provided by the circumstance that a great number of scholia in the Royal manuscript are excerpted from Isidore's *Etymologiae*; for example: *rubri maris* (lemma): *rubrum mare uocatum eo quod sit roseis undis infectum* (scholion in Royal D. 7. XXIV; cf. *Etymologiae* XIII. xvii. 2) or, *pelagi* (lemma): *pelagus latitudo maris sine litore* (scholion; cf. *Etymologiae* XIII. xvi. 10).[113] We have seen (above, pp. 165–71) that for the Old English glosses in the Brussels corpus the glossators also drew with some frequency on the *Etymologiae*.

What would be needed now (apart from an edition of the Latin gloss corpus) is a comprehensive and critical assessment of how competently the glossators of Royal 7. D. XXIV did their work, so that we would be in a position to form a reasoned judgement of Latin Aldhelm philology around the mid-tenth century. In any event, the number and nature of the Latin glosses in Royal 7. D. XXIV testify to the intensive study of Aldhelm's text in the years subsequent to Æthelstan's reign and perhaps (once the various strata of glosses will have been properly dated) as early as the 930s. What is clear thus far is that a glossing project of such immense scope (even if carried out in several instalments) must be viewed as a scholarly undertaking of considerable ambition. For our purpose of uncovering the historical and intellectual background of Æthelwold's possible involvement in the origin and promotion of vernacular Aldhelm glossing, it is of great interest that the vast Latin gloss corpus in Royal 7. D. XXIV should be found in a manuscript that has clear links with other manuscripts which in turn may reasonably be associated with King Æthelstan's household (namely Rawlinson C. 697 and CCCC 183), that the gloss corpus should be found in a manuscript, moreover, which (on the evidence of CCCC 183) was written and, arguably, glossed in a scriptorium enjoying royal patronage, perhaps Glastonbury.

Evidence of a different sort may perhaps point to immediate royal involvement in the production of Royal 7. D. XXIV as well. Such evidence could be furnished by Aldhelm's letter to Ehfrid, which is appended to the prose *De uirginitate* (162v–168r), and which was part of

---

[112] See above, p. 351 and nn. 64 and 65.

[113] For further examples, see Gwara, 'Manuscripts of Aldhelm's *Prosa de Virginitate*', pp. 150–3; the above quotations are taken from *ibid.*, pp. 150–1.

the original make-up of the manuscript. Among Aldhelm's correspondence, the transmissional history of this letter is remarkable: it is unique among Aldhelm's letters in being preserved in English pre-Conquest manuscripts. Of the thirteen letters of his correspondence (three of these addressed *to* Aldhelm) printed by Ehwald,[114] seven are found (in abbreviated form) only in William of Malmesbury's *Gesta pontificum*, four only in Vienna, Österreichische Nationalbibliothek, 751 (written at Mainz, s. ix^med) and one in both of these sources.[115] By contrast, the letter to Ehfrid is preserved in seven manuscripts, in all but one of these together with the prose *De uirginitate*.[116] As Ehwald noted, all extant copies of the letter are closely related, presumably all going back to a common archetype. The best texts are preserved in our Royal 7. D. XXIV and in Digby 146 (the Digby manuscript being derived from Royal 7. D. XXIV).[117] It is clear, therefore, that the letter to Ehfrid in Royal 7. D. XXIV is a text, copied with care and competence, which stands at the head of the English textual tradition. The care and competence of the scribe are worth mentioning, since the letter is a stylistic *tour de force*, remarkable even by Aldhelmian standards. As in the case of the Cuthbert Lives in CCCC 183, we cannot say whether the scribe of Royal 7. D. XXIV found the prose *De uirginitate* and the letter to Ehfrid together in one exemplar, or whether he first combined them from two different manuscripts. Even if he did find both texts in one exemplar, there may have been specific reasons why he should have copied out both *en suite* (reasons other than just faithful adherence to an exemplar). In order to understand what such reasons might have been we shall have to highlight a few details from Aldhelm's letter.

The identity of the letter's addressee is in doubt. Eadfrith, bishop of

---

[114] *Aldhelmi Opera*, pp. 475–503.

[115] See the brief discussion in Lapidge and Herren, *Aldhelm: the Prose Works*, p. 136, and Ehwald's *apparatus criticus*.

[116] See Ehwald, *Aldhelmi Opera*, pp. 487–8.

[117] See *ibid.*, p. 488 (and p. 222, for the text of the *De uirginitate*); for a discussion of the dependence of Digby 146 on Royal 7. D. XXIV (both the letter to Ehfrid and *De uirginitate*), see also Gwara, 'Manuscripts of Aldhelm's *Prosa de Virginitate*', pp. 137–42. There is a recent critical edition and commentary of the Letter and its accompanying (mainly Latin) glosses by S. Gwara, 'A Record of Anglo-Saxon Pedagogy: Aldhelm's *Epistola ad Heahfridum* and its Gloss', *The Journal of Medieval Latin* 6 (1996), 84–134. For a discussion of the textual relationships of the extant copies of the Letter (broadly confirming Ehwald's findings), see *ibid.*, pp. 100–8.

Lindisfarne from some point after 698 is one of the candidates who have been suggested, a suggestion which has, however, not been adopted by the recent translators of the letter.[118] In any event, at some point, the Ehfrid of the letter must have been Aldhelm's student: Aldhelm refers to him as 'your kindly Discipleship'.[119] Aldhelm's letter aims principally at a deprecation of Irish scholarship, of which its addressee (who is said to have returned from Ireland only recently) appears to have had some first-hand knowledge. In florid language Aldhelm propounds his firm belief that now that Archbishop Theodore (669–90) and Abbot Hadrian (d. 710) are active and flourishing in England, English scholarship is not only on a par with Irish learning, but brilliantly excels at every field where Irish scholarship has been applied. Interestingly, at one point in his panegyric on English learning, Aldhelm makes mention of former heathen practices: he commends the progress of Christianity through which dwellings for students and houses of prayer are constructed in places 'where once the crude pillars of the . . . foul snake and the stag were worshipped with coarse stupidity in profane shrines.'[120]

Judged in the context of King Æthelstan's reign, the inclusion of this specific letter in Royal 7. D. XXIV raises the suggestive possibility that the manuscript may originally have been conceived as a presentation copy for St Cuthbert's community, and that at some point this plan was abandoned in favour of CCCC 183, produced slightly later by the same scribe and the same artist. On this hypothesis, the letter would perhaps have been intended to serve an educational purpose. The king's advisers might well have thought fit to include in a manuscript destined for Chester-le-Street a letter which Aldhelm, renowned bishop of a southern

---

[118] See the brief discussion by Ehwald, *Aldhelmi Opera*, pp. 486–7, and Lapidge and Herren, *Aldhelm: the Prose Works*, p. 145. For a full review of the candidates who have been suggested, see A. S. Cook, 'Who was the Ehfrid of Aldhelm's Letter?', *Speculum* 2 (1927), 363–73. Cook's rejection of Eadfrith, bishop of Lindisfarne, on phonological grounds is not convincing. Even so, there are severe phonological problems involved in an equation of Ehfridus and Eadfrith. The matter would deserve fresh philological consideration. No precise dates for Eadfrith's episcopacy can be established; see Keynes, 'Episcopal Succession', p. 219.

[119] 'tuum affabilem discipulatum', Ehwald, *Aldhelmi Opera*, p. 491; Lapidge and Herren, *Aldhelm: the Prose Works*, p. 162.

[120] Lapidge and Herren, *Aldhelm: the Prose Works*, p. 160–1; 'ubi pridem . . . nefandae natricis ermula ceruulusque cruda fanis colebantur stoliditate in profanis', Ehwald, *Aldhelmi Opera*, p. 489.

see, had sent to one of his students (perhaps taken to be a bishop of Lindisfarne, St Cuthbert's monastery),[121] a letter, moreover, resounding with the praise of English scholarship and extolling English learning at the expense of the Irish. On this hypothesis again, the king's advisers might also have thought Aldhelm's remark on heathen practices very much to the point. It is well known that, in the tenth century, Christianity in the north was on the decline after a long succession of pagan Scandinavian rulers. An unmistakable testimony to this precarious state of Christianity in the north is provided by the Anglo-Saxon Chronicle. The D-version reports (s. a. 926) that when the Scandinavian, Celtic and English leaders of the north met *æt Eamotum* on 12 July 927 to acknowledge King Æthelstan's supremacy over the whole of Britain, they *inter alia* 'ælc deofolgeld tocwædon', 'forbade all idolatry'.

Such a hypothesis concerning the original plan for Royal 7. D. XXIV may be controlled by evidence of a different sort: the physical state of the manuscript. Royal 7. D. XXIV was apparently planned as a kind of *de luxe* edition of the prose *De uirginitate*, but work on the book was never completed. This is most evident in the unfinished full-page miniature on 85v. This miniature is thought to be a portrait of Aldhelm, modelled on a common type of Evangelist portrait.[122] Since the folio containing the miniature seems to have been trimmed to match the size of the other folios of Royal 7. D. XXIV, a case has recently been made that the miniature actually *is* an Evangelist portrait taken from elsewhere.[123] But

---

[121] Bishop Eadfrith no doubt held a place of honour among the Lindisfarne bishops: he is commemorated as the scribe of the Lindisfarne Gospels in a colophon entered in the manuscript (London, BL, Cotton Nero D. iv, 259r) by the glossator Aldred *c.* 970, that is almost 300 years after his episcopacy. (For Aldred's colophon, see, for example, Ker, *Catalogue*, p. 216 (no. 165)). It may also be noteworthy that Bede had dedicated his prose Life of St Cuthbert to this same Eadfrith and his *familia* at Lindisfarne, a dedication which in CCCC 183 (as in most other manuscripts of the Life) prefaces his *Vita* (ptd and transl. by Colgrave, *Two Lives of Saint Cuthbert*, pp. 142–7).

[122] See Temple, *Anglo-Saxon Manuscripts*, p. 36 (no. 4); for a reproduction, see *ibid.*, pl. 27.

[123] See J. A. Kiff-Hooper, 'Class Books or Works of Art?: Some Observations on the Tenth-Century Manuscripts of Aldhelm's *De Laude Virginitatis*', in *Church and Chronicle in the Middle Ages. Essays Presented to John Taylor*, ed. I. Wood and G. A. Load (London, 1991), pp. 15–26, at 16–18. This author suggests (*ibid.*) that because of its rather luxurious appearance but small size, the manuscript was intended as a presentation copy for some individual rather than a community; but see below.

even if this were so, by its insertion at the beginning of the prose *De uirginitate*, the compiler signalled that the picture was meant to serve as an author's portrait. (One might, perhaps, also note a certain parallel to the elaborate frontispiece in CCCC 183.) Furthermore, the book appears to have remained without a cover for a considerable time after it had been written: its outer folios (fols. 82 and 168) show signs of exposure and wear which would suggest this much.[124] Some errors in Digby 146, which derives (text and part of the glosses) from Royal 7. D. XXIV, may indicate that the Royal manuscript had already acquired such signs of wear on the outer folios (but on inner leaves as well) by the mid-tenth century, when a copy from it was made (which in turn served as the exemplar for Digby 146).[125] The small size of Royal 7. D. XXIV (*c.* 173 × 122 mm) need not preclude the possibility that its original destination could have been Chester-le-Street, when we recall that Æthelstan donated a gospelbook of even smaller dimensions to Christ Church.[126]

In short, some of the physical aspects of Royal 7. D. XXIV (its elegant layout and its unfinished state) give grounds for believing that, for some reason, an original prestigious purpose for the production of this manuscript had been given up before the book was brought to completion. Whether the original plans for Royal 7. D. XXIV were abandoned because, on second thoughts, the contents of CCCC 183 were deemed more appropriate for the purpose in question, or whether they were abandoned for some other reason, we cannot say. Royal 7. D. XXIV originally produced as a presentation copy for St Cuthbert's community must remain a tantalizing but unprovable possibility. But whatever the original purpose for the production of Royal 7. D. XXIV may have been, it is a book executed by the same scribe and (presumably) the same artist who subsequently did their work on CCCC 183 carrying out a royal commission. The Royal manuscript plays therefore a pivotal role in confirming our earlier inference that the careful and enthusiastic study of Aldhelm's works had been under way for some time when Æthelwold went to Glastonbury in 939 or thereabouts, and that the intellectual

---

[124] See Ker, *Catalogue*, p. 330 (no. 259).

[125] For some examples of such errors probably resulting from the worn state of the parchment, see Gwara, 'Manuscripts of Aldhelm's *Prosa de Virginitate*', pp. 141–2.

[126] London, Lambeth Palace Library, 1370, measuring *c.* 158 × 111 mm; for this donation, see Keynes, 'Æthelstan's Books', pp. 153–9.

milieu at King Æthelstan's court should be looked upon as the spring-
board for such study. It is also important to bear in mind that the
scriptorium where the royal commission concerning CCCC 183 was
carried out, and where, presumably, Royal 7. D. XXIV had been produced
slightly earlier, might well have been Glastonbury. This scriptorium
might also have been the place where over the following decades the vast
corpus of Latin glosses was added to Aldhelm's principal work, whereby
Royal 7. D. XXIV was transformed from an original prestige edition of
the prose *De uirginitate* into a genuine book for study.

BL, Cotton Cleopatra A. iii

With this manuscript of Latin–Old English glossaries we are at the
origins (as far back as they can still be traced) of the transmissional
history of the vernacular Aldhelm glosses of the post-Viking period. The
manuscript is dated unanimously to the mid-tenth century.[127] As we
have seen (above, pp. 151–4), the third glossary in Cleopatra A. iii (92r–
117r) is of great importance in that it furnishes external evidence
(through its textual affiliation and the date of the manuscript) for
confirming our suspicion that the huge corpus of vernacular glosses to the
prose *De uirginitate* which is transmitted in Brussels 1650 was in existence
in an earlier form by the mid-tenth century and that therefore our
association of these Brussels glosses (entered in the first half of the
eleventh century) with Æthelwold and his circle in the 940s need not rest
solely on verbal links without any manuscript evidence. The Third
Cleopatra Glossary (Cleo III) is an inventory of *glossae collectae* drawn from
a manuscript of the prose *De uirginitate* (and the *Carmen*) with interlinear
Old English (and a few Latin) glosses. There are reasons for believing that
Cleopatra A. iii was written at St Augustine's, Canterbury.[128] Concerning

---

[127] See Ker, *Catalogue*, p. 182 (no. 143), Bishop 'Notes on Cambridge Manuscripts',
p. 93, and cf. also *idem*, 'Notes on Cambridge Manuscripts', *TCBS* 2 (1954–8),
323–36, at 324–5, and Dumville, 'Square Minuscule' [*ASE* 23], pp. 137 and 139.

[128] The ascription to St Augustine's rests on a codicological link with London, BL,
Cotton Vitellius A. xix (s. x[med], probably from St Augustine's) and a shared scribe
with other manuscripts thought to be of St Augustine's origin and of mid-tenth-
century date; see the references given above, n. 127. For additional reasons for a
Canterbury association of Vitellius A. xix, see Lapidge, 'Prolegomena to an Edition of
Bede's Metrical *Vita Sancti Cuthberti*', p. 143.

a link with the manuscripts under discussion here, it should be recalled that T. A. M. Bishop thought that the hand of the second scribe in Cleopatra A. iii has some resemblance to 'some corrections in black ink' in Rawlinson C. 697.[129]

If, on the evidence of clear verbal links, it is reasonable to associate the origin of the Brussels glosses with Æthelwold, we have then, in view of a probable Canterbury origin of Cleopatra A. iii, interestingly, to assume that the nascent vernacular gloss corpus was copied (perhaps only in part) and disseminated to other centres within a short span after the original glossing had been done. In fact, the Third Cleopatra Glossary is almost certainly a copy and does not represent the original *glossae collectae* as they were culled from a glossed manuscript of Aldhelm's works. This much is suggested by its inclusion in a manuscript containing various glossaries, and is further indicated by the first glossary (Cleo I) preserved in Cleopatra A. iii (5r–75v), a glossary in a-order which re-uses (among other sources) material culled from Cleo III (see above, pp. 150–1). Since Cleo I comes first in the manuscript, Cleo III in the same manuscript, cannot reasonably have been its source. At least one further manuscript, from which Cleo III was copied and from which Cleo I culled its Cleo III glosses, must have existed. We have some direct manuscript evidence of such copying activities involving the early vernacular Aldhelm glosses: a manuscript (now London, BL, Cotton Otho E. i, s. x/xi, probably from St Augustine's) which may once have been a complete copy of Cleo I has survived the fire at Ashburnham House in 1731 in a badly damaged state.[130] In other words, a Canterbury origin of Cleopatra A. iii need in no way interfere with an assumed origin of the Brussels glosses in Æthelwold's circle. Rather, it could flesh out our skeletal information as regards the scholarly contacts which, by the mid-tenth century, existed between the leading Anglo-Saxon centres.

Conclusions

We leave our exploration of the evidence which may be gleaned from Rawlinson C. 697, CCCC 183, Royal 7. D. XXIV and Cleopatra A. iii with a number of suggestive possibilities, but with no firm notion or

---

[129] See Bishop, 'Notes on Cambridge Manuscripts', p. 93, and cf. above, p. 351.
[130] Cf. Ker, *Catalogue*, p. 238 (no. 184).

irrefutable proof concerning the way these manuscripts are related to each other and concerning the role they played in leading scholarly circles during the reign of King Æthelstan and that of his successors, Kings Edmund (939–46), Eadred (946–55) and Eadwig (955–9). An extreme case of elusiveness in this respect is Rawlinson C. 697 with its numerous possible links with other books and various persons and places. We have seen that this manuscript was arguably imported by one of King Alfred's helpers, thereby perhaps testifying to an interest in Aldhelm's works in the context of Alfred's educational programme. On account of the Æthelstan acrostic, the book still seems to have been connected with the royal household in the 920s and 930s. That it was closely studied is revealed by its glosses and annotations (some of these possibly by Dunstan, others, perhaps, pointing to a glossator in Royal 7. D. XXIV); it is also revealed by the circumstance that one of the Old English riddles is translated from Rawlinson's Latin text. A further link exists possibly with the youngest of the four manuscripts under inspection here (Cleopatra A. iii). All this suggests that Rawlinson C. 697 was studied over an extended period in various important Anglo-Saxon libraries after it had travelled to England from the northeast Frankish scriptorium where it was written.

In view of these confusingly intricate relationships between our manuscripts, it may be helpful to recall a letter written by one L to Archbishop Dunstan, probably between 974 and 984.[131] L is presumably to be identified with Lantfred, a Frankish monk from Fleury who had lived among Bishop Æthelwold's monks at the Old Minster for some time in the early 970s and had subsequently returned to Fleury. (While at Winchester, he composed for his hosts the *Translatio et miracula S. Swithuni*, occasioned by the translation of St Swithun on 15 July 971.) In his letter, L asks Dunstan for his help in having returned certain books which were formerly in his (L's) possession (and which he had probably brought with him to England). These books, L presumes, are now at Winchester. In particular, he mentions one book, now (in his view) in the possession of Abbot Osgar.[132] This Osgar was probably the student of

---

[131] For an edition, translation and discussion of this letter, see Lapidge, *The Cult of S. Swithun* (forthcoming). I am very grateful to Michael Lapidge for letting me consult his edition of L's letter, which is available in print only in Stubbs, *Memorials of St Dunstan*, pp. 376–7.

[132] For a possible link between L's request and manuscripts still existing, see J. P. Carley,

Æthelwold who had followed his master from Glastonbury to Abingdon (*c*. 954) and from there to Winchester in 963. He had returned to Abingdon within a short time and functioned as abbot of that house for the rest of his career (963/4 × 984).[133] The book L asked for in particular would therefore have been, in all probability, at Abingdon, not at Winchester (and note that L wrote to Dunstan at Canterbury to get his books back). In short, L's letter may serve as an excellent reminder of the close relationship between the principal proponents of the Benedictine reform, their intellectual pursuits and their exchange of books.

Our picture of the fate of the four books which have occupied us here may be only dimly realized. Nevertheless, the contents of Rawlinson C. 697, Royal 7. D. XXIV and CCCC 183 afford us a precious glimpse of some of the intellectual activities that were going on during Æthelwold's and Dunstan's formative years, intellectual activities in which they were playing an ever increasing role. The evidence of the Cleopatra glossaries enables us to understand vernacular Aldhelm glossing as part of these intellectual activities and to see how, once such glossing had been undertaken on a larger scale, it was handled in a scholarly fashion: the glosses were culled from glossed manuscripts of Aldhelm's works to form first-stage glossaries (or *glossae collectae* as in Cleo III), then recast and incorporated in alphabetical glossaries (Cleo I) and, in both forms, rapidly disseminated to various centres.

ARCHBISHOP ODA

Verbal links among the glosses in Brussels 1650 with works which can be associated with Æthelwold point unmistakably to his circle. However, we have seen (above, ch. 5) that the Brussels glosses are composite, comprising various layers and having attracted many accretions until they were assembled in the form in which they have reached us in Brussels 1650. It may therefore be worth asking whether other centres or persons could be identified as having been involved in the development of this massive corpus of glosses.

When we consider the origin of the glosses (during the 940s or early

'Two Pre-Conquest Manuscripts from Glastonbury Abbey', *ASE* 16 (1987), 197–212, at 209–10.

[133] See *Wulfstan: Life*, chs. 11, 17 and 21 (and notes to these chs.).

950s) Oda, archbishop of Canterbury (941–58) might be a suitable candidate. We have seen (above, pp. 339–40) that during the earlier stages of his career he may somehow have been associated with King Æthelstan's court, where he may well have acquired his taste for the hermeneutic style. Not much of Oda's literary activities has survived: a letter to his suffragan bishops and his *Constitutiones* (a set of canons pertaining to ecclesiastical law);[134] both texts are written in plain, unadorned but competent Latin. However, we have come to know Oda as an enthusiastic propagator of the hermeneutic style in the preface which he may have composed to Frithegod's *Breuiloquium* (above, p. 341). And it will be recalled that the Frankish scholar Frithegod probably came to England on Oda's personal invitation and, while there, composed his hermeneutic masterpiece at his patron's instigation. It is noteworthy that Oda and Frithegod agree in their particular brand of the hermeneutic style: a predilection for exceedingly obscure vocabulary, often neologisms coined on Greek elements[135] (as opposed, for example, to the more sober and more common grecisms employed in Winchester circles in the 970s).[136] In fact, the close agreement in vocabulary and style between Oda's prose preface and Frithegod's poem has been taken to suggest that Frithegod himself composed the preface in his patron's name.[137] Whatever the case, such agreement between the *Breuiloquium* and a preface going by Oda's name reveals that Oda and his protégé had shared common views on language and style. One may suspect, therefore, that when Frithegod at one point in his poem contemptuously refers to the *barbaries inculta* ('uncivilized rudeness') of the English language, this remark would not have met with any strong disapproval by his patron.[138] Nor (one may suspect) would Frithegod have ventured such a verdict if any vernacular glossing of a scholarly nature had been going on at Canterbury during his sojourn there.

Such a supposition may be borne out by the manuscript evidence for Frithegod's *Breuiloquium* (a poem – it would seem – in even greater need

---

[134] The letter (surviving only in an excerpt by William of Malmesbury, *Gesta pontificum* I, 16) is printed in *CS*, pp. 65–7 (no. 19); the *Constitutiones* (preserved in an eleventh-century manuscript) are printed *ibid.*, pp. 67–74 (no. 20).

[135] See Lapidge, 'Hermeneutic Style', pp. 116–19.

[136] See *ibid.*, pp. 124–7 and 139.   [137] See Lapidge, 'A Frankish Scholar', p. 168.

[138] *Breuiloquium*, line 96; cf. Lapidge, 'A Frankish Scholar', p. 177, n. 63, where this remark is cited as pointing to Frithegod's non-English extraction.

of glossing than Aldhelm's works). The *Breuiloquium* is preserved in three manuscripts, all closely related, all written presumably during Oda's episcopate, while Frithegod was still in England, in other words, before 958. All three manuscripts bear interlinear and marginal glosses and scholia, entered by various hands. These glosses and scholia, again, are closely related and contemporary with the main text. However, these glosses are far from being as dense as they are in some glossed Aldhelm manuscripts (such as Royal 7. D. XXIV), and there are almost no Old English glosses among them.[139] It may also be significant that Frithegod seems to have left England for Francia in search of a new patron in 958 (or thereabouts), which at least suggests that, after Oda's death, Canterbury no longer held much intellectual attraction for a scholar of his calibre.[140] Still, to judge from the competent Latin glossing done on the manuscripts of the *Breuiloquium*, we should not rule out the possibility that some *Latin* glossing in Aldhelm manuscripts was practised at Canterbury under the scholar-bishop Oda.

ABBOT DUNSTAN

On the evidence provided by Wulfstan and B, Æthelwold's and Dunstan's respective biographers (and confirmed by charter evidence) it is generally deduced that Æthelwold and Dunstan studied together at Glastonbury for more than ten years, between *c.* 939 and *c.* 954, when Æthelwold was appointed abbot of Abingdon.[141] We have seen (above, pp. 256–7) that

---

[139] See Lapidge, 'A Frankish Scholar', pp. 163–77, for a discussion of the manuscripts, glosses and scribes who wrote them (Frithegod himself may have been one of the scribes). For a notion of the density of the glossing, see *ibid.*, pls. II and V, and cf. these, for example, with pl. 54a (showing 124r of Royal 7. D. XXIV) in Warner and Gilson, *Catalogue* IV.

[140] For what can be conjectured about Frithegod's later career, see Lapidge, 'A Frankish Scholar', pp. 177–81.

[141] Wulfstan gives no date for Æthelwold's promotion to Abingdon, but states (ch. 11, *Wulfstan: Life*, pp. 18–22) that it took place during Eadred's reign, hence before Eadred's death on 23 November 955. The date 954 usually given (cf. e. g. Knowles *et al.*, *Heads of Religious Houses*, p. 50) is provided by the fourteenth-century chronicler John of Glastonbury, on what authority is not known; cf. *The Chronicle of Glastonbury Abbey*, ed. J. P. Carley (Woodbridge, 1985), p. 124; see also Lapidge, *Wulfstan: Life*, p. xlvi. However, since Wulfstan reports a visit by King Eadred to Abingdon (*Life*, ch. 12, pp. 22–4) implying that by then the building works had been going on there

Wulfstan's remark that, at Glastonbury, Dunstan acted as Æthelwold's tutor, probably reflects no more than the lifelong affection and *pietas* Æthelwold felt for his friend and coeval. In view of such a prolonged term of study which the future leaders of the Benedictine reform spent together, it may be worth asking whether any traces of the collaboration of Dunstan in the vernacular glosswork on Aldhelm's prose *De uirginitate* (or in the Royal Psalter gloss for that matter) can be detected. Again, the verbal links with the Old English Benedictine Rule point to Æthelwold, but it may not be unreasonable to assume that, as a result of their joint study, Æthelwold and Dunstan would have shared lexical predilections.

Unfortunately, it is not possible to test such a hypothesis. No works in Old English by Dunstan have survived or have as yet been identified – if such works were ever in existence. The corpus of Dunstan's surviving Latin writings is exiguous: a distich on 1r in what is now Oxford, Bodleian Library, Auct. F. 4. 32 ('St. Dunstan's classbook'), the first line of which is lifted from a poem by Hrabanus Maurus.[142] Next, three distichs inscribed on three gifts (an organ, a holy-water stoup and a little bell for the high table in the refectory) which Dunstan gave to Malmesbury abbey at some point during his episcopacy. They are preserved in the post-Conquest Life of Aldhelm by Faricius of Arezzo (d. 1117) and in William of Malmesbury's *Gesta pontificum* and give us a notion of Dunstan as an author of occasional verse, exhibiting some metrical proficiency.[143] We have further an exceedingly difficult acrostic poem of some thirty-six lines (the right-hand column spells out the words: *indignum abbatem Dunstanum Xpē respectes*). It is apparently indebted to Aldhelm's acrostic preface to his

for some time, a date somewhat prior to 955 should perhaps be assumed for Æthelwold's appointment. Dunstan apparently functioned as abbot of Glastonbury until he was driven into exile, probably in 956. On the charter evidence for the date of Dunstan's exile, see Keynes, *Diplomas*, pp. 49–68. B (as usual) gives no exact date for this event. For the date of Dunstan's appointment as abbot (*c.* 940), see below, n. 146. The implication of Wulfstan's narrative in ch. 9 of his *Vita* (*Wulfstan: Life*, p. 14) would seem to be that Dunstan had already been pursuing his studies at Glastonbury for some time prior to his elevation, and before he was joined there by Æthelwold, presumably in 939.

[142] See H. Gneuss, 'Dunstan und Hrabanus Maurus. Zur Hs. Bodleian Auctarium F. 4. 32', in his *Books and Libraries*, no. VIII, 136–148, with full bibliographical references. For a review of scholarly opinion on the famous line-drawing to which this distich is added, see Budny, 'St Dunstan's Classbook', pp. 116–23.

[143] The distichs are printed and discussed by Lapidge, 'Dunstan's Latin Poetry'.

metrical *De uirginitate*, and it has some Aldhelmian verbal echoes. The difficulties of Dunstan's acrostic lie principally in its ferociously convoluted syntax, but it parades some typically hermeneutic vocabulary as well, thereby revealing Dunstan as an eager reader of Aldhelm and practitioner of the hermeneutic style during his time at Glastonbury.[144] Aldhelmian echoes can also be found in a charter which has some claim to be regarded as having been composed and (at least in its original form) copied out by Dunstan at his Glastonbury scriptorium. The charter in question records the grant of the minster at Reculver in Kent to Christ Church, Canterbury. It is issued in the name of King Eadred and dated 949.[145]

Such possible evidence for Dunstan's literary activities being chanelled into the drafting of charters raises the question of how much leisure would have been left to the abbot of Glastonbury to join a glossing project on which Æthelwold (and perhaps some of his colleagues) had embarked. Dunstan was appointed abbot in 940 or thereabouts.[146] On B's account, which is supported (to some extent) by charter evidence, he must have been rather busy, acting as an influential member of the king's *witan* during the reigns of Edmund and Eadred.[147] The charter evidence for

---

[144] The poem has been printed, explained and translated by Lapidge, 'Hermeneutic Style', pp. 146–9; see also discussion *ibid.*, pp. 133–5. Aldhelm's prefatory acrostic is printed by Ehwald, *Aldhelmi Opera*, pp. 350–2.

[145] S 564 (BCS 880). Much has been written on this charter and its authenticity; see most recently (with further bibliographical references) Keynes, '"Dunstan B" Charters', p. 184. For an evaluation of the script of the two single sheets in which the charter survives, see Lapidge, 'Æthelwold as Scholar', pp. 185–6, and Dumville, 'Square Minuscule' [*ASE* 23], p. 146, n. 71. For the Aldhelmian diction, see Lapidge, 'Æthelwold as Scholar and Teacher', p. 186, n. 24. The attribution of the charter rests on its subscription: 'Ego Dunstan indignus abbas rege Eadredo imperante hanc domino meo hereditariam kartulam dictitando conposui et propriis digitorum articulis perscripsi', 'I Dunstan, an unworthy abbot, at the command of King Eadred composed this charter of inheritance by means of dictation and copied it out with the joints of my own fingers' (transl. Lapidge 'Æthelwold as Scholar and Teacher', p. 185). Note that, as in the acrostic, Dunstan is styled *indignus abbas*.

[146] The date 940 which is usually given for the beginning of Dunstan's abbacy (cf. Knowles *et al.*, *Heads of Religious Houses*, p. 50) is based on the impression created by B (*Vita*, ed. Stubbs, ch. 14, p. 25) that Dunstan was made abbot at some point early in King Edmund's reign. There is also a charter (preserved in two fourteenth-century cartularies) dated 940 and issued by King Edmund in favour of abbot Dunstan (S 466, BCS 752).

[147] See *Vita* (ed. Stubbs), chs. 13–14 and 19–20.

Dunstan's involvement in royal business is most impressive for the reign of King Eadred (that is from 946 onwards);[148] there are, however, clear indications that Dunstan and his Glastonbury scriptorium must have played an important role in royal administration already during the preceding reign of King Edmund.[149]

Our final piece of evidence which may have some bearing on the question of Dunstan's literary or scholarly activities are two remarks by B: first, that Dunstan corrected manuscripts.[150] It will be recalled that Dunstan's hand is thought still to be traceable in various manuscripts, most interestingly in annotations in Rawlinson C. 697 (Aldhelm) and in CUL Ee. 2. 4 (Smaragdus, *Expositio in Regulam S. Benedicti*).[151] Second, that Dunstan had skill in writing and illuminating manuscripts.[152]

The sum of this various evidence does not amount to much. We have, for example, no information whatsoever that Dunstan, upon his elevation to Canterbury, established there anything close to a school, dedicated to the study and production of Latin or vernacular texts.[153] Nonetheless, the circumstance that Canterbury seems to have been a centre for the

---

[148] Such evidence is provided by the so-called 'Dunstan B' charters, on which see most recently Keynes, '"Dunstan B" Charters'. This is a group of royal diplomas, clearly defined by their style (and standing outside the mainstream of tenth-century diplomatic), produced between 951 and 975. Their production is assigned to Glastonbury throughout, and their distinctive form is thought to derive from Dunstan himself. For a list of the charters in question, see Keynes, *ibid.*, pp. 173–9, for their stylistic distinctiveness, pp. 180–1, and for their association with Dunstan and Glastonbury, pp. 181–93. That in the closing years of Eadred's reign (953–5) the Glastonbury scriptorium should have been entrusted with issuing charters in the king's name, where the king is absent from the list of witnesses (presumably on grounds of his illness) may throw important light on the role played by Dunstan in royal politics during these years; see Keynes, *ibid.*, pp. 185–6.

[149] Two charters issued in King Edmund's name, in the production of which Dunstan was arguably involved, have clear links with the 'Dunstan B' charters and may serve to highlight Dunstan's position during these years. See Keynes, '"Dunstan B" Charters', pp. 182–5; the charters in question are S 509 (BCS 458, dated 946) and S 546 (BCS 880, dated 949, the Reculver charter, cf. above, n. 145). See, however, Brooks, 'The Career of Dunstan', p. 11, for a suggestion that Dunstan may have been kept deliberately out of court during Edmund's reign.

[150] *Vita*, ed. Stubbs, ch. 37, p. 49.   [151] See above, pp. 255 and 351.

[152] *Vita*, ed. Stubbs, ch. 12, p. 20.

[153] For an evaluation of what evidence we have for Dunstan's activities during his episcopate and his relationship with the two Canterbury communities, see Brooks, *Early History*, pp. 243–53, esp. 251–3. B vaguely remarks on the promotion of

production of glossed manuscripts of the prose *De uirginitate* (containing both Latin and vernacular glosses) in the late tenth and eleventh centuries[154] may be a reflex of Dunstan's interest and, perhaps, involvement in Aldhelm glossing. An adequate assessment of the Latin gloss corpora of the prose *De uirginitate* must await their publication. Our preoccupation here is with the origin of the vernacular glosses as preserved in Brussels 1650, and concerning the transmission of these glosses we are somewhat nearer to Dunstan's episcopacy with the bilingual glossaries in Cleopatra A. iii, arguably written at Canterbury (St Augustine's) by the mid-tenth century and containing a nucleus of the much larger Brussels gloss corpus. We may perhaps even permit ourselves to imagine that it was Dunstan who brought the exemplars for these glossaries to Canterbury. In sum, however, Dunstan as scholar and teacher remains a shadowy figure. Dunstan no doubt was the man whom Æthelwold loved and venerated above all others, with whom he had shared some of his formative experiences at King Æthelstan's court (such as their joint ordination as priests) and by whom he had subsequently been drawn to Glastonbury. The prospect of Dunstan and Æthelwold embarking together on an ambitious translation project is one which holds much attraction. But in the absence of any vernacular writings attributable to Dunstan and of any conclusive external evidence, such a prospect can be no more than an attractive possibility.

THE EVIDENCE OF LATER MANUSCRIPTS

We have seen that Canterbury was a centre where glossed manuscripts of Aldhelm were produced in later Anglo-Saxon England. As opposed to Canterbury, no manuscript of Aldhelm's prose *De uirginitate* with Old English (or Latin) glosses from one of the Winchester houses is extant. In evaluating this situation, we should, however, be aware of the fact that only comparatively few books written at Winchester appear to have survived, and that it has been shown that texts which demonstrably originated at Winchester are preserved in Canterbury, not Winchester

Dunstan's pupils to high ecclesiastical ranks (*Vita*, ed. Stubbs, ch. 15, pp. 25–6) but makes no mention at all of any instruction of an intellectual nature given by Dunstan.
[154] See Goossens, *Old English Glosses*, pp. 20–1, Gwara, 'Manuscripts of Aldhelm's *Prosa de Virginitate*', pp. 135–59, and *idem*, 'The Transmission of the "Digby" Corpus', *passim*; and cf. the list of manuscripts with Old English glosses, above, pp. 143–4.

copies. The Old English interlinear version of the *Regula S. Benedicti* in BL, Cotton Tiberius A. iii, the *Expositio hymnorum* (a prose paraphrase of the metrical hymns) and its Old English interlinear gloss in BL, Cotton Julius A. vi and Vespasian D. xii, or the Latin text of Æthelwold's *Regularis concordia* in Tiberius A. iii and BL, Cotton Faustina B. iii, would be a few more outstanding examples that come to mind.[155]

Brussels 1650, our most important witness for the vast vernacular gloss corpus in the origin of which Æthelwold was presumably involved, has been assigned to Abingdon by Neil Ker, both text and glosses (dated by him s. xi^{in} and s. xi^1 respectively). Ker's presumption of an Abingdon origin seems convincing; it is based on codicological and liturgical evidence, on the evidence of texts and inscriptions in Brussels 1650 and related manuscripts and on shared scribes and similarities of script between Brussels 1650 and other Abingdon manuscripts.[156] Ker further assumed that at Abingdon the Brussels gloss corpus was copied into Digby 146 (probably by s. xi^{med}; he did not pronounce on the origin of the Digby manuscript itself, dated by him s. x^{ex}).[157] However, interesting as such a possible origin of the Brussels and Digby glosses in the Abingdon scriptorium may be, an Abingdon origin of these glosses would surely be no proof that the gloss corpus itself originated there as well, since by the time both manuscripts received their glosses, Aldhelm had been securely established as the most important author in the late

[155] For the Winchester origin of the interlinear version of the *Regula*, see Hofstetter, *Winchester und Sprachgebrauch*, pp. 119–23; for the *Expositio hymnorum*, see Gneuss, *Hymnar und Hymnen*, pp. 133–4 and 186–8, and Hofstetter, *Winchester und Sprachgebrauch*, p. 102. For the Canterbury origin of Tiberius A. iii, see Ker, *Catalogue*, p. 248 (no. 186), and Gneuss, 'Origin and Provenance of Anglo-Saxon Manuscripts'; for Faustina B. iii, see Ker, *Catalogue*, p. 197 (no. 136), and Kornexl, *Die 'Regularis Concordia' und ihre altenglische Interlinearversion*, pp. xcix–cxi; for Julius A. vi and Vespasian D. xii, see Gneuss, *Hymnar und Hymnen*, pp. 91–101.

[156] See Ker, *Catalogue*, p. 7 (no. 8), p. 3 (nos. 2 and 3), and cf. also p. 38 (no. 24) and p. 47 (no. 34).

[157] See Ker, *Catalogue*, pp. 381–3 (no. 320). The attribution to Abingdon of the Brussels text and glosses and the Digby glosses has recently been challenged, and a Canterbury origin for both manuscripts and their glosses has been posited: see Gwara, 'The Transmission of the "Digby" Corpus', pp. 143 and n. 21, and 167 (for Brussels), and p. 141 and n. 9, and *passim* (for Digby). Note, however, the ascriptions for these manuscripts and glosses (different from the aforementioned and varying one from the other), given by Gwara in 'Manuscripts of Aldhelm's *Prosa de Virginitate*'; pp. 135–6, 142 and 156, and in 'The Continuance of Aldhelm Studies', p. 23 and n. 25, and p. 38.

Anglo-Saxon curriculum, and a manuscript encrusted with thousands of vernacular (and Latin) glosses would have been considered useful in any Anglo-Saxon school.

There is some other manuscript evidence for a sustained interest in vernacular Aldhelm glosses in Æthelwold's foundations. One such piece of evidence is provided by Oxford, Bodleian Library, Bodley 163, fols. 250–1, a bifolium now constituting the third part of this composite manuscript. The bifolium may be assigned to Peterborough, principally on grounds of a booklist which was copied onto 251r by *c.* 1100 and which probably catalogues books then belonging to the Peterborough library.[158] Onto 250r a small glossary (*glossae collectae*) containing some ninety-two entries has been copied in a hand dated by Ker to the mid-eleventh century.[159] Interestingly, this little glossary combines the – apart from the psalter glosses – two most important gloss traditions from Anglo-Saxon England: in its latter parts (almost exclusively Latin–Latin) it preserves many glosses drawn from the 'Leiden Family' of glossaries (particularly from the sections on the canons and decretals), and therefore ultimately deriving from the Canterbury school of Theodore and Hadrian.[160] The *interpretamenta* in the first third, however, are almost wholly Old English, and the lemmata derive largely from Aldhelm's prose *De uirginitate*.[161] They have clear links with the Brussels glosses and the Cleopatra glossaries. Note in particular the lemma *redimicula*, glossed by the exceedingly rare *cynewiððan* in Bodley 163 (Lendinara 508.16), in the Third Cleopatra Glossary (WW 513.25), and in Brussels 1650 (G 5121).[162] It is further noteworthy that this short glossary should transmit the entry *anagogen: gastlic andgit* (Lendinara 507.13). The *interpretamentum* is a phrase which was very possibly coined by Æthelwold, signifying allegorical biblical exegesis in general, or one of the fourfold senses of the Bible in particular. It occurs in the Brussels glosses for *allegoria* and in the First Cleopatra Glossary for *anagogen* (cf. above, p. 223). A few glosses in Bodley 163, however, do not appear in any other glossed

---

[158] See Ker, *Catalogue*, p. 358 (no. 304b); the booklist has been edited and discussed by Lapidge, 'Booklists', pp. 76–82.

[159] Ker, *Catalogue*, p. 358 (no. 304b).

[160] See Lapidge, *Biblical Commentaries*, ed. Bischoff and Lapidge, p. 179.

[161] The complete glossary has been edited by Lendinara, 'Il glossario'.

[162] For this gloss, see above, pp. 156–7.

manuscript or glossary of the prose *De uirginitate*,[163] which may serve to remind us that in spite of the vast vernacular gloss corpora our picture of Aldhelm glossing in Old English will never be complete.

A connection with an Æthelwold foundation (Abingdon again) may also be suspected for the youngest surviving manuscript of the prose *De uirginitate* to contain Old English glosses: Hereford Cathedral Library, P. I. 2. This manuscript has fifty-seven Old English glosses and *c.* 3700 scholia in Latin. Text and glosses are dated to *c.* 1200 (s. xii/xiii). The medieval provenance of the manuscript is Cirencester, about thirty miles west of Abingdon. Both Old English and Latin glosses are derived (presumably by an intermediary copy) from Digby 146, a manuscript which, as we have seen, arguably received its Old English glosses at Abingdon.[164]

Our final witness, possibly pointing to a long-lasting interest in vernacular Aldhelm glossing in Æthelwold's former sphere of influence, is again a glossary, this time to Aldhelm's *Carmen de uirginitate*, found in Oxford, Bodleian Library, Auct. F. 2. 14. This manuscript is a collection of Latin poetry, notably Wulfstan of Winchester's *Narratio metrica de S. Swithuno*, written in England, s. xi².[165] Its later provenance (and perhaps origin) is Sherborne.[166] The text of the *Narratio metrica* has a few Latin and Old English glosses which are also found in the second surviving manuscript of Wulfstan's poem: London, BL, Royal 15. C. VII, a book written at Winchester (Old Minster) around 996.[167] Since, according to

---

[163] See discussion by Lendinara, 'Il glossario', pp. 500–1.

[164] For the manuscript and textual affiliations of the Old English glosses in Hereford P. I. 2, see Ker, *Catalogue*, pp. 156–7 (no. 120), and Goossens, *Old English Glosses*, pp. 18 and 27. The Old English glosses are printed *OEG*, pp. 149–50 (no. 3); Napier (*ibid.*, p. xxv) noted already the dependence of these glosses on Digby 146. For the Latin glosses and scholia and their textual relationship, see Gwara, 'The Continuance of Aldhelm Studies'. For a description of the complete manuscript, see now R. A. B. Mynors and R. M. Thomson, *Catalogue of the Manuscripts in Hereford Cathedral Library* (Cambridge, 1993), pp. 73–4.

[165] See Ker, *Catalogue*, p. 354 (no. 295), and *idem*, *English Manuscripts in the Century after the Norman Conquest* (Oxford, 1960), p. 22 and n. 1, and Lapidge, *The Cult of St Swithun* (forthcoming).

[166] Cf. Ker, *Catalogue*, p. 354, and *idem*, *Medieval Libraries of Great Britain*, 2nd ed. (London, 1964), p. 179.

[167] For the Old English glosses in both manuscripts, see Ker, *Catalogue*, p. 354 (no. 295, art. b) and pp. 335–6 (no. 270); these glosses are printed *OEG*, p. 217 (no. 52). For the Latin glosses, and the date and origin of Royal 15. C. VII, see Lapidge, *Wulfstan: Life*, p. xxi.

Michael Lapidge, the text of the *Narratio metrica* itself in Auct. F. 2. 14 was copied from Royal 15. C. VII,[168] a Winchester origin for Auct. F. 2. 14 as well is at least possible.

In the margins of 11r–19v of Auct. F. 2. 14 a Latin–Old English glossary to the *Carmen de uirginitate* is entered in a hand dated by Ker *c.* 1100 (s. xi/xii).[169] This glossary is in a-order and comprises some ninety-six entries.[170] It is not possible to say whether the glossary was entered at Winchester, Sherborne or at some other place. However, as Napier has convincingly shown, it must have been copied from an earlier (eleventh-century) exemplar, since its phonology and morphology are pure West Saxon.[171] The occurrence of the entry *fastus: pryte* (*OEG*, no. 18B.29) may point to a Winchester ambit (see below, p. 420). Two points about this glossary are noteworthy: first, its ninety-six entries constitute a considerably larger gloss corpus to the *Carmen de uirginitate* than is found in any other glossed manuscript of that work.[172] In fact, the Bodleian Glossary is exceeded in number only by the section drawn from the *Carmen* in the Third Cleopatra Glossary (which marks the renaissance of Aldhelm glossing in the tenth century). Secondly, the Aldhelm lemmata have evidently been adapted for teaching purposes. This much is clear from the fact that, in most cases, grammatical information is provided for them, either by the addition of pronouns (thus indicating their gender), or by giving relevant inflexional endings. Cf., for example: *Hoc Gramma*: *Bocstæf* (*OEG* 18B.45); *Hæc Pira*: *Fyr* (76); *Phastus. sti*: *Boc* (70); *Faustus. ta. tum*: *God* (35); *Pullus. la. lum*: *Sweart* (75) *Findo. dis. it*: *Ic toclæfe ł dæle* (38); *Redoleo. les. redolui*: *Ic steme* (77). Here, if anywhere, we have Aldhelm adapted for elementary classroom instruction.[173]

The sum of this slender but suggestive evidence provided by the eleventh- and twelfth-century manuscripts and glosses of Aldhelm's works seems to point to an intrinsic interest in, and a strong tradition of, vernacular Aldhelm glossing in centres connected with Æthelwold; a

---

[168] See Lapidge, *The Cult of St Swithun*.   [169] See Ker, *Catalogue*, p. 354.

[170] It is printed *OEG*, pp. 186–8 (no. 18B).

[171] See A. S. Napier, 'Altenglische Glossen', *Englische Studien* 11 (1888), 62–7, esp. 63.

[172] For the glossed manuscripts of the *Carmen de uirginitate* which have survived, see above, p. 141, n. 27.

[173] This impression is confirmed by the fact that the same hand which copied the glossary also entered Latin and a few Old English glosses to Phocas, *Ars de nomine et uerbo* in the same manuscript; see Ker, *Catalogue*, p. 354 (no. 295).

tradition which apparently was carried on for several generations after that great master had first instituted it in his foundations. That the study of Aldhelm was continued here into an age with changing literary and scholarly preoccupations is, perhaps, a last reflex of the vigour with which such study was pursued in Bishop Æthelwold's schools.

CONCLUSIONS

Looking back from these last reflections of Aldhelm studies and glossing at Æthelwold's foundations to the origin of such studies at King Æthelstan's court, we have gone a long way in our attempt to understand why for Æthelwold, as well as for others of his generation, Aldhelm held such a great fascination. Given Æthelwold's well-attested interest in the vernacular and his delight in translating Latin texts into Old English ('Latinos libros Anglice ... soluere'),[174] it seems natural that for him the study of Aldhelm should include vernacular glossing. The confidence which he and his co-workers thereby placed in the intellectual potential, the pliability and the resourcefulness of the English language is revealed in the many coinages among the Brussels glosses trying to recreate the ingenuity and flamboyance of Aldhelm's vocabulary.[175]

We will probably never be in a position to single out from among the thousands of Old English glosses transmitted in Brussels 1650 a clearly defined group and identify this group as being devised by Æthelwold personally; and indeed it is doubtful if such a corpus ever existed. From their very beginnings, as these can be traced in the Third Cleopatra Glossary, the Brussels glosses appear to have been the result of some kind of Aldhelm seminar (much more so than the continuous and homogenous gloss to the Royal Psalter), a seminar in which Æthelwold will have played a leading part. Moreover, work on the Brussels glosses must have continued for several decades after its presumed beginning at Glastonbury in the 940s. The vocabulary of these glosses reveals that at least one of Æthelwold's foundations must have been involved in such continuation: the most important stratum of glosses in Brussels 1650, the CD corpus, was thoroughly revised and (one presumes) augmented in a centre where Winchester vocabulary was taught and employed, and at a time when this usage was fully-fledged, that is not before (say) the

---

[174] *Wulfstan: Life*, ch. 31, pp. 46–8.   [175] See above, pp. 158–83.

970s.[176] It will be even less possible to define which role precisely Æthelwold played in providing the thousands of Latin glosses and scholia to the prose *De uirginitate*, once they will have been fully published. Invaluable as these glosses and scholia are for recreating the intellectual milieu of the early stages of the reform, we may expect them to be wholly explanatory, never aiming to reproduce Aldhelm's lexical brilliance; and, as opposed to the vernacular glosses, conclusive verbal links with Æthelwold's known Latin writings are unlikely to be detected, since these writings themselves very much strive to emulate Aldhelm's style and diction. But we may suspect that, as with the Old English glosses, Æthelwold's influence in providing Latin glosses and scholia for Aldhelm's great work will have been pre-eminent.

As regards the hypothetical Aldhelm seminar at Glastonbury in the 940s and early 950s, we may have, in the form of a letter, a witness enabling us to draw an engaging picture of that seminar at work. The author of this letter[177] names himself as B, and he is presumably identical with B, the biographer of Dunstan, who (as we have seen) was educated at Glastonbury and subsequently seems to have been a member of Dunstan's personal retinue until *c.* 960. The letter is addressed to Æthelgar, who had been a monk at Glastonbury and one of Æthelwold's pupils. Æthelwold installed him as the first abbot of the reformed New Minster at Winchester in 964,[178] a post which Æthelgar held until 988, from 980 onwards in plurality with the see of Selsey. Upon Dunstan's death in 988, Æthelgar was appointed archbishop of Canterbury and held the metropolitan see until his own death in 990.[179] The letter in question dates presumably from some point in the 980s (Æthelgar is styled 'bishop'); it is written in heavily hermeneutic Latin, bristling with grecisms and neologisms.[180] In it B, *inter alia*, asks for permission to come to

---

[176] See Hofstetter, *Winchester und Sprachgebrauch*, p. 132, and above, p. 324.

[177] The letter is preserved in the eleventh-century collection of letters (s. xi^in, probably from Christ Church, Canterbury), now BL, Cotton Tiberius A. xv, 142r–173r. The letter is printed by Stubbs, *Memorials*, pp. 385–8. For an interpretation of its probable historical context and the identification of its author, see Lapidge, 'B. and the *Vita S. Dunstani*', pp. 283 and 286–8.

[178] See *Wulfstan: Life*, ch. 20, p. 36.

[179] On Æthelgar's career, see *ibid.*, n. 3, and Keynes, *Liber Vitae*, pp. 20, 31–2 and 90.

[180] For the diction of B's letter, see Lapidge, 'Hermeneutic Style', pp. 120–1; cf. also *ibid.*, p. 112.

Winchester in order to read Aldhelm's 'little book in praise of virginity',[181] and he states that he has been craving for such intellectual exercise for many years. The implication of this remark would probably be that B wanted to remind Æthelgar (whom he addresses in familiar terms) of their days at Glastonbury, when they had preoccupied themselves with the enthusiastic and intense study of Aldhelm's works, trying to make their way together through Aldhelm's *densa Latinitatis silva*.

[181] Cf. Stubbs, *Memorials*, p. 388: 'de parthenali laude libellum'.

10

French and German loan influence

From the exploration (undertaken in the three preceding chs.) of the historical and intellectual milieu in which the Benedictine Rule, the Royal Psalter and the Aldhelm glosses originated, let us return one last time to the study of words. In this concluding ch., we shall focus our attention on some loanwords, semantic loans and loan formations[1] from French and German, and we shall inspect in what way such loans may reflect an impact of the many foreigners who were attracted to King Æthelstan's court, and whether, possibly, these loans reveal traces of the activities of the foreign scholars who pursued their studies there.

Contacts between the Anglo-Saxon kingdoms or the English church and the Continent had been numerous before the reign of Æthelstan.[2] Yet in the tenth century (and perhaps throughout Anglo-Saxon England), Æthelstan's court culture marked the acme of such contacts in its readiness to absorb and assimilate both secular and clerical influence emanating from Francia and Germany. We are moderately well informed as regards the agencies through which such influence reached Æthelstan's

[1] For linguistic definitions of the terms semantic loan and loan formation, see Gneuss, *Lehnbildungen*, pp. 2–3 and 20–35, and (briefly) *idem*, 'The Old English Language', in *The Cambridge Companion to Old English Literature*, ed. M. Godden and M. Lapidge (Cambridge, 1991), pp. 23–54, at 42–3. In brief, a semantic loan is in question when a previously existing word adopts the meaning of a word from a foreign language (for example, OE *synn* 'crime' adopting the meaning of Latin *peccatum* 'sin'). By contrast, a loan formation is always a new term, coined after the model of a foreign word, and imitating its morphological structure in varying degrees of closeness (for example, OE *þriness* 'Trinity' after Latin *trinitas*, or OE *leorningcniht* 'disciple' after Latin *discipulus*).

[2] For a survey of such contacts, see most recently R. McKitterick, 'England and the Continent', in *The New Cambridge Medieval History II: c. 700–c. 900*, ed. R. McKitterick (Cambridge, 1995), pp. 64–84.

court. The links with the Continent have been explored as far as they can still be recovered; their story need not be rehearsed here. One thinks, for example, of the contacts formed by the marriages of four (? or five) of Æthelstan's half-sisters with continental rulers, of the embassy of Bishop Oda to Francia (presumably in 936, on which occasion Oda's link with Fleury may have been established), and of Bishop Coenwald of Worcester's trip to the Continent (probably 929 × 930, and presumably on royal business), when he visited 'all the monasteries throughout Germany', as the St Gallen confraternity book records. One also thinks of Theodred, bishop of London (900 × 926–951 × 953), who seems to have been in close contact with the king, and who, on the evidence of his name, was probably of German extraction, and, judging from the names of the clerics he mentions in his will, appears to have had a number of Germans among his clergy. One finally thinks of the foreign scholars and clerics in the king's entourage whose activities we have traced in the preceding ch.: Israel, Petrus and the anonymous scribe and poet of *Rex pius Æðelstan*.[3]

---

[3] For surveys of such contacts, see Stenton, *Anglo-Saxon England*, pp. 344–9 and 444, Wood, 'The Making of King Æthelstan's Empire', pp. 256–63, and Ortenberg, *The English Church and the Continent*, pp. 54–7, 61–6 and 229–32. On the contacts specifically with Germany, see K. Leyser, 'Die Ottonen und Wessex', *Frühmittelalterliche Studien* 17 (1983), 73–97, at 74–87 (transl. in his *Communication and Power in Medieval Europe: the Carolingian and Ottonian Centuries*, ed. T. Reuter (London, 1994), pp. 73–104). On the problem of how many of Æthelstan's half-sisters were in question (and who married whom), see Keynes, 'Æthelstan's Books', p. 148 and n. 27, and p. 191 and n. 232. On the unproblematic sisters Eadgyth (married to Otto I) and Eadgifu (married to Charles the Simple) and the impact these marriages may have had on the arrival of books in England, see. *ibid*., pp. 148–9 and pp. 191–3. Concerning the marriages of Æthelstan's sisters, see also the convenient genealogical table provided by Bullough, 'The Continental Background of the Reform', p. 32. For Bishop Oda's embassy to Francia, see above, p. 340; for his contacts with Fleury (where he allegedly received the monastic habit), see Byrhtferth, *Vita S. Oswaldi*, ed. Raine, *Historians* I, 413, and William of Malmesbury, *Gesta pontificum* I, 14 (ed. Hamilton, p. 22). For Bishop Coenwald's visit to Germany (probably in the context of the marriage proceedings of Eadgyth and Otto I), see Keynes, 'Æthelstan's Books', pp. 198–201 (the entry in the St Gallen confraternity book is printed *ibid*., pp. 198–9); see also *ibid*., pp. 158–9, for further evidence of a close connection between Coenwald and the royal court. On Bishop Theodred, his relationship with King Æthelstan and his suspected German extraction (and that of a number of his clergy), see D. Whitelock, 'Some Anglo-Saxon Bishops of London', in her *History, Law and Literature in 10th–11th Century England* (London, 1981), no. II, 3–35, at 17–20. (See *ibid*., p. 20, for the suggestion that Coenwald's visit to German monasteries may have been undertaken partly with the aim of recruiting clerics for the English Church.)

However, the evidence for an impact which such numerous and often close contacts may be supposed to have had on the English language seems surprisingly small.[4] This may in part be attributable to the fact that, in the tenth century, Latin was the *lingua franca* all over Europe. But then, what about contacts between secular nobles? Obviously, there must be further explanations. One such explanation may be that the surviving texts represent only some of the registers which Old English may reasonably be assumed to have possessed. In particular, the registers of poetic, religious or legal language are well attested, but hardly ever do we get a glimpse of the actual spoken language (where most of the loanwords which might have been adopted in a secular context would be expected to have been current first). There may yet be further reasons for the apparent paucity of French and German loans; some such possible reasons we shall consider shortly. The number of surviving loans from these languages which so far have been discovered is not only astonishingly small; with a very few exceptions, no attempts have been made to trace their origin back to a particular centre or sphere of influence.[5] However, given the

---

Theodred's will is printed and translated by D. Whitelock, *Anglo-Saxon Wills* (Cambridge, 1930), pp. 2–5 (no. 1); it is also translated in *EHD*, pp. 552–4 (no. 106). A reflex of the close contacts of Bishops Theodred and Coenwald with the king may also be seen in Æthelstan's charters, where both often attest in a prominent position; cf. Keynes, *Atlas of Attestations*, table xxxvii. For Israel, Petrus and the anonymous poet of *Rex pius Ædelstan*, see above, pp. 336–9. For two further foreign (probably German) members of the New Minster *familia* during Æthelstan's reign, see Lapidge, 'Latin Poems as Evidence', p. 81, n. 143. It is important to bear in mind, however, that other such German or French clerics or laymen may have left no record of their sojourn in Æthelstan's entourage. Also, a command of French as a second language is probably to be assumed in most of the many Breton clerics and nobles who had fled the political turmoils in Brittany and sought the refuge of King Æthelstan's court. On these, see, for example, Brett, 'A Breton Pilgrim in England in the Reign of King Æthelstan', pp. 43–50. On the early adoption of French by the leading classes in Brittany, see, for example, E. Ternes, 'The Breton Language', in *The Celtic Languages*, ed. D. Macaulay (Cambridge, 1992), pp. 371–5, at 373, and L. Fleuriot, 'Bretonische Sprache und Literatur', *LkMA* II (1982), 632–4, at 633.

[4] For a survey of the German and French loans which hitherto have been traced in Old English (with further literature on the subject), see Gneuss, 'Language Contact', pp. 131–7.

[5] For one of the rare attempts (concerning OE *sicor*, from Latin *securus*, which very probably reached English via Old Saxon), see Gneuss, 'Language Contact', p. 134.

probable date of composition of the three texts under inspection here (especially the Psalter and the Rule), it may be safe to say that any loans which are attested in them will have been adopted prior to the period when English speakers came into close and prolonged contact with personnel from the reformed monasteries in Francia and Germany. If we then reflect on the importance of Æthelstan's court culture for the intellectual foundations of the English Benedictine reform, it is entirely relevant to consider the introduction of such loans which are *first* attested in one of the works in question in the context of the presence of French or German nobles and scholars at the king's court.

One final point is worth mentioning: we have seen (above, pp. 51–2) that in the Rule and the Royal Psalter a number of *Latin* loanwords are first attested (and often employed with great consistency), and the suspicion must be that it was Æthelwold who was instrumental in their introduction into English. As an admirer of Aldhelm and a practitioner of the hermeneutic style, Æthelwold will have had an ingrained interest in words, and as a scholar who deeply concerned himself with the intellectual refinement of English, he no doubt will have paid close attention to any other vernaculars which he heard or read.

OLD SAXON AND OLD HIGH GERMAN INFLUENCE

During the early Middle Ages, two different yet closely related languages were spoken in Germany: Old High German and Old Saxon (or Old Low German (Altniederdeutsch) as it is more appropriately called in recent publications), distinguished most conspicuously one from the other by phonological differences.[6] Between Old Saxon (spoken in northern Germany) and Old English a high degree of mutual intelligibility must be assumed. Such mutual intelligibility will have been considerably reduced between speakers of Old English and one of the Old High German dialects. However, since Old High German belonged (together

---

[6] For philological surveys of Old Saxon and Old High German, see, for example, W. Krogmann, 'Altsächsisch und Mittelniederdeutsch', in *Kurzer Grundriß der germanischen Philologie bis 1500, I. Sprachgeschichte*, ed. L. E. Schmitt (Berlin, 1970), pp. 211–52, at 211–27, S. Sonderegger, 'Althochdeutsche Sprache', *ibid.*, pp. 288–346, G. Cordes, 'Altniederdeutsch', in *Lexikon der germanistischen Linguistik*, ed. H. P. Althaus *et al.*, 2nd ed. (Tübingen, 1980), pp. 576–80, and S. Sonderegger, 'Althochdeutsch', *ibid.*, pp. 569–76.

with Old Saxon and Old English) to the West Germanic branch of the Germanic languages, it may be safe to state that the differences between Old English and German in general are less marked than (say) between Old English and Old Norse (Old Norse belonging to the North Germanic branch).

Two literary texts are eloquent and famous testimonies to the intelligibility of Old Saxon to speakers of Old English, and to the interest such speakers took in German literary products.[7] The first of these texts is the so-called *Later Genesis* (or *Genesis* B), an Old English adaptation of an Old Saxon poem on the first book of the Pentateuch, produced by an Anglo-Saxon poet, perhaps by the end of the ninth century. The Old English adaptation has been inserted as lines 235–851 into an earlier, originally English, composition (*Genesis* A), as transmitted in Oxford, Bodleian Library, Junius 11 (s. x/xi, prob. Christ Church, Canterbury).[8] Of the original Old Saxon *Genesis* only a few fragments of a continental manuscript have survived.[9] On the evidence of the illustrations in Junius 11 and their art historical links with continental models, the Old Saxon poem may possibly have travelled to England as a lavish presentation copy, perhaps on the occasion of the marriage of King Æthelwulf of Wessex to Judith (daughter of Charles the Bald) in 856.[10] If so, then we may perhaps permit ourselves to imagine that such a copy was still extant in the royal household during the reign of King Æthelstan. The second of our witnesses testifying to an English interest in Saxon literature is a copy of the Old Saxon New Testament poem *Heliand* (in the original language)

---

[7] For surveys of Old Saxon and Old High German literature, see, for example, J. Rathofer, 'Altsächsische Literatur', in *Kurzer Grundriß der germanischen Philologie bis 1500, II. Literaturgeschichte*, ed. L. E. Schmitt (Berlin, 1971), pp. 242–62, S. Sonderegger and H. Burger, 'Althochdeutsche Literatur', *ibid.*, pp. 326–463, and W. Haubrichs, *Die Anfänge: Versuche volkssprachlicher Schriftlichkeit im frühen Mittelalter (ca. 700–1050/60)*, Geschichte der deutschen Literatur von den Anfängen bis zum Beginn der Neuzeit I, 2nd ed. (Tübingen, 1995).

[8] The *Later Genesis* has been printed most recently by A. N. Doane, *The Saxon Genesis* (Madison, WI, 1991). On some points concerning the relationship between Old Saxon and Old English poetry in general, see U. Schwab, *Einige Beziehungen zwischen altsächsischer und angelsächsischer Dichtung* (Spoleto, 1988).

[9] The Old Saxon fragments are printed *Heliand und Genesis*, ed. Behaghel and Taeger, pp. 241–56.

[10] See B. Raw, 'The Probable Derivation of Most of the Illustrations in Junius 11 from an Illustrated Old Saxon *Genesis*', *ASE* 5 (1976), 133–48, esp. 148.

written by an English scribe somewhere in southern England in the second part of the tenth century (now London, BL, Cotton Caligula A. vii, fols. 11–178).[11]

In other words, given the demonstrable interest in Saxon literature and the high degree of mutual intelligibility between English and Saxon, and given the close contacts which had existed between England and Germany ever since the Anglo-Saxon mission to the Continent, one might expect to find a considerable number of German loanwords, semantic loans or loan formations in Old English texts. However, as we have noted, such expectations are frustrated. So far, only a tiny number of German loans have been identified in texts other than the *Later Genesis*.[12] In addition to the aforementioned reasons of a more general nature, some further factors may serve to explain the scarcity of specifically German loans in Old English. Thus, apart from *Heliand* (some 5983 verses) and the *Genesis* fragments (some 337 verses) – both employing a distinctively poetic vocabulary – the corpus of surviving Old Saxon texts is exiguous, consisting principally of glosses or short religious pieces such as creeds;[13] and, in comparison with what has survived in Old English, the same must be said for extant texts in Old High German. The implication of this situation is that possibly some Old Saxon or Old High German loans in Old English may forever remain undiscovered. Furthermore, given the close affinity between Old English and Old Saxon, loanwords will not always be easily recognizable, and in the case of semantic loans or loan formations, it will often be difficult or even impossible to produce irrefutable proof. For example, among the words discussed below, the hypothesis that Old English *cildgeong* was formed as a loan translation after Old Saxon *kindjung* depends wholly on the distribution and frequency of *cildgeong* in Old English texts. Otherwise, there is no way of saying that *cildgeong* and *kindjung* could not have been coined independently of each other. The example *cildgeong* highlights another difficulty in evaluating potential Old Saxon loans in Old English. OS *kindjung* is attested only in *Heliand* (where it occurs several times). Was it a word

---

[11] For an edition of *Heliand*, see above, n. 9.

[12] Gneuss, 'Language Contact', pp. 133–4 lists no more than four such words.

[13] These texts have been printed by J. H. Gallée, *Altsächsische Sprachdenkmäler mit Faksimilesammlung* (Leiden, 1895), and again (more accurately) by Wadstein, *Kleinere altsächsische Sprachdenkmäler*. The texts in question are conveniently listed in Gallée, *Altsächsische Grammatik*, pp. 5–8.

restricted to poetry and recognized (and appreciated) as such by its Anglo-Saxon users, or did they hear (or read) it in other registers of Old Saxon as well? We do not know. By the same token, the paucity of surviving texts may prevent us from being more specific as to whether a loan was introduced from Old Saxon or from Old High German. An example would be *orgel* 'organ' (discussed below): a term for this musical instrument is not attested in Old Saxon, so there is no way of knowing whether, in the tenth century, the form with final *l* was restricted to Old High German or whether it occurred also in Old Saxon.[14]

Nonetheless, it would be worthwhile carefully searching Old English texts for words which were possibly borrowed from, or coined after, German terms, since such words and the way they are used in Old English writings are as precious a testimony to the cultural contacts betweeen England and Germany as is the gospelbook sent by Otto I to King Æthelstan. The few items which we will consider presently can be no more than preliminary to such a task. Even in the texts under inspection here, their number could probably be augmented. Only one of the following items (*ofearmian*) has previously been held to have been coined under continental (though not specifically German) influence.

Galsmære and *agælan*

The *hapax legomenon gālsmǣre* in the Rule (BR 30.8) meaning 'frivolous, facetious, jocose' and the two occurrences of *āgǣlan* 'to make light of' in the Royal Psalter (ps. LXXXVIII.32 and 35) stand out in that they do not belong to the semantic field 'sexual desire, wantonness, lust', to which the adjective *gāl* and its many derivatives almost invariably belong.[15] Hans Schabram has noted only two exceptions to this semantic range of *gal*, both occurring in the *Later Genesis*.[16] As he has shown, *gal* (line 327)

---

[14] For problems inherent in Old English–German language contacts, see also E. G. Stanley, 'The Difficulty of Establishing Borrowings Between Old English and the Continental West Germanic Languages', in *An Historic Tongue: Studies in English Linguistics in Memory of Barbara Strang*, ed. G. Nixon and J. Honey (London, 1988), pp. 3–16.

[15] For a discussion of *gālsmǣre* and *āgǣlan* in their contexts and as an important verbal link between the Rule and the Psalter, see above, p. 220.

[16] See Schabram, 'Die Bedeutung von *gāl* und *gālscipe* in der ae. Genesis B', *Beiträge zur Geschichte der deutschen Sprache und Literatur* 82 (1960), 265–74.

and *galscipe* (line 341) should there be assigned the meaning 'arrogant' and 'arrogance' respectively, and in the *Later Genesis* both words would accordingly belong to the semantic field of *superbia*, not to that of *luxuria* (as had hitherto traditionally been held on grounds of the usual meaning of *gal*). The most likely explanation for this strikingly unusual meaning of *gāl* and *gālscipe* in the *Later Genesis* would be that they are semantic loans from Old Saxon, translating *gēl* and **gēlskepi* which the (now lost) Old Saxon exemplar presumably had in the passages in question.[17] Lexicographers of Old Saxon unanimously assign the meaning 'in high spirits, frivolous' to Old Saxon *gēl* and its many derivatives.[18] The occurrence of *galsmǣre* and *agǣlan* in the Rule and the Psalter might indicate that Old Saxon *gel* had some broader influence on the meaning of Old English *gal* and its derivatives, at least at one point in Anglo-Saxon history and in one particular group of speakers, and that its influence was not restricted to a couple of isolated occurrences in a direct translation from the Old Saxon. It is possible that such broader influence of OS *gel* was reinforced by its Old High German equivalent *geil*. Unlike modern German *geil*, its Old High German predecessor does not appear to have had attested sexual connotations: 'frivolous, haughty, lofty' are the meanings given by the dictionaries.[19] Note that Holthausen (*Altenglisches etymologisches Wörterbuch*), as opposed to CHM and BTS, does not place the Old English unprefixed verb *gǣlan* (as well as *āgǣlan* or *tōgǣlan*) among the derivatives from *gāl*; he adduces ON *geila* 'to separate' or OHG *gīl* 'hernia' as etymological cognates. Whatever the philologically correct etymology of *(ā)gǣlan* may have been, given the acute interest revealed in the Royal Psalter (as in the Rule and the Aldhelm glosses) in sound relationships originally produced by i-mutation (see below, pp. 421–2), there can be little doubt that the Glossator would have noted that *gāl* and *āgǣlan* were bound together in the same sound pattern as (say) *brād* 'broad' and *brǣdan* 'to extend' or *lār* 'learning' and *lǣran* 'to teach'. To posit a semantic link between any two words connected by such sound patterns would have been only natural for him.

[17] See *ibid.*, pp. 271–2.

[18] See Sehrt, *Wörterbuch zum Heliand und zur Genesis*, and the glossary in *Heliand und Genesis*, ed. Behaghel and Taeger, s.v.v. *gel, gelmod, gelmodig, gelhert*.

[19] See, for example, Schützeichel, *Althochdeutsches Wörterbuch*, and Wells, *Althochdeutsches Glossenwörterbuch*, s. v. *geil*.

æwicness 'eternity'

This word (occurring in ps. CII.17) is a *hapax legomenon*; not even the most closely dependent D-type psalters follow the Royal Glossator in his choice. Old English *æwicness* is arguably a hybrid noun, consisting of the adjective *æwic*, from Old Saxon or Old High German *ēwig* 'eternal' and the Old English abstract noun suffix *-ness*.[20] There is no Old English word from which *æwic* might plausibly be derived.[21] Both in Old Saxon and in Old High German, the spelling and, presumably, the pronunciation of final *g* (as in *ēwig*) varied a good deal. Besides <g>, the spellings <h> and <c> are attested. The pronunciation would probably have been either a plosive or a fricative, that is /g/, /k/, /j/ or /ç/.[22] The substitution of *ǣ* in *ǣwicness* for *ē* in Old Saxon or Old High German *ēwig* might plausibly be explained in terms of the dialectal variants West Saxon *ǣ* and Anglian *ē* (representing West Germanic *ā*). Since there is reason to believe that the Royal Glossator drew on an Anglian A-type gloss, he would have been used to substituting WS. *ǣ* in Anglian forms like *slēp* 'sleep', *rēdan* 'to read' or *cwēdon* (pl. pret. of *cweþan* 'to say'). In other words, there are no phonological difficulties in assuming Old Saxon or Old High German *ēwig* behind Old English *æwic*.

The Glossator employs the hybrid loan *ǣwicness* in ps. CII.17 to translate the formula *in saeculum saeculi* 'world without end', 'to all eternity'. In all psalters, this formula (which is very common in psalms), is usually glossed word by word: *on worould worulde*. Such a literal rendition occurs in the Royal Psalter for example in pss. CI.13 and 29, CIII.5 or CXLIV.1. However, the Royal Glossator frequently employs a single word for translating the Latin phrase: *āworuld*, for example in pss. XVIII.10, XLIV.18, LI.10, LXXXVIII.30 or CXXXI.12. This is a

---

[20] Cf. Sehrt, *Wörterbuch zum Heliand und zur Genesis*, and *Heliand und Genesis*, ed. Behaghel and Taeger, s. v. *ēwig*, and Schützeichel, *Althochdeutsches Wörterbuch*, s. v. *(h)ēwīg*; for the etymology, see Kluge and Seebold, *Etymologisches Wörterbuch*, s. v. *ewig*.

[21] Cf. Holthausen, *Altenglisches etymologisches Wörterbuch*, s. v. *ǣwigness*, who does not give a concrete etymology. The explanation given by Roeder (basing himself on an etymology suggested by Karl Bülbring) is not convincing; cf. *Der altenglische Regius-Psalter*, p. 303.

[22] See Gallée, *Altsächsische Grammatik*, §§ 241 and 256, and W. Braune and H. Eggers, *Althochdeutsche Grammatik*, 14th ed. (Tübingen, 1987), §§ 148 and 149 and n. 4, and § 88c; cf. also the spellings *uuirðic* (German *würdig* 'worthy') and *fluhtik* (German *flüchtig* 'fugitive') in the Old Saxon *Genesis* (ed. Behaghel and Taeger), lines 74 and 75.

compound formed from *ā*, 'ever, always', and *woruld* 'world'; it was probably coined by the Royal Glossator himself, since it is scarcely attested outside the psalter glosses. The dependent psalters do not follow the Glossator in all instances where he employs *āworuld*, indicating thereby the unusual character of this compound. Since the compound is so obviously unusual, the *DOE* (s. v. *āworuld*) cautiously suggests in each of its quotations from the Royal Psalter that *aworuld* should perhaps be taken as two words. However, given the Royal Glossator's extraordinary resourcefulness in introducing striking neologisms, and given the fact that in all its occurrences in the Psalter *aworuld* is written as one word, there can be little doubt that the Glossator introduced *aworuld* as a compound which would ingeniously encompass both the meaning of the phrase *in saeculum saeculi* 'in all eternity' and (unlike Old English *ecness* 'eternity') the standard rendition of *saeculum* by *woruld*.

This is the context in which we must judge the even more striking *ǣwicness*, as a further testimony to the Glossator's attempts to find a suitable equivalent for *in saeculum saeculi*, a phrase which, in terms of modern linguistics, has been lexicalized, that is to say, its meaning cannot be captured by a word for word translation. The phonological similarity of *ǣwicness* to Old English *ēcness* 'eternity' and *ǣ* 'law', often 'divine law', will, perhaps, not have escaped the Glossator when he decided on this neologism. It is a phonological similarity to another Old English word-family which may have prevented *ǣwicness* from gaining any currency at all. The family in question is *ǣwisc* 'offence, shame, disgrace' and a number of derivatives (including *ǣwiscness* 'shameless conduct'). In view of the Royal Glossator's awareness of sound effects, the existence of *ǣwisc* (pronounced /æ:wiʃ/), could, in fact, indicate that he himself had learned *ǣwic* from native speakers of Old Saxon or Old High German, not from the study of written texts. Such speakers would have pronounced the final phonemes of *ewig* as /ik/, /ig/, /iç/ or /ij/, and the Royal Glossator must have had some such pronunciation in mind for *ǣwicness*. However, for any literate Anglo-Saxon without such contacts to native speakers of German, the spelling <ic> would have indicated the pronunciation /itʃ/,[23] a pronunciation which brought *ǣwicness* 'eternity' intolerably close to *ǣwisc* 'offence, shame'.

---

[23] See SB, § 206.3 and 8, and Campbell, §§ 428 and 433.

orgeldream

The triumphant last psalm of the psalter (ps. CL) begins: 'laudate deum (in sanctis eius)' repeated as 'laudate eum' in the beginning of each of the subsequent phrases. In this short psalm, a great variety of musical instruments is enumerated which (says the psalmist) should all join the human voice in giving praise to God; an organ is one of the instruments named here: 'laudate eum in ... organo' (ps. CL.4). The usual Old English equivalent for Latin *organum* or *organa* is the loanword *organa* or *organe*. This occurs already in the Vespasian Psalter and hence in other psalter glosses, and it is also attested in prose texts (for example in Ælfric). However, the Royal Glossator employs the compound *orgeldream* 'music produced by an organ', to translate *organum* in ps. CL.4. This compound is obviously another one of his many neologisms; only one of the later psalter glosses (Blickling) follows the Glossator's lead. Two others adopt his translation of *organum* by a compound, but substitute the ususal Old English form of the loan: *organdream* (Salisbury) and *orgena-dream* (Stowe; strictly speaking not a compound proper, but a substantive with an appositional noun in the genitive). The word *orgel* (or *orgeldream*) for 'organ' is recorded nowhere else in Old English.[24] The word corresponds precisely to Modern German *Orgel*.[25] Here, final *l* (instead of *n*, required by the etymology of the term) is explained either by a change *-en* > *-el* (*-en* being apparently understood as a suffix), or by a dissimilation originating in the plural forms (OHG *organan*, MHG *orgenen*). The forms with final *l* are first attested in twelfth-century glossaries, but there is no reason why they should not have been in existence in spoken language for some time previously, especially in view of their subsequent rapid and universal dissemination.[26] The word is not recorded in Old Saxon. Given the unique occurrence of *orgel* in Old English, it is unlikely that the substitution of original *n* by *l* should have occurred here independently;

---

[24] For Middle English, the *MED* records five instances of *orgel* (n. (2)) 'a kind of musical instrument, an organ'; OE *orgeldream* is given as its antecedent.

[25] BT (s. v. *orgele*) adduce one of the Middle English attestations (in explanation of *orgel* in *orgeldream*) and refer to OHG *orgela* (a form not attested in Old High German, see below) without, however, stating explicitly that they take *orgel* to be a loanword.

[26] See Wells, *Althochdeutsches Glossenwörterbuch*, s. v. *orgela*, and Kluge and Seebold, *Etymologisches Wörterbuch*, s. v. *Orgel*.

rather we may suspect that the Royal Glossator heard *orgel* from speakers of German and, on one occasion, employed it in his gloss.[27]

There is unequivocal evidence for the importance attached to organs in England in the second half of the tenth century, although it is not altogether clear on which occasions these organs were played. The most detailed description of an Anglo-Saxon organ is given by Wulfstan of Winchester in the 'Epistola specialis', prefaced to his *Narratio metrica de S. Swithuno* and addressed to Bishop Ælfheah (984–1005), Æthelwold's successor in office.[28] Here Wulfstan describes the organ of the Old Minster as it was enlarged by Ælfheah in the course of extensive building-works undertaken during his episcopate. This huge and impressively powerful organ was operated by as many as seventy men. For Æthelwold himself, we have the twelfth-century testimony of the Abingdon chronicle that he constructed the organ for the abbey church there *propriis manibus*.[29] In other words, there is no doubt that Æthelwold was familiar with organs, and that he held this instrument in great esteem. This in turn may give us a clue as to why he possibly coined the striking compound *orgeldream*, arguably based on a German loanword. *Organa* (or the singular *organum*) are polysemous in Latin. Apart from 'organ', they may denote any kind of musical instrument, as well as polyphony in song (the famous Winchester *organa*, for example).[30] In fact, in the only other occurrence of *organum* in the psalter, the word probably means 'harp', or at least a musical instrument which could be suspended from the willows *super flumina Babilonis*: 'In salicibus ... suspendimus

---

[27] The OHG attested forms for the nominative are *organa* and *orgina*; see Schützeichel, *Althochdeutsches Wörterbuch*. The presumed OHG forms with *l*-substitution would hence have been *orgala* or *orgila*. A substitution of *e* for *i* or *a* in an unstressed syllable would be expected in tenth-century English (cf. Campbell, §§ 369 and 377, and SB, § 44), and the inflexional ending would have been dropped in a compound such as *orgeldream* (cf. Campbell, § 341, n. 3, and SB, § 167 c).

[28] Lines 145–76; Wulfstan's prefatory letter is edited with translation and full commentary by Lapidge, *The Cult of St Swithun* (forthcoming). For the moment, see *Frithegodi monachi Breuiloquium et Wulfstani cantoris Narratio*, ed. Campbell, pp. 69–70.

[29] See *Chronicon Monasterii de Abingdon*, ed. Stevenson II, 278. (The remark is found in the tract *De abbatibus Abbendoniae*, appended to the *Chronicon* and dated s. xii/xiii.) For a brief survey of references to organs in late-tenth-century England and further literature on medieval organs and their use, see Lapidge, *The Cult of St Swithun*.

[30] For the various meanings of *organa*, see Holschneider, *Die Organa von Winchester*, pp. 135–9, esp. 138.

organa nostra' (ps. CXXXVI.2). As opposed to the A-type gloss (which here has *organa*), the Royal Glossator uses *dream* on this occasion. This (the determinatum in the compound *orgeldream*) originally means 'joy, bliss' and only in later texts came to denote 'music' and (rarely) 'musical instrument', meanings which arguably arose in the Royal Psalter gloss.[31] Perhaps these two occurrences of *organum* in the psalter and their glosses should be judged in combination. Unlike the A-type glosses, the Glossator avoids OE *organa* for an instrument which is not an organ, and he uses the fresh loan *orgel* (which as opposed to the older loan *organa* is not fraught with polysemy) where he wants to make it clear that an organ is the instrument in question.

There may be an additional reason why the Glossator should have decided on the neologism *orgeldream*, and this has to do with his pronounced penchant for paronomasia or word-play. There is a (rare) Old English word *orgel* (and a few derivatives from this such as *orgelness* or *orgelword*), meaning 'pride'. As far as I am aware, with one exception, this word and its derivatives are always used with negative connotations in Old English texts, implying 'arrogance' or 'haughtiness'.[32] However, Byrhtferth of Ramsey, a writer who evidently was infatuated with words and paid close attention to all their connotations, once employs the adverb *orglice* with an unambiguously positive meaning 'proudly':

Of þissum syx tidum wihst se quadrans swyðe wæwerðlice and forðstæpð wel orglice binnan feower wintrum, swylce hwylc cyng of his giftbure stæppe geglenged.[33]

It is noteworthy that in this passage Byrhtferth has a clear verbal echo of a gloss from the Royal Psalter: *giftbur* 'bridal chamber' is one of the Psalter's neologisms. Apart from Byrhtferth, the word occurs only in three dependent psalter glosses (Tiberius, Vitellius, Eadwine). In the psalter (ps. XVIII.6) *giftbur* glosses *thalamus* 'bridal chamber', whereas in the *Enchiridion*, *giftbur* translates *solium* 'throne'; it might therefore be considered less appropriate here. However, in his Latin text (which precedes his Old English translation of this text) Byrhtferth unambigu-

---

[31] Cf. above, pp. 189.

[32] Cf., for example, *orglice* 'arrogantly' in Ælfric, *Lives of Saints*, ed. Skeat I, 214.76.

[33] 'From these six hours the quadrant grows very beautifully and advances quite proudly over four years, as if some king came adorned from his bridal chamber'. *Enchiridion*, ed. Baker and Lapidge I. 1. 63–5.

ously adumbrates the psalm verse in question, cf.: 'et ipse tamquam sponsus procedens de thalamo suo' (ps. XVIII.6) and 'ex quibus quadrans surgit atque procedit uelut rex a solio suo'.[34] On the basis of this verbal reminiscence it is possible but not provable that Byrhtferth, when translating his Latin version into Old English, did not only recall the neologism *giftbur* which he would have found for *thalamus* in a glossed psalter, but perhaps also the even more striking compound *orgeldream* which he would have found elsewhere in the same manuscript, and which in turn would have prompted his employment of *orglice* in the present passage in the extraordinarily rare sense 'proudly'. (The glossed manuscript on which Byrhtferth drew would accordingly have been very closely dependent on the Royal Psalter.)[35] This hypothesis, in turn, could confirm the suspicion that the Royal Glossator, when coining *orgeldream*, did indeed intend to allude to *orgel* 'pride' (in a positive sense), an allusion which, perhaps, was not lost on Byrhtferth. It is uncertain, however, whether Byrhtferth would have understood *orgel* as a form of *organa*: for him *orgeldream* would perhaps have meant only 'proud music' or 'proud musical instrument' (a sense entirely appropriate in the ecstatic context of ps. CL).

In short, the Royal Glossator's coinage of *orgeldream*, arguably based on a freshly introduced loanword, would seem to have been called forth by his interest in musical terminology (amply attested elsewhere in his gloss, see above, pp. 188–200), by his flair for striking neologisms and by his predilection for paronomasia.

cildgeong 'young'

Our next example concerns a word in the Old English Rule (and its preface) for which Æthelwold seems to have had a predilection: *cildgeong*. It is possible that he coined the word as a loan translation after the Old Saxon compound adjective *kindjung*: the link between both terms is evident, there are no unequivocal attestations of *cildgeong* prior to the Rule, and the word is exceedingly rare in other texts. On one occasion,

---

[34] *Enchiridion* I. 1. 34–5. Attention is called to this verbal echo in the commentary, cf. *ibid.*, p. 253.

[35] For Byrhtferth's interest in the vocabulary of glosses, see *Enchiridion*, ed. Baker and Lapidge, pp. cvi–cxi; cf. also above, pp. 139–41 and 176.

the adjective is used to define *man* (*cildgeongum mannum*, BR 130.1), a collocation which is common in the Old Saxon *Heliand*.[36] No fewer than seven of the word's ten occurrences come from Æthelwold.[37] In the Rule, he employs it to translate Latin *infans* and (once) *puer*. In his Preface he refers by it to young King Edgar; cf. for example, 'gemundige his behates þe he on his æþelincghade cildgeong Gode behet' (*CS*, pp. 147–8), 'mindful of the promise which he had made as an atheling in his childhood'. It is noteworthy that the interlinear gloss to the *Regula* in Tiberius A. iii follows Æthelwold on no occasion: this gloss always has *cild* or *cniht*. It should further be noted that BT and BTS record only a few other compounds with *geong* as their second component, all of which are extremely rare. Æthelwold's penchant for this possible calque on an Old Saxon adjective also emerges from the fact that, on one occasion, he derives a noun from it: *cildgeoguþ* 'childhood'. This occurs in his Preface, again with reference to young Edgar: 'swa he ær behet on his cildgeogoðe' (*CS*, p. 148) 'as he had promised in his childhood'. The noun, too, is exceptionally rare: there are two occurrences in a later homily and one in Byrhtferth (to which we shall return presently).

It is possible that by introducing *cildgeong* and *cildgeoguþ*, Æthelwold had it somehow in mind to establish a specific Old English equivalent for the Latin term for the first of the four ages of man: *pueritia*. The ages of man (*pueritia*, *adolescentia*, *iuuentus*, *senectus*) were frequently referred to throughout the Middle Ages and explained in scholarly handbooks such as Isidore's *Etymologiae*.[38] Cf. for example: 'Cildgeongum mannum eal geferræden unþeawas styre, and hyra mycele gymene hæbben oð þæt

---

[36] Cf. Sehrt, *Wörterbuch zum Heliand und zur Genesis*, s. v. *kindjung*.

[37] The *DOE* notes twelve occurrences; two of these, however, have no independent value since they come from the Wells and Winteney versions of the Rule. The three non-Æthelwoldian attestations come from poetry; in two of these, however (*Crist* C 1424 and *Andreas* 684) it is uncertain whether *cildgeong* should not be taken as two words; the remaining instance is found in *Maxims* I, 48. The occurrences in the Rule are: BR 7.22, 61.10, 61.12, 115.7, 130.1, and in the Preface, *CS*, pp. 146 and 148.

[38] Although the fourfold division is common, there were other schemes such as a three- or a sixfold division. See A. Hofmeister, 'Puer, iuuenis, senex: Zum Verständnis der mittelalterlichen Altersbezeichnungen', in *Papsttum und Kaisertum*, ed. A. Brackmann (Munich, 1926), pp. 287–316. Isidore, for example, has a sixfold division (*Etymologiae* XI. ii. 1–8), whereas Byrhtferth adopts the fourfold division on several occasions (see *Enchiridion*, ed. Baker and Lapidge I. 1. 102–3 and IV. 1. 72–4); see also *ibid.*, p. 343, for further literature on the subject.

fifteoþe gear hyra ylde' (BR 130.1–2) 'The community shall correct any
improper behaviour in "child-young" men and shall supervise them
carefully until the age of fourteen'. Isidore (*Etymologiae* XI. ii. 3) states
that *pueritia* ends at the age of fourteen. In any event, Byrhtferth
unequivocally associated the expression *cildgeoguþ* with the ages of man. In
his discussion of the ages, he once adopts *cildgeoguþ* to translate *pueritia*;[39]
on two further occasions, I. 1. 120 and IV. 1. 73, he employs the more
common noun *cildhad* for the Latin term. It is interesting to note that the
hapax legomenon cnihtiugoð translates *adolescentia* in the same passage where
cildgeoguþ occurs (I. 1. 120). Once again, Byrhtferth's employment of
cildgeoguþ seems to indicate that he carefully read Old English texts,
searching them *mid scrutniendre scrutnunge* as he would have said, for
elegant words. We know that in his Latin writings (notably the *Vita S.
Oswaldi* and the *Vita S. Ecgwini*) Byrhtferth was a fervent practitioner of
the hermeneutic style, which in turn will have ignited his love for
recondite Old English words.[40] (In this respect, Byrhtferth and the Royal
Glossator seem to have been very much alike.)

Old English *cildgeong* and *cildgeoguþ* may serve to highlight the
difficulties with which we are confronted in trying to identify Old Saxon
(or Old High German) loan influence in Old English. If *kindjung* had not
been attested in Old Saxon, if the use of *cildgeong* and *cildgeoguþ* had not
been limited to practically one author, if *cildgeoguþ* had not attracted the
attention of Byrhtferth – there would have been no reason to suspect that
the Old English adjective might have been coined in imitation of an Old
Saxon model.

ofearmian, ofearmung (misereri, miseratio)

With our last examples we come back again to the Royal Psalter. The two
words belong to a small group of Christian terms on which much has
been written and surmised. The words of this group which are attested in
Old English are the loans for church, angel, bishop and devil and the loan

---

[39] *Enchiridion* I. 1. 121; the lemma *pueritia* is at I. 1. 103.

[40] For Byrhtferth's Latin style, see Lapidge, 'Hermeneutic Style', pp. 128–32, *idem*,
'Byrhtferth and the *Vita S. Ecgwini*', in his *Anglo-Latin Literature 900–1066*,
pp. 293–315, at 296–303 (orig. publ. 1979), and *idem*, 'Byrhtferth of Ramsey and the
Early Sections of the *Historia Regum* Attributed to Symeon of Durham', *ibid.*,
pp. 317–42, at 320–8 (orig. publ. 1981).

formations meaning 'heathen', 'to fast', 'to baptize', and (our verb) 'to pity'. Friedrich Kluge,[41] who was the first scholar to study the words in question as a group, posited that they had first been borrowed from Greek into Gothic, subsequently been introduced into southern Germany by Gothic missionaries, from there had travelled up the Danube and along the Rhine and had eventually reached England, perhaps already with St Augustine's West Frankish interpreters. The missionary activity through which these words were thought to have arrived in Germany has since come to be known to philologists as the 'Donaumission'. However, on close inspection, the hypothesis of such a 'Danubian mission' and its purported impact on the lexicon of several languages has not much to recommend it. And, as far as Old English is concerned, it has been shown that the words in question are not to be derived in direct line from any Gothic missionary activities on the Continent. [42]

Our sole concern here is with *ofearmian* and *ofearmung*, and for these two words there are grounds for believing that they indeed were modelled on corresponding German loan formations, certainly not in the wake of St Augustine's mission, but rather in the context of the cosmopolitan climate of King Æthelstan's court, and that they were arguably coined by the Royal Glossator himself. The words are not attested prior to the Royal Psalter. Here two occurrences of the verb have been noted so far (pss. XXXVI.21 and LXXVI.10, both translating *misereri*); to these should be added *feormað* for *miseretur* in ps. XXXVI.26 (note the proximity to the first attestation in ps. XXXVI.21). This is no doubt a corrupt form of *ofearmað*, as is indicated by the lemma, and by the fact that the dependent glosses in the Tiberius and Vitellius psalters translate the lemma by the correct form *ofearmað*. The noun (derived from the verb) *ofearmung* (for *miseratio*) is found on two occasions in the Royal Psalter (pss. XXIV.6 and CII.5). The usual equivalents for *misereri* and *miseratio* in the Royal Psalter (as elsewhere) are *miltsian* (for example pss. IV.2 or VI.3)

---

[41] See F. Kluge, 'Gotische Lehnworte im Althochdeutschen', *Beiträge zur Geschichte der deutschen Sprache und Literatur* 35 (1909), 124–60.

[42] For a brief survey of the problems inherent in the hypothesis of the 'Donaumission' (with full bibliography) and discussion of the Old English words in question, see Gneuss, 'Language Contact', pp. 120–3. The topic will be comprehensively addressed in the context of a full inventory and analysis of Greek loanwords in Old English in a dissertation by Helene Feulner (Munich, forthcoming).

and *miltsung* (for example pss. L.3 or LXVIII.17).[43] In Old High German the most frequent equivalent for *misereri* is *irbarmen* (German 'erbarmen'). As regards a suspected dependence of the English word on the German term, it has been pointed out that the prefix in *ir-barmen* is different from that in *of-earmian*;[44] and it might further be argued that a glossator as competent and ingenious as that of the Royal Psalter would have realized that *misereri* is derived from *miser* 'poor' and could therefore have coined a verb derived from Old English *earm* independently of any such calque existing in a cognate language. However, for an Anglo-Saxon glossator, coining an Old English word after Latin *misereri*, there was no reason to employ a prefix at all: *earmian* would have been a perfect rendering, and apparently no such verb (unsuitable by its established and potentially countervailing meaning) had existed previously. (Two recorded instances of *earmian* 'to pity' are from later texts.) By contrast, in Old High German the simplex *armēn* was in existence already, meaning 'to be or grow poor'. The German prefixed form *ir-barmēn* should therefore arguably be explained as an attempt to avoid polysemy of a confusing nature in *armēn*.[45] The Old English equivalent of the Old High German prefix *ir-* (in terms of etymology) would have been OE *or-* or *ā-*.[46] Of these, *ā* would have created a hiatus and might therefore not have appeared as a suitable choice, apart from the fact that presumably no native speaker of Old English would have recognized its relationship with German *ir-*. *Or-* is phonologically closer to *ir-*, but would not have appeared suitable on other grounds: it is not a common prefix, as a glance at the dictionaries will tell, and, more important, with verbs (as often with adjectives) it signifies negation, as in *ortruwian* 'to despair' or *georwyrðan* 'to disgrace'. Furthermore, German *ir-b-armen* actually has two prefixes, *b* being apparently a reduced form of *ab-* (the form *barmen* is in fact attested).[47] OHG *ab-* (OS *af-*) and OE *of-* are not

---

[43] For the rendering of *misereri* and *miseratio* in the psalter glosses, see Gneuss, *Lehnbildungen*, pp. 56–7.

[44] See Gneuss, 'Language Contact', p. 123.

[45] See Kluge and Seebold, *Etymologisches Wörterbuch*, s. v. *erbarmen*; see also the earlier edition of this dictionary: F. Kluge, *Etymologisches Wörterbuch der deutschen Sprache*, 20th ed. by W. Mitzka (Berlin, 1967). (From the editions revised by E. Seebold (22nd (1989) and 23rd (1995)) much useful etymological information has been omitted in order to gain space for additional headwords.

[46] See Meid, *Wortbildungslehre*, p. 39.

[47] Cf. Kluge and Seebold, *Etymologisches Wörterbuch* (and the previous editions by Kluge

only derived from a common Germanic ancestor;[48] more important, their phonological similarity is obvious, and the prefix is very common with Old English verbs, to which it often adds a perfective aspect (as in *ofgifan* 'to give up').[49] Usually, however, its meaning is rather vague, and it does not radically change the primary denotation of the verb (cf., for example, *seon* and *ofseon* 'to see' or *slean* and *ofslean* 'to kill'). In short, irrespective of whether the Royal Glossator heard or read a German form *abarmen or whether he only knew the usual *irbarmen*, the fact that he coined a prefixed verb (*ofearmian*) and not a simplex (*earmian*) to render *misereri* suggests that he somehow had come to know the German standard equivalent for *misereri*. In this connection we should recall the unique occurrence of the substantive *tofleam* for *refugium* in the Royal Psalter (ps. XCIII.22). The prefix in this *hapax legomenon* is no exact translation of the prefix in the Latin lemma, but it corresponds precisely to the prefix in one of the Old High German renderings of *refugium*, namely *zuofluht* (German 'Zuflucht', see above, p. 48).

It is obvious that *ofearmian* and *ofearmung* in the Royal Psalter are new terms and that they never gained any currency. They are not attested previously, and we have already noted the blunder which the scribe of Royal 2. B. V made on one occasion (*feormað*, ps. XXXVI.26). By the same token, on its first occurrence (ps. XXIV.6), *ofearmung* is combined with the usual *miltsung* in a doublet. Among the dependent psalter glosses, psalters EF have *ofearmian* in ps. XXXVI.21, G and H have it in ps. XXXVI.26, and FGHJ in ps. LXXVI.10. Of the two occurrences of *ofearmung*, only one (ps. CII.5) is found elsewhere, and in one only of the dependent glosses (Blickling Psalter). So even in the D-type glosses there is some hesitation in following their model. Outside the psalter glosses, *ofearmian* occurs no more than once, namely in the interlinear gloss to the *Regularis concordia* (glossing *misereri*).[50] Apparently the established terms *(ge)mildsian* and *mildsung* were eventually preferred as adequate renditions for one of the fundamental axioms of Christianity. Nonetheless, *ofearmian*

---

and Mitzka), s. v. *erbarmen*, as well as A. L. Lloyd and O. Springer, *Etymologisches Wörterbuch des Althochdeutschen* (Göttingen, 1988–) I, 478–80.

[48] Cf. Meid, *Wortbildungslehre*, p. 36.

[49] Cf., for example, R. Quirk and C. L. Wrenn, *An Old English Grammar*, 2nd ed. (London, 1958), p. 114.

[50] See Kornexl, *Die 'Regularis Concordia' und ihre altenglische Interlinearversion*, p. 49, line 592.

and *ofearmung*, which the Royal Glossator introduced to supplement *mildsian* and *mildsung* (the terms also favoured by himself), are further important witnesses to his intense interest in augmenting and refining the English language. That he possibly coined his new terms after a continental vernacular model affords us an intriguing glimpse of the intellectual milieu in which he did his work.

We may pursue this line of reasoning a step further. As opposed to *orgel* or the meaning 'frivolous' for *gal*, *ofearmian* and *ofearmung* are unlikely to have been adopted in the course of everyday and routine social communication between speakers of different languages. If the hypothesis is tenable, that *ofearmian* and *ofearmung* for *misereri* and *miseratio* were created after the model of German *(ir)barmen*, the necessary corollary would be that the Royal Glossator had either studied closely Old High German (or Old Saxon) translated or glossed versions of biblical texts, or that he had discussed possible ways of rendering crucial Christian terms with native speakers of these languages – or both. In this context, an Old Saxon version of the psalter – outstanding in its quality, but unfortunately preserved in a regrettably fragmentary state – deserves our notice. The two surviving fragments (dated s. x^ex) show this to have been a text which combined translation and commentary in continuous Old Saxon prose, following the text of the psalms verse by verse. By this technique, the Gernrode fragments (as they are called) actually represent a treatise on the psalms in the vernacular. In Appendix III we shall briefly return to this unique testimony to what must have been a remarkable tradition of scholarly translation in Old Saxon.

OLD FRENCH LOANWORDS AND WEST FRANKISH INFLUENCE

As in the case of German influence, the total number of loanwords in Old English which are of unequivocally French (in distinction to Latin) origin and which were incontestably borrowed before the Norman Conquest is exceedingly small.[51] Yet, the contacts between England (especially Wessex) and Francia were manifold and numerous, ever since the marriage

---

[51] See Gneuss, 'Language Contact', pp. 134–7, for a conspectus of the words which are in question and for a critical review of longer lists of such words, optimistically compiled by earlier scholars (often without considering a possible borrowing directly from Latin or taking into account an attestation in post-Conquest manuscripts only).

of Æthelwulf, king of Wessex (839–58, and father of Alfred the Great) to Judith, daughter of Charles II, the Bald, king of the West Franks (840–77), in 856. As we have noted, such contacts came to a first highpoint during King Æthelstan's reign and the marriage alliances of the English royal family with the Carolingians and Capetians. To an even greater extent than in the case of German loan influence, it is in everyday communication with native speakers of French, which such political and cultural ties will have brought with them, that we must see the principal channels through which French loans will have found their way into Old English. By the tenth century, no literature, and certainly no works of a scholarly nature in French were as yet in existence. On the other hand, the few extant texts in French dating from the ninth or tenth century leave one in no doubt that the language spoken in Francia by that time was clearly distinct from contemporary Latin. The earliest of the texts from which this much emerges are the famous 'Strasbourg Oaths', sworn in 842 by Charles the Bald and Louis the German (both sons of Louis the Pious) and their retainers to seal their alliance against their brother Lothair. The 'Strasbourg Oaths' are an important document for the French language as they are for German, inasmuch as they are the first witness attesting to the existence of two different 'official' vernaculars in the western and the eastern parts of the Carolingian Empire.[52]

For a full assessment of the number and nature of French or Gallo-Romance words which may have been known at least to an Anglo-Saxon elite, it would be necessary to look beyond Old English texts. Anglo-Latin texts would have to be scrutinized for possible French or Romance words contained in them. This has never been done on a comprehensive scale, and, to my knowledge, it has never occurred to Old English

---

[52] For a convenient survey of the development of Old French from its Vulgar Latin and Gallo-Romance prehistory up to the eleventh century, see P. Rickard, *A History of the French Language*, 2nd ed. (London, 1989), pp. 1–37; for the 'Strasbourg Oaths', preserved only in a tenth-century manuscript and still heavily influenced by Medieval Latin orthography, see *ibid.*, pp. 20–3; for these, see also H. Berschin, J. Felixberger and H. Goebel, *Französische Sprachgeschichte* (Munich, 1978), pp. 178–89. For a comprehensive linguistic treatment and comparison of the two earliest French texts, the Oaths and the sequence of St Eulalia (*c.* 880), see S. D'Arco Avalle, *Alle origine della letteratura francese. I Giuramenti di Strasbourgo e la sequenza di Santa Eulalia* (Turin, 1966).

philologists that Anglo-Latin sources might provide some useful information concerning Anglo-Saxon familiarity with Romance vocabulary. Hitherto, remarks on such vocabulary in Anglo-Latin texts are few and far between. For example, the obvious Romance origin of words such as *cambra* (Modern French *chambre*), *capellanus* (Modern French *chapelain*) or *senior* 'lord' (Modern French *seigneur*) in Bishop Asser's *Life of King Alfred* led the editor to posit that Asser had spent a period of study on the Continent,[53] but it has since been suggested that Asser might well have acquired such words in King Alfred's entourage.[54] Other texts containing an occasional word of Romance or French origin include a charter issued by King Edgar in 967 (S 755, BCS 1197) and the *Vita S. Eustachii*, a metrical life of that saint, possibly composed at Abingdon in the second half of the tenth century. Both texts use the word *uasallus* (Modern French, and English, *vassal*); in addition, the *Vita* attests Romance *caballus* (Modern French *cheval*).[55] And in one of the Latin poems attributable to Æthelwold's school at Winchester, the Old French word *blasmer* (Modern French *blâmer*, Modern English *to blame*) appears (with Latin inflexion) in lieu of *blasphemare*.[56]

It might be argued that these Romance words in Latin texts would not have been recognized as such by most of the literate Anglo-Saxons; but then, the French loans in Old English would not have been recognized by most of them either. Or, to put it differently, an Anglo-Saxon scholar (and perhaps a literate layman as well) who might have recognized the Romance origin of *prud* ('proud', on which see below) in an Old English text might also be credited with a knowledge of the Romance origin of (say) *caballus* in a Latin text. By the same token, there is no way of excluding the occasional employment of words such as *caballus* or *blasmer* in Old English as well. At all events, such Romance words testify to the impact which speakers of French had on the languages in use in Anglo-Saxon England.

[53] Cf. Stevenson, *Asser's Life*, pp. xciii–xciv.

[54] See Keynes and Lapidge, *Alfred the Great*, pp. 54–5, and cf. *ibid.*, p. 221, n. 112, where some further items of Romance origin are added to Stevenson's list.

[55] For the *Vita S. Eustachii* and its presumed origin, see Lapidge, 'Æthelwold and the *Vita S. Eustachii*'; for the Romance words, see *ibid.*, p. 222.

[56] See Lapidge, 'Three Latin Poems', p. 262, line 13, and pp. 263 and 486.

Iugelere, tudenard, coittemære

Such considerations should be borne in mind when evaluating these three loanwords, attested in the Brussels Aldhelm glosses. *Iugelere* (Old French *jougelere*, Modern English *juggler*) occurs four times, glossing *magus* 'magician' and similar terms.[57] While the French origin of *iugelere* has been accepted as probable from the end of the nineteenth century onwards,[58] the two other loans, probably borrowed from Old French as well, were discovered only more recently: *tudenard* 'shield' (from OF *toenart*) glossing *scutum* (G 812) and *parma* (G 4908), and *coittemære* 'boiled (and thereby reduced) wine' (from OF **cuite mere*) glossing *carenum* 'sweet wine' (G 203).[59] Of these three words, only *iugelere* is attested elsewhere.[60] By their nature, *iugelere*, *tudenard* and *coittemære* point to an adoption in court circles rather than in a clerical context; and there is no reason why *caballus* or *uasallus*, or other such words (attested in Anglo-Latin texts only) should not – in their French form – have been current as well in English conversation in the royal entourage. As regards the currency of *tudenard* and *coittemære* in court circles and their probable introduction through personal contacts, it should be noted that the presumed French antecedent for *coittemære* is not attested at all in French texts, whereas the occurrence of *tudenard* in the Aldhelm glosses predates the earliest attestation of the word in French by several centuries.[61] It should further be noted that *tudenard* in one of its two occurrences appears as *tude* in the manuscript (G 4908), a form which should probably be taken as a merograph, that is, an abbreviation which was deemed sufficient to recall the complete word (*tudenard* in this case) to the reader's mind. This in turn might suggest that the term was well established, at least with certain groups of speakers. It should finally be noted that

[57] Cf. G 3908, 3955, 3974 and 4354; on this word, see Gneuss 'Language Contact', p. 136 and n. 112.

[58] *Iugelere* occurs, for example, in the very small group of French loans listed by Campbell, § 567.

[59] *Tudenard* and *coittemære* were first identified as French loans by Mustanoja, 'Notes on Some Old English Glosses', pp. 53–4 and 59–60.

[60] Cf. Gneuss, 'Language Contact', p. 136, n. 112. Needless to say, the occurrence of *tudenard* and *coittemære* in glosses drawing on the Brussels corpus (such as those in Digby 146) cannot be counted as independent attestations.

[61] Cf. discussion by Mustanoja, 'Notes on Some Old English Glosses', pp. 54 and 59–60.

coittemære occurs in a passage in the *De uirginitate* where Aldhelm expressly points out that *carenum* ('sweet wine', the lemma glossed by *coittemære*) is a royal drink:[62] 'lento careni defruto, quod regalibus ferculis conficitur'.[63]

scrudnian (Lat. *scrutari*)

It is possible that West Frankish influence may also be detected in one of the outstanding verbal ties between the Royal Psalter, the Old English Rule, and the Aldhelm glosses: *scrudnian* 'to investigate, scrutinize, meditate on', and the noun *scrudnung* derived from the verb. We have considered these words and their importance for establishing a relationship between the three texts in question in some detail above (pp. 211–18). It will be sufficient here to rehearse only the most salient points which may indicate Frankish influence in the adoption of *scrudnian* and add some brief remarks on the usage and phonology of the word which may be pertinent. There are reasons to believe that *scrudnian* was introduced into Old English texts by Æthelwold and that he had been familiar with the word for some time before it appeared in the Psalter and the Rule. It is evident that Æthelwold had a great fondness for the word. It is employed in the Psalter for every occurrence of *scrutari*, and the Glossator derived the noun *scrudnung* from *scrudnian* as a gloss for *scrutinium*. Furthermore, both words occur in the Rule and its preface without being prompted by the corresponding Latin lemmata, and *scrutnian* glosses *scrutari* in the Brussels glosses. Apart from writings connected with Æthelwold – and apart from Byrhtferth again – *scrudnian* and *scrudnung* are scarcely attested at all. Whereas Byrhtferth took a delight in verb and substantive, comparable to Æthelwold's, there are only two attestations of *scrutnian* in

---

[62] On the meaning of Latin *carenum* and Old English *cæren* (the loan deriving from it), see C. E. Fell, 'A Note on Old English Wine Terminology: the Problem of *Cæren*', *Nottingham Medieval Studies* 25 (1981), 1–12; on the Aldhelm passage, see *ibid.*, p. 7 and n. 30.

[63] Ehwald, *Aldhelmi Opera*, p. 231. 17–18; 'with the treacly must of the sweet wine made for royal feasts', transl. Lapidge and Herren, *Aldhelm: the Prose Works*, p. 61. Interestingly, Byrhtferth adopts verbatim this definition of *carenum* in his *Vita S. Oswaldi* (thereby indicating that it was still valid at the turn of the millenium): 'caraenum quod regalibus conficitur ferculis', ed. Raine, *Historians* I, 465; cf. Fell, 'Wine Terminology', p. 7 and n. 31.

the vast corpus of Ælfric's writings, and even these have been replaced by other words in a number of manuscripts, perhaps as a result of Ælfric's own revisions of his homilies. The word is also avoided in later D-type psalter glosses. By contrast, in his *Enchiridion*, Byrhtferth employs *ascrutnian* frequently and always in passages where he is not translating Latin portions of his work (for example I. 2. 355; II. 1. 27; II. 1. 443; he always uses prefixed *ascrutnian* in finite verb forms). Like the Royal Glossator, Byrhtferth on several occasions indulges in elaborate word-play with the verb and its derivatives, both in English and Latin, as for example: 'synt to asmeagenne and synt eac to asmuganne mid scrut-niendre scrutnunge'.[64] There was no need to adopt *scrudnian*; Old English *(a)smeagan*, for example, would have been a perfectly adequate rendering of *scrutari* and is, in fact, employed in that sense in the Rule, the Royal Psalter, and by Byrhtferth. The sum of this various evidence suggests that *scrudnian* was a recondite word, fashionable in certain scholarly circles, and that because of this character it was thought fit by Æthelwold and by Byrhtferth to be adopted for embellishing the English language, in the fashion they felt this language should be embellished.

It is a phonological point which may tip the balance in favour of thinking that *scrudnian* owes its existence to contacts with Frankish scholars, rather than that it was drawn exclusively from Latin texts such as the psalter or Aldhelm. In the Royal Psalter, in all its frequent occurrences, the verb is consistently spelled with <d> (presumably pronounced /d/): *scrudnian* (as is the noun *scrudnung*). The spelling with <d> occurs also in the preface to the Rule, and it may have been the original spelling in the text of the Rule itself (cf. above, pp. 213–14). It might be objected that the actual pronunciation of original /t/ in *scrutari* by West Frankish speakers in the tenth century would have been /ð/, not / d/ (arguably in their pronunciation of Latin, and certainly when using the word in their vernacular). The development of Latin intervocalic /t/ in

---

[64] *Enchiridion* I. 2. 113–14, '[the days] must be examined, and must also be studied with scrutinizing scrutiny'. The Latin version of this is even more elaborate: 'perscrutandi sunt et scrutanti scrutinio inuestigandi' (I. 2. 66–7); cf. also the similar play in Latin in IV. 1. 77–8. Such word-play echoes ps. LXIII.7, translated by the Royal Glossator: 'hy scrudnodon unryhtwisnesse hy geteorodon scrudniende scrudnunge', cf. above, p. 211. It is also a verbal echo of a similar play in Aldhelm's prose *De uirginitate* (Ehwald, *Aldhelmi Opera*, p. 245. 2–3) and *De metris* I (*ibid.*, p. 62. 14); cf. *Enchiridion*, ed. Baker and Lapidge, p. 263.

Vulgar Latin, Gallo-Romance and Old French is generally described as follows: /t/ > /d/ in Vulgar Latin (probably by the fifth century) > /ð/ (for Old French attested, perhaps, already in the 'Strasbourg Oaths' sworn in 842); in Old French /ð/ is subsequently lost, presumably between the late ninth century and the eleventh.[65] The spelling <ð> for Latin /t/ or /d/ is occasionally found in earlier Latin loans in Old English where it presumably points to Romance influence; cf., for example, OE *senoð* < Lat. *synodus* 'synod' or *sæðerige* < Lat. *satureia* 'sage'.[66] However, the (Vulgar Latin) spelling <d (as in *abbod* < *abbatem* or *læden* < *latinus*) is clearly more frequent in such early loans. In Medieval Latin itself, intervocalic /t/ is occasionally spelled <d>, presumably indicating the pronunciation /d/ (perhaps /ð/) under the influence of spoken Latin and Romance vernaculars.[67] As regards the English form *scrudnian*, it should be noted that intervocalic <d> is also found in *tudenard*, for which no plausible etymology other than an Old French origin can be established (see above, p. 406). One might ask therefore whether the pronunciation of /ð/ by speakers of Old French might not have been noticeably different (the consonant was on the point of being dropped) from the pronunciation of OE /ð/ and that consequently Old English scribes did not see fit to render OF /ð/ by the graphs <ð> or <þ> they used for the Old English phoneme. Whatever the case, the consistent <d> spellings in *scrudnian* and *scrudnung*, in a gloss where in each instance the Latin lemma spelled with <t> stands beneath the Old English word, can hardly be satisfactorily explained without invoking the intervention of Frankish scholars: the words are of a learned character and do not occur prior to the Royal Psalter; therefore early Vulgar Latin phonology (as in early loans such as *abbod* or *læden*) is out of question. Apart from works connected with Æthelwold, the words are spelled with classical and Medieval Latin <t>: *scrutnian*, *scrutnung*, and, finally, there is no Old English sound change by which /t/ would be altered to /d/.[68] In other words, the orthography of

---

[65] See, for example, M. K. Pope, *From Latin to Modern French with Especial Consideration of Anglo-Norman* (Manchester, 1934), §§ 332, 335–6 and 346–7.

[66] See, for example, SB, § 199, n. 3; cf. also Campbell, § 530. Unfortunately, Old English grammars make only feeble attempts to differentiate between Vulgar Latin and Gallo-Romance (or even Old French) phonology.

[67] For this, see now P. Stotz, *Handbuch zur lateinischen Sprache des Mittelalters* III, *Lautlehre* (Munich, 1996), § 184. 1–3 (pp. 223–5).

[68] Cf. above, p. 218 and n. 82.

scrudnian, judged in combination with its absence from earlier texts, strongly suggests that the Royal Glossator (and the translator of the *Regula*) adopted the word not from written sources, but in the course of discussions with West Frankish scholars. Byrhtferth's predilection for *ascrutnian* and *scrutnung* may perhaps confirm such a deduction. Perhaps Byrhtferth was not only attracted to the words by their recondite character when he read them in glossed manuscipts, but also because he had often heard the Latin terms in conversations with his master, Abbo of Fleury. However, Byrhtferth (or Abbo) insisted on pronouncing (or at least writing) the words with correct Latin /t/.

Old English 'prud' and the terminology for 'superbia'

From the examples of German and French loan influence which we have inspected thus far it has emerged that King Æthelstan's court culture, so decisively influenced by foreigners (in its intellectual aspects as well as in the realia of life) may have left some intriguing reflexes in the vocabulary of the Royal Psalter, the Rule and the Aldhelm glosses. The case of *ofearmian*, very possibly formed by the Royal Glossator after German *irbarmen*, argues that such foreign influence could occasionally concern the terms for key concepts of Christianity for which an Old English terminology had long been established. An even more striking example for this is, perhaps, Old English *prud* (Modern English *proud*).

Prud occurs twice in the Aldhelm glosses, in nouns derived from the adjective: *prutscipe* (G 1158) and *prutung* (G 1215). The derivation of Old English *prut* and *prud*[69] from Old French *prud* ('valiant', cf. Modern French *preux*) has never been disputed since it was first posited by Friedrich Kluge in 1895.[70] The phonological and morphological aspects of the loan and its derivatives have been comprehensively examined by Hermann Flasdieck and Hans Schabram.[71] Old English *prud* is not only

---

[69] The forms with *t* are more frequently attested in Old English.

[70] Cf. F. Kluge, 'Ne. *Proud-Pride*', *Englische Studien* 21 (1895), 334–5. OF *prud* is an oblique form; Modern French *preux* reflects the nominative: OF *pruz, proz, prouz;* the word derives ultimately from Latin *prodesse* 'to be useful, to benefit'. For its cognates in Romance languages, see W. Meyer-Lübke, *Romanisches etymologisches Wörterbuch*, 3rd ed. (Heidelberg, 1935), p. 561, no. 6766.

[71] See Flasdieck, 'Studien zur Laut- und Wortgeschichte', pp. 257–71, and Schabram, *Superbia*, pp. 14–16.

one of the exceedingly few words for which an Old French origin and an attestation before the Norman Conquest are beyond question: it is also exceptional among these words by the frequency with which it occurs in Late Old English texts (the word-family based on *prud* occurs about fifty times in such texts). What is further striking about *prud* and its derivatives is that, with two notable exceptions (which we shall consider in due course), the words are always used in a pejorative sense, rendering the concept of *superbia* 'sinful pride'. With *prud* being employed in that sense, we are back to the heart of Winchester vocabulary, since the Old English terminology for *superbia*, *superbus* and *superbire* emanating from Æthelwold's school is precisely defined and distinctive.

Much work has been done on the Old English words for the concept of *superbia* and their distribution in Old English texts, yet several important questions concerning these words have never even been asked. Any comprehensive treatment of the matter is beyond the scope of the present book. Our sole concern here is with the questions of whether the introduction of *prud* into this semantic field would square with the concept developed in Æthelwold's circle for the translation of *superbia* and related terms, and whether the roots for such an employment of *prud* can be traced in the intellectual milieu of Æthelstan's court. In search for an answer to these questions, it will be necessary briefly to rehearse some essential facts which so far have been established concerning the Old English terminology for *superbia* and to point out some problems which are in need of further investigation. Hans Schabram, in his monograph on the Old English terminology for *superbia*, meticulously listed every occurrence of the relevant Old English words in all the texts then available in print.[72] (It should be said that this was done in the days before the Old English lexicon could be controlled with comparative ease by means of the *Microfiche Concordance*.) The most important result of Schabram's investigation was that no universally accepted terminology for the *superbia* field existed. He uncovered four word-families for the concept, the employment of which was, in his view, almost exclusively to be explained in terms of Old English dialectology. The four families in

---

[72] See Schabram, *Superbia* (Munich, 1965); for some additional material, see *idem*, 'Das altenglische *superbia*-Wortgut. Eine Nachlese', *Festschrift für Prof. Dr. Herbert Koziol zum siebzigsten Geburtstag*, ed. G. Bauer *et al.* (Vienna, 1973), pp. 272–9.

question (and their dialectal distribution according to Schabram) are as follows:

First, *oferhygd*, represented principally by the nouns *oferhygd* and *oferhyg(e)dness*, the adjectives *oferhygdig* and *oferhygd* and the verb *oferhygdgian*. This family occurs in Anglian texts (and texts with Anglian dialect features) throughout the Old English period.

Second, *ofermod*, represented primarily by the nouns *ofermōd(ness)*, *ofermōdigness*, *ofermēttu*, and *ofermēdu*, the adjectives *ofermōd* and *ofermōdig* and the verb *ofermōd(i)gian*. This family first appears in West Saxon texts from the time of King Alfred and continues to be used in West Saxon until the end of the Anglo-Saxon period.

Third, *modig*, represented principally by the noun *mōdigness*, the adjective *mōdig* and the verb *mōd(i)gian*. This family occurs in a number of Late West Saxon texts, beginning with Æthelwold's translation of the *Regula S. Benedicti*.

Fourth, *prud*, chiefly represented by the adjectives *prūd/prūt*, the nouns *prȳdo/prȳde* (spelled also with *t*), *prūtscipe* and *prūtung*, and the verb *prūtian*. This family occurs (sporadically, in comparison with the other three families) in Late West Saxon and other southern texts.[73]

Subsequent to Schabram's work, it has been demonstrated beyond reasonable doubt that the introduction and propagation of the *modig* family must be associated with Æthelwold and the usage taught at his school.[74] Such is, in brief, the present state of knowledge concerning the Old English terms for *superbia*. A few of the questions in this matter which have never been pondered but which would merit close attention are as follows: first, do the relevant Old English words occur (with any frequency or at all) outside the semantic field of *superbia*? So far, it is clear only that the *modig* family is amply attested in a positive sense, principally

---

[73] See Schabram, *Superbia*, esp. pp. 13–16 and 130–1. Note that I have not listed above all the members of each of the four families. It is interesting that the *modig* family is the one with the fewest members, and hence the most precisely defined group (only the three words listed above occur with any frequency), whereas the *prud* family (in spite of its rather sporadic occurrence) consists of twelve words (many of these *hapax legomena*).

[74] See Gneuss, 'Standard Old English', pp. 76 and 78, and Hofstetter, *Winchester und Sprachgebrauch*, esp. p. 17, and cf. *passim*, the tables and discussions of the texts employing Winchester usage. See also Hofstetter, 'Winchester and the Standardization of Old English Vocabulary', p. 150. For a list of the principal texts in question, see above, pp. 93–4. For discussion of the *modig* family as it is used in the Old English Rule, see Gretsch, *Regula*, pp. 351–3.

in poetry (meaning 'high-spirited, noble-minded, bold, brave').[75] Second, when employed in the semantic field of *superbia*, and when occurring in translations from Latin, do the words in question always render *superbia*, *superbus* and *superbire* or are they used for translating terms such as *fastus*, *elatio* and *arrogantia* as well? Information on this point would be invaluable, in view of the deep concern revealed by the Winchester school (and by some other authors, Byrhtferth for example) with connotations of words, or with specific senses or metaphorical meanings. Recall that, for instance, in the case of *wuldorbeag* for *corona* (meaning 'crown of life' etc.) or of *gelaþung* for *ecclesia* (meaning 'the congregation of faithful Christians') Winchester usage introduced a lexical distinction which does not exist even in Latin (cf. above, pp. 98–113). As regards the *prud* family, it is, for example, noteworthy that Ælfric, on the one occasion where he employs a member of this family, uses *pryte* to translate *arrogantia* in a passage where this lemma occurs in close proximity to *superbia*, which in turn is translated by his usual *modignes*.[76] By the same token, *ofermettu*, the older (Alfredian) translation word for *superbia*, is employed by Æthelwold for *exaltatio* (BR 23.9, *RSB* 7.7), not for *superbia*, for which he always uses *modignes*.[77] But matters will not always be as straightforward as in these two cases. Consider, for example, the two occasions where members of the *prud* family occur in the Aldhelm glosses. On both occasions, the lemma is not *superbia*: *prutscipe* glosses *arrogantia* (G 1158), and *prutung* glosses *fastus* (G 1215). However, both Latin lemmata are also glossed in Latin: *arrogantia* by *superbia*, and *fastus* by *elatio* and *superbia*. Do the Old English glosses aim to translate the lemmata or their Latin glosses or both? In these two instances we can say no more than that *prutscipe* and *prutung* are clearly employed in the semantic field of *superbia*. Nonetheless, Old English philologists should not be content with assiduously listing occurrences of the members of the four families without making at least an attempt to clarify possible connotations and perhaps subtle shades of meaning.

[75] See Schabram, *Superbia*, pp. 123 and 130, and cf. for example BT, s. v. *modig*, senses I ('of high or noble spirit, high-spirited, noble-minded') and II ('bold, brave, courageous').

[76] See *Catholic Homilies* II (ed. Godden), pp. 124.483–125.542; *pryte* occuring at 125.530, *modignes* at 125.31; and see the discussion (with recourse to Ælfric's sources for the passage in question) by Hofstetter, *Winchester und Sprachgebrauch*, p. 54.

[77] Cf. Gretsch, *Regula*, p. 352, and Schabram, *Superbia*, p. 57.

A third, and, in my view, a most rewarding, question which would merit investigation concerns whether any reasons may be detected as to why specific words were favoured or avoided in specific texts or groups of texts. The only explanations which so far have been adduced for the employment of the four families have to do with Old English dialectology and word geography: *oferhygd* is Anglian, *ofermod* West Saxon, and so on. Even for the choice of *modig* by Æthelwold's school the influence of certain West Saxon subdialects has been assumed.[78] One may well ask how plausible such a standard philological answer is when a central notion of Christianity is concerned. In what follows, I shall aim to uncover (as far as this can still be done) some of the reasons which may have determined the preference of specific words for *superbia* by Æthelwold and his circle and to see how the loanword *prud* would fit into this scheme.

We may best begin with the Royal Psalter. In order properly to assess the *superbia* terminology employed there, it will be necessary briefly to consider the Alfredian roots for this usage. In Alfred's translations (the *Regula pastoralis*, the Boethius, the *Soliloquies* and the prose Psalter) there is a striking uniformity in usage: *ofermēttu* is the noun principally employed, *ofermōd* the principal adjective and *ofermōdigian* the only verb.[79] Alfred clearly avoids the *oferhygd* family, which is by contrast exclusively employed by his bishop, Wærferth, in his translation of Gregory's *Dialogues*, as well as in the anonymous translation of Bede's *Historia ecclesiastica*, also associated with Alfred's circle.[80] Earlier still, the *oferhygd* family had been used exclusively in the Vespasian Psalter gloss.[81] I do not believe that Alfred's avoidance of the *oferhygd* words was determined primarily (if at all) by the presumed Anglian character of the family. Alfred does not appear to have suffered from any particular phobia about Anglian terms (see above, p. 319), and, in my view, there is no hard evidence for the supposed Anglian character of the *oferhygd* words in the ninth century, *inter alia* simply because we have no West Saxon texts from the period prior to Alfred to validate such a claim. For reasons which

---

[78] See, for example, Hofstetter, *Winchester und Sprachgebrauch*, p. 545. For the assumption that a great number of Winchester words are to be explained in terms of West Saxon subdialects, see E. Seebold, 'Winchester und Canterbury: zum spätaltenglischen Sprachgebrauch', *Anglia* 107 (1989), 52–60, esp. 53–4 and 59.

[79] See Schabram, *Superbia*, pp. 37–42 and 48–50.

[80] See *ibid.*, pp. 42–5 (for Wærferth) and 45–8 (for Bede).

[81] See *ibid.*, pp. 29–30, and the table at the end of the book.

cannot clearly be recovered now, Alfred felt the urge to create afresh the Old English *superbia* terminology. It is possible that he did this under the influence of John the Old Saxon, whose help in translating the *Regula pastoralis* he acknowledged in the preface to that work.[82] It should be recalled that Grimbald, whose help Alfred acknowledged there as well, originally had been a monk at Saint-Bertin in Flanders and therefore was presumably a native speaker of a language closely related to Old Saxon.[83] This is not the place to investigate the terminology for *superbia* in Old Saxon, but on the evidence of the Old Saxon *Heliand* and the Old Saxon *Genesis* as this can be reconstructed from its Old English adaptation (the *Later Genesis*), as well as on the evidence of other Old Saxon texts, there are grounds for thinking that the adjective *oƀarmōd* and the noun *oƀarmōdi* would have been the principal Old Saxon terms in this semantic field.[84] Old Saxon *oƀarmōd* and *oƀarmōdi* (*ō* in the noun presumably being pronounced /œ:/ through i-mutation)[85] would correspond almost exactly to Alfred's *ofermōd* and *ofermēttu*.[86] It is also possible that the importance Alfred attached to the concept of *mod* as he understood it (encompassing both the centre of human consciousness and Man's immortal soul) may have played a role in his choice of *ofermod* (and *ofermettu*). Recall that in his translation of the *Consolatio* he frequently presents personified *Mod* (in lieu of the Boethian first person pronoun) to carry on the discussion with Philosophy.[87] The likelihood is that the writings of King Alfred were

---

[82] See *Pastoral Care*, ed. Sweet I, 7. On John's career, see above, pp. 248 and 342–7.

[83] See *Pastoral Care*, ed. Sweet I, 7. On Grimbald's career, see above, p. 248.

[84] See Sehrt, *Wörterbuch zum Heliand und zur Genesis*, s.v. *oƀarmōd*; for the *superbia* terms in the Old English adaptation of the Old Saxon *Genesis*, see Schabram, *Superbia*, p. 128. For the influence of the Saxon *Genesis* on the wording of the Old English *Later Genesis*, see above, pp. 390–1. For the noun *oƀarmōdi* attested in an Old Saxon prose text, see Wadstein, *Altsächsische Sprachdenkmäler*, p. 16.12. For the Old Saxon terms, see also H. Gneuss, 'The Battle of Maldon 89: Byrhtnoð's *ofermod* Once Again', in his *Language and History*, no. X, 117–37, at 127–8 (orig. publ. 1976).

[85] In Old Saxon, i-mutation for velar vowels had probably taken place by the later ninth century, but it is only scarcely attested in writing. For i-mutation of *ō*, cf. Gallée, *Altsächsische Grammatik*, § 16 e (p. 21) and § 87 (p. 69). The grapheme <ƀ> represents a voiced fricative, presumably identical with OE /v/, spelled <f>, cf. Gallée, §163 (p. 126) and § 223 (p. 161).

[86] I shall return to Alfred's terminology for the *superbia* field on another occasion.

[87] For Alfred's concept of *mod*, see M. Godden, 'Anglo-Saxons on the Mind', in *Learning and Literature*, ed. Lapidge and Gneuss, pp. 271–98, at 274–7.

available at his grandson's court, and that, later on, they were closely studied in the circle where Æthelwold was active. Some sixty years later, Ælfric in fact refers to these writings as being easily accessible every-where.[88]

Like that of Alfred, the Royal Glossator's terminology is strikingly consistent. He uses *ofermod*, the adjective clearly favoured by Alfred, on all occasions of *superbus* in the psalter (thirteen times, e. g. pss. XVII.28 or LXXXVIII.11) and has Alfredian *ofermodigian* for the one occurrence of *superbire* (ps. IX.23). However, instead of *ofermēttu*, the noun favoured by Alfred, the Glossator invariably employs *ofermōdness* for all occurrences of *superbia* (nine times, e. g. pss. XVI.10 or XXX.19).[89] This noun, although attested in Alfred's writings, does not play an important role in the king's terminology. It is evident, therefore, that the Glossator's terminology is closely related to that of Alfred, a circumstance which (in view of other traces of Saxon influence in the Psalter) may lend substance to the suspicion that Old Saxon influence may have been a factor in Alfred's as well as the Glossator's choice of the *ofermod* words. But it is also evident that Alfred and the Glossator differ with respect to the noun they prefer (even so, the Glossator stays within the *ofermod* family). There may have been various reasons for such divergence. Influence of the A-type psalter gloss may have been one of these reasons. The Vespasian Psalter has consistently *oferhygd* as the noun, and almost exclusively *oferhygdig* as the adjective,[90] and the Royal Psalter's *ofermodness* and *ofermod* parallels this more obviously than *ofermettu* and *ofermod* would have done.[91] Another reason for the rejection of *ofermēttu* in the Royal Psalter may perhaps be sought in its phonological similarity to *ofermǣte* 'excessive, immoderate', *ofermǣtu* 'excess, presumption' or *ofermete* 'food in

---

88 See *Catholic Homilies* (ed. Thorpe) I, 2: '[the books] ðe Ælfred cyning snoterlice awende of Ledene on Englisc, þa synd to hæbenne'; 'which King Alfred discerningly translated from Latin into English; they are available'.

89 All occurrences of the *superbia* terms in the Royal Psalter and in all the other psalter glosses are conveniently listed in a table at the end of Schabram, *Superbia*.

90 See table at the end of Schabram, *Superbia*.

91 A noun *ofermod* would have been an even closer parallel to Vespasian's noun *oferhygd*, and such a noun is indeed (very rarely) attested in Old English. However, among the numerous compounds with *-mod* as their determinatum, listed by BT and BTS (s. v. *mod*), there are no further substantives, apart from *ofermod*. The implication is that a compound noun *ofermod* must probably be considered highly unusual in terms of Old English compounding with *mod*.

excess, a feast where there is food in excess'. We have had ample opportunity to observe the Glossator's awareness of, and interest in, sound similarities between different words.

A comparison with the Junius Psalter reveals the Royal Glossator's deep concern with the terminology for *superbia*. We have seen (above, p. 318) that the Junius Psalter is to some extent a Saxonization of an A-type gloss as represented in Vespasian A. i. It is interesting therefore that this psalter does not only retain all the instances of *oferhygd* and *oferhygdig* which occur in the Vespasian Psalter, but even substitutes *oferhygdig* on the three occasions where Vespasian has *oferhoga* for *superbus*.[92] This suggests that the *oferhygd* words were considered adequate translation equivalents in the *superbia* field by a West Saxon reviser in the first decades of the tenth century, which, in turn, may confirm our doubts about the presumed Anglian dialect character of the *oferhygd* family (at least for the early tenth century), and which makes the link between the Royal Glossator and Alfred stand out even more prominently.

A similar interest in the *superbia* terminology is evident in the Old English Rule with its deliberate introduction of the *modig* family into the field. There are nine occurrences of words from this family, all for *superbia* and derivatives (for example *modig* (BR 48.4), *modigness* (BR 22.14) and *modigian* (BR 125.10)), whereas the Royal Psalter's *ofermod* is retained on one occasion only (BR 17.15, for *superbus*), and Alfredian *ofermettu* also occurs once only (BR 23.9, translating *elatio*).[93] There were Alfredian forerunners for the use of *modig* in the field: Alfred's occasional use of the adjective *ofermodig* and the verb *ofermodigian*, and four occurrences of the adjective *modig* itself.[94]

Apart from their employment of the *prud* family, the Aldhelm glosses translate a few further lemmata from the *superbia* field by native terms. Here they show a transitional stage with *ofermodigness* (a hybrid of the types *ofermod* and *modig*) occurring twice (G 5043 and 5179).[95]

In view of the many attestations of the *modig* words in an unambiguously positive sense 'noble-minded, brave' (see above, pp. 412–13), the

---

[92] See table in Schabram, *Superbia*.
[93] See discussion in Gretsch, *Regula*, pp. 351–3.
[94] See lists in Schabram, *Superbia*, pp. 38–9.
[95] For comments on a correction in G 5179, presumably made to bring the gloss into greater conformity with the later Winchester preference of *modig*, see Hofstetter, *Winchester und Sprachgebrauch*, p. 130.

massive propagation of *modig* to express 'sinful pride', which begins with the Rule, is striking. It becomes even more striking when we reflect that (as far as we can see now) there was no lexical necessity to bend the originally positive meaning of *modig*: *ofermod* and *ofermodness* (or *ofermettu*) apparently captured the sense of 'sinful pride' in a satisfactory way and were used in texts (aside from those with Winchester connections) until the end of the Old English period. There is no way of explaining such usage of *modig* in terms other than a bold and rigorous re-evaluation of a heroic ideal from a Christian perspective. Such re-evaluation may be bold and rigorous, but it is not unparalleled in texts connected with Æthelwold.[96] We have seen (above, pp. 189 and 193) that the semantic change of *dream* (a term of crucial importance for a heroic lifestyle) from 'joy, rejoicing' to '(Christian) music, musical instrument' seems first to become manifest in the Royal Psalter (and the Rule), and that it is pervasive in the Aldhelm glosses. By the same token, *lofgeorn* 'eager for fame or praise', the very last word in *Beowulf* ('manna ... lofgeornost', line 3182), occurs three times in the Rule, in a somewhat vague sense, but with a clearly negative connotation: 'eager for praise (?obtained by being prodigal)'. The word is extremely rare: apart from the one occurrence in *Beowulf* and the three occurrences in the Rule, there are only three further independent attestations of *lofgeorn* (one from Ælfric and two from Wulfstan), all in a negative sense.[97] Therefore, Æthelwold is not only the first to use the word in prose, but also the author who employs it most frequently. The sense in which Æthelwold employs *lofgeorn* is vague *inter alia* because on

---

[96] Such a linguistic re-evaluation of heroic ideals as is evidenced in the Winchester school's employment of the *modig* words for 'sinful pride' has an interesting parallel in literature. Recently, A. Orchard (*Pride and Prodigies*, pp. 28–171 *passim*) has demonstrated that many of the human monsters and monster-slayers haunting the folios of BL, Cotton Vitellius A. xv qualified for their place in that anthology as exempla of excessive pride. Usually their pride is based on heroic exploits, and invariably it is judged and condemned in terms of Christian *superbia*.

[97] *Lofgeorn* occurs in fact twice in Ælfric, once in the *Lives of Saints* (no. xvi), ed. Skeat I, 356.302, and once in *De xii abusiuis*, ed. R. Morris, *Old English Homilies*, EETS OS 73 (1880), 297. Here, however, the passage in question is repeated verbatim from *Lives*, no. xvi, which leaves us with only one independent occurrence of *lofgeorn* in Ælfric. On the chronology of the two texts, see P. Clemoes, 'The Chronology of Ælfric's Works', in *The Anglo-Saxons. Studies in Some Aspects of their History and Culture Presented to Bruce Dickins*, ed. P. Clemoes (London, 1959), pp. 212–47, at 226 and 244. Ælfric uses the word in a description of *iactantia* ('boasting, ostentation').

all three occasions the word occurs in passages which translate rather freely. On two occasions, however, the Latin word to which *lofgeorn* seems to correspond is *prodigus* 'wasteful' (occurring in a list of qualities which the cellarer of a monastery should or should not have).[98] Such a translation of *prodigus* (referring to a wasteful cellarer) by *lofgeorn* seems to depend on an allusion to the heroic ideal of a chieftain being praised because of his generosity towards his retainers. This in turn would imply originally positive connotations for *lofgeorn*, connotations which must have had some currency. (In any event, the earliest attestations of *lofgeorn* in a prose text do not support any hypothesis concerning the *Beowulf*-poet's potentially critical attitude towards his hero.)[99]

If we now return to our point of departure, the French loan *prud*, a striking parallel to the sense development in the *modig* words can be observed: the employment of a term with positive connotations (very close to the original meanings of *modig*) in order to express 'sinful pride'. In view of the etymology of Old French *prouz* and its subsequent development to French *preux* 'valiant', a positive sense for *prouz* is to be expected, and, in fact, all attestations in Old French texts appear to have such positive meanings.[100] Our witness that such positive meanings were indeed extant after *prud* had been introduced into English is Byrhtferth once again. On the two occasions where he uses the adverb *prutlice*,[101] he does so in an unambiguously positive sense: 'proudly', once with the meaning 'wisely, prudently' implied: 'and eac hig [*i. e.* þa getyddustan boceras, 'the most learned scholars', II. 1. 432] prutlice gymað þæs miotacismus gefleard', 'and they proudly guard against the folly of *motacismus*' (II. 1. 456–7). *Prud* is not only extremely rare in Byrhtferth; from the context in which it occurs here, a certain exotic flair may be deduced for it. The passage bristles with Latin and Greek technical terms

---

[98] Cf. BR 54.9 = *RSB* 31.1 and BR 55.3 = *RSB* 31.12; the third occurrence is BR 18.18 = *RSB* 4.62 (without corresponding Latin lemma).

[99] Negative connotations for *lofgeorn* in *Beowulf*, on the evidence of its occurrence in prose, have been suggested by E. G. Stanley, '*Hæþenra Hyht* in *Beowulf*', in his *A Collection of Papers with Emphasis on Old English Literature* (Toronto, 1987), pp. 192–208, at 204–5 (orig. publ. 1963). On the meaning of *lofgeorn*, see also Orchard, *Pride and Prodigies*, pp. 54–5.

[100] Cf. Tobler-Lommatzsch, *Altfranzösisches Wörterbuch* (Berlin, 1915–43; Wiesbaden, 1951–), s. v. *pro* adj., esp. cols. 1922–6; for the etymology of OF *prouz*, see above, p. 410, n. 70.

[101] See *Enchiridion*, ed. Baker and Lapidge II. 1. 456 and III. 2. 33.

such as *motacismus* or *barbarolexis*, and it is heavily glossed in Latin.[102] More important, the passage presents two further French words: *sott* (II. 1. 452) and *sele* (II. 1. 454), and the adjective *Frencisc* occurs here with reference to the French language (apparently the sole unambiguous attestation for this meaning in Old English).[103] In other words, it is difficult not to see the usage of Byrhtferth's master, Abbo of Fleury, behind the employment of *prud* in the *Enchiridion* and the sense in which the word is employed there. Similarly, contacts with speakers of French may be presumed to have entailed positive connotations for *prud* for other Anglo-Saxons as well.

As regards the employment of *prud* to express sinful pride, the suspicion must be that Æthelwold, who had previously initiated a parallel semantic change in the *modig* family (a semantic change which always remained restricted to texts with Winchester connections), should have somehow been involved in the similar sense development of the *prud* family. A considerable number of the attestations of *prud* and its derivatives are found in texts exhibiting Winchester usage: Ælfric, the Lambeth Psalter, the Rule of Chrodegang (where the family is very common), and we have already noted the two occasions in the Aldhelm glosses. *Pryte* is also one of the *interpretamenta* in the short glossary to Aldhelm's *Carmen de uirginitate* entered in the margins of Bodleian Auct. F. 2. 14 (a manuscript with Winchester connections), written *c*. 1100, perhaps at Sherborne.[104]

There is yet a further pointer to Æthelwold's circle: the word-formation of the noun, *pryde/pryte*, first attested in Ælfric and the Rule of Chrodegang. The philological aspects of the word-formation of *pryte* have been exhaustively treated,[105] but, to my knowledge, the striking character of this derivation has called forth a comment only once.[106] We may safely assume that any literate Anglo-Saxon could have derived nouns such as *prutness* or *prutung* from *prud/prut*, but in the derivation of *pryte* we

---

[102] These Latin glosses are printed in *Enchiridion*, ed. Baker and Lapidge, p. 90.

[103] On *sott* and *sele*, see *ibid.*, p. 297; on *sott* and *Frencisc*, see R. Derolez, 'Language Problems in Anglo-Saxon England: *barbara loquella* and *barbarismus*', in *Words, Texts and Manuscripts*, ed. Korhammer, pp. 285–92, at 290–1.

[104] See above, pp. 379–80.

[105] See Flasdieck, 'Studien zur Laut- und Wortgeschichte', pp. 257–61, and Schabram, *Superbia*, p. 15.

[106] See Gneuss, 'Language Contact', p. 137.

have to assume an imitation of a sound change (i-mutation) which operated about 400 years earlier. *Prȳte* or *prȳde* are evidently formed after the model of *strong–strengu* ('strong–strength'), *brād–brǣdu* ('broad–breadth') or *hāl–hǣlu* ('healthy–health').[107] In these pairs, a feminine abstract noun is derived from an adjective by means of a Germanic suffix *-īn*, the suffix causing i-mutation of an originally velar vowel in the adjective.[108] Such derivations are rivalled by feminine abstract nouns formed from adjectives by means of the Germanic suffix *-iþō*; these nouns also undergo i-mutation. Examples would be *strong–strengþ(u)* ('strong–strength'), *earm–iermþ(u)* ('poor–poverty') and, interestingly, *ofermōd–ofermēttu*.[109] Note that in both types of derivation the pair /u:/–/y:/, as in *prūd–prȳde*, does not occur frequently; *hlūd–(ge)hlȳd* ('loud–noise') would be an example of the first type (in *full–fyllo*, 'full–fullness', the pair would be represented by short vowels), while for the second type *fūl–fylþ* ('foul–filth') and *cūþ–cȳþþ(u)* ('known–kinship') occur.

Now, unlike a modern philologist, a speaker of Old English could scarcely be expected to have been fully conversant with the ramification of i-mutation or details concerning the formation of Germanic abstract nouns by means of suffixes. Therefore the derivation of *prȳde* from *prūd*, which cannot be paralleled by any other such coinage in later Old English word-formation, testifies to a remarkably acute awareness of recurrent relationships between certain vowels. We have seen that an intrinsic interest in sound similarities between words and a penchant for exploiting such similarities for rhetorical embellishment is one of the distinctive traits of the Royal Psalter and the Rule. Especially noteworthy in this respect is a tendency in both these texts (and to some extent in the Aldhelm glosses) to employ a weak verb, class I (showing i-mutation) instead of a weak verb, class II (without i-mutation) to accompany the noun or adjective (with unchanged vowel) from which the verbs in question are derived: for example, *cēap* 'purchase, sale'–*becȳpan* 'to sell' (not *becēapian*; cf. above, p. 224), or *ēaðmōd* 'humble-minded'–*geēaðmēdan*

---

[107] The nom. sing. *prȳto* which would correspond precisely to *strengu* etc. (with later OE *o* for unstressed *u*) is indeed attested, even though the nom. *prȳte* is more frequent; cf. Schabram, *Superbia*, p. 15, n. 5, and Flasdieck, 'Studien zur Laut- und Wortgeschichte', p. 261.

[108] See SB, § 280, and Campbell § 589 (7).

[109] Cf. SB, § 255 (3), and Campbell, § 589 (6); in *ofermēttu*, *tt* results from original **ofermōdiþo* with *dþ* (after syncopation of *i*) being assimilated to *tt*.

'to humble oneself' (not *geēaðmōdian*, cf. above, p. 224). Further such pairs would be: *hosp* 'insult'–*hyspan* 'to mock', *gāl* 'frivolous'–*agǣlan* 'to make light of', *onāl* 'burning'–*onǣlan* 'to ignite' or *drēam* 'music'–*drȳman* 'to sing aloud'.[110] Often the weak verbs, class I, are decidedly less current than the corresponding class II verbs. Note also the extremely rare verb *lǣþan* 'to cause to loathe' (class I, derived from *lāþ* 'loath'), employed in the Rule, a formation which apparently was not understood and therefore replaced by common *lǣran* 'to teach' by the scribes of two manuscripts.[111] In other words, an interest in sound relationships and *figurae etymologicae* such as is characteristic of Æthelwold's circle should be sought behind the coinage of *prȳde* to accompany the loanword *prūd*. It is possible but not provable that the reminiscence embodied by the vowel alternation in *prud* and *pryde* of a similar alternation in *ofermod* and *ofermettu* (the pair favoured by King Alfred) may have played a role in the formation of *pryde*.

It remains to ask in what historical and intellectual situation *prud* may have found its way into Old English. Certainty is not attainable in this matter. However, given the positive meaning and often heroic connotations ('brave, excellent') which the word must have had for French speakers, French clerics living and working in English monasteries are, perhaps, not the first vehicle which comes to mind.[112] If we consider this original meaning of *prud* and the parallel sense development of *modig*, we may rather suspect that *prud* was first introduced in a courtly context. As in the case of *modig*, a certain currency in such circles would have lent more poignancy to the subsequent re-evaluation of *prud*. Naturally, King Æthelstan's court would not be the only centre where the adoption of the loanword in daily communication could have occurred. Nonetheless, if we reflect on what we know about the cosmopolitan atmosphere and the intellectual climate of that court, if we further reflect on the subsequent history of *prud* and *pryde* in Old English texts and the attitude towards the vernacular which underlies the formation of *pryde*, then it would seem

[110] See above, pp. 189–90, 210 and 390–1

[111] See BR 11.18 and cf. Schröer's *apparatus criticus*.

[112] Flasdieck ('Studien zur Laut- und Wortgeschichte', p. 270) considers an introduction of *prud* in a monastic context. He further purports that the meaning 'sinful pride' in OE *prud* derives from a careful study of French 'homiletic manuscripts' (and from conversation with French clerics). However, by the time when *prud* presumably was adopted, no French 'homiletic manuscripts' were in existence (cf. above, p. 404), and (as we have noted) the word's many attestations in Old French all bear a positive sense.

that Æthelstan's court has strong claims to be considered as the place where (perhaps together with *tudenard*, *jugelere* and *coittemære*) young Æthelwold first heard French *prud*. On this hypothesis, King Æthelstan's court and Bishop Æthelwold's school would have provided the English language with two terms of central importance: *proud* and *pride*.

CONCLUSIONS

We leave this discussion of the French and German loan influence in the Psalter, the Rule and the Aldhelm glosses with a clearer notion that a thorough knowledge of courtly and intellectual life in earlier tenth-century England is of crucial importance in estimating word usage in the three texts. We have seen in an earlier ch.[113] that Winchester words should be assessed in terms of Christian doctrine and spirituality (as these were understood by the chief proponents of the Benedictine reform) rather than in terms of standardization, let alone dialectology. The expressions for the concept of *superbia* must be reckoned among the most important, but also the most enigmatic, items of Winchester vocabulary. Our attempt to recreate the thought-world of Æthelwold and his circle may enable us to see reasons for the fluidity and eccentricity of their *superbia* terms. In the case of *ofearmian* (to recall a further striking example) we observe a lexical experiment in the field of another central Christian concept which not only testifies to the many contacts between England and Germany which the Royal Glossator will have witnessed in his youth, but also lets us glimpse how such contacts bore on the intellectual activities of Anglo-Saxon scholars.

None of the loanwords and loan formations reviewed here were 'necessary' (strictly speaking) in that they filled terminological gaps or were introduced together with previously unknown material objects or concepts. In this they are clearly distinct from the majority of the Latin loans in Old English. But the French and German loans in our three texts are distinct also from most of the Scandinavian loans adopted into Old English for which there was no need either. With the Scandinavian loans the explanation usually given is that they were adopted in daily contact occasioned by Danes and Anglo-Saxons living in the same neighbourhood, the implication being that these loans were taken over inadver-

---

[113] See above, pp. 98–113 and 324–5.

tently and haphazardly. By contrast, there appears to be a high degree of linguistic awareness in most of the French and German loans in our three texts. A strong case can be made for assuming that such loanwords and loan formations were consciously and experimentally introduced and employed by a distinct intellectual circle – Æthelwold's circle – in the course of their endeavours to forge, refine and embellish the vernacular so as to make it into a tool suitable for conveying complex ideas.

A corollary of our consideration of the intellectual endeavours of Æthelwold and his circle and the role there played by the French and German loans, but also the much more numerous Latin ones, is that it should be axiomatic for any philologist studying loanwords, loan formations and semantic loans in Old English to make every attempt to identify the historical and intellectual *ambiente* of their introduction and employment and not to be content with merely recording their earliest attestation and analysing their phonology and morphology. No doubt such analyses have an intrinsic interest for linguists, and they need to be made. They are even capable of providing important non-linguistic clues. Thus the most peculiar type of word-formation represented in *pryde* is, as we have seen, in itself a strong pointer to Æthelwold and his circle. But such analyses regularly need to be supplemented by historical evidence of all kinds. Only then will the study of loans establish itself on a par with the study of sources and manuscripts for a recreation of Anglo-Saxon literary culture and scholarship, and only then will the Old English loans speak to us with as clear a voice as the texts and manuscripts studied by the Anglo-Saxons.

11

Conclusion

It has often been remarked that by the time of the Norman Conquest, English libraries were deficient in their holdings of patristic texts and texts in use in the contemporary continental curriculum, especially those employed in the quadrivium. Such remarks are usually made with the implied corollary that, in 1066, Anglo-Saxon learning and scholarship was not only in intellectual backwaters, but presented itself to the scholars arriving from the Continent in a state of outright stagnation.

However, verdicts such as these are given from the point of view of the Norman and French abbots and bishops, inspecting the holdings of their monastery and cathedral libraries and canvassing the scholarship of their Anglo-Saxon monks and clerics. These continental abbots and bishops will have known nothing about the early-tenth-century roots of the English veneration for Aldhelm; for them, Aldhelm will simply have been a massive fossil in the antiquated English curriculum, and they will have looked upon the hermeneutic style, so indebted to Aldhelm and so universally practised in late Anglo-Saxon England, as a strange peculiarity, to say the least. Similarly, for them, the works of Ælfric and of Archbishop Wulfstan or the huge vernacular gloss corpora preserved in Anglo-Saxon manuscripts can have held no interest.

It is true that in our times the writings of Aldhelm, Ælfric and Wulfstan, as well as other Old English prose works and Latin hermeneutic texts, have attracted their share of attention (and moderate admiration) from Anglo-Saxonists in general. The vernacular gloss corpora, however, have thus far been considered of interest almost exclusively from a linguistic or textcritical point of view. In the case of the psalter glosses and the glosses to Aldhelm's prose *De uirginitate* (as in the case of the remaining gloss corpora), scholars have been concerned with their textual

425

affiliations, their dialect features in terms of phonology or word geography, their morphological dependence on their Latin lemmata in terms of loan formations, and so on. Important as such concerns are for an evaluation of the glosses, we have seen that there is far more to be learned from these glosses: they provide us with precious evidence of the intellectual preoccupations of the scholars who devised them. Apart from being directed towards the glossed texts themselves and their comprehensive exegesis, these preoccupations were turned in a decisive way towards the vernacular. The glossing is done in a highly competent fashion, coping effectively with the difficulties of the language of the psalms and of Aldhelm's diction. Furthermore, the glosses often aim to reproduce the poetic or extravagant, hermeneutic quality of the lemmata they translate; thus by their very nature they reveal the same interest in words which is so salient a feature of the hermeneutic style in Latin.

Such interest in a stylistic and intellectual refinement of the vernacular cannot be paralleled anywhere else in early medieval Europe. With regard to this unique role played by the vernacular in late Anglo-Saxon England, it has often been stated (no doubt with some justification) that the opulent tradition of vernacular prose had been triggered by King Alfred's translation programme and was decisively boosted by that king's authority. What is not sufficiently accounted for in such an explanation is the immense increase in flexibility and sophistication in the use of the vernacular which occurred between Alfred and Ælfric. Such flexibility and sophistication presupposes that in the interim a considerable amount of work had been done on English as a medium of literary and scholarly discourse. The Royal Psalter gloss and the Aldhelm glosses, produced in Æthelwold's circle and unequivocally bearing the impress of his mind and learning, allow us for the first time to form a more precise picture of the nature of such work on the English language and enable us to flesh out the skeletal account given by Wulfstan of Winchester, that his master always found it 'agreeable to teach young men and the more mature students, translating Latin texts into English for them' (ch. 31).

The origin of the glosses in Æthelwold's circle at Glastonbury (and perhaps Abingdon) also leave it beyond reasonable doubt that it was Æthelwold and Dunstan who were responsible for placing the study of Aldhelm in a central position in the late Anglo-Saxon curriculum, and that it was the intellectual milieu of King Æthelstan's court which inspired them to do so. By the same token, it becomes clear that the interest in lexical, grammatical and stylistic studies which the reading of Aldhelm and the imitation of his style required combined with the memory of King Alfred's achievements in English prose (no doubt still vivid at Æthelstan's court) to foster the enthusiasm for the refinement of English after the model of Latin, the language of learning and literature carrying a unique prestige for any Anglo-Saxon scholar.

As regards the distinctive 'Englishness' of the Benedictine reform in England, two features are traditionally pointed out: the institution of certain liturgical practices in the *Regularis concordia* (such as the regular prayers for the royal house) and the establishment of the monastic cathedral, a rarity on the Continent but fervently advocated by Bishop Æthelwold, and (it is thought) resulting, to some extent at least, from a careful study of the glowing account of monasticism in the early English church given by Bede in his *Historia ecclesiastica*. On the evidence of the Royal Psalter and the Aldhelm glosses, it is now possible to see that the English component in the Benedictine reform was deep-rooted and pervasive already in its nascent stage. The intellectual climate at King Æthelstan's court, shaped by the glorious achievement of the unification of England (and the resonance this had on the Continent), by the presence of numerous foreign scholars who brought their learning to bear in the service of the English king, by the veneration in which Aldhelm, the West Saxon bishop, scholar and man of letters, was held, by the memories of King Alfred and his achievements in polity and learning – this intellectual climate provided the formative experiences which young Æthelwold and Dunstan underwent in Æthelstan's court circles; experiences on which they built during their subsequent period of joint study at Glastonbury, experiences which permeated the school which Æthelwold eventually established at Winchester and which was to become the greatest school in late Anglo-Saxon England, the aftermath of its unrivalled vigour in many fields of scholarship being terminated only by the advent of the new learning introduced from the Continent subsequent to the Norman Conquest.

Æthelwold's life and career

The table printed below is based on Wulfstan of Winchester's narrative of major events in Æthelwold's biography; for each entry the relevant chapter-numbers in Wulfstan's *Vita S. Æthelwoldi* are given in brackets. For historical details concerning these events and for the rationale for the conjectural dates which may be assigned to events not precisely dated by Wulfstan, see the Introduction (pp. xxxix–li) and explanatory notes to the text in Lapidge and Winterbottom, *Wulfstan: Life*, and the references given there; cf. also *ibid.*, pp. xl–xlii for a fuller table of events pertaining to Æthelwold's life as related by Wulfstan.

904/5 × 909	Born in the reign of King Edward the Elder (899–924) (ch. 1).
924 × ?937/8	Stay at King Æthelstan's (924–39) household (ch. 7).
934/5 × 27 October 939	Ordained priest (together with Dunstan) by Bishop Ælfheah of Winchester (934/5–51), at some point before King Æthelstan's death and at the king's command (chs. 7 and 8).
?934/5 × ?939	At King Æthelstan's command, stay at Bishop Ælfheah's household to improve his education (ch. 9).
after 27 October 939	Æthelwold leaves Winchester (presumably after King Æthelstan's death) in order to join Dunstan at Glastonbury for a prolonged period of study. He is professed a Benedictine monk there (ch. 9, cf. ch. 10).
May 946 × 23 November 955	In the reign of King Eadred, Æthelwold plans to go overseas for purposes of study and to obtain a first-hand knowledge of continental Benedictinism. His plans are forestalled by Queen Eadgifu (d. 966/7), the king's mother and third wife of Edward the Elder (ch. 10).
before 23 November 955	In the reign of King Eadred, Æthelwold becomes abbot of Abingdon (perhaps in 954), which he refounds with the help of a number of monks from Glastonbury and other places (ch. 11).

29 November 963	Æthelwold is consecrated bishop of Winchester by Dunstan, archbishop of Canterbury (959–88), in the reign of King Edgar (957 (Mercia)/959 (Wessex)–975) (ch. 17).
19 February 964	Expulsion of secular clerics from the Old Minster, Winchester, and replacement with monks from Abingdon (chs. 17–18).
964	Expulsion of the secular clerics from the New Minster, Winchester, and instalment there of Benedictine monks (ch. 20).
964 or later	Establishment of the Nunnaminster, Winchester, as a house for Benedictine nuns (ch. 22).
?970	Refoundation of the monastery at Ely (ch. 23)
c. 970	Refoundation of the monastery at Peterborough; foundation of a monastery at Thorney (ch. 24).
15 July 971	Translation of St Swithun and establishment of his cult at the Old Minster (ch. 26).
before 8 July 975	Foundation of other monasteries with King Edgar's consent (ch. 27). In question are Chertsey and Milton Abbas (see *ASC* (A), s. a. 964) and St Neot's (probably c. 980, *i. e.* after Edgar's death; cf. *Liber Eliensis* II, 29, ed. Blake, pp. 102–3, and Lapidge, *Wulfstan: Life*, p. 1, n. 46).
before 980	Renovation of the Old Minster (ch. 34).
20 October 980	Dedication of the renovated Old Minster (ch. 40).
1 August 984	Death of Æthelwold in the reign of King Æthelred (978–1016) (ch. 41).
10 September 996	Translation of St Æthelwold under his successor, Bishop Ælfheah (984–1006; archbishop of Canterbury 1006–12) (ch. 43).

The Royal Psalter at Canterbury

Subsequent to its Winchester sojourn (see above, p. 265), Royal 2. B. V was at Christ Church, Canterbury, later in the eleventh and in the twelfth centuries, precisely from what time onwards is not clear.[1] The later Canterbury provenance of Royal 2. B. V can be deduced from the following evidence:

1. Six Old English prayers which were entered at the beginning and at the end of the manuscript in the course of the eleventh century. They present a text which is either identical with, or has been altered to conform with, the text of the same prayers as found in BL, Tiberius A. iii, written s. xi[med], presumably at Christ Church.[2]

2. Two of these prayers entered in Royal 2. B. V have been assigned to a Christ Church hand of s. xi[1].[3]

3. Notes in Old English (on 198v, s. xi, now partly illegible) point by their contents to Christ Church, Canterbury.[4]

4. The evidence of the Vespasian Psalter. In the first half of the eleventh century, a quire (now fols. 155–60) was added to Vespasian A. i (presumably a St Augustine's book). This quire contains the *Te Deum* (155r), the *Quicumque uult* (155r–156r) and various prayers.[5] The *Te Deum* and the *Quicumque uult* are

---

[1] See Ker, *Catalogue*, p. 320 (no. 249), and Sisam, *Salisbury Psalter*, pp. 53–4.

[2] See Ker, *Catalogue*, pp. 319 (no. 249, art. c–h) and 320. For Tiberius A. iii, see *ibid.*, pp. 240–8 (no. 186); for the presumed Christ Church origin of Tiberius A. iii, see now Gneuss, 'Origin and Provenance of Anglo-Saxon Manuscripts'.

[3] Cf. Ker, *Catalogue*, pp. 319 (no. 249, art. g and h) and 320.

[4] See *ibid.*, pp. 319 (no. 249, art. j) and 320, Sisam, *Salisbury Psalter*, p. 53, and P. P. O'Neill, 'A Lost Old English Charter Rubric: the Evidence from the Regius Psalter', *Notes and Queries* 231 (1986), 292–4.

[5] See *Vespasian Psalter*, ed. Wright, pp. 32–3 and 95–6, and Ker, *Catalogue*, pp. 266–7 (no. 203). The texts contained in the added quire are printed by Kuhn, *The Vespasian Psalter*, pp. 312–21.

provided with an interlinear gloss in Old English. The Latin text of the whole quire as well as the Old English gloss were written by the noted Christ Church scribe Eadwig Basan.[6] The Old English gloss to the Athanasian Creed (= *Quicumque uult*) is very closely dependent on the gloss for that text in Royal 2. B. V, and may well be a direct copy.[7] By the same token, twenty-two Old English glosses were added to the original psalter gloss in Vespasian A. i, apparently by the same scribe, Eadwig Basan. These added glosses are identical with those found in Royal 2. B. V for the *lemmata* in question.[8]

5. The evidence of the Eadwine Psalter. The *Romanum* version of the psalms in the psalterium triplex (*Romanum, Gallicanum, Hebraicum*) now Cambridge, Trinity College R. 17. 1 (written at Christ Church, Canterbury, *c.* 1155–60) is provided with an Old English interlinear gloss which in its first part (pss. I–LXXVII) has been heavily corrected after a D-type psalter gloss.[9] Of all surviving D-type psalters, these corrections agree most closely with the gloss in Royal 2. B. V. In fact, both glosses are so intimately related that the corrections in the Eadwine Psalter may well have been copied from Royal 2. B. V itself.[10]

---

[6] Cf. Wright, *Vespasian Psalter*, p. 42, Ker, *Catalogue*, p. 267, Bishop, *English Caroline Minuscule*, p. 22 (nos. 24 and 25), and Dumville, *English Caroline Script*, pp. 130 and 139–40.

[7] Cf. Campbell, 'The Glosses', p. 91; for the Athanasian Creed in Royal 2. B. V, see above, pp. 273–4 and 277–80.

[8] See Wright, *Vespasian Psalter*, p. 33, and Campbell, 'The Glosses', pp. 90–2.

[9] Sporadic D-type glosses, entered by a corrector, are also found in the lacunae left by the original scribe in the glosses to pss. XC.15–XCV.2. For this portion the English gloss in the Eadwine Psalter otherwise follows the text of the Old English metrical psalms; cf. P. S. Baker, 'A Little-Known Variant Text of the Old English Metrical Psalms', *Speculum* 59 (1984), 263–81.

[10] See K. Wildhagen, 'Zum Eadwine- und Regius-Psalter', *Englische Studien* 39 (1908), 189–209, at 191, Sisam, *Salisbury Psalter*, p. 57, and Baker, 'A Little-Known Variant Text', p. 265 and n. 7. For a recent assessment of the Old English gloss in the Eadwine Psalter and its relation to Royal 2. B. V, see O'Neill, 'The English Version', esp. pp. 131–2.

The Gernrode fragments of an Old Saxon psalm commentary

In 1856 or thereabouts, in Schloss Bernburg-Dessau (in the duchy of Anhalt) two badly damaged parchment folios were discovered. These had been used as an envelope for accounts from the former convent (Stift) of Gernrode (near Quedlinburg in the diocese of Halberstadt). The fragments, now dated to the late tenth century (see below), contain remnants of a psalm commentary (including a partial translation of the psalms) in Old Saxon. Since 1868 the folios have been kept in the former residence of the dukes of Anhalt at Dessau, Herzogl. Gipskammer, Bruchst. 2.[1] What is preserved are translations and commentaries pertaining to pss. IV.8–9, V.1–3 and 7–10. As the parchment had been in a state of advanced decay when discovered, many letters or words are illegible even within these few remnants. The fragments have been edited several times, their text having been emended and restored to a readable form. The most thorough and comprehensive edition is that by Elis Wadstein.[2] His text is also a variorum edition containing an annotated synopsis of conjectures suggested by previous editors. Wadstein first prints the text as he deciphered it in the manuscript. This is then followed by a readable edition, where illegible or lost letters and words are restored as far as the context or relevant passages from Latin psalm commentaries permit.[3] In an *apparatus fontium* Wadstein prints those passages from Latin psalm commentaries which he considered most relevant to the Old Saxon commentary. The Latin commentaries in question are the three which are relevant as well for the Royal Psalter (Cassiodorus, *Expositio psalmorum*, pseudo-Jerome, *Breuiarium in psalmos* (CPL, no. 629), Jerome, *Tractatus .lix. in*

---

[1] See S. Krämer, *Handschriftenerbe des deutschen Mittelalters*, Mittelalterliche Bibliothekskataloge Deutschlands und der Schweiz, Ergänzungsband 1. 1 (Munich, 1989), 292.

[2] *Kleinere altsächsische Sprachdenkmäler*, pp. 4–15 (no. 2, text) and 121–3 (editor's commentary).

[3] For facsimiles of the fragments, see J. H. Gallée, *Altsächsische Sprachdenkmäler* (Leiden, 1894), pls. 9a–c. However, the edition of the text prepared by Gallée is not very trustworthy.

psalmos (*CPL*, no. 592)), and, interestingly, a *catena* compiled from various commentaries, now preserved as Munich, Bayerische Staatsbibliothek, Clm. 3729, a tenth-century manuscript of unknown origin.[4] Of these several commentaries, none could have served alone as the source for the Old Saxon text; nor are the comments in Old Saxon entirely accounted for by these Latin commentaries, and (as in the case of the marginal scholia in the Royal Psalter) it is not clear whether the Old Saxon author himself, for his exegesis, drew on various treatises, or whether he translated a Latin compilation as yet unidentified. In order to create an impression of the remarkable intellectual and stylistic achievement of this unknown author, an achievement which can still be perceived in spite of the deplorable physical state of the surviving fragments, I print below two brief passages as edited by Wadstein. My first example is the exegesis for ps. V.2.[5]

> *Verba mea.*[6] Thiu heliga samnunga bidid mid theson vuordon that the salmsangas iro muthes gihoride uuerthen fan gode endi that fan imo fernoman vuerthe the vuillo thes thurugthigenon herton the alla thing ne fernimid mid then oron neuan mid themo liahte sinaro godhedies. (Wadstein, p. 13)

> *Verba mea.* The holy church prays with these words that the psalms chanted by their mouths may be heard by God and that the desire of the pious heart may be understood by Him who understands all things not through His ears but through the light of His Godhead.

As will be seen from a comparison of that passage with the following extract, the Old Saxon commentator is apt to vary the way he presents his material. Whereas in ps. V.2 he just gives the Latin *incipit* of the verse and then proceeds immediately to psalm exegesis, in the following example (ps. V.9), the Latin *incipit* is given again, this time supplemented by an Old Saxon translation of the complete psalm verse which in turn is followed by exegetical remarks.

---

[4] *Inc.* 'Generalis expositio psalmorum de diuersorum tractatibus auctorum deflorata'; cf. C. Halm *et al.*, *Catalogus Codicum Latinorum Bibliotheca Regiae Monacensis* III. 2, 2nd ed. (Munich, 1894), 128. Attention had first been drawn by E. Steinmeyer to the proximity of this *catena* to the Gernrode fragments; see Wadstein, *Kleinere altsächsische Sprachdenkmäler*, p. 122.

[5] Cf. Wadstein, *Kleinere altsächsische Sprachdenkmäler*, p. 13. In order to facilitate the access to the text, I have not reproduced in print Wadstein's intricate system of brackets and fonts whereby he indicates varying degrees of editorial intervention. Translations are my own.

[6] The complete verse (ps. V.2) reads as follows: 'Verba mea auribus percipe, domine intellege clamorem meum.'

Domine deduc me.[7] 'Vuola thu drohtin uthledi mik an thinemo rehte thuru mina fianda endi gereko minan vueg an thinero gesihti'. Vuola thu drohtin gereko min lif tuote thineru hederun gesihti thuru thin emnista reht tote then euuigon mendislon, thuru mina fianda endi thia heretikere endi thia hethinun. That is min te duonne that ik mina fuoti sette an thinan vueg, endi that is thin te duonne that thu minan gang girekos. Vuelik is the vueg ne uuari thiu leccia heligero gescriuo. (Wadstein, p. 15)

Domine deduc me. 'O my God, guide me through my enemies because of your justice, and direct my way under your eyes.' O my God, by your most perfect justice, direct my life to your radiant presence, to eternal joy, through my enemies and the heretics and the pagans. It falls to me to set my foot on your path and it falls to you that you direct my pace. Which is the way, if not the reading of the Holy Scripture?

What knowledge do we have concerning the historical circumstances of the origin and transmission of this commentary?[8] As we have seen, the surviving fragments come from Gernrode, a religious foundation for canonesses recruited from aristocratic families. It was established in 959 by Gero I, count of the Eastern March (d. 965), an important political figure at the court of Otto I (king of Germany, 936–73, and German emperor since 962).[9] Gernrode was lavishly endowed by its founder and, in 961, obtained important privileges and

---

[7] The complete verse (ps. V.9) reads as follows: 'Domine deduc me in tua iustitia propter inimicos meos, dirige in conspectu tuo uiam meam'.

[8] Wherever the Gernrode fragments are mentioned, praise is lavished on the translator's achievement; however, the question of the historical context in which he did his work has scarcely been asked. See, for example, W. Sanders, 'Gernroder Predigt', in *Die deutsche Literatur des Mittelalters. Verfasserlexikon*, 2nd ed., ed. K. Ruh *et al.* (Berlin, 1978–) II (1980), 1262, *idem*, 'Die Textsorten des Altniederdeutschen (Altsächsischen)', in *Sprachgeschichte. Ein Handbuch zur Geschichte der deutschen Sprache und ihrer Erforschung*, ed. W. Besch *et al.*, 2 vols. (Berlin, 1984–5) II, 1103–9, at 1107, and W. Haubrichs, *Die Anfänge: Versuche volkssprachlicher Schriftlichkeit im frühen Mittelalter (ca.* 700–1050/60), Geschichte der deutschen Literatur von den Anfängen bis zum Beginn der Neuzeit I, 2nd ed. (Tübingen, 1995), 208–9; but see H. de Boor, *Die deutsche Literatur von Karl dem Grossen bis zum Beginn der höfischen Dichtung, 770–1170*, Geschichte der deutschen Literatur von den Anfängen bis zur Gegenwart I, 7th ed. (Munich, 1966), 47 (de Boor, however, dated the manuscript, in accordance with an earlier view, *c.* 900, a date which is still given in the most recent edition of this book (9th, 1979, rev. by H. Kolb, p. 44), in spite of Bischoff's dating of the fragments to the end of the tenth century: see below).

[9] See Keynes, 'Æthelstan's Books', pp. 147–9, and above, pp. 337 and 385 and n. 3, for the cultural relationships between Otto's and King Æthelstan's courts.

exemptions from King Otto. The abbey church (Stiftskirche), dedicated to St Cyriacus and built subsequent to Count Gero having acquired a relic of that saint at Rome, is one of Germany's most imposing church buildings from the Ottonian era. Gero was buried there, and his daughter-in-law Hathui (d. 1014) became Gernrode's first abbess.[10]

Subsequent to their discovery, the Gernrode fragments had traditionally been dated to the end of the ninth century (s. ix/x).[11] Such a date seemed to rule out the possibility that the manuscript could have been written at Gernrode (founded only in 959). More recently, however, Bernhard Bischoff has dated the fragments almost a century later, to the last third of the tenth century.[12] This would open up the possibility that the manuscript was indeed written at Gernrode, a possibility which Bischoff himself had entertained.[13]

However, the date and possible origin of the manuscript provides us with no secure clue concerning the origin of the text itself. While it is conceivable that the treatise could have been composed at Gernrode (perhaps by one of the canons who acted as priests and spiritual advisers to the canonesses), on philological grounds an origin somewhere further west in Old Saxon territory has been assumed by some scholars. But the matter is not settled, and places as far apart as Werden (in the far west, in the vicinity of Essen) and Halberstadt (only a few miles north of Gernrode) have been suggested.[14] Needless to say, given the

---

[10] See *LThK* IV, 758, *LkMA* IV (1988), 1348–9, and esp. H. K. Schulze, *Das Stift Gernrode* (Cologne, 1965), pp. 1–21.

[11] See, for example, Wadstein, *Kleinere altsächsische Sprachdenkmäler*, p. 121, and cf. n. 8 above.

[12] See Bischoff, 'Paläographische Fragen deutscher Denkmäler der Karolingerzeit', in his *Mittelalterliche Studien* III, 73–111, at 107 (orig. publ. 1971). This date is confirmed in his *Katalog der festländischen Handschriften des neunten Jahrhunderts Teil I: Aachen – Lambach* (Wiesbaden, 1998), p. 216: 'X. Jh., ca. 3. Drittel'.

[13] See Bischoff, 'Paläographische Fragen', p. 107, and his *Katalog*, p. 216. For a brief survey of recent scholarship on book production and scriptoria under the Ottonians in general, see R. McKitterick, 'Continuity and Innovation in Tenth-Century Ottonian Culture', in *Intellectual Life in the Middle Ages. Essays presented to Margaret Gibson*, ed. L. Smith and B. Ward (London, 1992), pp. 15–24; cf. p. 20 for book production in female houses. The most important and comprehensive monograph study on the period is H. Hofmann, *Buchkunst und Königtum im ottonischen und frühsalischen Reich*, 2 vols., MGH, Schriften 30 (Stuttgart, 1986); a catalogue of manuscripts attributable to tenth- and eleventh-century German scriptoria is found at I, 126–516.

[14] See de Boor, *Die deutsche Literatur*, pp. 47–8; for references to earlier literature on the question, see G. Ehrismann, *Geschichte der deutschen Literatur bis zum Ausgang des Mittelalters* I, 2nd ed. (Munich, 1932), p. 273. For an origin at Werden, see recently Sanders, 'Gernroder Predigt', p. 1262, and *idem*, 'Textsorten', p. 1107 (as n. 8 above).

mutilated form in which the text is transmitted even in the short extracts which have been preserved, and given the paucity of surviving Old Saxon texts in general (see above, p. 389), philology can be of no help in establishing an approximate date for the original composition of the Gernrode commentary. In other words, as a result of the dismal state of the surviving fragments, we will never be in a position to pass a final judgement on the Gernrode psalm commentary as a whole and to evaluate satisfactorily the circumstances of its composition and transmission. Nevertheless, even those few passages in their appalling physical state attest to a remarkable competence and resourcefulness through which an unknown Old Saxon scholar reveals himself as a master of vernacular prose. Even if that scholar did not compile himself the Latin psalm commentary which underlies his text, but translated a Latin *catena* (thus far unidentified), we cannot but admire his skill in pressing his native language into service for conveying clearly and succinctly the essentials of typological psalm exegesis. It may not be fanciful to surmise that this impressive achievement was indebted to a tradition of vernacular translation of some standing, a tradition which has perished almost without trace.

As regards the possible traces of Old Saxon influence in the Royal Psalter which we explored in ch. 10, it is of great interest that the Gernrode fragments (which on palaeographical grounds must have been composed no later than the last third of the tenth century and which may have originated several decades earlier) present an amalgam of translation into the vernacular and condensed psalm exegesis, similar in many ways to the approach to the psalms offered by the Royal Psalter. This is not tantamount to assuming any direct link between both texts, the Royal Psalter and the Old Saxon commentary. The point simply is that the Gernrode fragments provide tangible evidence of an active interest in Old Saxon territory in translating biblical texts and expounding them in the vernacular, and of the remarkable level which such vernacular renderings had achieved there. This evidence may in turn confirm our earlier suspicion that words such as *ofearmian* and *ofearmung* (for *misereri* and *miseratio*) or *tofleam* for *refugium* (see above, pp. 399–403 and p. 48) may indeed have been coined by the Royal Glossator after Old Saxon models, and that he may have formed them as a result of discussions with scholars from Germany concerning adequate renderings of important Christian terms and, perhaps, as a result of a careful study of Old Saxon biblical translations such as represented in the Gernrode fragments.

Bibliography

Adriaen, M., ed., *Magni Aurelii Cassiodori Expositio psalmorum*, 2 vols., CCSL 97–8 (Turnhout, 1958)

Alexander, J. J. G., 'The Benedictional of St Æthelwold and Anglo-Saxon Illumination of the Reform Period', in *Tenth-Century Studies*, ed. Parsons, pp. 169–83

Baker, P. S., 'The Old English Canon of Byrhtferth of Ramsey', *Speculum* 55 (1980), 22–37

Baker, P. S. and M. Lapidge, ed., *Byrhtferth's Enchiridion*, EETS SS 15 (Oxford, 1995)

Bately, J. M., 'Old English Prose before and during the Reign of Alfred', *ASE* 17 (1988), 93–138

Bately, J. M., ed., *The Anglo-Saxon Chronicle. MS A*, The Anglo-Saxon Chronicle: a Collaborative Edition, ed. D. Dumville and S. Keynes 3 (Cambridge, 1986)

Behaghel, O. and B. Taeger, ed., *Heliand und Genesis*, 10th ed., Altdeutsche Textbibliothek 4 (Tübingen, 1996)

Berghaus, F.-G., *Die Verwandtschaftsverhältnisse der altenglischen Interlinearversionen des Psalters und der Cantica*, Palaestra 272 (Göttingen, 1979)

Biggs, F. M., T. D. Hill and P. E. Szarmach, ed., *Sources of Anglo-Saxon Literary Culture: a Trial Version*, Medieval and Renaissance Texts and Studies 74 (Binghamton, NY, 1990)

Bierbaumer, P., 'On the Interrelationships of the Old English Psalter-Glosses', *Arbeiten aus Anglistik und Amerikanistik* 2 (1977), 123–48

Bischoff, B., *Mittelalterliche Studien*, 3 vols. (Stuttgart, 1966–81)

Bischoff, B., M. Budny, G. Harlow, M. B. Parkes and J. D. Pheifer, ed., *The Épinal, Erfurt, Werden and Corpus Glossaries*, EEMF 22 (Copenhagen, 1988)

Bischoff, B. and M. Lapidge, ed., *Biblical Commentaries from the Canterbury School of Theodore and Hadrian*, CSASE 10 (Cambridge, 1994)

Bishop, T. A. M., 'Notes on Cambridge Manuscripts, Part V', *TCBS* 3 (1959–63), 93–5

'An Early Example of the Square Minuscule', *TCBS* 4 (1964–8), 246–52

'An Early Example of Insular-Caroline', *TCBS* 4 (1964–8), 396–400

English Caroline Minuscule (Oxford, 1971)

Blake, E.O., ed., *Liber Eliensis*, Camden Third Series 92 (London, 1962)

Brenner, E., ed., *Der altenglische Junius-Psalter*, Anglistische Forschungen 23 (Heidelberg, 1908)

Brett, C., 'A Breton Pilgrim in England in the Reign of King Æthelstan: a Letter in British Library MS Cotton Tiberius A. xv', in *France and Britain in the Early Middle Ages*, ed. G. Jondorf and D. N. Dumville (Woodbridge, 1991), pp. 43–70

Bright, J. W. and R. L. Ramsay, ed., *Liber Psalmorum: the West-Saxon Psalms, being the Prose Portion or the 'First Fifty', of the so-called Paris Psalter* (Boston, MA, 1907)

Brooks, N., *The Early History of the Church of Canterbury. Christ Church from 597–1066* (Leicester, 1984)

'The Career of St Dunstan', in *St Dunstan*, ed. Ramsay *et al.*, pp. 1–23

Brooks, N. and C. Cubitt, ed., *St Oswald of Worcester: Life and Influence* (Leicester, 1996)

Budny, M., '"St Dunstan's Classbook" and its Frontispiece: Dunstan's Portrait and Autograph', in *St Dunstan*, ed. Ramsay *et al.*, pp. 103–42

Bullough, D. A., 'The Continental Background of the Reform', in *Tenth-Century Studies*, ed. Parsons, pp. 20–36

'The Educational Tradition from Alfred to Ælfric: Teaching *utriusque linguae*', in his *Carolingian Renewal: Sources and Heritage* (Manchester, 1991), pp. 297–334 (orig. publ. 1972)

[Byrhtferth of Ramsey], *Vita S. Ecgwini*, ed. J. A. Giles, *Vita quorundum*[!] *Anglo-Saxonum* (London, 1854), pp. 349–96

Vita S. Oswaldi, in *Historians of the Church of York*, ed. Raine I, 399–475

Campbell, A., 'The Glosses', in D. H. Wright, ed., *Vespasian Psalter*, pp. 81–92

Campbell, A., ed., *Frithegodi monachi Breuiloquium uitae beati Wilfredi et Wulfstani Cantoris Narratio metrica de Sancto Swithuno* (Zurich, 1950)

Chamberlin, J., ed., *The Rule of St. Benedict: the Abingdon Copy* (Toronto, 1982)

Clemoes, P., ed., *Ælfric's Catholic Homilies: the First Series, Text*, EETS SS 17 (Oxford, 1997)

Colgrave, B., ed., *Two Lives of Saint Cuthbert* (Cambridge, 1940)

Colgrave, B. *et al.*, ed., *The Paris Psalter*, EEMF 8 (Copenhagen, 1958)

Colgrave, B. and R. A. B. Mynors, ed., *Bede's Ecclesiastical History of the English People*, Oxford Medieval Texts, rev. ed. (Oxford, 1992)

Crawford, S. J., ed., *The Old English Version of the Heptateuch, Ælfric's Treatise on the Old and New Testament and his Preface to Genesis*, EETS OS 160 (London, 1922; repr. 1969 with the text of two additional manuscripts transcribed by N. R. Ker)

Cubitt, C., *Anglo-Saxon Church Councils c. 650–c. 850* (London, 1995)

Darlington, R. R. and P. McGurk, ed., *The Chronicle of John of Worcester II: the Annals from 450 to 1066*, Oxford Medieval Texts (Oxford, 1995)

Davey, W., 'The Commentary of the Regius Psalter: its Main Source and the Influence on the Old English Gloss', *Mediaeval Studies* 49 (1987), 335–51

Derolez, R., ed., *Anglo-Saxon Glossography. Papers read at the International Conference Brussels, 8 and 9 September 1986* (Brussels, 1992)

Deshman, R., '*Benedictus Monarcha et Monachus*. Early Medieval Ruler Theology and the Anglo-Saxon Reform', *Frühmittelalterliche Studien* 22 (1988), 204–40

The Benedictional of Æthelwold (Princeton, NJ, 1995)

'The Galba Psalter: Pictures, Texts and Context in an Early Medieval Prayer-book', *ASE* 26 (1997), 109–37

Drögereit, R., 'Gab es eine angelsächsische Königskanzlei?', *Archiv für Urkunden-forschung* 13 (1935), 335–436

Dümmler, E., ed., *Epistolae Karolini Aevi II*, MGH, Epistolae 4 (Berlin, 1895)

Dumville, D. N., 'The Anglian Collection of Royal Genealogies and Regnal Lists', *ASE* 5 (1976), 23–50

'English Square Minuscule Script: the Background and the Earliest Phases', *ASE* 16 (1987), 147–79

'On the Dating of Some Late Anglo-Saxon Liturgical Manuscripts', *TCBS* 10 (1991), 40–57

Wessex and England from Alfred to Edgar (Woodbridge, 1992)

'The Anglo-Saxon Chronicle and the Origin of English Square Minuscule Script', in his *Wessex and England*, pp. 55–112

Liturgy and the Ecclesiastical History of Late Anglo-Saxon England (Woodbridge, 1992)

'The Kalendar of the Junius Psalter', in his *Liturgy and Ecclesiastical History*, pp. 1–38

English Caroline Script and Monastic History (Woodbridge, 1993)

'English Square Minuscule Script: the Mid-Century Phases', *ASE* 23 (1994), 133–64

Ehwald, R., ed., *Aldhelmi Opera*, MGH, Auctores antiquissimi 15 (Berlin, 1919)

Engelbert, P., 'Regeltext und Romverehrung. Zur Frage der Verbreitung der *Regula Benedicti* im Frühmittelalter', *Römische Quartalschrift* 81 (1986), 39–60

Fischer, B., *Lateinische Bibelhandschriften im frühen Mittelalter*, Vetus Latina: Aus der Geschichte der lateinischen Bibel 11 (Freiburg, 1985)

'Bibeltext und Bibelreform unter Karl dem Großen', in his *Lateinische Bibelhandschriften*, pp. 101–202 (orig. publ. 1965)

'Zur Überlieferung altlateinischer Bibeltexte im Mittelalter', in his *Lateinische Bibelhandschriften*, pp. 404–21 (orig. publ. 1975)

Flasdieck, H. F., 'Studien zur Laut- und Wortgeschichte. II', *Anglia* 70 (1951), 240–71

Frank, R., 'Some Uses of Paronomasia in Old English Scriptural Verse', *Speculum* 47 (1972), 207–26

'Poetic Words in Late Old English Prose', in *From Anglo-Saxon to Early Middle English. Studies presented to E. G. Stanley*, ed. M. Godden, D. Gray and T. Hoad (Oxford, 1994), pp. 87–107

Frere, W. H., ed., *The Winchester Troper*, HBS 8 (London, 1894)

Fry, T. *et al.*, ed., *RB 1980. The Rule of St. Benedict in Latin and English with Notes* (Collegeville, MS, 1981)

Funke, O., *Die gelehrten lateinischen Lehn- und Fremdwörter in der altenglischen Literatur* (Halle, 1914)

Gallée, J. H., *Altsächsische Grammatik*, 3rd ed., with corrections and bibliography by H. Tiefenbach (Tübingen, 1993)

Gameson, R., *The Role of Art in the Late Anglo-Saxon Church* (Oxford, 1995)

Gameson, R., ed., *The Early Medieval Bible* (Cambridge, 1994)

Gibson, M., T. A. Heslop and R. W. Pfaff, ed., *The Eadwine Psalter. Text, Image and Monastic Culture in Twelfth-Century Canterbury* (London, 1992)

Gneuss, H., *Lehnbildungen und Lehnbedeutungen im Altenglischen* (Berlin, 1955)

Hymnar und Hymnen im englischen Mittelalter, Buchreihe der Anglia 12 (Tübingen, 1968)

Language and History in Early England (Aldershot, 1996)

Books and Libraries in Early England (Aldershot, 1996)

'The Origin of Standard Old English and Æthelwold's School at Winchester', in his *Language and History*, no. I (orig. publ. 1972)

'The Study of Language in Anglo-Saxon England', in his *Language and History*, no. III (orig. publ. 1990)

'*Anglicae linguae interpretatio*: Language Contact, Lexical Borrowing and Glossing in Anglo-Saxon England', in his *Language and History*, no. V (orig. publ. 1993)

'Die Benediktinerregel in England und ihre altenglische Übersetzung', in his *Language and History*, no. VIII (orig. publ. 1964)

'Anglo-Saxon Libraries from the Conversion to the Benedictine Reform', in his *Books and Libraries*, no. II (orig. publ. 1986)

'Liturgical Books in Anglo-Saxon England and their Old English Terminology', in his *Books and Libraries*, no. V (orig. publ. 1985)

'Origin and Provenance of Anglo-Saxon Manuscripts: the Case of Cotton

Tiberius A. iii', in *Of the Making of Books: Medieval Manuscripts, their Scribes and Readers. Essays presented to M. B. Parkes*, ed. P. R. Robinson and R. Zim (Aldershot, 1997), pp. 13–47

'A Handlist of Anglo-Saxon Manuscripts' (forthcoming)

Godden, M. R., 'Ælfric's Changing Vocabulary', *English Studies* 61 (1980), 206–23

Godden, M., ed., *Ælfric's Catholic Homilies: the Second Series, Text*, EETS SS 5 (London, 1979)

Goetz, G., ed., *Corpus Glossariorum Latinorum*, 7 vols. (Leipzig, 1888–1923)

Goossens, L., ed., *The Old English Glosses of MS Brussels, Royal Library, 1650 (Aldhelm's 'De Laudibus Virginitatis')* (Brussels, 1974)

Greenfield, S. B. and D. G. Calder, *A New Critical History of Old English Literature. With a Survey of the Anglo-Latin Background* by M. Lapidge (New York, 1986)

Gretsch, M., *Die Regula Sancti Benedicti in England und ihre altenglische Übersetzung*, TUEPh 2 (Munich, 1973)

'Æthelwold's Translation of the *Regula Sancti Benedicti* and its Latin Exemplar', *ASE* 3 (1974), 125–51

'The Benedictine Rule in Old English: a Document of Bishop Æthelwold's Reform Politics', in *Words, Texts and Manuscripts*, ed. Korhammer *et al.*, pp. 131–58

'Der liturgische Wortschatz in Æthelwold's Übersetzung der Benediktiner-regel und sprachliche Normierung in spätaltenglischer Zeit', *Anglia* 111 (1993), 310–54

'The Language of the "Fonthill Letter"', *ASE* 23 (1994), 57–102

Gwara, S., 'Manuscripts of Aldhelm's *Prosa de Virginitate* and the Rise of Hermeneutic Literacy in Tenth-Century England', *Studi medievali*, 3rd ser. 35 (1994), 101–59

'The Continuance of Aldhelm Studies in Post-Conquest England and Glosses to the *Prosa de Virginitate* in Hereford, Cath. Lib. MS P. I. 17', *Scriptorium* 48 (1994), 18–38

'The Transmission of the "Digby" Corpus of Bilingual Glosses to Aldhelm's *Prosa de uirginitate*', *ASE* 27 (1998), 139–68

Hallinger, K., ed., *Initia Consuetudinis Benedictinae*, CCM 1 (Siegburg, 1963)

Hanslik, R., ed., *Benedicti Regula*, 2nd ed., CSEL 75 (Vienna, 1977)

Harper, J., *The Forms and Orders of Western Liturgy from the Tenth to the Eighteenth Century* (Oxford, 1991)

Heinzel, O., *Kritische Entstehungsgeschichte des ags. Interlinear-Psalters*, Palaestra 151 (Leipzig, 1926)

Hessels, J. H., ed., *An Eighth-Century Latin–Anglo-Saxon Glossary Preserved in the Library of Corpus Christi College, Cambridge* (Cambridge, 1890)

A Late Eighth-Century Latin–Anglo-Saxon Glossary Preserved in the Library of the Leiden University (Cambridge, 1906)

Higgitt, J., 'Glastonbury, Dunstan, Monasticism and Manuscripts', *Art History* 2 (1979), 275–90

Hoberg, G., *Die Psalmen der Vulgata übersetzt und nach dem Literalsinn erklärt*, 2nd ed. (Freiburg, 1906)

Hofstetter, W., *Winchester und der spätaltenglische Sprachgebrauch*, TUEPh 14 (Munich, 1987)

'Winchester and the Standardization of Old English Vocabulary', *ASE* 17 (1988), 139–61

Holschneider, A., *Die Organa von Winchester* (Hildesheim, 1968)

Holthausen, F., *Altenglisches etymologisches Wörterbuch* (Heidelberg, 1934)

Hughes, A., *Medieval Manuscripts for Mass and Office: a Guide to their Organization and Terminology* (Toronto, 1982)

Jaager, W., ed., *Bedas metrische Vita Sancti Cuthberti*, Palaestra 198 (Leipzig, 1935)

James, M. R., *A Descriptive Catalogue of the Manuscripts of Corpus Christi College, Cambridge*, 2 vols. (Cambridge, 1909–12)

Kastovsky, D., 'Semantics and Vocabulary', in *The Cambridge History of the English Language I: the Beginnings to 1066*, ed. R. M. Hogg (Cambridge, 1992), 290–408

Kendall, C. B., ed., *De arte metrica*, in *Bedae Venerabilis Opera*, pars I, *Opera didascalica*, CCSL 123A (Turnhout, 1975), 82–141

De schematibus et tropis, in *Bedae Venerabilis Opera*, pars I, *Opera didascalica*, CCSL 123A (Turnhout, 1975), 142–71

Kendall, C. B., ed. and transl., *Bede, libri ii de arte metrica et de schematibus et tropis. The Art of Poetry and Rhetoric* (Saarbrücken, 1991)

Ker, N. R., *Catalogue of Manuscripts Containing Anglo-Saxon* (Oxford, 1957)

'A Supplement to *Catalogue of Manuscripts Containing Anglo-Saxon*', *ASE* 5 (1976), 121–31

Keynes, S., *The Diplomas of King Æthelred 'The Unready', 978–1016* (Cambridge, 1980)

'King Æthelstan's Books', in *Learning and Literature*, ed. Lapidge and Gneuss, pp. 143–201

'Episcopal Succession in Anglo-Saxon England', in *Handbook of British Chronology*, ed. E. B. Fryde *et al.*, 3rd ed., Royal Historical Society Guides and Handbooks 2 (London, 1986), pp. 209–24.

'The "Dunstan B" Charters', *ASE* 23 (1994), 165–93

An Atlas of Attestations in Anglo-Saxon Charters, c. 670–1066, priv. ptd Dept. of Anglo-Saxon, Norse and Celtic, Univ. of Cambridge (Cambridge, 1995)

'Anglo-Saxon Entries in the *Liber Vitae* of Brescia', in *Alfred the Wise. Studies in*

Honour of Janet Bately on the Occasion of her Sixty-Fifth Birthday, ed. J. Roberts, J. L. Nelson and M. Godden (Woodbridge, 1997), pp. 99–119

'England 900–1016', in *The New Cambridge Medieval History* III, ed. T. Reuter (forthcoming)

Keynes, S., ed., *The Liber Vitae of the New Minster and Hyde Abbey Winchester: British Library Stowe 944*, EEMF 26 (Copenhagen, 1996)

Keynes, S. and M. Lapidge, *Alfred the Great. Asser's 'Life of King Alfred' and other Contemporary Sources* (Harmondsworth, 1983)

Kirschner, J., *Die Bezeichnungen für Kranz und Krone im Altenglischen*, Doctoral dissertation, Munich Univ. (Munich, 1975)

Kluge, F., *Nominale Stammbildungslehre der altgermanischen Dialekte*, 3rd ed., rev. L. Sütterlin und K. Ochs (Halle, 1926)

Etymologisches Wörterbuch der deutschen Sprache, 23rd ed. by E. Seebold (Berlin, 1995) (Kluge–Seebold)

Knappe, G., *Traditionen der klassischen Rhetorik im angelsächsischen England*, Anglistische Forschungen 236 (Heidelberg, 1996)

Knowles, M. D., *The Monastic Order in England. A History of its Development from the Times of St. Dunstan to the Fourth Lateran Council, 940–1216*, 2nd ed. (Cambridge, 1963)

Knowles, D., C. N. L. Brooke and V. C. M. London, ed., *The Heads of Religious Houses, England and Wales, 940–1216* (Cambridge, 1972)

Korhammer, M., 'The Origin of the Bosworth Psalter', *ASE* 2 (1973), 173–87

Korhammer, M. *et al.*, ed., *Words, Texts and Manuscripts. Studies in Anglo-Saxon Culture presented to Helmut Gneuss on the Occasion of his Sixty-Fifth Birthday* (Cambridge, 1992)

Kornexl, L., ed., *Die 'Regularis Concordia' und ihre altenglische Interlinearversion*, TUEPh 17 (Munich, 1993)

Koziol, H., *Handbuch der englischen Wortbildungslehre*, 2nd ed. (Heidelberg, 1972)

Kuhn, S. M., ed., *The Vespasian Psalter* (Ann Arbor, MI, 1965)

Lampe, G. W. H., ed., *The Cambridge History of the Bible II: the West from the Fathers to the Reformation* (Cambridge, 1969)

Lapidge, M., *Anglo-Latin Literature 600–899* (London, 1996)

Anglo-Latin Literature 900–1066 (London, 1993)

'The School of Theodore and Hadrian', in his *Anglo-Latin Literature 600–899*, pp. 141–68 (orig. publ. 1986)

'Old English Glossography: the Latin Context', in his *Anglo-Latin Literature 600–899*, pp. 169–81 (orig. publ. 1992)

'An Isidorian Epitome from Early Anglo-Saxon England', in his *Anglo-Latin Literature 600–899*, pp. 183–223 (orig. publ. 1988–9)

'Aldhelm's Latin Poetry and Old English Verse', in his *Anglo-Latin Literature 600–899*, pp. 247–69 (orig. publ. 1979)

'The Study of Latin Texts in Late Anglo-Saxon England', in his *Anglo-Latin Literature 600–899*, pp. 455–98 (orig. publ. 1982)

'Schools, Learning and Literature in Tenth-Century England', in his *Anglo-Latin Literature 900–1066*, pp. 1–48 (orig. publ. 1991)

'Some Latin Poems as Evidence for the Reign of Æthelstan', in his *Anglo-Latin Literature 900–1066*, pp. 49–86 (orig. publ. 1981)

'Israel the Grammarian in Anglo-Saxon England', in his *Anglo-Latin Literature 900–1066*, pp. 87–104 (orig. publ. 1992)

'The Hermeneutic Style in Tenth-Century Anglo-Latin Literature', in his *Anglo-Latin Literature 900–1066*, pp. 105–49 (orig. publ. 1975)

'St Dunstan's Latin Poetry', in his *Anglo-Latin Literature 900–1066*, pp. 151–6 (orig. publ. 1980)

'A Frankish Scholar in Tenth-Century England: Frithegod of Canterbury/ Fredegaud of Brioude', in his *Anglo-Latin Literature 900–1066*, pp. 157–81 (orig. publ. 1988)

'Æthelwold as Scholar and Teacher', in his *Anglo-Latin Literature 900–1066*, pp. 183–211 (orig. publ. 1988)

'Æthelwold and the *Vita S. Eustachii*', in his *Anglo-Latin Literature 900–1066*, pp. 213–23 (orig. publ. 1988)

'Three Latin Poems from Æthelwold's School at Winchester', in his *Anglo-Latin Literature 900–1066*, pp. 225–77 (orig. publ. 1972)

'B. and the *Vita S. Dunstani*', in his *Anglo-Latin Literature 900–1066*, pp. 279–91 (orig. publ. 1992)

'A Tenth-Century Metrical Calendar from Ramsey', in his *Anglo-Latin Literature 900–1066*, pp. 343–86 (orig. publ. 1984)

'Abbot Germanus, Winchcombe, Ramsey and the Cambridge Psalter', in his *Anglo-Latin Literature 900–1066*, pp. 387–417 (orig. publ. 1992)

'Surviving Booklists from Anglo-Saxon England', in *Learning and Literature*, ed. Lapidge and Gneuss, pp. 33–89

'Autographs of Insular Latin Authors of the Early Middle Ages', in *Gli autografi medievali: Problemi paleografici e filologici*, ed. P. Chiesa and L. Pinelli, Quaderni di cultura mediolatina 5 (Spoleto, 1994), 103–36

'Prolegomena to an Edition of Bede's Metrical *Vita Sancti Cuthberti*', *Filologia mediolatina* 2 (1995), 127–63

'Byrhtferth and Oswald', in *St Oswald of Worcester*, ed. Brooks and Cubitt, pp. 64–83

Lapidge, M., ed., *Anglo-Saxon Litanies of the Saints*, HBS 106 (London, 1991)

The Cult of St Swithun (forthcoming)

Lapidge, M. and H. Gneuss, ed., *Learning and Literature in Anglo-Saxon England. Studies presented to Peter Clemoes on the Occasion of his Sixty-Fifth Birthday* (Cambridge, 1985)

Lapidge, M. and M. Winterbottom, ed., *Wulfstan of Winchester: the Life of St Æthelwold*, Oxford Medieval Texts (Oxford, 1991)

Lapidge, M. and M. Herren, transl., *Aldhelm: the Prose Works* (Cambridge, 1979)

Lapidge, M. and J. Rosier, transl., *Aldhelm: the Poetic Works* (Cambridge, 1985)

Lendinara, P., 'Il glossario del ms. Oxford, Bodleian Library, Bodley 163', *Romanobarbarica* 10 (1988–9), 485–516

'The Old English Renderings of Latin *tabernaculum* and *tentorium*', in *Anglo-Saxonica. Beiträge zur Vor- und Frühgeschichte der englischen Sprache und zur altenglischen Literatur. Festschrift für Hans Schabram zum 65. Geburtstag*, ed. K. R. Grinda and C.-D. Wetzel (Munich, 1993), pp. 289–325

Lindelöf, U., *Studien zu altenglischen Psalterglossen*, Bonner Beiträge zur Anglistik 13 (Bonn, 1904)

'Die altenglischen Glossen im Bosworth-Psalter', *Mémoires de la Société Néophilologique à Helsingfors* 5 (Helsingfors, 1909), 139–230.

Lindelöf, U., ed., *Der Lambeth-Psalter*, 2 vols., Acta Societatis Scientiarum Fennicae 35.1 and 43.3 (Helsingfors, 1909–14)

Lindsay, W. M., ed., *Isidori Hispalensis Episcopi Etymologiarum siue Originum Libri XX*, 2 vols. (Oxford, 1911)

Logeman, H., ed., *The Rule of S. Benet. Latin and Anglo-Saxon Interlinear Version*, EETS OS 90 (London, 1888)

Lowe, E. A., *Codices Latini Antiquiores* II, 2nd ed. (Oxford, 1972)

Lübke, H., 'Über verwandtschaftliche Beziehungen einiger altenglischer Glossare', *Archiv für das Studium der Neueren Sprachen und Literaturen* 44 (1890), 383–410

Luick, K., *Historische Grammatik der englischen Sprache* (Leipzig, 1914–40; repr. with an index by R. F. S. Harmer, Oxford, 1964)

Machielsen, J., *Clavis Patristica Pseudoepigraphorum Medii Aevi*, CCSL (Turnhout, 1990–)

McNamara, M., 'The Text of the Latin Bible in the Early Irish Church. Some Data and Desiderata', in *Irland und die Christenheit*, ed. Ní Chatháin and Richter, pp. 7–55

Manitius, M., *Geschichte der lateinischen Literatur des Mittelalters*, 3 vols. (Munich, 1911–31)

Marsden, R., 'The Old Testament in Late Anglo-Saxon England: Preliminary Observations on the Textual Evidence', in *Early Medieval Bible*, ed. Gameson, pp. 102–24

The Text of the Old Testament in Anglo-Saxon England, CSASE 15 (Cambridge, 1995)

Meid, W., *Germanische Sprachwissenschaft. III: Wortbildungslehre* (Berlin, 1967)

Meritt, H. D., *Old English Glosses* (New York, 1945)

Fact and Lore about Old English Words (Stanford, CA, 1954)

Meyvaert, P., 'Towards a History of the Textual Transmission of the *Regula S. Benedicti*', *Scriptorium* 17 (1963), 83–110

Milfull, I. B., ed., *The Hymns of the Anglo-Saxon Church*, CSASE 17 (Cambridge, 1996)

Mitchell, B., *Old English Syntax*, 2 vols. (Oxford, 1985)

Morin, G., ed., *Sancti Hieronymi Tractatus sive homiliae in psalmos*, CCSL 78 (Turnhout, 1958), 3–352

Morrish, J., 'Dated and Datable Manuscripts Copied in England during the Ninth Century: a Preliminary List', *Mediaeval Studies* 50 (1988), 512–38

Mustanoja, T. F., 'Notes on Some Old English Glosses in Aldhelm's *De laudibus virginitatis*', *Neuphilologische Mitteilungen* 51 (1950), 49–61

Napier, A. S., 'Contributions to Old English Lexicography', *Transactions of the Philological Society* (London, 1903–6), pp. 265–358

Napier, A. S., ed., *Old English Glosses, Chiefly Unpublished* (Oxford, 1900)

Nelson, J. L., *Politics and Ritual in Early Medieval Europe* (London, 1986)

'Symbols in Context: Rulers' Inauguration Rituals in Byzantium and the West in the Early Middle Ages', in her *Politics and Ritual*, pp. 259–307 (orig. publ. 1976)

'The Earliest Royal *Ordo*: Some Liturgical and Historical Aspects', in her *Politics and Ritual*, pp. 341–60 (orig. publ. 1980)

'The Second English *Ordo*', in her *Politics and Ritual*, pp. 361–74

Ní Chatháin, P. and M. Richter, ed., *Irland und die Christenheit: Bibelstudien und Mission* (Stuttgart, 1987)

Nocent, H., ed., 'Ælfrici Abbatis Epistula ad Monachos Egneshamnenses Directa', in *Consuetudinum Saeculi X/XI/XII Monumenta non-Cluniacensia*, ed. K. Hallinger, CCM 7.3 (Siegburg, 1984), pp. 149–85

Noel, W., *The Harley Psalter* (Cambridge, 1995)

O'Keeffe, K. O'B., 'The Text of Aldhelm's *Enigma* no. C in Oxford, Bodleian Library, Rawlinson C. 697, and Exeter Riddle 40', *ASE* 14 (1985), 61–73

Oliphant, R. T., ed., *The Harley Latin–Old English Glossary*, Janua Linguarum, Series Practica 20 (The Hague, 1966)

O'Neill, P. P., 'Latin Learning at Winchester in the Early Eleventh Century: the Evidence of the Lambeth Psalter', *ASE* 20 (1991), 143–66

'The English Version', in *Eadwine Psalter*, ed. Gibson *et al.*, pp. 123–38

Orchard, A., *The Poetic Art of Aldhelm*, CSASE 8 (Cambridge, 1994)

Pride and Prodigies. Studies in the Monsters of the Beowulf-Manuscript (Cambridge, 1995)

'Artful Alliteration in Anglo-Saxon Song and Story', *Anglia* 113 (1995), 429–63

Ortenberg, V., *The English Church and the Continent in the Tenth and Eleventh Centuries* (Oxford, 1992)

Parkes, M. B., 'The Palaeography of the Parker Manuscript of the Chronicle, Laws and Sedulius, and Historiography at Winchester in the Late Ninth and Tenth Centuries', in his *Scribes, Scripts and Readers* (London, 1991), pp. 143–69 (orig. publ. 1976)

Parsons, D., ed., *Tenth-Century Studies. Essays in Commemoration of the Millenium of the Council of Winchester and 'Regularis Concordia'* (London, 1975)

Pfaff, R. W., ed., *The Liturgical Books of Anglo-Saxon England*, Old English Newsletter Subsidia 23 (Kalamazoo, MI, 1995)

Pheifer, J. D., ed., *Old English Glosses in the Épinal–Erfurt Glossary* (Oxford, 1974)

Planchart, A. E., *The Repertory of Tropes at Winchester*, 2 vols. (Princeton, NJ, 1977)

Pope, J. C., ed., *Homilies of Ælfric. A Supplementary Collection*, 2 vols., EETS OS 259–60 (London, 1967–8)

Pulsiano, P., 'Defining the A-type (*Vespasian*) and D-type (*Regius*) Psalter-Gloss Traditions', *English Studies* 72 (1991), 308–27

'Psalters', in *The Liturgical Books of Anglo-Saxon England*, ed. Pfaff, pp. 61–85

'The Originality of the Old English Gloss of the *Vespasian Psalter* and its Relation to the Gloss of the *Junius Psalter*', *ASE* 25 (1996), 37–62

Quentin, H. *et al.*, ed., *Biblia Sacra iuxta Latinam Vulgatam Versionem ad Codicum Fidem*, 18 vols. (Rome, 1926–94) (X: *Liber Psalmorum* (1953))

Quinn, J. J., ed., 'The Minor Latin–Old English Glossaries in MS Cotton Cleopatra A. III' (unpubl. PhD dissertation, Stanford Univ., 1956)

Rädle, F., *Studien zu Smaragd von Saint-Mihiel* (Munich, 1974)

Raine, J., ed., *Historians of the Church of York*, 3 vols., Rolls Series (London, 1879–94)

Ramsay, N., M. Sparks and T. Tatton-Brown, ed., *St Dunstan. His Life, Time and Cult* (Woodbridge, 1992)

Robinson, J. A., *The Saxon Bishops of Wells*, British Academy Supplemental Papers 4 (London, 1918)

The Times of Saint Dunstan (Oxford, 1923)

Roeder, F., ed., *Der altenglische Regius-Psalter*, Studien zur englischen Philologie 18 (Halle, 1904)

Sainte-Marie, H. de, ed., *Sancti Hieronymi Psalterium iuxta Hebraeos*, Collectanea Biblica Latina 11 (Rome, 1954)

Sawyer, P., ed., *Charters of Burton Abbey*, Anglo-Saxon Charters 2 (London, 1979)

Schabram, H., *Superbia I. Studien zum altenglischen Wortschatz* (Munich, 1965)

Schlutter, O. B., 'Zum Wortschatz des *Regius* und *Eadwine Psalters*', *Englische Studien* 38 (1907), 1–27

Schröer, A., ed., *Die angelsächsischen Prosabearbeitungen der Benediktinerregel*,

Bibliothek der angelsächsischen Prosa 2, 2nd ed. with a supplement by H. Gneuss (Darmstadt, 1964)

Schützeichel, R., *Althochdeutsches Wörterbuch*, 4th ed. (Tübingen, 1989)

Seebold, E., 'Was ist jütisch? Was ist kentisch?', in *Britain 400–600. Language and History*, ed. A. Bammesberger and A. Wollmann (Heidelberg, 1990), pp. 335–52

'Kentish – and Old English Texts from Kent', in *Words, Texts and Manuscripts*, ed. Korhammer *et al.*, pp. 409–34

Sehrt, E. H., *Vollständiges Wörterbuch zum Heliand und zur altsächsischen Genesis*, 2nd ed. (Göttingen, 1966)

Sisam, C. and K. Sisam, ed., *The Salisbury Psalter*, EETS OS 242 (London, 1959)

Skeat, W. W., ed., *Ælfric's Lives of Saints*, 4 vols., EETS OS 76 and 82 (London, 1881 and 1885), 94 and 114 (London, 1890 and 1900); repr. in 2 vols. (London, 1966)

Spannagel, A. and P. Engelbert, ed., *Smaragdi Abbatis Expositio in Regulam S. Benedicti*, CCM 8 (Siegburg, 1974)

Stenton, F. M., *Anglo-Saxon England*, 3rd ed. (Oxford, 1971)

Stevenson, J., ed., *Chronicon Monasterii de Abingdon*, 2 vols., Rolls Series (London, 1858)

Stevenson, W. H., ed., *Asser's 'Life of King Alfred'* (Oxford, 1904)

Stryker, W. G., ed., 'The Latin–Old English Glossary in MS Cleopatra A. III' (unpubl. PhD dissertation, Stanford Univ., 1951)

Stubbs, W., ed., *Memorials of St Dunstan*, Rolls Series (London, 1874)

Sancti Dunstani Vita Auctore B., in his *Memorials*, pp. 3–52

Sutcliffe, E.F., 'Jerome', in *Cambridge History of the Bible*, ed. Lampe, pp. 80–101

Sweet, H., ed., *King Alfred's West-Saxon Version of Gregory's Pastoral Care*, 2 vols., EETS OS 45 and 50 (1871–2)

Symons, T., '*Regularis Concordia*: History and Derivation', in *Tenth-Century Studies*, ed. Parsons, pp. 37–59

Symons, T., ed., *Regularis Concordia* (London, 1953)

Symons, T. and S. Spath, ed., *Regularis Concordia*, in *Consuetudinum Saeculi X/XI/ XII Monumenta non-Cluniacensia*, ed. K. Hallinger, CCM 7.3 (Siegburg, 1984), 61–147

Temple, E., *Anglo-Saxon Manuscripts 900–1066* (London, 1976)

Thorpe, B., ed., *The Homilies of the Anglo-Saxon Church. The First Part Containing the Sermones Catholici or Homilies of Ælfric*, 2 vols. (London, 1844–6)

Tolhurst, J. B. L., *Introduction to the English Monastic Breviaries*, HBS 80 (London, 1942)

Traube, L., *Textgeschichte der Regula S. Benedicti*, 2nd ed. by H. Plenkers, Abhandlungen der königlich bayerischen Akademie der Wissenschaften, philosophisch-philologische und historische Klasse 25.2 (Munich, 1910)

Turner, D. H., ed., *The Missal of the New Minster Winchester*, HBS 93 (London, 1962)

Vogüé, A. de and J. Neufville, ed., *La Règle de Saint Benoît*, 6 vols., Sources chrétiennes, 181–6 (Paris, 1971–2), vol. 7 (Paris, 1977)

Wadstein, E., ed., *Kleinere altsächsische Sprachdenkmäler* (Norden, 1899)

Walsh, P. G., transl., *Cassiodorus: Explanation of the Psalms*, 3 vols., Ancient Christian Writers 51–3 (New York, 1990–1)

Warner, G. F. and J. P. Gilson, *Catalogue of Western Manuscripts in the Old Royal and King's Collection in the British Museum*, 4 vols. (London, 1921)

Warner, G. F. and H. A. Wilson, ed., *The Benedictional of St Æthelwold*, Roxburghe Club (Oxford, 1910)

Weber, R., ed., *Le Psautier Romain et les autres anciens psautiers latins*, Collectanea Biblica Latina 10 (Rome, 1953)

Weber, R., R. Gryson *et al.*, ed., *Biblia Sacra iuxta Vulgatam Versionem*, 4th ed. (Stuttgart, 1994)

Wells, J. C., *Althochdeutsches Glossenwörterbuch* (Heidelberg, 1990)

Wenisch, F., *Spezifisch anglisches Wortgut in den nordhumbrischen Interlinear-glossierungen des Lukasevangeliums*, Anglistische Forschungen 132 (Heidelberg, 1979)

Whitelock, D., 'The Authorship of the Account of King Edgar's Establishment of Monasteries', in *Philological Essays: Studies in Old and Middle English Language and Literature in Honour of Herbert Dean Meritt*, ed. J. L. Rosier (The Hague, 1970), pp. 125–36

Wiesenekker, E., *Word be worde, andgit of andgite: Translation Performance in the Old English Interlinear Glosses of the Vespasian, Regius and Lambeth Psalters* (Huizen, 1991)

Wildhagen, K., 'Studien zum *Psalterium Romanum* in England und zu seinen Glossierungen', in *Festschrift für Lorenz Morsbach*, ed. F. Holthausen and H. Spies, Studien zur englischen Philologie 50 (Halle, 1913), 418–72

'Das *Psalterium Gallicanum* in England und seine altenglischen Glossierungen', *Englische Studien* 54 (1920), 35–45

Wildhagen, K., ed., *Der Cambridger Psalter*, Bibliothek der angelsächsischen Prosa 7 (Hamburg, 1910)

William of Malmesbury, *De gestis pontificum Anglorum*, ed. N.E.S.A. Hamilton, Rolls Series (London, 1870)

De gestis regum Anglorum, ed. W. Stubbs, 2 vols., Rolls Series (London, 1887–9)

Wilmart, A. and L. Brou, ed., *The Psalter Collects from V–VIth Century Sources*, HBS 83 (London, 1949)

Winterbottom, M., 'Aldhelm's Prose Style and its Origins', *ASE* 6 (1977), 39–76

Wood, M., 'The Making of King Æthelstan's Empire: an English Charlemagne?', in *Ideal and Reality in Frankish and Anglo-Saxon Society: Studies presented to J. M. Wallace-Hadrill*, ed. P. Wormald with D. Bullough and R. Collins (Oxford, 1983), pp. 250–72

Wormald, F., *Collected Writings I: Studies in Medieval Art from the Sixth to the Twelfth Centuries*, ed. J. J. G. Alexander, T. J. Brown and J. Gibbs (Oxford, 1984)

Wright, C. D., 'Hiberno-Latin and Irish-Influenced Commentaries, Florilegia and Homily Collections', in *Sources*, ed. Biggs *et al.*, pp. 87–123

Wright, D. H., ed., *The Vespasian Psalter (British Museum Cotton Vespasian A. i)*, EEMF 14 (Copenhagen, 1967)

Yorke, B., 'Æthelwold and the Politics of the Tenth Century', in *Bishop Æthelwold*, ed. Yorke, pp. 65–88

Yorke, B., ed., *Bishop Æthelwold: his Career and Influence* (Woodbridge, 1988)

Index of Old English words

This index contains words which are discussed as translations of Latin lemmata, but not words occurring in quotations or words cited exclusively for their phonological forms. The lemmata are usually given in the form in which they occur in CHM, but words occurring only in the Vespasian Psalter are given in the form attested there.

Index of Latin words glossed in
Old English or translated

abductio: 63
adeps: 326
adhaerere: 327
adolescentia: 399
adolescere: 154
adtendere: 38
aduersarius: 62
aemulus: 153
aequare: 61
aequitas: 327
algosus: 153
alienare: 60
allegoria: 378
Alpes: 168, 169
altare: 52
ambro: 154
ambulare: 50
anagoge: 223, 378
angustus: 114
anxiare: 60
arrogantia: 413
astronomia: 168
astute: 326
athleta: 153

barbarus: 326
beneplacitus: 326
bibliotheca: 9n
blasphemare: 405
breuis: 51

caballus: 405

calcar: 153
callositas: 154
calta: 153
cambra: 405
canticum: 51, 92
capellanus: 405
carenum: 406, 407
chorus: 52
christus: 72–9, 102, 112n, 304, 305,
    307
chronographus: 160, 162
circuitus: 62
ciuitas: 53
classicus: 153
cognoscere: 327
collidere: 96n
collocare: 51, 60
commouere: 37n
concidere: 68
confrequentatio: 56n
confringere: 81, 96n
congregatio: 108
conlaudare: 60
conlaudatio: 60n
consentire: 60
conterrere: 45, 96n
contradictio: 45
conuenticulum: 108
conuentus: 108
conuersio: 279
corona: 63, 98–102, 157, 161, 297, 298,
    303, 304, 324n, 413

460

General index